W9-DAZ-622

# SOVIET COMMUNISM:
# A NEW CIVILISATION?

# POLITICAL DIVISIONS

Baltic

FINLAND

A R C T

POLAND

WHITE
RUSSIAN
S.S.R.

Leningrad

KARELIAN
Aut. R.

Archangel

NORTHERN

Kiev

UKRAINIAN
S.S.R.

Odessa

WESTERN

IVANOVO

•Moscow

GORKI

SVERDLOVSK

R. F.

R. Ob

R. Yenisei

Kursk

Voronezh

CHUVASH
Aut. R.

CRIMEAN
Aut. R.

Black Sea

Rostov

Stalingrad

GERMAN
VOLGA
Aut. R.

TARTAR
Aut. R.

Volga

Samara

BASHKIR
Aut. R.

S.

U.

CHELIABINSK

Tobolsk

Omsk

Novo-
Sibirsk

WEST SIBERIA

Toms

Kuzr

R. Irtysh

•Astrakhan

R.

DAGHESTAN
Aut. R.

TRANS-
CAUCASIAN
S.F.S.R.

Caspian Sea

2

3  1

Aral
Sea

KAZAK   Aut. R.

KARA-KALPAK
Aut. R.

L. Balkash

1. Azerbaidjan
2. Georgia
3. Armenia

TURKOMAN S.S.R.

UZBEK S.S.R.

KIRGHIZ Aut. R.

P E R S I A

TADZHIK
S.S.R.

AFGHANISTAN

J.F.Horrabin

of the U.S.S.R.

# SOVIET COMMUNISM: A NEW CIVILISATION? BY SIDNEY AND BEATRICE WEBB.

VOL. I.

NEW YORK
CHARLES SCRIBNER'S SONS
1938

# PREFACE

This book calls, perhaps, for some explanation of its scope and plan, if not also of its length. It is not easy to appreciate either the magnitude of the Union of Soviet Socialist Republics (nearly one-sixth of the entire land-surface of the globe, with a population rapidly approaching 200 millions) ; or the variety, ranging from barbarism to a high degree of culture, of its hundred or more different races and languages. Its organisational structure is surely the most complicated known to political science. We ask the reader to gaze at the map (frontispiece), and at the two diagrams (pp. 456 and 460 of the Appendices of Part I.) giving precisely the main administrative areas and the principal organs of government of the USSR, which Mr. J. F. Horrabin has specially drawn, upon Mr. S. P. Turin's information, and generously contributed to this work. These diagrams, notwithstanding their wealth of symbols, can do no more than start the requisite impression of complication of federation within federation, and of tier upon tier of local governing bodies and central administrative organs. But in addition to all that is indicated by the map and those diagrams of the organisation of the citizens, the reader has to visualise the wholly different and not less complicated organisation of these same men and women in wealth production, whether as independent producers, or as wage or salary earners in their trade unions, or as groups of co-partners in agriculture, in hunting and fishing, or in manufacture. There is yet a third universal organisation of these 40 million families in their capacity of consumers, in which they become members of a hierarchy of some 45,000 local societies for the distribution among themselves of the foodstuffs and other commodities of their domestic housekeeping. And we have still to name a fourth pyramidal and equally ubiquitous organisation, the most unique and original, and some would say the most significant of all, made up of the extensive membership of what we have termed the Vocation of Leadership.

Even this is not the whole story. The degree of complication of the administrative, industrial and political structure of the USSR does but correspond with the magnitude and variety of

the functions for which the structure is elaborated : functions
which transcend in scope and range those consciously and deliberately undertaken by any other community. And, in each
department, structure and function are intertwined with each
other and with a wealth of voluntary associations and spontaneous
individual activities to constitute a highly integrated society which
definitely forms a synthesis. In all social history—that " endless adventure of governing men "—there has been no such a
colossal and so exciting an experiment. It takes us over 900
pages, constituting the six chapters and appendices of Part I.
and the first four chapters of Part II., to set forth all the welter
of structure and function making up what is, merely in magnitude, the biggest integrated social organisation in the world.

This widely comprehensive and, as it seems to-day, solidly
united mass organisation, is brand new, not yet twenty years old,
and is still rapidly developing. We suggest that, if it endures,
its eventual impact on the rest of the world must be considerable.
Its aims are grandiose and far-reaching. With what purpose are
its leaders and directors animated ? What is the philosophy on
which their lives are based ? Upon what motives and instruments do they rely for the attainment of their ends ? What
original conceptions of economics and political science, and what
new inventions in systems of wealth production and of social
relations, are being worked out in the Soviet Union, where, by
the way, they claim, by their novel adjustment of a planned
supply to a universally effective demand, to have definitely got
rid of involuntary unemployment ? Can it be true that there is
evolving, out of the incessant public discussions of the millions
of adolescents between the Baltic and the Pacific, a new ethical
system, with a code of conduct emerging from their actual experience of a transformed social life ? These issues are discussed in Chapters XI. and XII. Finally, we add a short epilogue raising the question whether what the world is witnessing
to-day in the USSR does not amount to a new civilisation,
differing from any that has hitherto existed ; and whether it is
likely to spread beyond its present borders.

But why undertake so great a task as a comprehensive description of the entire social order of the USSR ? The answer is
that it has been borne in on us by experience that the first step
to any competent understanding of what is happening in the

USSR is that the picture should be viewed as a whole. At the outset it may seem easier for each student to confine his investigation into his own particular speciality, and to write a detailed monograph upon what the USSR has done in that limited field. But unless and until the organisation of the Soviet Union has been studied as a whole, and some intelligent comprehension has been gained of its complicated structure and manifold activities ; of its aim and purpose ; of the direction in which it is travelling ; of its instruments and its methods ; and of its philosophy—no satisfying judgment can be passed upon any part of its work. No survey either of its achievements or of its shortcomings in wealth production or in artistic development, in education or in medicine, in changing the st ndard of living or revising the bounds of freedom, can be competently made without a grasp of the principles of multiformity and universalism that run through the warp and weft of every part of its texture. It is not the failure or the fulfilment of any one function that is significant, but the life of the whole ; and, be it added, not so much what the ever-moving mass is to-day, as whence it has come and whither it is tending. It is for this reason that we have, greatly daring, attempted to map the whole of what we may picture as the Eurasian Plain, in the belief that, however imperfect our survey, it will help other travellers to find their way in more detailed studies of their own specialities, by which our necessarily superficial sketches may be corrected, supplemented or superseded.

Contrary to common expectation, we have found the material for our work abundant and accessible. Of the vast outpouring of books in many languages since 1917, giving tourists' impressions of the land of the soviets, together with the better authenticated narratives of the resident newspaper correspondents, we need not speak. Among the more scientific studies of which we have been able to make substantial use in enlargement and correction of our own researches, we have to acknowledge that by far the greatest proportion stand to the credit of the United States—an outcome, we think, not only of the wider interest taken by that country than by Great Britain in a new social order, which is now attracting thousands of immigrants from the United States, but also of the large number of scholarships and fellowships enabling scientific researchers to spend a year or more in the USSR for the production of valuable monographs.

There are far too few such opportunities yet provided for the British student.

In addition to the stream of books affording descriptions by eye-witnesses of what they have seen in the USSR, there is available to the serious student an unusual output of printed documents by the Soviet Government through many of its departments ; by the ancient Academy of Sciences, and the thousand and one scientific research institutes, and the exploring expeditions that they send out ; by the trade unions ; by the Industrial Cooperative Societies ; by the Consumers' Cooperative Movement ; and, last but not least, by the Communist Party. These masses of reports and statistics are not all in Russian, nor yet in the languages of the various national minorities. Probably no other government in the world issues so large a mass of documents in languages other than its own (largely in English, French or German), whether as the proceedings of conferences or congresses, or the decrees and codes, or the speeches of its leading statesmen, or the reports of the discoveries of the scientific exploring parties, or the instructions to subordinate departments. In addition to these documents there is the large and always increasing soviet press, from such leading journals as *Pravda* and *Izvestia*, and their scores of local imitators, down to the innumerable news-sheets and wall newspapers of the factories and mines, of the collective farms, and of the state, municipal and cooperative plants and offices; whilst, for those who are interested in the personal life of the soviet citizen there are novels and plays, comic periodicals and all varieties of exhibition of the self-criticism in which the Russians delight. Nor are foreigners neglected. The Moscow press turns out daily and weekly organs, widely distributed throughout the USSR, in English, German and French. These journals, like all newspapers in the USSR, are almost entirely filled with information about the doings of the Sovnarkom, and the Central Committee of the Communist Party, or with detailed descriptions of the workings of mines, oilfields, factories and state or collective farms, statistics of the extent of fulfilment of the Five-Year Plan, and other instructional material. Meanwhile, the powerful wireless stations in Moscow broadcast the same kind of thing nightly to the world in no fewer than fourteen European languages, together with Esperanto.

Although we have aimed at precision in our references, we do

not indulge in a comprehensive bibliography. We have thought
it more likely to be helpful to students wishing to explore further
any of the topics with which we deal to give in each chapter a
list of the principal sources of information accessible to British
or American students (usually omitting therefore books existing
only in Russian or Ukrainian, even where we have had relevant
extracts from them translated for our own use).

Throughout our work we have had the valuable assistance of
Mr. S. P. Turin, lecturer at the School of Slavonic and East
European Studies and the London School of Economics and
Political Science in the University of London, who has not only
kept us continuously up to date about what is being published
in the USSR, but has also freely placed at our disposal much
additional information derived from his long study of his native
land both prior and subsequent to the Revolution. His recent
book *From Peter the Great to Lenin* supplies a valuable historical
introduction to the present labour movement. Mr. Turin has
enabled us to avoid many mistakes without necessarily sharing
either our viewpoint or our opinions ; and he is in no way responsible for our generalisations or our judgments.

We must mention also the assistance we have derived from
Dr. Julius F. Hecker, alike through his books, *Religion and
Communism, Moscow Dialogues, Russian Sociology* and others,
and through our illuminating discussions with him in Moscow
and London. Indeed, we must gratefully acknowledge the
continuous help we have received during the past four years from
friends too numerous to mention, scientific and literary, Russian
and non-Russian, residents in the USSR and also exiles of more
than one generation, and of all shades of opinion. At all times,
and notably during our visits to the USSR, the soviet authorities
have willingly answered our innumerable questions, and given
us every facility for going anywhere that we wanted to go ;
for seeing works, factories and farms, schools and hospitals, and
other institutions, as well as for admission to meetings that we
wished to attend. We have gathered much, not only from
officials but also from trade unionists, teachers, engineers,
doctors, peasants and fishermen, not omitting to take due note
of what we have been told by discontented intelligentsia and
disgruntled revolutionaries both inside the USSR and elsewhere.

What we have sought to present is an objective view of the

whole social order of the USSR as it exists to-day, with no more past history than is necessary for explanation, and with an intelligent impression of the direction in which it is travelling. We have not hesitated to criticise anything that seemed to us to call for criticism. We do not pretend to be without bias (who is ?), but we have tried to be aware of our bias, and have striven for objectivity.

The question will arise in some quarters : Why did two aged mortals, both nearing their ninth decade, undertake a work of such magnitude ? We fear our presumption must be ascribed to the recklessness of old age. In our retirement, with daily bread secured, we had nothing to lose by the venture—not even our reputation, which will naturally stand or fall upon our entire output of the past half-century, to the load of which one more book makes no appreciable difference. On the other hand, we had a world to gain—a new subject to investigate ; a fresh circle of stimulating acquaintances with whom to discuss entirely new topics, and above all a daily joint occupation, in intimate companionship, to interest, amuse and even excite us in the last stage of life's journey. This world we have gained and enjoyed. To use a theological term, this book is therefore to be received as a work of supererogation, which, as we understand it, means something not required, but spontaneously offered, which may be ignored or criticised, but which does not warrant blame, even if it be deemed (to use the words of Steele) " an act of so great supererogation as singing without a voice " ! Or, to take a humbler analogy, it may be taken as the etcetera, often thrown in as a gift by the salesman with a package of goods already paid for. As such we may present it unabashed to our British and American readers.

The reader will find at the end of Part I. (pp. $528^1$-$528^{26}$) an exceptionally accurate translation of the complete text of the New Constitution of 1936, by Mrs. Anna Louise Strong, to whom we are indebted for permission to reprint it. We give also a summary in the form of a new Declaration of the Rights of Man. At the end of Part II., after the Epilogue, we add a lengthy Postscript (pp. 1145-1216), dealing with the principal changes in the Soviet Union since 1934-5.

SIDNEY AND BEATRICE WEBB

# CONTENTS

## PART I. THE CONSTITUTION

PAGE

PREFACE . . . . . . . . . . vii

### CHAPTER I

THE CONSTITUTION AS A WHOLE . . . . . 3

Preliminary survey—Declaration of Rights of the Labouring and Exploited Peoples—Proclamation of the Soviet Union.

### CHAPTER II

MAN AS A CITIZEN . . . . . . . . 11

The Origin of the Soviet System—The Base of the Pyramid—The Village Meeting—The Village Executive—The City Soviet—The Method of Election—The Electors' Instructions—A Moscow Election—The Organisation of the City Soviet—The Rayons in the Cities—Indirect Election—The Rayon—The Oblast—The Seven Federated Republics—The RSFSR—The Ukraine—The White Russian and Transcaucasian Republics—The Formation of the Soviet Union—The All-Union Congress—The Central Executive Committee (TSIK)—The Council of People's Commissars (Sovnarkom)—The Council of Labour and Defence—The Commissariats—The Commissariats Dealing with Production and Trade—The People's Commissar of Finance—Banking and Saving—Insurance—The Commissariat of Defence—The Army as a School—The Commissariat of Foreign Affairs—The Commissariat of Internal Affairs—The Ogpu—The Supreme Court—The Procurator—The College of Advocates—The Problem of National Minorities—Cultural Autonomy—The Tartar Republic—The Jews in the USSR—A New Basis for Statehood.

## CHAPTER III

PAGE

MAN AS A PRODUCER . . . . . . . 161

*Section I.* Soviet Trade Unionism—History—Trade Union Structure in the USSR—Trade Union Elections—The Trade Union Factory Committee—Collective Bargaining in the USSR —The All-Union Congress of each Trade Union—The All-Union Congress of Trade Unions—Lateral Structure in the USSR Trade Unionism—The Trade Union Officials—The Transference of the Commissariat of Labour to the Trade Unions—The Shock Brigades and Cost Accounting Committees—Professional Associations—The Profintern—How does Soviet Trade Unionism compare with British Trade Unionism ?

*Section II.* The Associations of Owner-Producers.

(*a*) The Self-governing Workshop—The Members' Meeting— The Regional Council—The All-Union Council of Industrial Cooperatives.

(*b*) The Collective Farm—The Unproductive Peasant—The Crisis in Foodstuffs—The Prolonged Discussion as to Policy— The Policy of Universal Collectivisation—The Struggle for Efficiency in the Kolkhosi—State Machinery for Control : (1) The New People's Commissar ; (2) The New Agricultural Departments ; (3) Supervision by the Village Soviets—The Machine and Tractor Stations—The Work of the Policy Sections —Was there a Famine in the USSR in 1931–1932 ?—Life on a Collective Farm—Management—Democracy in Agriculture— The Commune—The Results in 1933–1935.

(*c*) Miscellaneous Associations of Owner-Producers—The Fishermen's Kolkhosi—Integral Cooperatives—War Invalids, etc.

(*d*) Associations of Artistic and Intellectual Producers. The World of Labour in the USSR.

## CHAPTER IV

MAN AS A CONSUMER . . . . . . . 304

The Hierarchy of Consumers' Cooperation—The Members' Meeting—The Committee of Management—The Rayon Union with the Rayon Council (Raisoyus)—The Oblast or Republic Union with its Council (Oblsoyus)—The All-Union Congress of Consumers' Cooperatives, with its Central Board for the USSR and the RSFSR (Centrosoyus)—The Mechanised Bakeries— Cooperative Education—The Rivals of the Consumers' Cooperative in Retail Distribution—Recent Encroachments on the Sphere of the Consumers' Cooperative Movement—Network of contracts for Supplies.

## CHAPTER V

THE VOCATION OF LEADERSHIP . . . . . . 339

How the Communist Party arose—The Party Membership—The Rules of the Order—The Meaning of Leadership—The Party Group (late fraction)—The Primary Party Organ (late cell or nucleus)—The District (Rayon) Conference—The Republic Congress—The USSR and RSFSR Party Congress—The Central Committee—The Motives for Party Membership—The Purging of the Party—The Internal Reorganisation of 1934—The Comsomols—The Pioneers and the Octobrists—The Comintern—The Nature of the Communist Party—Why in Soviet Communism National Leadership requires an Elaborate Organisation.

## CHAPTER VI

DICTATORSHIP OR DEMOCRACY ? . . . . . . 419

The Meaning of Dictatorship—Is the Party a Dictator ?—Is Stalin a Dictator ?—The Dictatorship of the Proletariat—Is the USSR an Autocracy?—In whose Interest does the Government Act ?—A New Social Form ?

## APPENDICES TO PART I

I. Diagram of the Political Structure of the USSR. Table I.—Administrative Structure . . . . . . 457

II. Diagram of the Organisational Structure of the USSR. Table II.—Political Structure . . . . . . 461

III. Appendix to Chapter I.—The Declaration of the Central Executive Committee of the Union of Soviet Socialist Republics of July 13, 1923 . . . . . . 462

IV. Appendix to Chapter II.—The Powers and Authorised Functions of the Village Soviet . . . . . . 465

V. Appendix to Chapter II.—The Sections and Commissions of the City Soviets . . . . . . 471

VI. Appendix to Chapter II.—Note Relating to the Commissariat for Workers' and Peasants' Inspection (Rabkrin, or RKI) . 474

PAGE

VII. Appendix to Chapter II.—The Internal Organisation of the
Narkomat of Sovkhosi . . . . . . 479

VIII. Appendix to Chapter II.—The Internal Organisation of the
Narkomat of Agriculture . . . . . . 485

IX. Appendix to Chapter IV.—List of the 154 Trade Unions among
which the Membership of the 47 Trade Unions of 1931 was distributed in 1934 . . . . . . . 492

X. The Duties and Functions of the Factory Committees . . 496

XI. Appendix to Chapter III.—The Collective Agreement (Kol-
dogovor) of the Fraising-Lathe Works at Gorki for the year
1933–1934 . . . . . . . . . 505

XII. Appendix to Chapter II. and VI.—The New Constitution
and Summary of the Rights of Man . . . . 528[1]

## PART II.  SOCIAL TRENDS IN SOVIET COMMUNISM

### CHAPTER VII

PAGE

THE LIQUIDATION OF THE LANDLORD AND THE CAPITALIST . 529

The Liquidation of the Agrarian Landlords by the Peasantry
—The Expropriation of the Capitalist—The Civil War and
Foreign Invasion—War Communism—The Famine of 1921—
The New Economic Policy—The Persecution of the Intelligentsia
—The Trial of the Industrial Party—The Trial of the Menshevik
Professors—Trial of the Metro-Vickers Engineers—Murder of
Kirov—The Liquidation of the Kulaks—The Activities of the
Tcheka and the Ogpu—The Organisation of the Ogpu—The Con-
structive Work of the Ogpu—The Procurator of the USSR—
Three Revolutions in One—Comparison with the English
Revolution.

### CHAPTER VIII

PLANNED PRODUCTION FOR COMMUNITY CONSUMPTION . . 602

The Episode of Workers' Control—The Supreme Economic
Council—The Emergence of the General Plan—Krassin's Exposi-
tion of Planning in 1920—Gosplan as Planning Authority—How
the Plan is Made—The Provisional Plan—The General Object of
Soviet Planning—The Division of the Nation's Income between
Current Consumption and Capital Investment—National Defence
—The Development of Education—Public Health and Housing—
The Final Plan—The Efficiency of a Planned Economy—The

World's Argument about the Plan—The Plan obviates both
Booms and Slumps—The Abolition of Involuntary Unemploy-
ment—The Abstract Economists' Criticism of a Planned
Economy—A Communist Reply to the Economists' Criticism—
How the General Plan might be Upset—" But Planning Means
Slavery "—Consumers' Control instead of Producers' Control—
Citizen's Control where that of the Consumer fails—The Supposed
" Coercion of the Consumer "—Greater Freedom of Choice for the
masses.

## CHAPTER IX

IN PLACE OF PROFIT   .    .    .    .    .    .    .    . 697

The Old Incentives Remodelled—Not Equality of Wages—
How Piece-work Rates are Fixed—The Grading of Wages—Pay-
ment According to Social Value—The Machinery of Arbitration
—Self-Employment as an Alternative to the Wage System—
Individual Self-Employment—Self-Employment in Manufactur-
ing Artels (Incops)—Self-Employment in Collective Farms (Kol-
khosi)—The Complicated Network of Agreements for Supplies—
The Bazaar—Socialist Emulation—Patronage—The Udarniki
(Shock Brigadiers)—Cost Accounting Brigades—Subbotniki, or
Voluntary Labourers—Public Honour and Shame—The Soviet
Orders of Merit—Public Dishonour—Encouragement of Inven-
tions by the Workers—Multiformity in Employment—The
Practice of Self-Criticism—Shortcomings and Achievements—
The Wasteful Costs of Inexperience—The Inefficiency caused by
Overlapping of Control—Where are the Captains of Industry?—
The Substitute for Profit-making—An Analysis of the Producers.

## CHAPTER X

THE REMAKING OF MAN .    .    .    .    .    .    .    . 805

(a) Health—The Woman—Motherhood—Infancy—Birth
Control—The Control of Abortion—Creating Health—How the
Health Service is Administered—The Staffing of the Service—
Hospitals—Health Centres in Factories—Rural Consultation
Points—The Flying Squad—The Campaign Against Tuberculosis
—The Night Sanatorium—Provision for Street Casualties—
Medical Research—A City of the Science and Art of Health.

(b) Economic Security—How the System of Economic
Security Developed—Death Benefit—Sickness Benefit—In-

validity and Old-Age Benefit—Maternity Benefit—Unemployment Benefit—Other Benefits—Rest Houses and Sanatoria—Personal Credit—Imperfections of the System.

(c) Education — Universalism — Polytechnikisation — The Organisation of Leisure—Physical Culture—Political Culture—Artistic Culture—Museums and Picture Galleries—Theatre and Ballet—Music—Holidays and Amusements—The Meaning of Culture—The Civilisation of a Whole Nation—Educational Shortcomings.

(d) Changing the Environment—The Service of Housing—Systematic Town Planning—Municipal Services.


CHAPTER XI

SCIENCE THE SALVATION OF MANKIND . . . . . 944

The Struggle with Nature—What Marxism Means—The Organisation of Scientific Research—How Research is Planned and Executed—The Academy of Sciences—The Communist Academy—Popular Participation—The Work of the Several Research Institutes—Mathematics and Physics—The Materials and Processes of Wealth Production—Agriculture—Genetics—The Fight for Health—The Central Institute of Roentgenology—The Leningrad Institute of the Brain—The Leningrad Institute of Experimental Medicine—The Moscow Institute of Endocrinology—The Campaign against Rheumatism—The Central Aero Hydro-Dynamic Institute—The Exploring Expeditions—The Unevenness in the Development of Science—The Need for Study of Social Institutions—The Science of Human Behaviour The Disease of Orthodoxy—" Anti-Godism "—The Campaign against Religion.

CHAPTER XII

THE GOOD LIFE . . . . . . . . . 1017

The Pursuit of Plenty—For the Whole Population—With Advanced Industrialism—In Social Equality—The " Classless Society "—A Compulsory Environment—Plan or No Plan ?—Where is Freedom ?—Unity in Action with Adventure in Thought—The Solution of the Problem—The Evolution of Communist Ethics—No Sense of Original Sin—No Absolute Morals—Ethics Emerging from Life—The Constant Service of the Community—The Payment of Debt—The Maximising of Health—Sexual Intercourse—Prostitution—What is " Not Done "—

Personal Acquisitiveness—The Duty of the Party Member—To
each according to his Needs—Ethical Progress in the USSR—
The Withering of the State—Contradictory Trends in Foreign
Affairs—The Policy and Activities of the Third International—
Soviet China—The Comintern Congress of 1928—The Change of
the Soviet Government from War to Peace—Joining in International Conferences and the League of Nations—Contrast between Comintern and Sovnarkom—The Comintern Congress of
1935—Prospects of greater Consistency—The Obstacle to Communist Propaganda of " Government from Moscow ".

## EPILOGUE

A NEW CIVILISATION    .       .      .       .      .      .    1119

What constitutes a Distinct Civilisation ?—Other Civilisa-
tions—The Eight Principal Novelties in Soviet Civilisation—
The Abolition of Profit-Making—The Planning of Production
for Community Consumption—Social Equality and Universalism—A Novel Representative System—The Vocation of Leadership—The Cult of Science—"Anti-Godism "—A New Conscience
for the Good Life—These make a Synthetic Unity in contrast
with Disintegrating Capitalism—Will it Endure ?—Will it
Spread ?


POSTSCRIPT TO THE SECOND EDITION .      .       .      .    1145

The New Constitution—Its Significance—The Moscow Trials
—The Stakhanov Movement—The Success of Collective Agri-
culture—The Retailing of Commodities—Soviet Currency—
The Control of Abortion—Some Criticisms—Inequality of In-
comes—Bureaucracy—Repression of Independent Thinking—
A New Civilisation.


INDEX OF PERSONS (with brief biographical details) .      .    . 1217
INDEX OF PLACES .     .       .      .       .      .      . 1235
INDEX OF SUBJECTS     .       .      .       .      .      . 1239

# PART I

## THE CONSTITUTION

" By constitution we mean, whenever we speak with propriety
and exactness, that assemblage of laws, institutions and customs,
derived from certain fixed principles of reason . . . that compose
the general system according to which the community has agreed
to be governed."

HENRY ST. JOHN, first Viscount Bolingbroke,
*Dissertation on Parties*, 1733, p. 108

# CHAPTER I

## THE CONSTITUTION AS A WHOLE

THE constitution of the Soviet Union differs, we think, from any adopted elsewhere during the past couple of centuries, in not having been the outcome of deliberate and usually prolonged study by political philosophers and jurists. At no time was there anything in the nature of deliberation by a constituent assembly. There was no formulated outline or plan either of the constitution as a whole, or of the relation between its several parts. Even its most prominent feature—the broad base of innumerable local elected councils universally known as soviets—was adopted, as we shall describe in the following chapter, without this having been thought of as the permanent base of a stable government eighteen months before. It is, in fact, one of the difficulties of intelligibly describing this continuously evolving constitution that, whilst it is nowhere given, as a whole, in any statute or official document, no part of it can be properly understood without having in mind all the rest. Thus, in the Soviet Union, what the western jurist is tempted to regard as the constitutional structure, namely, the pyramid of soviets, is plainly only a fragment of it, and, as some may say, not the most important fragment. Whether by statutory enactment or by accepted practice, the constitution of the USSR provides for the active participation of the people in the work of government in more than one way. It is therefore not only man as a citizen who is represented. He acts and votes separately in his capacity as a producer. Yet again, as a consumer, he also acts and votes separately. And, so far as concerns the millions who are members of the exclusive and highly disciplined Order or Companionship styled the Communist Party, which undertakes

3

the vocation of public leadership, we find these citizens acting
and voting also in a fourth capacity, which may be thought to be
the most influential of all.   Thus, in dealing with the structure
of the USSR, we must cast off, wholly and permanently, the
obsolete idea that the constitution of a nation is to be looked for
exclusively in some legislative enactment, or other authoritative
document.  We know now that in no nation, not even in the
United States, is the whole constitution to be found in any document ; just as in no nation, not even in the United Kingdom, is
the constitution wholly unwritten.  Whether or not we choose
to say, with Ferdinand Lassalle, that " the real constitution "
of any country is nothing more than " the actual relationships
of power ", we must, at any rate, always include, as part of the
working constitution, everything that operates as such.  Moreover, in the USSR, we must accept, once for all, the fact that no
distinction is made between the exercise of power that elsewhere
would be called legislation, and that which would be deemed
executive action or administration.  Every organ of administration in the USSR is capable of legislative and of executive action.
Every one of them is free to act, within its own area and for all
who find themselves within that area, very much as it thinks fit,
so long as it does not actually contravene any action or decision
by a superior authority.  But, equally, every one of them can
be peremptorily restrained, and may have its action vetoed and
cancelled, by any organ occupying a superior place in the hierarchy.

Can we venture on a brief summary of this elusive constitution before embarking on the description of its various parts ?
Such a sketch, whilst possibly suggesting more questions than it
answers, may help the reader to understand the necessarily
detailed pages that are to follow.  As we see it, the government
centred in the Moscow Kremlin is the apex of half a dozen
pyramidal structures covering the whole of the USSR, each of
them based, according to a common pattern, upon a vast number
of relatively small meetings of associated citizens for almost
continuous discussion, and for the periodical direct election of
primary representative councils.  Each of these structures rises
tier after tier, through successive stages of councils, governing
ever-widening areas and constituted by indirect election, up
to a group which is supreme for each particular mass.  These

half a dozen culminating groups, in different combinations, and by more or less formal joint consultations, constitute the source of all governmental authority, whether legislative or executive.

What are these half a dozen pyramidal structures ? There is first the hierarchy [1] of soviets, from those of the village and the city, through the district (rayon) and province (oblast) and constituent republic congresses or conferences, up to the All-Union Congress of Soviets of the USSR, with its Central Executive Committee (TSIK) and its Council of People's Commissars (Sovnarkom). In this hierarchy of soviets it is the citizen as such who is represented. But all citizens are assumed to be also producers by hand or by brain, or the non-able-bodied dependants thereof. A large and rapidly increasing proportion of them are actually wage or salary earners and members of their trade unions. All the producers thus paid are represented in the trade union hierarchy, equally based on innumerable small local workshop or office meetings of the members of each of the trade unions—now 154 in number—electing representative councils which rise, tier upon tier, up to separate central bodies for each of the several unions, and, yet further, to a supreme common assembly, the All-Union Congress of Trade Unions, acting for the whole aggregate of wage or salary recipients engaged in production or distribution of goods or services, by hand or by brain.

There are, however, other producers who are not remunerated by wages or salaries but are themselves owners, wholly or in part, individually or jointly, of the instruments with which they work, and of the product of their labour. Of these owner-producers, as such excluded from the trade unions, there are now

---

[1] Our use of the term " hierarchy " must not be misunderstood. No doubt the earliest usage, many centuries ago, was to employ this word with a theological implication, relating to the " heavenly host " ; or to this or that form of church establishment or priestly order. In English usage the term long ago came to be applied to non-theological organisations, but often with an implication of formation and control from the top. The use of the term in modern logic, or in contemporary science, now implies no necessary ascendancy or pre-eminence, any more than any theological reference, but merely " a body of persons or things ranked in grades, orders or classes, one above another " ; or " a system or series of terms of successive rank (as classes, orders, genera, species, etc.) used in classification " (*New English Dictionary*). It is in this purely neutral sense of classification, implying neither dictatorship nor popular election, that we use the term in this book.

several classes, among which two stand out as the principal. These two classes, numbering together more than half the active producers in the USSR, may be thought to be developing constitutionally into massive pyramidal structures parallel with those of the trade unions and the soviets, and formed on a similar pattern. Thus, there are the millions of kustar workers, joined in *artels*, now constituted as industrial cooperative societies of owner-producers (incops) which elect their own tiers of councils for districts and provinces, culminating in a central delegate body at Moscow. There are equally the millions of members of collective farms (kolkhosi, as distinguished from state farms or sovkhosi), the federal constitution of which is still only in germ, although it is already more developed in other instances, notably in the corresponding organisation of professional fishermen.

All these producers, whether they work for wages or salary, or as partners sharing a joint product, have, however, in common, not only their citizenship, acting through the hierarchy of soviets, together with their function of production, organised partly in the hierarchy of trade unions, and partly in the several hierarchies of associations of owner-producers, but also a separate and quite distinct interest as consumers. Accordingly practically the whole of them—over seventy millions of adults—are united in the 45,000 separate consumers' cooperative societies in each of which the membership elects its own board of management, whilst the societies are all united in district and provincial and republic associations, formed on substantially the common pattern of indirect election, and culminating in the Central Board of Centrosoyus, specifically representing the whole body of consumers throughout the USSR.

Finally, there is the remarkable Companionship or Order, termed the Communist Party, whose three million adult members and candidates, supported by its still larger junior organisations of Little Octobrists, Pioneers and Comsomols, are not abstracted from the several masses of citizen producers and consumers, but, on the contrary, whilst remaining citizens, assume the function and the duty, not merely, in so far as they are elected or appointed to office, of serving the community as its principal administrators, but also, in working at the bench or in the mine, of continuously educating, inspiring, guiding and leading the whole people among whom they live and work. It is interesting to find the internal organisation of this Companionship or Order following the common pattern running through all the rest of the constitution, with its base in the members' meetings of the 130,000 primary organs, and its tier upon tier of district and provincial and republic councils formed by indirect election, up to the supreme All-Union Congress of the Party, electing its Central Committee, which acts through its Politbureau, and its Orgbureau, and the extensive secretariat that it appoints.

What are not publicly formulated are the arrangements for the constantly shifting consultations and conferences which are perpetually taking place, not only, at each tier, between the intermediate councils and officials, but also between the several supreme bodies centred in Moscow and among their prominent leaders.[1] It is from these consultations and conferences that emanate the streams of orders and " directives " required for the government of so vast a country. The power needed for administration may be generated in the innumerable meetings of electors, producers, consumers and members of the Communist Party, which everywhere form the base of the constitutional structure. It is transmitted through the tiers of councils as by a mighty conducting cable, working, as it passes, the machinery of government in village and city, district (rayon) and province (oblast) and republic. It is this conception of an upward stream of continuously generated power, through multiform mass organisation, to be transformed at the apex into a downward stream of authoritative laws and decrees and "directives ", that is indicated by its inventors by the term " democratic centralism ".

If we had to name the principal distinguishing feature in this complicated constitution, unlike any other known to political science, we should say its all-pervading multiformity. This was more than once claimed by Lenin as one of the principal

---

[1] Does not a similar " blind spot " exist in the visions of other constitutions given by the political scientists ? It is never easy to evaluate, in one generation after another, the transient mouldings of the constitutional structure represented by the constantly shifting private consultations between different ministers, different departments and different administrative officials; not only with each other, but also with the Bank of England and the powerful associations of capitalist employers, representing, as they claim, all industry and commerce ; and, even if only formally, with the leaders of the Trade Union and Cooperative Movements.

merits of Soviet Communism. The very multiformity of the soviet administration, he said, " is a guarantee of vitality : it is a pledge that the common and single aim will be successfully fulfilled. The more varied, the better and the richer be the common experience, the truer and swifter will be the achievements of socialism, the easier will be the practical work, and only practical work will be able to evolve the best methods and means of struggle." [1]

What is the cause or the explanation of this multiformity ? The answer is that the working constitution of the USSR has necessarily to cover a much greater proportion of human life than that of any capitalist state, where so much is left to competitive profit-making. This all-inclusiveness was indicated in the " Declaration of the Rights of the Labouring and Exploited Peoples ", drafted by Lenin himself,[2] with which the Fundamental Law of July 10, 1918, opened. This declaration announced that—

" 1. Russia is declared a republic of soviets of workers, soldiers and peasants' deputies. All central and local authority is vested in these soviets.

" 2. The Russian Soviet Republic is established on the basis of a free union of free nations, as a federation of national soviet republics.

" 3. Within the fundamental aim of suppressing all exploitation of man by man, of abolishing for ever the division of society into classes, of ruthlessly suppressing all exploiters, of bringing about the socialist organisation of society and the triumph of socialism in all countries, the Third All-Russian Congress of Soviets of workers, soldiers and peasants' deputies further decrees :

" (a) In order to establish the socialisation of land, private ownership of land is abolished ; all land is declared national property and is handed over to the labouring masses, without compensation, on the basis of an equitable division giving the right of use only.

---

[1] Quoted in Shvernik's speech in *The Ninth Trade Union Congress*, Moscow, 1933, p. 3.
[2] Lenin doubtless had in mind, in emphasising collectivism, the " Declaration of the Rights of Man and of the Citizen " adopted by the French National Assembly in 1789, with its emphasis on individualism.

" (*b*) All forests, underground mineral wealth, and waters of national importance, all live-stock and appurtenances, together with all model farms and agricultural enterprises, are proclaimed national property.

" (*c*) As the first step towards the complete transfer of factories, works, shops, mines, railways and other means of production and of transport to the ownership of the workers' and peasants' Soviet Republic, and in order to ensure the supremacy of the labouring masses over the exploiters, the Congress ratifies the soviet law on workers' control of industry, and that on the Supreme Economic Council." [1]

The second document of this kind, formally adopted by the Central Executive Committee of the newly formed Union of Soviet Socialist Republics in 1923, is more lengthy and may be read in the Appendix at the end of Part I. It was addressed, doubtless in recollection of the American Declaration of Independence, " to all governments and all peoples of the earth ". Its purpose was to announce to the world the formation of the new federal state. " From the first moment of their existence ", runs this grandiloquent announcement, " the soviet republics were united by the bonds of close cooperation and mutual assistance, which subsequently assumed the form of treaties of alliance. The power of the workers and peasants united them into a single unit, with common needs, in their struggle against the attacks of foreign capitalist states, and against the internal counter-revolutionary attacks on the soviet form of society. The solidarity of the labouring masses united them in their common task of establishing fraternal cooperation between the liberated peoples. Together they emerged from the victorious proletarian revolution, having overthrown the power of their landowners and capitalists. Together they passed through the dire experiences of intervention and blockade, and emerged triumphant. Together they started the enormous task of restoring the national economy, on the basis

[1] *Soviet Rule in Russia*, by W. R. Batsell, New York, 1929, p. 81. It was given in Molotov's speech to the Central Executive Committee (TSIK) on January 23, 1933, as reported in *Moscow Daily News*, January 29, 1933. Molotov expressly said that this Declaration of 1918 was " written by the hand of Lenin ". A French translation of this " Declaration of the Rights of the Toiling and Exploited People, ratified by the Third National Congress of Soviets ", will be found in *Une Législation communiste*, by Raoul Labry, Paris, 1920.

of the new economic structure of society, after it had passed through unprecedented calamities.

" Whilst rendering to one another constant fraternal assistance with all their strength and resources, they nevertheless for a long time remained separate states only united by treaties of alliance.

" The further development of their mutual relations and the requirements of the international position have now led them to combine into one united state."

In the following chapters we seek to describe all the various parts of this constitution as they have grown, during the past eighteen years, into the organic structure of the hundred and seventy millions of people inhabiting the largest continuous geographical area in the world, comprising one-sixth of the entire land-surface of the globe.[1]

---

[1] It is the invariable custom in the USSR to describe its area as one-sixth of the land-surface of the earth. In the League of Nations *Statistical Yearbook* the area of the USSR is given as 21,176,000 kilometres (of which 5,999,000 kilometres are in Europe). The earth's land-surface is there given as 132,520,000 kilometres, of which the USSR forms, accordingly, 15·981 per cent, or somewhat less than one-sixth (16·666 per cent), but much more than one-seventh (14·285 per cent). We do not know whether all the soviet islands in the Arctic Ocean are included in the League of Nations *Statistical Yearbook* estimate.

# CHAPTER II

## MAN AS A CITIZEN

In this chapter we deal with the part of the constitution of the USSR, the pyramid of soviets, which was enacted as the " fundamental law " of the new state, and has therefore been accepted by many commentators as if it were the whole of the constitution. How mistaken is this view, and to what serious errors in interpretation it leads, will appear in the following chapters.

## *The Origin of the Soviet System*

" The soviet system ", it has been well said, " was one of those innumerable creations of the human mind which seem to owe their existence to a fortunate historical accident. It has survived because it proved to be peculiarly well adapted to become the organ of that dictatorship of the workers which lies at the foundation of communist theory and practice." [1]

By the word soviet, which originally meant any kind of council, is now understood a council of delegates or deputies chosen by the workers employed in the several factories and other establishments in an industrial city or district ; or by the soldiers in the various units of an army ; or by the peasants of a village or agricultural district or community ; or by any combination of these constituent groups. Its most obvious difference from other political entities is that it avowedly excludes the

---

[1] *How the Soviets work*, by H. N. Brailsford, New York, 1927, p. 57. This admirable, unpretentious little book, together with its predecessor *The Russian Workers' Republic*, New York, 1920, by the same author—though more complete and erudite volumes are now available—still afford, in brief, the best pictures known to us of the life of the USSR.

representation of the capitalist employers, landowners, shopkeepers, and persons of no occupation, even if these are of the
same tribe, race or nationality, or are resident within the area
concerned. Soviets of this nature were spontaneously created
in May and June of 1905 at Ivanovo-Voznesensk and Kostroma
to conduct strikes of textile workers.[1] They seem to have been
invented on the spur of the moment, owing particularly to the
absence of any independent and trusted trade union. These
working-class organs did not confine themselves to the strikes, and
assumed some of the functions of the decrepit local government.
It was, however, the soviet formed in St. Petersburg in October
1905 that gave a lead to the rest of Russia. At its first meeting,
on October 13, 1905, " it was only partly representative, consisting as it did of the factories from only the Nevsky district. A
proclamation was issued in its name which said : We propose
that every factory and every trade should elect a delegate for
every hundred workers. The delegates of each factory shall
form the factory committee. The delegates of all the factories
shall form the General Workers' Committee of St. Petersburg." [2]
In the course of the next two months similar soviets sprang into
being in a score of other Russian cities, from Reval to Baku,
but their prompt suppression allowed no opportunity for any
national congress of soviets to be convened.

The summary suppression of the soviets of 1905 did not prevent their remaining in the minds of the Russian workers. When,
in February 1917, the tsarist régime fell, almost of its own
rottenness, the workers in the Petrograd factories at once spontaneously formed a soviet, which did not concern itself specially
with any strike, but discussed and voted on all matters of public
interest. This example was quickly followed by the workers of
Moscow and those of many other industrial cities. Presently

---

[1] " It was the greatest strike ever witnessed in Russia. . . . Thus it was
that the first soviet of workers' delegates in Russia was formed between May 15
and 18, 1905. For the first time the workers came forward as a class for themselves, and no longer under the influence of the ' democrats ' as they had been
from the time of Gapon " (*Brief History of Russia*, by M. N. Pokrovsky,
translated by D. S. Mirsky, London, 1934, vol. ii. pp. 153-154, 189-190).

[2] *Ibid.* p. 166. Details will be found in the Russian work *On the History of
Soviets of Workers' Deputies in 1905*, by P. Gorin, second edition, Moscow,
1930.

See also, for further details, *From Peter the Great to Lenin*, by S. P. Turin,
1935.

the Petrograd soviet invited all the other city soviets to send delegates to constitute a congress of soviets, which appointed a standing committee to sit and act between one congress meeting and another. Here, it would seem, might be the basis for a workers' government of the whole state. But it does not appear that this was immediately recognised as a possible development of what had been originally mere strike committees. The Bolshevik Party was nominally still working for the Party programme of 1903, which had never been revised, and which, whilst emphasising the full collectivism of its economic side, contemplated, on the political side, the substitution, for the tsarist autocracy, of nothing more novel than an extremely democratic parliamentary assembly.[1] Lenin, it is true, at once recognised the importance of the novel form of " soviets of workers' deputies " of 1905, in which he saw " new organs of people's power". At the Fourth Congress of the Russian Social Democratic Party, in April 1906, a resolution was adopted explaining that the soviets, in the process of struggle, became transformed from " pure strike organisations into organisations of *general revolutionary struggle* ", and represented the " embryo of revolutionary power ", dependent for " their strength and significance entirely upon the strength and success of *the uprising* ". They were, in fact, at first regarded, as Lenin expressed it as late as November 20, 1915, merely as " *organs of rebellion* " (*Works*, vol. xviii. p. 312). There seems, accordingly, some warrant for the suggestion of an acute German historian, that, whilst Lenin had long foreseen the necessity of transforming the bourgeois liberal revolution into a socialist revolution, and had at once recognised the soviets as the weapon for effecting this transformation, it was only in March 1917, on receiving in Switzerland the first authentic news of the revolution in Russia, " that

[1] This programme asserted that " the first and immediate task put before itself by the Russian Social Democratic Party is to overthrow the tsarist monarchy, and to create a democratic republic, whose constitution would guarantee the following :

" 1. The sovereignty of the people, *i.e.* the concentration of all supreme state power in the hands of a legislative assembly, consisting of the people's representatives, and forming one chamber.

" 2. Universal, equal and direct suffrage for all male and female citizens, twenty years old or over, at all elections to the legislative assembly and to the various local organs of self-government : the secret ballot at elections : the right of every voter to be elected to any representative institution : biennial parliaments : salaries to be paid to the people's representatives."

he (Lenin) made a fateful discovery. He became convinced that the system of Soldiers' and Workers' Councils—soviets—was the modern expression of the inevitable socialist-democratic revolution. . . . In the soviet Lenin recognised the existence, in a weak and elementary form, of an entirely new type of working-class government which could only be compared historically with the Paris Commune of 1871. His study of the soviet convinced Lenin that everything which Marx had said in his famous essay on the constitutional and political aspects of the Paris Commune applied with equal truth to the Russian soviet in 1917." [1]

This is why, from the moment of his arrival in Petrograd, Lenin came more and more to speak of the soviets, as not only a means of checking and controlling the Provisional Government, and not merely as the instrument for the approaching overthrow of that Government, but even, occasionally, as the necessary basis of the new political constitution. It seems, however, that, right down to the actual seizure of power in October 1917, Lenin apparently thought it better that the Bolshevik Party should not commit itself definitely against a democratic parliamentary system as the political instrument for the administration of the socialist state that he intended.[2] This, however, did not prevent the launching of the slogan " All Power to the Soviets ".

By October 1917 Lenin had become enthusiastic about the soviets not merely as an " organ of rebellion " or an instrument

[1] *Geschichte des Bolshevismus*, by Arthur Rosenberg, 1932, translated as *History of Bolshevism*, 1934, p. 87.
In the third of Lenin's " Letters from Afar ", dated March 11/24, 1917, he discussed the rôle of soviets as organs, not merely of rebellion, but of proletarian democracy, as " the government of the soviets of workers' deputies " (*Works*, vol. ii. of English edition, p. 35). In the " Fifth Letter " he summed up that the next stage of the revolution must be the transfer of the state power to a new government which " must be organised on the model of the Soviets of Workers' and Peasants' Deputies " (*ibid.* p. 62, and see also pp. 99, 123, 128, dated April 1917).
[2] It is interesting to notice that, in May 1917, when Lenin was instructed to prepare for printing " all the material at the disposal of the Central Committee relating to a revision of the Party Programme "—this material consisting mainly of Lenin's own draft of the proposed new programme—he left unaltered the demand for a single supreme legislative assembly, elected by universal direct suffrage and secret ballot, merely adding proportional representation and recall by a majority of electors. His changing opinion is indicated only by the proposal to prefix a declaration asserting that " all representative parliamentary institutions would gradually give place to soviets of the people's

of revolution but also as " a step forward in the development of
democracy " ; though the terms in which he describes them
indicate that he had at that time a very inadequate vision of the
gigantic edifice of government that was destined to be erected on
this basis.[1] Finally, when the uprising had practically achieved
success, and the Second All-Russian Congress of Soviets was
deliberating, actually within sound of the guns, it was decided, at
his instance, by a large majority, that the supreme power should
be vested, not in any parliamentary assembly, but in the All-
Russian Congress of Soviets itself. In the course of its continuous
session of twenty hours the same congress appointed a provisional " workers' and peasants' government ", to be known as
the Soviet of People's Commissars (Sovnarkom), to act under the
control of the congress and its central executive committee
(TSIK) ; adopted Lenin's thundering declarations as to the
immediate conclusion of peace ; the transfer of the nationalised
land to the peasantry in usufruct ; and the election of workers'
committees in all industrial establishments ; and incidentally

representatives (from various classes and professions, or from various localities),
functioning both as legislative and executive bodies ".

(The old programme of 1903, and Lenin's proposed amendments, " written
in May 1917 ", will be found in vol. xx. bk. i. of the English edition of Lenin's
*Works*, p. 353. The revision was not proceeded with until 1919.)

[1] Lenin's words are worth quoting. " The soviets ", he wrote, " are the
new state apparatus, which in the first place represents the armed force of the
workers and peasants, a force which is not divorced from the people, as was the
force of the old standing army. . . . Secondly, this apparatus represents a
connection with the masses, with the majority of the people, that is so intimate,
so indissoluble, so readily verifiable and renewable, that nothing like it was even
approached in the former state. Thirdly, this apparatus, because it is elective,
and its personnel is subject to recall in accordance with the will of the people
without any bureaucratic formalities, is far more democratic than were the
former ones. Fourthly, it represents a firm connection with the most diverse
occupations, thus facilitating all sorts of radical reforms without any bureaucracy. Fifthly, it represents a form of organisation of the vanguard, *i.e.* of the
most class-conscious, most energetic, more progressive section of the oppressed
classes of the workers and peasants, whereby the vanguard can elevate, educate
and lead in its train the whole gigantic mass of these classes which until now
have stood absolutely outside all political life, outside history. Sixthly, it
makes it possible to combine the advantages of parliamentarism with the
advantages of immediate and direct democracy, *i.e.* to unite, in persons of
elected representatives of the people, both legislative and executive functions.
Compared with bourgeois parliamentarism this is a step forward in the development of democracy which has an historical world significance " (" Will the Bolsheviks retain State Power ? " written during October 1917 and published in
the first and only number of the new issue of *Prosveshchenie*, a monthly
journal. Included in Lenin's *Works*, vol. xxi. bk. ii. pp. 26-27, of the English
edition).

decided that the title of the new state should be the Russian
Soviet Republic.[1]

During the next few months the Sovnarkom of People's
Commissars, under the presidency of Lenin, governed the country
with a high hand, struggling with a mass of executive business
and issuing innumerable decrees on small matters and on great.
Meanwhile some of the People's Commissars and various small
committees were discussing the different items, and drafting the
clauses, of a systematic constitution.[2] All these suggestions
needed to be adjusted and combined, a task which the Central
Executive Committee entrusted early in April 1918 to a drafting
commission of fifteen, among whom were Sverdlov and Stalin,
but not Lenin himself. When the Fifth All-Russian Congress of
Soviets assembled in July 1918, the draft so prepared was,
without prolonged debate or serious challenge, immediately
adopted as the " constitution or fundamental law " of the Russian
Socialist Federative Soviet Republic (RSFSR). With many
minor amendments this fundamental law has remained to this
day (1935) substantially unchanged ; and in 1923 its provisions
were, in the main, adopted for the Union of Soviet Socialist
Republics (USSR).

## The Base of the Pyramid

The stability and permanence of a pyramid depend essentially
upon the width and soundness of its base. In the USSR the
electorate is at once more widely extended and more peculiarly
restricted than in any other country ; with the net result that it
constitutes by far the largest voting body in the world, having at
least as high a proportion of electors to the adult population as
the United Kingdom or the United States of America, whilst in
the USSR a much higher percentage of that electorate are actual
voters at elections than in either of those countries. The right to
vote, and with it the right of eligibility for office, is avowedly
based on active participation in socially useful work of one or

[1] *Soviet Rule in Russia*, by W. R. Batsell, 1929, pp. 52-53 ; *The Soviet State*,
by B. W. Maxwell, 1934, p. 18 ; *History of the Russian Revolution*, by L. Trotsky,
vol. iii., 1933, pp. 297-337 ; *La Révolution russe*, par Fernand Grenard, Paris,
1933, chap. xii. ; *History of the Russian Revolution, 1917–1921*, by W. H.
Chamberlin, 1935.

[2] A summary of the proceedings of this period, taken mainly from *Istoria
sovetskoi Konstitutsii*, and *Osnovy sovetskoi Konstitutsii*, both by G. C. Gurvich,
is given in *Soviet Rule in Russia*, by W. R. Batsell, 1929, pp. 57-65.

other kind, by hand or by brain; although not excluding those who, by age or infirmity, have ceased to be capable of such work. Every man or woman in the USSR who is not included in one or other of the legally disqualified categories finds himself or herself, at the early age of eighteen,[1] automatically entitled to vote, and to be elected to any position. The student of other electoral systems will be struck by the inclusiveness of this franchise. Apart from sheer incapacity to get to the meeting, there are practically none of the usual impediments to the actual exercise of the vote. Unlike every other political system, Soviet Communism does not exclude from its electorate residents living within its borders merely because they are of alien birth or nationality.[2] There is no disqualification by sex or marriage; by illiteracy or inability to speak or read any particular language; or by religious belief or lack of religious belief. Nor is there any requirement of independent occupancy or period of residence, which elsewhere so often excludes the mass of actually serving soldiers and sailors, domestic servants, lodgers in other people's houses and residents in hotels, boarding-houses and institutions; together with the majority of the different kinds of "transients". There is no disfranchisement of persons actually serving in any kind of public employment, such as sometimes disqualifies soldiers, revenue officers, policemen, postmen or other recipients of government pay or pension. Nor is there any disqualification for pauperism or the receipt of public assistance of any kind; nor for bankruptcy; nor (except where the deprivation of political rights for a stated term forms part of a judicial sentence) even for conviction of a criminal offence; though persons in exile, or actually detained in penal institutions, are disqualified for the period of their exile or detention.[3]

[1] The minimum age qualifying for the electoral franchise in different countries ranges from 18 to 25. The only countries, besides the USSR, allowing people of 18 to vote (and then men only) are Turkey, Argentina and (if married) Mexico. The minimum age for eligibility for elective office ranges from 18 (USSR only) to as much as 30. " No country in the world has yet thought of denying the franchise on the grounds of old age " (*Theory and Practice of Modern Government*, by Herman Finer, 1932, vol. i. p. 415).

[2] See p. 26 for an instance of an American citizen being allowed to vote. Among the members elected in January 1935 to the Moscow City Soviet is an American citizen (a negro).

[3] The " Instructions for the Election of Soviets and Delegates to the Congresses ", dated October 1, 1934 (printed in *Izvestia*, October 5, 1934), provide expressly, in the final paragraph of Article 14, that foreign " workers " have the right to vote; and that foreign " specialists " may be granted the right to vote if they are loyal to the soviet power.

## The Categories of the " Deprived "

On the other hand, there is compiled and publicly posted, in each electoral area, a list of local residents belonging to certain specified classes from whom both the right to vote and eligibility for elected office, and equally for trade union and consumers' cooperative society membership, are statutorily withheld. " The following persons ", enacts the " Fundamental Law " of the RSFSR,[1] which has formed the model for the laws of all the constituent republics as well as for that of the federation (USSR), " have neither the right to vote nor the right to be elected, even if they are included within one of the above-mentioned categories [of persons entitled to the franchise] :

[1] Fundamental Law of the RSFSR, ratified by the Fifth Congress, July 10, 1918, fourth section, chap. lxiv.; *The Soviet State*, by B. W. Maxwell, 1934, pp. 31-34; *Soviet Rule in Russia*, by W. R. Batsell, 1929, p. 92. This article was slightly modified in wording in 1925 and 1929 (becoming chap. lxix.), as given in French in *URSS : La Fédération soviétique et ses républiques*, by André Pierre, Paris, 1932, p. 26, and in the *Annuaire diplomatique* for 1933 (Moscow, 1933).

The decided cases show the following as held to be " deprived " : " Farmers, stock-raisers and mechanics who employ labour to an extent that enlarges their business beyond that of a toiler ; agriculturists and stock-raisers who also have trade and industrial establishments such as mills or shops with motor equipment, or those who manage them with permanent or seasonal outside help ; persons who rent out complicated farm machinery and motor equipment ; owners of large fishing-vessels who rent them out ; persons who loan money on security of stock, machinery, etc. ; persons who charge a land rent which is considered by rayon tax commissions as exorbitant ; persons who rent orchards or vineyards for purposes of exploitation (exceptions may be made when the tax commission does not consider the rents high enough to impose the unified individual and agricultural tax) ; owners and renters of undertakings who distribute work to individuals to be done at home, or lease or sub-lease these undertakings to a second party ; private traders, jobbers and middlemen, renters and owners of undertakings of factory-plant dimensions ; former officers and officials of the White Armies and leaders of counter-revolutionary bands ; all employees and agents of the tsarist police, especially of the corps of gendarmes, and all persons who were directly or indirectly connected with the former police ; ministers and officials of the old régime ; members of the imperial family ; former members of the prison staffs ; leaders of the nobility ; members of the prosecuting staffs and those who have held commanding positions in disciplinary battalions ; former and present employees of religious cults ; persons who have been exiled in an administrative manner for the duration of their exile and those who have been deprived of the franchise by judicial process, and persons in penal institutions " (*The Soviet State*, by B. W. Maxwell, 1934, pp. 32-33).

The latest statement of the categories of the " deprived " is that contained in the "Instructions for the Election of Soviets and Delegates to the Congresses", dated October 1, 1934, and printed in *Izvestia*, October 5, 1934.

" (a) Persons employing hired labour for the sake of profit.

" (b) Persons living on income not derived from their own labour, such as interest on capital, income from industrial enterprise, landed property, etc.

" (c) Private business men and trade commercial agents.

" (d) Monks and clergymen of all religious denominations.

" (e) Employees and agents of the former police, or of the special gendarme corps and secret police, and members of the former ruling dynasty of Russia.

" (f) Persons legally recognised as mentally deranged or imbecile, as well as those under guardianship.

" (g) Persons convicted of ' infamous or mercenary crimes ' for a period fixed by judicial sentence, according to law."

The percentage of members of these " deprived " categories has varied greatly from time to time and from locality to locality. In ten districts (uezds) of Pensensky gubernia in 1922, in which there were 892,244 electors, it was found by a statistical enquiry that the total number of the " deprived " was 9186, or just over 1 per cent of the electorate. Among them were 2070 traders and middlemen, 1187 rentiers and 581 employers, making a total of 3838 (two-fifths of the total exclusions) " deprived " on grounds of economic class. There were 1814 clergy and 1420 former members of the Tsar's police, making a total of 3234 (one-third of the exclusions), disqualified on account of professional occupation. Finally there were 1750 excluded by judicial sentence for crime, and 564 for unsoundness of mind.[1] On the other hand, it is alleged that in Leningrad, Kiev and Moscow there used to be, ten years ago, more than 10 per cent of the electorate in the " deprived " categories.

Of the numbers formerly excluded from the suffrage, many have died and others have been enfranchised by successive acts of leniency. At first the disqualification applied equally to persons who had at any time belonged to these categories, but had ceased to do so, and also to the spouses and to the sons and daughters of such persons. But it has for some years been possible for the local electoral commissions to remove from the

---

[1] *Soviets, Congresses of Soviets and Ispolkoms, being Materials for the Study of the Soviet Administration* (Russian), Moscow, 1924, p. 7.

list of the disqualified the sons and daughters who could show
that they are engaged in socially useful work, and have completed
five years' service in it. Recent laws and election instructions
have now admitted to the franchise all persons otherwise qualified who have reached the age of eighteen since 1925. A similar
opportunity of escape may be given to older persons who have
been for five years occupied in productive and socially necessary
labour, and have proved their loyalty to the soviet power, at
the discretion of the local commission responsible for the management of the elections, by whom the list of disqualified local
residents is annually prepared.[1] This local discretion is said to
be now exercised with reasonable leniency, each person being
dealt with according to what are deemed his present merits in
the way of socially useful occupation.

The result is that the numbers disqualified have been steadily
declining, partly owing to statutory amendments, partly as a
consequence of the trend of decisions on cases made the subject of
appeal, and partly owing to the increasing leniency of the local
electoral commissions.[2] The latest statistics as to the " deprived " that we have seen relate to the soviet elections of
1931 and were stated to cover between 80 and 90 per cent of the
whole USSR. Of the total population over eighteen an average
of 3·9 per cent were disqualified, as compared with 4·9 per cent
at the elections of 1929. In the cities the fall had been from

---

[1] By the " Instructions for the Election of Soviets and Delegates to the
Congresses ", dated October 1, 1934 (printed in *Izvestia*, October 5, 1934), it is
made clear that former kulaks working in the gold and platinum industry may
be reinstated in their right to vote after three years of productive labour ; and
udarniki among them even earlier.

[2] A recent careful enquiry into decided cases " shows that . . . the following
classes have the franchise : fishermen and peasants who sell the product of their
toil in the open market : owners of all kinds of undertakings such as dairies,
etc., who do not employ outside labour or distribute work to individual households : mechanics who do not employ outside labour, or who employ only two
apprentices and one journeyman and sell the product of their own toil only on
the open market : persons who live on the winnings of state lotteries or interest
on state bonds or savings which are deposited in state savings banks : persons
who receive aid from friends and relatives abroad, or insurance benefits from
abroad : invalids of toil and war who are conducting small businesses : janitors,
bellringers and similar employees of churches, and, strange as it may seem,
members of [church] councils: members of the free professions who perform public
useful labour, and children of those who have been disfranchised but who have
come of age since 1925, who may have been as minors dependent on their parents
but who are not performing useful work, although they still may be living with
their parents " (*The Soviet State*, by B. W. Maxwell, 1934, p. 32).

8·5 to 4·9 per cent, whilst in the rural districts it was from 4·1 to 3·7 per cent.[1] No fewer than 28·4 per cent of those "deprived" in the cities, and 43·4 per cent of those "deprived" in the rural areas, were dependants over eighteen of "deprived" husbands or parents. The decline is continuing. Counting by families, it is doubtful whether the exclusions, apart from unsound mind or judicial sentence, now average, in the rural areas, as many as 1 per cent of the families ; or, in the cities, as many as 2 or 3 per cent of the families. "In 1934", declared Molotov to the Seventh All-Union Congress of Soviets, "there were 2·5 per cent disfranchised persons from among the entire adult population, which amounts to a little over two millions. Compare that with the total number of voters to the Soviets, which amounted last year to 91 million persons." Within another decade it is anticipated that practically all those "deprived" on grounds of present or former occupation, together with their sons and daughters, will, with one exception, have disappeared from the lists.[2] The net result of the enfranchisements and disqualifications is now a colossal and ever-rising electorate, which in 1935 reached 91 millions of men and women, being 55 per cent of the census population : an electorate of which some 85 per

[1] The following table shows how each category contributes to the total:

| Category | Percentage of Total Disqualifications | |
| --- | --- | --- |
| | In Cities | In Rural Areas |
| Employers . . . . | 5·3 | 22·2 |
| Unearned incomes . . | 8·3 | 5·9 |
| Traders . . . . | 39·9 | 10·1 |
| Clergy . . . . | 4·9 | 6·8 |
| Former police . . . | 3·2 | 4·7 |
| Unsound mind . . . | 1·2 | 1·5 |
| Judicial sentence . . . | 8·8 | 5·4 |
| Dependants of above over 18 . | 28·4 | 43·4 |
| | 100 | 100 |

From Report of Presidium of Central Executive Committee (TSIK) of All-Union Congress of Soviets, 1931 ; see summary by Lazare Teper, in *American Political Science Review*, October 1932.

[2] The exception is that of the priesthood. Whether or not the number of ministers of religion continues to shrink, we cannot anticipate that they will entirely disappear from the USSR, nor can we speculate as to the possibility of a change of soviet policy when all anxiety about the continuance of the soviet régime has passed away.

cent actually participates in the voting, and which increases at
the rate of more than two millions per annum.[1]

## The Village Meeting

Whilst the electoral franchise is the same in the village as in
the city, the methods of election necessarily differ. We take
the village meeting first, not only because it represents three-
quarters of the whole population of the USSR, but also because
it is typically Russian in its characteristics.

The village meeting represents probably the oldest constitutional form in Russia ; and, as in various other countries, it
antedates alike representative assemblies and statute law. Like
the English parish vestry meeting of the fifteenth to the nineteenth
centuries,[2] and its seventeenth-century offspring, the New England
town meeting, the village meeting in Russia cannot be shown
to have had any statutory origin. Whilst it has been legally
regulated and restricted from time to time, and also has had
additional functions assigned to it, there has never been any
precise or complete delimitation of its powers. At the height of
its authority, as the Mir, towards the close of the eighteenth
century, it could apparently discuss any subject of local interest,
apart from such as might be regarded as " political questions ".
It could declare the will of the village ; direct any action to be
taken within the village that the assembled villagers agreed upon ;
redistribute the holdings of land ; alter the conditions of tenure ;
extract pecuniary contributions from any or all of the villagers ;
and even decide that recalcitrant members should be exiled to
Siberia, a decision carried out by the tsarist police. On the
other hand, the Mir was always subject to arbitrary control
whenever the Tsar's Ministers chose to interfere. In particular,

[1] After each general election, the Central Executive Committee (TSIK)
publishes a report (Ossnovnye itogi raboty Pravitelstva). The latest totals (in
round numbers) are as under :

|      | Electorate | Voters | Percentage of Electorate |
|------|------------|--------|--------------------------|
| 1927 | 77,800,000 | 39,000,000 | 50·2 |
| 1929 | 81,300,000 | 51,600,000 | 63·5 |
| 1931 | 85,900,000 | 60,900,000 | 70·9 |
| 1934 | 91,000,000 | 77,000,000 | 85·0 |

[2] See The Parish and the County, by S. and B. Webb, 1907.

its members ran the risk of punishment by local official or judge for coming to "decisions not within the competency of the assembly". Moreover, by a ukase of December 24, 1905, any decision come to after the drinking of vodka might be declared to be invalid ! [1]

The village meeting in the USSR, now including all residents or occupiers male or female, over eighteen, not being among the "deprived" categories, has lost some of the powers of the Mir, but is still unfettered by any precise limitation of what it may do. It may, however, now discuss any matters relating to the government, central or local. We are here concerned only with its position as the base of the pyramid of soviets. Whilst the meeting can still be held as often as is desired, and may, in practice, discuss anything in which its members are interested, a new and important function (if it has not less than 300 inhabitants) is the triennial election of the village soviet (selosoviet). This is conducted by an independent electoral commission, the president of which is appointed for each electoral area by the presidium of the rayon. This president is assisted by ten members nominated by the village soviet itself. The commission fixes the date at which the election is to take place ; appoints a chairman for each meeting ; revises the existing list of persons excluded from the franchise, and causes this to be publicly posted in the village ; and sees to it that the electors are, five days in advance, personally notified to attend, as a quorum of 40 per cent of the electorate must be present to avoid an adjournment. The chairman of the meeting, who is supported by two assessors whom the meeting itself elects, announces the total number of electors in the electoral area and also the number present at the meeting, so as to demonstrate that there is the requisite quorum, and declares how many persons the meeting is called upon to elect. This is fixed by statute at one for each hundred of the population, with presumably one for the excess fraction over even hundreds—roughly equivalent to one for every fifty electors—but with a minimum of three members. The provision fixing a maximum of fifty members was omitted from the Election Instructions of 1931 and 1934. In addition, one-third of the number are to be elected as "candidates",

---

[1] The Mir was confined to heads of households belonging to the local community, and women were usually not permitted to participate. It could not appoint to public office any person neither owning property within its area, nor permanently resident there.

meaning substitutes or alternates. The electoral meeting has also to elect a revision or auditing committee distinct from the soviet itself. Men and women are then nominated (either by themselves or by their friends), sometimes without recommendation, but often in speeches of fluent if rude eloquence. Wherever there is an active cell or nucleus of the Communist Party, this will usually prepare a " slate " of recommended candidates, seldom confined to Party members ; usually putting these forward only for a certain proportion of the places to be filled, and often deliberately including ten or fifteen persons in excess of the places. At one stage it was officially ordered that, except in the districts practically covered by collective farms, there should be held, prior to the election meeting, a meeting of poor peasants (bednyaki) in order that they might prepare their own nominations. The vote is taken, as has been immemorially the custom, by show of hands, usually in a lengthy process of rejecting one by one those candidates whom the meeting does not support. Finally, the candidates who have received the votes of a majority of the meeting—the number having been thereby reduced down to the number of places to be filled—are put simultaneously to the vote, now usually unanimous, and declared by the chairman to be elected. Apparently the Russian peasant has never known such devices as " proportional representation ", the " second ballot ", or even any system of " exhaustive voting ". On the other hand, it seems to have always been assumed, and is now invariably the rule, that the electoral meeting, and indeed any electing or appointing body, is empowered at all times to " recall ", by its votes at a subsequent meeting at which 40 per cent of the electors form a quorum, any person whom it has elected, and to substitute for him, for the remainder of his term of office, as for anyone who dies or voluntarily resigns, any person from the list of those elected as " candidates " or substitutes.

### A Discussion Forum

At this point it is well to remember that these meetings of the village electors are summoned, not merely triennially to elect the selosoviets,[1] but also frequently throughout the three years,

---

[1] The election of the soviets at first took place annually. A few years ago it was directed to be held every two years. Now it is, in village, rayon, oblast and republic alike, triennial. The recall can be exercised at any time by the electing body.

often six or eight times within twelve months. These meetings are habitually, though not invariably, held in the evening, and are reported to be numerously attended, often by more than half the total electorate, and not infrequently by nearly as large a proportion of women as of men. The discussions range over the whole field of public interests, full expression being given to local desires. So many people wish to speak that the meeting is occasionally adjourned to a subsequent date. Resolutions may be passed for transmission to other authorities, but most of the speaking is directed towards impressing the audience, and especially those members who have been or who are likely to be elected to the soviet; and who are expected to be present to supply information and to answer questions. The village meeting may pass resolutions in the nature of suggestions or instructions on any subject whatsoever, addressed either to the village soviet or to any higher authority. Thus the meeting may voice the popular desire for a public bath-house or a village hall, or for the establishment or closing of the government vodka shop.[1] All this helps to make the discussion interesting. Whether or not the resolutions are carried out, they have always to be forwarded to the rayon soviet, and they may be sent to any other authorities concerned; and their repetition in the same or in other localities becomes influential.

Thus, it seems that the working constitution of the USSR—taking, for the moment, only that part of it which lives in the villages and is represented in the pyramid of soviets—is rooted in an almost inconceivable amount of public discussion, in literally a million or two of small local meetings in the course of each year. Whether or not the vociferous debaters at these innumerable meetings get all the attention they desire, the political student will note, not only the amount of political education, but also the sense of continuous participation in public administration that such discussions create.

We have not ourselves had the opportunity of attending any village election meetings; and we have found hardly any detailed description by eye-witnesses. But the following, by a competent

[1] We have been told that, in one case in which a resolution to close the vodka shop was carried, the women electors rallied at the next meeting and got it reversed—not because they approved of the men's drinking habits, but because they thought the closing would only lead to the men journeying, or sending their wives, to the nearest vodka shop 16 versts away!

American observer, gives what we believe to be a characteristic sketch.

"I was present", writes Karl Borders, "at the election at Maslov Kut [1] in 1926, and even voted (for all resident workers of the country above the age of eighteen are eligible to vote whether actually Russian citizens or not). . . . As soon as the registration of those present was verified, the meeting opened with a speech by an organiser from the county centre. The visitor urged the selection of good, honest workers to the soviet, and particularly asked that some women be elected. . . . A caucus had previously prepared a complete list of candidates for the thirty-six places on the soviet, and this slate was first offered *in toto* to the assembly. With very slight parley this overture was almost unanimously rejected, and it was decided to make nominations from the floor. . . . One by one the names were shouted up to the secretary, who entered them as candidates. Sometimes a few identifying remarks were made, but for the most part all of those suggested were well known and needed no such introduction. . . . The wish of the voter, as of old, is expressed by the raising of the hand. Nearly a hundred years ago the Tsar's government attempted to introduce the ballot-box in the village assemblies, but the peasants called it ' playing marbles ', and would have nothing to do with it. Again the soviets have simply used an ancient custom, and have not invented one for the occasion. It is true that this open method of voting makes clear the political persuasion of the voters. But in this instance it seemed to deter freedom of expression very little. The little bloc of richer peasants voted together as a man. The few women stood manfully by the members of their sex who were nominated. The whole yard turned against the candidates offered from the workers of the sovkhos, reflecting clearly the effects of the land dispute between the village and the government farm which had been hanging in the courts for many months. Hour after hour the process moved on in the Russian way. As in the old village Mir, discussion ran free and high. . . . At times a candidate was asked to mount the verandah so that he might be seen by all. One was pronounced too young. Others

---

[1] *Village Life under the Soviets*, by Karl Borders, New York, 1927, pp. 111-115. The author is an American graduate, who spent over a year in the USSR, after long experience of Russians in Chicago.

Maslov Kut is a village in the rayon of Archangelskoe in the North Caucasus, with a population of 3600 in 750 houses or courtyards.

were refused election on the basis of their indifferent records. The kulaks voted solidly against the women. My own political enthusiasm waned after two or three hours . . . but the villagers . . . used the rest of the mid-winter day to select the whole quota of candidates and the auditing commission, which by law must be chosen separately at the time of the general election. The final result showed that of the thirty-six members elected to the soviet three were women, five communists and remainder non-Party peasants of the village. . . . On the whole, one is impressed with the ' essential democracy ' of these . . . meetings, and is certainly not aware of any intimidation on the part of the authorities. There is an intimacy about the smaller unit of the village, with its old-entrenched families, that makes little political hoodwinking possible. . . . Certainly the great emphasis on getting out the vote does not argue for the widely believed fiction that the communists are afraid of the will of the peasant. The daily conduct of public business is the only form of politics in which the peasant is interested."

The total number of rural electoral areas electing selosoviets was officially stated in 1931 as 71,780 when the number of villages and hamlets was given as 599,890, so that, on an average, eight or nine of these were united in each selosoviet. The village in some parts of the USSR has usually only a few hundred inhabitants, whilst in other parts it runs up to as many as 10,000.[1]

[1] "The agricultural population of the USSR is settled mostly in villages. Isolated farms are found only in the northern and north-western regions of the Union; generally speaking, in the forest districts north and north-west of the blacksoil zone. Here the population is settled on isolated farms or in small villages. The average population of the rural villages in these regions is small, about 100 persons ; in some regions a little below (70 to 90) ; and in some regions a little above (120 to 150). But in the blacksoil area there are very few isolated farms, and villages are larger. Here the average size of a village is from 400 to 500 inhabitants. In Ukraine, however, the typical village has from 1000 to 2000, or from 2000 to 5000 and from 5000 to 10,000. Large villages are characteristic of all the blacksoil zone, particularly of the prairie regions. The villages in the regions of new colonisation, such as Western Siberia, often are large, with about 1000 to 2000 inhabitants. Of the new regions of colonisation, only in the dry steppes of central Asia are small villages typical, perhaps because here the native population is semi-nomadic, and crop raising is of secondary importance " (*Agricultural Russia and the Wheat Problem*, by Vladimir P. Timoshenko, Stanford University, California, 1932, pp. 33-41).

There is noticeable a tendency to take out of the areas of the village soviets (selosoviets) a considerable number of more or less urbanised or industrialised places, either as containing a large proportion of wage or salary earners, whether in isolated factories or workshops, motor-tractor stations, collective farms (kolkhosi) or state farms (sovkhosi), or as suburban districts destined to be more

But it may be doubted whether throughout this huge territory
there is any exact or complete enumeration of the separate
settlements or hamlets. Wherever a new settlement arises in a
previously unsettled part of the forest or the steppe, the inhabitants spontaneously begin meeting to discuss their local affairs,
and they may presently obtain recognition as a separate voting-
place for the selosoviet in the area of which they reside. Indeed,
it is the practice, as outlying hamlets grow up apart from the
main village, for the electoral commission itself spontaneously
to arrange for them to have separate meetings at which to elect
their own quota of the village soviet. For the RSFSR, which
has 53,000 village soviets, or five-sevenths of the whole, we have
been informed that the number of such separate " curia " or
" election points " was, in 1929, 275,000 as compared with 207,000
in 1927. The number increases annually with the constant
growth of population. Thus, it may be assumed that, for the
whole USSR, the total number of separate meetings simultaneously electing members of village soviets in 1935 must be
something like 400,000, plainly the most extensive electoral
machinery known to political science. The total number of
members elected to village soviets was stated in 1932 to have
increased from 1,112,000 in 1927 to 1,510,800 in 1932. In 1935
it will approach nearer to two millions : a colossal representation
of rural opinion by direct popular election !

### Administration by the Village Soviet

It is difficult to discover and to describe, in terms of British
and American constitutional usage, either the exact degree of
legal autonomy or the customary sphere of action of the 70,000
selosoviets of the USSR. We print as an appendix to this volume
a recent formulation of their statutory duties.[1] The Soviet

closely connected with the rapidly growing cities. These abstracted areas have
their own elected soviets, and choose their own delegates either directly to the
rayon soviet (ispolkom) or to the soviet of the neighbouring city, at the rate of
one for every sixty electors (equal to about 115 population).

[1] Decree of February 7, 1930, of USSR TSIK : included in RSFSR decree of
January 1, 1931, and in corresponding decrees of the other constituent republics.
For an able summary see *The Soviet State*, by B. W. Maxwell, 1934, pp. 83-99.

Note that a new election of the whole selosoviet is to be held (*a*) if more
than half the elected members have resigned or left the district, and there is an
insufficient number of " candidates " (substitutes) ; (*b*) if two-thirds of the

Government is not content that the village soviet should deal only with the questions of local or village importance ; and the newest decree insists that every selosoviet should consider and discuss also affairs of rayon, oblast, republic and even USSR importance. It is laid down, in a general way, that, within its territorial limits, the village soviet has control of the execution by all citizens and officials of the laws and instructions of the government. The village soviet is to prevent all interference with the execution of the measures taken by the central government, or with the policy from time to time prescribed. The village soviet may, within its wide competence under the statute, issue obligatory ordinance and impose administrative penalties and fines. It may establish village courts, with jurisdiction over disputes as to property or conditions of employment and over petty offences. And the village soviet is expressly directed to support the great voluntary association, elsewhere described, having for its object the widest possible participation of the whole population in the measures taken for national defence. But perhaps the most interesting enlargement of the sphere of the village soviet is the range of duties assigned to it in connection with the newly developed kolkhosi or collective farms within its area. The village soviet is to instruct, to supervise, to inspect, to audit, to insist on the fulfilment of all obligations, and on obedience to all laws and regulations. Moreover, it is equally part of the duty of the village soviet to keep an eye on the operations of the state manufacturing and trading departments in its locality, and on those of the consumers' cooperative societies, in order that the village customers may not be baulked in getting what they desire, and so failing to swell the receipts by their purchases.[1] Within the village itself, there is practically nothing

members request a new election ; (c) " if a selosoviet does not follow the proletarian class-policy, or if it includes in its membership people who do not adhere to the above policy, or if it has manifested a general inactivity " (decree of January 1, 1931).

[1] The People's Commissar of Finance for the RSFSR—the Chancellor of the Exchequer for a republic of more than a hundred million inhabitants, who happens to be a woman (Varvara Nikolaievna Yakovleva)—called attention, in her " Budget speech " to the Central Executive Committee of the RSFSR, to the financial deficit ; and insisted on the need, not for reductions in public expenditure, but for greater attention by the Government trading departments and the consumers' cooperatives to the desires of their customers, so as to increase the receipts. " The local soviets ", she declared, " *will have to watch more carefully the work of the trade organisation* " (*Moscow Daily News*, December 20, 1933).

that the soviet may not organise, regulate or provide at the public expense, from roads and water supplies, through club-houses and dance floors, up to schools, theatres and hospitals.

To the British reader, accustomed to the narrow range of work allowed to the parish or rural district council, the lengthy and varied catalogue of duties prescribed for the local authority of the village in the Russian steppe or Siberian forest will seem absurdly pretentious, all the more so when he is told by the soviet jurists that within the village the selosoviet is "sovereign"; meaning that nothing which it does requires the sanction of any higher authority before it is put in operation.[1]  This does not look as if the Soviet Government was afraid of the peasant, or dis-trustful of popular democracy !  Nor does the Government seem to grudge any amount of public expenditure on raising the stan-dard of life of the mass of the people.  Every public department at the republic capital, or at Moscow, is, in fact, genuinely eager to stir all the 70,000 village soviets into the utmost public activity.  Far from wanting to concentrate everything in the ministerial commissariats of the USSR, or even in those of the several constituent republics, the widest scope is given to each of the directly elected councils of the 70,000 villages between the Baltic and the Pacific, to do all it can for its own people. The view taken by the central authorities is that it is only by the widely dispersed efforts of the local bodies—in fact, only by the active participation of the people themselves in their incessant meetings which the village soviet obeys—that the frightful social backwardness of the countryside can be, *within this generation*, overcome.  The government of the USSR is perhaps unique among governments in this determined refusal to postpone rural social reform to a distant future.

It is, of course, not to be supposed that the immense cata-logue of duties decreed in 1930, and recited summarily in the appendix to this volume, are actually being performed by the village soviets.  Probably no selosoviet is dealing with all the matters prescribed, and the majority are doing but little.  What is significant is that they are all empowered to take any action they choose in all these directions ; and that they are being

---

[1] Or, as an American author puts it, " the village soviet is the highest governmental organ within a given territorial limit " (*The Soviet State*, by B. W. Maxwell, 1934, p. 89).

frequently exhorted to use this liberty to make their own decisions. Thus, what even the downtrodden Russian peasant is gradually acquiring is a sense of political freedom.

## Administrative Safeguards

The student of administration will ask how the Soviet Government can afford to allow this unprecedented freedom to 70,000 village councils, without such safeguards as prior enquiry and sanction, a statutory maximum for local expenditure and a limit to local taxation ; without even an official expert audit or the requirement of a report. And this in a country supposed to be enveloped in red tape ! The answer is to be found in the characteristic soviet constitution about to be described. The principle may be summed up as freedom to err, subject always to veto and reversal by superior authority. Any decision or action by the village soviet will be, when it is heard of, summarily vetoed and reversed whenever it has contravened any specific prescription or action by any higher authority. Moreover, any decision or action by the village soviet may be vetoed and reversed by any higher authority, such as the ispolkom, or executive committee of the rayon, and will certainly be so treated by the highest constitutional authority of the constituent republic or of the Soviet Union, if it is thought to be seriously inconsistent with, or inconveniently obstructive of, the policy laid down by superior authority. And there is a further safeguard. Although there may be, as yet, less than 100,000 cells of the Communist Party among the 400,000 village or hamlet separate meetings—there must, in fact, be a large number of " electoral points " at which there sits not even one member of the Party or a single Comsomol —yet the Party influence is widespread. Party guidance will not long be wanting if any village soviet shows signs of going astray ; and the advice and instruction given by inspector or other official, or even by a visitor who is a Party member, will, if unheeded, in due course be supported and enforced by superior authority. And although a large proportion of the 400,000 electoral meetings must be uncontrolled by the presence of even one Party member or Comsomol, it is significant of the character and popularity of the Party that, out of 59,797 village soviets at the 1931 election, 35,151 chose a Party member as elected

president, who is always a member of the local presidium, whilst
3242 others elected a Comsomol.[1]

### The Village Executive

Just as the Mir had its starosta, so the selosoviet has its
president, with other executive officers, in addition to the
secretary (who may or may not be a member of the soviet) whom
it appoints.  These executive officers, by a recent decree, are to
number one for every seventy-five households in areas of complete
collectivisation, and one for every fifty households in areas of
incomplete collectivisation.  They are appointed by the soviet
for a term of two or three months, the persons qualified as electors
and under fifty in the case of men, and under forty-five in the case
of women, being taken by rotation.  If they are members of a
kolkhos, or collective farm, or employed in any public office at a
wage or salary, they are entitled to take " time off " for their
public service under the selosoviet without loss of income.  Others
may receive pay for their term of service at a rate fixed by the
soviet ; a tax to cover the expense being levied upon all persons
in the village who are disqualified from holding the office, either
as being for one or other reason disfranchised or disqualified by
judicial sentence from holding positions in state institutions, or
else as awaiting trial for some criminal offence.  The duties of
these village executives are to keep order ; to protect public
property ; to keep open the highways and supervise sanitation ;
to report all violations of law, and to carry out the decisions of
the village courts ; as well as to perform any other functions that
the soviet may put upon them.

The soviet is required by decree to appoint besides its ispolkom,
or executive committee, also [2] a number of sections or committees
to deal with separate parts of the work, and it is strongly urged
to associate with its own members on these sections a large
proportion of the village residents.  This is in accordance with
the fundamental principle of Soviet Communism of ensuring the
participation in government of as large a proportion of the people
as possible.  It is left to the legislatures of the several constituent

---

[1] Report of Central Electoral Commission of the USSR on the elections to
the soviets in 1931, and composition of the organs of power, p. 9 (in Russian).

[2] In large villages, where the soviet consists of more than fifteen members,
it appoints a presidium instead of an ispolkom.

republics to prescribe exactly which sections must be appointed. In the RSFSR it is ordered that every selosoviet shall appoint at least seven sections, for agriculture, women's work and interests, education, cultural developments, finances, trade and cooperatives, and finally, for the general communal life. In the numerous settlements or hamlets apart from the main village and entitled to elect their own quotas to the village soviets, settlement sections are to be appointed. In addition, selosoviets appoint special committees to deal with particular collective farms, or to collect taxes, and also such officers as statisticians, harvest controllers, etc. Over and over again the decrees insist on the duty of the soviets to incite, persuade and press the apathetic toiling masses, and particularly the women, to take interest in public affairs, to join the sections, to attend the meetings, and to vote. Village and settlement meetings are to be held every few months. Three times a year must the soviet render an account of its stewardship to specially convened meetings which every elector is urged to attend.

At first the village soviets had no separate budget, and their receipts and expenditure formed part of the budget of the volost (now rayon).[1] Now each selosoviet is ordered to make its own budget in the way prescribed by the constituent republic. In the RSFSR it is ordered that the village budget must include the expenditure of the soviet on all its functions or duties ; and the mere recital of its liabilities for maintenance and repair of every

[1] As recently as 1925, in six important districts, only about 13 per cent of the selosoviets had their own budgets.

| District | Total Number of Selosoviets | Number of them having Budgets |
|---|---|---|
| North Caucasus  .    .    . | 1911 | 252 |
| Vladimirsk .    .    .    . | 1411 | 71 |
| Stalingradsk.    .    .    . | 926 | 13 |
| Briansk    .    .    .    . | 598 | 66 |
| German Volga    .    .    . | 287 | 287 |
| North Dvinsk    .    .    . | 236 | 18 |
|  | 5369 | 707 |

(*Local Soviet Apparatus* (in Russian), by A. Luzhin and M. Rezunov, of the Institute of Socialist Construction and Soviet Law, Moscow Communist Academy).

conceivable public concern within the village territory is a reminder to the soviet itself of how diverse those functions and duties actually are. Its revenues include the income derived from local public property and enterprises, the local taxes and dues collected within the village territory, including the agricultural tax and contributions to local revenues under various laws and agreements with the state, the constituent republic and the collective farms ; and lastly, the " self-assessments " levied by the village soviet itself. These latter require the majority decision of a special meeting at which not fewer than 50 per cent of the entire electorate must be present. The assessments most frequently levied are, we are informed, those for the building and maintenance of educational, health and cultural institutions ; the improvement of communications by roads ; veterinary and other agricultural institutions ; fire protection ; public baths and water supply from wells and ponds ; the provision of a new burial-ground ; and the employment of a village watchman. The information is that the number of village soviets actively undertaking local work, and the aggregate revenue and expenditure of the village soviets in the USSR, are both increasing annually by leaps and bounds.[1]

As is usual in the Soviet Union, it is the spirit in which the village is dealt with that is more important than the language of the laws. We cannot sum up our description of the organisation and activities of the village soviets better than by quoting at length from an address by M. I. Kalinin, the president of the Central Executive Committee (TSIK) of the USSR, to a conference of chairmen of village soviets of the western province of the RSFSR in 1933. " It is ", he declared, " no easy task to lead a village soviet. You must always remember that, on the one hand, a village soviet is a government organ, an organ represent-

---

[1] The activities of the village soviets were even stimulated in 1933 in a way which has not yet occurred to the British Minister responsible for village life. A contest for the best village soviet in the USSR was announced by the All-Union Central Executive Committee (TSIK), which set aside 50,000 roubles for premiums to be awarded to those adjudged the best. The winner of the first prize in this contest, which will last the whole of the year, will be that village soviet which gives the most active assistance to the state and collective farms ; which best organises labour in their establishments ; which works most energetically among individual peasants ; and whose farms lead in fulfilment of the spring sowing campaign and the harvest season.

As a further measure, a series of educational classes for presidents of village soviets were instituted in 1935 at several urban centres.

ing the government in the village ; and that, on the other hand, the village soviet is an elective organ, which represents the workers of the village. Upon you, as the chairmen of village soviets, hard and very complicated tasks devolve.

" Our biggest trouble is that many of our village soviets are inclined to resort primarily to administrative measures. A weak chairman of a village soviet tries to do everything through administrative orders ; and the weaker he is, the more frequently does he resort to this method. On the other hand, the more politically developed a chairman of a village soviet is, the more authoritative he is among the collective and individual farmers, the less frequently does he have to resort to administrative methods, to the employment of methods of coercion.

" Take the following example. A chairman of a village soviet issues an official order that on such and such a day all must appear to do some social work. Such orders are given by strong as well as by weak chairmen of village soviets. In both cases they appear on paper in the same form, signed by the respective chairmen. But in the case of a good chairman the piece of paper would merely inform all citizens when and where to meet. The good chairman would organise his men, and make all preparations in advance ; and his official order would merely announce a decision about which everybody already knows. The order merely gives the signal to start, to get into action. It is the same as a bugle call, or the commandant's order in the army. All units are given the signal to start, and the whole army moves as one man. That is how things work when the village soviet chairman knows his job. His order falls on the ears of a prepared audience. The people know in advance what has to be done, and they get together in order to do it.

" But how does it work out if the chairman is weak ? With a weak village soviet chairman, the order is the first step he takes. A notice is put up announcing the order ; and the citizens reading it begin to query what it is all about, and what good it will do.

"It is clear, therefore, that in the first case the order would be carried out promptly because the masses would be prepared for it by soviet methods, by Party methods. In the second in- stance nothing would have been done in advance, the announce- ment would be the first step taken, and naturally things would be done haphazardly ; stern orders would be necessary, and resort to administrative measures would be called for.

"This is the difference. The first method is the soviet method, which is distinguished from methods used in any bourgeois capitalist state. Our orders, our decrees, if we regard them externally, may resemble the orders of any municipal government of a capitalist country ; or the orders of some land administration in any part of the world. But preparatory work, the preparation of the people, that is the essence of soviet work. That work is performed at meetings of your communists, at Party meetings, at meetings of active citizens, and general meetings, and the like.

"I need not go into this at great length. You know about it very well. Herein lies the essence of our democracy. Our Soviet democracy is not expressed in our official edicts. Our Soviet democracy is expressed in broad activity, when every decision is worked out by the masses, criticised hundreds of times by the collective farmers, by the individual peasants, from every possible angle. Herein lies the difference and the intricacy of the work of leaders of village soviets." [1]

### The City Soviet [2]

The thousand or so urban communities naturally require governing authorities essentially different from those of the seventy-odd thousand areas into which the half a million or more rural villages, hamlets and settlements are grouped. But city soviets and village soviets have this in common, that they

[1] *Moscow Daily News*, weekly edition for September 22, 1933.

[2] The constitution and organisation of city government, with the decrees under which it works, are given, to name only works in English, in *The Soviet State*, by B. W. Maxwell, 1934, pp. 48-82 ; and *Soviet Rule in Russia*, by W. R. Batsell, 1929, pp. 663-687. Much additional information as to municipal administration will be found in *The Socialist Reconstruction of Moscow and other Cities in the USSR*, by L. M. Kaganovich, 1931, 125 pp., and *The Construction of the Subway and the Plan of the City of Moscow*, by the same, 1934, 58 pp. Detailed description of the municipal organisation of Moscow and Leningrad will be found at pp. 52-54.

The decree of January 20, 1933, defining the constitution and powers of the city soviets, together with a verbatim report of the discussion in the third session of the Central Executive Committee (TSIK), and a popular exposition of the terms of the decree, were published (in Russian) in a pamphlet entitled *The Tasks of the City Soviets in the Light of the New Decree*, by A. Kisselev, 64 pp., Moscow, 1933.

are the only governing bodies in the USSR that are directly elected by the inhabitants at large. Together they constitute the broad base of the pyramid by means of which man as a citizen expresses his will and his desires.

## The Method of Election

The city soviet is elected at relatively small open meetings of electors in much the same manner as the village soviet. But the electoral meetings in the thousand or so urban municipalities in the USSR differ essentially from the village meetings. When, in 1905, at whose suggestion we know not, the workmen employed in the principal industrial establishments in Leningrad almost simultaneously held meetings inside the several factories to choose their own delegates to form a workers' soviet for the conduct of the general strike, they invented a form of organisation—unprecedented in any country, and at that time extralegal—which has become, by reason of the dominating influence of the city proletariat, the foundation stone of Soviet Communism. These electoral meetings at the factories (to which similar meetings have been added for all kinds of offices and institutions, cultural as well as industrial) have, it will be seen, not a territorial but an occupational basis. The electors are summoned to attend, not as residents within the city or within a ward, precinct or parish of the city, but, irrespective of their place of residence, as persons employed in a particular factory or other institution. If the establishment is large, there are separate meetings for the several departments, branches, brigades or shifts.[1] If it is very small, it is grouped for purposes of meeting

---

[1] The great tractor factory at Stalingrad in 1932 had about 130 such electoral group meetings, which, it was said, were attended by more than 95 per cent of the total number employed.

On the other hand, Narkomindel (the government department at Moscow corresponding to the British Foreign Office) is grouped together for election meetings, not only with Gosbank (analogous to the Bank of England) and several other offices, but also with a watch-repairing artel, or industrial cooperative society.

Nevertheless, though small factories or institutions may be joined together for election meetings, each establishment chooses its own member or members of the soviet, without interference by the electors from other establishments at the same meeting. Thus, in the example cited above, the staff of Narkomindel, though not numerous enough to have a meeting of their own, chose by their own votes one member and one candidate for the city soviet, with two members and one candidate for the rayon soviet.

with other small establishments of similar character.  Those who work in the particular factory or institution, as soon as they become eighteen years of age, whatever their grade or salary or craft or sex—the manager, the technicians, the skilled artisans, the labourers, the factory doctors and nurses, the cleaners and the canteen cooks—all attend the same meeting.  It should be noted that this is not trade union representation.  All the employees are entitled to vote, and are eligible for election to the city soviet, irrespective of whether or not they are members of a trade union.  Factories and other establishments or institutions, urban in character, which are situated outside the city boundaries, elect their members to soviets as if they were within a city.[1]

Thus, in marked contrast with the constituencies of western Europe and America, the actual unit of the electorate in the urban communities of the USSR is everywhere a relatively small assembly of persons, usually a few hundreds and seldom exceed-

[1] In 1929 the number of cities was officially given as 704, whilst other industrial centres and workers' settlements treated as of urban type (such as isolated workshops and factories in rural areas and motor tractor stations) numbered 478; in 1931, 730 and 530 respectively.

It should be mentioned that there has been of recent years, especially in connection with the abolition of the former division called the Okrug, a marked tendency to include, as within the area of the city, a large number of surrounding villages, each with its own selosoviet, but sending delegates, not to the rayon council, but to the city soviet.  For instance, the area already assigned to the rapidly growing city Dnieprostroi (which may possibly take the name of Electropolis) with 270,000 population, rapidly doubling its numbers, is at present governed by 62 village councils, which elect representatives to the city council to sit with directly elected representatives of the workers in the urbanised part.  It is proposed eventually to have six city districts each with its own directly elected council, together with an indirectly elected council to control the whole area.  We learn, incidentally, that in the Middle Volga Krai in 1930 five cities, between 50,000 and 200,000 population, had had added to them no fewer than 229 selosoviets, comprising 1185 villages and hamlets, raising the aggregate population under the five city soviets from 513,000 to 950,000.

| Name of City | City Population (in thousands) | Village Population (in thousands) | Total | Number of Selosoviets | Number of Villages and Hamlets |
|---|---|---|---|---|---|
| Samara | 176 | 68 | 244 | 37 | 193 |
| Orenburg | 123 | 102 | 225 | 65 | 364 |
| Pensa | 92 | 106 | 198 | 52 | 278 |
| Ulyanovsk | 72 | 105 | 177 | 52 | 205 |
| Syzran | 50 | 55 | 105 | 27 | 145 |

(Article, " The Liquidation of Okrugs in the Middle Volga Krai ", in *Soviet Construction* (in Russian), Nos. 10, 11, 1930.)

ing one thousand, who, wherever they reside, or whatever their grade, or industrial status, or particular craft, or vocation, are, for the most part, *habitually meeting each other in daily work*. The employees of all establishments whether manufacturing or mining, distributive or transporting, educational or medical— the theatre and the concert-hall, the hospital and the university, the bank or the government office—are for electoral purposes dealt with in the same way.

The number of members to be elected was fixed by a statute of October 24, 1925, on a complicated scale, varying with the city population, in proportion to the number of electors entitled to attend each electoral meeting. Thus—taking only a few examples of the scale—in cities not exceeding 1000 in population each meeting was to elect one delegate for each fifteen electors entitled to be present; in cities not exceeding 10,000 in population one delegate for each fifty electors; in cities not exceeding 100,000 in population, one delegate for each one hundred and fifty electors; in Leningrad, one delegate for each 400 electors; and in Moscow, where there is so large a proportion of office workers, one delegate for each 400 factory workers and one for each 400 office workers.[1] These numbers are varied from election to election, as the population and the number of separate establishments increase, so as to keep down the number of elected persons to a reasonable figure.

It should be added that provision is made for taking separately the votes, and for hearing the views, of electors not attached to any factory, office or institution. These include the non-working invalids and the men and women superannuated or retired from age or infirmity; the home-keeping wives not working in factory, office or institution and others employed in domestic service; such independent workers, male or female, as "freelance" journalists or foreign newspaper correspondents;[2]

[1] Law of October 24, 1925; *The Soviet State*, by B. W. Maxwell, 1934, pp. 53-63; *Soviet Rule in Russia*, by W. R. Batsell, 1929, p. 672. By the RSFSR Election Instructions issued in October 1934 cities with between 400,000 and 450,000 inhabitants will to their city soviet elect one delegate to every 400 to 500 electors. In Moscow and Leningrad the city soviet will have one delegate for every 1500 electors.

[2] But of these only such whose attitude to the USSR " proves the fullest loyalty to the Soviet Government ". In such cases the franchise is conferred by decision of the city soviet and the higher election committee, whilst no entry is made with regard to the others in the published list of the disqualified (Election Instructions for RSFSR, 1931, p. 13).

authors, dramatists and musical composers not in salaried employment, independently working artists and scientific researchers of all kinds, together with such remnants of individual producers as the droshky drivers, shoeblacks and peddlars, casual washerwomen and dressmakers, etc. For all these, in each urban centre, many district meetings are held, often one in each street, having powers and functions identical with the meetings of citizens working in factories or institutions of any kind. In a great city these "non-organised" electors run into tens of thousands, and in Leningrad and Moscow even to hundreds of thousands, so that the electoral meetings summoned in order to hear their views and record their votes have to be held in all parts of the city, to the number of several hundreds.[1]

[1] Here is an interesting table, showing the statistics for the city of Leningrad of all these electors in their several categories, the number of members elected by them, and the proportions of Party and non-Party persons so elected :

MEMBERSHIP OF LENSOVIET AND RAYSOVIETS
(Deputies elected from non-organised population in 1930–1931)

| Groups of Population | Number of Electors | ELECTED | | | | | | | | | | Total Elected to both Lensoviet and Raysoviet |
| | | To the Lensoviet | | | | | To the Raysoviets | | | | | |
| | | Total | Men | Women | Party Cand. and Members | Non-Party | Total | Men | Women | Party Cand. and Members | Non-Party | |
| --- | --- | --- | --- | --- | --- | --- | --- | --- | --- | --- | --- | --- |
| Housewives . | 222,396 | 251 | 56 | 195 | 120 | 131 | 516 | 122 | 394 | 230 | 286 | 767 |
| Independent artisans . | 801 | 3 | 3 | .. | 3 | .. | 5 | 4 | 1 | 2 | 3 | 8 |
| Peasants . | 720 | .. | .. | .. | .. | .. | 1 | 1 | .. | 1 | .. | 1 |
| Invalids . | 21,949 | 30 | 26 | 4 | 23 | 7 | 46 | 35 | 11 | 24 | 22 | 76 |
| Members of artels (industrial co-operative). | 55,183 | 89 | 81 | 8 | 84 | 5 | 205 | 142 | 63 | 141 | 64 | 294 |
| Others . | 2,020 | .. | .. | .. | .. | .. | 9 | 4 | 5 | 8 | 7 | 9 |
| TOTAL . | 303,069 | 373 | 166 | 207 | 230 | 143 | 782 | 308 | 474 | 405 | 377 | 1155 |

(*Gorodskoy Soviet Na Novom Etape* (The New Stage of the City Soviet) (in Russian), Moscow, 1932, p. 126.)

Lensoviet means the municipal authority for the whole city of Leningrad ; raysoviet that for each of the eight wards or boroughs into which the city is divided. Note the very large number of housewives not occupied as wage-earners.

Another table supplied to the authors by the President of the Leningrad City

## The Election Procedure

There are, it must be remembered, in the USSR no political parties, using the term in the sense in which it is understood in all other countries, and consequently there is none of the usual party activity in the elections to the soviets. Nominations of individual candidates are made orally, either by themselves or by friends or admirers, there being always considerable competition and usually not a little personal rivalry. There is, of course, almost invariably a " slate " or list of candidates recommended by the local members of the Companionship or Order styled the Communist Party, often including non-Party persons, and usually covering only a certain proportion of the vacancies ; and there may be other lists.

What is not usually understood by foreign observers is that there is, at each election, not one election meeting, but (as often in the village elections) several successive election meetings for the same electoral unit, at which candidates are nominated, discussed and either successively eliminated or carried forward to the final meeting when the last vote is taken. This, the only decisive vote, is usually unanimous (or more strictly, what in England is called *nemine contradicente*), a fact which has often led to the inference that there has been no real exercise of choice by the electorate. On the contrary, the procedure is one of elaborate preliminary sifting of the nominations by various, often many,

Soviet gives particulars as to the voters in each of the rayon soviets at the 1931 election :

| RAYONS | Number of Electors who have taken part in the Election | In Them | | | | | |
|---|---|---|---|---|---|---|---|
| | | Men | Women | Work-men | Clerks | House-wives | Others |
| Vassileostrovsky | 111,085 | 60,201 | 50,884 | 57,332 | 20,167 | 21,126 | 12,460 |
| Volodarsky . | 108,419 | 64,448 | 43,971 | 64,231 | 22,997 | 16,006 | 5,185 |
| Vyborgsky . | 130,012 | 80,793 | 49,219 | 87,569 | 12,929 | 11,321 | 18,193 |
| Moskovsky . | 83,904 | 49,440 | 34,464 | 59,787 | 10,786 | 7,818 | 5,513 |
| Narvsky . . | 141,449 | 89,451 | 51,998 | 102,055 | 24,630 | 10,659 | 4,105 |
| Oktyabr'sky . | 117,300 | 57,230 | 60,070 | 32,094 | 26,628 | 26,203 | 32,375 |
| Petrogradsky . | 122,536 | 53,334 | 69,202 | 55,983 | 22,355 | 29,502 | 14,696 |
| Smol'ninsky . | 258,445 | 130,974 | 127,471 | 82,829 | 98,755 | 53,692 | 23,169 |
| | 1,073,150 | 585,871 | 487,279 | 541,880 | 239,247 | 176,327 | 115,696 |

successive votes at the previous meetings, by which the less popular candidates have been eliminated.

### The Electors' Instructions

There is, moreover, another function of the successive election meetings of the electors of each electoral unit, which is regarded, as we think, rightly, as of no less importance than the actual choice of members of the soviet. This is the passing of resolutions in the nature of instructions—perhaps we should say suggestions —to the deputies or delegates to be elected, or to the soviet as a whole, or even to higher authorities. These resolutions may be proposed by any elector, but they are usually put forward by groups of electors and often by those representing particular factories or institutions. In the large cities the aggregate number of such resolutions passed at one or other of the innumerable meetings of electors runs into thousands, the subjects being of extreme diversity. They vary in importance from the most trivial details of administration, and the smallest of improvements, up to issues of municipal policy of far-reaching character. Apparently nothing is formally excluded, but we imagine that anything " counter-revolutionary " or fundamentally in opposition to the communist régime would not be risked by any opponent, or if risked, would not be tolerated by the meeting. We are told that factories vie with each other as to which can bring forward the largest number of valuable suggestions, or of suggestions that will secure the support of a majority of the meeting. We are told also that the resolutions adopted, and even those largely supported though not adopted, are carefully noted by the authorities ; and that those which are most frequently moved or adopted usually lead to appropriate action being taken, whether by the soviet or by some other authority, to remedy what is recognised as a widely felt grievance, or to meet what has been shown to be a popular desire.

It is hard for the foreigner to realise how extensive is the use made of this opportunity of the electorate to tell their delegates what they are to do ! Fortunately the Secretary of the Moscow Committee of the Communist Party gave a lengthy analysis of these instructions. " During the elections to the Moscow Soviet in 1931," declared L. M. Kaganovich, " no fewer than one hundred thousand additions to the instructions were put forward . . . [their subjects being] housing and city enterprises, 10 per cent; city transport, 11 per cent; education, 16 per cent; food supply, 18 per cent. . . . The main demands were : (1) Break up the housing trusts into cooperatives (276 enterprises, 290,000 electors); (2) eradicate illiteracy (90 large enterprises); (3) introduce polytechnical methods in all the schools (3 large enterprises); (4) enlarge the number of closed retail stores (595 enterprises, 400,000 electors); (5) improve the quality of bread (313 enterprises); (6) increase the number of hospitals (210 enterprises); (7) goods transport to work at night (80 large enterprises); (8) the organisation of means of transport for workers and employees, for the delivery of fuel, and for the service of the population generally (80 enterprises); (9) facilitate exchanges between workers employed in similar enterprises with the purpose of bringing the places of living of the workers nearer to their places of work. *Most of these suggestions have already been carried out.*" [1]

There is, however, throughout the whole proceedings, and, as it seems, in all the multitudinous speeches, no formulation of opposing or competing programmes, to which the candidates proclaim allegiance; but only a common profession of desire for efficiency in the building up of the socialist state, possibly with emphasis on the achievements or shortcomings of particular departments, and sometimes on the candidate's own qualifications

[1] *The Socialist Reconstruction of Moscow and the other Cities in the USSR*, by L. M. Kaganovich, Moscow, 1932, pp. 78-81. The same speech also specified a dozen of the concrete demands made at the same election. The first two of these were as follows : " (1) the public baths to work on the uninterrupted work system from 9 A.M. to 9 P.M.; establish a children's day at the baths; build special baths for children; instal mechanical laundries at the baths, so that the bather's clothes may be washed while he is bathing. (2) The construction of new tramway routes; at each tramway stop a strict schedule to be displayed of the movements on that route; express tram routes from the outskirts to the centre without stop; children under fifteen to be permitted to enter the cars from the front platform; double-deck buses to be introduced " (*ibid.* p. 79).

It is to be noted that the village meetings are equally prolific of instructions or suggestions. A report embracing a large number of village meetings throughout the RSFSR, excluding Moscow and Leningrad, during the election campaign of 1931, and those succeeding it during the ensuing two years, down to January 1, 1933, shows that these meetings sent up 26,000 concrete demands or proposals. Out of these, it is reported that more than 17,000, being about 60 per cent, were more or less carried into effect (" Mass Work of the Soviets in the Third and Fourth Years of the First Five-Year Plan " (in Russian), pp. 25-26, by the accounting information department under the presidium of the Central Executive Committee (VTSIK) of the RSFSR).

for office or personal predilections.  In this respect, the soviet contests seem to resemble the British and American electioneering of primitive times, before the development of the party system ; a state of things still lingering in Great Britain in nearly all the country parishes, many of the urban or rural districts and some of the smaller municipalities, which the national party organisations have not yet reached or from which they have been deliberately excluded.  What is remarkable in the soviet elections, in the absence of what Britain and America mean by party strife, is the width of public interest that they excite, the amount of discussion that takes place, and the very high percentage of the electorate that records its vote.  We are told, for instance, that in the USSR there is never such a thing as an uncontested election, either for the village or the city soviets.[1]

### A Moscow Election

We may cite, as an outstanding example of these soviet elections—doubtless an extreme instance, not necessarily typical of the smaller cities—that of the choice of the Moscow City Soviet and of its eight rayon soviets in 1931.  There were 2542 members (or substitutes in case of absence)[2] to be elected to the governing bodies of this city of some three million inhabitants.  The total number of men and women more or less formally nominated is not recorded, but they evidently numbered many thousands.  The percentage of votes cast to the total electorate

[1] British readers will be aware that in the United Kingdom a large majority of the elections for parish councils are uncontested ; of the elections of rural district councils a considerable proportion are always uncontested ; of those for urban district councils many are uncontested.  The same is true of the elections for the town councils in a considerable number of wards in the municipal boroughs, and of those for the county councils in most of the rural county districts, as well as in many of the electoral areas in London for county and metropolitan borough councils.  Even for the House of Commons there are always a number of constituencies in which the election is uncontested.  Such an absence of the opportunity of " participation " would be considered in the USSR to be gravely " undemocratic ", as well as socially injurious.

[2] It is customary for the electors to elect, especially to bodies of importance, not merely the prescribed number of members, but also a certain number of substitutes or alternates, usually termed " candidates " (not exceeding one-third of the number of members), who may automatically be appointed as members in place of members disabled or prevented from attendance.  Such substitutes or alternates are entitled to attend the meetings of the elected body as guests, and even to obtain their expenses of travelling to the place of meeting, although they cannot vote.  They may be consulted and give advice, and they may even be allowed to volunteer their opinions.

is given as 94·1, which we should take the liberty of calling an incredible figure, if it were calculated as it would be in Britain or America.[1] What is more interesting is the detailed description of the efforts made both to educate the electors to and induce them to vote. The city evidently resembled, during several weeks, a British city in the last days of a hotly contested parliamentary election. There was the same elaborate display of printed and illustrated posters. There were flashing electric signs and illuminated statuary groups in plaster emphasising particular slogans. Besides the innumerable small meetings in the factories and institutions of all kinds, there were many large meetings in all parts of the city, open to all comers, at which speeches were made by candidates and other " spellbinders ". The achievements and projects of the various departments of the municipal administration were described. The extensive shortcomings and patent errors were usually not explained away but frankly admitted and criticised. Questions were answered and complaints noted. There were processions through the streets, with banners and bands. In every factory or workshop, every school or college, every hospital or institution of any kind, repeated personal appeals were made to every elector to cast his vote. Foreign residents, we are told, asked with amazement why so much trouble was taken, and so much expense incurred, when no party issues were at stake, no party feeling was involved and no party gain could be made. The answer was that Soviet

[1] Explanations of such an apparently impossible percentage of voters to electorate may be found in the fact that there is, under Soviet Communism, as already explained, no such obstacle to universal voting as a register of electors always more or less " stale ". In the United Kingdom no one can vote at an election whose name is not included in a register now made up only once a year, on the basis of the completion of three months' residence at a specified address, and the arrival of the elector's twenty-first birthday, both prior to a fixed date, which may actually prove to be seventeen months previous to the election day ! A large percentage of the registered electors are always found to have died or removed from the district, whilst newcomers and persons who have newly reached the qualifying age cannot vote. In the United States, although the method of compiling the register is different from that in the United Kingdom, the effect, in preventing a large proportion of those over twenty-one from voting, is substantially similar. In the USSR the man or woman reaching eighteen on the day of the election, and actually working on that day in the factory or institution, can at once vote ; whilst those who have died or removed do not clog the electorate, or affect the percentage of actual voters to the electorate.

It is reported that the average percentage of voters to the electorate, in all the cities of the USSR, was 84. In the several constituent republics the percentage varied between 70·9 in that of Uzbekistan and 90·6 in the Ukraine.

Communism was based on universal participation in public administration—participation by intelligent understanding of the whole function of the state, in which the casting of a vote for this candidate or that, according to personal preference, was but the final and conclusive act. " Such ", it was declared, " was soviet democracy, then in its fourteenth year. How much more real ", it was asserted, " than parliamentary democracy in other lands ". In the end, out of the 2542 members or substitutes elected, either to the city soviet or to the rayon soviets, it was reported that 604 were women ; 358 were doctors, engineers or clerical workers ; and the rest, about 1400, were manual workers. Just about two-thirds of the total were members, or candidates for membership, of the Communist Party or of the League of Communist Youth (Comsomols) ; whilst about one-third were " non-Party ", that is to say, unconnected with this dominant Order.[1]

It is, of course, not denied that the members of the Communist Party, together with its probationary members (called candidates), and the League of Communist Youth (Comsomols), make up the bulk of the " activists ", to whose zeal and exertions the " liveliness " of the elections is due. At Moscow in 1931 it was they who saw to it that two-thirds of all the candidates who survived to the final votes belonged to the all-powerful communist organisation, and it was doubtless to their special efforts that these nominees owed their success. But it was evidently by intention that room was left for a substantial minority of " non-Party " candidates to be elected.[2] The membership of the soviets is practically never wholly composed of docile adherents of the government. There are, indeed, constantly recurring complaints of the extent to which disaffected persons, or even " counter-revolutionaries ", find their way into these councils, especially the rural soviets, to such an extent as even to impair their efficiency in " building up the socialist state ". But though such persons may become candidates, may canvass quietly for votes among their friends, and may even secure

[1] Summarised from article on " The Soviet Elections " by D. Zaslavsky (of Moscow) in *International Press Correspondence*, 1931, pp. 90-91.

[2] The statistical table in the footnote to p. 40 shows that, in the Leningrad election in 1930, slightly more than one-half of the members elected by the " non-organised " electors (namely, those not voting at the factories or other establishments) were Party members.

election, they do not, in their candidatures, stand as opponents of the established order of things, or proclaim their preference for any contrary policy. When—as occasionally happens even in the cities, and more frequently than not in the rural soviets [1] —they even find themselves in a majority, they may hang back and cause trouble, leading often to their partial elimination at a subsequent election.

We add to the foregoing description an account of a previous Moscow election as seen from a textile factory, and of the procedure of electing its delegates to the Moscow City and rayon soviets, by an experienced British publicist who had more than once visited the USSR. This investigation took place in 1926 prior to the Five-Year Plan; at a time of the New Economic Policy, when many of the workers were being sweated by small profit-making employers and the Labour Exchanges were busy trying to place demobilised Red Army men and others who had failed, during this partial reversion to private enterprise, to get work. " On the walls of the factory when I visited it, some days before the actual election, two lists of candidates had been posted, who sought election to the Moscow City Soviet, and to the less important rayon [ward] soviet. There were also shorter lists of ' substitutes ' who would take the places of the elected members in case of death or prolonged absence on other duties. The factory had the right to return one delegate for each 600 of its workers ; its allowance was, in fact, fourteen members. The

---

[1] The total number of members of the Communist Party in the village soviets was stated in a report to amount in 1932 to no more than 15 per cent (225,582 out of a total of 1,510,800), and this was an increase over the 9 per cent at which it stood in 1927 (116,774 out of 1,112,000). In 1935 they numbered 18·9 per cent (236,853 out of a total of 1,252,134).

In the city soviets, of which there now are over one thousand, there were reported to be 166,900 members in 1932 as compared with 122,572 in 1927. Among these the proportion of members of the Communist Party was just upon one-half ; their number having risen in the five years from 54,927 to 82,952. Rather more than two-fifths of these various totals were reported to be manual working wage-earners, the remaining being mostly clerical employees of various grades, or engineers and other technicians, with a few doctors, journalists and lawyers. In 1935 the proportions of Party members and Comsomols in the city soviets were provisionally given as 43·1 per cent and 11·2 per cent respectively.

It should be added that women are now members of nearly every soviet, whether rural or urban, to the aggregate number, as it was officially reported in 1932, of 316,690 (as compared with 151,298 in 1927), being 21 per cent of the total membership (as compared with less than 14 per cent in 1927). In very many cases women are elected to the presidency of the soviet.

singularity of this list was that it contained fifteen names. At
their head stood Lenin. He had been their member while he
lived, and they still paid to his memory this touching homage.
They would have laughed unpleasantly at the orthodox conception of immortality but for them the dead hero still lived in his
works, and in the hearts of his followers. I thought of the
Greek fishermen of the Aegean isles, who will hail one another,
after a storm, with the traditional greeting ' Alexander lives and
reigns '. After Lenin's name came that of Rykov, his successor
as chairman of the Council of Commissars (the Russian cabinet).
This factory had been the pioneer in the revolutionary struggle,
and it claimed the honour of returning the active head of the
Soviet administration as its senior member. The remaining
names were all those of workers or former workers in the factory.
Seven of the fourteen were, as the list showed, members of the
Communist Party ; one was a member of the Communist League
of Youth, and the rest were ' non-Party '. Three of the fourteen
were women.

" Here, then, was the official list, containing a bare majority of
professed Communists presented to the electors for their ratification. There was no alternative list. By what method had it
been compiled ? The first step is that each member of last year's
soviet (the elections are annual) [1] who desires to stand again,
presents a report on his or her activity. A meeting then takes
place between the Works Council [this is the factory committee]
and the 300 delegates, who represent small groups of the various
categories of workers. At this meeting names are put forward,
and there often follows a thorough discussion of the record and
reputation of each. There is usually a vote on each name. In
this way the first draft of the official list is ' compiled '.under the
supervision of the Works Council [factory committee]. It then
goes before separate meetings of the various crafts [query work-
shops] in the factory, and at these it may be modified. In its
final form it is a selection presented by the Works Council to a
general meeting of all the workers in the factory. At this general
meeting it is still theoretically possible to oppose any name in
the list and to put forward another name to replace it ; but of
this right the electors rarely avail themselves, for the good reason
that the preliminary procedure by which the list is prepared does

[1] Now triennial (1935).

furnish some guarantee that it corresponds, on the whole, with the wishes of the electors.  They are not consciously settling big issues of national policy, nor are they even directly choosing legislators.  They are choosing average, trustworthy citizens, who will see that the administrative machine of the city runs efficiently for the common good of the working population.  The atmosphere of the election and, indeed, of debates in the soviets themselves, is strangely remote from ' politics ' as western democracies conceive them.  A big family, animated by a single purpose, sits down on these occasions to administer its common property.

" The factory produces its own newspaper, *The Spur*, which appears fortnightly and is written entirely by workers under the direction of its branch of the Communist Party.  Its contents during the election week are, perhaps, as good a sample as one could find of soviet politics, as the average town worker sees them.

" The number opens with a leading article in which every elector is summoned to take part in the elections. . . . ' Comrades, remember Il'ych's [Lenin's] watchword.  The time is ripe for every servant-girl, while she is still in the kitchen, to learn how to govern Russia.  The tasks before us are the practical work of building houses and increasing our output.  We have many a hardship still to endure, and Russia needs you all.  If you feel yourselves ill-off, then elect active members of the soviet to better your case.  You are yourselves responsible for your own lot.  Don't leave the work to others.  Be bold, choose conscientious men who will carry out Lenin's ideas, and then be sure that your hardships will vanish and poverty disappear.'

" The heavy, business-like part of the election literature consisted in the official report of the Communist Party on the year's work of the Moscow Soviet.  It claimed that the Party had fulfilled its promises.  It had increased the output of industry, bettered the conditions of the workers, and kept alive the unity between workers and peasants. . . .

" The peroration of this very practical document boasted that these results were due to the participation of the ' broad masses ' (a characteristic Russian phrase) in the work of government, ' a thing possible only under the soviet system '.

" The similar report on the work of the Ward Soviet was on much the same lines.  It contained one reference, however, to the aesthetic side of life—trees had been planted to beautify the streets. It noted considerable activity in summoning small private employers (kustari) for breaches of the labour code. The rest of the election news consisted of the reports of some of the retiring members of the soviet. . . .

" ' No. 1 [a woman] was responsible for inspecting the houses of the old-age pensioners. She got their daily ration of white bread increased by half a pound, and saw that better meals were provided for the consumptives. She was distressed by conditions at the Labour Exchange ; many demobilized Red Army men had failed for two years to get work ; some workers fainted while waiting at the Exchange ; the present manager is not the right man for this post.

" ' No. 2 [a man] occupied himself with education, and stressed his insistence that preference should always be given to the children of the workers.

" ' No. 3 [a woman] claims that, as the result of her inspection of eighteen schools, the expenditure on food, per month, per child was raised from fifteen to twenty-three roubles.

" ' No. 4 [a man] worked in the health section. He advocated a dispensary for venereal diseases and an increase in the number of beds both for adults and children. He was responsible for sending sick children to Yalta in the Crimea, and got an additional dispensary opened for the tuberculous, making the thirteenth in our district. He got a workshop for winter use built in the home for children addicted to drugs (these pitiable little wretches are mainly orphans of the civil war and the famine, who for a time ran wild in the towns). He also insisted that less monotonous work (" fancy " sewing instead of making sacks) should be provided for the women who are being reclaimed in the home for prostitutes.

" ' No. 5 [a woman] insisted that bed-linen should be changed fortnightly instead of monthly in the eye hospital.

" ' No. 6 [a man] found many cases in small private workshops in which lads under eighteen were working over eight hours ; the employers were prosecuted.

" ' No. 7 [a woman] inspected five factories and found one in which there was no hospital. The workers had to walk seven versts to the nearest. This was remedied.' " [1]

[1] *How the Soviets Work*, by H. N. Brailsford, 1927, pp. 34-40.

## The Organisation of the City Soviet

The method of election adopted from the start for the city soviet—the separate choice of one or more delegates by the staff of each enterprise—even the smallest—has given that body a membership and a character entirely different from those of the municipal councils of Great Britain or the United States. In any considerable city of the USSR the city soviet is composed of an unwieldy mass of men and women delegates without fixed total, the numbers increasing at each election with the perpetual multiplication of establishments of every kind. With the addition of 33 per cent of candidates or substitutes, who are entitled to attend, the plenum of the city soviet runs into hundreds, and in the cases of Moscow and Leningrad to more than two thousand. Such a body has necessarily to entrust its powers and functions to an executive committee, which, again, is too large for executive action, and therefore leaves the daily work to a presidium of something like a dozen members, in whom the day-by-day administration of the city resides, and who give their whole time and attention to their municipal duties.

On the other hand, again in contrast with the western municipalities, much less use is made in the cities of the USSR of that trained, permanent and salaried staff by whom in most other countries the actual work of municipal administration is conducted. In the absence of such a staff, which is only now beginning to appear in the USSR, the city soviets have made the most of that principle of the widest possible participation of the whole people in the work of government which is so characteristic of Soviet Communism. The city soviet appoints an ever-increasing number of sections or committees, each consisting of a small proportion of the elected members or candidates, to whom are joined an indefinite number of volunteers drawn from outstanding and "activist" citizens of either sex and of the most varied positions and occupations. Each section consists of several scores of members; occasionally even of hundreds, and in Moscow and Leningrad sometimes running up to a thousand or so; all of whom undertake to spend hours every week in their own localities in gratuitously doing detailed administrative work, much of which would in England and America be carried out by a salaried staff of inspectors, relieving officers, investigators, school attendance officers, collectors and what not.

It must be said that the organisation of the city soviets is still inchoate, ranging from Moscow and Leningrad downwards to quite primitive conditions in some of the smaller cities. " The decree of 1925 and subsequent legislation provided for . . . six permanent committees (or sections), namely, communal economy, financial budgetary business, education, public health, cooperative trade and workman-peasant inspection. Other committees (or sections) may be appointed by local soviets in accordance with their needs. In most city soviets there are ten or more additional committees (or sections) and they are known as administrative, cultural, sanitary, judicial, trade, social security, etc. Deputies (or delegates) may select the committees (or sections) they prefer to join, but under some conditions they may be appointed to committees (or sections) not of their own choice." We must content ourselves with descriptions of Moscow and Leningrad.

### Moscow

The plenum of the Moscow City Soviet consisted, in 1934, of 2206 triennially elected members, with half a dozen others added by the presidium, and with 450 elected candidates or substitutes. About 1750 were Party members, whilst about 900 were non-Party. This plenum meets ten or twelve times a year.[1] It elects an Executive Committee (Ispolkom) of 50 members, which is summoned to meet at irregular intervals about three or four times a year, when some special business requires its attention. But the effective municipal executive is the presidium of fifteen members, with six candidates or substitutes,

[1] " The difference between our soviets and bourgeois democratic municipalities consists not only in the fact that it is not the nobles, manufacturers, bankers and houseowners, and their lackeys, who sit on our soviets but working men and working women, but also in the very methods of working. The soviet is a permanently functioning legislative organisation, which controls and supervises not only the enterprises belonging to the city, but all other economic activities carried on within its territory. Much has been done in recent years to reconstruct the work of the soviets. The sections of the soviets are bodies that supervise and direct the various branches of city enterprise. . . . The work must be raised to higher levels. Ceremonial plenary sessions are still widely practised in our soviets : this practice must be discontinued " (*The Socialist Reconstruction of Moscow and other Cities in the USSR*, by L. M. Kaganovich, Moscow, 1931, pp. 78-79).

elected by the Executive Committee (Ispolkom), subject to the approval of the plenum, and meeting regularly nearly every week. Practically all important decisions are taken by the presidium. On a few issues of special importance or difficulty, the presidium consults the Executive Committee, which sometimes has matters under enquiry and consideration for several months.[1] Usually the decisions of the presidium are reported direct to the plenum, by which they are almost invariably ratified, although sometimes not without considerable discussion.

The majority of the members of the plenum man the sections, or, as we should say, the committees, which supervise the various branches of municipal administration. Every member is required to serve on at least one section, according to his choice, the numbers being unlimited, and varying with the popularity of the subject. In 1934 there were twenty-eight such sections, concerned respectively with finance, education, theatres and cinemas, health, housing, building projects, allocation of sites, supplies and trade, municipal shops, the municipal farms, city planning, construction, municipal heating, militia (police) and fire brigade, courts of justice, establishment, archives, statistics, the legal department, and sundry other matters; together with half a dozen charged with the supervision of the special trusts, or boards, to which is delegated the routine administration of such municipal enterprises as the tramways, the main drainage system, the underground railway works, the licensing of automobiles, and the management of dwelling-houses. Each section has a membership varying from about 40 to three or four times that number. All of them meet about once a month, but each elects a bureau of a few members who meet once every five days.

### Leningrad

The Leningrad City Soviet, which is housed in the Smolny Institute, of revolutionary fame, has an even larger membership than that of Moscow. Its plenum consists of over 3000 triennially elected deputies, with about 1000 elected candidates or substitutes. It has a presidium of 17 deputies and 8 candidates, which meets nearly every week. Unlike Moscow, Leningrad has

[1] This was the case with the project for *metrostroi*, the extensive underground railway, which the city soviet is constructing by direct employment, and which was under examination for many months.

now no executive committee (Ispolkom) ; and the presidium reports in all cases direct to the plenum. There are nearly 30 sections or committees, among which the members of the plenum distribute themselves according to choice. In the summer these sections meet once a month, but in the winter only three times every two months.[1]

It should be added that in Moscow and Leningrad, and often in other cities, the members and candidates elected to the municipal soviet by the several brigades, shifts or workshops of a large factory habitually combine into an extra-legal standing committee, which takes under its special care the municipal interests of all the workers employed in the factory as a whole, with those of their families. They see to the housing, the sanitation, the medical services, the arrangements for holidays and organised recreation, the provision of nurseries and kindergartens, schools and technicums. They deal with every sort of complaint or criticism. It is interesting to note that they do not confine their activities to what are essentially subjects of municipal government. They invade the sphere of action of the factory committee, with which they nevertheless cooperate without friction or jealousy. They investigate cases of waste or breakdown. They press for continuity and increase of output. They deal with absenteeism and complaints against foremen. In every respect they act in the factory as an additional influence for contentment and efficiency.

## The Rayons in the Cities

But this is not all the complication of the municipal structure. In nearly all the cities having populations of 100,000, and in a few others by special authorisation of the Central Executive Committee (TSIK) of the constituent or autonomous republic (or autonomous krai or oblast), subordinate rayon soviets may be elected by the several rayons (or, as we should say, wards or boroughs) into which the city can be divided for this purpose. Thus, Moscow has 10 rayon soviets, Leningrad 8, Baku 7 and Gorki (formerly Nizhni-Novgorod) 8. In some cases (as at Gorki) one or other of the rayons may include new industrial districts growing up outside the city boundary. In other cases, on the principle of cultural autonomy, the rayon may be formed out of

[1] See table on opposite page.

DISTRIBUTION OF MEMBERS OF THE LENINGRAD SOVIET ACCORDING TO THEIR SOCIAL STANDING (1934)

| LENSOVIET | Total | Total Number of Workmen | In Them | | Clerks | Students | Housewives | Kustars | Peasants | Red Army Men | "Kompolits" | Unemployed | Invalids | Udarniks | Others |
|---|---|---|---|---|---|---|---|---|---|---|---|---|---|---|---|
| | | | Industrial Workmen | Employed in Administration and Public Institutions by Election and Udarnichestvo | | | | | | | | | | | |
| Members | 2282 | 1524 | 810 | 714 | 391 | 89 | 121 | … | … | 28 | 120 | 2 | 7 | 1718 | … |
| Candidates | 1202 | 685 | 510 | 175 | 223 | 62 | 156 | … | … | 25 | 40 | 1 | 4 | 872 | 6 |

SOCIAL STANDING

an area within the city inhabited mainly by the racial " national minority ". Elections to the rayon soviets are held quite independently of the election to the city soviet itself, but on the same franchise ; and, for convenience, within the period of the same election campaign, and often on the same day. It is permissible but unusual for the same person to be elected to both city and rayon soviet. The rayon soviets are charged by the city soviet with much of the detailed municipal administration of their own areas, especially the supervision and management of the local institutions, and of the local sanitation. Each rayon soviet appoints its own presidium of a few members, and various sections of local inhabitants for specific functions, exactly like those of the city soviet.[1] Their finances form part of the budget of the city soviet; and this control over finance involves their general subordination to, and control by, the financial organisation of that body. The competition of the different rayons among themselves in order to obtain approval for their several projects of additional local amenities, leads to keen discussion in the plenum and Ispolkom.

It must be said that, although great improvements have been made, there is considerable dissatisfaction with the administration of the city rayon soviets and their sections. Kaganovich did not shrink, in 1934, from publicly declaring that " the district soviets are still working poorly on the improvement of their districts ; they still do not show, and they do not feel themselves, that they are the masters of their districts in the full sense of the word. A most important task is to bring the district soviets closer to the masses of the population which they serve. In every corner of the district there must be a master, who would know all the needs of the district and make them his daily concern. There should be a master who pays attention to the good order of his street and house ; there should be a master who, loving his section, his street, would make it his concern to fight against hooliganism, bad house management, untidiness and lack of culture. If the Moscow soviet and the district soviets are to begin this big undertaking, it is apparent that sub-district soviets must be created. The districts containing up to 400,000 population are too big—each district is a whole large city in itself. It is hard to cover and keep account of the needs of such a big district from one centre. If there are sub-district soviets covering several streets, if the soviet deputies and

[1] See table on opposite page.

**THE DISTRIBUTION OF MEMBERS OF THE LENINGRAD RAYON SOVIETS ACCORDING TO THEIR SOCIAL STANDING**

(Election of 1931)

| RAYON SOVIETS | Total | Total Number of Workmen | In Them: Industrial Workmen | In Them: Employed in Public Administrative and Economic Institutions by Election and Udarnichestvo | Clerks | Students | Housewives | Kustars | Peasants | Red Army Men | "Kompolits" | Unemployed | Invalids |
|---|---|---|---|---|---|---|---|---|---|---|---|---|---|
| **Members of the Soviets:** | | | | | | | | | | | | | |
| Vassileostrovsky | 454 | 262 | 218 | 41 | 109 | 39 | 32 | : | : | 12 | : | : | : |
| Volodarsky | 478 | 370 | 287 | 83 | 51 | 8 | 34 | : | 2 | 13 | : | : | : |
| Vyborgsky | 598 | 373 | 315 | 58 | 158 | 44 | 23 | : | : | : | : | : | : |
| Moskovsky | 347 | 231 | 196 | 35 | 80 | 7 | 10 | : | : | 18 | : | : | 1 |
| Nevsky | 563 | 421 | 325 | 96 | 101 | 6 | 23 | : | : | 3 | : | : | 9 |
| Oktyabr'sky | 512 | 208 | 149 | 59 | 195 | 47 | 31 | 2 | : | 29 | : | : | : |
| Petrogradsky | 412 | 194 | 166 | 28 | 137 | 20 | 38 | 1 | 1 | 21 | : | : | : |
| Smol'ninsky | 1078 | 559 | 277 | 282 | 334 | 72 | 71 | 5 | : | 37 | : | : | : |
| **TOTAL** | 4442 | 2618 | 1933 | 682 | 1165 | 243 | 262 | 8 | 3 | 133 | : | : | 10 |
| **Candidates of the Soviets:** | | | | | | | | | | | | | |
| Vassileostrovsky | 164 | 87 | 87 | : | 33 | 13 | 22 | : | : | 9 | : | : | : |
| Volodarsky | 172 | 113 | 96 | 17 | 27 | 5 | 19 | : | : | 7 | : | : | 1 |
| Vyborgsky | 192 | 121 | 111 | 10 | 37 | 18 | 16 | : | : | : | : | : | : |
| Moskovsky | 129 | 82 | 81 | 1 | 31 | 1 | 8 | : | : | 6 | : | : | 1 |
| Nevsky | 214 | 149 | 126 | 23 | 38 | 4 | 16 | : | : | : | : | : | 7 |
| Oktyabr'sky | 164 | 58 | 48 | 10 | 59 | 13 | 24 | : | : | 10 | : | : | : |
| Petrogradsky | 152 | 90 | 81 | 9 | 30 | : | 24 | : | 2 | 6 | : | : | : |
| Smol'ninsky | 346 | 158 | 114 | 44 | 119 | 17 | 43 | : | : | 9 | : | : | : |
| **TOTAL** | 1533 | 858 | 744 | 114 | 374 | 71 | 172 | : | 2 | 47 | : | : | 9 |

the soviet section leaders work actively in the sub-district soviets, becoming fighters for their street, their sidewalk, their court, the improvement of Moscow will go on apace." [1]

## The Subbotniki in the Cities

Both city soviets and, in the larger cities, rayon soviets, together with the numerous sections that they appoint, are constantly falling behind in the vast work involved in any municipal administration unprovided with an extensive and competent salaried staff. These shortcomings are, to some extent, made good by the spasmodic outbursts of energy by the subbotniki ("Saturday-ers"), who, as we shall describe in a subsequent chapter,[2] volunteer gratuitously to clear away accumulations of work which would otherwise not be done in time. It is estimated that in the aggregate, apart from such salaried staff as exists, as many as 50,000 citizens are, at any moment, participating in the municipal administration of Moscow, and nearly as many in that of Leningrad.[3]

## Indirect Election

In describing the basic foundation of the soviet hierarchy we have had a lengthy but a relatively easy task. Much more difficult is it to describe, or even precisely to understand, the complicated political edifice that has been erected on that foundation. The first few congresses to which the People's Commissars reported their proceedings, and to which they addressed their orations, consisted only of delegates from an indefinite number of city and village soviets, being such as found themselves able to attend at the capital. They were drawn during the Civil War from a comparatively small and shifting area, which at one time sank

[1] *The Construction of the Subway and the Plan for the City of Moscow*, by L. M. Kaganovich, 1934, pp. 56-57.

[2] "In Place of Profit", Chapter IX. in Part II.

[3] It should be added that the members of the city and rayon soviets receive no payment for their services as members. The majority of them, being employed at wages or salaries, are entitled to take "time off" from the employment, without loss of pay, whenever they are engaged on their municipal duties. Those of them who have no wage or salary (such as the independent handicraftsmen) may receive from the soviet compensation for "lost time" at rates fixed by the soviet authorities. Housekeeping wives, supported by their husbands, continue to be supported by them, and are assumed (like the wage-earners) merely to take "time off" for their municipal duties, which they perform as part of the voluntary social work expected from every loyal citizen.

to little more than a relatively narrow corridor of territory between Leningrad and Moscow. The available territory was, in fact, not only restricted by the political separation of the Ukraine and Transcaucasia, but also dependent month by month, during two whole years, on the fluctuating success of the Red Army in pushing back the various White Armies, subsidised and strengthened, as these were, by the munitions, officers and military contingents supplied by half a dozen foreign governments. But when, at the end of 1920, nearly the whole territory of what is now the USSR was cleared of hostile forces,[1] Lenin and his colleagues were confronted with the problem of constructing a firm and stable government from the whole continent extending from the Baltic to the Pacific, and from the Arctic Ocean to the Black Sea, with more than a hundred millions of inhabitants, two-thirds of the whole unable even to read, belonging to many different races, languages and religions, including numerous nomadic and barbaric tribes without any written language, some of them still in the stage of animism and magic. Even if the Bolsheviks had been enthusiastic believers in western liberalism, with its faith in a parliament directly elected by universal suffrage and the ballot-box, such a political constitution was plainly impracticable for the vast heterogeneous hordes with which they had to deal. But the Bolsheviks had become fervent believers in the plan of basing the whole constitution, not on the anonymous mass voting of huge electoral constituencies, but on a large number of relatively small meetings of neighbours and associates in work, at which there could be an intimate discussion of the issues in which the people were interested, and about which they had views of their own. At these meetings the people could choose, to represent their wishes, someone whom they actually knew. Only in this way, Lenin believed, could all these " deaf villages " and primitive communities be taught the art of representative government, and at the same time be held together a unitary state. Many persons thought, at first, that it would suffice to constitute a federal republic of city and village soviets, to be governed by an All-Russian Congress of delegates or deputies from the innumerable little soviets throughout the whole area. This, in fact, was what was indicated in the resolutions " on the federal institutions of

[1] The Japanese did not evacuate Vladivostock until 1922, and the northern half of the island of Sakhalin not until 1925.

the Russian republic " adopted by the " Third All-Russian Congress of Workers', Soldiers', Peasants' and Kazaks' Deputies ", on January 18, 1918, as the plan on which the Central Executive Committee (TSIK) was to draft " these fundamental principles of the constitution " for submission to the next All-Russian Congress.[1] When, however, the drafting committees got to work, it became evident that such a conception was unduly simple. To represent directly in any central congress all the small meetings in so huge an area, with so colossal a population, was plainly impracticable. Moreover, the administration of provincial affairs affecting more than one local soviet had also to be provided for, and this mass of detail could not be brought to Moscow. Further, many of the districts, both small and large, clung desperately to their local autonomy, which had perforce to be conceded. Yet it was no less indispensable to establish a supreme government of strength and stability, if only to deal with such subjects as foreign relations, defence, transport and communications, and so on. Moreover, the Bolsheviks attached paramount importance to their peculiar conception—never before considered by framers of constitutions—of an economic community based upon the suppression of the landlord and the capitalist, and all forms of profit-making. This could be ensured only by a powerful and supreme central authority. To harmonise and achieve all these ends involved protracted consultations before even the first fundamental law was agreed to on July 10, 1918. It took four more years of congresses and discussions to get adopted the successive elaborations and amendments out of which emerged in 1922–1923, in relatively stable form, the constitution of the Union of Soviet Socialist Republics.

The solution of the unprecedented constitutional problem with which the Bolsheviks were faced was found, as early as the spring of 1918, in the adoption, in the manner and on a scale

---

[1] *Soviet Rule in Russia*, by W. R. Batsell, 1929, p. 789. We may perhaps regard this conception as an echo of the idea of Bakunin that, when the strong central governments of the European states had been overthrown, they would be succeeded only by congeries of free associations of the workers in each neighbourhood, which might be loosely federated in groups for common purposes. We are told that Prince Peter Kropotkin, who had re-entered Russia after the 1917 revolution, and who sympathised with Bakunin's ideas as to the necessary minimum of governmental organisation, had formed in Moscow a committee of his friends to discuss the proposed constitution, and their views were forcibly urged on others who were influentially concerned with the drafting.

never before attempted, of the principle of indirect election, which has continued unchanged down to the present day (1935) ; but of which a drastic alteration is now under consideration. As adopted in 1918, the directly elected primary soviets in addition to governing their own areas were to choose deputies or delegates to higher congresses of soviets governing larger areas. Each of these higher congresses of soviets, besides administering the affairs of its own district—whether we think of it as county, canton or province, *kreis* or *département*—was to choose deputies or delegates to yet higher assemblies, governing even larger areas ; and these again ultimately sending their own representatives to constitute the All-Union Congress of Soviets, which was to be the supreme governing authority for the whole Soviet Union.

This sounds, to a Briton or an American, a complicated scheme for providing for the representation of " Man as a Citizen". But there are many more complications yet to be unravelled. The soviet constitution, as will be seen, includes not only an assembly for the government of the whole undivided community inhabiting one-sixth of the entire land-surface of the globe, but also a graded hierarchy of local governing bodies, at once legislative and executive, for the administration of the affairs peculiar to areas of different magnitudes and diverse character- istics. And it does more than this. It provides also a series of independent assemblies for the separate governments of areas, large or small—whether we think of them as tribes or nations, states or republics—inhabited by peoples who feel themselves to constitute distinct nationalities. We have, in fact, in the USSR a unique constitutional form which combines, in one and the same hierarchy, the organs of both local and central govern- ment, of both legislature and executive, of both unitary state and federation.

### How the Pyramid was built

We need not trouble the reader with the successive changes since 1918 in the details of the indirectly elected hierarchy. The tsarist local governing authorities, whether gubernia, zemstvo, uezd or volost, quickly fell to pieces at the Revolution. For years chaos reigned in varying degree from place to place ; and each soviet, in city or village, assumed whatever powers it wanted, and dealt with the affairs of its own area as it chose.

Gradually things were straightened out by the central govern ment, and formulated by successive All-Union Congresses ot Soviets. Municipal authorities were established for the cities. The village soviet (selosoviet) entirely replaced the Mir. The three old divisions of tsarist local government, whether gubernia (province), uezd (county) or volost (rural district), were eventually superseded by two new ones, formed, to some extent, along lines of economic characteristics, and termed oblast or krai,[1] and rayon.[2] No less important, as we shall presently describe, was the vital policy of cultural autonomy and, wherever practicable, native self-government for the scores of separate nationalities scattered over the Eurasian continent. What is of interest is that all these different kinds and grades of governing bodies find places in the main soviet hierarchy, and spring ultimately from the same base of primary soviets. The simple pyramid, springing by indirect election from the broad foundation of some 75,000 directly elected primary soviets of village or city, turns out to have, not merely one supreme apex in the All-Union Congress of Soviets, but also a number of separate minor apices, not only in the congresses of soviets of the autonomous republics or oblasts, but also in those of the seven (or rather nine) federated constituent republics,[3] of which we must give some description before tackling the supreme government of the Union.

---

[1] The terms oblast and krai are applied indiscriminately, according to local usage. But we are told that, strictly speaking, an oblast is a newly established district containing no autonomous area. Where an autonomous area peopled mainly by a national minority exists as an enclave within the district the proper term is krai. The North Caucasian krai contains as many as seven autonomous areas.

Among other works in Russian we may cite *The Soviet State : the Origins and the Development of the Constitution of the USSR*, by V. I. Ignatiev, 1928, 146 pp.; *The USSR, and the Union's Republics*, by S. A. Kotlyarevsky, 139 pp.; *The Soviet Autonomous Oblasts and Republics*, by K. Arkhipov, 123 pp

[2] There was at first an additional tier of councils, termed the okrug soviet, for an area roughly corresponding to that of the old volost, in which both village soviets and city soviets were represented. This was found inconvenient, as leaving too little scope for the development of the rayon soviet in enlivening the village soviets; and as encouraging too much bureaucratic control, to which the city soviet especially objected. It was decided by the Central Committee of the Communist Party by a decree of July 6, 1930, to " liquidate " the okrugs and to wind them up by October 1, 1930. The decision was ratified by the Sixteenth Party Congress (*Political Report to the Sixteenth Party Congress of the Russian Communist Party*, by Josef Stalin, 1930, pp. 125-129). But, in the vast area of the USSR, such changes take time to become universal. In 1934 there were still functioning 22 okrugs.

[3] These are the RSFSR (Russia proper with Siberia); the Ukraine ; White

## The Rayon and the Oblast

There are, accordingly, two main strands in the closely knit constitutional fabric of Soviet Communism : the direct choice, by adult suffrage, at open meetings of fellow-workers or neighbours, of people's deputies or delegates ; and the formation, by indirect election from below, of a pyramidal series of superior authorities. We may observe in passing that, as we shall presently describe, the same two strands run through all the four divisions of the representative system of Soviet Communism, whether it is dealing with " Man as a Citizen ", or with " Man as a Producer ", or with " Man as a Consumer ", or with " Man as a Super-citizen engaged in the Vocation of Leadership ".

We now resume our description of the government of Man as a Citizen in the successive tiers of councils above the village or small city soviet,[1] through those of the rayon and the oblast, and

Russia ; the Transcaucasian Federation (which is a union of three—Georgia, Azerbaijan and Armenia) ; Turkestan ; Tadzhikistan and Usbekistan.

The trouble about a metaphor is that it is never completely accurate as a description ! One of the authors objects that it is a peculiarity of the soviet pyramid that its supreme apex is not flanked by parallel minor apices ; these are all actually included inside the supreme apex, which they help to support, and moreover some of these minor apices have other still smaller pyramidal apices within themselves ! A chart will enable the student to get a clearer vision of this amazingly complicated constitution than is practicable through the written word (see the diagram in the Appendix to Part I.).

[1] It adds to the complication that the names and areas of the tiers of councils have been, during the past few years, in process of change. This economic " rayonising " of the USSR was contemplated immediately after the end of the Civil War, but was not seriously undertaken until 1928, when it was needed for the most effective formulation of the First Five-Year Plan. It was based on the conception of four different types. There were to be industrial rayons (as in the Leningrad oblast, or in the Donetz Basin of the Ukraine). There were to be agricultural rayons (as in the Black Soil region, the Middle Volga, the south-west part of the Ukraine or in Kazakstan). There had also to be mixed rayons, which were necessarily both industrial and agricultural (as in North Caucasus, the Lower Volga krai, the Crimea). There were also timber rayons (as in Northern Asia). (See an instructive section, in Russian, in *The Five-Year Plan of the National Economy Construction of the USSR*, vol. iii., " The Rayon Divisions of the Plan ", 1929.) Under this " rayonising ", what were, under the tsarist régime, 56 gubernia (provinces), 476 uezd (cantons or counties) and 10,606 volost (rural districts), have been reorganised into 100 oblasts (or krais) and about 3000 rayons. An intermediate council for the okrug, standing between the rayon and the oblast, was designed ; but this was abandoned in 1930. This reorganisation is now nearly completed ; and for the sake of clearness we shall limit our description to the new general system, although the old continues to exist temporarily in a few places.

With the abolition of the okrug, the cities having populations of more than 50,000, and some others of great industrial importance, have been, in the six smaller constituent republics, taken out of the rayon, and made directly sub-

those of the autonomous and the constituent republic, up to the supreme authority of the All-Union Congress of Soviets, with its bicameral Central Executive Committee (TSIK), its Cabinet of Ministers (Sovnarkom) and its various other derivatives.

## *The Rayon*

Among the innumerable and apparently unlimited powers of the selosoviet and the small city soviet, there is one universal duty which stands out, that of electing people's deputies or delegates to the congress of soviets of the rayon.   The rayon, now formed mainly on lines of economic production, is a new area comprising a number of adjacent villages and what in England would be called hamlets, together with such small cities or urban settlements as happen to be intermixed with them. The geographical extent and the population of the rayon differ from place to place according to local circumstances, and may be varied from time to time by decrees of any superior authority.[1] It may thus comprise any number of villages, from a few dozen to many score, with half a dozen times as many dependent hamlets, with or without one or more cities and urban settlements.   The soviet of each of these annually elects one (or if large, several) people's deputies or delegates to constitute the rayon congress of soviets, which meets at the principal centre of the rayon.

ordinate to the Sovnarkom (Cabinet) and TSIK (central executive committee) of the constituent republic within which they are situated.   In the RSFSR, however, these major cities are subordinated also to the executive committee (ispolkom) of the oblast or krai.   The other cities, having populations below 50,000, remain within the rayons, but with an autonomy greatly exceeding that enjoyed by the villages.   Such cities, for instance, fix their own local taxes and settle their own budgets, which are adopted by the city soviet, and only passed through the rayon ispolkom for general concurrence, and submission to the oblast ispolkom.

For exact information as to local government constitution in the USSR, the student must go to the decrees themselves, but these are summarised in *The Soviet State*, by B. W. Maxwell, 1934, chap. vii., " Provincial Government ", pp. 100-108 ; where the Russian sources are indicated (pp. 347-348). See also *Soviet Rule in Russia*, by W. R. Batsell, 1929, chap. xi., " Local Administration " (pp. 663-687), which does not clearly give the more recent changes.

[1] Actually the 3000 rayons appear to include, on an average, about 23 selosoviets and perhaps one small city or urban settlement apiece, with an average population of about 45,000 ; which is analogous to that of an English rural district council in its much smaller area.

In the RSFSR and the Ukraine the village soviet elects these delegates at the rate of one for every 300 inhabitants. The soviets of the small cities and urban settlements within the rayon elect delegates at the rate of one for each unit of 60 electors of these soviets (approximately equal to 120 inhabitants). Thus, as is usual in the soviet bodies, the total number of members of the rayon congress of soviets is not fixed, and with the increase of population it is always growing. It elects a president, with some other members to form a presidium, and also a standing executive committee (ispolkom) not exceeding 45 members, together with one-third as many candidates or alternates.

When we enquire what are the powers and duties entrusted to the rayon congress of soviets, we are met with the same difficulty as that with which we were confronted in the case of the village soviet. The list of these powers and duties, as expressly laid down in the RSFSR decree of January 1, 1931, is indeed substantially similar to that relating to the village soviet, which we give as an appendix to this volume. These powers and duties range from the consideration and discussion of the loftiest matters of policy and administration of the USSR as a whole, in which the rayon congress of soviets, like the village soviet, is invited and desired to participate, and which it is expressly directed to put in operation within its own area, down to the minutest details of parochial administration. It is, indeed, not to be supposed that the entire conglomeration of these subjects are even discussed by any of the 3000 rayon congresses of soviets, any more than they are by the 70,000-odd village soviets. But in startling contrast with the narrowly limited and precisely defined functions of the British or American local governing body, there is practically nothing in the world that the rayon congress of soviets, equally with the village soviet, is not authorised and indeed invited to deal with, so far as its application to the denizens of its area is concerned. On the other hand, again in contrast with the British or American local authority, the rayon congress of soviets, like the village soviet, has no legal rights on which it can insist against the will of any superior administrative authority. It may at any moment find its decisions overruled, and its actions cancelled and reversed by the oblast congress of soviets which it joins with other rayons in creating; or by the oblast ispolkom (or executive committee); or by the republic congress of soviets or its Central Executive Committee ; or by the sovnarkom, or the People's Commissar, of the constituent or autonomous republic within the area of which it is situated ; or by the All-Union Congress of Soviets or its TSIK (or Central Executive Committee); or, indeed, by the presidium of any of these bodies ; or by the USSR Sovnarkom of People's Commissars.  Thus, the rayon congress of soviets has a practically unlimited sphere of action, so far as its own area is concerned, subject always to the liability to be sharply pulled up and overruled whenever it does anything contrary to the policy or the will of any authority higher than itself.  It has absolute freedom to participate in government, and it is encouraged and strongly urged to participate in any way it chooses ; but it is no less sternly warned that whenever it " goes off the rails ", its action will be cancelled and reversed ; and if the local body persists, it will be summarily disbanded, and a new election will be called for.  In order to enable this superior authority to be exercised, all obligatory decrees of a lower authority—indeed the minutes of proceedings themselves—have to be forwarded immediately to the next higher authority, as well as to the appropriate People's Commissariat of the USSR and that of an autonomous republic. We gather that, in practice, the rayon congress and its executive, like the village soviet, usually errs by default rather by excess of zeal ; and that drastic interference from above, though unhesitatingly undertaken when required, is, to put it mildly, not of incessant occurrence.

The relation of the rayon congress of soviets to the various village and small urban soviets within its area is mainly one of supervision and control.  Thus, the rayon congress appoints for each village the president of the electoral commission of ten local members to supervise the election of the village soviet ; to compile and post up publicly the list of persons excluded from the electorate ; and to provide an independent chairman for the various election meetings.

On the other hand, an essential function of the 3000 rayon soviets is that of concentrating in a single body the representation of the large number of village soviets within their several areas, occasionally amounting, as it seems, to more than one hundred, in such a way as to render practicable the election of delegates to the next higher council in the hierarchy.

The organs of local administration of the rayon congress of soviets, acting under the supervision and direction of the rayon ispolkom, or executive committee that' the plenum elects, and of the presidium that the ispolkom appoints, consist of a number of sections (six of them being obligatory [1]) on each of which there serve some members of the rayon congress and ispolkom, together with a varying number of inhabitants whom the ispolkom invites to act as a civic obligation. We are informed that the object of forming these sections is that of associating as large a proportion as possible of the " toiling masses " in the work of government. Meetings are held in the various factories and workshops, clubs and reading-rooms, throughout the rayon, where the members of the rayon congress of soviets, the " militia " (local constabulary) and the local courts of justice attend; where active workers are enlisted for the sections, and where the " concrete problems " of the work of the rayon congress are discussed. The obligatory sections are those dealing with " soviet construction and control of execution " ; " industry, labour and supplies " ; agriculture ; health ; education, the rayon's share in the General Plan, and the rayon's financial budget.

The rayon section dealing with the General Plan, so far as it relates to the rayon area stands in an interesting relation to Gosplan, to which it is subordinate. National planning is now based largely upon constituent rayon planning. The rayon has to prepare each year its own preliminary plan for all the enterprises within its area in accordance with the general economic considerations of which it is advised. This has to be submitted to each local enterprise, productive or cultural. Each considers the quota assigned to it, and either approves or prepares a counter-plan. The whole are then submitted to the higher authorities to be further revised and finally enacted.[2]

The only other part of the administration of the rayon calling

[1] Namely, those on (1) Soviet Construction and control of execution ; (2) Industry, Labour and Supply ; (3) Agriculture ; (4) Finance and budget; (5) Popular Education ; (6) Public Health (RSFSR decree of January 1, 1931, section 38). To these there has been added, for all but the smallest rayons, a section on the General Plan, in subordination to the Union State Planning Commission, which we describe in our chapter on " Planned Production for Community Consumption ".

[2] From paper by V. Kuibyshev, head of Gosplan, in *Planned Economy*, April 1931. We deal with the whole subject in our subsequent chapter entitled " Planned Production for Community Consumption ", Vol. II.

for attention is that of finance.  The rayon congress has annually
to settle the budget of local receipts and expenditure for the
ensuing year, which has to be submitted to the oblast ispolkom
for approval, and for inclusion in the oblast budget, with a view
to its ultimate incorporation in the budget of the autonomous or
constituent republic, and, indeed, finally in that of the USSR
itself.  Thus there is, in principle as well as in form, no effective
local autonomy in finance in any grade of council from the
smallest selosoviet up to the All-Russian Congress of Soviets of
the RSFSR.  In practice, however, there is a great deal of
financial autonomy.  To begin with, the amount of expenditure
to be undertaken by the lower authorities, whilst it can be summarily restrained by any higher authority, cannot effectively be
increased otherwise than by exhortation and persuasion.  On the
other hand, if the lower authorities choose to incur larger expenditure at their own cost, they are usually permitted to add a
surtax to one or other of the taxes levied within their area by any
of the higher authorities.

Elaborate provision is made by law as to the rayon being
served by half a dozen organised departments of permanent
officials, who are required to possess technical qualification and
training.  In fact there is as yet, in the vast majority of rayons,
nothing more than a skeleton staff of officials of the very minimum
of training.  A marked feature is the extreme youthfulness of
nearly all of them, few being over thirty, or having more than a few
years' office experience.  We understand that measures for the
special training of administrative officials are under consideration.

### *The Oblast*

Above both the rayon congresses of soviets of the rural
districts and the soviets of the small cities, and superseding the
ancient gubernia or province, stands, in the RSFSR and the
Ukraine, the authority of the krai or oblast.  The oblast congress
of soviets is formed by delegates from the rayon congresses of
soviets, representing the village soviets, at the rate (in the
RSFSR) of one for every 12,500 inhabitants (equal to about one
for every 7000 electors) ; and also by delegates elected directly
by the soviets of the small cities (together with those of the urban
settlements, factories and collective farms outside civic bound-

aries) at the rate of one delegate for each 2500 electors. Any autonomous republic or autonomous area within the territory is entitled to elect its own delegates at the rate of one for each 2000 electors from urban centres and one for each 10,000 inhabitants from rural settlements. It will be seen that the city soviets enjoy the usual disproportionate representation (more than twice as great as that of the rural villages). This disproportionate representation of the population of the cities, in comparison with that of the villages, does not prevent most, if not all, oblast congresses of soviets from containing far more representatives of villages than of city dwellers, because the proportion of the latter to the whole population of the area is still only as one to five or six.

The area over which the oblast congress of soviets presides, the number of its members, and the nature and extent of its functions, appear to differ in different parts and to be still in course of settlement. The population within the different oblasts varies enormously, even as much as from one to ten millions. In the RSFSR the approximate average appears to be nearly four millions. If we take the autonomous republics in the USSR, which are classed with the oblasts properly so-called, we see that their average population is only about a million and a half, whilst their average area is no less than 650,000 square kilometres. On the other hand, the average population of the fourteen oblasts properly so-called, exceeds five millions, although their average area is roughly the same as that of the autonomous republic.[1] In the Ukraine the average population and area are both smaller. The five lesser constituent republics have no oblasts, the rayon congresses of soviets being directly under the republic congress of soviets, its central executive committee and its sovnarkom.

In the RSFSR there are, we gather, twenty-six territories ranking as oblasts, including the areas of the twelve autonomous republics within its boundaries which have the same constitutional form as other oblasts, except that they call their ministerial heads of departments People's Commissars and their council a sovnarkom. Thus there are the fourteen newly delimited oblasts of Moscow and Leningrad, the Ivanovo industrial area, the Northern ter-

---

[1] Thus the autonomous republic in the RSFSR, whilst having a large area, is comparable in population to the half-dozen most populous administrative counties of England. The oblasts of the RSFSR, on the other hand, usually surpass in population the most populous of the English administrative counties, and some even that of Ireland or the administrative county of London.

ritory, the Western territory, the Central Black Earth area, the Gorki (late Nizhni-Novgorod) territory, the Ural territory, that of the North Caucasus, the two territories of the Middle and Lower Volga, and the two of East and West Siberia, together with the Far Eastern territory. With them are ranked the twelve autonomous republics, namely, those of the Crimea, the Tartars, the Volga Germans, Kazak, Yakut, Kirghiz, Chuvash, Karelia, Buryat, Bashkir, Karakalpak and Daghestan. In each of these divisions there is a Congress of Soviets electing an executive (termed either ispolkom or sovnarkom) which directs a varied and extensive local administration.

In the Ukraine, some of the oblast areas are particularly large, there being only half a dozen so called for the whole republic.[1] But in the Donetz industrial area the population is so dense, and the amount of work so great, that each rayon soviet is accepted as equivalent also to an oblast soviet. In the other parts of the Ukraine, the rayon congress of soviets, either each year or every two years, elects representatives to the oblast congress of soviets at the rate of one for each 15,000 of the population, amounting in each case to several hundred delegates.

Wherever it exists, the oblast congress of soviets is an important authority. It is, indeed, the supreme local organ of power within its own area, with a competence extending to all matters of government. It has, however, to coordinate its activity with the policy and administration of the central executive committee (VTSIK) and the Sovnarkom of the constituent republic, whilst the USSR sovnarkom and its presidium also have the right to suspend or reverse, in case of need, anything done by the oblast authorities. It has the right to control all public institutions within its area, not being those of the USSR ; and even these it has a right to supervise and report upon. It can veto any regulation or decision of any of the city soviets or any of the rayon or selosoviets within its area. It controls all the elections within the oblast. Finally, it has the right to propose to the authorities of the constituent republic the enactment and promulgation of any laws and regulations relating to the oblast that are required.

---

[1] Namely, those of Chernigov, Kiev, Odessa, Dniepropetrovsk, Kharkov and Vinnitsa, with which must be ranked the Moldavian Autonomous Republic, and, as explained in the text, all the separate rayons of the Donetz Basin.

But the oblast congress of soviets meets as a plenum, usually, only once a year, when it elects a president, and his assistant, who both give their whole time to the work, and also an ispolkom, or executive committee, of about one hundred members, who receive only their expenses and a free pass over all the railways within the oblast. In the case of the autonomous republics, the congress of soviets elects, in lieu of an ispolkom, a sovnarkom of People's Commissars who themselves control the various branches of administration. In both cases the USSR Government is directly represented in the oblast executive by officials of such USSR People's Commissariats as Railroads and Posts and Telegraphs, The ispolkom of an ordinary oblast is supposed to conduct its administration through its presidium and four organised departments of officials (a secretariat, an organisation department, a planning commission termed obplan, and a " commission of execution "). But the work which has to be performed falls under fifteen or more heads, of which we may mention a " regional council of people's economy " ; agriculture ; trade or distribution of commodities ; finance ; communal department ; education ; health ; social welfare ; military ; political ; and archives ; together with the department of justice. In many oblasts the lack of an adequate official staff has led to the appointment of a number of sections each containing a selection from the members of the oblast congress of soviets and the ispolkom, together with other active or representative citizens appointed by the ispolkom. Each of these sections is charged with the supervision and actual administration of one department of the work of the oblast. It should be said that, in the matter of local taxation and the budget of the oblast the oblast ispolkom has the right to participate in the discussion both of the budget of the constituent republic and of that of the USSR itself, in so far as these relate to its own area.

### The Seven Federated Republics

The next tier of councils, above that of the oblast or krai, where they exist, and of the autonomous republics, is that of the seven Union or constituent republics of the RSFSR, the Ukraine, White Russia, the Transcaucasian Federation (itself a federation of three distinct republics), Turkmenistan, Uzbekistan and

Tadzhikistan, all of which are directly joined together in federation as the USSR.

## The RSFSR

The first and by far the most important of these republics, the Russian Socialist Federal Soviet Republic, although expressly termed a federation, is and has always been essentially a unitary state. Notwithstanding its title, and an express declaration in the first article of its Fundamental Law in 1918, what was established by that law, without subsequent revision, was a soviet hierarchy, or pyramid, of the pattern that we have so often described. The RSFSR was to have a supreme All-Russian Congress of Soviets, made up of deputies or delegates elected by provincial congresses of soviets under various designations ; and these provincial congresses were made up of deputies or delegates from smaller district congresses of soviets, themselves consisting of deputies or delegates from village or urban soviets, who were directly elected at innumerable small gatherings of electors, associated either in work at particular establishments or as neighbours in rural villages. From top to bottom of this pyramid of councils, each tier has complete authority over all below it, and is itself completely subject to all above it. This system of " Democratic Centralism ", as it is fondly called, which is universally characteristic of Soviet Communism, seems to us to have nothing in common with the curtailed but inviolable autonomy of the various units that is understood by federalism.[1]

It is, indeed, remarkable how small and relatively unimportant have been the changes since 1918 in the constitutional structure

[1] In the discussions leading up to the formulation and adoption of the " Fundamental Law " during the first half of 1918, the slogan of " All Power to the Soviets " was so strongly insisted on, that the very first article had to assert that " Russia is declared a republic of soviets of workers', soldiers' and peasants' deputies. *All central and local authority is vested in these soviets.*" The state that was established as the Russian Soviet Republic, and then styled the RSFSR, was conceived, by at least some of its most energetic advocates, as nothing more than a federation of all the urban and rural soviets throughout the country.

In article 10 it is again expressly declared that " all authority within the boundaries of the RSFSR is vested in the entire working population of the country, *organised in the urban and rural soviets* " (Fundamental Law of the RSFSR, ratified by the Fifth All-Russian Congress of Soviets on July 10, 1918, First section, chap. i., article 10 ; *Soviet Rule in Russia*, by W. R. Batsell, 1929, p. 81). But the Fundamental Law, taken as a whole, established, as we now see, a state of the very opposite character.

of the RSFSR, notwithstanding the development of autonomous republics and autonomous areas within it, and the formation of the USSR about and above it.[1] Its capital is still Moscow, where the RSFSR ministerial departments are cheek-by-jowl with those of the USSR. The "All-Russian Congress of Soviets" now meets only every few years, usually just prior to the All-Union Congress, to which the same delegates immediately proceed. It is composed of delegates elected by the congresses of soviets of the several oblasts or krais, autonomous republics and autonomous areas, and the larger cities, in the proportion of one to every 125,000 population of rural areas, and one to every 25,000 city electors (equal to about 45,000 population). The Central Executive Committee (VTSIK) of the RSFSR, now increased in size from 200 to 400, meets only once a quarter. The Sovnarkom no longer includes as many as eighteen People's Commissars, seeing that all the "questions of national importance" specified in articles 49 and 50 of the Fundamental Law, with the departments of foreign affairs, armed forces, foreign trade, heavy industry, forestry, state farms, railways and waterways, posts and telegraphs, and food industry, have passed to the USSR ; and these departments are now represented in the RSFSR Sovnarkom only by the delegates or agents of the USSR People's Commissars. There are, however, in the RSFSR Sovnarkom, still eight People's Commissars, under a president, with two vice-presidents, namely, those for Finance, Interior, Justice, Education, Health, Social Welfare, Agriculture, and Light Industries, together with the president of the RSFSR Gosplan.[2]

When it is remembered that the population of the RSFSR exceeds one hundred millions, and that the territory stretches from the Gulf of Finland to the Pacific Ocean, it will be seen

[1] Incidentally we may note that the territory of White Russia, and thus of the USSR, was reduced under the Treaty of Riga (1921) ending the war with Poland, by a strip along the western frontier, which was ceded to Poland. In 1929 the extensive but scantily peopled district of Tadzhikistan was taken out of the RSFSR, and promoted to the status of an independent constituent republic of the Soviet Union, entitled, like the RSFSR itself, to representation by five members in the Soviet of Nationalities, forming part of the bicameral Central Executive Committee of the USSR.

[2] Agriculture now has a USSR People's Commissar, who has, in the RSFSR, as in other federated republics, considerably reduced the autonomy of local People's Commissars. The departments of the Commissariat for Labour have been transferred to the AUCCTU, and there is accordingly now no People's Commissar of Labour.

that even these nine government departments represent an immense task of administration. The civil service of the RSFSR may exceed in number the federal staff of the USSR itself, apart from the defence forces and the establishments in foreign countries. With the more significant features of this vast administration we shall deal in subsequent chapters. The RSFSR Sovnarkom is still busy in developing schools and medical services over the vast area that it controls. It has to carry on the great retailing business in Moscow, Leningrad and Rostov that we shall describe in a later chapter. Its responsibility— save for the occasional spasmodic intervention that we shall presently describe of the USSR Supreme Court—for the administration of justice, the prevention of crime and the maintenance of prisons within the whole area of the RSFSR may be circumscribed by the creation of the new USSR People's Commissar for Internal Affairs. The observer cannot resist the feeling that, whilst the local government of the cities, and that of the krais and oblasts, rayon and selosoviets, within the RSFSR, is growing in magnitude and activity, the various central organs of the RSFSR at Moscow have lost ground to the other central organs located in the same city, belonging to the federal government of the USSR that we have still to describe.

## The Republic of the Ukraine

The second in importance among the seven constituent republics now forming the USSR and the only one of a magnitude and a population, a productivity and an aspiration at all comparable with the RSFSR, is that of the Ukraine. Here we have a population of thirty millions (nearly one-third of that of the RSFSR), concentrated, to the extent of 150 to the square kilometre, on an area comparable with that of Sweden, having its own language appreciably differing from Russian ; its own ancient cultural centre at Kiev ; and its own traditions of former national autonomy under an elected hetman. Although these traditions had been interrupted by centuries of Tsarist tyranny, it needed little incitement from the German military authorities in 1916-1917 to induce a large proportion of the Ukrainians to struggle, not merely for the destruction of Russian dominion, but also, with some expectation of sympathy from Ukrainian (otherwise called Ruthenian) minorities in Austria, Poland and Roumania, for an independent Ukrainian Republic. This was proclaimed on December 27, 1917. There was, however, never any chance for a political union of the whole Ukrainian race, one-fifth of which, outside the USSR, remains to this day firmly held within the four neighbouring states, Poland, Czechoslovakia, Hungary and Roumania. Accordingly, when between 1917 and 1922 the foreign armies and the widespread banditry were got rid of, there was established, within the Ukrainian part of Tsarist Russia, a reasonably well-organised government on the common pattern of the hierarchy of soviets, in a friendly " military and economic alliance " with the RSFSR, which was formally proclaimed in December 1920, and converted into a federal union in 1922–1923.[1]

The supreme authority in the Ukraine is the All-Ukrainian Congress of Soviets, which now meets for about a week, usually once every few years, just before the All-Union Congress of Soviets at Moscow. It consists of about a thousand delegates and " candidates " (being substitutes or alternates) chosen by the plenums of the six oblast congresses of soviets, together with that of the Autonomous Republic of Moldavia and the congresses of soviets of each of the Donetz rayons. This All-Ukrainian Congress of Soviets hears speeches, approves drafts of decrees and administrative resolutions laid before it, and appoints a president of the Ukraine Congress, with an Assistant, together with a Central Executive Committee, and a sovnarkom of People's Commissars.

The Central Executive Committee of about 400 members, who all receive a free pass over the railways in the Ukraine, meets usually once a quarter for about ten days, and exercises supreme authority between the infrequent sessions of the All-Ukrainian Congress. A meeting is usually held immediately before each meeting of the Central Executive Committee (TSIK) of the USSR at Moscow, in order to consider the business coming before that meeting, and if necessary to concert a Ukrainian policy.

The Ukrainian Sovnarkom consists of a president, several vice-presidents and a secretary, with People's Commissars for Finance, Internal Affairs, Agriculture, Justice, Light Industries, Educa-

[1] See *National States and National Minorities*, by W. C. Macartney, 1934.

tion, Health and Social Welfare, and a local Planning Commission practically subordinate to Gosplan.

The Ukrainian People's Commissars dealing directly with industry have exceptionally heavy departments to administer. The industrial developments in the Ukraine during the past few years have been enormous in amount and range ; and whilst most of the work has fallen first to the USSR Supreme Economic Council, and on its abolition to the People's Commissars for Heavy and Food Industries respectively, the Ukrainian Government has retained and developed some of its own undertakings. It has its own steelworks and machine-making factories, conducted in dutiful compliance with the General Plan, but as enterprises of the republic.[1]  The Ukrainian Sovnarkom also conducts, in supplement of the efforts of Centrosoyus and the increasing work of the Ukrainian Co-operative Societies, a very extensive business in retailing household commodities of all kinds, in the relatively well-appointed government shops at Kharkov, Kiev, Odessa, Dnieprostroi and other cities.

Beneath the All-Ukrainian Congress of Soviets, with its Central Executive Committee and Sovnarkom of People's Commissars, there stands the usual hierarchy of soviets of the oblasts, rayons, cities and villages according to the common pattern which we have just described. Some peculiarities of the Ukraine may, however, be mentioned. Its villages are usually exceptionally large and populous, many having between five and ten thousand inhabitants, so that the electors have exceptionally often to be divided into settlements or wards, for each of which a separate meeting (election point or curia) has to be held to elect members to the village soviet (selosoviet). Similarly, as we have already mentioned, the rayons in the densely populated industrial area of the Donetz Basin have so great a number of electors, and local government functions of such importance, that they rank and are treated also as oblasts, and directly elect their own delegates to the All-Ukrainian Congress of Soviets.

The Ukraine retains among its intelligentsia a strong national feeling, and energetically develops its own Ukrainian culture,

[1] When, in 1932, the Supreme Economic Council of the USSR was, as we shall presently describe, replaced by new People's Commissars for Heavy, Food and Timber Industries respectively, careful provision had to be made to preserve to the Ukrainian Sovnarkom its control over the enterprises that were Ukrainian.

which is very nationalist in form, although communist in essence, in books and newspapers, theatres and universities. The USSR authorities wisely respect the racial susceptibilities of this important republic. It is as a concession to these susceptibilities that it was in 1934 decided to retransfer the capital which has for the past decade been at Kharkov, to the ancient metropolis of Kiev. But whatever may happen in learning and literature the industrial development is so predominantly " All-Union " in its influence, and the Communist Party in the Ukraine is so definitely directed from Moscow, that, in spite of repeated attempts of the *emigrés* centred in Paris and Prague to incite to rebellion, it is impossible to ignore a tendency to a more complete unification.[1]

## The White Russian and Transcaucasian Republics

We need not go into detail about the White Russian Soviet Socialist Republic (capital Minsk) on the western border of the USSR, adjoining Latvia, Lithuania and Poland ;[2] or about the combined Union republic of the Transcaucasian Socialist Soviet Federation, which has its capital at Tiflis, for its three constituent republics wedged between the Black and Caspian Seas, and adjoining Turkey on the southern border.[3] Both have

[1] The Moldavian Socialist Soviet Republic, on the left bank of the Dniester river, which forms the frontier of Bessarabia, was made an autonomous republic under Ukraine on October 12, 1924. This exclusively agricultural community (capital Balta) with a population of 600,000 upon an area of only 8288 square kilometres—about as large as the North Riding of Yorkshire or the canton of Berne—may perhaps be regarded as a lasting embodiment of the protest of the USSR against the Roumanian seizure of Bessarabia, which, it is hoped, may one day be enabled, as South Moldavia, to unite with the northern half of what is claimed to be a single community. With this view, the Moldavian Republic maintains a sovnarkom of People's Commissars, but is for many purposes dealt with as if it were merely an oblast of the Ukraine.

[2] The White Russian Socialist Soviet Republic has an area of 126,790 square kilometres—three times that of Switzerland—with a population slightly exceeding five millions, four-fifths of whom speak the White Russian dialect, whilst Jews attain the relatively high proportion of 10 per cent. The constitution is almost identical in form to that of the RSFSR, with which it finds its activities coordinated.

[3] The three constituents of this federation are Azerbaijan (capital Baku), which established its soviet republic in April 1920 ; Armenia (capital Erivan), which did so in December 1920 ; and Georgia (capital Tiflis), in which a soviet government was established by the Bolshevik army in February 1921. On March 19, 1922, these three governments, strongly influenced by the Communist Party, agreed to unite in a Transcaucasian Federation, with a common president, congress of soviets, a central executive committee of no fewer than

governments organised upon the common pattern, with central executive committees several hundreds strong and sovnarkoms administering the local affairs. Both retain strong feelings in favour of local autonomy based on racial and linguistic, as well as (especially in the case of Georgia) historical associations, and are accordingly left in undisturbed enjoyment of the cultural autonomy that they value. Both find their industries developed, continuously and extensively, at the expense of the whole Soviet Union, and their agriculture directed according to the USSR General Plan; whilst in both the strictly unitary Communist Party everywhere exerts a potent influence in promoting a common economic policy and in gradually developing a new common sentiment as constituent parts of the larger whole.

## The Formation of the Soviet Union

With the final defeat of the " White " armies, and the withdrawal of the last of the contingents of the foreign powers, the time came for the establishment of a common rule for the whole territory of what was left of Tsarist Russia.[1] The capitalist governments did not relinquish their hostility with the withdrawal of their forces, and the necessity for union for common defence had been made sufficiently obvious. Its importance for economic and social planning could not be missed. The influence of the widely dispersed membership of the essentially unitary Communist Party worked powerfully in the same direction. Already by December 28, 1920, Lenin and Chicherin, for the RSFSR, had agreed with Rakovski, president of the Ukrainian Sovnarkom, and also its People's Commissar for Foreign

485 members and Sovnarkom of People's Commissars. Each of the constituent republics has also its own government for local affairs, and maintains its own cultural autonomy, especially the use of its own language in its own schools, law courts and public offices. The population of the federation now exceeds six millions in a largely mountainous area four times as great as Scotland. For the three other " Union Republics ", namely Turkmenistan, Uzbekistan and Tadzhikistan, see p. 82.

[1] The so-called Border States (whether Estonia, Latvia and Lithuania ; or Finland and Poland), by 1918 established as independent states, were never included in the RSFSR ; whilst Bessarabia was seized by Roumania, and a further strip on the west was ceded to Poland on the conclusion of the war in 1921 (Treaty of Riga, 1921). The Ukraine, White Russia, Georgia, Azerbaijan and Armenia were, between 1918 and 1921, at various times enjoying a nominal independence under a shifting domination by foreign armies or local banditry.

Affairs, on a Treaty of Alliance which embodied the main outlines of the eventual Treaty of Union. The World International
Conference, to which the Moscow Government had gladly accepted an invitation, was about to meet at Genoa, and agreements were hastily concluded by the RSFSR with White Russia
and the Transcaucasian Federation, as well as with the Ukraine,
providing that they should accept, as their representatives at
the World Conference, the delegation of the RSFSR, and support
the proposals in the common interest that would be put forward.
The proceedings at Genoa proved to be of little interest or importance for the Soviet Government; but Chicherin was able
to conclude with Germany, to the consternation of the other
diplomats, the important separate Treaty of Rapallo, in which
were included, for the first time, all four soviet states. This was
followed, after months of negotiation, by the agreement of these
four governments, in December 1922, to constitute the Union
of Soviet Socialist Republics. Stalin was in a position to report
to the Tenth All-Russian Congress of Soviets, which opened at
Moscow on December 23, 1922, that resolutions had been received from the supreme congresses of soviets of the Ukraine,
of White Russia and of the Transcaucasian Federation, urging
the necessity and advantage of creating a single federal union.
A special delegation representing all four republics was appointed
to draw up the necessary treaty, upon much the same basis as
had been agreed with the Ukraine in 1920. The draft had
already been prepared. Within three days the " Declaration
of Union " was formulated ; adopted by the " First Congress
of Soviets of the USSR ", and duly proclaimed by the Executive
Committee which that Congress had appointed. All that was
needed was a formal constitution. The new Central Executive
Committee of the Union (TSIK), which was, in fact, dominated
by the members who belonged to the Central Executive Committee of the RSFSR, prepared a draft which did little more than
reproduce, for the Union, the scheme of government of the RSFSR
itself. At this point the Communist Party publicly intervened
with a more statesmanlike proposal. The Twelfth Congress of
the Party was in session (April 1923) ; and its Central Committee formally recommended to the presidium of the All-
Union Central Executive Committee (TSIK) that the draft
required amendment. The proposed constitution did not, the

Communist Party protested, afford by its terms sufficient assurance to the three smaller republics that the autonomy to be allowed to them would be protected against the dominance of the RSFSR. Moreover, so Stalin urged, it did not provide for putting on a genuinely federal basis the autonomous republics and autonomous oblasts that he had been establishing, inside the RSFSR, for the principal nationalities. The " counter-plan " of the Communist Party embodied a new ideal, that of the " Unnational State ", in sharp contrast with the consciously "National " states into which Europe had become divided in the course of the past four centuries, this stream of tendencies coming more recently to a climax in the Italy of Mussolini and the Germany of Hitler. The project of the Communist Party, which resulted in the present federal constitution of the USSR, seems to us so novel, and fraught with consequences so important, that we give in full its fundamental propositions. It was essential, the Party declared :

" (a) To secure, during the establishment of the central organs of the Union, the equality of rights and duties of the individual republics in their mutual relationship with each other, as well as in regard to the central authority of the Union.

" (b) To establish, in the system of supreme organs of the Union, a representation of all national republics and regions on principles of equality, with possible representation of all nationalities living in these republics.

" (c) To construct the executive organs of the Union on principles which would secure a real participation therein of the representatives of these republics, and a real satisfaction of all needs of the peoples in the Union.

" (d) To allow for the republics sufficiently liberal financial, and in particular, budgetary rights, which would enable them to show their own state-administrative, cultural, and economic initiative.

" (e) To man the organs of the national republics and regions chiefly from amongst the local population, who would know local customs, language, etc.

" (f) To issue special laws which would secure for them the right to use their native language in all state organs and institutions serving the local national minorities—the laws which would prosecute and punish with full revolutionary severity all violators of national rights, and in particular of rights of national minorities.

" (g) To promote educational work in the Red Army in the sense of cultivating therein the ideas of brotherhood and solidarity of the peoples composing the Union and to take practical measures concerning the organisation of national armies, at the same time taking care that the defensive structure of the republic shall always be kept adequate." [1]

A special committee, in which the RSFSR had only 14 members out of 25, thereupon drew up a new constitution, in which Stalin's plan of a " Soviet of Nationalities ", with no greater representation (5) of the RSFSR than of any other constituent or autonomous republic, but with the addition of single representatives also from all the other autonomous areas within the constituent republics, was adopted as part of a bicameral Central Executive Committee. At the same time the autonomy of each constituent republic was safeguarded by suitable phrases introduced at appropriate places. The new draft was approved by the Central Committee of the Communist Party, and after formal agreement in the three other capitals, it was adopted at Moscow by the Central Executive Committee of the USSR (TSIK) on July 6, 1923, when it came immediately into force ; to be finally ratified by the Second All-Union Congress of Soviets on January 31, 1924.

## The Federal Union

We are thus brought, at long last, to the central federal organs of the gigantic Soviet State. But we cannot refrain from the observation that this seven-starred constellation, brilliant and

[1] *Soviet Rule in Russia*, by W. R. Batsell, pp. 281-282 ; *Fifteen Years of Soviet Construction, 1917–1932* (in Russian), 1932, p. 63. The novelty and the importance of the new conception, to which we recur at the end of this chapter, are handsomely recognised in the remarkable work, *National States and National Minorities*, by W. C. Macartney, 1934.

In the concluding section of this chapter we describe in some detail the steps taken in the USSR to establish, under the " Unnational State ", complete political, economic and social equality among a population of 170 million persons, comprising nearly 200 different races at markedly different stages of development—Slavs and Teutons in sundry varieties of Christendom and paganism ; Scandinavians of sorts, with Finns and Esquimaux ; Mongols of every grade of civilisation ; Jews and Syrians and gypsies ; Turks and Armenians ; with Siberian and central Asiatic tribes of the most varied character, from Buddhists and Bahaists and the " Shiahs " and " Sunnis " of Islam to magic-mongers and animists.

powerful though it be—now filling, indeed, almost the whole
soviet sky—is not and has never been a federation of participants
of anything like equal status. The Union of Soviet Socialist
Republics was a leonine partnership. What happened in 1922
was that the RSFSR, with an elaborate parade of federal forms,
and a genuine concession of cultural autonomy, virtually annexed
to itself the three other fragments of Tsarist Russia which had
been, by the Bolshevik forces with the active cooperation of a
large proportion, if not a majority, of the inhabitants, cleared of
hostile armies and insurgent banditry, and thus in effect con-
quered. To these have since been added three communities on
the south-eastern Asiatic border, of vast area but small population, which have been set up as additional constituent or Union
republics.[1]  It must always be remembered that the prime mover
in these transactions, the RSFSR itself, holds sway over a territory extending from the Baltic to the Pacific, in area twelve
times as large as all the other six constituent or Union republics
put together, and twenty-three times as large as the next biggest
among them. It has a population twice as great as the aggregate
of all the other six, and three times the total of the next greatest
among them. It had at that date an army (and an armed police
force) which had lately suppressed every attempt in any of the
territories to set up or maintain any government hostile to that
of Moscow. Above all, it possessed, in the Communist Party, a
ruling order or companionship, at that time mainly concentrated
in the RSFSR, which dominated the whole. When we consider
how preponderant were those influences, the successive treaties
of union themselves, and all the façade of federation that was set
up, might easily be imagined to be unimportant, if not illusory.

[1] These are the Uzbek SSR (formerly Bokhara, capital Samarkand), the
Turkoman SSR (capital Askhabad) and, promoted to independence from
having been merely part of the RSFSR, the Tadzhik SSR (capital Stalinbad),
all bordering on Persia and Afghanistan. The first two were formally admitted
by the USSR Congress of Soviets in May 1925, and the third in October 1929.
In area the three republics are nearly a million square kilometres, more than that
of Germany, Austria, Holland, Belgium and Denmark combined. Their inhabitants, now numbering over seven millions, are almost all Mohammedans, but
unlike the Persians, Sunnis, not Shiahs. Notwithstanding this religious difference, it was apparently feared that they might be drawn into union with Persia
or Afghanistan ; and special efforts have been made to strengthen their loyalty
to the USSR, with which they are now all connected by railway and river, air
lines and telegraphs as well as by new motor roads, whilst agriculture, industry
and commerce have been greatly developed. (See the able survey in *The
National Policy of the Soviet Union* by A. Rysakoff.)

How far such a judgment would be accurate we shall now be able to examine.

### The All-Union Congress of the USSR

The supreme body in the soviet hierarchy is the All-Union Congress of Soviets, which is made up of delegates from every part of the USSR. These are specially elected just before each such congress, which is now convened only every three or four years. These delegates have hitherto been chosen, not merely by the highest congress of soviets of each of the seven constituent republics of the Union, but also, at the rate of one delegate for every 125,000 population, by the congresses of soviets of the autonomous republics and autonomous areas within any of these seven constituent republics ; and also by the soviets of the more populous cities and urban settlements at the rate of one delegate for each 25,000 electors, equivalent to about one for each 5000 of population. The number of delegates varies, being roughly proportionate to the several census populations. At the congress in March 1931 the total (including 833 " candidates ", being substitutes or alternates) was 2403, about three-fourths being members of the Communist Party, or candidates for membership. At the next congress, in 1935, there were 2200 delegates with deciding votes, the total including candidates or alternates reaching some 3000. Of the delegates 74 per cent were Party members or candidates, or Comsomols. About one-sixth were women. More than half of the whole were attending for the first time. This huge assembly, made up of delegates of scores of races speaking different tongues, who meet only for a week or so and then " surrender their mandates ", and do not even know in advance each other's names, cannot, of course, develop the corporate life of a Parliament, or deal adequately with the details of legislation or administration. The Congress has been described, in fact, as little better than a picturesque " biennial picnic " in Moscow for locally elected visitors from all parts of the USSR, whose whole expenses are provided from USSR funds.[1] Even if this were true, it would

---

[1] " During the congress of the soviets, which assembles from time to time in Moscow, I have watched the delegates from these far-flung territories assemble in the ' Big Theatre ' which serves as meeting-place for the Congress until such time as the Palace of the Soviets is completed. Mongolians, Tadzhiks, Bashkirs, Uzbeks, Yakuts and some scores of other nationalities, representing peoples of

not imply that the Congress is of no political importance. On the contrary, its periodical meeting is one of the most useful parts of the USSR constitution. Although so large and heterogeneous a gathering is of no effect as a legislature, and not even very well fitted to be a forum of debate, its very existence is a potent factor of unity. It would be difficult to overestimate the value in this respect of bringing together some three thousand local personalities from a thousand cities and villages all over the USSR, to be entertained for a week or so in Moscow, which many of them have never before visited, and to be made to feel that it is upon them that the whole government depends. The delegates listen to the lengthy reports laid before them, and to the not less lengthy orations of the leading statesmen. In the end the delegates unanimously give a general sanction to the outlines of policy and legislation expounded to them. But they do much more than this. Probably no foreign observer sits through all the prolonged and sometimes heated discussions that, continued day after day, make the " picnic " a very strenuous exercise. Fortunately a shorthand report of the speeches is published. At the Fifth All-Union Congress in 1929, there spoke, on the general report presented by the Government, no fewer than 90 delegates ; on the combined reports of the People's Commissar of Agriculture, the Grain Trust (Zernotrest) and the cattle-breeding state farms (sovkhosi), 40 delegates; and on the report upon the organisation of collective farms (kolkhosi), 41 delegates. At the Sixth All-Union Congress in 1931, there took part in the discussions on the Government's general report, 57 delegates ; on the report dealing with the position and prospective development of industry, 31 delegates ; and on that about the main tasks of agriculture in connection with the whole " people's economy ", 40 delegates. The mere fact that no delegate is " denied the floor ", even if there is no effective voting, makes so representative a gathering of real political importance.

### The Soviet " Reform Bill "

The sensation of the Seventh All-Union Congress in 1935

almost every creed, stand together in respectful silence as the ' International ' is played. Later in the proceedings they pass a unanimous vote of confidence in their Central Executive Committee " (*Moscow, 1911–1933*, by Allan Monkhouse, 1934, p. 135).

was the proposal by V. M. Molotov, the president of the USSR Sovnarkom, speaking on behalf of the Central Committee of the Communist Party, for a complete change in the system of election. At a time, it was said, when in the capitalist countries parliamentary democracy was becoming more and more discredited, soviet democracy was evolving to the fullest electoral development. The Congress was invited to substitute " equal elections for not entirely equal, direct election for indirect, and secret for open elections ". It was explained that, as the kulaks were now crushed and the kolkhosi had achieved victory, the basis of representation in village and city (hitherto differing as between one delegate per 125,000 *inhabitants* and one per 25,000 *electors*) might safely be equalised. " All soviet organs from city and village soviets to the Central Executive Committee of the Union of Soviet Socialist Republics " are to be chosen by direct election. The right of the voters to recall their deputy from any organ is to be preserved. There is to be participation of non-Party organisations and groups of toilers in the nomination of candidates. All elections are to be by secret balloting. With these far-reaching reforms the evolution of soviet democracy would be completed. This important " Reform Bill " was enthusiastically adopted by the Congress, the whole of the delegates standing to give Molotov an ovation with no dissentient voice. Molotov's opening speech was broadcast from more than 60 radio stations to all parts of the USSR to be picked up by a couple of million wireless sets in homes, and many thousands of loud-speakers in factories and offices, as well as on the streets and squares of every city. It must have been heard by literally millions of citizens.[1]

By the Congress the proposal was immediately referred with unanimity to the Central Executive Committee (TSIK) with instructions to have the scheme of reform worked out by a Constitutional Commission, for approval at a subsequent session of the Central Executive Committee, and for use at the next regular election of " the organs of soviet power ". The very next day this Constitutional Commission was appointed, consisting of 31 members, under Stalin as chairman, and including all the seven

[1] Telegrams reported " good reception " and attentive listening crowds at all parts. Those " workers of Moscow factories and mills . . . of the morning shifts, who have no radio sets in their homes, remained at the plants till evening in order to hear the reports from the large Kremlin Palace " (*Moscow Daily News*, January 30, 1935).

presidents of the Union republics, Kaganovich, Molotov and
Litvinov, Radek and Bukharin, and a number of other leading personalities of the Party, representing all shades of opinion.
At its first meeting, on July 7th, the Commission appointed eleven
sub-committees to deal with as many separate departments of
its work, together with a twelfth, the editorial sub-committee,
consisting of the chairmen of all the others, under Stalin himself.

We understand that the new electoral system is now (1935)
being actively worked out by the sub-committees of the Constitutional Commission : but nothing is yet known of the means
by which the difficulties will be overcome.  The methods of
election of the village and city soviets, and of the rayon, oblast
and republic congresses of soviets, have to be considered, equally
with those of the All-Union Congress of Soviets ; but there seems
no actual need for complete identity of device in all these cases.
Will the characteristic use of small meetings of the electors be
given up ?  If anything like a couple of thousand delegates are
to be directly elected to the All-Union Congress by single-member
constituencies, approximately equal in populations, with electorates of between 40,000 and 50,000, the constituencies in the
rural districts must be of great superficial area, entailing some
difficulty in voting and in collecting the votes for counting.
But in Queensland and Western Australia similar difficulties have
been successfully overcome.  In the USSR the date of the
election might have to be changed from winter to summer.
More difficult may be the adoption of secret voting.  It is hard
to imagine what system can be successfully adopted for an
electorate soon to reach one hundred millions in number, dispersed over so huge an area.  If individual ballot papers are used,
the amount of paper required will be considerable; and if, as is the
case at present, all the elections are contested, the task of counting the votes will tax the arithmetical powers of the local officials.
The political world will watch with interest so colossal an experiment in taking the vote.  We do not ourselves believe that the
outcome of the election in the USSR under direct, equal and
secret voting will be substantially different from that under
the present system of indirect election.  The principal result may
be a new demonstration of the very widespread acquiescence of
the population in the existing régime, whose recent economic
and political achievements have become highly appreciated.

Equally striking will be the demonstration that the existing Soviet Government does not fear the peasants' votes, and has no need of the dictatorial powers conferred by law upon Mussolini and Hitler.

## *The Organs of the Congress*

Of the routine decisions of the Congress, the principal is the election of the Central Executive Committee (TSIK), to which is entrusted all legislative and executive power until the meeting of the next All-Union Congress. This executive is a curiously constructed bicameral body, which we shall presently describe in detail, consisting of the "Union of Soviets" of 607 members in 1935 (437 in 1931) elected by the Congress in proportion to the census population of the areas represented, at the rate of something like one to each 300,000 inhabitants ; and of the " Soviet of Nationalities " of 150 members, being five representing the highest congress of soviets of each constituent republic or autonomous republic within a constituent republic, and one by the like body of each other autonomous area.[1]

With regard to the distribution of powers between the federal government and the governments of the constituent parts, there may seem, at first sight, practically nothing that is unusual in federal states.[2] To the federal authority fall (1) all foreign relations (representation, treaties, declarations of war and peace, alteration of the external frontiers) ; (2) all the armed forces ; (3) transport, posts and telegraphs and radio ; (4) currency and credit systems, also weights and measures and statistics ; (5) the issuing and management of all state loans, internal or external ; (6) conditions of citizenship ; (7) the right of general amnesty ; and (8), more ambiguously, what is called the establishment of the bases and fundamental principles in respect of civil and

---

[1] In practice, we are told, the actual choice of these representatives of the several autonomous parts of the federation—at any rate for the " Union of Soviets "—is sometimes made by the group of delegates from each part who find themselves together at Moscow attending the Congress. Each delegation nominates to the Congress the particular member of its delegation whom it wishes to see elected to the " Union of Soviets " (about a quarter or one-third of its own delegation to the Congress). The Congress elects without question the nominees put forward in the name of each republic.

[2] Batsell could even state that " The specific categories of power . . . declared to fall within the exclusive purview of the Union . . . conform very closely to section 8 of article 1 of the constitution of the United States " (*Soviet Rule in Russia*, by W. R. Batsell, 1929, p. 284).

criminal codes, courts of justice, education, public health and labour protection, and of the development and use of land, waters, mineral deposits and forests. What is unmistakably novel is (9) the concession to the federal government of everything relating to imports and exports to or from the Soviet Union, under which all foreign trade has become a centralised state monopoly ; and (10) " the establishment of the foundations and the general plan of the whole people's economy of the Union ", meaning the collective organisation of the whole production and distribution of commodities. These last two categories of federal government are, however, not gained at the expense of the constituent authorities, which never wielded these powers. They represent the deprivation of the individual landlord or capitalist of his private power over the means of production, distribution and exchange. Their assumption by the federal government, together with the enormous development of industrialisation during the past decade, have increased beyond all expectation the dominance of the USSR administration over that of even the largest of the associated republics.

### *The Central Executive Committee (TSIK)*

The great powers of the federal government, whether legislative or executive, are shared between the bicameral Central Executive Committee (TSIK), with various commissions that it appoints, on the one hand, and on the other, the Sovnarkom, or Council of People's Commissars, which it also appoints, but which occupies a position of exceptional administrative authority requiring a separate description.

The Central Executive Committee, usually referred to as TSIK, and consisting of the Union of Soviets and the Soviet of Nationalities in two separate chambers, is a standing body, existing from congress to congress, and meeting three or four times annually,[1] principally to discuss and ratify the decrees and

---

[1] It was stated that, of the TSIK members in 1933, 18·4 per cent were actually manual working wage-earners in industrial enterprises. It is habitually found that all but 1 or 2 per cent are members of the Communist party. All members of the TSIK wear a silver badge, and enjoy the privilege of a free railway pass over the whole country. They receive, in addition, the whole of their expenses in attending the meetings at Moscow.

A member of TSIK cannot be arrested or prosecuted without the permission of the presidium of TSIK. They are empowered to attend any meetings of any

decisions formulated, either by its own presidium or arrived at by the USSR Council of People's Commissars (Sovnarkom), which corresponds approximately to the Cabinet of Ministers of western democracies. Its agenda, which the committee itself can alter, is drawn up by its presidium.

One of the functions of the Central Executive Committee and the one to which it owes its bicameral form, seems to have lost some of its significance. The Soviet of Nationalities is unique among political bodies in its remarkable basis of numerically equal representation (5 each), not only of the 9 constituent republics (the Transcaucasian Federation counting as 3), which vary in population from one to one hundred millions, but also of the numerous " autonomous republics " which are actually situated within divers of these constituent republics ; to these the other " autonomous areas " (oblasts or krais), also within the territories of the constituent republics, each add one representative. The two chambers of this bicameral body have equal rights as regards legislation. Each chamber must separately assent to every new law. In case of disagreement the issue is referred to a Conciliation Committee formed of an equal number of each chamber, with a president taken from among the members of TSIK, who may be in either chamber. The committee's decision is formally submitted to both chambers, and if either refuses to accept it, the measure is held to be rejected. However, either chamber may then appeal to the All-Union Congress, whose decision is final.

Thus, there is reason for the two chambers to meet separately and, when they have a joint session, even to vote separately. They must hold a joint meeting for the election of the presidium of TSIK, which is about the most influential organ of the constitution.

But we believe that the twofold nature of TSIK has, so far, never been called upon to resist either the increasing tendency to centralisation of authority, or the unmistakeable predominance of the area (the RSFSR) within which both Moscow and Leningrad are situated. It was devised, it is said, by Stalin himself, as part of the inducement by which the Ukraine, Transcaucasia

public body in the USSR, and visit any institution. But they are forbidden to address any meeting on behalf of TSIK, or speak in its name, without its special permission.

and White Russia were brought into federal union. With the liberal recognition of " cultural autonomy " and, very largely, of the principle of confiding the government of each locality to officials belonging to its own race, no serious cleavage along racial or geographical lines seems to have developed. Whilst differences of opinion naturally arise among members, and sectional grievances find spokesmen in both chambers of TSIK, it is understood that the Soviet of Nationalities, as such, has never voted differently from the Union of Soviets as such, so that the joint meetings of the two chambers, with which each session of TSIK terminates, and which are marked by unanimous votes in both parts of the joint body, have become purely ceremonial.

It would, however, be a mistake to regard the Central Executive Committee as merely a ratifying body. It evidently plays an important part in the discussion of general policy, alike by way of criticism of executive action and in the formulaion and adoption of new measures to cope with changing circumstances. Its members from all over the USSR bring information, both of local needs and of local opinion, to bear upon the minds of potentates necessarily resident in Moscow itself. If current gossip is to be trusted, it is the discussions in TSIK that have more than once determined a change in policy. Moreover TSIK takes an important part in administration, by the various commissions which it appoints, and which report directly to itself. Thus it has a Budget Commission, which reports on the finances of the whole USSR, and a Central Election Commission, which sees to the regularity of all the multifarious elections throughout the Union. It has a standing commission on the care of the central archives, and another on general questions of administrative organisation. There is a committee on scientific research and progress ; a central technical education commission, and also a committee on the higher colleges, all of them dealing with the organisation and geographical distribution of university and other institutions necessarily transcending the purview of the several constituent republics and autonomous areas, to which all education had been allotted as one of the subjects of " cultural autonomy ". Somewhat analogous functions are entrusted to commissions, entitled respectively the Supreme Council of Physical Culture and an All-Union Council of Communal Economy. Finally, there is the Supreme Court of the USSR, with the all-important Procurator's Department, and the newly appointed Procurator for the USSR, whose duties appear to include a new and increased supervision of the activities of the Ogpu itself, to which we shall recur. The aggregate of all these departments, directed by members of TSIK and immediately responsible to its plenum, make it one of the most important parts of the whole state organisation.

## The Presidium of TSIK

The presidium of TSIK, consisting of 9 members from the presidium of the Union of Soviets, 9 from that of the Soviet of Nationalities, and 9 elected by a joint session of these two chambers, is a standing representative of TSIK itself. It chooses seven presidents, one from each constituent republic, to preside on successive days of the sessions alike of TSIK and of its presidium. All draft decrees of new taxes, or increases of old ones, have to be first submitted to this presidium. All decisions relating to the alteration or abolition of regulations as to any of the TSIK's, or their presidiums, in any of the constituent republics of the Union are invalid without the sanction of the presidium of the TSIK of the USSR.

## Federal Machinery

The constitutional relations of the central federal organs of the USSR—such as the biennial All-Union Congress of Soviets, the Central Executive Committee (TSIK) and the Sovnarkom of People's Commissars—with the several governments of the constituent parts of the federal state, are in many respects unique. By the " fundamental law " the " sovereignty " of the seven constituent or " Union " republics is not only to be recognised by the USSR but is also to be protected by the federal power. This state sovereignty is expressly declared (in the Fundamental Law of the USSR of July 6, 1923) to be " restricted only within the limits stated in the present constitution, and only in respect of matters referred to the competence of the Union. *Beyond these limits each Union republic exercises its sovereign authority independently*. . . . Each Union Republic retains the right of free withdrawal from the Union . . . and for modification [or] limitation of [this provision] the agreement of all republics forming the USSR is required." [1]

Each of the seven constituent republics accordingly has its own congress of soviets of the republic, with its own Central Executive Committee and its own Council of People's Commissars, as "supreme organ of authority" within the limits of its own territory. But it can have no People's Commissars for foreign affairs, defence, trade beyond the USSR, mercantile marine, transport by rail or river, or posts and telegraphs, because these are subjects entirely reserved to the federal administration. What is unusual, if not unique, in federal constitutions, old or new, is the statutory provision that the responsible cabinet of ministers (sovnarkom) of each constituent republic, shall admit, as members, the official agents, delegates or "plenipotentiaries" of the People's Commissars of the USSR for each of these exclusively federal departments, "with either an advisory or decisive voice", according as the Central Executive Committee of the constituent republic may determine. There is an exactly similar representation of these USSR commissariats in the sovnarkom of each of the 15 autonomous republics. In the majority of cases, we are informed, the "voice" is advisory or consultative only.

Accordingly, in the great Russian Socialist Federal Soviet Republic (RSFSR), which has over a hundred millions of inhabitants, there sat in 1935, in its cabinet of 24, no fewer than 9 of these federal officials of the USSR. Among the 23 members of the cabinet of the Ukraine, there were also 9 such officials of the federation. In that of the White Russian Socialist Soviet Republic there were also 9 out of 23. In that of the Transcaucasian Socialist Federated Soviet Republic, with a total membership of no more than 17, these officials of the federal government at Moscow (9) constitute an actual majority. [2] The specific function of these federal officials is doubtless to see that nothing

---

[1] Chap. i. of "Fundamental Law of the RSFSR adopted for the USSR, July 6, 1932"; see *Soviet Rule in Russia*, by W. R. Batsell, 1929, p. 308; and pp. 297-298, where an obviously incorrect interpretation of the statute is given.

[2] In the three smallest constituent republics the representation of the USSR is equally strong. In the Uzbek Republic Sovnarkom there sit 9 delegates of federal commissars in a sovnarkom of 23. In that of Turkmenistan there were also 9 out of a total of 23. In that of Tadzhikistan there were 9 out of 22. In the 15 autonomous republics the numerical proportion of delegates of federal commissariats is similar.

is done or even initiated by the constituent or autonomous republic that would be inconsistent with federal policy in federal affairs. But it is stated that, as members of the local sovnarkoms or cabinets, they do not confine themselves to any specific class of questions, and that they take part in all the cabinet's deliberations. It is clear that their mere presence in the local cabinet in such numbers, even with no more than an " advisory " or a consultative voice, must necessarily exercise a constant influence towards unity of policy and action throughout the whole of the USSR.

This peculiar official interpenetration goes even further than the local cabinets of the constituent or autonomous republics, which necessarily meet at the local republic capitals. In a dozen or so other cities of the USSR, especially those at which any foreign consuls are stationed, or which are near an important frontier, or which are much frequented by foreign travellers, there will be found resident a responsible officer of the USSR People's Commissar for Foreign Affairs at Moscow.[1] Doubtless the primary function of this " diplomatic agent " is to keep an eye on the activities of the foreign consuls, and to prevent any questions arising with regard to the treatment of foreign nationals. But it is of interest in this connection to notice that these official agents of the USSR federal government are usually, as a matter of course, made members of the highest administrative council meeting in the cities in which they reside. Thus the one at Leningrad is a member of the presidium of the executive committee of the soviet of the city of Leningrad ; and the one who, down to 1934, resided at Kiev was a member of the corresponding body for the great oblast of Kiev—in both cases taking full part, and naturally exerting a great influence, in all the deliberations of these local authorities.[2]

[1] Such "diplomatic agents " are stationed at Leningrad, Vladivostock, Alexandrovsk (Sakhalin), Alma Ata and Khabarovsk in the RSFSR; at Kharkov and Odessa in the Ukraine ; at Baku, Batoum and Erivan in the Transcaucasian Federation ; at Kerki and Kouchka in Turkmenistan ; and at Termez in Uzbekistan. To these have lately been added Arkhangelsk, Blagovestchensk, Chita, Okla (Sakalin), Kamchatka and Verkhneudinsk.

[2] There is still a further official interpenetration to be mentioned. On the executive of the oblast in the RSFSR and the Ukraine, whether ispolkom in the oblasts properly so called, or sovnarkom in the autonomous republics, there sit officials representing the USSR People's Commissariats of Land Transport (railways) and Posts and Telegraphs. (See *The Soviet State*, by B. W. Maxwell, 1934, p. 106.) Similar important officials of these and other federal departments

Equally serviceable in ensuring unity of policy and action must prove the practice of what in the joint stock world is known as " interlocking directorates ". Thus the seven presidents of the Central Executive Committee of the USSR, who are generally the most influential of the 27 members of its presidium, were in 1932, all of them simultaneously, either the presidents of the Central Executive Councils of the several constituent republics or of their sovnarkoms of People's Commissars. Among the other 20 members of this all-powerful central presidium at the same date were 6 other People's Commissars or cabinet ministers of the constituent republics, not one of which was thus without an influential representative actually inside the most important federal body, of the membership of which they together made up one-half. The position remains substantially the same in 1935.

There is yet another variety of this official interpenetration. Under the statutory constitution the various public departments, for the administration of which each constituent republic is responsible in its " sovereign capacity ", are classified as " unified " and " non-unified ". The unified departments are now those of finance and light industries, together with the recently added separate USSR Commissariat for the collective farms (kolkhosi), with the still surviving independent peasantry. For these departments the People's Commissars of the federal government do not, as a rule, set up offices of their own in the constituent or autonomous republics, but are required, by statute, to make use of the local official staff, which is of course appointed and directed by, and immediately responsible to, the several People's Commissars of the different constituent or autonomous republics. In order to make this statutory provision work smoothly, the federal government has established a convention with the governments of the several constituent or autonomous republics, under which the official head of the local department concerned—usually but not necessarily a local " native " or resident—is always chosen after private consultation between the two governments, so that each may feel assured that the new officer will be faithful in the discharge of

sit on such powerful municipal soviets as those of Moscow and Leningrad, either by direct election in their capacity as citizens, or, where they are not thus elected, by cooption at the instance of the presidium.

his curious double responsibility.[1]  A similar unpublished convention is said to exist even with regard to the appointment of the People's Commissar himself, at any rate in finance, where the nomination is said to require the private sanction of the People's Commissar of Finance of the USSR.

There remain the non-unified departments, significantly enough, those directly connected with the " cultural autonomy " which is what the local " national minorities " are most concerned to maintain against the centralising and unifying encroachments of a federal administration.  Over these departments, such as education, health and social welfare,[2] the People's Commissars of the several constituent or autonomous republics have, at least in theory, sole authority, in each case subject only to his own Sovnarkom of People's Commissars and his own Central Executive Committee and Congress of Soviets.  They have, however, all to realise that the formulation by the federal government of " basic principles " in these subjects, and its determination of the form

[1] It is not without interest to find that this unpublished convention was described differently by the two parties to it.  From one side it was said that, on the occurrence of a vacancy, the choice made by this state government was submitted to Moscow for concurrence.  From the other side it was said that the choice made by the federal government was submitted to the state capital for concurrence.  It was also remarked that such arrangements should not be too closely scrutinised !

[2] With regard to education, as already mentioned, there is now a commission on university and higher technical institutes ; another on technical education generally and a third on scientific research and progress, all three appointed by and responsible to the Central Executive Committee (TSIK) of the USSR, in order to deal with such questions as the allocation of new institutions which transcend the view of any local authority, and new scientific developments in the way of exploration and important experiments.

Two of the non-unified commissariats in the constituent and autonomous republics have lately been suppressed.  That for labour has been transferred to the All-Union Central Committee of Trade Unions and its subordinate hierarchy of local trade union councils.  The inspectorial activities of the Workers' and Peasants' Inspection have been similarly transferred to the trade union hierarchy.  But the disciplinary and other action taken as a result of these activities have been given to a new Control Commission responsible to the USSR Sovnarkom, in close collaboration with another new Control Commission appointed by the Central Committee of the Communist Party.

Two others of the non-unified commissariats in the constituent and autonomous republics have been either suppressed or brought much more under federal control.  These are those for agriculture, which have, as above stated, been placed essentially in the position of unified departments, subordinate to the new USSR People's Commissars for State Farms (sovkhosi) and for collective farms (kolkhosi) together with the remaining independent peasantry.  And the work of the Commissariat for Internal Affairs has been partly transferred to the new USSR People's Commissar for Internal Affairs (Narkomvnutdel), and partly subordinated to him as a unified department.

of the economic organisation, together with its conduct of the whole of the nationalised industries and of foreign commerce—along with such all-important matters as finance and taxation and land and water transport—must not be hampered or interfered with.

It should be added that, whilst, as we have seen, the federal government is very powerfully represented in the cabinet of each constituent or autonomous republic, as well as in all the " unified " departments, and in many of its great cities, the governments of the constituent and autonomous republics have not, under the constitution, the reciprocal privilege of being formally represented either at the federal capital of Moscow or at the capitals of the other constituent republics. All the constituent republics do, in fact, maintain their own offices in Moscow, at which some of their own officials reside for convenience of making any necessary enquiries or representations concerning any part of the federal administration.[1] But such enquiry agents have no formal status under the constitution, and they apparently do not exist at any other capital than Moscow.

### The Council of People's Commissars (Sovnarkom)

The greater part of the higher executive work in the USSR is entrusted, by the Central Executive Committee (TSIK), to the Council of People's Commissars (Sovnarkom), which directs the action of the principal government departments much as the groups of Cabinet Ministers do in parliamentary democracies. " What shall we call ourselves ? " Lenin is reported to have asked Trotsky,[2] when, on finding themselves, in October 1917, in command of the state, they had to allot the offices among their

---

[1] Their names are printed in the official *Annuaire Diplomatique* published in French by the Commissariat of Foreign Affairs (Narkomindel) of the USSR. The 12 autonomous republics within the RSFSR are stated to be similarly represented at Moscow, but this is not mentioned in the *Annuaire*.

[2] " Not Minister, that is a repulsive designation." " We might say Commissar," suggested Trotsky, " but there are too many Commissars now." " Perhaps Chief Commissars. . . . No, ' chief ' sounds too bad. What about People's Commissars ? Well, this may be all right." " And the Government as a whole, the Soviet of People's Commissars," continued Lenin ; " this will be splendid, it smells of revolution."

The anecdote circulates in various versions. See *Soviet Rule in Russia*, by W. R. Batsell, 1929, p. 544 ; *Lenin*, by L. Trotsky, p. 132 ; *My Life*, by the same, 1930, pp. 337-338.

colleagues. The designation " Minister " was rejected because of
its association with tsarist autocracy and parliamentarianism.
" People's Commissar " was viewed more favourably, and, after
some discussion, adopted, at first for the RSFSR and then, successively, for all the constituent republics and even for the
" autonomous republics " within them. The same designation
was adopted in 1923 for the USSR. We need not trace the
repeated changes made during the past eighteen years in the
number and in the functions of these People's Commissars.
For the USSR there are now People's Commissars for the following departments :

(1) Foreign Affairs (NKID).

(2) Defence (NKOBORONY).

(3) Foreign Trade (NKVNESHTORG).

(4) Means of Communication (Railways) (NKPS).

(5) Heavy Industries (NKTYAZHPROM).

(6) River Transport (NKWT).

(7) Posts, Telegraphs and Radio (NKSVYAZ).

(8) Forestry and Wood Industries (NKLES).

(9) Light Industries (NKLEGPROM).

(10) Agriculture (NKZEM)—added to the federal organisation
in 1932, specially for the collective farms (kolkhosi) in addition
to the commissariats for agriculture in the several constituent
autonomous republics.

(11) State Farms (NKSOVKHOSI).

(12) Food Industry (NARKOMPISHCH).

(13) Internal Trade (NARKOMVNUTORG).

(14) Finance (NARKOMFIN).

(15) Internal Affairs (NARKOMVNUTDEL).[1]

There are, in addition, half a dozen other government departments of great importance, which are always represented in

[1] The above list is the outcome of various changes. Thus there was, until
November 26, 1932, a People's Commissar for Foreign and Home Trade, until
a decree of that date replaced him by a People's Commissar of Supplies and a
People's Commissar of Foreign Trade. In 1934 the former was relieved of
wholesale and retail trading for which a separate People's Commissar of Internal
Trade was appointed. Similarly, the burden of the People's Commissar for
Transport was lightened on January 30, 1931, by transferring maritime and
river transport, with ports and harbours, to a new People's Commissar for
Water Transport. Later in 1931 a new central administration was set up for
road transport in the USSR, assisted by similar central administrations for the
main roads in each of the constituent republics.

the Sovnarkom, although their heads are not styled People's Commissars.

There is, to begin with, (16) the Office of Administrative Affairs, a department which has the duty of seeing to it that all the decisions of the Sovnarkom are promptly and accurately put in course of operation.[1]

There is the very important State Planning Commission (Gosplan) with a president and six vice-presidents, which is represented in the Sovnarkom by its president.

There is the Council of Labour and Defence (STO) consisting of a president, three vice-presidents and six other members ; and the " Commission of Fulfilment " of this Council, consisting of a president, a vice-president and three members—both these departments being at present represented in the Sovnarkom by their common president (Molotov).

There were also, in 1934, various other boards for special purposes, such as a State Yield Committee and a State Arbitration Committee, a Central Board for Road Transport and another for the Civic Air Fleet, a Concessions Committee and a Control Board of the North Sea Route. Some of these were only temporary. They may not enjoy representation in the Sovnarkom : their presidents may be summoned when their representative subjects come up for discussion.

Finally, but by no means least important, there was, until July 1934, the Union State Political Administration (the Ogpu or GPU), whose permanent president, with his immense and almost uncontrolled authority within the wide sphere of his department, might be described as a facultative member of the Sovnarkom, as he went to its meetings whenever he chose to do so. This position was regularised, in July 1934, by the establishment of an All-Union People's Commissariat for Internal Affairs (Narkomvnutdel), with its own People's Commissar in the Sovnarkom, under whose direction was placed the control and direction of the

---

[1] We are informed that there is now no separate Director of Administrative Affairs. But the " Bureau of Administration " was expressly charged in order to secure "the exact and timely execution" of ordinances of the Sovnarkom by all institutions and officials thereof (decree of February 17, 1924, of the Sovnarkom ; *Soviet Rule in Russia*, by W. R. Batsell, 1929, p. 605).

We do not know whether the Sovnarkom has followed the new practice of the British Cabinet since 1914 of keeping regular minutes of even the most secret decisions.

Ogpu as " the Chief Department of State Security ", alongside of five other " chief departments ".

Lastly, we have to note the establishment in February 1934, at the instance of the Communist Party and in super-session of the Workers' and Peasants' Inspection, of a new and powerful organ of the USSR Sovnarkom, entitled the Commission of Soviet Control, consisting of sixty tried and trusted Party members nominated by the Central Committee of the Party. Its president will always be one of the vice-presidents of the Sovnarkom itself. This Commission of Soviet Control is charged specifically with seeing to it that every important decree or directive of the Central Executive Committee (TSIK) or Sovnar-kom is actually complied with and carried into execution in every part of the USSR.[1] For this purpose it will have its own in-spectors, accountants and other agents, who will reside per-manently in the various republics, krais and oblasts of the Union and will be independent of any local authority. It will act in close conjunction with a Commission of Party Control, appointed by the Communist Party, which will apply disciplinary action to Party members, whilst leaving to the Sovnarkom and the several People's Commissars to do what is required to remedy the de-fects and deficiencies discovered.[2]

This score or so of ministers of state form at present the All-Union Council of People's Commissars (Sovnarkom), which may be taken to be the highest executive authority in the USSR, nearly corresponding to the cabinet in the governments of the western world ; although it is by no means exclusively executive, and can enact decrees subject to ratification by the Congress. In fact, in the USSR no small proportion of the constant stream of new decrees, definitely legislative in character and normally subject to eventual ratification by the All-Union Congress of Soviets, bear the signature of Molotov, as president of the All-Union Sovnarkom : this being often coupled with that of Kalinin, as president of the Central Executive Committee (TSIK) of the All-Union Congress of Soviets; and, since 1930, even more usually with that of Stalin, as general secretary of the Communist Party.

[1] Its basic object is described as " the systematic, concrete and operative verification of the execution of the most important decisions of the government by all branches of the soviet and economic apparatus from top to bottom".

[2] See, for this decree, *Pravda*, February 28, 1934.

This USSR Sovnarkom, or one or other of its committees, is almost daily in session in the Moscow Kremlin all the year round. Its actual procedure is wrapped in a secrecy exceeding even that of the British Cabinet. No minutes or records of proceedings are ever published. Apart from its formal decrees or "directives", commanding action to be taken, the Sovnarkom of the USSR issues no *communiqués* to the public or the press. Political gossip—which is rife and rank in the diplomatic circle at Moscow, and among the foreign journalists there—is severely discouraged among all grades of soviet officials. Although the foreign correspondents are, from time to time, addressed by one or other of the Commissars, or on their behalf, the soviet newspapers are strictly forbidden to give currency to political gossip, or even to mention unauthorised rumours about what the Soviet Government is discussing or intending. The foreign correspondents are asked to conform to this rule. On the other hand, almost every department publishes its own weekly or monthly journal, which is full of reports of all branches of departmental work. Every office has its own "wall newspaper" written by its own staff about the internal life of the office. Moreover, in no country do statesmen so frequently take the public into their confidence by the publication in full, in the widely circulating newspapers, of long and detailed "resolutions" come to by the Central Executive Committee (TSIK) or by the Sovnarkom, going into all sorts of financial and technical details. Moreover, the newspapers are constantly being filled by verbatim reports of the lengthy addresses of ministers to conferences and meetings of all kinds, about the vicissitudes of the innumerable government undertakings, the new projects about to be put in operation and the general progress of the "Five-Year Plan".

Of the way in which the ministerial organisation actually works, there is (as is normally the case in all countries) little available information. No one can describe the frequently changing relations that exist between the Sovnarkom and its president (Molotov) ; or between it and its other members ; or between it and the presidium of the Central Executive Committee (TSIK) of the All-Union Congress of Soviets ; or between it and such important bodies as the Commission of Labour and Defence (STO), in which Stalin and another important official of the Communist Party sit with eight People's Commissars ; or the secret working of the State Planning Commission (Gosplan) ; or the position of the Union State Political Commission (Ogpu) in its new form of People's Commissariat for Internal Affairs under the new commissar. It will be observed that among the People's Commissars, or the members of the USSR Sovnarkom, we do not find the name of Kalinin, who acts as, and is commonly styled, president of the USSR, to whom the foreign ambassadors present their credentials and who is certainly one of the most influential of the presidents of the All-Union Congress of Soviets and of its Central Executive Committee (TSIK), and also of the presidium thereof. Nor do we find the name of Stalin, who is general secretary of the Communist Party, but who long held no government office other than that of one among the ten members of the Commission of Labour and Defence (STO). In 1935, however, Stalin was elected a member of the Central Executive Committee (TSIK), and likewise a member of its presidium, at the same time becoming chairman of the special commission for the revision of the electoral system. Menzhinsky, until his death in 1933 the president of the Ogpu, though not a member, was definitely stated to have the right of attending the Sovnarkom whenever (and this was said to be rarely) he wished to do so. Probably Stalin and Kalinin have, in practice, the same privilege, and more frequently exercise it. Harmony among all these personages, and unity of action among the departments they control, are usually well maintained ; but serious, and sometimes prolonged, public controversies over policy, with peremptory removals from office, and drastic exclusions from the Party, have taken place from time to time. Whatever changes of personnel may occur, no careful observer can doubt the essential stability of the government as a whole, and even its continuity of fundamental policy, coupled with a remarkable capacity for sudden changes in the forms and methods of its application, according to the lessons of experience.

We need not seek to detail the organisation of all the government departments which the ministers direct and control. One distinctive feature of the constitution has been, until 1934, that each People's Commissar was required, by statute, to have, besides one or more Assistants, a collegium of several persons of position and experience, with whom he was required confidentially to discuss all important proceedings or proposals.[1] This was professedly designed to ensure that he might take into account all relevant considerations, obtain all the available information and listen to the best advice. These colleagues of the minister were apparently not chosen always by himself, or even privately suggested for his approval, but were nominated by the Sovnarkom as a whole, sometimes deliberately as a check on too independent action. By a remarkable provision in the decree formally regulating the Sovnarkom, the collegium of each People's Commissar, and any member thereof, was given " the right of appeal " from any decision of the Commissar, " without suspending its execution, to the Sovnarkom as a whole ".[2] We do not know whether this formal right of appeal was ever exercised, or how often. The members of the collegium were usually prepared at any time to act as deputies for the Commissar, or to take his place if he was absent or incapacitated by illness.

Upon a decision of the Central Committee of the Communist Party in 1934 that the collegia should be given up, these have been, one by one, abolished by separate decrees of the Central Executive Committee, which effected, at the same time, a certain amount of reorganisation of the business of each commissariat.

The authority of the All-Union Sovnarkom and its People's Commissars extends all over the USSR. With regard to the so-called All-Union or federal narkomats (or, as we should say, ministries) such as those dealing with foreign affairs ; military and naval affairs (now styled defence) ; foreign trade ; land transport ; water transport ; posts, telegraphs and radio ; and now heavy industries, forestry and supplies, the very considerable staffs throughout the entire area of the USSR, as well as those maintained in foreign countries, are appointed and directed by the several All-Union People's Commissars, to whom these locally resident officials are solely responsible, without regard to the government of the particular republic in the territory of which they may be serving. Moreover, as we have mentioned, each People's Commissar for an All-Union or federal narkomat sends a delegate or plenipotentiary to each constituent and each autonomous republic, who has the right of sitting as a member in the

[1] The collegium of the People's Commissar for Foreign Trade had more than a score of members.

[2] Decree of November 12, 1923, of the Central Executive Committee (TSIK) ; *Soviet Rule in Russia*, by W. R. Batsell, 1929, pp. 599-604.

local sovnarkom, with either a " consultative " or a " decisive " voice, according as the Central Executive Committee of that republic may have decided. The delegate so appointed by the All-Union Commissar is normally entrusted by him with the direction and control of the local staff of the All-Union narkomat. In the case of the " unified narkomats ", now only three (Internal Trade, Agriculture and Finance), the All-Union People's Commissar has, apart from the persons actually employed in the numerous " nationalised " enterprises, no office staff exclusively his own in any of the constituent or autonomous republics, over and above that attached to the narkomat office at Moscow ; members of which may, however, be detached for travel or temporary residence. For the local executive work of his narkomat in the several constituent or autonomous republics, including the RSFSR, he has to rely on a " unified staff " which is appointed and controlled by the corresponding People's Commissar of each such republic, but which is required to carry out any instructions received from the People's Commissar of the USSR. In order to make such an arrangement work smoothly there has grown up the remarkable private convention between the two governments that we have already described, namely, that the head of each department of the constituent republic's " unified " staffs, and sometimes the local People's Commissar, should be chosen and appointed by the two governments in joint private consultation, in order that each of them may be assured of his necessarily bipartite loyalty.

The non-unified narkomats are those dealing with the subjects in which the constituent republics have been conceded " cultural autonomy ". For these subjects (which have long comprised justice and police—except for the sporadic intervention of the USSR Supreme Court and the Ogpu—education [1] and public

---

[1] With regard to universities and the higher technical institutes and the promotion of scientific research, which have more than a local significance, it has been found convenient, as already mentioned, to give the local People's Commissars for Education the assistance of three federal commissions appointed by the Central Executive Committee (TSIK).

The position with regard to internal affairs was changed in July 1934 by the establishment of a USSR People's Commissar of Internal Affairs (Narkomvnutdel), who takes over much of the work formerly done by the local commissariats of Internal Affairs. Such a local commissariat had been abolished in January 1931, when its work in each constituent or autonomous republic was temporarily placed, partly under the local sovnarkom, and partly under a " chief office of communal authority ". These functions are, from July 1934, discharged by the new USSR People's Commissar of Internal Affairs.

health) there are no All-Union People's Commissars and no All-Union staffs of officials, and each constituent and autonomous republic has its own, which are subject only to the supervision and control of each republic's own Sovnarkom, Central Executive Committee and Congress of Soviets.   But it must not be overlooked that the All-Union Congress of Soviets and its Central Executive Committee (TSIK)—not to mention the Central Committee of the Communist Party—exercise a great influence upon the nominally independent organs of the various constituent republics, so far at least as the " general line " and the " basic principles " of legislation and administration are concerned.

It should be added that USSR Sovnarkom has always appointed standing committees from its own membership, often with the addition of a few other persons.   The number, and also the activities, of these standing committees have varied from time to time ; and some of them have lingered in existence, taking up one subject after another as required, long after their main purpose had been fulfilled or become exhausted.   Committees of this sort were at their height during the period of war communism, 1918–1921, and they have declined in importance as the system of administration has become more settled.[1]

### The Council of Labour and Defence

The oldest of the standing committees of the USSR Sovnarkom is now the Council of Labour and Defence (STO),[2] which was

---

[1] The most important of these was the Supreme Economic Council, which, from 1918 to 1932, was in charge of the greater part of the industrial reconstruction ; and to which we shall recur in our subsequent chapter on " Planned Production for Community Consumption".

[2] See the decree of August 21, 1923, of the Sovnarkom as to the Council of Labour and Defence (STO), in *Soviet Rule in Russia*, by W. R. Batsell, 1929, pp. 620-622 ; also the incidental references in *Soviet Russia*, by W. H. Chamberlin, 1930, pp. 135-136 ; *Moscow, 1911–1933*, by Allan Monkhouse, 1934, p. 184 ; " The Organisation of Economic Life", by W. H. Chamberlin, in *Soviet Economics*, edited by Dr. G. Dobbert, 1933, p. 27.

The competence of the STO is defined as under :

(*a*) The consideration and practical carrying through the appropriate organs of the economic and financial plans of the Union of SSR.

(*b*) The consideration of problems concerning the defence of the country and the taking of measures for improvement of military affairs.

(*c*) The consideration of the condition of various provinces of the economic life of the country (finance, industry, trade and transport) which are of All-Union

appointed by the Sovnarkom's decree of August 21, 1923, embodied in the Code of Laws, 1932, " in order to carry on the economic and financial plans of the USSR, to verify them in accordance with economic and political conditions, as well as for the purpose of close direction of the commissariats of the Union in the sphere of economic activities and defence ". It was from the outset placed permanently under the chairmanship of the president of the Sovnarkom for the time being. It is essentially a joint-committee of those People's Commissars who are principally concerned with economic issues and national defence. It now consists of a dozen members, specially appointed by the Sovnarkom, and including the People's Commissars for finance, railways, agriculture, food supplies, heavy industry and defence ; the president of the planning department (Gosplan) ; the principal assistant of the People's Commissar of finance, who is also president of the state bank ; and last but certainly not least, Stalin, who is the general secretary of the Communist Party.

The resolutions of STO come immediately into operation, but they must be forwarded at once to the Sovnarkom, which has the right to suspend or cancel any of them. Moreover, each member of STO, and also any People's Commissar of the Union, has a right to appeal to the Sovnarkom within three days ; and the Sovnarkom of any constituent republic may also appeal without any time limit.

The student of the work of the Council of Labour and Defence will, we think, conclude that its work has been steadily decreased in scope and importance by the growth of other authorities, sometimes those springing directly from itself. For instance, the State Planning Department (Gosplan), with which we shall deal elaborately in our chapter entitled " Planned Production for Community Consumption ", originally appointed by STO, and regularly established by statute of August 23, 1923, has become a gigantic and virtually independent department, directly represented by its president in the Sovnarkom, as well as in the

significance, and the taking of measures necessary to bring about their development.

(*d*) The direction of People's Commissariats of the USSR in the field of state economy and of the defence of the republic.

(*e*) Direct direction of economic councils (conferences) of union republics, of standing commissions and committees attached to the STO and consideration of their reports (as laid down in the Code of Laws, 1932, No. 15, article 85, par. 1).

(Decree of August 21, 1923.)

Council of Labour and Defence. By the steadily improving
plans that it lays for ratification before the Sovnarkom, the Central
Executive Committee and the Central Committee of the Communist Party, it practically formulates the course for the year
of every economic factor in the USSR. The Council of Labour
and Defence (STO) still continues to be appointed annually,
and to be an important influence, but its duties appear now to
consist largely of odds and ends not assigned to any particular
People's Commissar ; such as appointing committees on particular subjects of economic importance ; and acting from time
to time as a mediating or arbitrating body between the competing projects or differing opinions of two or more of them.[1]
Among the busiest of its several departments seems to be the
Bureau for Inventions (BRIZ), which deals with the extraordinarily large number of suggestions and inventions and other
improvements in industrial and other administration, which are
submitted by workmen and others to the managements concerned. Naturally, their examination takes time, and is possibly
sometimes perfunctory. The result is much complaint, and a
more or less formal appeal of which the Bureau of Inventions
(BRIZ) takes cognisance.

### The Commissariats

So much for the constitution of the Sovnarkom as a whole,
and its relation to the Central Executive Committee and the
All-Union Congress of Soviets, on the one hand ; and, on the
other, to the governments of the constituent and autonomous
republics and the autonomous areas. The volume and importance
of its work has naturally steadily increased with the growth of

---

[1] " For example, in February 1932 it elected the committee for the holding-
ready of agricultural products, a committee formed to conduct the campaign
for the accumulation of agricultural stocks, formerly a work for which each
economic commissariat was held responsible " (" Organisation of Economic
Life ", by W. H. Chamberlin, in *Soviet Economics*, edited by Dr. G. Dobbert,
1933, p. 27).

Other standing committees of STO may be mentioned, such as that on the
development of the " sub-tropical " areas within the USSR ; that on the provision of agricultural products (storage); that on the kustar industry and the
incops ; that on standardisation ; that on merchandise funds and trade
regulations ; that on reserve foodstuffs ; that on goods traffic difficulties ; that
on the shortage of live-stock ; that on grain elevators ; and that on the metric
system.

industrialism and the development of collectivism among the peasantry as well as among the factory workers. The life of a People's Commissar of the USSR is one of continuous labour and worry in coping with the difficulties with which every department is confronted. " It is commonly said in Moscow that there is hardly a commissar whose health has not been undermined as a result of overwork." [1] The cabinet ministers in other countries, for the most part, find time for a great deal of social intercourse in the wealthy society of the capital and the country houses, often interspersed with sport and amusements, and even occasional travel. So far as the authors have been able to form an opinion, the work of the USSR People's Commissars is more continuous and unremitting, as well as far less highly paid, than that of ministers elsewhere.

This is involved, we suggest, in the fact that the government of the USSR undertakes a task that no other government has ever undertaken. In every other country, the government, whilst mildly interested in this or that particular reform that may, from time to time, seem to be required, habitually assumes that its business is to maintain the *status quo*. No government outside the USSR has ever frankly taken as its task the complete recasting of the economic and social life of the entire community, including the physical health, the personal habits, the occupations and, above all, the ideas of all the millions for whom it acts—in short, the making of a new civilisation.

We need not trouble the reader by describing each of the score or more of ministerial departments or commissariats, but, in order to bring out the difference between them and the ministries of western Europe, we are compelled to comment on the peculiarities of some among them.

### The Commissariats dealing with Production and Trade

The greatest distinction between the Sovnarkom of the USSR and the cabinets of capitalist countries is in the nature of the

---

[1] " Captains of Soviet Industry ", by Professor Heinrich Poppelmann, in *Soviet Economics*, edited by Dr. G. Dobbert, 1933, p. 81. The German professor adds " coupled with privation ". The People's Commissars, like all other Party members, have to live simply and sparely ; but we doubt whether their health has suffered from anything to be properly termed privation. It would have been most unwise and imprudent for the USSR government not to have seen to it that its ministers were adequately fed, clothed and housed.

business dealt with. In the capitalist countries by far the greater part of the production and distribution of commodities and services is conducted by private persons, with the object of making profit for themselves ; and not by public departments aiming directly at the service of the community. In the Soviet Union, on the other hand, practically the whole of the heavy industries, and the larger part of the light industries, together with nearly all transport and foreign commerce, are conducted by public departments, which are in the main established, controlled and directed by the federal government.[1] The members of the Sovnarkom of the USSR accordingly find themselves charged with work of great magnitude and variety, with which the cabinet ministers of capitalist countries have little or nothing to do. The People's Commissars of the USSR are responsible, jointly or severally, not only for the railways and waterways, the posts and telegraphs, the currency and the taxation of an immense and widely scattered population, but also for the direction of the ten thousand or more separate manufacturing establishments in the USSR ; the five thousand or more state farms (sovkhosi) ; the thousand or more mines of coal, ironstone, manganese, lead and other metals ; the gigantic oil-plants, steelworks, electric generating stations, the considerable foreign trade, the growing mercantile marine, and what not.

For the greater part of this work of what the capitalist world would regard as business administration, eight separate People's Commissars are now, after many successive changes, individually responsible. The whole of the exporting and importing of any commodities whatsoever, to or from any place outside the USSR, is directed by the People's Commissar of Foreign Trade (Narkomvneshtorg), who has his own subordinate commissions, or (in accordance with the law of the foreign countries concerned) even joint-stock companies, and his own network of commercial agents, all over the world. A large part of the service of food production and distribution for the population of the USSR was for several years under the People's Commissar for Food Supplies (Narkom-

---

[1] The enterprises of the various associations of owner-producers in industry and agriculture, and those of the consumers' cooperative societies, are described in the chapters relating to those subjects. The extent to which independent self-employment prevails in the USSR, and the spheres assigned to free trade and free competition, are described in the chapter "In Place of Profit", IX. in Part II.

pishch).  He has been replaced by two People's Commissars, one of Food Industry, dealing mainly, not with grain, but with all other food-stuffs (and with alcoholic drinks and tobacco) which need processing, preparing or canning ; and the other of Internal Trade, charged with the organisation or control of all distribution of commodities, whether wholesale or retail.  There is also a People's Commissar for the State Farms (sovkhosi), which are administered as if they were factories of grain, flax or cotton, beet, livestock or dairy produce.  The difficulties in getting in the harvest, especially in .the North Caucasus and in certain parts of the Ukraine, led, in 1932, to the subordination of all the seven People's Commissars for Agriculture in the constituent republics to a separate All-Union People's Commissar for Agriculture (including the kolkhosi as well as the supervision of the surviving independent peasantry), in order to organise and direct the extensive " drive " on the incompetent, negligent or recalcitrant peasants in the collective farms from one end of the USSR to the other.  The " heavy " industries, which include the mining of coal, peat and lignite, and of iron, manganese, lead and other ores ;  the extraction of oil and the manufacture of numerous oil products ;  the making of pig-iron and steel ;  and the manufacture of machinery of every kind, are placed under the new narkomat of Heavy Industries (NKTYAZHPROM).  The " light " industries, principally engaged in making commodities from textiles or leather for household use, are now subject to a new narkomat for Light Industries (Legprom).  Another new narkomat, that for timber industries, directs the exploitation of the forests (les), which, it is believed, can be economically combined, at different seasons, with the agricultural work on the collective farms (kolkhosi) ;  and the same People's Commissar will direct the manufacture of paper and other timber products, on the one hand, and of innumerable articles of furniture on the other.

In accordance with the directions of these eight People's Commissars, and of the State Planning Commission (Gosplan), the full description of which we reserve for a subsequent chapter, all the innumerable separate industrial establishments in the USSR (other than those of the consumers' cooperative societies, and those of the artels organised in industrial cooperatives) are grouped under boards or commissions called sometimes trusts and sometimes combines.[1] These boards or commissions are appointed by the People's Commissar in each case. The usual form has been a board consisting of a president, a secretary and from three to a dozen other members, all of whom give their whole time to their duties, which combine those of a director and a manager in an important English industrial company. The aim has been to secure, among these members of each trust or combine—so an American enquirer was informed in 1932—"a 'Red' director, a technical director, a factory director, a commercial director and a general director. All except the 'Red' director must have had experience in the industry ",[2] qualifying each of them for supervision and direction from their several angles of vision. But the exact forms of the trusts, as well as their grouping under particular commissariats, are frequently changed, as experience indicates defects in organisation or improvements in efficiency.

The industrial enterprises in the USSR are, on the average, much larger than those of other countries (even the United States), many having over 20,000 employees and some over 50,000 (comparable rather with Imperial Chemical Industries, Limited, or the United States Steel Corporation). Each com-

---

[1] We gather that the term trust is now usually employed in the USSR for what is, in our language, a " horizontal " combination, in which factories or other establishments producing similar commodities are united for management and sales. The term combine or combinat seems to be used for what in our language is a " vertical " combination in which establishments are included which produce materials or components that other members of the combination require, as coal-mines may be united, on the one hand, with forests producing pit props, and, on the other, with blast furnaces and waggon works.

A useful source of information is the British Government S.O. Paper of 1931, " The Organisation of Foreign Trade of the USSR", by G. Paton, C.B.E. See also *Fifteen Years of the Foreign Trade Monopoly of the USSR*, by A. P. Rosenholz, People's Commissar of Foreign Trade, Moscow, 1933, 30 pp.

[2] *Russia in Transition*, by Elisha M. Friedman, 1933, p. 240.

Stalin thought that too much of the detailed management of the industries was assumed by the board itself and done by writing minutes one against the other. In his address of June 1931, to a meeting of industrial leaders, he said : " It is necessary that our combines should replace management by collegium with individual management. The position at present is that in the collegium of a combine there are ten or fifteen men, all writing papers, all carrying on discussions. To continue to manage in this way, comrades, will not do. We must put a stop to paper leadership, and adopt genuine, business-like Bolshevik methods of work. Let a chairman and several deputy chairmen remain at the head of the combine. That will be quite enough to take care of its management. The remaining members of the collegium should be sent to the factories and mills " (*New Conditions: New Tasks*, by Josef Stalin, 1931, p. 20).

bine unites a number of enterprises that produce for other members of the combine. Each trust has to manage a number of factories manufacturing the same class of commodities, either in a particular region or else widely dispersed throughout the whole USSR. Each trust or combine, with more or less confirmation by the People's Commissar, and with the concurrence of the workers in their several trade unions, appoints, for each factory or plant, a general manager ; and often assigns to the enterprise particular specialist technicians, either Russian or foreign. The general manager, often styled director, with more or less consultation with his leading officials and recruiting committees, appoints the whole staff of the factory, and, with many responsible heads of departments, continuously directs all their operations, including every associated section, such as that of medical supervision and treatment of all the employees, and that of the canteen and restaurant which serves their meals ; and (by a recent decree) also the former "consumers' co-operative" attached to the enterprise, which now produces for consumption by the employees all sorts of farm produce, and retails to them nearly all the other commodities that they purchase.

We reserve for our subsequent chapter on "Planned Production for Community Consumption" detailed analysis of how all this governmental enterprise works. But we may observe, at this point, that, vast as is the aggregate of business in the USSR, its organisation and management by a hierarchy of boards and directors will not appear, to the American financier, as novel or as impracticable as it does to the British economist or banker. It is comparable to nothing more extraordinary than the organisation of one or two hundred industrial leviathans like the United States Steel Corporation or Imperial Chemical Industries, Limited ; and their subjection to a supreme co-ordinating directorate of half a dozen "supermen"—a consummation easily imagined by the potentates of Wall Street ! It is the purpose of the enterprise in the USSR, not the method of its organisation, that is so novel. To provide for the well-being of the whole people, on a steadily rising standard of life rather than the securing of profit for a relatively small minority, is the fundamental purpose of the Sovnarkom of People's Commissars.

## The State Planning Commission (Gosplan)

What has become one of the most important departments of the Soviet Government, the State Planning Commission, had its start in Lenin's conception of a vast plan of electrification covering the whole area of the USSR. This became a programme by its adoption by the Eighth All-Union Congress of Soviets in December 1920. A commission, appointed in April 1921, was transformed by a decree of December 22, 1922, into a permanent State Planning Commission, and by another decree of August 21, 1923, its scope was extended to the whole of the USSR. The modestly named " control figures " of Gosplan were, in 1927, given the form of a Five-Year Plan of Production for the USSR, which was formally adopted by the Fifteenth Congress of the Communist Party in 1928, and by the Central Executive Committee (TSIK).

Gosplan, which now consists of a president and seven other members or assistants, has a staff of statistical and technical experts that exceeds a thousand in number. In every constituent republic and every autonomous republic or oblast, and in every town having more than twenty thousand inhabitants, there are planning commissions subordinate to the central department at Moscow. We reserve our account of this unique administration for Part II. of this book.

## The People's Commissar of Finance

There can be no doubt of the commanding position in the soviet economy that is held by the USSR Commissariat of Finance;[1] but this position is not easy to define in the terms employed by western governments. The People's Commissar

[1] Voluminous as are the Russian sources for taxation and finance, there is relatively little about the actual organisation and working of the soviet departments themselves. Of what is easily accessible to the western student, the most important work is that entitled *Soviet Policy in Public Finance, 1917–1928*, by G. Y. Sokolnikov and associates, edited by L. Hutchinson and Carl C. Plehn, 1931. The most systematic and complete survey is that given in *Das Steuersystem Sowjet Russlands*, 1926, and *Die Finanz und Steuerverfassung des USSR*, 1928, both by Paul Haensel, of which a popular summary, very critical in tone, was published by him as *The Economic Policy of Soviet Russia*, 1930. See also the articles on " Taxation in Soviet Russia " and " Financial Reform in Soviet Russia " and " The Financing of Industry in Soviet Russia ", by Margaret S. Miller, in *Slavonic Review* for 1925, 1927, 1930, 1931 and 1932 ; *Russian Economic Development since the Revolution*, by Maurice Dobb, 1928 ; *Currency*

of Finance may be relatively quite as powerful as the British Chancellor of the Exchequer or the American Secretary of the Treasury ; but his sphere of action differs markedly from that of either of them. The huge Budget of income and expenditure that he annually presents to his ministerial colleagues includes much that is not under his control. Even much of the taxation is assessed and collected, not by any service under his own command, but by officers on the financial staffs of the governments of the constituent republics. And he has to submit his Budget proposals for the concurrence of the president of the Planning Department even before he can lay them before the Sovnarkom. These are vital differences in financial structure that call for analysis.

The first peculiarity of the Budget of the Soviet Union is that it is not confined to the public services of the Union itself, but includes, in addition to every department of federal administration, all the departments of the several Union and autonomous republics, the complete Budgets of which have to be incorporated by the USSR People's Commissar in his own. In a sense, indeed, it comprehends and covers much more. For though the Budget of each Union or autonomous republic does not include separately every item of receipts and outgoings of every subordinate authority,[1] from the autonomous area, the krai or the oblast down through the rayon and city to the village soviet itself, the Budget of each constituent republic depends in the main on the finances

---

*Problems and Policy of the Soviet Union*, by L. N. Yurovsky, 1928 ; *Die russische Währungsreform des Jahres 1924*, by H. J. Seraphim, Leipzig, 1925 ; *Russian Currency and Banking*, 1914–24, by S. S. Katzenellenbaum, 1925 ; *Russian Debts and Russian Reconstruction*, by Leo Pasvolsky and H. G. Moulton, 1924.

Detailed figures as to finances are to be found in the *Soviet Year-Book* for 1930 (the last published in English), pp. 380-446 ; and in the corresponding volumes annually published in Russian. A good description (in German) by the People's Commissar of Finance (G. F. Grinko) himself will be found in *Das Finanzprogramm des USSR für das vierte und letzte Jahr der ersten Piatiletka*, Moscow, 1932, 62 pp.

[1] By the decrees of August 21, October 10 and December 10, 1921, it was sought to separate the Budgets of the local authorities from those of the central government, on the principle of " covering local expenditure from local resources ". By further decrees of May 25 and 26, August 17 and 31 and November 16, 1922, the financial obligations of local authorities were further defined. On November 12, 1923, the so-called " Temporary Regulations ", modified by the law of October 29, 1924, and the " ruling " of April 25, 1926, systematically organised both income and expenditure. But the desired end of securing a balance between the two sides of the account was attained only by a continuous increase in the grants, allocations and surcharges, by which the burden was largely assumed by the finances of the republics.

of the local authorities below it.  They all possess a large measure of practical autonomy in local expenditure on education and health, roads and bridges, agriculture and the needs of labour, and they keep for themselves most of what they locally collect. But they are mainly dependent on the grants that they receive, or the allocations (or deductions) which they are allowed to retain out of the centralised taxes, together with the surcharges which they obtain permission to make for their own benefit on certain of them.  Their separate Budgets have to be approved by their immediate superior authority, and these Budgets are expected to balance.  But the balance is usually reached only by increasing the aforesaid grants, allocations and surcharges made out of the aggregate revenues of each republic as a whole.  Rather more than half the total expenditure of the RSFSR, the Ukraine and the other constituent republics goes in this way in subventions to their subordinate local authorities.[1]  And thus it is the USSR Commissariat of Finance that has, in effect, to meet the net charge of all the public expenditure of every authority in the USSR.

This situation is all the more peculiar to western eyes in that the USSR Commissariat of Finance has no staff of its own in the innumerable areas of all the selosoviets, rayons, cities, oblasts and republics whose financial needs ultimately fall upon the USSR Budget.  Finance is a subject standing between those which are exclusively federal in administration (such as railways and foreign trade) and those which are exclusively local in administration (such as those of elementary education and local sanitation). Finance is committed in each union or constituent republic to a " unified " commissariat, appointed by and responsible to the People's Commissar of Finance of the republic ; but directed equally to carry out the instructions, in matters interesting the Soviet Union generally, of the USSR People's Commissar of Finance.  In order to make this arrangement work smoothly, there has come to be, as we have already explained, a convention that the chief permanent official of each unified commissariat shall be appointed only after consultation between the two People's Commissars, to whom the official will owe a peculiar loyalty.

[1] See the figures from 1924–1925 to 1927–1928 in *Soviet Policy in Public Finance*, by G. Y. Sokolnikov, 1931, pp. 405-406.

It should be added, however, that the USSR People's Commissar for Finance is dependent on the administrations of the several Union or constituent republics only for a relatively small part of his resources. Apart from taxation, there are the large receipts from the railway service and those from the post office and telegraphs, which are managed centrally by his own colleagues on the Sovnarkom, the People's Commissars for those departments. He has also at his command the extensive proceeds of the federal government's mines and oilfields, and of its enormous manufacturing and trading enterprises. These receipts, on which he has only to agree with his ministerial colleagues in charge of the various departments, amount to several times as much as is raised directly by taxation, either by the federal government or by any of the local governments.

When the single Budget for the Soviet Union has been drawn up, incorporating the separate Budgets of the Union or constituent republics—and this is the work of the Budget Department of the USSR Commissariat of Finance—it is not the People's Commissar of Finance who has the last word, either on the items of expenditure to be incurred or on the taxation to be levied. The draft has first to be submitted to Gosplan (the State Planning Commission), which goes over every item on both sides, scrutinising it from the standpoint of the economic prospects for the ensuing year. For instance, the quantities involved in the various enterprises, alike of materials, components and labour force, have to be brought within the anticipated total output. The cost of any imports required has to be provided for by a corresponding value in exports, which will involve a deduction from the amount of commodities that would otherwise have passed into internal consumption. " This ", it is authoritatively stated, " is the subject, every year, of frequent and warm controversies between the Narkomfin (People's Commissariat of Finance) and the Gosplan, when the control figures are being fixed." [1] Gosplan is practically in a position to insist on whatever modifications in the Budget that such considerations involve. Then, at last, the Budget, so modified, can be laid before the USSR Sovnarkom, which will decide any difference of opinion on the Budgets between the People's Commissars of Finance of the several Union or

[1] *Soviet Policy in Public Finance*, by G. Y. Sokolnikov and others, 1931, p. 338.

constituent republics, or between any of them and the USSR People's Commissar of Finance. Finally, the USSR Budget, together with those of the several Union or constituent republics incorporated in it, will be ratified and become law by decision of the Central Executive Committee (TSIK) of the USSR.

Notwithstanding all this complication of authorities, and this dispersion of powers, the USSR Commissariat of Finance has, in the past eighteen years, secured a vast improvement in financial accounting, supervision and control. The Budget figures, once finally decided, cannot be departed from without express authority. Transfers (virements) from item to item are allowed only sparingly and then by the highest authority only. The principle is generally enforced that all the revenues derived from various sources must be paid to the single treasury of the USSR under the People's Commissar of Finance ; and this treasury becomes the source of all state expenditure, both of the Soviet Union and of the separate republics. As far as possible, it is insisted that all receipts of every public authority should be immediately paid in to one of the numerous branches of the State Bank. To see to all this, and to keep things straight, the Commissariat of Finance has become a huge congeries of departments, including those for (1) the Budget ; (2) Currency ; (3) State Revenue ; (4) Taxation ; (5) Economics and Finance ; (6) Control and Audit ; (7) Local Finance, together with (8) Central Administration. In addition, the Commissariat includes (9) the State Savings Bank ; (10) the State Insurance Department (Gosstrakh), insuring against death, fire, hail, cattle plagues and loss of goods in transit ; and (11) the office for note and currency issue, with its printing works and mint.

We need say little of the system of taxation properly so called. It is, of course, avowedly based, not on principles of " equality of sacrifice " or maximum yield, but on those of " building up the socialist state ", by penalising any remnant of profit-making enterprise (which is regarded as criminal) ; and as even Jeremy Bentham recommended, by drastically taxing relatively large incomes and inheritances, whilst exempting from any direct imposts the mass of poor folk. The main direct taxes are now few and simple. The principal is a tax on the output or turnover of all industrial enterprises of any magnitude, which are now all state-owned ; coupled with a single agricultural tax on all agricultural enterprises according to their size or importance. In both cases the assessment is mitigated in various ways in favour of the collectivised concerns, and of those enterprises which it is part of public policy to encourage, to the detriment of the surviving individual peasant or producer. Along with these main instruments of revenue rank the taxes on incomes [1] and on inheritances, which are drastically progressive, so as to operate in a similar direction. The indirect taxation, including excise (mostly on alcoholic drinks and tobacco), customs (very small in yield) and stamps on legal transactions, has been steadily modified in the direction of simplification and (with the great exception of sugar) concentration upon undesirable luxuries and upon expenditure not much incurred by the mass of the people.[2]

Where the USSR People's Commissar of Finance is free from

[1] The rates of Income Tax are extremely complicated, varying not only with the income, but also according to the category in which the taxpayer is placed. The lowest rates are those payable by workers and salaried employees, which are from 80 kopecks per month to (for those getting over 500 roubles per month) $3\frac{1}{2}$ roubles per month for the excess over 500 roubles. The rates for persons of the " first category ", including authors, artists and inventors, rise from 1 per cent to (for income in excess of 20,000 roubles monthly) 38 per cent. In the second category are kustars, not employing hired labour ; dentists, holders of patents, etc. These pay from $2\frac{1}{2}$ per cent up to (for excess over 24,000 roubles per month) 50 per cent. In the third category come non-cooperative kustars employing hired labour ; retail traders ; the clergy and others living on unearned income. Their tax rates rise from 5 per cent up to (for excess over 24,000 roubles per month) 87 per cent (Regulations of May 17, 1934, in (Russian) *Economic Life*, May 24, 1934). The high incomes are, of course, extremely rare ; though popular authors, dramatists and singers occasionally obtain very large amounts.

[2] " The general plan [of taxation] may be stated simply as follows :
" (1) The authority for any and all taxes (and purposes of expenditure) emanates by legislation on decrees from the central government. (2) Certain taxes are uniform throughout the country, but old local taxes, deep rooted in the local history, are maintained. (3) The republics, the component commonwealths of the Union, are permitted (a) to retain a large part, even up to practically all, of certain taxes collected within their boundaries (this is what is called the ' method of deductions '), and (b) to levy surtaxes or rates over and above the Union tax rates, on certain other taxes which are primarily for the Union (this is called the ' method of additions '). . . . (4) A number of purely local taxes have been continued, with modifications, for the use of the republics or of their local subdivisions. Finally there are the ' grants in aid ', handed down by the central government and by the republics, for designated government purposes, such as schools. There are in addition, the grants to industries for the ' development of ' national economy ; which are spoken of as non-governmental outlays, since there are few corresponding direct grants of that sort in other countries " (*Soviet Policy in Public Finance*, by G. Y. Sokolnikov and associates, 1931, p. 394, footnote by the American editors).

interference by the governments of the several constituent republics is in the important domain of currency and banking, where he has his own mint and issue department, handing out the notes printed at his own printing establishment. We need not describe the efforts that were necessary to rise from the swamp of a universal depreciation of the rouble through unlimited printing of paper money during the Civil Wars. Under the able direction of Mr. G. Y. Sokolnikov, who became People's Commissar of Finance in 1924, the rouble was rehabilitated through the chervonetz; and has now, it is claimed, attained a new status of its own superior to that of the dollar and the pound. What is remarkable and peculiar is the soviet policy of secluding its currency from contact with that of any other country. No rouble or kopeck can lawfully be taken out of the USSR, and none can be brought in. Whatever is purchased from abroad is paid for in *valuta*, procured by exporting sufficient commodities to realise in *valuta* the amount of the obligations to foreigners. It is thus only that the variations in world prices of the oil, timber, furs, manganese and wheat that the USSR exports (whether these variations are caused by over-production or by any other factor) trouble the USSR People's Commissar of Finance, not the fluctuations in the foreign currencies themselves. The catastrophic fall in the world price of textiles, whether due to Japanese economies in production costs or to the depreciation of the yen, do not disturb the USSR Government, which buys just as much or as little of Japanese textiles as it finds convenient.

## Banking and Saving

The complete control over currency and credit is facilitated by the federal government's monopoly of banking. The State Bank of the USSR (Gosbank), with its couple of thousand branches all over the country, has now become the only bank at which any of the state industrial enterprises is allowed to have a current account. Gosbank is now required to limit its overdrafts or other accommodations, not only to the amounts prescribed for each enterprise in the General Plan, but also to the separate operations that have to be undertaken at each season of the year. All sales by the enterprise must be paid for not in currency but by transfer, by the purchaser, of the price to the seller's current account. Immediately the bank notices any falling behind in receipts, or any excess in expenditure, beyond the figures in the Plan, this has to be notified to the Sovnarkom, by whom instant notice is taken. The other banks operating in the USSR have been reduced to four, confined respectively to the special purposes of affording long term credit to state enterprises for industry and electrification, or for agricultural improvements in the sovkhosi and kolkhosi, and for carrying out the financial transactions involved in foreign trade.

The State Savings Bank with its own 20,000 branches, and its use of the local post offices in all the cities and substantial villages of the USSR in which it has no branch, is also under the People's Commissar of Finance. The number of depositors, and the total sum standing to their credit, increases annually at a great rate. These popular savings, in 1934 amounting to more than one thousand million roubles, by twenty-five million depositors, are encouraged by interest at the rate of 8 per cent, and by total exemption of such deposits from income tax, inheritance tax and various stamp duties. The total assets of the Savings Bank are invested in the USSR Government loans.[1]

### *Insurance*

A useful department of the USSR Commissariat of Finance, of which little is heard abroad, is that of insurance, which in the USSR is a state monopoly. Insurance has long been compulsory, outside the cities, on buildings against fire, on crops against storms of hail, and on horned cattle and horses against disease. In the cities it is optional on buildings and their contents, as well as against losses in transit upon goods of all kinds. Life insurance is also undertaken on an entirely optional basis.

In order to make the economic security of the village as com-

[1] The following statistics will be of interest :

| Year | Number of Branches and Sub-offices | Depositors' Balances in millions of roubles | Number of Individual Depositors in thousands |
|------|------|------|------|
| 1929 | 20,364 | 315·8 | 7172·1 |
| 1931 | 35,184 | 494·4 | 13671·7 |
| 1933 | 57,556 | 974·0 | 23903·3 |
| 1934 | 48,573 | 1192·6 | 25120·0 |

plete as possible the system of compulsory insurance was reformed and greatly extended by a decree of the USSR Sovnarkom
in July 1934.[1] This provides for the compulsory insurance of
property, crops and stock, in collective farms, hunting, fishing and
other primary producers' cooperatives in village districts. The insurance is to apply to all buildings, equipment, tools, etc., means
of transport, agricultural products for consumption or sale, raw
materials and stores of goods. These are insured against fire,
flood, earthquake, landslides, storms, hurricanes, cloudbursts,
lightning and boiler explosions. Greenhouses are insured against
hailstorms ; seedings and plantings of orchards, vineyards, etc.,
against hailstorms, cloudbursts, storms and fire ; plantings of
crops and vineyards against freezing, heating and flooding; special
and technical plants, as listed, against elemental destruction,
insect and other pests and plant diseases ; plantings of flax and
hemp against drought ; seedings of red clover against drought
and freezing ; stock 6 months old and over against the risk of
death ; horses, camels, asses, mules, hinnies and reindeer from
1 year old up, and pedigreed stock from 6 months up, against
death ; sheep, goats and hogs from 6 months, against death ;
hunting- and fishing-boats against elemental destruction while
afloat and on stocks ; and hunting- and fishing-equipment and
gear against elemental destruction. Collective farm members,
individual farmers, workers, employees, cottage (kustar) workers
and trade workers must insure their individual buildings and
workshops against fire, flood, earthquake, etc., in the same way
as collective property, and their crops, plantings, orchards, vineyards, stock, hunting- and other boats, on the same basis as those
belonging to collectives. This extraordinarily complete insurance is to apply in all sections of the country where similar insurance has been in force hitherto, and may be adopted in other
districts where it has not prevailed. Industrial and special crops
other than those listed may also be insured against elemental
destruction by agreement between the governments of the constituent republics and the Gosstrakh (State Insurance Agency).
They may also arrange higher rates for an insurance against

---

[1] The decree will be found in (Russian) *Economic Life*, July 20, 1934 ; and
in *Russian Economic Notes* of the United States Department of Commerce,
August 30, 1934. Notwithstanding the government monopoly, the consumers'
cooperative societies are allowed to have mutual insurance funds of their own
for insuring their own property against fire.

deterioration of quality of tobacco and makhorka as the result of hailstorms.

Property belonging to " kulak " households and to individuals rated in category III. of the Income Tax schedule, also to others deprived of the vote, may not be insured.

The decree lists in detail the amounts paid in case of loss, also the premiums to be paid by collective farms and farmers, showing an average reduction of 7 per cent from the rates in force in 1934. Young stock up to 6 months or 2 years, according to kind, are insured without premium, as are areas seeded above the seeding plan. As an encouragement to cattle-raising and increasing the market supply of animal products, a 20 per cent reduction is made in premiums for pedigreed animals and for stock on stock-farms. Collectives with approved fire protection, and showing a good record in raising and caring for stock, enjoy reductions in premiums of from 25 to 50 per cent, according to equipment. A 50 per cent reduction also applies for the first year for colonists moving to a new settlement. Special reductions of part or all of premiums apply to collectives and individual farmers in the nomadic and semi-nomadic districts of Turkmenistan, Tadzhikistan, the Kazak and Kirghiz republics, the Kalmyk oblast, and the Far North. A similar reduction is made for certain classes of collective farmers, as " heroes of the Union ", former and present military and other similar servants and families of those who have fallen in the struggle with the kulaks or of forest workers killed on duty. Collectives and individuals who have suffered from elemental destruction in districts where insurance did not prevail may be granted partial reductions in premiums, according to the circumstances, but not more than 90 per cent of the premiums.

Unfortunately we have no recent statistics as to the amount of property thus insured, but it is known to have been steadily increasing. The compulsory insurance of peasants' buildings against fire, which had long existed under the zemstvos, covered in 1928 over twenty million homes at an average of 302 roubles. At the same date sixty million desyatins or hectares were insured against hail, and thirty million horned cattle and nine million horses against disease. About 12 per cent of these, being those of the poorest peasants, were insured without premium. But whereas the average fire premium charged by the zemstvos was, in

1914, 1·08 per cent, that charged by the Government in 1927–1928 was only 0·72 per cent. The total sum thus compulsorily insured against these various calamities was in 1928–1929 over 11,000 million roubles, the annual premium receipt over 109 million roubles, and the total payments for losses 95 million roubles.

The various branches of voluntary insurance have increased even more than those under compulsion. Premiums paid for voluntary fire insurance in 1927–1928 amounted to 57 million roubles, and those for voluntary insurance of goods in transit to 7½ million roubles. Life insurance proceeds more slowly, but the 145,900 persons insured for 97 million roubles in 1925–1926 had grown to 385,000 for 214 million roubles in 1928.[1]

## The Commissariat of Defence

One of the USSR Commissariats that is both like and unlike the corresponding ministry in a western country is that dealing with the armed forces. The People's Commissar for Military and Naval Affairs—a post held in succession by Trotsky (1918–1923), Frunze (1923–1926) and, since 1926, by K. E. Voroshilov—stood formerly at the head, not of an ordinary collegium, but of a " Revolutionary Council of War ", consisting of ten members, appointed by the Sovnarkom mainly from among officers of experience in the various branches of the service. In 1934, in accordance with the general decision to abolish all

---

[1] Another branch of popular finance, widely extended in Western Europe—that of pawnbroking, *mont de piété*, or " lombard "—is not much in evidence in the Soviet Union. We are told that pawnbroking offices, dating from tsarist times, are maintained only in about twenty-six cities, and there exclusively by the city soviets. They are now nominally under the supervision of the USSR Commissariat of Finance, but are not regarded with favour. Pawnbroking, as carried on for profit, necessitates the periodical sale by auction of unredeemed pledges. This practically involves the existence of a class of dealers who make a practice of buying such unredeemed pledges, in order to sell them at a profit— a practice which has, in the USSR, been made a criminal offence. Hence the surviving municipal pawnshops find a difficulty in disposing of their unredeemed pledges. Their occasional auctions are sometimes held inside the great factories, where the only purchasers are the workmen buying for family use. Sometimes admission to the auction is confined to persons presenting a card of trade union membership. We gather that it is hoped that pawnbroking can eventually be superseded, on the one hand, by the friendly loans of the Mutual Aid Societies (see pp. 882-884), and, on the other, by the numerous retail shops maintained by the city municipalities for the sale of unwanted commodities on a commission of 25 per cent. The practice of pawning winter clothing on the advent of spring, in order to get it protected from theft or moth during the summer months, may be superseded by a system of communal storage.

the collegia attached to the USSR Commissariats, the Revolutionary Council of War was brought to an end ; at the same time —perhaps as a gesture, emphasising the conclusion of so many Pacts of Non-Aggression—the commissariat was given the new title of People's Commissariat of Defence.[1] The Revolutionary Council of War has been replaced by a purely advisory Military Council consisting of 80 members, over whose meetings the People's Commissar himself presides. This council includes the principal commanders of the various departments of the defence forces, including specifically the Far Eastern Army and the Military Air Fleet, together with the president of the great voluntary organisation called Osoaviakhim.

This Commissariat of Defence has, of course, an extensive organisation of its own throughout the whole Union, for the maintenance, training and education of the nine hundred thousand men under arms in the army, navy and air force. We can ourselves say nothing useful as to the military efficiency of these three forces, which are combined in a single administration. It is a mere matter of observation that the troops seen in the streets or travelling by train or steamboat, in camp or in barracks, are obviously not only well fed and well clothed but also relatively intelligent and well behaved. Military experts declare these forces to be competently drilled, well armed and highly mechanised ; some even going so far as to say that the USSR is at least as well prepared for war as any other nation.[2] The air force appears to be exceptionally formidable and in a state of great efficiency.

The Commissariat of Defence is organised in two main divisions, administrative and operative. Under them there are half a dozen separate branches, each headed by a commander

[1] Decree of USSR Central Executive Committee (TSIK) of June 20, 1934 ; in pursuance of decree of March 15, 1934, on governmental and industrial organisation by the same authority, in conjunction with the USSR Sovnarkom ; and the resolutions of the Seventeenth All-Union Congress of the Communist Party. The *Moscow Daily News* of June 22, 1934, comments on the change significantly.

[2] It is curious that some of the critics of the USSR, who declare that the government and the workers alike show hopeless incompetence and inefficiency in industrial production, transport and agriculture, often go on to say that the highly mechanised and scientifically equipped army of the Soviet Union, with its extensive service of home-made automobiles and aeroplanes, as well as guns and munitions of every description, has reached a degree of technical efficiency so great as to render it a menace to the rest of the world !

of a competence proved in long service. The Commissariat is specially represented by confidential agents in the various constituent and autonomous republics.

## The Army as a School

The feature in which the military forces of the Soviet Union seem to us to differ most significantly from those of western Europe (and also of Japan)—a feature that may well be of the greatest importance to the community—is the rôle that this part of the social structure plays in the cultural development of the whole people.[1] " The Red Army ", it is officially stated, " is not only a military school ; it is also a school of culture." " The Red Army ", it is also declared, " is essentially a school of citizenship." Nothing is more resented by the communist than the conception of an army trained only as a military force, separate and apart from the mass of the people. Thus, in the Red Army the greatest care has been taken to prevent the upgrowth of anything approaching to a military caste. Neither the commanders (meaning the officers), even of highest grade, nor the rank and file think of themselves as separate from, or in any way superior to, other people who are serving the community in industry or in agriculture, in medicine or in civil administration. Whilst serving their time with the colours, both commanders and men temporarily suspend their membership of their trade unions and associations ; but they take part as citizens in all elections, and with equal votes choose their own members for the soviets, wherever they happened to be stationed. They form their own cooperative societies, which elect their own committees of management, and belong to Centrosoyus, the apex of the whole movement. They are encouraged to keep up their correspondence

---

[1] Apart from the abundant Russian material, the most accessible information as to the Red Army will be found in the *Military Year-book of the League of Nations*, 1932 ; and in the chapter entitled " The Army " in *The Great Offensive*, by Maurice Hindus, 1933, pp. 222-234 ; chap. i., " The Redarmyist ", in *Making Bolsheviks*, by S. N. Harper, 1931, pp. 132-152 ; *Eastward from Paris*, by Edouard Herriot, 1934, pp. 228-234 ; and (for an earlier and more critical view) *La Révolution russe*, par Henri Rollin, Paris, 1931, vol. ii. pp. 133, 343, etc.

See also the anonymous pamphlets published in Paris, entitled *Le Soldat de l'armée rouge*, 1929 ; and *L'Armée rouge et La Flotte rouge*, the latter with preface by P. Vaillant-Couturier, 1932.

with their relatives in the villages and cities from which they have been drawn ; and even to act as local correspondents to the newspapers. They not only remain citizens whilst serving in the ranks ; they become even influential citizens. The peasant who is serving in the army can always command a hearing. Many are the instances in which a son who is a " Red Army man " (the word soldier is not used) has been able, by intervening from a distance, to obtain redress for his father and family who have been suffering from some petty tyranny or injustice at the hands of a local official.

The Red Army is, like all Continental forces, recruited by compulsory service. It is strictly confined to the offspring of " workers and peasants ", no child of the former nobility or *bourgeoisie* being admitted. Service (for the infantry) is for two years, for the air force three years, and for the navy five years. Only about one-third of those eligible to serve and sound in health are taken for the Red Army.[1] What is unusual is to find the conscription not unpopular. This is partly due to the unique informative and propagandist methods of the recruiting department. Prior to each annual conscription a specially selected commander (the word officer is not used) visits the village and convenes a meeting of the young men, and such of their elders as choose to attend. He explains, not at all as a person of superior class or rank, but in an atmosphere of comradeship, the rôle of the Red Army, the conditions of service, the educational and other advantages provided, and the varied amenities of the life ; and then he invites questions, which are put by the score, and answered to the best of his ability, as between friends and equals. The result is that, in marked contrast with the practice in tsarist times, those on whom the lot falls mostly go, not only without reluctance or amid the tears of their families, but willingly. Many who are not conscripted actually volunteer for service. They find the army conditions, in fact, superior to those of the independent peasant or the miner, the factory

[1] All the rest are placed in a territorial militia, in which they retain their civil employments, but are called out for instructional service for a few weeks at a time. In the course of five years they will have served in this way for eight or ten months. When so called up, their civil situations are guaranteed to them ; they continue all their social insurance benefits, whilst they receive two-thirds of the wage they have been earning. Up to the age of 24, all are in the first reserve ; from 24 to 40 in the second reserve, to be called up only in the greatest emergencies.

operative or the worker on the oil-field. The commanders, and even those whom we should call non-commissioned officers, treat the Red Army man with respect. All ranks address each other as equals. In the field, as at drill, or on manœuvres, prompt obedience to orders is enforced, discipline is strict, and some formality is observed. But off duty all ranks meet together on equal terms, sit next to each other at places of amusement, travel together, and even play games and engage in amateur theatricals together; the wives of the commanders often playing parts along with members of the rank and file! To the Red Army man his commander is merely a man of special knowledge, who, when all are on duty, has the function of leader, just as the manager of a factory has in the industrial field.

Probably such an army could achieve no military efficiency unless all ranks were educated. Accordingly, in the Soviet Union, as much care is taken in the appropriate education of the rank and file as in the specialised training of the commanders. At every military centre there are club-houses, school-rooms, lecture courses, libraries, theatres and cinemas. The aggregate number of volumes now included in the thousands of libraries of the defence forces is reported to be somewhere about twenty millions. If any men still join as illiterates, they are promptly taught to read and write both their own vernacular and Russian. All are put through an educational course lasting throughout their whole service, in which not only geography and history, but also economics and " political grammar " (naturally Marxian), are imparted by instructors trained to be both simple and interesting in their expositions. All men are taught to sing, and, as many as desire it, to play one or other musical instrument. There are a number of special newspapers for the defence forces with an aggregate circulation of a quarter of a million. The men have also a quite exceptional amount of vocational training, for which the modern mechanised army offers abundant opportunity. Moreover, as this under Soviet Communism offends no private interest, the troops are continually being called out to help, not only in the agricultural operations of the locality, but also in all sorts of industrial work in which extra labour force is urgently needed, to avert a breakdown or prevent injurious delay, whether in such operations of civil engineering as roads and bridges, railways and embankments, or in repairing buildings, restoring telegraphic communications, or mending machines of every kind. Incidentally it may be said that considerable attention is paid by the Communist Party to the promotion, among all the recruits, of the orthodox Marxian faith. There are one or more cells of the Party in every military unit or barrack, as well as one or more groups of the League of Youth (Comsomols), to the number, in the aggregate, of more than 10,000.[1]

Every year nearly half a million Red Army men, who have completed two or more years of this training, return to their homes and resume their civil occupations. As there are some 600,000 villages, hamlets and cities in the USSR, this means that, during the past decade, an average of three or four such men have re-entered each village and hamlet between the Baltic and the Pacific; about forty to the area of each selosoviet. These young men in the early twenties, relatively well informed and widely read, trained to good habits and filled with a sense of order and efficiency, easily become presidents of many of the 70,000 village soviets; delegates to congresses and conferences; managers of cooperative societies or collective farms; and in various ways influential leaders of the local community. In another decade their number in each village will have been doubled. It is, we think, impossible to over-estimate the importance of this continuous impregnation of what used to be the " deaf " villages of the remote steppe or the Siberian forest, alike in the promotion of national unity, in the stimulation of rural thought, and in the universal penetration of the communist faith.

[1] These cells are busy " coordinating the activity of the 120,000 communists (that is, Party members) in the official total of 562,000 Red Army-ists; a total now raised to nearly a million. The Communist League of Youth has an even larger representation, numbering 150,000. In the senior commanding personnel, and among the ' political workers ' in the Red Army, the percentage . . . is even higher. Every year several tens of thousands of new Party members are recruited from the Red Army-ists in active service " (*Making Bolsheviks*, by S. N. Harper, 1931, p. 135). In 1934 the proportion of Party members was placed as high as 60 per cent (*Eastward from Paris*, by Edouard Herriot, 1934, p. 231). Such a figure, however, applies more correctly to the officer corps. Among regimental commanders the proportion of Party members in 1935 reached 72 per cent, among division commanders, 90 per cent, and among corps commanders, 100 per cent. Among the rank and file, 49·3 per cent were members of the Party or Comsomols (Speech by Tukhachevski, Assistant People's Commissar of Defence, at Seventh All-Union Congress, *Moscow Daily News*, February 2, 1935).

## The Commissariat of Foreign Affairs

The Commissariat of Foreign Affairs (Narkomindel), which has been presided over successively by Trotsky (1917–1918), Chicherin (1918–1930) and, since 1930, by Litvinov, who had long been assistant to Chicherin, has gradually become an extensive and elaborately organised department, at least as well equipped for negotiations and for the orderly maintenance of international relations as the corresponding departments of other governments.[1] The People's Commissar has still two assistants or deputy commissars, but was, in 1934, relieved of his collegium. Besides the usual branches for the protocol, for archives, for the press, for the staff of diplomatic couriers, and for the consular service (in 1934 stationed at eighty-six foreign cities) there is a legal department and an economic department, both of which have manifested their competence. Continuous relations are maintained with the score of representatives or diplomatic agents in the chief cities of the USSR. In constant communication with the thirty soviet embassies or legations abroad,[2] there are five separate departments dealing with the relations with particular governments. Three of these departments manage the intercourse with the western world ; the first taking Poland and the Baltic and Scandinavian states ; the second Germany, Czechoslovakia, Austria, Hungary, Roumania, Bulgaria, Yugo-

---

[1] With the gradual resumption of diplomatic relations with other governments, the necessity was felt of a systematic analysis of the position of the USSR as a socialist island in a capitalist ocean.  This was worked out in two treatises (in Russian), the first-named translated into German, namely, *International Law in the Transition Period, as the Basis for the International Relations of the Soviet Union* (1929), by E. A. Korovin, professor of the University of Moscow ;  and. *The Law as to Ambassadors and Consuls in the Soviet Union* (1930), by Professor A. Sabanin, head of the Legal Section of Narkomindel. See *Le Caractère et la situation internationale de l'Union des Soviets*, by Professor Otto Hoetzsch, 1932, pp. 46, 49, 103 ; *Die völkerrechtliche Anerkennung Sowjetrusslands*, by Peter Kleist, Berlin, 1934 ; and *The Soviet Union and International Law*, by T. A. Taracougio, New York, 1935.

Since 1927 there has been an *Annuaire Diplomatique* issued by the Commissariat of Foreign Affairs (Narkomindel) at Moscow, giving a mass of particulars likely to be useful to the diplomatic circle.  A useful account of Narkomindel will be found in *The Soviet State*, by B. W. Maxwell, 1934, pp. 120-121.

[2] It may be added that the USSR is now (1935) recognised *de jure* by all the governments of Europe (except Switzerland, Holland, Portugal and Yugoslavia), and by all those of Asia (except Iraq and Siam), as well as by that of the United States.  Of the states of Central and South America, only Uruguay has yet (1935) entered into formal relations with the USSR.

slavia and Greece ; and the third the United Kingdom and all its dependencies, France, Italy, Spain, the United States and South America. Two departments tackle the eastern world ; the first dealing with Turkey, Arabia, Yemen, Persia and Afghanistan ; and the second with Japan, China and Mongolia.

## *The Commissariat of Internal Affairs*

In 1934 a new All-Union People's Commissar for Internal Affairs (Narkomvnutdel) was appointed (the office being revived from its former existence in the RSFSR down to 1922), principally to take over the functions that have, during the past dozen years, developed upon the Ogpu, which had always been a federal department. This development had long been in contemplation. As long ago as January 1931, so a leading Ukrainian exile complains, " Moscow suppressed the commissariats of Internal Affairs in all the Union republics, alleging that ' in the circumstances of the socialist reconstruction of national economy these commissariats had become superfluous ballast in the soviet apparatus ' ". The duties of the liquidated commissariats were entrusted partly to newly created " chief offices of communal economy " and partly to the " Central Executive Committees of the separate Union republics, their Councils of (People's) Commissaries, and the commissariats of labour and justice " [1] The completion of this process was delayed until it was convenient, after the death of Menzhinsky, its president, in April 1934, to suppress also the separate existence of the Ogpu. By decree of July 11, 1934, the long-expected All-Union Commissariat for Internal Affairs (Narkomvnutdel) was established, with functions stated to be " the guarantee of revolutionary order and state security, the protection of socialist property, the registration of civil acts (births, deaths, marriages, divorces), and the protection of the frontiers ". The new commissariat consists of six principal departments, namely " the Chief Department of State Security, the Chief Department of Workers' and Peasants' Militia, the Chief Department of Frontier and Internal Protection, the Chief Department of Corrective

---

[1] " Ukrainia under Bolshevist Rule ", by Issac Mazepa, in *Slavonic Review*, January 1934, p. 341.

Labour Camps and Labour Settlements, the Department of Civil Acts, and that of Administrative Business " [1]

It is difficult, without further experience of the actual working of the new commissariat, to appreciate, with any accuracy, the extent and nature of the constitutional change that has been effected. We may, however, note, at once, an increasing centralisation of authority and administration. The constituent and autonomous republics, together with the municipalities and the other local authorities, hand over to the USSR People's Commissar what had hitherto been their sole control and administration of the " militia " [2]—that is to say what in western Europe and the United States is called the local constabulary or police force. The control of the local constabulary has now to be shared between the city soviet and the new central authority. The same may be said of the registration of births, deaths, marriages and divorces, which now becomes a function of the USSR Commissariat of Internal Affairs, though the local soviet retains a share in the administration.

## *The Ogpu*

The supersession of the Ogpu, which has hitherto been directly responsible to the USSR Central Executive Committee (TSIK) ; and the assumption of its functions by the new USSR People's Commissar of Internal Affairs, is not a case of increased centralisation. There may well be administrative advantages in placing, in separate branches of the commissariat, equal in independent status, such distinct functions as " guaranteeing revolutionary order and state security " on the one hand, and, on the other, the control of the local constabulary forces in the several localities, the frontier guards, and " the corrective labour camps and labour settlements ", all of which the Ogpu submerged in a single, secret administration. But apparently the principal change involved in the absorption of the Ogpu in the new commissariat is the splitting off of its strictly judicial functions, which are to be transferred, in accordance with the legal require-

[1] For the decree of July 10, 1934, see *Pravda*, July 11, 1932 ; and *Russian Economic Notes* of the United States Department of Commerce, August 30, 1934.

[2] This was foreshadowed in 1933 when, on the institution of permits of residence (called passports) in Moscow and some other cities, the issue of those permits was entrusted to the militia, who were placed under the direction of the Ogpu for this purpose.

ments, to the competent judicial organs to which all the cases investigated by the new commissariat in any of its sections are to be sent for trial and judgment. Cases under the " Department of State Security " (the former Ogpu) are to be directed to the Supreme Court of the USSR ; whilst all cases of high treason and " espionage " will go to the military collegium of the Supreme Court, or to the competent military tribunals. That a substantial transfer of work on these lines is contemplated may be inferred from the published intention to increase the judicial staffs of the Supreme Court of the USSR, the supreme courts of the constituent and autonomous republics, the provincial and regional courts and the military tribunals.

On the other hand, it is apparently not intended completely to separate administrative from judicial proceedings. A " Special Conference " is to be organised under the People's Commissariat of Internal Affairs, which, on the basis of definite regulations, is to be empowered to apply, by administrative order, such decisions (which will apparently not be called judicial sentences) as banishment from or to particular localities within the USSR, or exile beyond its frontiers, or detention in corrective labour camps for a period not exceeding five years. It is to be feared that this provision will cause critics to declare that it is only the name of the Ogpu that has been changed ! It will be fairer to await experience of the action taken under the new decree.

## The Supreme Court of the USSR

We have still to deal with what is, from one standpoint, the most important branch of the federal power, namely the Supreme Court of the USSR, together with the powerful department of the Procurator. This should involve a complete survey of the system of law and justice under Soviet Communism (for which we have no competence) and an examination of the conception of prisons for ordinary criminals as institutions not punitive but exclusively reformatory. We shall recur to the activities of the Ogpu in Part II. of this book, and we must content ourselves here with a brief account of the judicial structure from the federal angle.[1]

[1] An excellent summary description will be found in " The Russian Legal System ", by D. N. Pritt, K.C., in *Twelve Studies in Soviet Russia*, edited by

The administration of justice, like the prevention of crime and
the maintenance of prisons, is, in the constitution of Soviet
Communism, not one of the subjects assigned to the federal
government. There is, accordingly, in each of the nine constituent republics (including the three united in the Transcaucasian Federation), a People's Commissar for Justice, with
a system of courts, police and prisons under his direction ;
a Procurator with an extensive staff ; and also a corresponding
department, with that or some equivalent designation, in each
of the autonomous republics and autonomous areas, great or
small. But among the authorities appointed by and directly
responsible to the Central Executive Committee (TSIK) of the
USSR is the Supreme Court, which has jurisdiction over the whole
territory. This USSR Supreme Court "has power to review
by way of supervision . . . the judgments of the Supreme Courts
of the seven [nine] constituent republics ; it has original jurisdiction (which it has never yet been called upon to exercise)
over disputes between constituent republics ; and it exercises
criminal jurisdiction in rare cases involving either persons of
high position or charges of exceptional importance ; by its
military department it also exercises original jurisdiction over
military officers of high rank, or exceptionally important charges
against military defendants, as well as cassational jurisdiction
over the decisions of the military courts. The Supreme Court
has, strictly speaking, no other judicial functions ; but the plenum
[that is to say, the general meeting] of the court, consisting of the

M. I. Cole, 1933, pp. 145-176 ; see also Mr. Pritt's article " The Spirit of a
Soviet Court ", in *The New Clarion*, December 24, 1932. A later account is
*Justice in Soviet Russia*, by Harold J. Laski, 1935, 40 pp. The subject is dealt
with in greater detail in *Soviet Administration of Criminal Law*, by Judah
Zelitch, of the Philadelphia Bar (Pennsylvania University Press, 1931, 418 pp.).
The civil law will be found (in French) in *Les Codes de la Russie soviétique*, by
J. Patouillet and Raoul Dufour, 3 vols., 1923-1928 (Bibliothèque de l'Institut
du droit comparé de Lyon) ; or (in German) in *Das Zivilrecht Sowjetrusslands*,
by Heinrich Freund, Berlin, 1924, or *Das Recht Sowjetrusslands*, by N. Timaschew,
N. Alexejew and A. Sawadsky (Tübingen, 1925). These valuable codes do not
yet seem to have engaged the serious attention of British lawyers, but we have
heard them spoken of by continental jurists with admiration.

As is so often the case in Soviet Communism the law and the courts of justice
in the USSR ignore the classifications and the categories of the rest of Europe.
There is no distinction between civil and criminal courts, and very little between
the procedure in civil and criminal actions.

A convenient summary of the history of the Russian law prior to the
revolution will be found prefixed to vol. i. of *Les Codes de la Russie soviétique*, by
J. Patouillet and Raoul Dufour (1923).

president, the deputy president, the three departmental presidents, four of the ordinary judges of the court selected for the purpose, and the president of the supreme court of each of the constituent republics [these not being members of the Supreme Court, but making the so-called plenum up to 18] issues explanations and interpretations of law and of legislation, and exercises certain limited powers of review both over the acts and decrees of the central executive committees (the ostensible seats of direct executive and legislative power) of the constituent republics, and over the decisions of their supreme courts ".[1]

The judges of the Supreme Court, as of all other courts in the USSR, are, like those in other countries of continental Europe, not appointed from the professional advocates, as they are in Great Britain. So far as they are " whole time ", and, so to speak, permanent, they are, as in other European countries, professionally qualified members of what we should call the Civil Service. Almost every court of first instance in the USSR consists of one permanent judge, appointed from year to year at a fixed salary about equivalent to that of the earnings of a highly paid skilled mechanic ; and two co-judges (narodnye zasedateli, literally people's co-sitters), drawn for about a week at a time from a panel of persons, mostly manual-working men or women, normally in industrial employment, but carefully instructed in their judicial duties ; and compensated merely for their loss of earnings during the week in which they sit. Although in theory these co-judges possess equal rights with the permanent judge, and can therefore outvote him on the bench, they serve, in practice, very much the same purposes as a British jury.[2]

---

[1] A cassational court, practically corresponding with our court of appeal, consists only of three permanent judges.

[2] " The Russian Legal System ", by D. N. Pritt, K.C., in *Twelve Studies in Soviet Russia*, edited by M. I. Cole, 1933, p. 148.

It is explained by Mr. Pritt that " cassation is the quashing or setting aside for some informality or irregularity, as opposed to appeal, which is, in theory, a rehearing. In Russia there is technically no appeal ; but the grounds of cassation are so wide, both in definition and in practical application, that the distinction is immaterial " (*ibid.* p. 148). . . . " Side by side with the provision as to cassation, there exists a somewhat remarkable power in the courts to reverse or modify erroneous decisions of lower courts through ' review by way of supervision '. At any stage of a case, however early or however late (even after cassation is barred by lapse of time, and when a case has long been finally concluded in the inferior court), the president or the procurator of a court may call upon any inferior court to produce the record of any case, and they examine

Now it is interesting to find that the same principle is adopted in the constitution of the Supreme Court of the USSR. The permanent judges, including the presidents, deputy president and thirty others, as members of this Court (and likewise the judges of the military courts), are appointed directly by the presidium of the Central Executive Committee (TSIK), from among persons possessing the electoral franchise and qualified by their legal attainments, and by previous service in the judicial hierarchy for a prescribed minimum period. But they do not sit alone. In every court of three, even for cases of the greatest importance, one member (the people's co-sitter), is a layman, although this co-judge is, for the USSR Supreme Court (as for the RSFSR Supreme Court) taken from a special panel of forty-eight co-judges, approved by the presidium of the Central Executive Committee. The Supreme Court of the USSR sits whenever required, normally in public (though with power to hold sessions in camera if the court thinks necessary) ; and not always in Moscow, but in special sessions wherever may be thought convenient.

## The Procurator

Side by side with the Supreme Court in each of the constituent republics of the USSR, is a department which is unfamiliar to the Englishman, namely that of the Procurator. The Procurator, who is, in every continental country, one of the principal officers of the Minister of Justice (in the RSFSR he is the Deputy People's Commissar), is all that we mean by Public Prosecutor, together with much of what we mean by Attorney-General, and a great deal more besides. In the RSFSR, and in the other constituent republics, where both he and his deputy are appointed by the presidium of the Central Executive Committee, he has " the general duty of supervising in the public interest the operation of all government organs, in the widest sense of the phrase ; and to enable him to fulfil this duty he is placed in a position of virtual independence of all departments ",[1]

the whole proceedings, and if necessary set aside the decision itself or any preliminary step or decision. . . . The procedure is constantly invoked, and leads directly to the correction of wrong verdicts, and indirectly, no doubt, to much greater efficiency and vigilance " (*ibid.* p. 153).

[1] " The Russian Legal System ", by D. N. Pritt, K.C., in *Twelve Studies in Soviet Russia*, edited by M. I. Cole, 1933, p. 160.

though always in general subordination to the People's Commissar for Justice. He is responsible (as no official in England is) for the state of the law, with the positive duty of suggesting to the Sovnarkom or the Central Executive Committee any new legislation that is required, or any repeal or amendment of existing laws. He is supposed to keep a continuous watch (which no one in England is charged to do) on the activities of all judges, investigating officers, advocates, the local police and others connected with the administration of justice ; and to institute proceedings against them, either administrative or disciplinary or criminal, whenever required.[1] He may intervene in civil actions when he thinks necessary, in order " to safeguard the interests of the state and of the toiling masses ". But the largest part of the work of the extensive department of the Procurator is concerned with the investigation, in preparation for possible criminal proceedings, of deaths or physical casualties, damage or destruction of property, and mere pecuniary loss, so far as concerns any cases in which it is alleged or suspected that there has been a serious breach of the criminal law. The judicial systems of all civilised countries make more or less systematic provision for investigations of this kind, partly in order to ensure that no criminal goes undetected and unprosecuted, and partly in order to sift out, from the mass of trivial causes of assault, petty larceny or contravention of bye-laws, those calling for more drastic treatment. The English system is exceptional in leaving this function in the main, partly to the

---

[1] " It is not an uninteresting feature of the Procurator's duties that he is particularly active in connection with prison administration. He has to see that sentences are properly carried out, that any persons unlawfully detained are released, and that prisons are properly managed. He visits prisons regularly, generally as often as once in six days, and receives and investigates complaints by individual prisoners. The public are earnestly encouraged to take their complaints to his active and powerful organisation, and they are not slow to do so " (*ibid.* p. 160). Over a thousand such visits to prisons each month of the year were paid in 1923 and 1924 by the members of the Procurator's Department (*Soviet Administration of Criminal Law*, by Judah Zelitch, 1931, p. 124).

Incidentally, as we are informed, this continuous inspection of the prisons by the Procurator's department leads to a considerable number of discharges or remission of sentences. Each constituent or autonomous republic has an item in its budget for prison expenses, which it is loth to exceed. When the prisons get full, an excess on the year is threatened. As a practical expedient, the number of prisoners is then reduced by the Procurator recommending for immediate discharge a sufficient number of those whom he thinks most likely to be favourably affected by such leniency.

local police forces, rarely specialised into a Criminal Investigation Department (in cases of death, also to the ancient coroner) and partly, if he can afford the expense, to the private person aggrieved, who may now, in serious cases, sometimes be able, by comparatively recent reforms, to enlist the services of the Treasury Solicitor or the Public Prosecutor, if not of the Attorney-General. In the constituent republics of the USSR, as in most other countries, this work is undertaken as a matter of course by the government, in an extensive department known as that of the " Procurator ". [1] In all allegations or suspicions of certain classes of crime, and in any other case in which it is thought desirable, the Procurator's Department makes an investigation, in which every person supposed to be able to give relevant information, whether or not suspected of being the criminal, and including experts as well as witnesses, is interrogated in private by a qualified judicial officer, called in the USSR an inquisitor or investigator. At this stage, no person is accused (although a person strongly suspected may be detained in prison) and no one can legally be compelled to answer questions ; whilst anyone may appeal, summarily and without expense, to the Procurator himself, against any sort of maltreatment at the hands of the investigator. The enquiries and interrogations are, in many cases, necessarily searching and prolonged (as we have lately learned about those in similar cases made by our English policemen). But there is reliable testimony, so far as the RSFSR is concerned, that efforts are made to bring out impartially the whole of the relevant facts, whether or not pointing to a crime having been committed, and whether for or against any suspected person. The idea seems to be that, if a crime has been committed, it ought to be " reconstructed " from the facts before a decision is come to that any particular person should be prosecuted as the probable criminal. When

---

[1] The student will find this function of the USSR Procurator precisely described in minute detail in *Soviet Administration of Criminal Law*, by Judah Zelitch, 1931, chap. vi., " Proceedings prior to the Trial ", pp. 153-196.

Until July 1933 the Procurator, and his extensive department, was exclusively a branch of the administration of justice of each constituent republic, the USSR itself having none. There has now been appointed a Procurator for the USSR, having all the wide powers and functions of the Procurator for the RSFSR. In addition, this new federal Procurator (Akulov) is charged with the " supervision. . . . of the legality and regularity " of the activities of a most important federal department, the Ogpu, to which we have already referred.

this " reconstruction " has been made, to the satisfaction of the Procurator, he decides whether the facts point to any particular person as the probable criminal, and if so, the case is then remitted to the court for trial. Only at this stage is the indictment, which for the first time specifies precisely the breach of the criminal law that is alleged to have been committed, drawn up and communicated to the defendant, who can then obtain the assistance of an advocate and prepare his defence.

Whether this system of preliminary official investigation by searching interrogation in private—which prevails all over the European continent—is or is not more efficacious than the peculiar British arrangement in like cases, either in securing the conviction of criminals, or in protecting the innocent from annoyance or danger, we do not presume to judge.

## The College of Advocates

It is instructive to notice the reasons assigned for the fact that the profession of advocacy plays a smaller part in the USSR than in other countries. " The simplicity ", we are authoritatively told, " of the procedure ; the greater thoroughness in criminal cases of the preparatory work done before the case comes to court ; the absence of rules of evidence and of similar technicalities ; the greater certainty of the law arising from the absence of a vast fungus of reported cases ; the freedom from all the hindrances that excessive wealth, on one side or the other, can place in the way of justice—all tend to make it less essential to employ an advocate. Nevertheless advocates are frequently employed, and the organisation of the profession is interesting." [1]

After passing through various vicissitudes during the first five years of the revolution, the legal profession in the USSR (which does not distinguish between solicitors and barristers, any more than between these and jurisconsults, notaries or conveyancers) is, by the Advocacy Law of 1922, organised as a College of Advocates.[2] Admission is open to anyone (not belonging to one of the " deprived " categories) who qualifies, either

---

[1] " The Russian Legal System," by D. N. Pritt, K.C., in *Twelve Studies in Soviet Russia*, edited by M. I. Cole, 1933, p. 158.

[2] Law No. 36 of 1922, since slightly amended by the Judicature Laws of 1923, 1924 and 1926 ; *Soviet Administration of Criminal Law*, by Judah Zelitch, 1931, pp. 140-144.

by two years' service in the soviet judiciary system in a grade not lower than that of an investigator, or by graduating at the Institute of Soviet Law, or even by studying at evening classes and passing an examination. Since 1926 the number of members has been restricted. On admission as a member of the College, he or she becomes available for consultation by anyone seeking legal advice, or for assignment to act for any litigant, in civil or criminal action. The applicant for advice or the litigant requiring advocacy is, if recognised as " poor ", such as a non-working invalid or aged pensioner, charged no fee. Industrial workers, peasants, clerks and handicraftsmen may be charged a small sum, which may be made payable by instalments. Any-one pecuniarily better off pays a fee according to a fixed scale, dependent partly on the amount of service rendered and partly on the pecuniary position of the client. But these fees, what-ever they may be, are taken by the College of Advocates.[1] Its members receive fixed salaries, which are reported to vary ac-cording to their several abilities and to the amount of work required from them. Professional discipline is maintained by the College, or rather by its presidium which the members' meeting elects, always subject to appeal to the Provincial Court. In the USSR, advocates, as well as judges, are, at least in theory, liable to suspension, disqualification and even criminal prose-cution, for any breach of professional duty, even if no more than neglect, by reason of which any litigant or other client, suffers loss or injury. It is to be noted that most of the ad-vocates, like most of the doctors and many of the authors, do not seek to become Party members. This is not, in most cases, because they are not communists in opinion and sympathy, but because there is a feeling that the demands of Party dis-cipline might prove incompatible with full performance of their duty to their clients and their profession. Thus, it is said that 85 per cent of the members of the College of Advocates are non-Party. Although the contrary has been stated, without evi-dence, at least one competent observer reports that advocates are quite free to present the cases of their clients fearlessly and without smarting for their freedom.[2]

[1] Apparently anyone wishing to do so may agree with the advocate to pay him a special and additional fee.

[2] " One of the most eminent advocates, who had appeared for many persons accused of counter-revolutionary activities, stated that he never felt the least

## The Problem of National Minorities

We have yet to add to our description of the pyramid of soviets, an account of how the Bolsheviks believe that they have solved the problem presented by the existence, in the vast territory for which a constitution had to be provided, of a hundred or more distinct nationalities. One of the difficult problems presented to political science by the geographical unity of the Eurasian plain has always been that of the extreme diversity of the population found upon it, in race, religion, language, degrees of civilisation and culture, habits of life, historical tradition and what not. The continuity of land surface from the Gulf of Finland to the Pacific Ocean prevented the rest of the world from recognising in the tsarist régime what was essentially a colonial empire, ruled from St. Petersburg by the upper class of a superior race—not without analogy to the colonial empire of Holland, ruling its East Indian dependencies from the Hague ; or indeed to that of the Britain of the eighteenth century, ruling its heterogeneous colonies from Westminster. The systems of the Dutch and the British appealed to the Bolsheviks no more than those of the Spanish and the French. The compulsory " russification " aimed at by the Russian autocracy was not only manifestly impracticable, but also in the highest degree unpopular.

Lenin and his colleagues in the Social Democratic Party of Russia had not failed to notice, from the very beginning of the twentieth century, how strong and persistent was the popular discontent caused by the tsarist insistence on the " russification " of all the national minorities within the Empire.[1] Ignoring the indications in the Communist Manifesto of 1848, as to proletarian supremacy leading to the passing away of national differences, and resisting the growing feeling through Europe in favour

embarrassment or difficulty in presenting his case as strongly as he thought fit " (" The Russian Legal System ", by D. N. Pritt, K.C., in *Twelve Studies in Soviet Russia*, edited by M. I. Cole, 1933, p. 159).

[1] Already at the London Conference of 1903, Lenin got carried a resolution stating that " The Conference declares that it stands for the complete right of self-determination of all nations " ; to which the Second Congress of the Party in August 1903 added the important words " included in any state ". The Central Committee of the Party, at the meeting of September 25, 1913, emphasised the necessity of guaranteeing " the right to use freely their native language in social life and in the schools ".

of united nationalist states, Lenin insisted that the Bolsheviks should declare themselves in favour, along with the right of self-determination of even the smallest nationality, also of the concession of " cultural autonomy " to national minorities included within states. This proved to be an important factor, so far as the national minorities of tsarist Russia were concerned, in securing their participation in the revolutions of February and October 1917.

How were the insistent demands of the various nationalities to be met ? The Provisional Government had left this problem, along with so many others, to the prospective Constituent Assembly. But in October 1917 Lenin and his colleagues found themselves in power, before anyone had worked out any scheme of organisation that would satisfy the national minorities without endangering the strength and unity of the central authority. This did not prevent the new government from issuing a flamboyant proclamation promising autonomy in return for support.

" Mohammedans of Russia," it began, " Tartars of the Volga and Crimea ; Kirghiz and Sartes of Siberia and Turkestan ; Turks and Tartars of Transcaucasia, your beliefs and customs, your national institutions and culture, are hereafter free and inviolable. You have the right to them. Know that your rights, as well as those of all the peoples of Russia, are under the powerful protection of the Revolution, and of the organs of the soviets for workers, soldiers, and peasants. Lend your support to this revolution, and to its government." [1]

The working out of the problem of national minorities was entrusted to Stalin, who, as a member of one of the innumerable tribes inhabiting the Caucasian mountains, had long had a personal interest in the subject. In 1913, indeed, he had published a pamphlet in which he endeavoured to reconcile cultural autonomy with the supremacy of the whole proletarian mass.[2] He was made People's Commissar for Nationalities, with the opportunity of concentrating his whole energy on the task.

---

[1] *Soviet Rule in Russia*, by W. R. Batsell, 1929, p. 109. A French translation will be found in " Le Bolshevisme et l'Islam ", by Castagne, in *Revue du monde musulman*, Paris, vol. xxxi, pp. 7-8.

[2] *Marxism and the National Question*, by Josef Stalin, 1913 (in Russian).

## Cultural Autonomy

It took Stalin four years to get his ideas even formally embodied in the constitution. He had first to secure the confidence of the national minorities in European Russia, a task which was, in the turmoil of the civil war, for a long time impossible. " In its earlier years ", it has been well said,[1] " the Commissariat of Nationalities was an agency for the propagation of the communist faith among the non-Russian peoples." It was, as well, " the arbiter of differences arising between autonomous states and the guardian of the interests of the national minorities, and was generally active in promoting cooperation among the several self-governing peoples. . . ." " As early as March 1918, Stalin signed a decree calling for the formation of a Tartar-Bashkir Republic. The civil war intervening, the measure remained a dead letter. The first ethnic group actually to achieve autonomy were the German settlers on the Volga, who, even under the old régime, had had certain privileges. They were organised in 1918 as a so-called ' Labour commune ', which later became an autonomous republic. The establishment of the Bashkir State followed a year later. This was the first soviet state with an Oriental, that is, Turkish and Moslem, population. Upon soil once ruled by the khans of the Golden Horde the Tartar Republic was proclaimed in 1920. The Volga Tartars are the dominant nationality here, and the ancient city of Kazan is the administrative and cultural centre. About the same time the Karelian Republic was formed on the Finnish border, while the territories occupied by the Kalmyks, the Votyaks and the Mari were given the status of autonomous regions. Within the next two years the Crimean Republic came into being, the Komi people of the north was allotted a spacious region of its own, and the Chuvashian territory, now a republic, also became an autonomous region. Thus, by 1922 all the more important ethnic groups in the European part of the Russian federation had become masters of their own houses." [2]

In the Fundamental Law for the RSFSR, which was adopted on July 10, 1918, provision had been made for the possible com-

---

[1] *The Jews and other National Minorities under the Soviets*, by Avrahm Yarmolinsky, 1928, pp. 131-133.

[2] *Ibid.*

bination or union of the soviets of "regions which are distinguished by a particular national and territorial character ". It was even foreseen, by Article II., that these autonomous regional organs might "enter into the RSFSR on a federal basis ". But none of them existed at the time, and (perhaps because they were at all times already inside the unitary state) none of them ever did "enter into the RSFSR on a federal basis ".

Nevertheless the work done by Stalin, during his four years' tenure of office as People's Commissar for Nationalities, was of great and lasting importance. What he worked out in the vast domain of the RSFSR was not federalism (which came only in 1922–1923, when the nationalities outside the RSFSR joined with it in the federal USSR) but the concession of "cultural autonomy ", coupled with an actual encouragement of the admission of members of the national minorities to the work of local administration. The autonomous republics and autonomous regions established within the RSFSR during the years 1918–1922 do not seem to have had in law any powers or duties, rights or functions differing essentially from those of the local authorities of the remainder of the territory of the RSFSR. They were, in practice, between 1918 and 1922, as they are to this day, dealt with by the central authorities at Moscow, *apart from matters of cultural autonomy*, almost exactly as if they were simply krais or oblasts. And when we realise that the most important of these enclaves had less than three millions of inhabitants ; and that the aggregate population of the whole couple of dozen of them did not, at the time, exceed five millions ; whilst the rest of the RSFSR had nearly a hundred millions, we shall not be inclined to take too seriously their several pretensions to federal status.

What the People's Commissar for Nationalities achieved between 1918 and 1922 was to stretch the provisions of Article II. of the Fundamental Law to cover the organisation of particular "regional unions of soviets " into what were called, in a dozen of the more important localised communities, "autonomous republics ", and in another dozen cases "autonomous areas ". Their regional congresses of soviets were recognised as having authority over all the soviets of the villages or cities or other districts within the territories assigned to these newly created "autonomous" parts of the RSFSR. Such of them as were called autonomous republics have even been allowed, in flat contradiction of the Fundamental Law,[1] to call their principal officials People's Commissars, and to group them into a sovnarkom, or Cabinet of Ministers. This harmless concession to regional pride was safeguarded by the express stipulation in the decree that, for all the " unified " narkomats or ministries [2] the appointment of People's Commissar was to be made only after consultation with the corresponding People's Commissar at Moscow. There was not even any concession of "cultural autonomy " explicitly embodied in the instruments constituting the new local authorities. It was, however, granted in administration. Stalin had sufficient influence with his ministerial colleagues, and with the Central Executive Committee, to induce them to refrain from using their powers of disallowance and cancellation in such a way as to interfere with the practical autonomy of these autonomous areas in purely cultural matters of local concern.

So far the important concession of cultural autonomy had involved little or no difference in political structure between the areas recognised as occupied by distinct nationalities and the other parts of the RSFSR organised in congresses of soviets for provinces (gubernia), counties (uezd) and rural districts (volost). The various minorities were, in fact, induced to adopt, in substance, the same constitutional structure as the rest of the RSFSR. What the concession of cultural autonomy amounted to between 1918 and 1922 was merely that the central authorities of the RSFSR did not, in practice, prevent those of each autonomous republic and autonomous area from adopting its own vernacular as the official language ; or from using it in councils and courts of justice, in schools and colleges, and in the intercourse between government departments and the public.

[1] Article 48 declares that " the title of People's Commissar belongs exclusively to the members of the sovnarkom who administer the general affairs of the RSFSR, and cannot be adopted by any other representative of the central or local authorities " (Fundamental Law of July 10, 1918, Article II. ; *Soviet Rule in Russia*, by W. R. Batsell, 1929, p. 88.)

[2] The " unified " commissariats, narkomats or ministries comprise the more important of the departments under local administration (see p. 103), such as those of finance, food supplies and light industries, and (until 1934) also labour, and workers' and peasants' inspection. To these was added in 1934 the commissariat of agriculture dealing with the kolkhosi and the independent peasantry.

The local authorities could give preference to their own nationals as teachers and local officials, and were even encouraged to do so. Their religious services were not interfered with by the Central Government. They could establish theatres, and publish books and newspapers in their own tongues. These were exactly the matters in which local autonomy was most warmly desired.[1]

A further stage in dealing with the problem of nationalities was marked by the reorganisation of Stalin's own Commissariat (Narkomat) by decrees of May 19 and December 16, 1920. There was then created (but merely as a part of Stalin's own ministerial department) a " soviet of nationalities " consisting of the presidents of delegations of the various autonomous republics and areas, who were to sit with five of Stalin's own nominees under his presidency. This body was merely to advise the minister in his duties, which were on the same occasion defined anew, without mention of federation, as " all measures guaranteeing the fraternal collaboration of all the nationalities and tribes of the Russian Soviet Republic ". This taking directly into council the heads of the national minorities within the RSFSR was an act of statesmanship ; but how far this " fraternal collaboration " was from federalism, or even genuine autonomy, may be seen from the fact that the People's Commissar for Nationalities was expressly empowered to appoint his own resident agent to the capital city of each autonomous region " to watch over the execution of the decrees of the federal central authority of the Russian Soviet Republic ".

[1] The limits to this " cultural autonomy " should be noted. Apart from the highly important matter of local administration by the natives, it is mainly a matter of permitting the use of the vernacular for all activities that are lawful in the Soviet Union ; not a new right to conduct any activities that may be alleged to have been part of the vernacular culture. Thus it must not be assumed that the Ukrainians, the Georgians or the Germans, in the autonomous areas of the USSR, were to be given unlimited freedom to maintain or enter into relations with persons of the same nationality outside the USSR, including *émigrés* or exiles. In the concession of cultural autonomy within the USSR loyalty to the régime of the country was presupposed. In short, cultural autonomy (as distinguished from native government) was a reversal of the tsarist policy, of " russification ", and nothing more. " The Soviet Government," it has been said, " is not Russian, but proletarian : it does not seek to russify the peoples of the Union, but to train them as communists like the Russian people itself, partners in the building up of socialism " (*Nationalism in the Soviet State*, by Hans Kohn, 1934, p. 112).

## The Adoption of Federalism

The high constitutional importance of Stalin's work as People's Commissar of Nationalities was, however, not adequately realised until the time came in 1922 when steps could be taken for the federal union between the RSFSR on the one hand, and the Ukraine, White Russia and the Transcaucasian Federation on the other. Then, as we have described, the autonomous republics and autonomous areas which Stalin had established within the RSFSR were all accorded independent and equal representation, nominally upon the same basis as the incoming independent republics, and indeed, as the RSFSR itself, in the federal organ entitled the Soviet of Nationalities, which is one limb of the bicameral Central Executive Committee (TSIK) of the USSR.[1]

It remains to be said that, during the dozen years since the formation of the Soviet Union in 1923, the position of nearly all these autonomous republics and autonomous areas has been largely transformed. It is not that there has been any important alteration in their political structure, or in their nominal relation to the central authorities of the constituent republics within which they are situated, or to those of the Soviet Union. Their position of cultural autonomy has, indeed, been strengthened, not only by long enjoyment of their privileges, but also by the scrupulous care taken at Moscow always to treat the minority cultures with respect, even on occasions when counter-revolutionary aspirations of a nationalist character have had to be sternly repressed. This policy has not been maintained without an occasional struggle. From time to time it has been complained that the recognition of all these national minorities and their cultures was costly in money and detrimental to educational and administrative efficiency;[2] and, worst of all, that it was

---

[1] The functions of the Commissariat of Nationalities included " (*a*) the study and execution of all measures guaranteeing the fraternal collaboration of the nationalities and tribes of the Russian Soviet Republic; (*b*) the study and execution of all measures necessary to guarantee the interests of national minorities on the territories of other nationalities of the Russian Soviet Federation; (*c*) the settlement of all litigious questions arising from the mixture of nationalities " (Decree No. 45 of May 27, 1920; see also that of No. 99 of December 25, 1920; *Soviet Rule in Russia*, by W. R. Batsell, 1929, pp. 118-119).

[2] The State Bank, in 1925, issued a circular to its numerous branches forbidding their use of the various vernaculars in the books of account or in correspondence with Moscow or with each other. This attempt to " establish for

admittedly made use of occasionally as a cloak for " separatist " machinations. But the Communist Party declared against such " Pan-Russian chauvinism ", as being even more subversive than " local nationalism ".[1]

The number of autonomous republics and autonomous areas has been, in fact, from time to time increased. Even the Jews, who are dispersed all over the Union, have been encouraged and assisted to form locally autonomous groups, especially in Southern Ukraine and the Crimea, and have been formally granted an autonomous oblast (in due course to be promoted to an autonomous republic) at Biri Bidjan in Eastern Siberia. The Soviet Government has even begun to " settle " the gypsies, who swarm restlessly in the USSR as elsewhere.[2]

It would be too much to expect the reader to examine, in detail, the varying developments of the twenty-seven autonomous republics and autonomous areas.[3] No fewer than twelve

---

itself a common language for its bureaucracy " was objected to by a delegate to the Third All-Union Congress of Soviets in 1925, who declared that " such projects should not be introduced " (Shorthand report of the Congress, p. 133 ; *Soviet Rule in Russia*, by W. R. Batsell, 1929, p. 649).

[1] *Nationalism in the Soviet Union*, by Hans Kohn, 1934, pp. 103-107 ; see also *How the Soviet Government solves the National Question*, by L. Perchik, (Cooperative Publishing Society of Foreign Workers in the USSR, Moscow, 1932, 68 pp.)

[2] " In Moscow there live 4000 members of this ancient and mysterious race. In other countries they are left to themselves ; the Soviet Government has formed a club among the few active elements in the gypsy youth ; it is called in the gypsy language " Red Star ". It has some 700 members, of whom until quite recently only about 5 per cent could read and write. It is active in the liquidation of illiteracy, arranges lectures, organises excursions to factories and museums, and issues the first wall-newspaper in the gypsy language. Alongside this cultural activity an attempt is being made at the economic reorganisation of gypsy life. The gypsies have been given land. Under the leadership of the Moscow club, 7000 gypsy families have been settled on holdings ; workshops have been started ; and an obstinate struggle has begun against the past life of the gypsies. In harmony with the efforts of the Soviet Government on behalf of national cultures, the popular gypsy songs and dances have been developed and freed from the elements which had been interpolated in them through performance in places of public entertainment. The first play staged by the club in the gypsy language dealt with the transition to a settled life " (*Nationalism in the Soviet Union*, by Hans Kohn, 1934, p. 130).

[3] Actually the first to be granted cultural autonomy as a region in 1918, and as a republic in 1923, with the right to give preference in filling local offices to its own nationals, was the Autonomous Socialist Soviet Republic of the Volga Germans, a settlement founded as long ago as 1764. This has now 631,300 inhabitants, mostly peasants, of whom two-thirds are German by extraction and language, one-fifth Russians and one-eighth Ukrainians. Fifteen years ago 15 per cent of the families owned 75 per cent of the land, more than three-quarters of the whole having to work as wage-labourers. The 15 per cent who

of the autonomous republics are within the RSFSR ; and these autonomous republics alone extend to more than eight million square kilometres out of the total area of that constituent republic of less than twenty million kilometres, though including only sixteen and a half million inhabitants out of more than one hundred million.[1]

## The Tartar Republic

We must content ourselves with a particular account of a single specimen, in its progress perhaps the most remarkable of all : the Tartar Autonomous Republic which the authors had the advantage of visiting in 1932. Twenty years ago its present area was an indistinguishable part of the vast gubernia or province of Kazan, with a poverty-stricken agricultural

had added field to field had a higher standard of farming and education, and more sustained industry and thrift, than their indigent neighbours ; and they were long reluctant to cooperate in collective farms, to unite their scattered plots into fields permitting mechanisation, and to adopt methods of joint working which allowed the fuller use of an improved equipment. After pleading in vain to be let alone, or to be permitted to emigrate *en masse*, those who were not deported as recalcitrant kulaks (whose sufferings had in many cases been great) were eventually compelled to accept the kolkhos system, of which they have apparently made an economic success. There are now 361 kolkhosi, 431 sovkhosi, with 99 machine and tractor stations, and over 90,000 peasant householders. The republic, the area of which is now almost wholly collectivised in sovkhosi or kolkhosi, is divided into 12 rayons, in six of which the language in use is German ; in two, German and Russian ; in two, German and Ukrainian ; and two others, German, Russian and Ukrainian. Whereas fifteen years ago there were said to be only some 200 volumes of books in the whole republic, there are now 82 libraries, 178 village reading-rooms and tens of thousands of volumes. The nationality law of the republic of the Volga Germans is described in two publications in German, which also give a valuable account, though not unbiassed, of the general nationality policy of the Soviet Government (Rudolf Schulze-Molkau, *Die Grundzuge des wolgadeutschen Staatswesens im Rahmen der russischen Nationalitatenpolitik*, Munich, 1931; and especially Manfred Langham Ratzenburg, *Die Wolgadeutschen, ihr Staats und Verwaltungsrecht in Vergangenheit und Gegenwart, zugleich ein Beitrag zum bolschewistischen Nationalitatenrecht*, Berlin, 1929. And see, generally, *Nationalism in the Soviet Union*, by Hans Kohn, 1934, p. 125).

[1] The one autonomous republic in the Ukraine extends to only a small part of its total area ; and those of the Transcaucasian Federation to no great proportion of its total area. White Russia contains no autonomous republics or areas. On the other hand, the three newest constituent republics (Turkmenistan, Uzbekistan and Tadzhikistan) may be considered to be wholly composed of national minorities.

" The autonomous republics in the RSFSR have a total area of 8,054,855 square kilometres and a population of 16,782,047 ; without these republics, the RSFSR has an area of 11,693,441 square kilometres and a population of 84,075,538 " (*Territorialnoe i administrativnoe delenie SSSR*, 17; *Soviet Rule in Russia*, by W. R. Batsell, 1929, p. 631).

population almost entirely of Tartar race ; 85 per cent illiterate ; the women veiled ; and the whole people completely debarred from self-government ; and indeed, outside the city, left almost without administrative organs of any sort. There were a few dozen small elementary schools of the poorest kind, and only three places of higher education, in which but ten Tartar students, none of them the sons of peasants or wage-earners, were to be found. To-day there are over 1700 elementary schools, with more than 99 per cent of all the children of school age on the register, including girls equally with boys. The vernacular colleges and institutes of higher education are numbered by dozens, and filled with Tartar students, the great majority coming from peasant or wage-earning homes, whilst many more are to be found in colleges in other parts of the USSR. All the women are unveiled, and are taking their share in every department of public life. When the authors interviewed the Sovnarkom of People's Commissars (all of Tartar race) we found one of them a woman, who was Minister of Education. The health service for the village is an entirely new creation. Doctors (mostly women) and small hospitals (including lying-in accommodation), now cover the whole rural area, whilst at the capital, the city of Kazan, there are not only specialist central hospitals, but also a completely reorganised medical school, now filled mainly with Tartar students. More than two-thirds of the peasants have joined together in collective farms, which cover three-quarters of the entire cultivated area, and which, alike in 1932, 1933 and 1934, were among the first in the Union to complete their sowing, whilst they harvested more than 100 per cent of the planned yield. Fifteen years ago Tartar industry was practically non-existent ; in the years 1931 and 1932 the planned industrial output was respectively 239 and 370 million roubles ; and in each of the past three years the plan was more than fulfilled. The Tartar People's Commissar of Health, evidently a competent medical practitioner, explained how the crude death-rate for the republic as a whole had steadily declined year by year, whilst the infantile death-rate had been halved. There are, as we saw, still a few Mohammedan mosques functioning in Kazan, but the great majority of the population appear to have dropped Islam, almost as a spontaneous mass movement. There is a flourishing state publishing house, which pours out a continuous stream of Tartar books and pamphlets, for which there is a large sale. There are Tartar theatres and cinemas, Tartar public libraries, and a well-frequented museum of Tartar antiquities and modern art products. In all sorts of way the Tartar autonomous republic demonstrates how proud of itself it has become !

## The Jews in the USSR

We cannot omit to mention one important and peculiar minority, racial and religious rather than national, with which the Soviet Union has had to deal, namely that of the Jews. Under the Tsars their oppression had been severe and unrelenting.[1] " When the autocratic régime fell, the crash reverberated in Jewish ears as though all the bells of freedom were ringing. With a stroke of the pen the Provisional Government abolished the complicated network of laws directed against the Jews. Suddenly their chains fell off. Disabilities and discriminations were cast on the refuse heap. . . . The Jews could straighten their backs and look to the future without fear." [2]

Unfortunately there were still to be undergone the three or four years of civil war and famine, during which, at the hand of the contending armies, the bulk of the Jewish population suffered the worst excesses. All that can be said is that, on the whole, the White Armies were the most brutal, whilst the Red Army did its best to protect these poor victims, notwithstanding

[1] It is manifestly impossible for us to cite the extensive literature relating to the three centuries of history of the Jews in Lithuania, Poland and tsarist Russia. There have been Jews in the Ukraine for 1000 years ! The student will find more than enough references in such works as *History of the Jews in Russia and Poland*, by S. M. Bubnov, translated from the Russian by I. Friedlander, 3 vols., Philadelphia, 1916–1920 ; *A History of the Jewish People*, by M. L. Margolis and A. Marx, Philadelphia, 1927 ; *Economic Conditions of the Jews in Russia*, by I. M. Rubinov, Washington, 1908 ; *The Jews of Eastern Europe*, by A. D. Margolis, New York, 1926 ; *The Jews of Russia and Poland*, by I. Friedlander, New York, 1915. For conditions since the revolution see the admirable succinct account *The Jews and Other National Minorities under the Soviets*, by Avrahm Yarmolinsky, New York, 1928, 194 pp. ; *The Slaughter of the Jews in the Ukraine in 1918*, by E. Heifetz, New York, 1921 ; the documents of the Jewish Distribution Committee, 1921, etc. ; and those of the Jewish Colonisation Society of the USSR (OZET), 1928–1935]; *On the Steppe*, by James N. Rosenberg, New York, 1927 ; " Les Colonies juives de la Russie meridionale ", by E. Despreaux, in *Le Monde juif*, June 1927 ; " Biro-Bidjan ", by Lord Marley, in *Soviet Culture* for March 1934.

[2] *The Jews and other National Minorities under the Soviets*, by Avrahm Yarmolinsky, New York, 1928, p. 48.

the fact that, for one or other reason, the majority of the Jews were, for some time, not sympathetic to the Bolshevik Government. Its condemnation of profit-making trading, as of usury, bore harshly on the Jews of White Russia and the Ukraine, whose families had been for centuries excluded alike from agriculture and the professions, and confined to the towns of the Jewish Pale. In 1921 the New Economic Policy temporarily enabled many of them to resume their businesses ; but by 1928 the all-pervading collectivist enterprises of the trusts and the cooperative societies, aided by penal taxation and harsh measures of police, had killed practically all the little profit-making ventures to which the Jewish families were specially addicted. The handicraftsmen were somewhat better off, and the younger ones, at least, could obtain employment in the government factories.

The Jewish problem, as it presented itself to the Soviet Government, was twofold. It was important to rescue from misery, and to find occupation for, the families of the ruined traders and shopkeepers of the small towns of White Russia and the Ukraine. Moreover, it was obviously desirable to secure the loyal allegiance to the Bolshevist régime of the whole three millions of Jews of the USSR. For the economic rehabilitation of the Jews—apart from those whose education and ability enabled them to obtain official appointments or entrance to the brain-working professions—the main resource was placed upon the establishment of Jewish agricultural settlements, at first in Southern Ukraine and the Crimea, and latterly in the extensive territory allocated for this purpose at Biro-Bidjan on the Amour River, in eastern Siberia. Largely by Government help with land and credit, assisted by a whole series of philanthropic associations promoted by the Jews of the United States (notably the Jewish Distribution Committee), as well as those of the USSR in the great voluntary Jewish Colonisation Society (OZET), something like forty thousand Jewish families, comprising a hundred and fifty thousand persons, have within the past fifteen years, been added to the agricultural population of the Soviet Union,[1] one-fourth of them in Biro-Bidjan, which has already been made an " autonomous region ", ranking as an oblast, and

---

[1] This is at least twice as many as the number, mainly from Poland, settled on the land in Palestine during the same period.

will become a " Jewish autonomous republic" as soon as it obtains
a sufficient population.[1]

To all the aggregations of Jews, although not recognised as
a nation, the Soviet Government concedes the same measure
and kind of cultural autonomy as it accords to the national
minorities properly so called. "Jewish soviets exist wherever
there is a considerable Jewish group. They have been formed
in the Crimea as well as in White Russia. Here there are eighteen
petty soviets, four of them rural. In the Ukraine . . . a minimum
of 1000 Ukrainians or 500 non-Ukrainians is entitled to form a
soviet. No less than 25,000 Ukrainians or 10,000 non-Ukrainians
may elect a regional soviet. On April 1, 1927, there were 115
Jewish soviets of the lowest category, both rural and semi-urban,
and one Jewish regional soviet in the Kherson district. The
seat of the latter is in the old colony of Seidemenukka, now renamed Kalinindorf for the president of the Union. It was convened for the first time on March 22, 1927, and the session was
the occasion of much rejoicing. . . . The area of the rayon is
57,636 dessiatines, 27,000 of which are occupied by Jewish
settlers ; and the population of 18,000 includes some 16,000
Jews, all farmers. Delegates to this regional soviet come from
seven rural soviets, six of which are Jewish. . . . There is a
Jewish police commissioner, with a force of three men at his
command, not to mention a ramshackle two-roomed jail. . . . It
is expected that more such soviets will come into existence in
the near future in the districts of Krivoi-Rog, Zaporozhie and
Mariupol. . . . In the Jewish soviets practically all the
transactions, both oral and written, are in Yiddish ; it is
the language of the sessions, of all instruments and of the
correspondence. . . . There are also a number of lower courts

[1] For a recent description of Biro-Bidjan—a territory half as large as England—traversed through its centre by the Trans-Siberian Railway ; practically vacant of indigenous inhabitants ; well-adapted to agricultural settlement,
and apparently amply supplied with mineral resources as yet unworked—see
Lord Marley's article in *Soviet Culture* for March 1934. "In order to encourage
settlers, the Soviet Government has offered free transport, free housing and free
land to suitable Jewish families in good health and trained in agriculture, or in
one of the professions or industries available in the new republic, who are willing
and desirous of settling in Biro-Bidjan, and would be willing to participate in
the normal communal life of that area " (*Ibid*, p. 5). There are already nearly
a hundred primary schools, some fifty collective farms, seventeen small hospitals,
and about fifty medical practitioners or assistants, for a total population of about
50,000, largely Jewish where not indigenous.

(36 in the Ukraine and 5 in White Russia) where the business
is conducted entirely in Yiddish. . . . Yiddish is, of course,
the language in which Jewish children get their schooling,
and is also employed in a number of Jewish homes, where
Jewish children are cared for. . . . Of the Jewish population . . .
a little over ten per cent in the Ukraine elects its own
soviets." [1]

The policy of the Soviet Union with regard to its Jewish
population has not been universally approved by the leaders of
that community throughout the world. The condition of
thousands of Jewish families in White Russia and the Ukraine
is still one of poverty, relieved only by the alms of their co-
religionists. The old people cannot make a new life for themselves. But they suffer, not as Jews but as shopkeepers and
moneylenders, whose occupation has become unlawful. They
are protected from violence as never before. They retain
their synagogues and their vernacular speech. Their sons and
daughters find all branches of education, and all careers, open
to them. Many thousands of families have been assisted to
settlement on the land. Wherever there is a group of Jewish
families together they have their own local government and
their cultural autonomy. They are not prevented from maintaining their racial customs and ceremonies. But all this falls
far short of the ideals cherished by so many of the Jews in the
USSR as elsewhere. "The Jewish Soviet Republic ", it has been
said,[1] " envisaged by the orthodox communists, differs fundamentally from Herzl's polity in Zion, as well as from the Terri-
torialists' Homeland. It is not intended to furnish the Jewish
race throughout the world with the political life that it has lacked
for so long. Nor is it intended to become the seat of the putative
civilisation of the race. . . . For the present, the state extends
to the Jewish masses what it offers to the other minorities :
government institutions using their own language, and instruction entirely in their own tongue. In spite of the fact that everything relating to religion is excluded from the schools, the children
who pass through them are imbued with the Jewish spirit. The
racial experience is transmitted to them through the medium
of the Yiddish writers on whose works they are brought up ;

---

[1] *The Jews and other National Minorities under the Soviets*, by Avrahm
Yarmolinsky, New York, 1928, pp. 105-106.

and whose language they use, not only in the home but also in the classroom."

Nevertheless, it cannot be denied that all the blessings of security from pogroms and freedom to enter professions that the USSR accords to the Jews involve, in practice, their acceptance of the soviet régime ; and make, on the whole, for assimilation. The policy of the Soviet Union accordingly meets with persistent opposition, and even denigration, from the world-wide organisation of the Zionists, among whom the building up of the " national home " in Palestine brooks no rival.

## The Solution of the Problem

It is, we think, owing to the whole-hearted adoption of this policy of cultural autonomy, and even more to its accompaniment of leaving the local administration to be carried on mainly by " natives ", that the Soviet Union, alone among the countries of Eastern Europe, can claim, with a high degree of accuracy, that it has solved the difficult problem presented by the existence of national minorities within a strongly centralised state.[1] It has found this solution, not, as France has done, along the road of absorbing the national minorities by the creation of an overpowering unity of civilisation from end to end of its territory ; nor, as tsarist Russia sought in vain to do, along that of forcibly suppressing all other national peculiarities in favour of those of the dominant race ; but by the novel device of *dissociating statehood from both nationality and race*. In spite of the numerical dominance of the Russian race in the USSR, and its undoubted cultural pre-eminence, the idea of there being a Russian state has been definitely abandoned. The very word " Russia " was, in 1922–1923, deliberately removed from the title of the Soviet Union. All sections of the community—apart from those legally deprived of citizenship on grounds unconnected with either race or nationality—enjoy, throughout the USSR, according to law, equal rights and duties, equal privileges and equal opportunities. Nor is this merely a formal equality under the law and the federal constitution. Nowhere in the world do habit and custom and public opinion approach nearer to a

[1] See, for the whole problem, *National States and National Minorities*, by W. C. Macartney, 1934.

like equality in fact. Over the whole area between the Arctic
Ocean and the Black Sea and the Central Asian mountains,
containing vastly differing races and nationalities, men and
women, irrespective of conformation of skull or pigmentation
of skin, even including the occasional African negro admitted
from the United States, may associate freely with whom they
please ; travel in the same public vehicles and frequent the same
restaurants and hotels ; sit next to each other in the same colleges
and places of amusement ; marry wherever there is mutual
liking ; engage on equal terms in any craft or profession for
which they are qualified ; join the same churches or other
societies ; pay the same taxes and be elected or appointed to any
office or position without exception. Above all, these men and
women denizens of the USSR, to whatever race or nationality
they belong, can and do participate—it is even said that the
smaller nationalities do so in more than their due proportion—
in the highest offices of government and in the organised vocation
of leadership ; alike in the sovnarkoms and central executive
committees of the several constituent republics and in those of
the USSR, and, most important of all, in the Central Committee
of the Communist Party (and its presidium), and even in the all-
powerful Politbureau itself. The Bolsheviks have thus some
justification for their challenging question : Of what other area
containing an analogous diversity of races and nationalities can a
similar assertion be made ?

The policy of cultural autonomy and native self-government
is, indeed, carried very far. It is not confined to the more
powerful national minorities, nor even to groups of magnitude.
Wherever a sufficient minimum of persons of a particular race
or culture are settled together, the local administration allows
for their peculiar needs.[1] Hardly any of the distinct races or

---

[1] " There is scarcely a people in the Soviet Union which has no members
who form a minority in one, or very often in many member states or regions.
The Soviet Union has accordingly enacted very elaborate minority legislation,
assuring to the minorities their schools and the employment of their mother
tongue ; wherever minorities live together in villages or districts they have been
brought together in administrative units in which their language and their
national characteristics have full play " (*Nationalism in the Soviet Union*, by
Hans Kohn, 1934, pp. 69-70).

" The lower steps in the ladder of soviet national (minority) political organisation are the ten national (minority) circuits (or oblasts), 147 national (minority)
rayons, and about 3200 national (minority) soviets (in village or city). These
units represent small national (minority) groups in the midst of larger units

cultures, not even the Russians who count so large a majority, are without their local minorities, dwelling amid alien local majorities. On the other hand, some of the races are wholly dispersed, and are to be found everywhere. Hence the autonomy has to be, and is, carried so far as to secure, for even the smallest minority group, its own autonomy, as regards primary school and local officials, even against the dominant minority culture.

## The Maintenance of Unity

Yet the state as a whole maintains its unity unimpaired, and has even, like other federal states, increased its centralisation of authority. It is only in the USSR that this centralisation involves no lessening of the cultural autonomy of the minorities, and even occurs concomitantly with the strengthening of the various regional cultures. This unbroken unity, and this increasing centralisation of authority, is ensured in ways that will become plain as our exposition proceeds. It will suffice for the present to note, first, that, legally and formally, the powers of the superior authorities in disallowance and cancellation, are the same over the autonomous republics and autonomous areas as over other oblasts, rayons, cities and villages ; the cultural autonomy, though formally established in principle by general law, being essentially a matter of administrative

that are permitted to develop their own national (minority) cultural life. In fairness to the soviets, it must be said that the national minorities are given every opportunity to develop their cultural interests " (*The Soviet State*, by B. W. Maxwell, 1934, p. 26).

" For example, in the RSFSR there are ten national districts, 147 national regions and 3200 national village soviets. In the Ukrainian SSR, among the 380 regions, there are 25 national regions : 8 Russian, 7 German, 3 Bulgarian, 3 Greek, 3 Jewish and 1 Polish. Among the great number of national village soviets of the Ukrainan SSR there are 16 Moldavian, 10 Czech, 4 White Russian and even 1 Swedish and 1 French. In the Abkhdazian SSR there is even a negro soviet" (*How the Soviet Government Solves the National Question*, by L. Perchik, Moscow, 1932, p. 27). It is currently asserted in 1935 that there are in the the USSR, 5000 national soviets.

The existence of a negro village, with a soviet of its own race, is, we imagine, unique in Europe. Persons of African descent, though relatively few in number in the USSR, are more than is usually supposed. Besides the scattered workmen in many occupations who have drifted in from the United States, and a small number of highly educated negro specialists who have been engaged to assist in cotton-growing, etc., there are, about the shores of the Black Sea, quite a number of descendants of the African slaves whom the wealthy used to buy in the slave market of Constantinople. It will be remembered that Pushkin, the first great Russian poet, was of negro descent.

practice. Next, the great levelling influence of the economic
relations exemplified in widespread industrialisation and collectivism, which operate irrespective of race or nationality, or any
geographical boundaries, constitute a silent but continuous
unifying factor. Finally, the ubiquitous guidance and persuasion of the essentially unitary Communist Party, composed
of members of every race and every distinctive culture in the
USSR, ensures not only unity but also all the centralisation that
is necessary.

Alongside this maintenance and strengthening of the minority
cultures, there has been an unmistakeable rise in the level of
civilisation. Note first, and perhaps as most important, a
marked increase, among the national minorities, of their own self-
respect. It is, indeed, the many backward populations, which
had suffered so much under tsarist repression that they had
nothing that could be destroyed, which have gained most from
the nationalities policy of the Soviet Government. They have,
to a considerable extent, already lost their " inferiority complex ",
and gained in confidence and courage. The women, in becoming
literate, have become effectually free, alike from the veil and
from the control of husband or father. The children have
been almost universally got to school, and have been provided
with technical institutes and colleges of university rank, using
the vernacular. The health of the whole people has been improved. With hospitals and medical services, epidemics have
been got under, and the death-rate has everywhere been greatly
reduced. All this has been carried out by the local administration, largely in the hands of " natives ", but with the constant
guidance of the various commissariats of health and education,
and of the Communist Party, with abundant encouragement
and financial assistance from Moscow, always under conditions
of " cultural autonomy ". Even more influential in change has
been the economic development. The nomadic tribes have, to
a great extent, become settled agriculturists, grouped in collective farms ; the peasants have been helped to new crops ;
the collective farms have been mechanised ; the surplus of
labour has been absorbed in extensive industrial enterprises in
mining and manufacturing, largely in the various localities themselves ; additional railways have been constructed ; and dozens
of new cities have sprung up. This has been, in the main, the

outcome of the First and Second Five-Year Plans of 1929 and 1933.

## A New Basis for Statehood

Fundamentally what the Bolsheviks have done, and what Stalin may be thought to have long been looking for, is something which does not seem to have occurred as a possibility to western statesmen. In devising the federal organisation that we have described, they threw over, once for all and completely, the conception that statehood had, or should have, any connection with race or nationality. Political science had, for the most part, come to see, during the nineteenth century, that statehood need have nothing to do with the colour of the skin or with the profession of a particular creed. It had even sometimes contemplated the possibility of doing without a dominant national language. But right down to the resettlement of European boundaries according to the Treaty of Versailles and its fellows in 1919, the political scientists have allowed statesmen to cling to the value, if not the necessity, of a unity of race as the basis of perfect statehood. This conception is connected with, if not consciously based upon, that of an inherent and unalterable superiority of one race—usually one's own race—over others ; and with the belief, for which neither history nor biological science knows of any foundation, that what is called " purity of blood " is an attribute of the highest value. The Bolsheviks put their trust in a genuine equality of citizenship, as completely irrespective of race or language as of colour or religion.[1] They neither undervalued nor overvalued the national minority cultures. What they have sought to do is to develop every one of them, in its own vernacular and with its own peculiarities. They refused to accept the assumption that there is any necessary or inherent inferiority of one race to another. They declared that scientific anthropology knows of no race, whether white or black, of which the most promising individuals could not be immeasurably advanced by appropriate education and an improvement in economic and social environment. The Bol-

---

[1] " Their way of dealing with Home Rule and the nationalities is a masterpiece of ingenuity and elegance. None of the able statesmen of to-day in other lands has attempted to vie with them in their method of satisfying the claims of minorities " (*Russia To-day and To-morrow*, by E. J. Dillon, 1928, p. 228).

sheviks accordingly invented the conception of the unnational
state. They abandoned the word "Russia". They formed a
Union of Socialist Soviet Republics in which all races stood on
one and the same equal footing. And just because it is not a
national state, belonging to a superior race, the Soviet Union
has set itself diligently, not merely to treat the " lesser breeds
within the law " with equality, but, recognising that their backwardness was due to centuries of poverty, repression and en-
slavement, has made it a leading feature of its policy to spend
out of common funds considerably more per head on its backward races than on the superior ones, in education and social
improvements, in industrial investments and agricultural reforms. The record of the USSR in this respect during the past
eighteen years stands in marked contrast with the action towards
their respective lower races of the governments of Holland or
France, and even of that of the United Kingdom, which has
been responsible for the government of India, and many of the
West Indian islands, and much of Africa, for more than a century.

It is interesting to notice how the absorption of such a heterogeneous population as that of the Soviet Union into a strong and
in many respects centralised state has been facilitated by the
system of soviets, using the expedient of indirect election, instead of a parliament directly elected by mass votes. No widespread empire has yet found it possible to establish a parliament
effectively representing its whole realm ; [1] just as none has yet
attempted to carry on its whole production and distribution of
commodities and services by a cabinet responsible to a single
popularly elected parliamentary assembly. But the USSR finds
it quite practicable and useful to let each village in Kamchatka or Sakhalin, or beyond the Arctic circle, elect its own
selosoviet, and send its own deputies to the rayon congress of
soviets, and so to the congress of soviets of the oblast or autonomous republic, and ultimately to the All-Union Congress of
Soviets at Moscow, in exactly the same way, and with exactly
the same rights, as a village in the oblast of Moscow or Leningrad.
Such a remote and backward village, it must be remembered.

---

[1] No one can seriously suggest that the admission to the French Senate and
Chamber of Deputies, and even, very occasionally, to minor ministerial office,
of members nominally elected by the people of Martinique, Guadaloupe, Reunion,
Pondicherry, Guiana, Senegal or Cochin China (omitting Algeria, Tunis, Mada-
gascar, etc.), amounts to any solution of the problem.

which uses its own vernacular in its own schools and its own court of justice, enjoys, likewise, the privilege of filling the local offices, even the highest of them, with its own people. And what is of even greater importance, its residents are eligible, equally with persons of any other race or residence, for the Order or Companionship undertaking the Vocation of Leadership, which their leading members are encouraged and even pressed to join, and for which, as we shall hereafter describe, they are provided gratuitously with the necessary intensive training, returning to their homes equipped for filling any of the local offices, and even for promotion to the highest places in the Union. Not without reason, therefore, is it claimed that the soviet system has, for a far-flung empire, certain advantages over that of a directly elected parliamentary assembly.

In the foregoing lengthy analysis of the soviet organisation for the representation of " Man as a Citizen ", and for his participation in the administration of public affairs, the reader might assume that he has had placed before him the constitution of the USSR. Needless to say this would be a mistake. Not all the solidity of the base of the pyramid of soviets—not all the varied specialisation of its successive tiers of councils and the administration organs connected with them—not all the centralisation of supervision and direction in the highest governing groups of statesmen, would have enabled the Soviet Union to carry through successfully, either the extensive and rapid industrialisation of so heterogeneous a country, or the extraordinary transformation of agriculture now in progress over one-sixth of the earth's land surface, without an equally elaborate organisation of " Man as a Producer ", in the trade union hierarchy of all kinds of wage or salary earners, and in the various associations of owner-producers ineligible for trade union membership. There will then still remain to be considered the representation, through the consumers' cooperative movement, of " Man as a Consumer ", in order to secure the maximum practicable adjustment of the nation's production to the needs and desires of every member of the community. Moreover, we suggest that not even these three particular forms of democracy, through which, as it is claimed, every adult in the USSR, with small and steadily dwindling exceptions, finds a threefold place in the constitution, would have sufficed for such a unique task as that undertaken by the Bolsheviks—the transformation, from top to bottom, of the economic, social and cultural life of the whole community of the USSR—if provision had not also been made in the constitution, by remarkable forms hitherto unknown to political science, for the continuous exercise of the Vocation of Leadership ; that leadership without which there can be no consistent or continuous government of any populous state, however democratic may be its character and spirit. Before the reader can adequately appreciate the part of the constitution of the USSR that deals with " Man as a Citizen ", he must take into account also the parts dealing with " Man as a Producer " and " Man as a Consumer " ; and, last but certainly not least, also that dealing with the Vocation of Leadership, all of which are described in the ensuing chapters. What we have given here is therefore not a summary of the soviet constitution : this has necessarily to be reserved for the final chapter of Part I., entitled " Democracy or Dictatorship ? "

# CHAPTER III

## MAN AS A PRODUCER

THROUGHOUT the USSR man as a producer is organised in two separate groupings, differing widely in their political, economic and social characteristics. First and foremost there are the trade unions, with inner circles of professional and craft associations, in conception derived from western Europe, more especially from Great Britain and Germany. Secondly, there are the associations of owner-producers, which—ignoring for the moment certain miscellaneous forms [1]—may be either manufacturing or agricultural, springing out of the old Russian artel or mir. These two types of mass organisation, though on friendly terms and frequently helping each other, are mutually exclusive. No member of any association of owner-producers can be a member of a trade union.

## SECTION I

### SOVIET TRADE UNIONISM

The important place held by the trade union as a part of the constitution of the USSR has been explicitly affirmed by no less an authority than Stalin himself. Stalin was describing the various mass organisations, each of them extending from one end of the country to the other, and serving—to use his own terms —as " belts " and " levers " and " guiding forces ", all essential

---

[1] Such as the fishermen and the peculiar group of " Integral " cooperatives in the Far North, together with some special groups like the " war invalids " (partially disabled ex-soldiers), to be described in a subsequent section of this chapter.

161

to what Lenin had described as the " broadly based and extremely powerful proletarian apparatus " of a federal constitution, rendering it both " supple " and effective.   " What are these organisations," Stalin continued.   " First of all there are [not, be it noted the soviets, but] the trade unions, with their national and local ramifications in the form of productive, educational, cultural and other organisations.   In these the workers of all trades and industries are united.   These are not [Communist] Party organisations.   Our trade unions can now be regarded as the general organisation of the working class now holding power in Soviet Russia.   They constitute a school of communism.   From them are drawn the persons best fitted to occupy the leading positions in all branches of administration.   They form a link between the more advanced and the comparatively backward sections of the working class, for in them the masses of the workers are united with the vanguard.

" Second [only secondly, be it noted] we have the soviets with their manifold national and local ramifications taking the form of administrative, industrial, military, cultural and other state organisations, together with a multitude of spontaneous mass groupings of the workers in the bodies which surround these organisations and link them up with the general population. The soviets are the mass organisations of those who labour in town and country. . . .

" Thirdly, we have cooperatives of all kinds with their multiple ramifications. . . . The cooperatives play a specially important part after the consolidation of the dictatorship of the proletariat, during the period of widespread construction.   They form a link between the proletarian vanguard and the peasant masses whereby the latter can be induced to share in the work of socialist construction. . . .

" Lastly, we come to the party of the proletariat [the Communist Party], the proletarian vanguard.   Its strength lies in the fact that it attracts to its ranks the best elements of all the mass organisations of the proletariat.   Its function is to *unify* the work of all the mass organisations of the proletariat, without exception ; and to *guide* their activities towards a single end, the liberation of the proletariat.   Unification and guidance are absolutely essential.   There must be unity in the proletarian struggle ; the proletarian masses must be guided in their fight for power and for the upbuilding of socialism; and only the proletarian vanguard, only the party of the proletariat, is competent to unify and guide the work of the mass organisations of the proletariat." [1]

## Trade Union History in the USSR [2]

We need not describe the slow beginning of Russian trade unionism in the last decades of the nineteenth century under conditions of illegality and constant police persecution.[3] It is sufficient to note that, in the revolutionary movement of 1905, combinations of industrial wage-earners spontaneously arose in

---

[1] *Leninism*, by Josef Stalin, vol. i., 1928, pp. 29-31. We need not take too seriously the relative positions that Stalin assigned to the various blocks of the constitutional structure of the USSR—either when he puts the trade unions first, or when he puts the Communist Party last !

[2] The book and pamphlet literature on soviet trade unionism during the past sixteen years has been enormous. We may cite first the publications of the International Labour Office of the League of Nations, such as *The Trade Union Movement in Soviet Russia* (1927, xii and 287 pp.); and *Wages and Regulations of Conditions of Labour in the USSR*, by S. Zagorsky (1930, viii and 212 pp.). To these may be added *Selection of Documents Relative to Labour Legislation in Force in the USSR* (British Government Stationery Office, 1931, 200 pp.). Perhaps the most informative book down to 1927 is the admirable monograph entitled *Soviet Trade Unions*, by Robert W. Dunn (1928, New York Vanguard Press, ix and 238 pp.); and down to 1931, *The Soviet Worker*, by Joseph Freeman (1932, vii and 408 pp.); and *Die russischen Gewerkschaften; ihre Entwicklung, ihre Zielsetzung und ihre Stellung zum Staat*, by Michael Jakobso (Berlin, 1932, 188 pp.). See also "Wages Policy in Soviet Russia," by S. Lawford Childs and A. A. Crottet, in *Economic History*, January 1932; "The Transformation of Soviet Trade Unions," by Amy Hewes, in *American Economic Review*, December 1932; *The Trade Unions, the Party and the State*, by M. Tomsky (Moscow, 1927, 22 pp.); and *The October Revolution and the Trade Unions*, by A. Abolin (Cooperative Publishing Society of Foreign Workers in the USSR, Moscow, 1933, 54 pp.). Much is to be learned from *After Lenin*, by Michael Farbman, 1924; *Civic Training in Soviet Russia*, 1929, and *Making Bolsheviks*, 1932, both by Professor S. N. Harper; *Soviet Russia*, by William G. Chamberlin (1930, viii and 453 pp.); and *The Economic Life of Soviet Russia*, by Calvin B. Hoover, 1931. *The Report of the Ninth All-Union Congress of Trade Unions* (in English, Moscow, 1933) is invaluable. Several of the above give extensive lists of Russian documents and works.

[3] The earliest attempts at trade unionism in Russia appear to date only from 1875, when Zaslavsky, "an organiser and propagandist of talent", established at Odessa a "Union of the Workers of Southern Russia", having industrial as well as political aims, which was promptly suppressed with severe punishment, no word about it being allowed to appear in the newspapers. In 1879 a similar "Union of the Workers of Northern Russia" was established at St. Petersburg by a carpenter named Stevan Khaltourine, whose efforts were suppressed in 1881 (*Histoire du parti communiste de l'URSS (parti bolchevik)*, par E. Yaroslavski, Paris 1931, pp. 24-25; see also *From Peter the Great to Lenin*, by S. P. Turin, 1935, p. 34).

all the industrial areas. These trade unions, together with the contemporary soviets of " workers and peasants ", were, in fact, the organs of the popular upheaval. In 1905, and again in 1906, an All-Russian Trade Union Conference was held in Moscow, representing some 600 separate unions, with about 250,000 members. In 1907 a second conference opened up relations with the trade union movement in western Europe, and actually sent a delegation to the International Labour and Socialist Congress at Stuttgart. All this activity was summarily suppressed by the Tsar's police in 1908, when 107 unions were dissolved by a single ukase, and in the following years the Russian trade union movement was practically destroyed.[1] Various industrial centres, however, kept alive " underground " groups of " illegal " propagandists. " The industrial boom," Trotsky tells us, " beginning in 1910, lifted the workers to their feet and gave a new impulse to their energy. The figures [of strikes] for 1912–1914 almost repeat those for 1905–1907, but in the opposite order ; not from above downwards but from below upwards. On a new and higher historical basis—there are more workers now, and they have more experience—a new revolutionary offensive begins. The first half-year of 1914 clearly approaches, in the number of political strikes, the culminating point of the year of the first revolution. But war breaks out and sharply interrupts this process. The first war months are marked by political inertness in the working class, but already in the spring of 1915 the numbness begins to pass. A new cycle of political strikes opens, a cycle which in February 1917 will culminate in the insurrection of soldiers and workers." [2]

It has been estimated, however, that, on the outbreak of the revolution in February 1917, the total membership of all the trade unions throughout the Russian empire cannot have exceeded a few tens of thousands. During the interval between the February and October revolutions, trade unionism spread

[1] " The unions were prohibited from assisting strikers ; they were closed down for attempting to intervene in the great strike movement ; members of the executives were arrested and exiled to Siberia ; funds were confiscated, and books were taken to the police stations ; police were present at all meetings, which were closed down on the slightest pretext, and very often without any reason at all. . . . The iron fist of the victorious reaction ruthlessly crushed the labour organisations at their birth " (*Trade Unions in Soviet Russia*, by A. Losovsky, p. 15 ; *Soviet Trade Unions*, by Robert W. Dunn, 1927, p. 16).

[2] *History of the Russian Revolution*, by L. Trotsky, 1932, vol. i. p. 55.

with startling rapidity through all the industrial areas. By June 1917 there were already 967 separate organisations, with an aggregate membership of a million and a half. In that month the third All-Russian Conference of Trade Unions was held, when a standing committee or executive board was appointed to guide the policy of the movement. By October 1917 the total trade union membership had come to exceed two millions.

Meanwhile there had developed a sharp rivalry between the trade unions, based on organisation by trades and directed mainly by the Mensheviks, and the " Soviets of Workers' and Soldiers' Deputies ", based on organisation by factories which were being permeated and presently dominated by the Bolsheviks. Both the trade unions and the new soviets were intimately connected with the factory committees, which had sprung up spontaneously in most of the large establishments in Leningrad and Moscow. We give the issue in the words of a subsequent trade union leader. In June 1917 he writes : " At the Third All-Russian Trade Union Conference (the first after the February revolution of 1917), the trade unions split into two wings on one of the fundamental questions of Leninism—that of the bourgeois-democratic revolution growing into a socialist revolution. The Mensheviks, the Bundists [the separate organisation of the Jewish workmen] and the Social Revolutionaries, mainly representing the non-industrial unions and the small urban centres (of the industrial unions, the only one which constituted a firm bulwark of the Mensheviks, and that only temporarily, was the printers' union), based their argument on the premiss that the revolution which was developing, both in its objective political sense and in its content, was a bourgeois revolution ; and they therefore held that the only tasks of this revolution were those of bourgeois democratic reform. The Bolshevik premiss was the opposite. The Bolsheviks held that the growing revolution was a proletarian and socialist revolution, and that it would also incidentally complete the tasks of a bourgeois-democratic revolution." [1]   In his admirable work entitled *Civic Training in Soviet Russia,* Professor S. N. Harper has described this internal feud and its relation to the structure of soviet trade unionism. " An All-Russian Conference of Factory Committees was held on the very eve of the

[1] *The October Revolution and the Trade Unions,* by A. Abolin, p. 7 (Cooperative Publishing Society of Foreign Workers in the USSR, 1933, 54 pp.).

October revolution. It was called on the initiative of the Bolsheviks, to compete with the executive board set up by the trade union conference of June (1917), at which the Mensheviks had the majority. This struggle between the rival party factions for the control of the organisations of the workmen was decided by the October revolution. After the victory of the Bolsheviks, the factory committees and the trade unions were combined, the former becoming the primary units of the latter." In January 1919 the first All-Russian Congress of Trade Unions was convened in Petrograd. It claimed an authority superior to that of the previous conferences. It decided to support the " dictatorship of the proletariat " established by Lenin, and to assist vigorously in building up the socialist state throughout the RSFSR. " For this purpose," it declared, " factory committees must become local organs of the union, and must not carry on an existence separate and apart from the trade union." [1] The central committee of the factory committees was therefore to be abolished. Some of the unions, records Professor Harper, or at any rate some of their branches, such as that of the Moscow printers, " would not recognise the congress ", continuing for a time their independent existence, as a protest against the Bolshevik seizure of power.

During the ensuing decade the position and functions of the trade unions in the soviet state became the subject of acute controversy. If we are to realise where they now stand in the constitution, we must briefly summarise the successive stages of this hotly contested dispute. For the first few months after October 1917, as we shall subsequently describe, the workmen assumed that they were, by their committees in the several

[1] In addition to Professor S. N. Harper's *Civic Training in Soviet Russia*, the student should compare, for this controversy, the valuable summary in *After Lenin*, by Michael Farbman, 1924, p. 142, etc.; and the interesting pamphlet by A. Abolin, *The October Revolution and the Trade Unions* (Cooperative Publishing Society of Foreign Workers in the USSR, Moscow, 1933, 54 pp.). The last-named work gives the following statistics showing the gradual triumph of the Bolsheviks : "At the Third Conference of Trade Unions, held in June 1917, the Bolsheviks and their adherents constituted 36·4 per cent, whilst the Mensheviks and their adherents constituted 55·5 per cent. At the First Congress of Trade Unions, held in January 1918, the Bolsheviks and their adherents represented as much as 65·6 per cent, whilst the Mensheviks and their adherents were only 21·4 per cent. At the Fifth Congress of Trade Unions, the Mensheviks and their sympathisers were represented by only 2·2 per cent, while the Bolsheviks numbered 91·7 per cent " (*ibid.* p. 13).

factories, to take over the whole function of the owners and managers of the enterprises in which they were employed. In some cases, the workers' committee formally appointed, not only the foremen, but also the previous proprietor, whom they made their manager. Nor was this conception confined to the Petrograd factories. There was a brief period during which the running of the trains on the Petrograd-Moscow railway was decided by the station staffs. Even on vessels of the Soviet mercantile marine, the captains took their navigation orders from the committee elected by the ship's company. Within six months, however, Lenin decided that such a form of workers' control led only to chaos, and that there must be, in every case, a manager appointed by and responsible to the appropriate organ of the government. But for a long time the workers' committees in the factories retained a large measure of control. They had to be consulted by the manager on every matter in which they felt an interest. In many cases they appointed the manager's chief assistant. Even the captain of a ship had such an assistant, who scrutinised every decision. But the workmen's most effective control over industry was afforded by the fact that the government's boards or commissions had, in their membership, a large proportion of the leaders of the trade unions. The trade unions were strongly represented on the Central Executive Committee and the Supreme Economic Council. They nominated the People's Commissar for Labour. It was very largely they who manned the Workers' and Peasants' Inspection.

Upon this confusion of powers and responsibilities there supervened the Civil War, which submerged all controversy. The trade unions threw themselves whole-heartedly into the struggle, and supplied a large part of the government's fighting forces. The union offices became principally recruiting centres, whilst the work of nearly every industrial establishment was concentrated on supplying the needs of the Red Army. The unions became, in substance if not in form, government organs. Membership was, by mere majority vote in each factory, made compulsory for all those at work. Trade union dues were simply stopped from wages, and any trade union deficit was met by one or other of the forms of government subsidy.[1]

[1] " During the period of War Communism, we went through a stage of inflation, falling currency, and we could not collect our trade union dues

With the final expulsion from soviet territory of the last of the hostile armies, and the oncoming of the great famine, there came in 1921, as the only means of providing the necessaries of life whilst the government was building up the heavy industries, the New Economic Policy (NEP), temporarily allowing a limited amount of private capitalist enterprise for individual profit. What, then, was to be the position of the trade unions ? Trotsky argued, from his military experience, that the industrial workers could best be organised as a labour army, and that the trade unions should be formally incorporated in the state machinery as government organs, through which common action could be ensured and industrial discipline maintained. Lenin, on the other hand, objected to this as a monstrous extension of bureaucracy. He realised also that NEP would inevitably produce the old trade disputes, for dealing with which an independent trade unionism was indispensable. Moreover, in the large enterprises, which were to remain governmental, there could be no going back from management by qualified technicians and administrators, who must be appointed by such state organs as the trusts. Lenin argued that the unions would have their hands full, at least for some time to come, with defending the interests of the workers against exploitation by the private " Nepmen ", even more than against the evils of bureaucracy in the governmental trusts. It was accordingly officially decided, in December 1921, that the trade unions should be made independent of government machinery and control, and that, whilst they should continue to be essentially schools of communism, their specific function should be to improve their members' material conditions, both by resisting exploitation by private employers, and " by rectifying the faults and exaggerations of economic bodies so far as they proceed from a bureaucratic perversion of the machinery of the state ". " The chief task of the trade unions," it was stated, is, " from now

regularly . . . at that time we took money from the state. The state subsidised us. Now we have a stable currency, we take no subsidies from the state, except that which is provided for by the constitution and the law, and which flows logically from the very nature of the proletarian state. The code of labour laws, paragraph 155, runs : ' In accordance with statute 10 of the constitution of the RSFSR, all organs of the state must render to the industrial unions and their organisations every assistance, place at their disposal fully equipped premises to be used as Palaces of Labour, charge reduced rates for public services, such as posts, telegraphs, telephones, railway and shipping rates, etc.' These are the privileges and subsidies afforded to us " (*The Trade Unions, the Party and the State,* by M. Tomsky, Moscow, 1927, p. 20).

onward, to safeguard at all times in every possible way, the class interests of the proletariat in its struggle with capitalism. This task should be openly given prominence. Trade Union machinery must be correspondingly reconstructed, reshaped and made complete. There should be organised conflict commissions, strike funds, mutual aid funds and so on." [1]

It will be seen that, in setting up the several trade unions as independent defenders of the material interests of their members, primarily against the newly revived profit-making employers, their relation to the government as employer was left in some ambiguity. It was therefore natural that each trade union should push for higher wages for its own members, irrespective both of the effect on the workers in other industries and of the wider interests of the community as a whole. So long as the profit-making capitalism of NEP continued, this ambiguity in the trade union relation to government employment remained undecided. The trade unions did not object to the view that, whilst the working day should be shortened, the total output had to be augmented. They willingly agreed to an almost universal adoption of piecework rates, under which both output and individual earnings were increased. But when the policy of NEP was reversed, and government or cooperative employment became universal, it was not easy for the workers to realise that they, as a class, had no enemy left to fight. Any further increase in their wages, beyond that accompanied by an equivalent increase in production, could no longer be taken from the income of a private profit-maker. It now involved a definite encroachment on the amounts to be set aside for the social services and for the desired multiplication of factories and increase of machinery, development of electrification and so on, which, to the whole community of workers, were, in the long run, as necessary as their wages.

With the introduction of the Five-Year Plan matters came to a crisis. At the Eighth All-Union Congress of Trade Unions, in 1928–1929, a sharp conflict took place. Tomsky, who had been President of the All-Union Central Council of Trade Unions (AUCCTU), the supreme organ of the whole trade union movement, bluntly put the position of the trade unions in the USSR as

---

[1] Report of commission (of which Lenin was a member) of December 1921, summarised in *Soviet Trade Unions*, by Robert W. Dunn (New York, 1927), pp. 26-27.

being substantially the same as in the capitalist states.  He emphasised the importance of the complete freedom of each of the trade unions to press, as far as it could, for further and further improvements in the material conditions of its own members, on the assumption that it was in such increases in wages in particular industries that the prosperity of the nation consisted.  It was not for the trade unions, he declared, to press for improvements in factory technique, even if these would lead to increased productivity.  He (or one of his supporters) is reported to have said that the government must indeed be hard up if it wanted " socialist competition " among the workers to increase output !  He did not see how the trade unions could control the industries on the basis of commercial accounting, and be at the same time the representatives and defenders of the interests of their own members.

Against Tomsky's view of trade union function,[1] the whole influence of the Communist Party was thrown.  It was not for such an anarchic scramble after rises in wages by the strongest trade unions, irrespective of their effect on the required universal increase of industrial productivity, that Lenin had restored trade union independence.  The very existence of the Soviet State, it was held, depended on the bound forward of industrial productivity being universal ; and, even if only from the standpoint of permanently securing higher wages for their own members, it was this universally increased production that it was the duty of the trade unions to promote.  At the very congress, in December 1928, at which Tomsky, then making his last stand, so bluntly expressed his own views, the majority of the delegates were induced to elect to the all-powerful presidium of the AUCCTU, L. M. Kaganovich, an assistant secretary of the Communist Party, who had been specially selected for this service, and who devoted himself for the next two years to a continuous educational cam-

---

[1] Tomsky's view of the task of trade unionism seemed, in 1927, quite satisfactory to an exceptionally competent and sympathetic American observer. " ' As long as the wage system exists in any country,' says Chairman Tomsky of the AUCCTU, '. . . the worker will naturally demand higher wages than he receives.  It is the duty of the trade unions to know the industry and *each factory unit and its possibilities for meeting the demands of the workers* ' " (*Soviet Trade Unions*, by Robert W. Dunn, 1927, p. 82).  But soviet theory holds that the demands of the workers should not be related to the productivity of " each factory unit ", but to that of the industry as a whole ; and not even to that of a particular industry, but to that of soviet industries in general, preferably advancing as nearly as possible uniformly all along the line.

paign among the committee-men and other " activists " in trade unionism, leading to a far-reaching reorganisation of trade union executives in personnel as well as in policy. This was accompanied, at the beginning of 1930, by a general purge in all departments of the state, as a result of the suspicion aroused as to lack of cordial cooperation in soviet policy by persons not sprung from the manual labour class. It was found that " on January 1, 1930, only 9 per cent of the personnel of the AUCCTU were of working-class origin. The percentage of former members of other parties to the total number of communists [Party members] was as follows : In the AUCCTU 41·9 per cent ; in the central council of metal workers 37 per cent ; in the central council of printers 24 per cent, etc. The purge exposed 19 persons of alien class origin in the newspaper *Trud*, persons originating from among the merchants, nobles, priests, etc. There were 18 descendants of nobles and merchants in the central committee of the trade union of soviet employees. In eleven central committees of trade unions 53 personages were found who, in the past, were actively alien and hostile to the proletariat." [1]   These disaffected elements were eliminated..

When the time came for the Ninth All-Union Congress of Trade Unions, in 1931, the current of opinion among the organised workers had been changed. Tomsky had, in the interval, on other grounds, fallen out with the Central Committee of the Communist Party ; and had retired in 1929 from trade union leadership, at first from ill-health, eventually taking another honourable but less influential office.[2]

After the Congress of 1928–1929, the All-Union Central Committee of Trade Unions (AUCCTU), under Kaganovich's influence, enjoined all trade unionists to " face production ", and look to the output, not merely of their own factory, or even of their own industry, but of soviet industries as a whole. The Sixteenth All-Union Congress of the Communist Party, in 1930, decided that it was the duty of the trade unions actually to take the lead in promoting "socialist competition", and also to organise " shock brigades " (udarniki) in order to raise to the utmost the

---

[1] *Report of Ninth Congress of Trade Unions, 1931*, pp. 25-26.

[2] He was appointed in 1931 to be director of Gosisdat (subsequently called Ogiz), the great state publishing establishment of the RSFSR. The struggle is summarised in *Die russischen Gewerkshaften*, by Michael Jakobson, 1932, pp. 141-143.

productivity of the whole community. Not unnaturally, this lesson was hard to learn. It has taken nearly a decade to persuade the strongest defenders of trade unionism that its function as an " organ of revolt " against the autocracy of each capitalist employer, and as an instrument for extracting from his profits the highest possible wage for the manual workers whom he employed, had passed away with the capitalist employer himself.[1] It required long-continued instruction to convince all the workmen that when they, in the aggregate, had the disposal of the entire net product of the nation's combined industry, it was not in the " profits " of each establishment, but in the total amount produced by the conjoined labours of the whole of them, that they were pecuniarily interested ; and that what trade union organisation had to protect was, not so much the wage-rates of the workers in particular industries, as the earnings, and, indeed, the whole conditions of life, inside the factory and outside, of all the wage-earners of the USSR.

### Trade Union Structure in the USSR

We are now in a position to appreciate the difference between the structure of the trade unions in Soviet Communism from that of those of Britain or the United States. The British or American trade union, being formed to fight the employers in each industry against any lowering of the wage-rates of particular crafts, and using for this purpose the device of collective bargaining to prevent the cut-throat competition among unemployed workmen for particular jobs, takes the form of a combination of workers of a particular craft, or, in the alternative, of a particular industry, seizing every opportunity for extracting higher wages from the employers of the particular establishments in which the members

---

[1] This has to be perpetually impressed, not only on young recruits but also on experienced foreign trade unionists working in the USSR. " The primary task of the trade unions in the Soviet Union ", declared Shvernik, the Secretary of the All-Union Central Committee of the Trade Unions, in an address to 130 foreign worker delegates, in the Moscow Palace of Labour (*Moscow Daily News*, November 12, 1932), " is to make workers realise that, as the sole owners of the means of production, they must learn to take responsibility for the maintenance of these means." Hence, he continued, " the soviet trade union is not an isolated body, but an integral part of the entire soviet system, assisting in the fulfilment of production programmes by organising socialist competition and shock brigades, and attending to the cultural and economic requirements of the workers ".

are employed. Each craft or industry, desperately anxious to save its own members from the morass of unemployment, accordingly fights for its own hand, irrespective of the effect on the cost of production of the establishment as a whole, or on the wage-rates of other crafts or industries. The soviet trade union, on the other hand, is not formed to fight anybody, and has no inducement to prevent the competition among workmen for particular jobs. The pecuniary interest of its members is found in the productivity of soviet industry in general, which is made up of the productivity of all the factories in which they work ; and it is this aggregate productivity, not anybody's profits, on which the standard wage-rates of all of them will directly depend. Moreover, apart from money wages, the soviet trade union is interested in its members' protection against industrial accidents, and the amenity and healthfulness of their places of work ; in discussing and advising on the plans on which the factory is carried on ; in conducting the comrades' courts in which the members themselves deal with minor delinquencies of their own number ; in the amount of food and other commodities that, in the "factory cooperative" (including the newly developed factory farms), can be got for the money wage ; in the administration of the sickness and accident and old-age pension insurance, which is entrusted to the local committee that the factory elects ; in the "legal bureaux" which it maintains for the aid of its members in obtaining their rights ; in the housing accommodation secured for the personnel ; in the club-house which the factory provides for the members' recreation and education ; in the holiday resorts, opportunities for travel, and tickets for theatre and opera that the union secures for its members. It will be noted that in all this large and ever-growing sphere of trade union functions, the trade union acts as an organisation not of producers, for its members do not produce these services, but of consumers, in which all the workers in the enterprise are equally concerned.

This brings us to the most important difference in structure between trade unionism in the USSR and that in other countries : as the soviet trade unions have not to fight profit-making employers, but to share in the organisation of the industry in which they are engaged, it is the establishment as a whole, not any particular craft within it, and the whole of the establishments turning out the same kind of product, not any particular branch of the industry, that is made the unit of trade union structure. And as all those working in the establishment are cooperatively creating the product, and not only those of any particular craft, or grade, or age, or sex, trade union membership logically embraces the whole staff or personnel of the establishment, from the general manager to the office-boy, from the foreman to the apprentice, from the most scientifically qualified specialist to the least skilled general labourer.[1]

Hence the trade union in the USSR is neither a craft nor an industrial union. It is nearest to what has been called, in Great Britain, an employment union, in its most ideal comprehensiveness in a national monopoly. All those who work within any one establishment—the manager, the technicians, the clerks and book-keepers, the foremen, the artisans and labourers, the factory doctors and nurses, and even the canteen cooks and cleaners, and this entire personnel in all the establishments producing the same commodity or service throughout the USSR—are included in one union, whether the object of the nation-wide enterprise be extracting, manufacturing, transporting or distributing commodities, or rendering administrative or cultural services of any kind.

A further principle, following from that of looking to the product instead of to the profit, is that of nation-wide organisation by establishments. All the tens of thousands of establishments in the USSR are grouped together for trade union purposes according to their several predominant products. This involves that all the wage-earners in each establishment should belong to the particular trade union in which the establishment is included. There are now no local trade unions, any more than craft or industrial unions. The number of separate unions, which has varied from time to time, was brought down to 23 ; then raised in 1931 to 47 ; and on the comprehensive reorganisation in 1934, further increased to 154, having memberships ranging from less than a hundred thousand to half a million or

[1] It is to be noted that " the one-shop one-union principle " was laid down as axiomatic at the Second Trade Union Conference of 1906, and has ever since been increasingly believed in (*Soviet Trade Unions*, by Robert W. Dunn, 1927, pp. 13-14). The railway workers' union (AZRG), which was the first effectively to establish a union for the whole country, included from the outset all grades of railway employees, in all districts, from the highest superintendents to the lowest firemen (*Die russischen Gewerkschaften*, by Michael Jakobson, 1932, p. 9).

so. We may add that, at the end of 1933 the aggregate contributing membership of the trade unions amounted to about eighteen million persons—far more than in the trade unions of all the rest of the world put together—representing a total census population of something like forty millions, being at least one-fourth of that of the whole of the USSR.[1]

The aggregate membership in past years is given as under :

| 1917 | . | . | 1,475,000 | 1920 | . | . | 5,122,006 |
| 1918 | . | . | 1,946,000 | 1921 | . | . | 8,418,362 |
| 1919 | . | . | 3,706,779 | | | | |

The total then fell to 5,846,000, largely due to the exclusion of individual independent handicraftsmen (kustari) and members of cooperative associations of owner-producers, or of the old artels. It continued to decline until 1923. It then rose as under :

| 1924 | . | . | 5,822,700 | 1926 | . | . | 8,768,200 |
| 1925 | . | . | 6,950,000 | 1927 | . | . | 9,827,000 |

[1] The non-unionists among the wage-earners, of whom at any particular date there may be as many as four or five millions, comprise in the main : (*a*) newly engaged peasants fresh from the farms, and other recruits for the first three months of their service ; (*b*) seasonal workers returning periodically to peasant households, though some sections of these, like the Leningrad dock labourers, are strongly unionised ; (*c*) workers in newly established isolated factories distant from industrial centres, to which trade union organisation has not yet spread ; (*d*) isolated wage-earners or small groups, engaged at wages by kustar artels or on peasant farms; (*e*) a steadily diminishing proportion of boys and girls under sixteen ; and (*f*) an uncertain number of the " deprived " categories, statutorily excluded from trade union membership, but unobtrusively allowed to continue in employment at wages or on salaries, sometimes because their services are particularly useful.

In September 1934, Shvernik (Secretary of the All-Union Central Committee of Trade Unions), in propounding the scheme of reorganisation, complained that 22 per cent of all those employed for wages or salary in the USSR were outside the trade unions ; he said that the agricultural state farm workers' union had only 49 per cent, and the stock-breeding state farm workers' union and that of the peat workers only 54 per cent of the persons employed, whilst the railway-construction workers had no more than 61 per cent. Even the machine-tractor station workers had only 73 per cent, the building trades workers only 74 per cent, and the miners only 77 per cent in their respective unions (*Moscow Daily News*, September 10, 1934).

The rules for admission, as revised in September 1931 by the All-Union Congress of Trade Unions (AZRG), run as follows : All permanent wage (or salary) earners may join a trade union during the first days of employment. Seasonal workers may be admitted as soon as they have completed two months' uninterrupted work, and this waiting period may be waived if they were engaged as seasonal workers in the previous year. Members of collective farms engaging in industrial, transport or building work as wage (or salary) earners may at once join the appropriate union (*Ekonomischeskaja Zhizn*, September 16, 1931).

The trade union hierarchy—we use this word, as already explained, without any implication of dependence upon a superior authority—like the other parts of the USSR constitutional structure, is built up, in each trade union, by a series of indirect elections based at the bottom upon direct popular election by the members of that union, whether paid by wages or salaries, irrespective of sex, craft, vocation, grade or amount of remuneration ; assembled in relatively small meetings of men and women actually associated in work, whether by hand or by brain, in any kind of industrial or other establishment. This trade union organisation has been only gradually formed into a broadly based pyramid, uniform in its constitution in all trade unions all over the USSR, and this evolution has even now not reached complete identity. As it stood in 1933 it was well summarised in a speech by Shvernik, the General Secretary of the All-Union Central Committee of Trade Unions (AUCCTU). " We have at present ", he said, " forty-seven unions, each headed by its own central committee. The central committees . . . have regional committees . . . under them ; then come the factory committees [fabkom] and the local committees [mestkom] in soviet institutions ; and in addition to these the trade union group organisers. This principle of building up the trade unions . . . has enabled us to bring all enterprises, all soviet and [trading] business institutions within the sphere of trade union organisation. [There are now 513,000 trade union groups, but] the basic nucleus . . . is the factory committee [fabkom] and the local committee or *mestkom* in soviet and [commercial] business organisations. There are 186,640 . . . committees of this kind. There are 888 regional departments . . . and . . . 47 central committees of trade unions. . . . All branches of national economy are covered by the trade union organisations, which unite in their ranks 75 per cent of the total number of those working [for wages or salaries] in our national economy." [1]

The basis of the trade-union hierarchy is the meeting or

---

[1] *Speech of Welcome to Foreign Delegates*, by N. M. Shvernik, General Secretary of the AUCCTU, delivered May 8, 1933 (Moscow : Cooperative Publishing Society of Foreign Workers in the USSR, 1933, p. 6). The number of trade union groups given in Shvernik's speech to the ninth All-Union Trade Union Congress itself ; see " The Soviet Trade Unions on the Threshold of the Second Five-Year Plan " in *Report of the Ninth Trade Union Congress* (same publishers, p. 94).

meetings for the choice of the factory committee (fabkom) which, in government offices and trading establishments and in all non-industrial institutions, is called the local committee (mestkom). The rule is to have one such committee covering the whole of each establishment. But in the great cities there are enterprises so small that several of them have to be grouped together to elect one factory committee. Such a tiny unit is, however, more characteristic of the non-industrial establishments, such as hospitals or other medical institutions; schools, colleges and universities, and research institutions; and the local offices of government departments. As was the case also before the revolution, the characteristic industrial establishment (or " plant ") in the industry of the USSR has thousands of workers employed in its various departments, in numerous separate buildings erected upon an extensive site, which often exceeds in area a square mile. Thus the Rostselmash Agricultural Machine Works at Rostov-on-Don, which is not by any means the largest plant, but which employs as many as 13,000 workers, has 32 separate shops, in which there are no fewer than 481 " brigades ".[1] Each brigade has its own meetings for discussion, and also for the election of its own trade-union organiser and " educational organiser ", these being usually unpaid officers. There should also be an unpaid " dues-collector " for each, and one or more " insurance " delegates. Each shop also holds its own shop meetings, at one of which a " shop committee " of seven members is elected for the ensuing half-year, with a president and a secretary. For the factory committee in this great establishment the trade union members assemble half-yearly in their several " shops ", 32 in number, each of which elects one delegate, or in the larger shops two or three, making 51 altogether. The total number of members of the 186,640 fabkoms and mestkoms in the USSR is estimated at something like two millions, to which must be added another million or so of members of the various sub-committees or commissions working under these committees. Thus, apart from the officers, paid and unpaid, at least 15 per cent of the trade union members are actively engaged in committee work.[2]

---

[1] A brigade may be a particular shift, or a group engaged on a common job.

[2] It may be noted that these popular meetings for trade union business (including elections of delegates to other councils and committees) differ in the following respects from the meetings of workers, also held in the factories, offices or institutions but separately and at different dates, from which emanate

## *Trade Union Elections in the USSR*

It must not be supposed that these trade-union elections are tame and lifeless affairs. The resolutions of the Sixteenth All-Union Congress of the Communist Party, repeated in substance at the Fifth Plenum of the AUCCTU in 1931, went into elaborate detail as to the steps to be taken, in every establishment in every trade union in every part of the USSR, to make the election an occasion for a stirring campaign among all the wage-earners, in which the "activists"—those who actually took part in the campaigning work—numbered more than two millions; in Moscow alone more than 160,000.[1]

Nor was the trade-union election campaign of 1931 an excep-

the soviet hierarchy. The trade union meeting (*a*) admits workers under eighteen, but is confined to those of all ages contributing to the trade union; (*b*) its decisions within its own sphere of action, and not contrary to law, can be vetoed only by the higher authorities of the trade union hierarchy, not by those of the soviet hierarchy; (*c*) it has nothing corresponding to the non-factory meetings where the so-called unorganised workers, being either domestic workers or those who are not working for wage or salary,'can vote for the soviet.

The trade union meetings are invariably held on the premises of the factory, office or institution, which have to be placed gratuitously at the disposal of the trade union for this purpose, either in the evening or at some other time outside working hours that is most convenient to those entitled to attend. Although the minimum age for admission to trade union membership is sixteen, only those who have attained the age of eighteen are entitled to vote at elections. Those employed part time in more than one factory, office or institute may attend the meetings of all of them, but may vote only once at any election.

[1] See Shvernik's speech to Ninth All-Union Trade Union Congress (" The Soviet Trade Unions on the Threshold of the Second Five-Year Plan ", 1933, p. 96). As an immediate outcome of this campaign throughout the USSR no fewer than 1,200,000 applications were made for trade union membership, more than 150,000 for membership of the Young Communist League (Comsomols), and 160,000 for membership of the Communist Party. " The ranks of the shock-workers were reinforced by the addition of 920,000 new workers. 130,000 new shock-brigades and business-accounting brigades were organised, and 250,000 workers' recommendations submitted (to the managements). . . . As a result of this campaign a number of enterprises began to overhaul their industrial and financial plans. Summing up the work of the trade unions in connection with the election campaign we must say outright that in no other country save the USSR, in no other trade unions save those of the soviets, is there such a highly developed trade union democracy " (*ibid.*).

In the " collective agreement campaign " at Dniepropetrovsk in 1933, " in preparation for the approaching Ninth Congress of Trade Unions ", " the 40,000 workers of the Dniepropetrovsk steel plant responded . . . with great enthusiasm. During this period 282 new shock-brigades and 98 cost-accounting brigades were organised. The Communist Party recruited 286 new members; 60 joined the trade union. More than 75 per cent of the workers attend technical schools " (pamphlet by L. Kaufmann, published by the Cooperative Publishing Society of Foreign Workers in the USSR, 1932: see also *Moscow News*, weekly edition, March 23, 1932).

tional effort. In 1933 we find the AUCCTU, which is the apex
of the trade union pyramid for the whole USSR, again issuing
detailed instructions for a still greater campaign.[1] It commands
that, for 1933, these elections " must be made the occasion for
resolute proletarian self-criticism, both through voluntary 'check-
up' brigades of the workers, reviewing the work of their representatives, and through ' mass-accounting' meetings, where every
trade union official, from the group dues-collector to the president
of the factory (or ' plant') committee, must report, to union
members and non-members alike, what he has accomplished during
the year. The ' election campaign' must help in the drive against
absenteeism, in training new workers and taking them into the
union, and in spreading knowledge of constructive achievements.
It should give a new impulse to socialist competition and shock-
brigade work, as well as in action for improving workers' living
conditions. . . . All the work of the election campaign should be
based on socialist competition between the various trade union
groups within the plant (establishment), and between plants, for
the best mobilisation of the working masses to carry out the
Plan ; the greatest improvement in living conditions ; 100 per
cent attendance at election meetings ; enrolment of new workers
into the union." Prior to the actual election meetings, there are
to be preliminary " accounting " meetings, when every officer and
representative must give an account of his stewardship ; and also
discussion meetings in the groups formed by brigades or shifts.
The account of the work done must be put in the " wall newspapers ", which should be renewed daily whilst the campaign
lasts ; and full use must be made of the radio, the movies, the
local press, " evenings of questions and answers ", meetings of
wives and children of workers, and so on, in order to " mobilise
the masses " to take part in the elections and to understand the
problems. To draw up the programme of the election campaign,
and to fix the dates of the various meetings, together with the
publication of the names of candidates and the actual conduct of
the election, will be the work of special election commissions for
each shop and for the whole establishment, chosen by trade union
members at the accounting or special meetings, and confirmed by

[1] See the lengthy and detailed instructions for the " election campaign "
published in the official trade union organ *Trud*, of which a summary appeared
in the *Moscow Daily News*, December 12, 1932.

the next higher trade union authority. Nominations may be made orally at a meeting, or by handing in a signed list of names. Five days before the election, the list of candidates must be posted in all main shops, departments, clubs, " Red Corners ", residential barracks and workmen's trains, together with the production experience of, and the social work accomplished by each candidate, with the name of his nominator. At the election meeting there must be 75 per cent present of the trade union members actually working on that date. Voting is by show of hands, to be counted by special counters elected by the meeting. To be elected, a candidate must be approved by at least 60 per cent of the voters present. A mere plurality cannot elect.

We have no information as to the extent of the " liveliness " of these trade-union election campaigns throughout the whole country ; and it may well be that, over so vast an area as the USSR, with electorates of very different habits and capacities, the well-meant instructions emanating from the highest trade union authority will not always be fully obeyed. But we have been impressed by various testimonies on the subject. The workers' meetings are frequent and well attended, to the extent of 50, and sometimes even 75 per cent of the whole body, and by women as well as by men. They are the occasions for much unrestrained discussion of persons, as well as of industrial policy, and local conditions of life. There is a laudable desire to encourage the newer and younger members, and to recruit the committees with new blood. And—what seems to us very noteworthy—the members of the Communist Party, who undoubtedly constitute most of the " activists " giving liveliness to an election campaign, do not monopolise the places. On the contrary, they definitely promote the election of a considerable number of " non-Party " candidates, in order, as they quite frankly say, to bring them effectively into the work of administration, which to be successful, needs to be based upon proper representation of the whole people.[1]

The total number of meetings in the USSR for the election of factory committees, even within each of the 154 trade unions, has not been ascertained, but is evidently very large—in some of these

[1] For the Rostov Agricultural Machine Works (Rostselmash) we happen to have the figures. Of the 51 members of the factory committee, only 24 were, in 1932, members of the Communist Party. Much the same proportion was found in the 32 shop committees, and among the 400 trade-union officials (mostly unpaid).

unions running into tens of thousands. For the entire eighteen
million membership of the whole 154 unions, the number of such
meetings concerned in the election of no fewer than 513,000
groups, brigades or shifts, and about one-third of that member of
committees, must run into something like a million. As these
members' meetings are held at intervals throughout the year—
though only once or twice a year for the purpose of electing the
factory committee—their aggregate number, in the whole USSR,
must be in the neighbourhood of five millions in every twelve-
month—certainly a broad popular base for the trade-union
hierarchy !

But these members' meetings are much more than the base of
a hierarchy. The political science student must not allow the
excitement of the election campaigns in the trade unions to obscure
the more solid daily work of the various committees and commissions, regional councils and central committees of each union, in
which, as we have seen, apart from the salaried officials, not fewer
than a couple of million members are continuously engaged. It
must be remembered that the fabkom and mestkom have a large
part to play in the current administration of the factory, office or
institution. The meetings for these purposes are frequent and
lengthy, often with elaborate agendas, which differ from enterprise to enterprise. The manager or director, with the technicians
most nearly concerned, meet, on terms of equality, the representatives of every grade in the establishment. Often more striking
to our western eyes than a factory meeting is the administration,
by such a committee (mestkom) of a non-industrial institution.
We ourselves attended, during our voyage, a meeting of the
" ship's soviet ", belonging to the Seafarers' Trade Union, at
which the captain laid the ship's accounts before the meeting of
the entire crew and explained the items. One of the electricians
presided, and all sections of the ship's company, including several
women, were represented. As the accounts indicated a loss on
the voyage, various criticisms were made on the expenses. One
sailor asked why the ships used such a costly wharfage site on the
Thames. The captain replied that it was worth the rent to be so
near the butter market. One of the stewards asked why such a
high speed had been maintained on the last voyage ; only to be
told that a better price was expected for the cargo if it could reach
the Thames before a specified day. Many other questions and

answers followed.  It was impossible not to be impressed with the educational value of the discussion, as well as by the complete sense of comradeship among all ranks, and the feeling of being engaged in a common task.

We add another sample, in an account by an American nurse, of an ordinary meeting of the Medical Workers' Union in a Leningrad hospital.  " The routine meetings of these unions are apt to be vivid occasions, with a picturesque red-kerchiefed laundry worker in the chair, a woman doctor graduated from the Sorbonne as recording secretary, and committees including the tolerant, humorous-eyed director of the institution, who may have been a famous specialist fifteen years ago, an excitable young doctor who is equally enthusiastic for communism and for medical research, a sleepy stove-man whose high boots reek of poorly cured leather, and several rows of whispering, stolid nurses and orderlies.  The meetings last long into the night, as much of the detailed administration of the hospital or clinic is discussed and decided here. Complicated technical details have to be put into slow and simple language, a process often exacting heavy toll from the patience of the nimble-witted doctors, but when the session is at last over there has usually been worked out a rather remarkable understanding of the situation, together with the intelligent cooperation of different groups among the staff.  These union meetings are a real school of democracy." [1]

### The Trade Union Factory Committee

The trade union factory (FZK) or institution committee (fabkom or mestkom) of between 5 and 50 members, has important, varied and continuous functions.  Its plenum meetings may not be more frequent than once a quarter,[2] but it always elects annually a president and secretary, who in all the larger units generally give their whole time to trade union work ; and a presidium of half a dozen to a dozen members, which usually meets every week or two.[3]  It undertakes, as regards all those employed in the

---

[1] *Health Work in Soviet Russia*, by Anna J. Haines, p. 33.

[2] In the large industrial plants the committees of the various shops, shifts or brigades, to which reference has already been made, usually meet three or four times a month, independently of the meetings of the fabkom.

[3] Among the usual subcommittees or commissions under the factory committee are those (1) for the protection of workers and the promotion of their health, including safeguarding of machinery, housing, day nurseries, rest-

factory, office or institution, the detailed administration of the various branches of social insurance ; the arrangements for sending workers to convalescent or holiday homes ; the management of the factory club, the factory canteen or dining-rooms, and any factory cultural undertakings, and even the allocation among the workers of theatre and concert tickets placed at their disposal. For any or all of these duties separate commissions may be appointed, on which trade union members not elected to the factory committee may be asked to serve.[1] The officers and presidium of the committee are in constant relations with the management of the factory, office or institute, over which they have no actual control, but which must always inform the factory committee of proposed changes, discuss with them any of the workers' grievances, hear their suggestions, and generally consult with them as to the possibility of increasing the output, lessening waste and diminishing cost. It is the factory committee which organises shock-brigades, and, on behalf of the workers, enters into " socialist competition " with other factories, offices or institutions, as to which can achieve the most during a given period.

### Collective Bargaining in the USSR

The soviet trade unions play such a large part in social administration, and have so many different functions, that the foreign observer is apt to underestimate the amount and the importance of their work in collective bargaining. Far from there being less collective bargaining in the USSR than in Great Britain or the United States, or in Germany before the Hitlerite dictatorship, there is actually very much more than in any other country in the world. To make this clear we must anticipate what will be explained in greater detail in our subsequent chapter entitled " Planned Production for Community Consumption ".

In the USSR, as in every country in which trade unionism has passed from the stage of small local combinations to that of

houses, etc.; (2) for " cultural-educational matters ", including technical classes, libraries, wall newspapers, theatre tickets, etc.; (3) wage assessments and disputes ; (4) production, including all possible improvements in productivity ; (5) auditing ; (6) finance ; (7) international workers' relief ; (8) cooperative society ; (9) club management, and often many others.

[1] Those who give their whole time to trade union duties receive from trade union funds salaries equal to their earnings in the factory. All others are allowed " time off ", without any objection by the management, without loss of pay, to perform any duties for which their fellow-workmen have chosen them.

national unions comprising whole industries, the standard time-rates in each industry are settled, not by the several establishments or localities in which the industry is carried on, but in negotiations between committees representing respectively the whole of the workers and the whole of the managements in the country. So far as concerns the basic rates of time wages in each union, and the coefficient of increase to be applied to these for the ensuing year throughout the whole of soviet industry, this collective bargaining is concentrated, in the main, in one prolonged and manifold discussion, in the early months of each year, between the AUCCTU and the central committees of all the 154 trade unions, on the one hand, and the representatives of the Sovnarkom and the managements of the various trusts and public services on the other. The note in these discussions is not one of conflict and struggle between two hostile parties, each endeavouring to deprive the other of something to which it clings for its own benefit, but rather one of objective examination of the statistical facts and the considerations of public policy, to which both parties agree to defer. " The peculiar feature of the soviet collective agreements " said a trade union representative, " is the absence of the enemy party ". It is, indeed, not so much a new rate of wages that has to be determined as the " General Plan " of soviet industry for the ensuing year or years, in which, as will be explained in a subsequent chapter, the amount of wages is only one of several determining factors. The collective bargaining of the trade unions is far from being merely series of tussles between " labour " and " capital ", as to the shifting boundary-line between wages and profits. What emerges from the discussions is specific allocation of the entire net product of the community's industry, arrived at by agreement as to the nature and amount of the aggregate sums to be set aside for particular objects of common concern. Although there is no tribute of rent or profit to be abstracted, it is recognised that the whole produce cannot be distributed as " personal wages ". A substantial part must annually be devoted not only to repairs and making good the depreciation of plant, but also to the extension of the nation's industry, and the building and equipping of additional mines, factories, ships and railways. This expansion is universally recognised as necessary, not merely to meet the clamorous demand of the workers themselves for additional com-

modities but also in order to make the USSR as far as possible
independent of the hostile capitalist states. There is no limit
within view to this effective demand for more goods, and better ;
and as we shall show, in a subsequent chapter, there is no reason
to suppose that any such limit will ever appear. It is, indeed,
one of the essential conditions of " Planned Production for Community Consumption " that it provides for the popular demand
being always " effective demand ", either for commodities and
services, or for holidays and a shortening of the hours of labour.
But the annual increase of industry is necessarily limited by the
forces then and there available, and in particular by the labour
power of the ever-increasing population, swollen by the peasants
whom the mechanisation of agriculture is constantly dispensing
with. Here the statistics annually worked out by the State
Planning Commission carry irresistible weight. It is to no one's
interest to waste any of the labour force that will be available,
and thus allow unemployment to recur. Then there are the
necessary " overhead charges " of the nation to be provided for ;
the cost of all the government departments, national defence, and
the administration of justice, together with a matter in which
the workers of the USSR are more keenly interested than those of
any other country, namely, scientific exploration and research.
Here, too, the calculation is largely a matter of statistics of how
much can be immediately undertaken out of the programme
already decided on by the people's representatives. Finally
there is the total estimated cost of the extensive and ever-expanding social services, including not only the whole educational and
" pre-school " system, with all its maintenance scholarships ;
the far-flung state medical service in its innumerable forms ; the
endless task of sanitation and rehousing for the whole population ; the constantly growing social insurance to which the
workers make no individual contribution ; the publicly organised
provision for physical and mental recreation of every kind, and
so on. This whole expenditure—now amounting to about 50 per
cent of what the workman draws in cash as his wages—is significantly known as the " socialised wage ". It is always the subject
of trade union pressure, but of pressure for its increase, notwithstanding the obvious fact that every kopek of increase lessens
the balance that is available for distribution as " personal wages ".
For it is the whole of what remains, after the above-named " cuts "

have been made from the estimated product of the year, that the trade unions accept as the lump sum available for the personal wages of the whole aggregate of workers by hand or by brain. It is the amount of this residue divided by the total number of workers that enables the coefficient of increase of standard time wages—the percentage by which last year's wage-rates can be augmented—to be calculated.

Exactly how this aggregate wage-fund shall be shared among the whole army of workers employed at wages or salaries is left, very largely, to be worked out by the central committees of the 154 trade unions, in consultation with their joint body, the All-Union Central Committee of Trade Unions (AUCCTU). We can give here only a brief summary of the way it is done, leaving to our subsequent chapter entitled " In Place of Profit " a fuller exposition alike of principle and practice. It must here suffice to say that the trade unionists in the USSR, after various experiments in the nature of " trial and error ", agree in a common system of grading, which is continually being better adjusted to the technical peculiarities and the changing circumstances of the various localities in which each industry is carried on. Separate provision has to be made for the remuneration, on the one hand, of apprentices and other novices, and such indispensable but non-material workers as gatekeepers and clerks ; and, on the other, for that of specialist technicians and administrators, all of whom, it will be remembered, are members of the trade union concerned. In all these cases it has become plain to all concerned that the decisive factor is the necessity of attracting to each industry and each locality the necessary " cadres " of each kind of skill and ability. The problem is not one of trying how little the indispensable people can be got for, but of discovering by what inducements and special provision for training the existing shortage in these " cadres " can be most effectively diminished. Then the main body of manual workers are divided into eight or more grades, as may be found most suited to the industrial processes ; grades not according to craft or function, but according to degrees of skill or capacity, very largely based on its relative scarcity. The grades are, in fact, grades of wage-rates ; fixed according to what is called " social value ", which means, in effect, according to the relative scarcity of any particular kind of capacity to perform the operations required. These graded wage-rates rise by

steps from one for the unskilled worker to two, four or eight times
that amount per month for different degrees of skill or capacity.
Any worker may enter any grade for which he can perform the
work. The zealous and ambitious young man in the lowest grade
(say grade one) may at any time claim to be promoted to grade
two. " Very well," is the response, " you can have a fortnight's
trial. If in that time you make good, to the satisfaction of the
management and of the trade union official, you will remain in
grade two, and draw its higher rate of wage. If not, you will
revert to your lower grade." Presently the workman claims to
be able to proceed to grade four, when the same procedure is
gone through. The result is that a very large proportion of the
young workers—in one factory we were told, it ran up to 90 per
cent—are found to be voluntarily studying in evening classes
(which charge no fees), endeavouring to " improve their qualifications ". As there is no risk of unemployment, and as all the
workers in each industry are in one and the same union, there are
no " demarcation " disputes. As every increase in skill and
capacity means increase of output and decrease of " spoilage " or
waste, the management, and equally the trade union, has nothing
but welcome for its unskilled labourers turning themselves into
skilled mechanics, and even into scientifically educated engineers.
All that is essential is that the growth of net output should at
least keep pace with the increased wage-bill.

So much for the principles and methods by which the collective
bargaining over the national wage rates is conducted. But in all
industries, and in every country, the sphere of collective bargaining comprises much more than the national scale of wage-rates.
Over all the rest of the field, it is the local organisations of each
union in the USSR that enter into protracted discussions with the
management of the particular factory in which the members are
working. In the first place, there is the perpetual business of
fixing the piecework rates for each task or process. Here the
national timework rate for each hour's work has to be translated
into an equivalent payment for each job, so that any worker
accepted for employment, and not subject to any physical disability, should be able, with ordinary diligence, to earn at least
the standard rate for each month. What is indispensable in
fixing piecework rates is equality as between different tasks or
processes. Those workers who work more quickly or more

efficiently, than the common man will, with the full approval of
the management, and to the eventual advantage of every person
in the factory, take home higher earnings, which are amply compensated for by the increased output by which everybody gains.
In the USSR it is the trade union's own official, the rate-fixer for
whose training in the principles and practice of rate-fixing the
trade union has often paid, who has the initiative and the greatest
influence in fixing the piecework rates, on the basis of equality
between different jobs, and of equivalence, for the common man
of ordinary diligence, of the earnings by time and by the piece.
The management has its own officials, who may object to any
proposed rate as not conforming to these principles. If the
experts on each side cannot agree, the matter goes to arbitration.
But, in the USSR, the management has no pecuniary inducement
to "cut" the rates!

We have, however, far from completed the exploration of the
sphere of collective bargaining in the USSR. For the workman
in that land of proletarian dictatorship, the factory is not merely
the place in which he earns a toilsome wage. It is very largely
the centre of his life. It often provides his dwelling-place and his
club, his children's nursery-school and kindergarten, his own and
his wife's technical classes, their excursions on free days and their
annual vacations, their extensive and varied social insurance.
All these things and much else are dealt with by the trade union.
What is novel and unexpected is to find them matters of collective
bargaining with the factory management, to be provided, wholly
or partly by the management itself, as part of the overhead charges
of the undertaking, though almost entirely administered by the
trade-union committees. The foreign observer is surprised to find
the safety and amenity of the places of work, the provision of
hospital and sanatorium beds, the measures taken for the prevention of accidents, the provision of additional or better dwelling
accommodation for the persons employed, the establishment of
crèches and kindergartens for the young children ; the workmen's
clubhouse and the technical classes provided to enable them to
improve their qualifications—and many other matters of importance to the workmen's daily life, dealt with in the detailed agreement (kol-dogovor) drawn up annually in March between the
management and the various workmen's committees, in time to
allow the management to provide, in the budget for the factory

operations, the necessary increases in factory expenditure, which have all to find their place in the General Plan. These increases are sometimes considerable. " Four million roubles ", we read, " have been granted for workers' housing by the Petrovsk and Lenin metal plant of Dniepropetrovsk, according to the Planning Department of the AUCCTU. Two more children's nurseries will be built. The workers, in turn, agree to increase output 38 per cent. Their wages will go up 24 per cent. Metal workers up to now have occupied the nineteenth place on the wage list. In the present wage revisions they will be elevated to third place."[1] As there are no tributes to private persons of rent or profit out of which these expenses can be drawn, the argument turns on the necessary limits to such a disposal of the aggregate product, and the mutual relation of the shares allotted respectively to these " socialised wages " and the " personal wages ".

In these annual discussions with the management of each factory, it is astonishing to see how large is the proportion of the workmen who are drawn in to take part. In March 1932 Shvernik said : " The attendance of workers and employees at the meetings where drafts of the new collective agreements were discussed has, in a number of enterprises, been as high as 95 or 100 per cent. The number of workers who took part in drawing up the collective agreement at the ' Hammer and Sickle ' plant amounted to 98·6 per cent ; at the Stalingrad Tractor plant, 97 per cent ; at the ' Red October ', 97 per cent ; at the Yaroslav Brake plant, 100 per cent ; at the Shinsky Textile plant, 100 per cent."[1] Even if this participation in the collective bargaining, of practically the entire local membership of the trade union, amounts to no more than attendance at the meetings, listening to the speeches, occasionally asking questions, and then unprotestingly adopting a unanimous decision, this must be admitted to be in itself no little political education, and not a bad method of arousing in the rank and file that " consciousness of consent " which is necessary to effective democracy. Moreover, the treaty is never unilateral. " An agreement made by soviet workers ", writes a trade union representative, " is in reality a promise they make

[1] Pamphlet by L. Kaufmann (Cooperative Publishing Society of Foreign Workers in USSR, 1932); see *Moscow News*, weekly edition, March 28, 1932.

to themselves and their fellow-workers to fulfil certain self-determined conditions. No outside coercive power exists. . . . In capitalist countries collective agreements are the armistice terms of two hostile forces. In the negotiations the employers strive to force the worst possible conditions on the workers. . . . Here there is no enemy. No one tries to give as little as he can for as much as he can." [1]

Apart, however, from the annual discussions, there is a great deal of collective bargaining going on throughout the whole year. New determinations of piecework rates have to be made for novel jobs ; there may be special bonuses to be given for particular jobs or exceptional service ; and there is the inevitable stream of complaints from individual workmen about real or imaginary ill-treatment, expressing discontent with the piecework rates for their particular jobs, or appealing against dismissal or other disciplinary action. Actual suspension of work by a strike is, by this time, practically unknown ; but this does not mean that there are no divergences of view between the management and whole groups of workmen. As we have already mentioned, any such dispute is promptly referred to what is popularly termed " the triangle ", an arbitration court within the factory, office or institution, formed for each occasion and composed of a representative of the management, a leading official of the trade union within the establishment and the local official of the cell or group within the establishment consisting of members of the Communist Party. This informal domestic tribunal almost invariably settles the dispute on common-sense lines, in a way that is accepted by the disputants. Either party could, however, always appeal to the RKK (workers' control commission) on which there sit members of the trade unions as well as officers of the trusts ; or, indeed, to the Commissariat (ministry) of Labour of the constituent republic within the territory of which the establishment is situated, and even, ultimately, to the People's Commissar for

[1] Shvernik's speech in *Report of Ninth Trade Union Congress, 1933*, pp. 64-65.

These " kol-dogovor ", or annual agreements between the factory employees and the factory management, are elaborate and lengthy printed documents. That of the " Red Plough " works at Moscow for 1933 ran to 70 pages, 16mo ; that of the Electrocombinat to 59 pages ; that of the First State Factory of Spare Parts to 44 pages ; and that of the Railway Transport Workers Union to 64 pages. We print in the appendix a slightly abbreviated translation of the kol-dogovor of a large factory at Gorki.

Labour of the USSR.[1] Now that these People's Commissars, whom the AUCCTU has always nominated, have been superseded by the AUCCTU itself, it is to this highest trade union body that such an appeal would be made.

It is, however, one thing to get the obligations of the management to the workers and those of the workers to the management enshrined in a " kol-dogovor ", or mutual agreement for the year, and quite another thing to get these reciprocal obligations exactly and punctually fulfilled. " There are still ", observed Shvernik at the Ninth All-Union Trade Union Congress in 1932, " a number of very real defects in the way of collective agreements to be handled. The most important of these defects is the absence of a systematic method of checking up the fulfilment of the obligations undertaken under the collective agreement both by the workers and by the administration. Many trade union organisations do nothing from year's end to year's end but record the fact that both parties to the agreement have failed to fulfil their obligations, thus limiting their activities to the campaign for the conclusion of a new agreement—a campaign which is conducted but once a year. This sort of thing must be put a stop to once and for all. It should be the everyday duty of all trade union organisations to check up the way the collective agreements are being fulfilled. We must succeed in making both our economic bodies and our trade union organisations fulfil all the obligations of the collective agreement. Only then can the collective agreement become a real weapon in the struggle of the whole working class for the fulfilment of the industrial and financial plan, for raising the productivity of labour and for improving the material and general living conditions of the workers." [2]

Thus the factory committee has extensive and important duties throughout the year. For all this business, including the desk work and interviewing by its officers, and committee and members' meetings, the enterprise which it serves is required to

---

[1] In 1928–1929 there were still as many as 47 strikes sent up for consideration by the People's Commissar for Labour. In 1929–1930 there were only 7 (*Die russischen Gewerkschaften* by Michael Jakobson, 1932, p. 164.)

In both years the number was insignificant for so vast an area as the USSR, and for so many millions of trade unionists, employed in ten or fifteen thousand separate establishments.

[2] Shvernik's speech in *Report of Ninth Trade Union Congress, 1932*, pp. 64-65.

allocate convenient and properly furnished premises with heating and lighting, all free of charge.[1]

The factory committee, by means of volunteer " dues collectors " collects the trade union contributions of the whole of the trade union members within the factory, office or institution. These contributions—at one time paid by the management as a charge on the undertaking—are now fixed by the highest delegate congress of each union, and may include extra subscriptions for special funds for educational activities, various sorts of " mutual aid " and sundry voluntary associations, to which only a part of the trade union members belong.[2] By new regulation of the AUCCTU, dating from September 1, 1933, the trade union dues have been universally reduced to a fixed one per cent of wages,

---

[1] The Labour Code of 1932, section 15, ordains that " the management of the undertaking, institution or enterprise shall grant the committee (fabkom) the use of a room free of charge, with the necessary equipment, heating and lighting, both for the business of the committee itself and for general and delegate meetings."

[2] " Where the system of individual payment of contributions is in force (now nearly universal) it is generally considered necessary to have one collector [presumably thus engaged only after his day's work] for every 20 or 30 members. The collector makes one round a month. Besides the trade union contributions properly so-called, he also collects other contributions (clubs, mutual aid societies, various associations) and gives a temporary receipt to the payer, whose account book he takes and transfers to the factory committee concerned. The factory committee subsequently issues official receipts for the payments made. In many organisations, however, these arrangements work badly ; in certain cases, in order to simplify the work of the collectors, proposals and experiments have been made in paying contributions by means of stamps specially issued for the purpose " (*The Trade Union Movement in Soviet Russia* ; I.L.O., League of Nations, 1927, p. 82).

It took a long time to put on a proper footing all trade unions and in all parts of the USSR the system of individual payment of trade union dues, in substitution of the former system of automatic deductions from wages. Not until the Seventh All-Union Congress of Trade Unions (1926) could it be reported as completed. The scale then fixed was 30 kopeks per month for all receiving not exceeding 25 roubles per month earnings, rising gradually to 10 roubles per month on earnings exceeding 400 roubles per month. The trade union may, with the consent of the All-Union Congress of the particular union (AZRG), add a supplement not raising the total contribution to more than 4 per cent of the highest grade of earnings. This supplement is often from one-half per cent to two per cent of the monthly earnings, and is usually devoted to the expenses of the fabkom or mestkom. Of the regular dues, 10 per cent is usually allocated for the expenses of the lateral or inter-union organisations, whilst the remainder provides for the upper stages of the vertical hierarchy, particularly the All-Union Congress of each trade union, and the central committee which it elects (ZK). There are often small special funds for cultural activities, and (now less frequent) for unemployment and the occasional small strikes (*Die russischen Gewerkschaften*, by Michael Jakobson, 1932, p. 127 ; *Soviet Trade Unions*, by Robert W. Dunn, 1927, p. 70).

whilst the number and amount of other contributions are cut down to a minimum. Trade union members may belong to several societies, but may not pay subscriptions to more than two.[1] Membership dues are now universally collected by the sale of stamps to be affixed to the members' trade union cards.

Not without warrant can it be claimed by an American observer that " the trade union fabkom is a growing force in the Soviet Union. It brings workers not only into the unions, but into the whole economic activity of the country. It is the principal organ of workers' democracy in a government and an industrial system operated by and for workers. In no other country does this type of workers' council have so much power. . . . In no other country does it have such varied and important functions. Nowhere do its members have so much freedom and responsibility as in the USSR. It acts as the fundamental contact point through which the worker begins to take part in factory as well as in social life, to exercise his rights as a worker in this community ; and to participate in building up the nationalised industries." [2]

### The Regional Council of the Trade Union

The next stage to the factory committee in each trade union hierarchy in all but the smaller unions is now the regional council, representing all the establishments belonging to the particular trade union within a particular area, which is generally coterminous with the soviet area of the oblast, or in the case of the largest cities, with the city itself, but is sometimes demarcated so as to correspond more conveniently with the geographical distribution of the establishments belonging to the union.[3] Altogether there

[1] Resolutions of the TSIK, Sovnarkom and VTSSPS of August 16, 1933 : see *Izvestia*, August 17, 1933. Trade union members' dues to the Communist Party (to which between one and two millions of them belong) were at the same time fixed as under :

| | | | |
|---|---|---|---|
| 20 kopeks on a wage or salary up to 100 roubles | | | |
| 60 ,, | ,, | ,, | of 101 to 150 roubles |
| 1 rouble | ,, | ,, | ,, 151 to 200 ,, |
| 1·50 roubles | ,, | ,, | ,, 201 to 250 ,, |
| 2 ,, | ,, | ,, | ,, 251 to 300 ,, |
| 2 per cent | ,, | ,, | ,, 301 to 500 ,, |
| 3 ,, | ,, | ,, | ,, above 500 ,, |

[2] *Soviet Trade Unions*, by Robert W. Dunn, 1927, p. 45.
[3] It was laid down at the Second Trade Union Congress in 1919 that " the type of organisation which best corresponds to the fundamental duties of the

are, among the hundred larger trade unions, approximately 900 regional councils.

The trade union regional council is elected by a delegate meeting representing the factory committees of all the establishments belonging to that particular trade union within the region. This delegate meeting meets as a plenum very infrequently, and usually only when it has to elect its president and secretary, who always give their whole time to their trade union work, with a presidium of half a dozen members, for whose deskwork and meetings the regional council of each trade union maintains everywhere its own regional office.

The most interesting function of the regional council of each trade union and one to which we shall presently refer may be that of entering into lateral relations with the other unions within the region.

### The Republic Council of each Trade Union

The highest stage of the trade union hierarchies within the six smaller constituent republics (not in the RSFSR) is the congress of delegates elected, in the hundred or so larger unions, by all the regional councils which the particular union has within the area of the republic ; and in the forty-nine smaller unions which have no regional councils by the factory or institution committees. Such trade unions may thus enjoy several " republic " congresses, being one for each of the smaller constituent

---

trade union movement must embody All-Russian central unions, with sections and sub-sections in the provinces (linked up by inter-trade union councils based on the formation of the All-Russian council and factory committees, or employees' committees in non-industrial undertakings). The territorial division into sections and sub-sections is to be determined by the central organ of the All-Russian trade union concerned, and every attention is to be given to the geographical distribution and numerical importance of the various industrial groups. At the same time the division into groups must correspond as far as possible with the administrative areas of the country " (*The Trade Union Movement in Russia*, International Labour Office, League of Nations, 1927, p. 57).

We gather that in each trade union the subsectional council has been abandoned and the sectional councils are now styled regional councils, above which there are, in the smaller constituent republics, for some of the trade unions, republic councils, which (together with the regional councils of the RSFSR) elect an All-Union Congress of the particular trade union (AZRG), from which a central committee for the union (ZK) is chosen.

In the reorganisation of 1934, so far as concerns the 49 smaller unions, the regional council has gone the way of the subsectional council, thus bringing the central committee of each of these unions in immediate contact with all its fabkoms or mestkoms.

republics in which the particular trade union has a considerable and completely organised membership.

### The All-Union Congress of each Trade Union [1]

Each trade union has still to create its central organ for the administration of the affairs of its whole USSR membership from the Baltic to the Pacific. Each trade union accordingly has its own " All-Union " congress, formed of delegates chosen by its several congresses of the highest grade, in the RSFSR those of the regions, whether cities or oblasts or, in the six smaller republics, those of the constituent republics over which its own membership is spread. This All-Union delegate congress (AZGR), which varies in size according to the magnitude of the aggregate membership of the trade union, meets usually only every other year for a few days' general discussion and for the election of a standing central council (ZK) and of the usual president, secretary and presidium, by whom the supreme administration of the trade union is practically conducted. It is this authority by which, in close consultation with the USSR joint trade union organ still to be described (AUCCTU), are arranged the dozen or two grades of wage-rates applicable to as many grades of workers, among which, with some local variations and various exceptional cases, the entire membership of the trade union finds itself working. Moreover, it is this All-Union authority for each trade union that, in similar close consultation, actually conducts on behalf of its entire membership between the Baltic and the Pacific—so far as concerns the standard wage-rates in the several trade unions ; the coefficient of increase to be adopted for the ensuing year, and the aggregate of wages and salaries in the USSR—the collective bargaining between the trade union and the organs representing the Sovnarkom of People's Commissars for the USSR, together with Gosplan, and the various trusts directing the nationalised industries. It was authoritatively laid down in 1932 that " the central committees of the unions must concentrate their efforts primarily upon questions of regulating wages and settling rates and categories, upon the organisation of labour and production, upon housing construction, upon the

---

[1] The term " All-Union " invariably means the whole of the USSR ; never all trade unions.

improvement of the working and living conditions of their members ".[1]

But although this hierarchy of trade union councils, from the brigade or shift or shop, through the factory or institution committees, and the regional councils, right up to the trade union authorities of each republic and those for the whole of the USSR, undoubtedly serves to unite the whole membership of each union, and to concentrate its final influence, it must not be supposed that there is any corresponding dissipation of authority in the settlement of policy. It was quite definitely laid down by the Ninth All-Union Congress of Trade Unions that " the republican, regional and district councils of trade unions, while not renouncing responsibility for problems of wages, production, etc., must give up the duplication and replacement of union organisation, and *concentrate their major attention upon checking the fulfilment of the directives of the Party, the government and the All-Union Central Committee of Trade Unions* (AUCCTU) ".[2]

### The All-Union Congress of Trade Unions

There is, it will be seen, yet a higher and in some ways even more important body than the supreme USSR authority for each trade union, namely, a congress acting, not for one union only, but for the whole of the 154 unions, and for their aggregate membership throughout the USSR. This joint congress, the authority for soviet trade unionism as a whole, is made up of a couple of thousand delegates elected approximately in proportion to trade union membership, by the several congresses, whether regional or republic or All-Union, of the 154 trade unions, or rather by their highest elected committees. This All-Union Trade Union Congress meets only every other year, for general discussion and for the election of an All-Union Central Committee of Trade Unions (AUCCTU), and of the invariable president, secretary and presidium.

The All-Union Congress of Trade Unions is, however, no mere parade, but a live forum of popular discussion. We quote a description by an American observer in 1926. " Walk into a congress of Russian workers, the last (seventh) All-Union Con-

---

[1] *Report of Ninth All-Union Congress of Trade Unions, 1932*, p. 386.
[2] *Ibid.*

gress of the AUCCTU for example. One finds about 1500 delegates present. They are not, as in many countries, all the representatives of the central committees of national unions. In fact
all of them were elected at provincial congresses, and two-thirds
of them are men and women from the provinces. About one-
sixth of them have come directly from the lathe and the
loom and the plough. Only one-sixth are officials from the
higher ranks of the national unions, who have been selected
at provincial congresses. Some thirty-three nationalities are
represented, and nearly one hundred women delegates are
present." [1]

But important and influential as may be the discussions at the
All-Union Congress of Trade Unions, the fact that it meets only
every other year necessarily throws all its powers into the hands
of the central committee (AUCCTU) that it elects. Although
this central committee itself meets as a plenum only every few
months,[2] the officers, instructed and supervised by the presidium,
and giving their whole time to the work, are almost continuously
engaged throughout the year, largely in dealing with minor issues
that arise between the different unions, and in adjusting differences and divergences likely to become injurious or acute. But
the most important function of these inter-union officers is to
centralise and supervise the collective bargaining between the
central representatives of the several trade unions and the
committees and officials representing the Sovnarkom (or Cabinet)
of People's Commissars, Gosplan, and the various state trusts and
other enterprises, especially in the annual settlement, and the
continuous detailed adjustment, of the General Plan. It was this
body, for instance, that made the momentous collective agreement with the Supreme Economic Council in September 1931, for
the fundamental remodelling of the wage scales in the coal and
iron and steel industries, by which the difference between the
earnings of skilled and unskilled workers was greatly enlarged
and the higher grades were better remunerated, as a means of

[1] *Soviet Trade Unions*, by Robert W. Dunn, 1927, p. 162.

[2] There were six plenums of the AUCCTU between the Eighth All-Union
Trade Union Congress in 1928–1929 and the Ninth All-Union Trade Union
Congress in 1931, during a most important period of reorganisation.

The plenum was, in 1934, directed to meet regularly every two months. Its
membership was at the same time reduced from 502 to 338, in spite of the
division of the 47 trade unions into as many as 154.

increasing the total productivity.[1]  It is, in fact, this body as the repository of the power conveyed from the (literally) millions of members' meetings all over the USSR, through the whole hierarchy of councils of each of the 154 gigantic trade unions, that exercises the effective government of the trade union movement. " The All-Union Central Committee of Trade Unions (AUCCTU)", it was authoritatively declared, " must base all its work directly upon the work of the central committees of the trade unions, furnishing them with concrete aid, and constantly checking and providing concrete leadership for their activity. . . ."  "The congress instructs the AUCCTU to take all necessary measures toward improving financial discipline, insisting on prompt payment of membership dues, and improving the financial relations between the central committees of the trade unions and the AUCCTU, in the direction of increasing independence of the industrial unions." [2]

And the AUCCTU does not hesitate to strike hard when it is necessary.  When the Central Committee of the Union of Workers in the Sugar Industry had allowed the organisation of that union to go to pieces, and had failed altogether to prevent all sorts of malpractices in the state farms of Soyuzsakhar, where so many of its members were employed, the AUCCTU itself discovered what was going on.  The presidium of the AUCCTU presented a damning report to the plenum of the Central Committee of the Union of Workers in the Sugar Industry, in which a drastic change in leadership was demanded.  The members of the union plenum

---

[1] *New Methods of Work, New Methods of Leadership*, by J. Grabe (Cooperative Publishing Society of Foreign Workers in USSR, Moscow, 1933), p. 31.

[2] *Report of Ninth All-Union Congress of Trade Unions, 1932*, p. 387.  A recent development of the AUCCTU has been the formation of a " Foreign Bureau " (Insnab) in order to maintain a closer contact with the foreign workers employed in the USSR and to investigate their complaints.  Such a trade union Foreign Bureau exists actively in Moscow and is supposed to exist in every trade union District or City Council in which there are foreign workers with an " Insnab Control Commission " elected by the foreign workers themselves.  These are not to interfere with the functions of other trade union organisations, but to bring the foreign workers into closer contact with these organisations, and to see to it that all their grievances are promptly dealt with (*Moscow Daily News*, May 10, 1932).

The work of the AUCCTU in 1934 was reorganised into 9 departments, namely : (1) Responsible Instructors or Organisers ; (2) Planning of Wages ; (3) Bureau of Social Insurance ; (4) Labour Inspection ; (5) Clubs and Cultural Work ; (6) Accounting ; (7) Finance ; (8) General Administration ; and (9) Physical Culture.

were convinced, and substituted a new presidium for that which had so hopelessly failed.[1]

### *Lateral Structure in USSR Trade Unionism*

So far we have described only the vertical hierarchy of the trade unions, by which the stream of power may be said to pass from the 186,640 factory and local committees (fabkom and mestkom), elected in the innumerable members' meetings, right up to the 154 central committees of the several unions and the single central committee representing all of them, the AUCCTU— there to be transformed into the authority by which the whole eighteen million trade unionists between the Baltic and the Pacific are governed. We have, however, yet to notice the equally elaborate lateral structure at each stage of the vertical hierarchy, by means of which the activities of the various trade union committees within each local area are coordinated, and inter-union conflicts are avoided. The factory and local committees (fabkom and mestkom) of the establishments belonging to one trade union within the area of a city or a district may send delegates to a city or district committee for that particular trade union. But such an organisation will deal only with matters relating to the one trade union, and is not universal. What is universal, in every large city and every industrialised district outside the cities, is a district trade union council, formed of delegates, either from the city or district committees of particular trade unions where such exist, or, more usually, from the factory or local committees (fabkom and mestkom) of all the establishments within the area, to whatsoever trade unions they belong. There seem to be nearly 3000 of such inter-union district or city councils in the USSR. In this way, something analogous to the organisation of the local trades councils of the British trade union movement is formed, dealing, however, not with municipal politics, which occupy so large a proportion of the attention of the British trades councils, but almost entirely with trade union matters. When it is remembered that nearly all the 154 soviet trade unions include some workers of the same craft or vocation—whether general labourers or unspecialised clerks ; or such craftsmen as carpenters, engineers and electricians common to nearly all industries ; or

[1] *Report of Ninth All-Union Congress of Trade Unions, 1933*, p. 27.

professional specialists such as doctors and nurses—and that these are incessantly moving from one establishment to another, frequently thus transferring to other trade unions, it will be seen that innumerable questions must arise between them.

These lateral connections exist at each stage of the trade union hierarchy. There are about 70 republic or regional councils of the various trade unions, having each its own office with its own officials. In some of the republics at least (as in the Ukraine) this organisation (OVWR) exists for combined action of all the trade unions within the particular constituent republic.

### The Trade Union Officials

So extensive an organisation, operating over so vast a territory, naturally requires a considerable army of officials. As we have already indicated, the bulk of the work of collecting the subscriptions, managing the elections and administering the local business, is performed voluntarily without remuneration by duly elected unpaid officers and committee men, possibly as many as a million in number, in their leisure hours. But in every industrial establishment of any magnitude, trade unionism requires the whole-time service of one or more experienced officials, to whom the union pays salaries approximately equal to the earnings of skilled mechanics. The lateral inter-union organisations, as well as the central committee of each union, employ whole staffs of similar officials. It is, however, the work of the most important body, the All-Union Central Committee of Trade Unions (AUCCTU), that calls for the most extensive and responsible civil service. It is in this part of the trade union bureaucracy that the scheme of reorganisation of 1934 has wrought the greatest changes. In its relations with all the unions, the AUCCTU had gradually developed an elaborate " functionalism ", each branch of the work having its own specialised officials, by whose written communications and personal visits the fabkoms and mestkoms were being perpetually harassed. In 1934 Shvernik got adopted a reform by which these specialised or " functional " officials were wholly replaced by a single service of " instructors "—who in England would be termed organisers or inspectors—who are to be for all purposes the channel of communication between the central body on the one hand and both the separate trade unions and the innumerable fabkoms or mestkoms on the other. Henceforth it will be these trained " instructors " who will both supervise or inspect the work of the 154 unions and their local organs, and convey to them the criticisms or "directives" of the AUCCTU. In the larger unions the central committees will have, in addition, their own staff of similar " instructors ", assisting and controlling their various branches and local committees in all the details of their work. The colossal industrial establishments, having each tens of thousands of members, may even find " instructors " permanently assigned to each of them. This far-reaching reconstruction of the trade union civil service, by which it is hoped to economise in the total numbers employed, will plainly make more effective the influence of the central body representing all the 154 unions, as well as that over the local organs exercised by the central committee of each union. The reform may be expected to bring to the assistance of the local administrators the advantage of consistency in policy, and the lessons of a larger experience than any one of them can command. But how far this increasing centralisation of authority will increase trade union efficiency as a whole must be left to experience to reveal.

### The Transference of the Commissariat of Labour to the Trade Unions

With the growth of trade union membership to eighteen millions, the work falling on the trade union administrators had become colossal. It was destined to be still further increased. In 1933 a momentous addition was made to the trade union business: by a decision and decree of the Central Committee of the Communist Party and the Central Executive Committee (TSIK) of the All-Union Congress of Soviets, the office of the USSR People's Commissar of Labour together with those of the People's Commissars of Labour of all the constituent and autonomous republics were summarily abolished. Practically all the functions of these commissariats were transferred to the All-Union Congress of Trade Unions, and to its elected Central Committee of Trade Unions (AUCCTU), with its subordinate hierarchy of committees and officials. The duties thus transferred from the soviet part of the constitution to the trade union part are of considerable magnitude and importance. They include the supreme direction of all branches of social insurance ; the whole responsibility for factory inspection ; the provision and management of the rest-houses and convalescent homes enjoyed by the trade union membership, with the farming enterprises for their "self-supply" that have lately been developed ; and, in supersession of the labour exchanges, now abolished along with involuntary unemployment, the organisation of all labour recruiting for the constantly expanding industries.

This constitutional change is a remarkable recognition of the position that trade unionism holds in the soviet state. The magnitude of the funds, outside the members' subscriptions, which will now be administered by the trade union organisation is impressive. The social insurance budget for 1933 totalled 4432 million roubles, levied by a contribution upon every kind of enterprise of $1\frac{1}{2}$ or 2 per cent of its wage-total ; and providing 814 million roubles for sickness, 532 millions for old-age and infirmity pensions, 203 millions for rest-homes, 35 millions for dietetic restaurants for the sick, 930 millions for hospitals, 189 millions for crèches and 600 millions for workmen's dwellings. These services, moreover, are growing by leaps and bounds. The 1934 budget of the All-Union Central Committee of Trade Unions (AUCCTU), *without including the expenditure of the 154 trade unions themselves upon their accustomed functions,* amounted to no less than 5050 million roubles. It provided 1514 million roubles in sick pay and invalidity pensions ; 1040 millions in repayment of the cost of medical services and hospitals ; 57 million roubles for special diets for sick workers ; 215 millions for their rest-houses ; 327 millions for nursery schools and kindergartens to set the mothers free for industrial service ; 750 millions for education ; 885 millions for workers' dwellings ; 41 millions for factory inspection ; 50 millions for insurance administration ; and 170 millions for the necessary working balance or reserve. The corresponding budget for 1935 amounted to no less than 6079 million roubles. The administration of such extensive services—in which, be it noted, the trade unions act as organisations of consumers or users of the services, not as producers—throws a great work on their active members, even more onerous and responsible than their previous duties in the administration of the wage agreements.[1]

---

[1] The transfer was accompanied by a great change in the machinery for payment of the cash benefits. Each trade union has now its own head paying

This vast addition to the work and influence of the soviet trade unions has been curiously misunderstood in some quarters, as a degradation of their position to nothing more than friendly societies ! But the trade unions retain and continue to exercise all the influence and authority in the administration of the factory and in the settlement of wages that they have possessed for the past fifteen years. The new control over social insurance and the entire administration of funds and services of such magnitude can hardly fail to strengthen the trade unions in their work of raising the standard of life of the workers, and even to knit more closely together their far-flung membership.

Those foreign critics, on the other hand, who are appalled at the idea of handing over to the trade unions such vast funds, not derived from the contributions of their members, may, we think, be reassured. The constitutional change, important as it is, will not make so much difference to the administration of social insurance as might be imagined by those conversant only with the constitutions of western Europe or America. It is not, for instance, in any way comparable to the abolition, in the United Kingdom, of the Minister of Labour, and the transfer of his functions, with regard to unemployment insurance and wages boards, to the British Trade Union Congress and its General Council ! The People's Commissar for Labour was, it is true, in every republic and in the USSR itself, a member of the Sovnarkom, and thus, as we should say, a Cabinet Minister. But he had long been appointed on the nomination of the AUCCTU, with whom he was always in the closest relations.[1] Thus the

and accounting office, dealing through its branches exclusively with its own members. There are, accordingly, more than 150,000 pay stations. At the same time each union became responsible for the continuous " inspection " of its members on benefit, in order to prevent abuse. This has involved the appointment of 80,000 members as inspectors, many of whom have not yet become efficient.

[1] Moreover, the officials of the Commissariat of Labour have long been nominated by the trade unions. " The trade union councils of the various republics select the labour commissar for their area of their respective congresses. All lower officials of the labour commissariat are likewise selected by the corresponding subordinate trade union body. The local trade union council selects the labour inspectors, who must be trade union members, and the sanitary and technical inspectors employed by the Commissariat of Labour. These inspectors work in close cooperation with the trade unions and report to their congresses. The unions are well represented in the social insurance departments throughout the country. All labour legislation, including all

change might even be taken to involve, in one of its aspects, the exclusion of a direct representative of trade unionism from the highest councils of the state. The actual work of the Commissariat for Labour, voluminous in magnitude and detailed in its nature, has long been dealt with in an extensive official department, which must necessarily continue in existence. What has been transferred is the supervision and direction of this department, for which a responsible chief is now appointed by the AUCCTU, instead of being only nominated by that body for inclusion in the Sovnarkom. In the various constituent and autonomous republics there has been a corresponding transfer of direction and authority, from a local official partly responsible to the People's Commissar for Labour at Moscow, to the highest organ of each trade union within the area, whose chief official will, we assume, have a like double responsibility, to his own trade union by which he is appointed, and to the director at Moscow appointed by the AUCCTU.[1] The change accordingly represents a great increase of responsibility for trade unionism in the USSR, without, necessarily, any great alteration in current administration. The practical abolition of involuntary unemployment in the USSR, which we shall describe in a subsequent

laws which affect labour in any way, is drawn up in consultation with the trade unions " (*The Soviet Worker*, by J. Freeman, 1932, p. 122).

[1] See *New Functions of the Soviet Trade Unions : the Merger of the People's Commissariat of Labour in the AUCCTU* by N. Shvernik, 1933.

An experienced American observer refers to this change in the following terms : " With very little ado and practically no press comment, an edict has merged the Commissariat of Labour into the All-Soviet Trade Unions, so that control of the many-billion-rouble social-insurance fund, the sanatoria, rest-homes, all workers' medical services, and the protection of labour passes from the hands of the government to the trade unions. Thus, formally at least, the process by which, under socialism, the state dies a slow death through attrition has advanced another step. Back in 1920, Trotsky advocated a reverse development : the suppression of the unions and the organisation of official labour battalions. Nevertheless, as usual, some foreign observers have styled the recent Soviet decree a ' Trotskyist move '. Professional anti-Trotskyists, on the other hand, viewing the 1920 Lenin-Trotsky trade union controversy in the new light of Italian and German fascism, find ideological points of contact between the Duce, Hitler and the sage of Prinkipo. While these salon polemics rage, we shall wait to see whether the latest change, which gives the unions broader functions, also gives them greater independence " (" Russia's last Hard Year ", by Louis Fischer, in *The Nation* (New York), July 12, 1933).

It is interesting to the constitutional student to find this decree was signed not only by M. Kalinin, as president of the Central Executive Committee (TSIK), and V. Molotov, as president of the Sovnarkom, but also by N. Shvernik, as secretary of the All-Union Central Council of Trade Unions (AUCCTU). See the text in *Moscow Daily News*, September 17, 1933.

chapter, and the consequent cessation of unemployment benefit, probably renders the change less open to criticism than other countries might be disposed to imagine.

### The Office-work of USSR Trade Unionism

No one can adequately realise the magnitude, the ubiquity or the activity of this complicated trade union organisation who has not seen something of its work in different cities of the USSR. Yet so vast is the area that no one person can catch more than a glimpse. We may appreciate something of the volume of the work when we learn that the aggregate number of salaried full-time officials in the service of the 154 trade unions, and of their joint or federal bodies, throughout the USSR, in spite of the attempt of the AUCCTU to reduce the number of this salaried bureaucracy, exceeds 30,000, whilst the number of unpaid or part-time officials, apart from members of committees, is estimated to amount to at least ten times as many. We add something to the definiteness of the impression when we merely look at the structural accommodation that has had to be provided for their offices and meetings. It was, we think, a wise statesmanship that saw to it that the whole trade union organisation should be decently housed at the public cost.[1] For every structural requirement of the trade union work within each establishment, whether factory, office or institution, the establishment itself has to provide, as we have mentioned, free of charge, including rooms for permanent office use, and others transiently for members' meetings, with lighting, heating and ordinary furniture. But all the couple of hundred thousand district, regional, republic and central committees and councils and All-Union congresses require offices and meeting-halls. These have been provided free of charge, and a free telephone service added, by the Soviet Government itself, in one or other of its grades, or by one or other of its departments. We do not think it is usually understood how greatly the efficiency of trade unionism may be increased, and its very character raised to the height of a service of public utility, merely by the provision of

---

[1] Exceptionally, in the densely peopled industrial district of the Donetz Basin, where few wealthy people had deigned to live, the coal-miners' trade union has built for itself a dozen " labour temples " (*Soviet Trade Unions*, by Robert W. Dunn, 1927, pp. 2-3).

structural accommodation equal in dignity to that of a government department, in which all the several unions in each locality
may be worthily housed together. The Soviet Government was
fortunate in finding in its hands, in every city, an array of deserted
buildings suitable for this purpose. Among the very first acts
of Lenin's administration was the assignment to the trade union
movement of some of the best and stateliest of the buildings left
derelict by the flight of the nobility and the wealthy. At Leningrad and Moscow the splendid palaces of the nobles' clubs and
similar magnificent premises were thus transferred to new uses,
rightly regarded as of public character. In other cities, great and
small, the best available buildings, previously used as residences
of the rich merchants or manufacturers, or as clubs or hotels for
their use, or as boarding-schools for their daughters, were, between
1918 and 1920, similarly converted into central trade union offices
for the locality. All around these cities we find suburban or rural
homes, once occupied by capitalist families, now placed gratuitously at the disposal of the trade unions, and used, either as
convalescent homes on medical order or as rest-homes, by their
tens of thousands of members on their weekly rest days or their
annual holidays. No less remarkable is the accommodation provided for the trade unions in the smaller cities. At Vinnitsa, in
the Ukraine, an obscure city of 11,000 inhabitants, an American
observer [1] found the trade union offices occupying the whole of
the tallest building in the city, and the only one with six stories,
formerly the best hotel ; and subsequently discovered this to be
" fairly typical of Labour Palaces throughout the Soviet Union.
. . . Every room housed some busy trade union branch, some
department of union life—the offices of the 23 unions of the
district as well as the local trades council ; the district social
insurance department, with union appointees in charge of it ; a
dining-room ; the workers' students section ; the educational
department ; a library ; committee rooms and a meeting-hall.
We found union members coming to the building in connection
with all sorts of matters touching their daily lives—rents, jobs,
dues, insurance, vacation allowances, cooperatives, doctors' permits, transportation, rest-home recommendations, scholarships
and the scores of needs and benefits that are somehow related to
union membership in the USSR."

[1] *Soviet Trade Unions*, by Robert W. Dunn, 1927, p. 2.

### The Shock Brigades and Cost Accounting Committees

The work of the trade unions is greatly assisted by a number of subsidiary organisations. In nearly every industrial establishment of any magnitude there have been formed one or more " shock brigades ", the members of which (udarniki) are recruited from volunteers among the trade unionists. These shock brigades take as their function the acceleration of production, coupled with improvement in quality and lessening of cost. They undertake collectively special tasks in their own establishment, or they may volunteer to go to some other establishment which has fallen behind. They bring to their work exceptional energy, speed or skill ; they labour more assiduously than is common ; or they put in extra time in subotniki (voluntary work). They do this out of zeal, for which they receive honour and applause. They seldom or never have a higher wage-rate and usually no extra bonus, though when working by the piece their increased output automatically brings higher earnings. They often receive preference in the allocation of places in the holiday rest-houses, and, where necessary, in the convalescent homes, as well as in the distribution of the theatre tickets allotted to their trade union. They are put forward as candidates for the factory committee or for the local soviet. The outstanding ones may be awarded the Order of the Red Banner. And as an expression of the honour and applause which are spontaneously accorded to them, they are often given their meals in a separate apartment of the factory restaurant, in a comfortable, quiet privacy, with the highest grade of rations, and such little amenities as tablecloths and flowers, and occasionally special dainties.[1] Of these shock-brigaders, or udarniki, there are reported to be, in the USSR, many millions.

A special application of shock-brigading began early in 1931 when a foundry worker in the great " Lenin " factory at Leningrad suggested in a letter to *Trud*, the weekly journal of the AUCCTU, which has a circulation of several hundred thousands, the advisability of " narrowing down the work of the brigade to certain specific tasks or operations ", with the definite intention of lessening cost by improvements in method, following on the adoption of precise cost accounting. The project was

[1] *Die Russischen Gewerkschaften*, by Michael Jakobson, 1932, p. 147.

energetically pushed by *Trud*, and was presently approved by the All-Union Central Council of Trade Unions.[1] It spread like wildfire. Within a couple of years there had been formed, in the USSR, no fewer than 150,000 cost accounting brigades, which are reported to have effected a whole series of improvements in the methods of working, by which the production costs of thousands of different articles have been appreciably reduced.[2]

This spontaneous development of an elementary form of "costing", by which a particular brigade discovers the cost in material and labour time of each part of its own process, and is thus enabled to discover where time might be economised and "scrap" diminished, is, in the USSR, as in most of capitalist industry, only just beginning to be applied by comparative costings of every process in all the establishments turning out the same product. This, we gather, is being taken up in the statistical branch of Gosplan, now transformed into a Cost Accounting Department.

In January 1933 there was an "All-Union Udarnik Day" at Moscow, when about 80,000 shock-brigaders, from about 120 separate industries or trades throughout the USSR, were brought together to be fêted and exhorted, and incidentally to confer among themselves as to the shortcomings still characteristic of soviet production, and how these can best be made good. In preparation for this great celebration, the All-Union Central Council of Trade Unions (AUCCTU) had directed the trade union committees everywhere to call together the various shock brigades and cost accounting committees in each establishment, which were not only to sum up their achievements and to talk over their plans for the ensuing year, but also to designate for

---

[1] *Moscow Daily News*, June 23, 1932.

[2] "On February 1, 1931, we could number only ten business accounting brigades in the USSR, comprising 130 persons. By April 1, 1932, their number had increased to 155,000, comprising one and a half million workers. The number of plants, and still more of separate shops, where there is hundred-percent business accounting is continually increasing. Leningrad takes the first place. It was in Leningrad that the first initiative towards organising business accounting brigades took its rise, and now no less than 70 per cent of the workers there are included in business accounting brigades. In the Moscow district, there are 30,000 business accounting brigades in the Ukraine, comprising 300,000 workers" (Ninth All-Union Congress of Trade Unions, 1932, speech by Shvernik, general secretary, p. 31).

The work of a business accounting brigade is described in detail in *A Business Accounting Brigade*, by A. Nikolayev, a worker in the Baltic shipyards (Moscow, Cooperative Publishing Society of Foreign Workers in the USSR, 1932, 40 pp.).

special honours (including portrait painting, and exhibition at the cinemas) their own leading udarniki. The All-Union Council wanted reported to this Moscow celebration " the state of labour-productivity, labour discipline, socialist competition and shock work, and cost accounting brigades. They should determine whether the 1932 industrial and financial plan is being carried out as regards both quantity and quality ; whether the udarniki are carrying out their pledges, whether lack of responsibility and equality of wages for unequal work have been rooted out. They should test whether the enterprise, as well as its departments and units, its restaurants, farms, cooperative store and management, are ready to accomplish the 1933 programme." [1]

### Professional Associations within USSR Trade Unionism

The trade union organisation, in which all those employed by each enterprise, and all the enterprises in the USSR, having the same predominant purpose, are associated in a single trade union, irrespective of craft or vocation, is accompanied, at any rate for certain crafts or vocations, by a certain amount of separate organisation, irrespective of establishment or industry, in which workers of the same craft or kind throughout the USSR are associated together. Thus the medical practitioners employed at salaries in all the various factories and farms, hospitals or institutions, who are, along with the nurses and ward maids, practically all members of the Medical or Public Health Workers' Trade Union, one of the meetings of which we have already described, are also united in an exclusively medical organisation —nominally only a section of that union, but having its own regional branches and an All-Union congress, at which are discussed all the subjects in which the medical practitioners have a special interest. [2]

[1] *Moscow Daily News*, December 28, 1932.
    See also *ibid.*, January 3, 1933, for report of meeting of shock-brigaders at the Moscow Auto Plant (Amo), which had over 16,000 of its workers taking part in socialist competition.
[2] In pre-war times, from 1870 onward, the various grades and sections of medical practitioners (doctors, pharmacists, midwives, nurses, etc.) formed professional societies for mutual aid. By 1905 there were nearly a score of such societies, most of which united in publishing the *Medical Workers' Journal*. In the subsequent years of repression these organisations declined in membership and activity. In 1918 most of the societies of the humbler grades dissolved themselves in order to form the All-Russian Medical Workers' Union. The pharmaceutical workers' society merged into this in 1920, together with the

In the same way the brain-working specialists in applied science, whether engineers or electricians, chemists or biologists —more than half of whom are now " soviet-trained "—employed in mines, power stations, factories, oil-fields or farms, anywhere in the USSR, have their own associations, supplementary to their membership of the several trade unions in which their establishments are included. These intellectuals are reported to be " organised into sections at all levels of the trade union structure. They are united at the top into a central body known as the Inter-Union Bureau of Engineers and Technicians of the All-Union Central Council of Trade Unions. Membership is entirely voluntary, and funds are set aside from the dues of these members to cover their particular work. They usually have their own special technical magazines. . . . These sections hold their own conferences nationally as well as provincially ; they have executive bureaux elected at these congresses. . . . Over 500 delegates attended one of the congresses convened in 1927. . . . Reports to this congress show over 105,000 members in the sections." [1] Another congress, still more numerously attended, and claiming to represent an enrolment of 125,000 members, was held in 1932, when it was welcomed by both governmental and scientific dignitaries. It is significant that the principal oration was entrusted to Shvernik, the general secretary of the AUCCTU, who addressed the congress at great length, urging on them the continuous study of industrial technique, with a view to its further improvement. "The local trade union groups ", he urged, " should strengthen their links with the engineers and other specialists, and support their work, keep them from being snowed under with petty routine, so that they can give real leadership. And the unions should see that these intellectual leaders get better living conditions." [2]

veterinary workers and the sanitary inspectors. The doctors still stood out, insisting on retaining their separate association. In 1920 the now powerful All-Russian Medical Workers' Union appealed to the Central Council of Trade Unions (which became the AUCCTU); and this body compulsorily dissolved the doctors' separate society, and insisted on the Medical Workers' Trade Union being recognised as the sole authority for all grades and sections of the profession. Many doctors joined at once, but others long resisted, considerable ill-feeling resulting. This gradually subsided when a special section for medical practitioners was formed within the Union (*Health Work in Soviet Russia*, by Anna J. Haines, New York, 1928, pp. 30-32).

[1] *Soviet Trade Unions*, by Robert W. Dunn, 1927, p. 67.
[2] *Moscow Daily News*, November 23, November 27, December 3, 1932.

The most ancient, and in the intellectual world the most important, of these associations of intellectual specialists is the Academy of Science, under the presidency of the aged Karpinsky, now over eighty, which counts on the assistance of more than a thousand scientific professors and researchers in ninety institutes. These are scattered throughout the USSR, though predominantly in Leningrad, Moscow, Kiev and Kharkov. In equipment and resources many of these institutes excite the envy of scientists of other countries. Besides its numerous scientific meetings, at which papers are read on every branch of science, the Academy now holds a certain number of public receptions, at which less technical addresses are given on particular subjects of general interest. " Zaslavsky ", we are told, " vividly describes the scene. In the body of the hall the proletariat, fresh from factory, plant, technical school, docks. On to the spacious stage file the academicians amid thunderous applause from the gathering. Here are names famous throughout the world in astronomy, physiology, biology, geology and other sciences. Here, leonine frosted heads, broad stooped shoulders, many of the traditional figures of the scientists of the bygone era. Some still wear the ancient frock coat of ceremony, with the traditional contempt of their kind for clothes." [1] The Academy of Science—not without some struggle—has accepted the régime of Soviet Communism. In so far as its members receive salaries from their institutes, as most of the academicians do, they are eligible for membership of the trade union to which their institute belongs, many of them have joined, and some of these have now become active members of the trade unions with which the academy had formerly no connection.

There are, however, other academies. Thus the Academy of the History of Material Culture unites a membership of 10,000 archaeologists,[2] mostly employed in museums and universities in the various parts of the USSR, where they are members of the trade unions to which their institutions belong. Besides local meetings and periodical national congresses for the promotion of its studies, this academy equips and sends archaeological expeditions to various parts of the USSR, and undertakes or supervises excavations.

[1] *Moscow Daily News*, November 27, 1932.
[2] *Ibid.*, November 27, 1932.

We are unable to give anything like a complete list of these professional associations of intellectual workers ; not, as in Britain and the United States, parallel with and scarcely conscious of the trade union organisation, but forming integral parts of it ; superimposed nationally, so to speak, on the universal organisation by establishments. There is a central association of teachers ; there is a press writers' section of the typographical trade union, and a scientific workers' section of the educational workers' trade union. There is a special section for statisticians and accountants in the commercial workers' trade union. The professors and scientific workers in museums, libraries and laboratories have a section of their own, with a membership (in 1927) of 14,000, organised in fifty branches in as many cities. The authors have been organised in several societies ; one of them was confined to members of the Communist Party, which tended to a certain asperity against " non-Party " writers. By a decision of the Central Committee of the Party, in April 1932, this exclusive organisation was dissolved, in order that all authors who support the soviet régime, and who attempt to participate in socialist construction, whether or not they are Party members or candidates, may constitute a single society of soviet authors.[1] There is an All-Union Sectional Bureau of Engineers and Technicians (YMBIT), which at the instance of Shvernik, secretary of the AUCCTU, resolved to participate actively in the " agricultural machinery repairing campaign " on the 32 repair-shops of the machine-tractor stations ; and also in the " drive for technical education for Comsomols ".[2] There is also a Society of Soviet Architects, founded in 1932, with 6 branches in the RSFSR and a monthly journal of its own.[3] All these segregations of professionals, formally authorised by the Seventh All-Union Congress of Trade Unions in 1926, have for their object the promotion of their special cultural activities ; not forgetting, however, the raising of their members' salaries, the improvement in their housing conditions and the establishment of special pension systems.[4]

On the general trade union reorganisation in September 1934,

[1] *Manchester Guardian*, May 1, 1932.
[2] *Moscow Daily News*, October 28, 1933.
[3] *Ibid.*, August 17, 1933.
[4] *Soviet Trade Unions*, by Robert W. Dunn, 1927, pp. 67-69.

Shvernik, the secretary of the AUCCTU, fully recognised the utility and importance of these professional associations uniting for specific purposes the members of various trade unions. It was, he explained to the present writers, contemplated that there would be several such sectional associations associated within most, if not all, of the 154 trade unions among which the 47 older unions were distributed. It had, however, not been possible to complete this organisation by September 1934, and it would have to be postponed until 1935.

This specialist segregation within the trade union organisation is not confined to the intellectual workers. The limitation in 1931 of the number of unions to 47 involved the association in one union of many different kinds of artisans and labourers. The trade union of food workers, for instance, united operatives in flourmills with those in slaughter-houses, candy factories, bakeries, fish canneries and tobacco factories. In many cases, accordingly, at the instance of the Central Committee of the Communist Party, specialised sections have been formed, especially with a view to a more detailed study of processes as a means of increasing productivity, as well as to a better-instructed collective bargaining on behalf of particular kinds of workers throughout the USSR. " Parallel with the establishment of these sections," said the C.C.C.P., " the holding of special meetings and production conferences according to trades must be put into practice (foundry workers, moulders, machinists, examiners, mechanics, stopers, tractor mechanics, assistant foremen, cotton printers, etc.); and in the shops a delegate representing the leading trade must be designated along with the shop delegate." [1] We find the AUCCTU, whilst dutifully promulgating this policy of sectionalisation, not forgetful of the possible danger to the trade union organisation of such " particularisms ". " The sections ", the Trade Union Bulletin of the AUCCTU had pointed out as early as 1926, " must not be regarded as an initial step towards dividing the unions, or turning the sections into independent bodies. The sections must be created within a union, as auxiliary bodies which can better examine into the special industrial and living conditions of the members and serve them more satisfactorily." [2]

[1] *Report of Ninth All-Union Congress of Trade Unions, 1933*, p. 110 (Kaganovich's report). A stoper is a miner working a stope or layer.

[2] *Soviet Trade Unions*, by Robert W. Dunn, 1927, p. 69.

Similarly, in the case of the Inter-Union Bureau of Engineers and Technicians, to which we have already referred, it has been ordered that decisions of section bodies have to be submitted to and confirmed by the governing body of the particular union to whose members they relate before they become effective.[1]

### The Profintern

The preceding description of the complicated trade union organisation of Soviet Communism does not complete the analysis of the pattern. As we have seen in the case of the soviet hierarchy, and as we shall presently describe in the case of the Communist Party, what is contemplated is membership of a far-reaching international organisation which is eventually to be world-wide. For man as a wage-earning producer there is to be eventually a world trade unionism of the soviet pattern. The whole trade union organisation of the USSR accordingly belongs to the International Council of " Red " Trade Unions, commonly known as Profintern, which was formally established at an international gathering at Moscow summoned by the AUCCTU in 1921.[2] There was already in existence an International Association of Trade Unions, centred at Amsterdam, which had secured the adhesion of the great bulk of European trade unionism, irrespective of political opinions. With the spread of social democratic views among the workmen, this " trade union

---

[1] *Soviet Trade Unions*, by Robert W. Dunn, 1927, p. 67.

[2] The published reports and pamphlets relating to the " Red International " (Profintern) are very numerous, and many of them exist in English, French and German versions. A useful list with an elaborate chronicle of proceedings (down to 1926) will be found in *The Trade Union Movement in Soviet Russia* (International Labour Office, League of Nations, 1927, pp. 262-263). A later list appears in *Handworterbuch des Gewerkschaften*.

Among those available in English, French or German, see, in particular, *Resolutions, Proclamations and Manifestos of the First Congress of Trade and Industrial Unions*, Moscow, 1921 ; *Minutes of the International Council of Red Trade Unions*, Moscow, 1921 ; *The Red Trade Union International*, Moscow, 1921-1926 ; *The World Trade Union Movement before and after the War*, 1924, and *Moscow or Amsterdam ?* 1924, both by A. Lozovsky ; *World Communists in Action*, by G. Piatnitsky, 1931 ; and *Les Questions vitales du mouvement révolutionnaire internationale*, Paris, 62 pp., by the same. The British Government Blue Book (Cmd. 2682 of 1926) contains a miscellaneous mass of documents of the Red International seized by the London police in October 1925. Many similar documents may at any time be found published in Inprecorr (*International Press Correspondence*). See also *Soviet Trade Unions*, by Robert W. Dunn, 1927, pp. 222-252 ; *Soviet Russia*, by W. H. Chamberlin, 1930, pp. 267-274.

International" had become associated with the "Second International", the alliance of Labour and Socialist societies established in 1889, at Paris, to which the socialist parties of western Europe were affiliated. These very generally took up an attitude of hostility to Bolshevism, principally because of its intolerance of opposition and its suppression of the Menshevik section of the social democratic party. Hence, just as the Comintern was set up at Moscow in opposition to the "Second International", so the Profintern was set up there in opposition to the "Amsterdam International".

The Profintern is professedly governed by an annual congress of delegates from the several national organisations of communist trade unions. Such congresses were, for nearly a decade, held at Moscow, but opinions differ as to the extent to which they can be said ever to have been effectively either international or representative of trade unions as such. At the congress held in 1927, for instance, when the " Red Trade Union International " claimed to speak for 13,862,209 members of affiliated organisations, 10,248,000 were trade unionists of the USSR, and 2,800,000 were members of Chinese societies of various kinds, which were promptly dissolved or have simply faded out. The other three-quarters of a million included a few communist trade unions, chiefly in Germany, France and Czecho-Slovakia, but was mainly composed, as Losovsky himself reported, not of trade unions at all but of a varied array of nondescript bodies, including minority groups, illegal associations and miscellaneous committees in some forty or fifty other countries, including North and South America, Australia and New Zealand, India, and Africa,[1] hardly any of which had sent anyone to Moscow expressly as delegates to the congress. The subsequent congresses have been of the same kind. The delegates consist of those appointed by the AUCCTU of the USSR, together with a tiny number of persons actually sent for the purpose by foreign trade unions, supplemented by others sent by the nondescript

[1] The character of the affiliations was described by the President of the Congress in 1930. " You know that the trade union movement which is united in the Profintern is most varied in so far as organisational structure is concerned. Independent organisations, illegal trade unions, semi-legal organisations, and further, trade union oppositions, or minorities inside trade unions, all belong to the ' Profintern ' " (Extract translated from A. Losovsky's report to the Moscow Conference of Active Workers in Trade Unions, September 9, 1930, on " The Results of the Fifth Congress of the Profintern ").

groups above mentioned, as well as by communist trade unionists of foreign birth or nationality, residing and working in Moscow, and even stray visitors of like opinions who happen to be there. This congress appoints an executive council, with presidium, president and secretary, most of them habitually resident in Moscow. The representative validity so far as foreign trade unions are concerned and the practical effectiveness in other countries of an international organisation of this kind appears to be of the slightest. We do not wish to imply that the Profintern does not express the views of large numbers of communists in other countries, who have occasionally gone to the ballot-box in millions, and who exercise in their respective countries an influence, not only among the unemployed, but also in trade union memberships and meetings, which have, except in a few instances, as yet not achieved control of the trade unions themselves. It is the claim of the Red International to represent foreign trade unions as such which is disputed, not its representation of the opinions of the communist members of the wage-earning class.

The Central Council of the Profintern is a body including four of the leading members of the Communist Party of the USSR, with two persons belonging to each of the large industrial countries. The real work is done by an Executive Bureau of seven members, two of them belonging to the USSR. The proceedings of the Executive Bureau, though often lacking in accurate knowledge of the position of labour in other countries, have not been without vigour and dexterity. There is a polyglot secretariat, paid for out of the dues levied by the Profintern on its affiliated bodies, and thus largely by the trade unions of the USSR. This secretariat is departmentally organised by countries, and includes communists belonging to one or other of the principal nations dealt with. Its extensive correspondence with all sorts of communist organisations in the different countries has, in the past, frequently included detailed " directives " as to how these bodies ought to proceed. These instructions, the tone of which excites some resentment, have been, in the past, occasionally accompanied by substantial remittances under various disguises, usually in aid of strikes. Since 1929, however, it is believed that these subsidies have, except in some cases when communist officials have required legal defence in criminal prosecutions, dwindled to minute sums, designed more to maintain connection than with any idea of fostering a world upheaval.

The story of the proceedings of Profintern during the past dozen years is largely taken up with the continuous controversy with the " Amsterdam International ", which, in 1932, commanded the allegiance of many millions of trade union membership in nearly all countries except the USSR (also, for other reasons, except the United States of America), and with its satellites, the 27 international federations of the trade unions of separate industries. Profintern has been tireless in its incessant attempt to arrange for what it calls a " united front " against capitalism throughout the world. It cannot, however, bring itself to unite with an organisation formed on the basis of trade unionism as it exists in capitalist countries which, in the present interests of these members as wage-earners, avowedly forgoes any attempt to overturn by force the existing order in which these members actually find their living. On the other hand, the Amsterdam International refuses to make any kind of alliance, or undertake any common enterprise, with a body which glories in existing for purposes definitely criminal under the laws of the states in which the trade unionists live, and which is avowedly directed from Moscow, and is universally supposed to be under the control of the Politbureau of the Communist Party of the USSR. Apart from usually fruitless manoeuvres for a " united front ", the Red International does all it can to encourage and support strikes and industrial disturbances in all capitalist countries, and, wherever possible, the active propaganda of communism itself. Its vision of a future world organisation of trade unions, *under a universal communist régime*, is not without merit. But in the meantime, with trade unionism facing capitalist employers and unfriendly governments, we cannot help thinking that, as in the case of the Comintern, the avowed interference of Moscow in the internal affairs of other countries actually militates, by the nationalist resentment that it creates, against the progress of communism itself.

*How does Soviet Trade Unionism compare with British Trade Unionism ?*

Trade unionism in the USSR, it will have been realised, is a large and powerful organisation, more extensive than trade unionism in any other country, more busily engaged in a wider range of functions, and more closely connected with the other organs of the state. It is, we think, unique in the intense interest that it takes in increasing the productivity of the nation's industry; in its inclusion within its own membership of the directors and managers who have taken the place of the capitalist employers, and in its persistent desire to reduce costs. We shall describe in a subsequent chapter how cordially it has accepted the various arrangements—in substitution for the capitalist's incessant desire to increase his profits—for securing the utmost possible output at the lowest possible expense to the community.[1] But what, it may be asked, does the trade union in the USSR retain from its model in British trade unionism ? Put summarily, it may be answered that the soviet trade union, like the British, is emphatically the organ of the wage-earners as such : it is based on optional individual membership and subscription ; it appoints and pays its own officials and manages its business by its own elected committees ; it conducts, through its highest committees and its national officials, the collective bargaining with the employing organisations by which the general scheme and standard rates of wages are fixed ; piece-work rates are settled in each factory, job by job, after discussion with the union's local officials and not without their consent ; these officials may actually be specialist " rate-fixers ", for whom the union organises special training ; it takes part, through its chosen representatives and appointed officials, in almost every organ of government; finally, its essential function is that of maintaining and improving the worker's conditions of life—taking, however, the broadest view of these, and seeking their advancement only in common with those of the whole community of workers.

Not so easy to explain is the relation of the soviet trade union to the other organs of the Soviet State. " Are the trade unions ", asked Tomsky in 1927, " dependent on or independent of the state ? If this is to be understood in the formal interpretation which Western European trade unions usually give to the question, then, of course, we are independent, for the trade unions are managed by their own democratically elected organs, have their own funds, and are in no way subject to the state. In the wider meaning of the word, in the sense of class politics, the

[1] See Chapter IX. in Part II., " In Place of Profit ".

unions are dependent, as organs of a united class, for the state is our state. But this dependence is based on mutual dependence, for equally the Council of People's Commissars and the Central Executive Committee of the Soviet Government is dependent upon the trade unions. How can they be independent when we have 4 representatives in the Presidium of the Central Executive Committee of the Soviet Government and 60 representatives in the Central Executive Committee of the Soviets itself; when we have a consultative vote in the Council of People's Commissaries on every question that arises therein; when the Council of People's Commissaries cannot decide a single question concerning the life of the workers without our final decision in the matter; when we have the right to remove from the agenda of any high state organ any question whatever, by a mere telephone call saying, ' Just a moment. You want to discuss such and such a matter : but you have not asked us our opinion. We have something to say on the matter. Be good enough to postpone that item'? And we know of no case when this has been refused us. The trade unions have the right to call upon any of the People's Commissaries to appear before them to make a report, and no one of them has the right to refuse us on the grounds that he is not formally responsible to the unions in question." [1]

We suggest that the relation of soviet trade unionism to the other organs of the soviet state cannot be accurately estimated until the position and influence of the Communist Party is appreciated. To this we devote a subsequent chapter entitled " The Vocation of Leadership " (Chapter V. in Part I.).

## SECTION II

### THE ASSOCIATIONS OF OWNER-PRODUCERS

It was characteristic of Lenin's genius that he set superlative value on the principle of multiformity in social organisation, not only for the sake of that universal participation in government which, as he held, could alone make democracy real, but also as a " guarantee of vitality . . . a pledge that the common and single aim will be successfully achieved ". Only on this principle, it

---

[1] *The Trade Unions, the Party and the State*, by M. Tomsky, Moscow, 1927, pp. 18-19.

was urged, could men and women of diverse temperaments and talents, antecedents and circumstances, be all enrolled for the supreme task of building the socialist state. Hence we find, in the USSR, alongside the trade union of the wage and salary earners employed by state, municipal and consumers' cooperative enterprises and institutions, an entirely different—one might almost say a contradictory—type of organisation, the self-governing workshop or collective farm. In this type the members are not recipients of salary or wage ; indeed, not employed under any contract of service at all. They are, individually or jointly, owners or part owners not only of the instruments of production but also of the products of their labour. This method of organising man as a producer has been, in western Europe, for over a century, continuously advocated, and frequently practised under the name of cooperative production, as a desirable and practicable alternative to the organisation of industry under the capitalist profitmaker. As such it has been the subject of heated controversy ; is it either a desirable or a practicable alternative to the wage system ? Incidentally, it may be said that the present writers replied in the negative,[1] at any rate within the framework of the capitalist system. Hence we have been all the more interested to discover that, within the framework of Soviet Communism, associations of owner-producers, of one or other kind, have, within the past decade, become actually the predominant type in the agriculture of the USSR ; whilst they have apparently demonstrated their advantages in various branches of manufacturing industry, and in such widespread methods of earning a living as hunting and fishing.

### (a) THE SELF-GOVERNING WORKSHOP

We start our analysis of the constitutional structure of associations of owner-producers in the USSR, not with the largest and in every way the most important group, namely, that of the collective farms, but with that which stands in most marked contrast with what we have described in our preceding section on trade unionism, namely, the associations of owner-producers in

---

[1] See *The Cooperative Movement in Great Britain*, by Beatrice Potter, 1891 ; *Industrial Democracy*, by S. and B. Webb, 1898 ; *The Consumers' Cooperative Movement*, by the same, 1922.

manufacturing industry, or what in England is called the Self-Governing Workshop.[1]

The typical "manufacturer" of Russia in the nineteenth century was neither the capitalist entrepreneur nor the wage-paid artisan, but the individual handicraftsman, working alone or in a family group, on the wood or iron, wool or flax, bone or leather that he made up into commodities for household use, to be sold for his own subsistence. At all times a group of these handicraftsmen would unite in a labour "artel" (the word dates from the twelfth century). "This", we are told, "was a temporary association of individuals for a definite industrial undertaking, usually of a temporary character, conducted on a basis of joint management and responsibility." It was unrecognised by the law, and enjoyed no official or legal protection; but was habitually not interfered with by the government. Many artels were formed for work at building construction or manufacturing in the cities. Others existed in the villages for the production of commodities for sale. Many were formed "annually for each year's campaign, and dissolved after the accounts for the goods delivered and sold in the season had been settled".[2] A small proportion of them latterly took a more durable form as cooperative societies for production. On the other hand, a much larger

[1] For information as to the past and present of the kustar handicraftsmen, their artels and their cooperative societies, the most accessible sources are *The Cooperative Movement in Russia during the War*, by E. M. Kayden and A. N. Antsiferov (Economic Social History of the War, Yale University, New Haven, 1929, 436 pp.); *Les voies du développement de la coopération de production en URSS*, par W. Tikhomirov, 1931, secretary of central council of cooperative societies; see also by the same, *Die Genossenschaften in socialistischen Aufbau* (Berlin), 1927, pp. 36; *The Soviet Worker*, by T. Freeman, 1931, pp. 238-240, gives a useful summary. How it appeared to the Russian orthodox economist (and to the Tsarist Government) will be seen in the report of the Commission impériale de Russie à l'Exposition Universelle de Paris, 1900, entitled *La Russie à la fin du 19ᵉ siècle*, ouvrage publié sous la direction de M. W. de Kovalevsky (Paris, 1900, pp. 652-658). There is a useful collection (in Russian) of all the decrees on handicraft cooperation and kustar industries by I. A. Selitsky and I. R. Koisky, edited by Professor D. M. Genkin, Moscow, 1928. With this must be read the important decree and resolution of July 23, 1932, by the Central Executive Committee and Sovnarkom of the USSR, rearranging the whole organisation.

Other works in Russian are *Zakonodatelsvro o promcooperatzii* (The Legislation on Incops), by D. M. Genkin, Moscow, 1933; *Ten Years of Incops in the USSR*, by V. Gnoussov and I. P. Chernyshev, Moscow, 1932; *Pavlovo* (a collection of stories and essays on Incops in Pavlovo), by V. Korolenko and K. Pazhitnov.

[2] *The Cooperative Movement in Russia during the War*, by E. M. Kayden and A. N. Antsiferov, 1929, pp. 4, 367.

proportion had, by 1914, lost their economic independence, and had fallen into the hands of capitalist middlemen, who either gave out their own materials to be made up at a " sweated " rate, or sold them on credit to the associated handicraftsmen, taking back the product in furniture, toys, leather goods, textile stuffs or articles of clothing at ruinously low prices.[1] In 1914 the aggregate number of these owner-producers in industrial pursuits was given as five and a quarter millions, constituting a census population of some fifteen or twenty millions, representing as much as one-eighth of tsarist Russia at that date. Their gross output was estimated at 2400 million roubles, equal to one-half of that of the factory industry of the time. During the seven years of war and civil war, 1914–1920, although some of the unions of artels " achieved important results in the service of the country and the army ",[2] two-thirds of this population of handicraftsmen faded away, the bulk of the survivors being found, in 1921, in the more remote villages which suffered least from the ravages of the contending armies.

Under the Soviet Government these independent owner-producers have been, from 1919 onwards, and especially since 1932, revived and encouraged, as an approved alternative form of production (particularly for household supplies) to that of employment at wages in the industries conducted by government or trust, municipality or consumers' cooperative society. Lenin's original policy was " to maintain and develop energetically cooperative production ", not only as a way of alleviating the condition of the peasants, but also as the means by which the small industry could, as he then believed, " develop into mass production, on the basis of free associations of workers ".[3] Consequently the handicraftsmen were, from the outset, enabled freely to form productive cooperative societies, which have been, at times, granted state credit for the purchase of materials at the lowest possible prices. Sometimes small factories or workshops, abandoned by their owners, were handed over to such

[1] *Les voies du développement de la coopération de production en URSS*, par W. Tikhomirov, 1931.

[2] *The Cooperative Movement in Russia during the War*, by E. M. Kayden and A. N. Antsiferov, 1929, p. 366.

[3] *Les voies du développement de la coopération de production en URSS*, par W. Tikhomirov ; quoting from vol. xx. p. 466 of the Russian text of Lenin's *Works*.

societies. In other cases they have been helped to buy machinery and workshop equipment. Occasionally the experts of a trust, or of a particular modernised plant, have assisted one of the larger artels to change its whole system of production in such a way as greatly to increase its output.[1]

The various government departments, central or municipal, together with the manufacturing trusts and the consumers' cooperative societies, have, during the past decade, willingly supplied their own needs by contracting to take from the manufacturing associations of owner-producers (incops), at agreed fixed prices, a large proportion of their output, thus ensuring for long periods a profitable market for their wares. Nor have the isolated independent handicraftsmen been left entirely unaided. The incops have been asked to do everything possible to bring them into the network of organisations, and meanwhile to assist them by contracting to take their individual products so as to assist their marketing.[2] Especially since the establishment of the Five-Year Plan in 1928 have these manufacturing associations of owner-producers multiplied and developed. The result has been, not only the progressive revival of the great bulk of the kustar industry,[3] but also the enlargement of its scope, and its assumption of definite constitutional forms according to the pattern common throughout the soviet system. By a remarkable decree of July 23, 1932, by the Central Executive Committee and the

[1] " Thus, upon the paper's (*Trud*) initiative, a factory let us say manufacturing shoes, undertakes to assist a shoemaking artel in improving and increasing its output. An artel is a cooperative enterprise, which unites sometimes as many as five or six hundred artizans who formerly worked in their own little shops. Although in numbers these artels often present sizable factories, the method of work too often remains as of old, each man doing a complete job without attempting to sectionalize the work. Under the guidance of experts from a factory employing modern production methods, it has been possible to so arrange the work of the artels as to increase the output many times " (*Moscow Daily News*, June 23, 1932).

[2] When unemployment was rife, the labour exchanges occasionally pressed a cooperative society, whose little factory was manufacturing successfully, to admit as additional members individual handicraftsmen who had failed to maintain themselves by independent production; or to accept unemployed youths as additional apprentices and eventual members; sometimes selecting one half from sons of existing members and the other half from the labour exchange.

[3] So greatly has the nationalised and municipalised industry increased that all the handicraft industry accounts only for one-fifth of the manufacturing production of the USSR, in 1933, instead of the one-third of that of tsarist Russia with which it was credited in 1913.

Sovnarkom of the USSR, the whole system was further developed and drastically reorganised.[1]

At the beginning of 1932, in addition to an uncounted host of isolated individual handicraftsmen who still exist, in the cities as well as in the villages, to the aggregate number of a million or more, the number of definitely organised cooperative societies of this kind was estimated at about 20,000, with 30,000 workshops or other establishments, having a total membership of 2,350,000 men and women, representing a census population of seven or eight millions, with an aggregate gross production of commodities valued at about four and a half thousand million roubles. Another calculation of later date, and including a wider range of societies, puts the amount, in 1932, of " output of the producing cooperative associations, including invalids and timber-working cooperatives " (to which we refer elsewhere), at " 6230 million roubles, calculated at planned prices of 1932 ".[2] Whereas before the war the great majority of the handicraftsmen worked at home, now fewer than a third do so, and of the members of the cooperative societies fewer than one-eighth. These societies, in half a dozen instances, now run small coal pits, producing, in the aggregate, more than two million tons per annum, and, in one case, at Rechesk in the Urals, even a blast furnace.[3] There are, in Kazakastan, lead mines under incops ; elsewhere various small machine-making factories ; many quarries, brickfields and lime-kilns, and even

---

[1] These associations of owner-producers in industry (incops) have been classified as under by the latest Russian authority on the subject (*The Legislation of Incops*, by D. M. Genkin, Moscow, 1933) :

(1) Associations for Supply and Sale, in which every member works at home, but sells the whole or part of his output through the society, from which he obtains his raw material and adjuncts. Members, who must themselves work, enjoy a reduction of income tax on the part of their output sold through the society.

(2) Associations for Joint Production, in which the members all work at home, but materials and product alike belong to the society, and not to individual members.

(3) Artels, which maintain a common workshop in which members are associated in a particular craft or branch of industry (the law forbidding an artel composed of workers in different crafts).

[2] *Summary of Results of the First Five-Year Plan* (Gosplan, 1933, p. 61).

[3] The Rechesk plant, in the Urals, produces 15,000 tons of pig-iron a year, practically all of which supplies the needs of other incops. In other cases there are rolling mills, which refashion scrap iron and steel obtained from the plants under the direction of the Commissariat of Heavy Industries. The coal-mines of the incops in the Donbas and elsewhere in the Ukraine and in East Siberia supply indifferently other incops, or the local industries, or USSR enterprises.

small chemical plants producing soap, acetic acid, iodine, nicotine and various radio supplies.[1] But the incops mainly devote them-selves, to the extent of more than half their work, to the pre-paration of various kinds of food products and to the production and repair of all sorts of commodities for household use, such as furniture and kitchen equipment, boots and shoes, barrels and baskets, every description of textile stuffs and made-up clothing, mats and rugs of all kinds, toys, leather goods, artistic wood and iron work, pottery, and even hand-painting on wood, by those who formerly produced religious icons. For sale to the public in the cities, these cooperative societies have over a thousand shops, and more than that number of stands. Their members, indeed, have come to form an important element in the urban population. Whereas, in 1926, the handicraftsmen in the cities numbered only half a million, or 2·1 per cent of the population, in 1931 the urban registration disclosed their numbers as about two millions, or 6·2 per cent of the population.[2]

### The Members' Meeting

The base of the constitutional hierarchy, in which these organ-ised groups of industrial owner-producers are represented, is everywhere the meetings of members of their several incops or industrial cooperative societies, which may each include anything from a few dozen to a thousand or more workers; the average being a little over a hundred. In the smaller incops these meet-ings, which every member over 18 years of age is expected to attend, take place frequently, according to the rules of the particular society, usually every few weeks. The course of the incop's business is reviewed by the president, manager or other official, and any subject of interest to the members can be dis-cussed. Once a year the president—often also a manager—and, to constitute the presidium half a dozen other members, are elected, together with the prescribed number of delegates to other

---

[1] Much of the work of timber-cutting, as well as that of fashioning the timber into planks, doors, plywood, etc., is done by groups of workmen associated in artels. These, however, are not included in the incops organisation, but have a union of their own (Vsekopromlessoyus), which works in conjunction with the newly formed Commissariat of Timber (Narkomles). These timber artels are grouped, not by the Union republics but by oblasts or krais; and, in some special cases, by autonomous republics.

[2] *Summary of Results of the First Five-Year Plan* (Gosplan, 1933, p. 189).

bodies.  The incops in a given locality, and manufacturing the
same kind of commodities, may also join together in a specialised
" union " for common convenience, as for the joint supply of
tools, raw materials or auxiliary components, or joint representation in dealings with state departments.  But the principal
delegation is to the regional council, to which all incops within
the region (usually an oblast or krai), irrespective of the particular
commodity that they manufacture, are now required to belong.
The members' meeting elects also in each case a committee of
revision, whose main duty is to audit the accounts.  According to
law this committee ought to include in its membership some
members of other incops.  It is this committee of revision that
decides the occasional disputes that arise in the society, subject to
appeal to the regional council.  If the membership of the incop
does not exceed 300, it is the ordinary meeting of members which
makes this election of delegates.  If, however, as is increasingly
coming to be the case in the large cities, the incop has many
hundreds of members, the aggregate meeting is held only annually,
to elect a smaller executive council of a few dozen members ; and
it is this executive council which chooses alike the incop's own
officers and its delegates to the regional council.

Under the revised arrangements of 1932, the regional councils
(soviets) whilst aiding the incops by instruction, planning, advice,
and settlement of disputes, do not themselves have any operative
functions.  They do not, that is to say, themselves engage in
production or distribution,[1] nor are the incops in any way
hampered in their several industries.  Each incop is freely to
obtain for itself the materials that it requires, with the exceptions
of wool, cotton, flax, hemp, silk cocoons and hides other than
pig-hides.  These may be obtained how the incop pleases, but
only within the geographical districts prescribed by the Supplies
Committee of the Council of Labour and Defence (STO).  Each
incop is also to be free to acquire from any of the state enterprises
such industrial remnants, waste and refuse (including metal scrap,
textile waste, rags, rejects and waste timber) as it may need, and
all state enterprises are directed to enter into contracts for these
supplies at prices to be agreed upon.  The incops are to be free to

---

[1] There seems to be one exception.  The Vsekopromsoviet has under it a
"metalpromsoyus ", or group of incops working in metal, which itself performs
" operative functions " in conjunction with these incops.

obtain from the state bank the credit that they require, and to sell their products as and wherever they choose, including the open markets in the towns and their own retail shops. Except when working on materials provided from state funds, the incops are no longer required to dispose of any part of the output to any state department, but all state departments are directed to place with the incops such orders as they can. Orders for its own manufactured products may now be sought and obtained by each incop direct from the consumer's cooperative movement, or from state or municipal departments, or from any of the government trusts, as well as from individual purchasers. Prices are left to be settled by agreement or contract in each case. The one transaction that is strictly prohibited is " speculation ", meaning buying commodities with the intention of selling them again at a profit—in other words, the incops are not to engage in mere dealing. It should be noted that, although the incops are founded on the principle of a partnership of the workers themselves, they are allowed, by way of exception, to employ non-members at wages, as specialists (such as engineers) or as subsidiary or seasonal workers, to the extent of not more than one-fifth of the membership, or than 30 per cent of the combined total of members and candidates for membership. The non-members thus employed at wages, who are generally members of their respective trade unions, must all receive the rates current in their several industries ; as agreed to by the trade unions. Nothing in the nature of undercutting is allowed.

### The Regional Council of Incops

The decree of July 23, 1932, whilst abolishing various intermediate and All-Union federal bodies of industrial cooperative societies,[1] established an obligatory association of the incops within a given region ; not for the purpose of control or of inter-

---

[1] Thus the decree peremptorily " liquidates " the All-Union Federation of Food Industry Cooperatives, the All-Union Federation of Heavy Industry Cooperatives, and the All-Union Federation of Industrial Cooperatives ; and lays down that " under no circumstances is it permitted to create in the regional councils of incops cumbersome apparatus, once the organisation has been permitted in the structure of the All-Union Federation of Incops of specialised groups for the fundamental forms of the incops ". Republic Associations of the heavy metal industry are to continue ; and also the All-Union Cooperatives of the Timber Industry, but " without creating associations of these cooperatives in the various republics ".

ference with their business enterprises—in which they were to enjoy an enlarged independence—but solely for their assistance in fulfilling the tasks which they had undertaken. The region for this purpose was to be either each of the six smaller constituent republics, or else, in the RSFSR and in other districts of highly developed industry, the oblast or krai, or an area specially defined. Each such region has now a council of delegates from its constituent incops, which are represented approximately in proportion to their several memberships, as fixed by the council itself from time to time. This council no longer decides on the levy to be made upon the funds of each incop for regional and All-Union administration and other purposes. All such levies are to be kept down to a minimum, and to be made by a special meeting for the purpose, at which specially delegated representatives of the several incops within the region will confer with representatives of the regional council. That council will be responsible for supervising the audit of the societies' accounts by their own committees of revision, and, where necessary, for supplying competent auditors to assist any society. The regional council is also responsible for supervision of the general direction of the incops' several activities but solely for the purpose of securing the due fulfilment of the obligations undertaken by each of them. The greatest possible independence in management is to be left to each incop, on the understanding that they are, for the most part, primarily to supply the household commodities needed by the rural community, to the extent at least of 70 per cent of their production. The incops declare that their aim is to make this percentage at least 75 per cent, but it is admitted that this amount has not yet been reached.

### The All-Union Council of Industrial Cooperatives

In place of the Central Federation (Vsekopromsoyus) established in 1922, as a directing and coordinating centre, there is now established an All-Union Council of Incops (Vsekopromsoviet), to which all the regional councils send representatives, and which also acts as republic council for the RSFSR. It is expressly laid down in the decree that this " Council of the Incops of the USSR and RSFSR shall not perform operative functions of any kind ". It is to be supervisory, not executive. What is to this council expressly " reserved " is " the organising work, accountancy, directorial, and prospective planning and representation of the incops in government organisations (concerning credits, funds of supply, protection of state laws, grants to the incops) ".[1]

In 1932 was held the first All-Union Congress of the reorganised producers' cooperatives [2] (incops), at which some 200 delegates attended. Such a Congress will presumably be held every few years, but had, in 1934, not yet been repeated. The Congress elected an executive council to meet as a plenum once in every few months, with a president, and other members of a presidium, by whom the work of supervising the whole 20,000 incops is done. During 1933 and 1934 the executive council invited to Moscow for consultation the heads of most of the incops from time to time.

There has never been a People's Commissar for cooperative production, any more than for the consumers' cooperative movement. Such supervision and attention as has been given to the subject by the government at the Kremlin has come within the province of the Council of Labour and Defence (STO). It is interesting that the president for the time being of the All-Union Council of Incops (Vsekopromsoviet) is admitted, when he chooses to attend, to the meetings of the Central Executive Committee (TSIK), the Sovnarkom and the Council of Labour and Defence (STO) ; in each case with only a consultative voice. Perhaps the most important relation into which the All-Union Council enters is its participation with the officials of Gosplan in the annual settlement and the almost continuous adjustment of the General Plan, so far as concerns the societies forming its membership. The preliminary plan is drawn up by Gosplan itself, but it is based on the separate reports which the Executive Committee obtains from every one of the 20,000 incops, stating

---

[1] The membership of the central federation for previous years is given as :

|  |  |  |  |
|---|---|---|---|
| 1922 | . | . | 84,000 |
| 1923 | . | . | 187,000 |
| 1924 | . | . | 248,000 |
| 1925 | . | . | 344,000 |
| 1926 | . | . | 457,000 |
| 1927 | . | . | 599,000 |
| 1928 | . | . | 1,004,000 |
| 1929 | . | . | 1,454,000 |
| 1930 | . | . | 1,944,000 |
| 1931 } 1932 | . | . | 2,353,000 |

[2] *Moscow Daily News,* December 28, 1932.

what they have produced during the preceding year, and what they think they can produce for the ensuing year. The provisional decision by Gosplan of what kind and what amount of production should be undertaken by the incops, arrived at in consultation with the Executive Committee, after consideration of the needs of the USSR as a whole, is then submitted to the several regional councils, who pass on each part of it, with criticisms and suggestions, to the several incops, whose officials and committees have promptly to give it their serious consideration, and return it with any objections or counter-proposals. If any incop finds a difficulty in undertaking the manufacture of any of the commodities that the Plan requires from it, the regional council may arrange for the technical instruction of some of its younger members at a special district school maintained for the purpose.

The educational provision made by the incops for their own members and their families, apart from and in addition to that made by the soviets under the People's Commissars of Education in the several constituent or autonomous republics, is extensive and steadily increasing. In 1934 no less than 98 million roubles was appropriated for this purpose by the Executive Committee. All the larger units maintain their own trade schools and evening technical classes. In some of the principal cities there are university colleges, exclusively for members of incops or their sons and daughters—that at Leningrad had, in 1934, 2400 students all over eighteen, pursuing five-year courses. In addition, more than sixty technicums are maintained. Three quarters of the students are provided with stipends, sometimes more liberal than those of the students of the state institutions. There are special club-houses for incop members. Their new " Palace of Culture " at Leningrad cost ten million roubles, and claims to be the best in the city. The incops have also their own holiday homes and sanitoria.

Members of the incops are not covered by the general scheme of social insurance. The All-Union Council has accordingly provided its own fund, by a levy on all the incops, in which the whole membership is included, including the wage-earners whom they employ. This fund had in 1933 an accumulated capital of over a hundred million roubles, being eight times as much as in 1929. The fund provides medical attendance and medicines, and secures admission to hospitals and convalescent homes, for all the members and their wives and children throughout the USSR. All confinements are treated in hospital, with sixteen weeks full wages, as in the state scheme. This is wholly independent of the People's Commissars of Health, except that the assistance of the state medical service is obtained, on a contract involving the payment of forty million roubles annually, in districts in which the number of incop members is insufficient to warrant an independent medical service.

We see, in this reorganisation of the old kustar artels, an extraordinarily rapid development of what has again become, alongside the state and municipal factories, an important element in the industry of the USSR. It is one more example of the tendency to multiformity affording opportunity for ever-wider participation in the organised life of the community. The report of the State Planning Commission (Gosplan) in 1933 may rightly claim that " cooperative industry . . . in which the form of handicraft associations predominates . . . plays a great part in the industrial life of the country. It is in connection with state industry, and supplements it in a number of ways (supplies supplementary raw material, produces auxiliary materials, works up state raw materials and semi-finished goods, produces articles for the general market, etc.). At the same time the industrial cooperative industry comes forward as the special means for the socialist remoulding of the small home worker, and, on the basis of the cooperative organisation of production, draws him into the common socialist channel of industrial development." [1]

It is interesting to witness, in the Soviet Union, the successful adoption of a form of industrial organisation which has been extensively tried, during a whole century, in various capitalist countries, but seldom with any considerable or lasting success. Neither in Great Britain nor in France, neither in Germany nor in the United States, nor yet in any other country of advanced industrialism, have manufacturing associations of owner-producers, themselves jointly owning the actual product of their daily labour—that is to say, self-governing workshops—been able to make any considerable headway against systems of industrial production in which the working producers do not own the product of their labour, but are remunerated only by wages or salaries. Why is it different in the USSR ? We suggest that

---

[1] *Summary of Results of the First Five-Year Plan* (Gosplan, 1933, p. 61).

the answer is to be found partly in the different environment provided in a country from which the profit-making capitalist has been entirely eliminated ; and partly in the deliberate limitation and regulation of the sphere allotted to the cooperative associations.  It is noticeable that the incops of the USSR seldom or never compete in the market with the state trusts or municipal enterprises.  On the contrary, these latter are on the most friendly terms with the artels and incops, which are accorded a function of their own, duly recognised and specified in the General Plan, and are constantly being helped to fulfil it.  In other countries the associated workers find themselves ruthlessly competed with and undercut even to the point of extinction, by the mass-production of gigantic establishments eager to obtain a monopoly of the markets.  But experience shows that associations of producers in capitalist countries also succumb in another way.  Here and there, very exceptionally, usually by creating a speciality of their own, or attaching to themselves a special clientele, they have successfully withstood the warfare of their capitalist rivals, even to the point of sometimes making considerable incomes for the cooperating members.  These have then, almost invariably, sooner or later, limited their numbers, and shrunk into small partnerships, including shareholders who are not working members, and employing non-members at wages.  Tempted by what are, in effect, high profits, they eventually become indistinguishable from the capitalist profit-makers themselves.  In the Soviet Union this process of degeneration is watched and effectively prevented.  When an incop shows signs of closing its body of members to recruits from outside, it finds itself unostentatiously required to fill up vacancies so as at least to keep up its number.  When it becomes too prosperous, so that its members could share among themselves incomes markedly in excess of those secured by the trade unions for their own members in state industry, it is sharply reminded that this is against the law under which incops are formed.  The excess profits may be carried to a reserve fund, or added to the insurance fund, but they may not be shared among the members.  In most cases a new arrangement of prices takes place, either in the rates at which the incop buys its materials and components, or in the prices it obtains from the purchasers of its wares.  When a manufacturing association of producers obtains most of its materials from the Government, and sells much of its product either to some branch of the Government, or to one or other department of Centrosoyus, it is not difficult to prevent the annual shares of the members in their own products from rising substantially above the earnings of similar workers in the state factories or the consumers' cooperatives. Moreover, the members are required always to work at piece-work rates, as the basis of the advances that they receive in lieu of wages : and there is no provision allowing payment of interest or profit to non-workers. Thus protected and safeguarded, the manufacturing associations of owner-producers in the USSR do no harm to the collectivist organisations, in the interstices of which they live. On the contrary, by the positive addition that they make to the aggregate of commodities and services brought to market, they benefit the community as a whole. And they can add the further boon of an ever-widening variety in the supply of the commodities and services that they contribute. It is a net gain to associate for handicraft production during the winter, the members of one or more collective farms ; or the dock labourers of an ice-bound port. Nor are the incops confined to production by manual labour. There are incops of artistic workers of more than one kind, including painters and sculptors. Associations of writers are formed to do their book production and publishing. There seems no reason why this form of organisation should not afford a socially useful means of livelihood to members of the " deprived" categories, who are admitted as members if they are prepared to work loyally with their hands ; and who might, at their option, unite among themselves to form new incops to render some special service calling for individual taste or skill, or not yet performed by any state or municipal enterprise.[1]

## (*b*) THE COLLECTIVE FARM

It is with a sudden acceleration of " Bolshevik tempo " that we pass, in the survey of the organisation of man as a producer, from the associations of owner-producers in industry to associa-

---

[1] There is reason to believe that somewhere in the neighbourhood of 4000 or 5000 persons belonging to the " deprived " categories are to be found among the membership of the incops, though they have not as yet formed societies of their own. The " social structure " of the membership of incops making returns

tions of owner-producers in agriculture.[1]  In industry, as the reader will have realised, the new and predominant type is the trade union, including all kinds and grades of workers by hand or by brain.  In agriculture, though state farms, with the appropriate trade unions, are increasing in number and variety, it is the millions of individual owner-producers associated in collective farms that occupy the centre of the picture.  Moreover, whilst the development of the kustar artels into industrial cooperative societies (incops) has been pursued without serious controversy, and without a trace of civil disorder, the advent of the collective farm (kolkhos), as the pattern organisation for the vast hordes of peasant cultivators on one-sixth of the earth's surface, has been accompanied, not merely by heated controversy, both public and

on April 1, 1931 (these covering 719,000 members, or 45 per cent of the aggregate), was as under :

|  | City Incops, per cent | Village Incops, per cent |
| --- | --- | --- |
| Former workmen or landless peasants  .  . | 26·2 | 6·25 |
| Members of kolkhosi  .  .  .  .  . | 8·6 | 23·8 |
| Poor peasants  .  .  .  .  .  . | 12·7 | 23·95 |
| Middle peasants and kulaks not employing hired labour  .  .  .  .  .  . | 45·3 | 44·4 |
| Former employees  .  .  .  .  . | 5·4 | 0·6 |
| Former kulaks employing hired labour  .  . | 1·1 | 0·2 |
| Kulaks, traders, employers and " deprived " persons | 0·7 | 0·2 |
|  | 100·0 | 100·00 |

(See *Ten Years of Incops in the USSR* (in Russian), by V. Gnoussov and I. P. Chernischer, Moscow, 1932, p. 24.)

[1] The information available on agriculture in the USSR, even apart from that only in Russian, is as great in bulk as it is uneven in accuracy or relevance. The history and the geographical conditions of Russian agriculture are elaborately described in the erudite monograph by Vladimir P. Tomshenko, *Agricultural Russia and the Wheat Problem* (Leland Stanford University, California, 1932, p. 571); also in *Rural Russia under the Old Régime*, by C. G. Robinson, 1932 ; *The Russian Peasantry*, by Stepniak, 1895, should also be read in this connection. The problem and its difficulties are well stated in the chapter " Russian Agriculture ", by R. G. Tugwell, in *Soviet Russia in the Second Decade*, edited by Stuart Chase, R. Dunn, and R. G. Tugwell (New York, 1928). *Russia, Market or Menace*, by Thomas D. Campbell, 1932, gives a valuable report by an American expert on large-scale wheat-farming. Upon the peasant psychology, the four books by Maurice Hindus, *Broken Earth, Humanity Uprooted, Red Bread* and *The Great Offensive*, are invaluable. See also *The Russian Land*, by A. R. Williams (New York, 1928) ; *Collective Farm " Trud "*, a moving recital by a peasant woman, Eudoxia Pazukhina, of how she started a collective farm (London, 64 pp.); *Red Villages*, by Y. A. Yakovlev (London, 1930, 128 pp.) ; and *Collective Farming in 1932* (Moscow, 1932), by the same.

private, but also, among the peasants themselves, by widespread sullen resentment, and not a little recalcitrance, which cannot be assumed to have yet (1934) been completely overcome. Indeed, it might almost be said that the partially enforced collectivisation and mechanisation of agriculture during 1929–1934 represents the final stage, not yet completed, of the rural uprisings of 1917, that effectually liquidated the private landlord.[1] The question inevitably arises, why did the Soviet Government of 1928, in face of prolonged and heated discussion within the Communist Party itself, attempt so drastic, and as it seemed, so hazardous an experiment. The answer is that the situation was such as, within their framework of reference, to leave no other course open to them.

Stalin's own account of the policy from 1929 to 1931, together with the " model statutes ", is given in *Building Collective Farms*, by J. Stalin (New York, 1931, 184 pp.). A valuable description of the internal organisation of the collective farms is given (in Russian) in *Distribution of Income in the kolkhosi*, by N. Tataev (Partizdat, Moscow, 1932). A well-informed and generally adverse criticism will be found in the chapter on " Agriculture " by Professor Dr. Otto Auhagen, in *Soviet Economics*, edited by Dr. Gerhart Dobbert (1933). For recent hasty glimpses over a wide area, see the chapter on agriculture by John Morgan in *Twelve Studies in Soviet Russia*, edited by M. I. Cole (1933) ; *From Peasant to Collective Farmer*, by N. Buchwald and R. Bishop (1933) ; the five articles contributed to the *Manchester Guardian*, October 17–21, 1933, by its then correspondent W. H. Chamberlin; and *Reise durch 100 Kollectivwirtschaften*, by L. F. Boross (Moscow, 1934, 190 pp.). The publications in German are voluminous, and apparently of greater *expertise* and authority, if also more critical, than those in English. Those of Dr. Otto Schiller, the agricultural expert attached to the German embassy in Moscow, are published in *Berichte uber Landwirtschaft*, the latest being (Sondesheft 79) *Die Krise der sozialistischen Landwirtschaft in der Sowjetunion* (1933, 82 pp.). See also his previous articles, " Die Kollectivisirung der russischen Landwirtschaft " and " Die landwirtschaftliche Problems der Sowjetunion, 1931–1932 ". These lengthy and valuable reports, although very critical, do not, in our opinion, support the adverse conclusions of the pamphlet entitled *Collectivised Agriculture in the Soviet Union*, published by the School of Slavonic Studies (London, 1934, 32 pp.). More impartial, and therefore specially cogent, is the able historical summary contained in two issues of the *Political Science Quarterly* (New York, January and June 1934), entitled " Collectivisation of Agriculture in the Soviet Union ", by W. Ladejinsky. Other recent works are *Die Getreidewirtschaft in den Trockengebieten Ruslands*, by B. Brutzkus, W. von Poletika and A. Von Ugrimoff ; and *Das Agrarexperiment Sowjetrusslands*, by Dr. H. Zorner. *Die Bilanz des ersten Funfjahrplanes der Sowjetwirtschaft*, by Dr. Otto Auhagen (Breslau, 1933, 75 pp.) gives great place to agriculture.

[1] Three substantial books recently published should be added, especially as each author takes a different view of what one of them has termed the " first revolution in agriculture anywhere since the bourgeois industrial revolution made the serf a peasant and a farmer ". These are *Russia's Iron Age*, by W. H. Chamberlin, 1935 ; *Soviet Journey*, by Louis Fischer, 1935 ; and *Economic Planning in Soviet Russia*, by Boris Brutzkus.

*The Unproductive Peasant*

Candid observers of the Russian mujik during the past half-century, whilst differing in their estimates of his " soulful " qualities, agree in the testimony that as an agriculturist he has hitherto been, in the mass, either per head or per hectare, the least productive of all the peasantries of Europe. Whether as the result of nature or of nurture ; of climate or of race ; of centuries of oppression and illiteracy ; or of generations of virtual slavery and peonage ; or of a religion that imposed no code of conduct and amounted to little more than propitiatory rites, the typical mujik—when not under coercion by landlord, tax-collector, usurer or employer—failed to grow enough food, taking bad years with good, even to maintain his own family in full health and strength.[1] And the " bad years " recurred with fatal frequency. During the first half of the nineteenth century, from 1800 to 1854, there are reported to have been no fewer than 35 years in which there was a more or less serious failure of the crops. In the 20 years from 1891 to 1910, there were only 4 good harvests, with 13 poor harvests, and 3 famine years. During the first decade of Soviet rule, 1918–1927, there were only 3 years of good harvests, 5 years of poor harvests and 2 famine years. This habitual unproductivity of the Russian peasant was masked, to the uncritical observer, by the fact that, so long as the landlord was in a position to exact his rent, the tax collector his taxes and the village usurer and employer the profits that they could squeeze out of their impecunious neighbours, some grain was always sent to market, even if the village starved. Moreover, a considerable proportion of the aggregate area, was, down to 1917, cultivated in the large farms of the improving landowners, and in the smaller but often substantial holdings of the kulaks, who

---

[1] Let us, in fairness, briefly recapitulate some of his difficulties. His holding was, on the average, minute in area ; and in the repeated redistributions, actually becoming smaller year after year. It was usually made up of numerous small strips, often miles apart, which had to be cultivated according to the common practice of his neighbours. He had hardly ever any adequate equipment (one-third of all the holdings had no iron plough, but only a wooden stick ; at least one-fourth had no horse or ox with which to plough). Manuring of any kind was at a minimum, and artificial fertilisers were scarcely known. There was next to no rotation of crops. The minimum of labour was spent on weeding. Reaping was by the sickle, and thrashing by the flail ; marketing practically limited to the passing visits of the grain dealer. To sum up, as compared with the peasant of France or Flanders, South Germany or the Tyrol, the majority of the Russian mujiks were, in 1900, still in the fourteenth century.

had " added field to field " by their oppression of the poorer villagers. Thus, so long as the landowners remained, and the tax collector used force, and the kulaks' characteristic " thrift " was unrestrained, there could be, in all but the worst years, not only an adequate supply for the relatively small city populations but also, occasionally, a substantial export. Meanwhile the poor peasant was being increasingly " driven off the land " ; and in bad years—during the past century, every other year—the infants, the aged, and often the nursing mothers were dying by thousands of inanition, typhus or enteric. We shall describe in a subsequent chapter [1] how frequently, in the present century, the peasants rose against their most obvious oppressors, the landlords ; whose mansions they burnt, whose stores they plundered and whose land they divided. This almost continuous *jacquerie* was not the work of the Bolsheviks, who were not yet in office. Nor did it result in any substantial or lasting improvement in the condition of the mass of poor peasants, or in any increase of marketable foodstuffs. It did not even enlarge the area of the average peasant holding, nor give him an iron plough, nor any horse or ox to draw the plough. In 1917, with the swarming back of the men from the armies, and the workers from the factories, all demanding shares of the land of the village to which they belonged, the redistribution of the large estates merely increased the number of starveling peasant holdings from some fourteen or fifteen millions in 1916 to some twenty-four or twenty-five millions in 1926.

### The Crisis in Foodstuffs

Ever since the Bolshevik seizure of power, the maintenance of the food supply for the population of the cities and the Red Armies had been a constant preoccupation of the Soviet Government. This perpetual anxiety as to how the people could be saved from hunger, to which the British and French Governments in times of peace never gave a thought, was not directly due to any socialist measure taken by Lenin and his colleagues. On the contrary, it sprang from their inability, during a whole decade, to deal with the extreme individualism and primitive conditions of Russian peasant agriculture. During the years of War Communism, all the grain that could be discovered was

[1] See Part II. Ch. VII., "The Liquidation of the Landlord and Capitalist ".

simply taken by force for the feeding of the Red and the White Armies, which naturally led to the peasants limiting their cultivation either to what sufficed to feed themselves or what they saw their way to hide. The situation became desperate enough to drive Lenin to the New Economic Policy of 1921, under which a revival of limited capitalist enterprise, with market prices left free to be settled by "supply and demand", encouraged the kulaks to bring out their hidden grain in exchange for the commodities that they desired. It could not, however, avert the serious famine of 1921, which was the result, not merely of adverse weather conditions, but also of the widespread desolation wrought by the Civil Wars. The subsequent opening of the "scissors" —the disparity between the exchange values of primary products and manufactured articles—had grave consequences on the peasant mentality.[1] The great bulk of the peasantry, whether poor or relatively prosperous, had supported the Bolsheviks in overthrowing the Provisional Government, because this collapse of authority enabled the peasants, including the kulaks, to drive away the landowners and share their estates among the villagers. On similar grounds the peasantry had everywhere eventually supported the Red Armies against the Whites, because these latter threatened to reinstate the landlords in their possessions. But once that danger had disappeared, the peasants, poor, middle or kulak, now imagining themselves proprietors of the land they tilled, demurred to parting with their produce to feed the cities, even at free market prices, so long as these prices did not enable them to obtain the manufactured commodities they desired at something like the old customary rates. The peasants, moreover, even the very considerable proportion of them to whom the revolution had given land for nothing, resented, like peasant proprietors all over the world, the levying on them of any direct taxes. Nor did the marked development, in the village, of the

---

[1] The obstinate divergence between the general level of exchange values for household commodities and that of exchange values for grain—the persistent wide opening of the "scissors"—was doubtless aggravated by the determination of the Soviet Government, for good and sufficient reasons of general policy, to press on the erection of new factories and the increase of machinery, rather than the immediate production of additional clothing and household necessaries. But it must be remembered that the phenomenon of markedly higher exchange values for manufactures than for primary products has been, since 1921, common to all the world, irrespective of communist or any other policy, or even of currency systems or fiscal devices.

characteristic peasant vices of greed and cunning, varied by outbursts of drunkenness and recurrent periods of sloth, produce
anything like general prosperity, nor even any common improvement in agricultural methods. What became apparent was that
the peasant, formerly servile, was becoming rebellious.

Mr. Maurice Hindus, who was born and bred in the Russian
village, vividly describes his own astonishment at discovering, in
a village meeting, the typically rebellious mujik.[1] The chairman
of the village soviet had been speaking to an audience which gave
him rapt attention. " Of a sudden, somewhere from the fringe
of the audience, there boomed out a deep voice as startling as a
thunderclap. ' Words, words, words—only words ! ' It was an
elderly mujik speaking. Barefooted, bareheaded, with a flowing
beard and in a soiled linen shirt, he raised his arms high as though
to quiet the murmur of protest that his interruption had called
forth. ' All for the benefit of the foreign visitor ', he drawled
mockingly. ' Showing off. Look at me, *inostranetz*,' and he
pounded his fists on his bulging chest. ' I am the truth, the sole
putrid truth in this beastly land.' Denunciations hailed on him
from every direction, but he paid no heed to them. ' I am sixty-
five years of age. The soviets did give me land, but what shall
I do with it ? Can I eat land ? I have no horse and what can
I do on land without a horse ? ' The chairman himself, and
several of his associates, sought to quiet him, but he raced on
unperturbed. ' In the old days,' he shouted, raising his voice
above the tumult that had broken out, ' we had a Tsar, landlords,
exploiters, and yet I could always buy a horse if mine died, and
boots too, and all the calico I could pay for. And now there is no
Tsar, there are no landlords, there are no exploiters, and yet—
no horse, no boots, no calico, nothing. Remember that, stranger.'

" I stared at the mujik, at the disturbed chairman, at the
heaving mob. It seemed so unbelievable that anyone in Russia
would dare to lift his voice in such haughty disdain, in such
flaming defiance of the proletarian dictators—least of all a mujik.
I remembered him so well in the old days, this lowly miserable
creature of a mujik. How meek he seemed in the presence of
officials. How humbly he would bow before a man in a uniform,
or sometimes only in city clothes. With what alacrity he would
remove his hat before anyone he deemed his superior. Shy he

[1] *Humanity Uprooted*, by Maurice Hindus, 1929, p. 149.

was, this unwashed, hairy, big-boned mujik, and cautious in his choice of words, in voicing a grievance, lest he give offence to the man representing *praviletstvo*—government—and when he noted in the expression of the official's face a sign of annoyance or disapproval he shrank back, apologized, begged for forgiveness.  In his heart he may have cherished only hate for the official, but when face to face with him he was all meekness and docility.  But now in this desolate village, I witnessed the extraordinary spectacle of a bedraggled, mud-bespattered mujik, actually denouncing and haranguing officials—all government—with no more restraint or compunction than as if he were scolding his son or whipping his horse.  It seemed so terribly unreal, so unbelievably heroic ! " This mujik proved to be typical of many in the succeeding years.

Matters were made not better but worse by the growing prosperity in the village of the more thrifty and more industrious, but also the more cunning and more oppressive of the agriculturists, to whom the opprobrious name of kulak (fist) was applied. The inequality of conditions, to which Stolypin's reforms had given an impetus, was not removed by the multiplication of starveling holdings and not lessened by the monopoly of resources by a minority of hated usurers.  Though the kulaks might be climbing steadily into capitalists, the army of the landless was rapidly growing.  What was, however, most serious of all was that the national food supply was rendered thereby not less but even more precarious than before.  Whenever the harvest was relatively good, practically all the peasants consumed a larger and took to market a smaller proportion of the yield.  In years of threatened scarcity, the kulaks had the cities at their mercy.

### Experimental Improvements

It would, however, be unfair to the mujik, and an inaccurate description of the dilemma of the statesman, to ignore the various experiments in agricultural organisation which had been, in one locality or another, pretty extensively tried between 1917 and 1927.  In the first place, there had been, among the more prosperous of the peasants, a great extension of agricultural cooperation of the ordinary type.  Voluntary cooperative associations of independent peasants abounded in 1927, to the aggregate number, it was reported, of some 80,000 societies for several dozens of different purposes with literally millions of members.[1] This once powerful voluntary movement has now almost entirely ceased to exist. Its place has been taken by the so-called kolkhosi, or collective farms, in which the members united either the whole or some of their resources in capital and labour, in order to share among themselves as copartners an increasing output. Of these collective farms, of which some thousands had spontaneously come into existence between 1918 and 1927, with varying degrees of success, we may distinguish three types. There was, first, the association of members merely to the extent of combining their labour forces for joint tillage ; for working in company in ploughing, sowing and harvesting a particular crop upon their several holdings of land, and sharing the proceeds among themselves. A second type, usually styled an artel,[2] was that of the association in which were united not merely the labour force but also the ownership of the capital employed (the landholdings, the implements and the farm buildings), but only in so far as concerned the production of cereals or other specified crops, sometimes also with a common flock or herd ; leaving in individual occupation and management the dwelling-houses, the garden grounds, the poultry, the bees, the domestic pig and sometimes a cow, for the particular care and profit of the several families. The third type was called the commune. In this, not only the fields and buildings connected with cereal cultivation,

[1] This agricultural progress had started, under Stolypin's reforms, even before the Revolution ; but after 1917 it was greatly extended. By 1927 there were, in the USSR, no fewer than 80,000 agricultural cooperative societies, of nearly fifty different kinds—credit societies, marketing societies, creameries, societies for purchasing machinery and forty different kinds of specialist societies for developing particular crops or animal products. These 80,000 entirely voluntary cooperative societies numbered, in the aggregate, ten million members (many in more than one society). There were nearly 10,000 kolkhosi of the joint labour type, some 10,000 of the artel type, and more than a thousand communes. But all this enterprise, much of which is now superseded by the systematic organisation of sovkhosi and kolkhosi, left two-thirds of the peasant population almost untouched.

[2] The form of the artel was used for cooperative associations in agriculture (apparently for the first time) towards the end of 1895 by N. V. Levitski, in the province of Kherson, afterwards spreading to Simbirsk, and some parts of Siberia, not in all cases extending to joint cultivation, and mainly for joint purchase of implements and other necessaries, and generally the use of cooperative credit (*La Russie à la fin du 19e siècle*, par M. W. de Kovalesky, 1900, p. 656). In its simplest form, the association for joint tillage, it reminds the student of the voluntary working " bee " of the American pioneer farmers, except that the latter deals successively with individual holdings, instead of simultaneously with all of them.

but also all the other rural enterprises, were owned and administered in common, and the whole proceeds were shared, together with the dwelling-houses and all the improvements and amenities for common enjoyment that the settlement could afford. Some of these communes, in various parts of the USSR, had already proved remarkably successful over periods of several years, reaching a level of productiveness, and sometimes of amenity, amounting to what the western world would deem civilisation, superior not only to the average of the peasantry, but even to most of the collective farms of the artel type. It appeared, however, that the commune, to be permanently successful, required in its necessarily voluntary membership a considerably higher level of personal character, and also of managerial capacity, than other forms of village settlement, a level which could not reasonably be expected to become universal, or even to be commonly attained, within a generation. If it was necessary to obtain, over the USSR as a whole, any considerable increase in the quantity of marketable grain even in good years—still more, if it was imperative, in the interest of the whole community, to ensure that there should be no actual shortage in the bad years that were certain to come—it did not seem possible for the government to sit down with folded hands to await the slow and gradual extension, to the entire peasantry, either of agricultural cooperative societies or of collective farming of any type whatsoever. Some way of quickening the tempo and enlarging the area of agricultural improvement had to be found. On the other hand, the state farms (sovkhosi), which the Soviet Government had managed to retain in its own administration, and had been for nearly a decade struggling to cultivate exclusively with wage-labourers, had so far failed to produce, after their staffs had been fed, even in good years, more than a small net addition to the aggregate of marketable grain. It seemed impossible, in the near future, to transform these " grain factories " into an effective and, in bad years, a certain source of the nation's food supply.

### The Prolonged Discussion as to Policy

The problem for the Soviet statesmen was desperately difficult. It may surprise those who assume the existence of a dictatorship, and deny that of free speech, to learn that, for nearly three years (1925–1928), the issue was the subject of heated public controversy in articles, pamphlets and books, widely circulating in large editions, as well as prolonged committee debate in the Central Executive Council and within the Communist Party. There were those (such as Trotsky) who declared that the growth and development of the kulaks (here meaning merely the more prosperous minority of peasants, who employed wage labour) was, by rebuilding capitalism, endangering, if not destroying, the whole achievement of the Revolution. This faction demanded the most drastic measures for the suppression of the kulaks, but failed to make clear by what means it proposed to increase the agricultural output of the minute holdings of the majority of poor peasants otherwise than by the slow spread of one or other form of voluntary cooperation. There were those who laid more stress on the multiplication of state farms (sovkhosi), employing labourers at wages as in the state factories, which, it was said, would prove the only efficient and reliable source of the foodstuffs required. But no one showed how to develop state farms at a rate that would avert the peril of mass starvation. Accordingly, those for whom Bukharin and even A. I. Rykov were for some time the spokesmen urged that, as the state farms would take a long time to develop to the extent required, and as it was hopeless to look for agricultural improvements to the great mass of tiny holdings, it was only the more energetic and enlightened of the peasants, who had already obtained the use of relatively considerable holdings of land, with superior equipment and improved agricultural systems, who could promptly make any appreciable contribution to the increased aggregate production that was immediately needed. These, therefore, it was said, though often oppressive kulaks, should be encouraged and assisted to enlarge their enterprises, as the only available means of national safety, even at the price of temporarily reducing many more of the poor peasants to the position of wage labourers.[1]

### The Policy of Universal Collectivisation

In the end, the Central Executive Committee of the All-Union Congress of Soviets (TSIK), in conjunction with the Central

[1] It is interesting to notice that Stepniak (*The Russian Peasantry*, 1895), though hating the kulak, could at that date see no better prospect for the peasantry as a whole than being driven off the land by the kulak class, in order

Committee of the Communist Party, hammered out during 1927 an alternative policy, for which, we think, Stalin deserves most of the credit. As proclaimed by him in 1928, the decision of these committees prescribed, for immediate execution, nothing less than a second agrarian revolution, in which the whole of the individual peasantry would be transformed within less than a decade. This was to unite (a) the utmost rapid development of the state farms (sovkhosi) with (b) a far more extensive gradual combination of the poorer and middle peasants, under government persuasion, in collective farms (kolkhosi) of the artel type ; [1] in both cases in order that (c) agriculture might be universally mechanised by tractors and harvesting combines to be supplied by the government ; whilst (d) the output upon the enlarged farms could be further increased by rotation of crops and the use of fertilisers. Practically the whole of the individual peasantry was to disappear, and to become workers on relatively large amalgamated areas, either as cooperative owner-producers (in kolkhosi) or (in sovkhosi) as farm labourers at wages. Only in this way, it was suggested, could the twenty-five or twenty-six million tiny holdings be merged within the necessary time into a few hundred thousand relatively large farms on which the use of machinery would be practicable. Only in this way, it was urged, could the whole peasant population, and not merely an exceptional minority, be raised to the comprehension of improved systems of agriculture. Meanwhile, the kulak was to be taxed more severely, denied the use of the new government tractors, and harried in every possible way, with a view to his complete

that, in some distant future, they might, as landless proletarians, be inspired to revolution. This, too (though without contemplation of even a future revolution), was virtually the line of Stolypin's great agricultural reforms of 1907-1910.

[1] See, for instance, the explicit descriptions of the three types in "Dizzy with Success", reprinted from *Pravda* of March 2, 1930, in *Leninism*, by Joseph Stalin, vol. ii. pp. 283-284, 1933. " Is it the Associations for Joint Tillage ? No, it is not. The Associations for Joint Tillage, in which the means of production are not yet socialised, represent a stage in the collective farm movement which has already been passed. Is it, perhaps, the agricultural communes ? No, it is not the agricultural communes. The communes are still isolated phenomena in the collective farm movement. The conditions are not yet ripe for the agricultural communes as the predominant form, in which not only all production but distribution also is socialised. The key link in the collective farm movement, its predominant form at the present moment, which we have now to seize hold of, is the agricultural artel. . . . It is on this that the ' Model Statute ' for collective farms—the final text of which is being published to-day —is based."

" liquidation " as a class, within a few years. It is this policy which has, since 1928, covered all parts of the USSR with collective farms, formed by peasants who have, nominally voluntarily, but often after intense propaganda, and at times under considerable local pressure, merged their little holdings in larger units, belonging to themselves jointly instead of to themselves individually. In this way, there has been created, for agriculture (at the cost of driving out the universally hated kulaks and the recalcitrant Ukrainians or Don Cossacks by tens or even hundreds of thousands of families), something analogous to the kustar artels, or cooperative societies of owner-producers in manufacturing industry, that we described in the preceding section.

We may pause to consider the magnitude and the difficulty of this transformation. To convert, within less than a decade, even two-thirds of a population of 120 millions of peasantry steeped in ignorance, suspicion and obstinacy, accustomed for centuries to individual cultivation of the little holdings that they now deemed their own, with all the cunning and greed that such a system develops, into public-spirited cooperators working upon a prescribed plan for a common product to be equitably shared among themselves, might well have been deemed hopelessly impracticable. At least, it would have been said, by anyone acquainted with a peasant population, that such a transformation —the " real agrarian revolution in Russia " [1]—must require a whole generation of persistent effort.

### The Struggle for Efficiency in the Kolkhosi

The past five years have, indeed, seen a tireless struggle in nearly all parts of the USSR, to induce the gigantic membership

[1] " The truth is, the real agrarian revolution in Russia occurred towards the end of 1927, as an outcome of the enactments of the 15th Congress of the Party " (" Agriculture ", by Professor Dr. Otto Auhagen, in *Soviet Economics*, edited by Dr. Gerhard Dobbert (1933), p. 212).

The 15th Party Congress did, in fact, adopt a report from the Central Committee containing the following passage : " Where is the way out ? The way out is in the passing of small disintegrated peasant farms into large-scale amalgamated farms, on the basis of communal tillage of the soil ; in passing to collective tillage of the soil on the basis of the new higher technique. The way out is to amalgamate the petty and tiny peasant farms gradually but steadily, not by means of pressure but by example and conviction, into large-scale undertakings on the basis of communal, fraternal collective tillage of the soil, supplying agricultural machinery and tractors, applying scientific methods for the intensification of agriculture. *There is no other way out.*"

of the kolkhosi, which had often been achieved only by considerable governmental pressure, to remain loyally in membership, and to work their cooperative enterprises with honesty and adequate efficiency. At first, by widespread propaganda and reckless promises of tractors and harvesters, improved ploughs and selected seeds, the process of conversion was altogether too quick. Whilst only 20 per cent of collectivisation had been contemplated during the first year, something like 55 per cent was attained. For so rapid a transformation the Soviet Government was not prepared ; and more than half the new collective farms could not be given the aid of tractors. The zeal of the government agents had led, on the one hand, to something very like compulsion of the hesitating peasants to join the collectives ; and, on the other, to unduly large and repeated levies upon such of them as were successful, representing what was claimed to be the government share of the harvest. The middle peasants, feeling themselves condemned to a merger that was repugnant to them, in many instances slaughtered, in 1929–1930, their cattle and horses, sheep and pigs, rather than bring them into the common stock.[1] So widespread was the outcry that the central

[1] The magnitude of this holocaust of live stock is seldom realised. The following table shows that, in one year, 1929–1930, more than sixty million animals were slaughtered, being one-quarter of the whole ; and in the course of the next three years, 1931–1933, over eighty millions more. In 1933, the total live stock was less than four-ninths of the total in 1929.

LIVE STOCK IN THE USSR

(In millions of head)

|  | 1916 | 1929 | 1930 | 1931 | 1932 | 1933 |
|---|---|---|---|---|---|---|
| Horses . . . | 35·1 | 34·0 | 30·2 | 26·2 | 19·6 | 16·6 |
| Large-horned cattle . | 58·9 | 68·1 | 52·5 | 47·9 | 40·7 | 38·6 |
| Sheep and goats . . | 115·2 | 147·2 | 108·8 | 77·7 | 52·1 | 50·6 |
| Pigs . . . . | 20·3 | 20·9 | 13·6 | 14·4 | 11·6 | 12·2 |
|  | 229·5 | 270·2 | 205·1 | 166·2 | 124·0 | 118·0 |

(Stalin's report on the work of the Central Committee of the Communist Party in the Soviet Union, in *Proceedings* (in Russian) *of the Seventeenth Congress of the CPSU*, 1933, p. 30.) See, in confirmation, *Die Krise der sozialistischen Landwirtschaft in der Sowjetunion*, by Dr. Otto Schiller, 1933 ; and *Economic Planning in Soviet Russia*, by Boris Brutzkus, 1935, p. 211.

This colossal slaughter, repeated in successive years, has been subsequently excused as having been due to lack of wheat or oats for fodder, owing to government exactions. But why did they slaughter sheep and pigs, and even goats ?

committees were driven to instruct Stalin to issue his manifesto entitled "Dizzy with Success", in which the zeal of the government agents was rebuked ; the voluntary character of membership of the collectives was emphasised ; permission to withdraw was conceded ; and proper consideration of the varying stock brought in by different members was insisted on. Nevertheless the animals continued to be slaughtered and the total membership to fall off. Partial failures of crop in 1931 and 1932 deepened the discontent. This was especially the case in some parts of the once-favoured community of the Don Cossacks, where the loss of the special privileges, in which a large proportion of the population had shared under the Tsars, was still resented. The recalcitrance took on the gravest aspect in some parts of the Ukraine, where the aspirations of some of the intelligentsia after national independence had been kept alive by continuous incitement and occasional secret emissaries from the Ukrainian exiles at Paris and Prague. The whole organised movement for an independent Ukraine was, we are told, from 1928 onwards, directed towards stimulating the peasants to resist collectivisation. The forms taken by this resistance, it has been frankly stated by one of the Ukrainian émigrés, " have greatly varied. At first there were mass disturbances in the kolkhosi, or else the communist officials and their agents were killed ; but later a system of passive resistance was favoured, which *aimed at the systematic frustration of the Bolshevik plans for the sowing and gathering of the harvest.* The peasants and workers, seeing the ruthless export by their Bolshevik masters of all food produce, began to take steps to save themselves from starvation in the winter time, and to grasp at any means of fighting against the hated foreign rule. This is the main reason for the wholesale hoarding of grain and the thefts from the fields—offences which, if detected, are punishable by death. The peasants are passive resisters everywhere ; but in Ukrainia the resistance has assumed the character of a national struggle. *The opposition of the Ukrainian population caused the failure of the grain-storing plan of 1931, and still more so, that of 1932.* The catastrophe of 1932 was the hardest blow that Soviet Ukraine had to face since the famine of 1921-1922. The autumn and spring sowing campaigns both failed. Whole tracts were left unsown. In addition, when the crop was being gathered last year, it happened that, in many areas, especially in the south, 20, 40 and even 50 per cent was left in the fields, and was either not collected at all or was ruined in the threshing." [1]

Towards the close of 1932, when the extent of this continuous deliberate sabotage had become manifest; when the too persistent rains of the summer had ruined the prospect of an abundant harvest, even where the agricultural operations had been loyally carried out; and when it was realised that the reserves had been specially depleted owing to the measures taken in order to stave off a Japanese invasion, the food situation again looked desperate. There is reason to believe that those in authority did not know where to turn. Finally, in January 1933, Stalin announced an administrative campaign, designed to reach the nerve-centres of every one of the 225,000 collective farms; a campaign which for boldness of conception and vigour in execution, as well as in the magnitude of its operations, appears to us unparalleled in the peace-time annals of any government. The desperate situation had to be saved. And, aided fortuitously by good crops in 1933 and 1934, it was saved. How this was accomplished will appear in the following pages.

### The Magnitude of the Problem

We must first emphasise the magnitude of the problem. The rush of some seventy million people into the collective farms had not been accompanied by any sufficient provision of agricultural machinery, seeds and fertilisers even for those who were loyal; and certainly not by any adequate means of supervision and control of such of them as might be disloyal or recalcitrant. The total number of collective farms of all types in the USSR, which was less than 20,000 in 1927, had grown by the first quarter of 1933 to 211,000, actually cultivating about 85 million hectares, or an average for each enterprise of over 400 hectares (1000 acres).[2] The total number of households is variously stated as

---

[1] "Ukrainia under Bolshevist Rule," by Isaac Mazepa, in *Slavonic Review*, January 1934, pp. 342-343. The writer was Premier of the Ukrainian Republic of 1919, and is now professor at the Ukrainian Agricultural College at Prague.

[2] The Moscow Narodny Bank's *Monthly Review* (vol. vi., April 1933, No. 4) gives a convenient summary of the statistics showing the number of peasant households united in collective farms and the percentage they form of the total

between 14 and 15 millions, making a population of some 70
millions, and giving an average for each collective farm of
between 65 and 70 households. We may contrast these statistics
of collective farms with those of the village soviets (selosoviets).
The number of village soviets in the USSR is about 70,000,
governing some 600,000 villages and hamlets—thus there are,
on an average, three collective farms in the area of each village
soviet. But as in some districts the collective farms are still
scanty, the average per village soviet in the rest of the USSR
must be much higher than three; and as some of the areas of
the village soviets have more than ten times the population of
others, there must be areas under a single village soviet which
each contain six or even a dozen collective farms. Collective
farming " is most complete in the rich grain districts of southern
and south eastern Russia, and least advanced in the northern
provinces, with their poorer soil, and in some of the autonomous
republics inhabited by non-Russian nationalities ".

households in each of the principal agricultural areas in the USSR, in the first
quarter of 1933 :

| Area | No. of Peasant Households | Percentage of Total |
|---|---|---|
| *Producing areas* (areas which produce a surplus over their own requirements) : | | |
| Ukraine . . . . . | 3,100,000 | 70 |
| Northern Caucasus . . . | 960,000 | 70 |
| Lower Volga . . . . | 660,000 | 80 |
| Central Volga . . . . | 930,000 | 78 |
| Urals . . . . . | 700,000 | 68 |
| Western Siberia . . . . | 750,000 | 63 |
| Central Black Soil Region . . | 1,300,000 | 68 |
| Bashkiria . . . . . | 350,000 | 68 |
| Crimea . . . . . | 65,000 | 80 |
| | | |
| *Consuming areas* (areas which do not produce enough for their own requirements) : | | |
| Moscow Province . . . | 650,000 | 55 |
| Western Provinces . . . | 530,000 | 47 |
| Gorky (Nizhni-Novgorod) . . | 600,000 | 45 |
| White Russian Republic . . | 330,000 | 45 |

" The average cultivated area per collective farm is over 400 hectares,
which compares favourably with that of well-to-do peasants who, in the past,
used to cultivate from 15 to 20 hectares per household. The total number of
collective farms now exceeds 211,000."

*The State Machinery for the Control of the Collective Farms*

(a) The New People's Commissar

The new policy of universal collectivisation involved a far-reaching reorganisation of the machinery of government.[1] The first step was the establishment of federal control. Hitherto agriculture had been a subject retained by the several Union or constituent republics, in each of which (and also in the autonomous republics) there had been, since 1923, a People's Commissar of Agriculture, responsible only to his own Sovnarkom (cabinet of ministers) and central executive committee. There were now appointed by the USSR Government two new People's Commissars to deal with agriculture throughout the whole Union. One of these, the People's Commissar for state farms (sovkhosi), took complete command of these wherever they were or might hereafter be established. The other, the People's Commissar for Agriculture, was to deal both with the collective farms (kolkhosi) of all types, and with the still surviving individual peasantry. The existing People's Commissars of Agriculture in the several constituent or autonomous republics were not removed, nor were their offices abolished. What happened was that, at one fell swoop, the whole score of them were stripped of a large part of their autonomy ; passing suddenly from governing, as they chose, " non-unified " departments (like that of health), which were responsible solely to themselves, to presiding over " unified " departments (like that of finance), in which they had to follow the plans and execute all the orders received from the USSR Peoples' Commissar, and in which their local staffs were required to render loyal service both to the local People's Commissar, and also to his superior, the USSR People's Commissar.

---

[1] This " radical change in agricultural administration " was described by Kalinin at the Third Session of the Central Executive Committee of the USSR (TSIK) in January 1933. " Formerly ", he said, " we had only the national People's Commissariats [for agriculture, in each of the seven Constituent Republics], which were each adapted to the local peculiarities of a scattered rural economy which they assisted to improve. Everything was reversed with collectivisation [in collective and state farms], which raised the last layers of rural backwardness with the strengthening of agriculture and the coming of tractors and combines. The old [and during the Revolution one year counts as ten] organisation structure had outlived its usefulness. The production of agricultural goods was rapidly mechanised, and this required more centralised direction on an All-Union scale " (*Moscow Daily News*, January 26, 1933).

### (b) The New Agricultural Departments

In each of the constituent republics, there had existed a Land Department, descended from the various Land Committees which were supposed to direct the division among the peasantry of the land of the monasteries and the Tsar's family, and those estates from which the landlords had been expropriated. These offices had become somnolent with the completion of the division, and actually fulfilled few functions. They were now reorganised into Agricultural Departments, having in charge the supervision alike of the independent peasantry and of the rapidly growing kolkhosi of various types. These departments had much to do with the adjustment of boundaries of the several kilkhosi, and with the settlement of disputes. Their whole work was brought under the supervision and the orders primarily of the People's Commissar of Agriculture of the republic ; but with the obligation of loyally carrying out any commands and instructions of the USSR People's Commissar.

In the autonomous republics, as in the oblasts or krais of the RSFSR and the Ukraine, there are also Agricultural Departments subordinate to those of the several constituent republics. In the case, however, of the very extensive oblasts or krais of the RSFSR, such as those of East and West Siberia and the Urals, and in the case of the larger among the autonomous republics, it became the practice for their Agricultural Departments to be in direct communication with the USSR People's Commissar of Agriculture at Moscow, where there had been a special kolkhos centre, obtaining all statistical and other information about the kolkhosi throughout the whole USSR. This kolkhos centre became a part of the new USSR Commissariat of Agriculture.

Beneath the oblast or krai, or autonomous republic, there was also a Land Department for each rayon. These had apparently wholly gone to sleep, to be rudely stirred by Kaganovich at the Seventeenth Party Congress. " Our rayon Land Departments ", he said, " are in a state of neglect, they are in an interregnum as it were, they do not seem to be able to grasp what their functions are. Very often the planning work of the rayon Land Department resolves itself into their mechanically distributing the production quotas among the collective farms without taking into account their traction facilities, their labour power, and their economic possibilities. The rayon Land Departments must be organised in such a way that they may know the situation in every collective farm." [1]

### (c) Supervision by the Village Soviets

Then the village soviets (selosoviets) were made to realise that it was an important part of their duty to watch the administration of all the collective farms within their several areas, so as to prevent them from going so far wrong as to threaten a failure of supply. It was pointed out that the kolkhos, even more than the individual peasant, owed a positive duty to the state, in the form of the utmost production of foodstuffs on the nationalised land that had been entrusted in usufruct to each little community ; and that the performance of this duty had to be enforced. The president of each village soviet was reminded that he was personally responsible for the proper conduct of each collective farm within the area under his charge, so far at least as using all his personal influence was concerned, with instructions to report without delay when he perceived anything going wrong.

### *The Soviet Hierarchy grips the Collective Farm*

This soviet hierarchy now took hold of the administration of the collective farms. From one end of the USSR to the other, every kolkhos had to be firmly gripped—to be merely supervised, aided and praised, if its agriculture was successful ; to be admonished and warned and threatened, if the sowing, the weeding, the reaping, the threshing and the warehousing of the grain was not loyally and efficiently conducted ; and in all cases to be helped and instructed and supplied with seed, fertilisers and machinery. The problem, Kaganovich had pointed out as early as 1930, was to bring the state machinery as close as possible to the villages and hamlets, of which there were, as we have mentioned, no fewer than 600,000. " At present ", he continued, " the centre of gravity of collective farm construction has been shifted to the rayon. Here are gathered up the threads of collective farm organisation and all other economic work of the villages, cooperative and soviet, credit and supply. Are the

---

[1] *Proceedings of Seventeenth Congress CPSU*, speech of Kaganovich, pp. 67-69.

rayon organisations sufficiently equipped with the necessary workers to deal with all this varied work ? There can be no doubt that they are extremely inadequately supplied with workers. Where is the way out ? "

What was done in 1930 was to decree the abolition of the okrug (the intermediate council between the oblast and the rayon) ; and to distribute its staff among the congresses of soviets of both the latter authorities. In addition some 25,000 selected Party members were sent to " the agricultural front". This, however, proved during 1931 and 1932, even when the active help of the village soviet could be secured, insufficient to watch over the administration of every collective farm.

### The Machine and Tractor Stations

An effective lever for lifting to prosperity every collective farm that was not deliberately wrecking its own agriculture was presently found in the Machine and Tractor Station (MTS), in which the supply of machinery to the farms had gradually been concentrated. Between 1930 and 1933 the number of these M. and T. stations was increased to over 2600, with nearly 700 repairing shops and 80,000 tractors ; [1] their repairing shops were raised to a high level of efficiency ; and their administration was made the means of persistent supervision of all the fifty to one hundred farms within the area, averaging about fifteen square

[1] See *What are MTS (Machine and Tractor Stations)?*, by L. Valersctein and A. Leontiev (Moscow, 1932, 24 pp.). "During the last three years there have been created 2600 machine [and] tractor stations, which include 1306 stations serving grain farms, 329 stations for sugar-beet farms and 217 stations for cotton farms. The value of their equipment now exceeds 600 million roubles. It includes 80,000 tractors, which are operated by about 200,000 drivers ; 2000 combines ; thousands of other improved implements, including reapers and so on. In connection with the machine [and] tractor stations, some 685 repair-shops have been established to maintain the agricultural tractors in good repair " (Moscow Narodny Bank's *Monthly Review*, vol. vi. No. 4, April 1933).

The above statistics were left far behind by the great campaign of 1933. Stalin announced to the Seventeenth Congress of the Communist Party on January 26, 1934, that there were then in the field " 204,100 tractors ; with a capacity of 3,100,000 horse-power ; 25,000 combines ; 30,101 motors and traction engines ; 58,000 threshing machines ; 1505 installations for electric threshing ; 24,400 motor lorries and 4600 cars ". (This represents something like a fourfold increase of machines of all kinds within three years.) " At the same time," continued Stalin, " the government had trained and sent into agriculture 111,000 technicians and agronomists, over 1,900,000 tractorists, combine operators, drivers, etc., and more than 1,600,000 men and women for managerial and administrative posts."

miles, that each station served. Their activities were described by an adverse critic in the following terms. " The erection of Machine [and] Tractor Stations, the first of which was set up in the Odessa region in 1927, had a significant influence on the subsequent developments. These stations may (each) have on hand as many as 100 tractors and more, together with all the necessary accessories, as well as threshing-machines, repair shops and technical personnel. Each station undertakes to draw up agreements with near-by village communities or collectives on the basis of a share in the harvest in exchange for technical assistance. To-day these stations are the so-called heavy artillery of the ' forced ' collectivisation ; they are established by order of the government ; and instructions are given to ensure that the peasants within the working radius of each station are linked up with them. It is arranged for each station to have a maximum field of operation of 50,000 to 60,000 hectares. For the year 1930 there were 313 stations in operation ; by 1931 this figure had increased to 1400, and in 1932 it is planned to have 3100. One-third of the summer and winter sowings in 1932, roughly about 48 million hectares, are to be carried out with the assistance of these stations." [1]

During 1933, the relations of the Machine and Tractor Stations with the collective farms within their several districts were reorganised in the light of the experience of the previous years. Whilst the thousands of tractor drivers and mechanics that descended on the villages necessarily exercised a considerable missionary effect, their relations with the collective farms were to be strictly on the basis of a business contract mutually agreed to. In addition to advice and help in preparing plans, so many tractors or other machines, kept constantly in good working order, bringing their own petrol, would execute so much work in ploughing, sowing, reaping and threshing, including fallow-land and winter sowing, in return for fixed and specified percentages of the yield mutually agreed to, the percentages for each group of collective farms being fixed with some regard to its prospective harvest. The percentage for threshing was henceforth to be calculated not on the amount of wheat brought to be threshed, but on the actual amount of the yield in grain. And when the

[1] " Agriculture ", by Professor Dr. Otto Auhagen, in *Soviet Economics*, edited by Dr. Gerhard Dobbert, 1933, p. 130.

work for each collective farm is completed, the management
board of the farm, in conjunction with the MTS, is to draw up
jointly a special protocol showing exactly the work done and its
results in quality as well as quantity, and the amount due.
Similar arrangements to those of the 1192 MTS serving grain
farms would be made by the 348 in sugar beet regions, 246 in
flax, 238 in cotton, 151 in vegetables and 85 in potatoes.[1]

### The Soviet Hierarchy is reinforced by the Communist Party

It was, however, not enough to reorganise, from top to bottom,
the soviet departments responsible for agriculture, and not
enough even to place in their hands the lever of 3000 or 4000
Machine and Tractor Stations, with an aggregate park of artillery
of 200,000 tractors and combines, served by thousands of competent drivers and mechanics, provided with unlimited petrol.
In the USSR, perhaps even more than in western countries,
there is always an immense " lag ", alike in time and in space,
between the creation or reorganisation of a government department, and the actual accomplishment—everywhere and completely—of the task that it is set to do.  In so vital a matter
as the food supply, Kaganovich, with Stalin's full support, was
taking no risks.  He turned to the zealous and trustworthy
members of the Communist Party to see that, not only the
immense soviet organisation, from the USSR People's Commissariat, down to the most remote village soviet and the furthest
flung Machine and Tractor Station, but also the 225,000 collective
farms with their several boards of management and their fifteen
million families, all of them actually did their duty.  It was
decided by the Central Committee of the Communist Party to
create some 3000 new local organs, termed " politotdeli ", being
special sections or committees of selected Party members,
charged with seeing to it, in the several regions assigned to them,
that the government policy was actually put in operation by the
persons immediately responsible for each part of it.  These
" Policy Sections " as we shall call them—the usual translation
of " Political Sections " being, we are told, not precisely accurate,
and certainly misleading—represent a unique projection from
Moscow of the highly centralised Communist Party.

[1] *Moscow Daily News*, weekly edition, February 5, 1933.

*The Work of the Policy Sections*

This throwing into the field, all over the USSR, of a " hand-picked " and trustworthy second army of some 25,000 members of the Communist Party, chosen, we are told, out of a much larger number of eager applicants for the adventure, and seconded out of all sorts of departments and factories for this special service, and especially their organisation in some 3000 Policy Sections, was acclaimed as a master-stroke of policy, which, as we read the evidence, contributed more than anything else to the marked success of the agricultural campaigns of 1933 and 1934. The members of these Policy Sections were carefully instructed in their duties by Kaganovich himself, and despatched in batches from Moscow to some 3000 chosen centres in all parts of the USSR. Each Policy Section consisted of at least five persons and often more, including a director, an organiser of Party work, another of work by the Comsomols, with a woman to organise the women workers ; together with an editor, not only of posters and leaflets, but also of the little local newspaper that was every-where started.[1] The duty of each section, with the assistance of all the Party members and Comsomols in the area, was primarily and specifically to see to it that everyone—whether on the staff of the Machine and Tractor Stations, or in the service of the oblast or rayon, or of a village soviet, or in that of a collective farm—did his or her duty. Many of the Party members thus sent to " the agricultural front " also undertook one or other office, either in the Machine and Tractor Station, or in the village soviet or in the management of a collective farm. This attitude of inspection and control, coupled with the actual filling of particular posts, naturally brought the members of the Policy Sections into delicate and somewhat ambiguous relations with the local soviet officials on the one hand, and, on the other, with the Party fractions and provincial Party agents, with the result of not a little friction and some open quarrels, which had to be straightened out. We get a vision of the difficulties and dangers encountered by these missionaries in the correspondence of one

[1] We have been told that the tens of thousands of members of the politotdeli were all carefully selected by the official staff of the special commission of the Communist Party ; and even that they were all personally interviewed by Kaganovitch himself—perhaps this applied only to the director of each politotdel —who rejected those of whose capacity and fidelity he was not satisfied.

of those who went out in the first batch in 1930. Gregor Injevat-kine, who, after bringing to a high degree of organisation the district of Turkestan to which he was sent, was eventually assassinated by a group of recalcitrant peasants. His letters to his wife, to his comrades in the Moscow factory in which he had been employed, and to the Party authorities afford a moving picture of the life of these devoted Party missionaries.[1] The establishment of the Policy Sections, and the selection in 1933 of a second army of Party members to man them, arose, we are told, directly out of the disclosure to the Central Committee of the Communist Party of the continued recalcitrance and sabotage in the North Caucasus. Their instructions were briefly summed up on the phrase that what they had to do was to " make the kolkhosi bolshevist and the members thereof more prosperous ".[2]

We are able to give a useful account of the actual methods and results of a politotdel at work as a whole in a recent description by an American student who was spending a year among the kolkhosi. " As each collective farm completes [its harvesting], the Policy Section issues directives regarding grain deliveries to the government [and] the past, present and future activities of the farm. These sum up the accomplishments and failures . . . discuss its special problems and give instructions for the future . . . stating whether the directives need to be discussed with the kolkhos board of the district executive committee before being carried out. The directives begin with a statistical report on the fulfilment of grain deliveries, and a statement of the success of the collective in relation to its own history and the achievement of other collective farms in the district. The kolkhos is reminded of its contract with the Machine and Tractor Station, that it must pay the MTS in kind a percentage of the crop for the use of the machines. The directives then take up the collective needs of the kolkhos, the needs of special groups within it, and, finally, special directives are given in regard to families and individuals. A fund must be laid aside for seed and insurance, arrangements made for invalids and orphans and a kolkhos social fund created. . . . Care is exercised to secure justice for groups of individuals.

[1] *One of the 25,000 : the Story of a Shock Worker*, by A. Isbach (Moscow, 1931) ; *Un des 25,000 : la brigade de choc de la collectivisation : documents rassemblés par A. C. Izbasch* (Paris, 1931, 72 pp.).
[2] *The Politotdel* (in Russian), by M. Karavai (Moscow, Partizdat, 1934, 150 pp.).

The collective farm which has accomplished specially fine work sometimes receives a tractor or a truck as an award from the MTS. On one farm where repairs were urgently necessary, and there were not sufficient funds to care for the whole kolkhos, the policy section has directed that the cottages housing the largest families should be repaired first. Faithful and efficient farm members, or a brigade which surmounted great difficulties, are credited with a 10 or 20 per cent increase on their work days. Very careless workers receive a like deduction. Where a collective farm worker has retrieved a bad reputation, his deduction may be cancelled or cut in half. Those kolkhos udarniks who are without a cow are singled out to receive a calf from the kolkhos dairy. In one instance a family had received no payment last year because of the kulak sabotage which disrupted the farm ; this year the political section has ordered a 15 per cent increase in its work days [addition to its units of sharing] in partial restitution. . . . The directives deal with innumerable other details, with every phase of kolkhos life ; ploughing, bee-keeping, poultry-keeping, etc." [1]

### *Was there a Famine in the USSR in 1931–1932 ?*

From one end of the USSR to the other we must visualise the Agricultural Departments of the oblasts and rayons, with the village soviets and the Machine and Tractor Stations, continuing to supervise and assist the couple of hundred thousand collective farms, the whole organisation being guided and directed by the 3000 Policy Sections, inspired and driven by the incessant activity of Kaganovich at the head of the Agricultural Department of the Central Committee of the Communist Party. What has been the result of this attempt to cope with climatic difficulties on the one hand, and on the other with the inertia, the ignorance and the suspicion of the peasantry of the immense area that had to be dealt with ? Was there or was there not a famine in the USSR in the years 1931 and 1932 ?

Those who think this a simple question to answer will probably already have made up their minds, in accordance with nearly all the statements by persons hostile to Soviet Communism, that

[1] Article by F. E. Hurst, on the Ustiabinsk Machine and Tractor Station, North Caucasus, in *Moscow Daily News*, October 15, 1933.

there was, of course, a famine in the USSR ; and they do not hesitate to state the mortality that it caused, in precise figures— unknown to any statistician—varying from three to six and even to ten million deaths.[1] On the other hand, a retired high official of the Government of India, speaking Russian, and well acquainted with tsarist Russia, who had himself administered famine districts in India, and who visited in 1932 some of the localities in the USSR in which conditions were reported to be among the worst, informed the present writers at the time that he had found no evidence of there being or having been anything like what Indian officials would describe as a famine.

Without expecting to convince the prejudiced, we give, for what it may be deemed worth, the conclusion to which our visits in 1932 and 1934, and subsequent examination of the available evidence, now lead us. That in each of the years 1931 and 1932 there was a partial failure of crops in various parts of the huge area of the USSR is undoubtedly true. It is true also of British India and of the United States. It has been true also of the USSR, and of every other country at all comparable in size, in each successive year of the present century. In countries of such vast extent, having every kind of climate, there is always a partial failure of crops somewhere. How extensive and how

[1] Scepticism as to statistics of total deaths from starvation, in a territory extending to one-sixth of the earth's land-surface, would anyhow be justified. But as to the USSR there seems no limit to the wildness of exaggeration. We quote the following interesting case related by Mr. Sherwood Eddy, an experienced American traveller in Russia : " Our party, consisting of about 20 persons, while passing through the villages, heard rumours of the village of Gavrilovka, where all the men but one were said to have died of starvation. We went at once to investigate and track down this rumour. We divided into four parties, with four interpreters of our own choosing, and visited simultaneously the registry office of births and deaths, the village priest, the local soviet, the judge, the schoolmaster and every individual peasant we met. We found that out of 1100 families three individuals had died of typhus. They had immediately closed the school and the church, inoculated the entire population and stamped out the epidemic without developing another case. We could not discover a single death from hunger or starvation, though many had felt the bitter pinch of want. It was another instance of the ease with which wild rumours spread concerning Russia " (*Russia To-day : What can we learn from it ?* by Sherwood Eddy, 1934, p. xiv).

We had this investigation described to us in detail by one of the interpreters who took part in it, and who had the not inconsiderable task of arranging the transport for a journey of a hundred kilometres away from the railway over almost impossible highways. It became well known among Russian journalists at the time (see, for instance, *Reise durch hundert Kollectivwirtschaften*, von F. L. Boross, Moscow, 1934, pp. 161-163), but no British or American correspondent seems to have mentioned it.

serious was this partial failure of crops in the USSR of 1931 and 1932 it is impossible to ascertain with any assurance. On the one hand, it has been asserted, by people who have seldom had any opportunity of going to the suffering districts, that throughout huge provinces there ensued a total absence of foodstuffs, so that (as in 1891 and 1921) literally several millions of people died of starvation. On the other hand, soviet officials on the spot, in one district after another, informed the present writers that, whilst there was shortage and hunger, there was, at no time, a total lack of bread, though its quality was impaired by using other ingredients than wheaten flour; and that any increase in the death-rate, due to diseases accompanying defective nutrition, occurred only in a relatively small number of villages. What may carry more weight than this official testimony was that of various resident British and American journalists, who travelled during 1933 and 1934 through the districts reputed to have been the worst sufferers, and who declared to the present writers that they had found no reason to suppose that the trouble had been more serious than was officially represented. Our own impression, after considering all the available evidence, is that the partial failure of crops certainly extended to only a fraction of the USSR; possibly to no more than one-tenth of the geographical area. We think it plain that this partial failure was not in itself sufficiently serious to cause actual starvation, except possibly, in the worst districts, relatively small in extent. Any estimate of the total number of deaths in excess of the normal average, based on a total population supposed to have been subjected to famine conditions, of sixty millions, which would mean half the entire rural population between the Baltic and the Pacific (as some have rashly asserted), or even one-tenth of such a population, appears to us to be fantastically excessive.

On the other hand, it seems to be proved that a considerable number of peasant households, both in the spring of 1932 and in that of 1933, found themselves unprovided with a sufficient store of cereal food, and specially short of fats. To these cases we shall recur. But we are at once reminded that in countries like India and the USSR, in China, and even in the United States, in which there is no ubiquitous system of poor relief, a certain number of people—among these huge populations even many thousands—die each year of starvation, or of the diseases endemic under these conditions ; and that whenever there is even a partial failure of crops this number will certainly be considerably increased. It cannot be supposed to have been otherwise in parts of the southern Ukraine, the Kuban district and Daghestan in the winters of 1931 and 1932.

But before we are warranted in describing this scarcity of food in particular households of particular districts as a " famine ", we must enquire how the scarcity came to exist. We notice among the evidence the fact that the scarcity was " patchy ". In one and the same locality, under weather conditions apparently similar if not identical, there are collective farms which have in these years reaped harvests of more than average excellence, whilst others, adjoining them on the north or on the south, have experienced conditions of distress, and may sometimes have known actual starvation. This is not to deny that there were whole districts in which drought or cold seriously reduced the yield. But there are clearly other cases, how many we cannot pretend to estimate, in which the harvest failures were caused, not by something in the sky, but by something in the collective farm itself. And we are soon put on the track of discovery. As we have already mentioned, we find a leading personage in the direction of the Ukrainian revolt actually claiming that " the opposition of the Ukrainian population *caused the failure of the grain-storing plan of 1931, and still more that of 1932*". He boasts of the success of the " passive resistance which aimed at a systematic frustration of the Bolshevik plans for the sowing and gathering of the harvest ". He tells us plainly that, owing to the efforts of himself and his friends, " whole tracts were left unsown ", and " in addition, when the crop was being gathered last year [1932], it happened that in many cases, especially in the south, 20, 40 and even 50 per cent was left in the fields, and was either not collected at all, or was ruined in the threshing ".[1]

[1] " Ukrainia under Bolshevist Rule ", by Isaac Mazepa, in *Slavonic Review*, January 1934, pp. 342-343. One of the Ukrainian nationalists who was brought to trial is stated to have confessed to having received explicit instructions from the leaders of the movement abroad to the effect that " it is essential that, in spite of the good harvest (of 1930), the position of the peasantry should become worse. For this purpose it is necessary to persuade the members of the kolkhosi to harvest the grain before it has become ripe ; to agitate among the kolkhos members and to persuade them that, however hard they may work, their grain will be taken away from them by the State on one pretext or another ; and to sabotage the proper calculation of the labour days put into harvesting by the

So far as the Ukraine is concerned, it is clearly not Heaven which is principally to blame for the failure of crops, but the misguided members of many of the collective farms.[1]  What sort of " famine " is it that is due neither to the drought nor the rain, heat nor cold, rust nor fly, weeds nor locusts ; but to a refusal of the agriculturists to sow (" whole tracts were left unsown ") ; and to gather up the wheat when it was cut (" even 50 per cent was left in the fields ") ?

The other district in which famine conditions are most persistently reported is that of Kuban, and the surrounding areas, chiefly inhabited by the Don Cossacks, who, as it is not irrelevant to remember, were the first to take up arms against the Bolshevik Government in 1918, and so begin the calamitous civil war. These Don Cossacks, as we have mentioned, had enjoyed special privileges under the tsars, the loss of which under the new régime has, even to-day, not been forgiven.  Here there is evidence that whole groups of peasants, under hostile influences, got into such a state of apathy and despair, on being pressed into a new system of cooperative life which they could not understand and about which they heard all sorts of evil, that they ceased to care whether their fields were tilled or not, or what would happen to them in the winter if they produced no crop at all.  Whatever the

members of the kolkhosi so that they may receive less than they are entitled to by their work " (Speech by M. Postyshear, secretary of the Ukraine Communist Party, to plenum of Central Committee, 1933).

[1] It can be definitely denied that the serious shortage of harvested grain in parts of southern Ukraine was due to climatic conditions.  " In a number of southern regions, from 30 to 40 per cent of the crop remained on the fields. *This was not a result of the drought* which was so severe in certain parts of Siberia, the Urals and the Middle and Lower Volga regions that it reduced there the expected crops by about 50 per cent.  *No act of God was involved in the Ukraine.* The difficulties experienced in the sowing, harvesting and grain collection campaign of 1931 were man-made " (" Collectivisation of Agriculture in the Soviet Union ", by W. Ladejinsky, *Political Science Quarterly* (New York, June 1934, p. 222).  " It is evident ", writes another of the leaders of the Ukrainian émigrés at Prague, himself the Foreign Minister of the short-lived Ukrainian Republic of 1919, "*that this famine was not the result of natural causes.* . . . The peasants are absolutely hostile to a system which runs counter to all their habits for centuries past. . . . The Ukrainian peasant has always been an individualist . . . and *sees no reason why he should work for the profit of others* " (" Ukraine and its Political Aspirations ", by Alexander Shulgin, in *Slavonic Review*, January 1935).

Mr. Chamberlin himself now ascribes at any rate some part of the relative failure of the harvests of 1931 and 1932, not to any climatic conditions, but " largely as a result of the apathy and discouragement of the peasants ", which made the yield " much lower than it would have been in normal years " (" Russia Through Coloured Glasses ", in *Fortnightly Review*, October 1934).

reason, there were, it seems, in the Kuban, as in the Ukraine, whole villages that sullenly abstained from sowing or harvesting, usually not completely, but on all but a minute fraction of their fields, so that, when the year ended, they had no stock of seed, and in many cases actually no grain on which to live. There are many other instances in which individual peasants made a practice, out of spite, of surreptitiously " barbering " the ripening wheat ; that is, rubbing out the grain from the ear, or even cutting off the whole ear, and carrying off for individual hoarding this shameless theft of community property.[1]

Unfortunately it was not only in such notoriously disaffected areas as the Ukraine and Kuban that these peculiar " failures of crops " occurred. For instance, the Machine and Tractor Sections that were sent to far-off Turkestan found, as we learn from the intimate private letters of the martyred Party member that we have already cited,[2] just the same recalcitrance among the ignorant and suspicious peasants, whether nominally enrolled in collective farms or persistently obstructing their formation.[3] These were the dupes and victims of the ceaseless machinations of the kulaks and others, whose position was threatened with destruction.

[1] The practice led to the employment of children (members of the " Pioneers " organisation) to guard the growing crops against thieves. Presently it was found necessary in some places to erect wooden watch-towers and to post sentinels night and day, in order to prevent the whole crop from being looted. (In China, one member from each family habitually watches the household plot as soon as the plants appear above ground, to prevent their being stolen.)

[2] *One of the 25,000 : the Story of a Shock Worker*, by A. Isbach (Moscow, 1931).

[3] Much the same recalcitrance had been manifested in 1927–1928 when the wide opening of the " scissors " caused the relatively well-to-do peasants to withhold their grain from the market. " A genuine and severe economic tug-of-war between the Soviet Government and the more prosperous peasants occurred during the winter of 1927 and the spring of 1928, and seems likely to go on indefinitely, perhaps in milder forms. As early as the fall of 1927 it became evident that the peasants were holding back their grain to a degree which not only destroyed any possibility of exporting it but even *seriously menaced the bread supply of the cities.* How did this ' grain strike ' come about ? It is very hard to answer this question. There is certainly no widespread secret organisation among the peasants which could coordinate their activity or instruct them all to do the same thing at the same time. And yet they sometimes display an uncanny faculty for apparently unconscious spontaneous action, as when they deserted from all parts of the front and swarmed on the landlords' estates in 1917. Something of this faculty must have come into play in the autumn of 1927, when in Siberia and Ukrainia, in Central Russia and the North Caucasus, the same phenomenon of peasant unwillingness to part with grain made itself felt " (*Soviet Russia*, by W. H. Chamberlin, 1930, p. 195).

How serious the situation appeared to Kaganovich we may gather from the lurid denunciation that he made in January 1933.[1] To any generally successful cultivation, he declared, " the anti-soviet elements of the village are offering fierce opposition. Economically ruined, but not yet having lost their influence entirely, the kulaks, former white officers, former priests, their sons, former ruling landlords and sugar-mill owners, former Cossacks and other anti-soviet elements of the bourgeois-nationalist and also of the social-revolutionary and Petlura-supporting intelligentsia settled in the villages, are trying in every way to corrupt the collective farms, are trying to foil the measures of the Party and the Government in the realm of farming, and for these ends are making use of the backwardness of part of the collective farm members against the interests of the socialised collective farm, against the interests of the collective farm peasantry.

" Penetrating into collective farms as accountants, managers, warehouse keepers, brigadiers and so on, and frequently as leading workers on the boards of collective farms, the anti-soviet elements strive to organise sabotage, spoil machines, sow without the proper measures, steal collective farm goods, undermine labour discipline, organise the thieving of seed and secret granaries, sabotage grain collections—and sometimes they succeed in disorganising kolkhozi."

However much we may discount such highly coloured denunciations, we cannot avoid noticing how exactly the statements as to sabotage of the harvest, made on the one hand by the Soviet Government, and on the other by the nationalist leaders of the Ukrainian recalcitrants, corroborate each other. To quote again the Ukrainian leader, it was " the opposition of the Ukrainian population " that " caused the failure of the grain-storing plan of 1931, and still more that of 1932 ". What on one side is made a matter for boasting is, on the other side, a ground for denunciation. Our own inference is merely that, whilst both sides probably exaggerate, the sabotage referred to actually took place, to a greater or less extent, in various parts of the USSR, in which collective farms had been established under pressure. The partial failure of the crops due to climatic conditions, which is to be

---

[1] Report of Kaganovich on Resolution of the Joint Plenum of the Central Committee and the Central Control Commission of the Communist Party, in *Moscow Daily News* (weekly edition), January 20, 1933.

annually expected in one locality or another, was thus aggravated, to a degree that we find no means of estimating, and rendered far more extensive in its area, not only by " barbering " the growing wheat, and stealing from the common stock, but also by deliberate failure to sow, failure to weed, failure to thresh, and failure to warehouse even all the grain that was threshed.[1] But this is not what is usually called a famine.

What the Soviet Government was faced with, from 1929 onward, was, in fact, not a famine but a widespread general strike of the peasantry, in resistance to the policy of collectivisation, fomented and encouraged by the disloyal elements of the population, not without incitement from the exiles at Paris and Prague. Beginning with the calamitous slaughter of livestock in many areas in 1929–1930, the recalcitrant peasants defeated, during the years 1931 and 1932, all the efforts of the Soviet Government to get the land adequately cultivated. It was in this way,[2] much more than by the partial failure of the crops due to drought or cold, that was produced in an uncounted host of villages in many parts of the USSR a state of things in the winter of 1931–1932, and again in that of 1932–1933, in which many of the peasants found themselves with inadequate supplies of food. But this did not always lead to starvation. In innumerable cases, in which there was no actual lack of roubles, notably in the Ukraine, the men journeyed off to the nearest big market, and (as there was no deficiency in the country as a whole) returned after many days with the requisite sacks of flour. In other cases, especially among the independent peasantry, the destitute family itself moved away to the cities, in search of work at wages, leaving its rude dwelling empty and desolate, to be quoted by some incautious observer

---

[1] " The peasant resisted by frauds, exaggerating their demand for seeds and cattle food, under-estimating their crops. They fought very hard against compulsion. Moreover, when they saw that they had to give over a great part of their output, they diminished the output, with the result that there was an immense slaughtering of the cattle, and a very serious diminution of the crops. The régime had the great good luck of the great harvest in 1933. Before that there was hunger in large sections of the country " (" An Economist's Analysis of Soviet Russia ", by Arthur Feiler, in *Annals of the American Academy of Political and Social Science*, July 1934, pp. 153-157).

[2] " In general, the harvesting and threshing processes were carried out by the collectivised peasantry of the Ukraine in such a manner that from 34 to 36 million quintals of grain were wasted in the fields. *This amount alone could have covered two-thirds of the grain the Ukraine was to have delivered to the State* " ("Collectivisation of Agriculture", by W. Ladejinsky, *Pol. Sci. Quarterly*, p. 233).

as proof of death by starvation.  In an unknown number of other cases—as it seems, to be counted by the hundred thousand—the families were forcibly taken from the holding which they had failed to cultivate, and removed to distant places where they could be provided with work by which they could earn their subsistence.

The Soviet Government has been severely blamed for these deportations, which inevitably caused great hardships.  The irresponsible criticism loses, however, much of its force by the inaccuracy with which the case is stated.  It is, for instance, almost invariably taken for granted that the Soviet Government heartlessly refused to afford any relief to the starving districts.  Very little investigation shows that relief was repeatedly afforded where there was reason to suppose that the shortage was not due to sabotage or deliberate failure to cultivate.  There were, to begin with, extensive remissions of payments in kind due to the government.[1]  But there was also a whole series of transfers of grain from the government stocks to villages found to be destitute, sometimes actually for consumption, and in other cases to replace the seed funds which had been used for food.[2]

Of the enforced removals there have been two kinds.  In 1929 and 1930 drastic measures were taken against those elements in the villages which were seriously interfering with the formation of kolkhosi, often by personal violence, and wilful damage to buildings and crops.  These disturbers of the peace were in many cases forcibly removed from their homes.  " The usual assumption outside the Soviet Union ", writes one who witnessed the proceedings of 1930, " is that this exiling occurred through

---

[1] " The basic decree, promulgated on May 6, 1932, states that the grain collections from the collectives and the individual farms must be decreased by 43·2 million quintals in comparison with the 1931 programme " (" Collectivisation of Agriculture in the Soviet Union ", by W. Ladejinsky, in *Political Science Quarterly* (New York), June 1934, p. 231).

[2] Thus : " On February 17, 1932, almost six months before the harvesting of the new crop the Council of People's Commissars of the USSR and the Central Committee of the Communist Party directed that the collective farms in the eastern part of the country, which had suffered from the drought, be loaned over six million quintals of grain for the establishment of both seed and food funds " (*ibid.* p. 229).

Later, we read : " Certain areas, such as the Ukraine and North Caucasus which . . . had to consume all the available grain, remained with little or no seed funds.  In this case the Soviet Government loaned to the collectives of the Ukraine almost 3·1 million quintals of seed, and to those of North Caucasus, over 2 million quintals " (*ibid.* p. 243).

drastic action by a mystically omnipotent GPU. The actual process was quite different : it was done by village meetings of poor peasants and farm hands who listed those kulaks who ' impede our collective farm by force and violence ', and asked the Government to deport them. In the hot days of 1930 I attended many of these meetings. There were harsh, bitter discussions, analysing one by one the ' best families ', who had grabbed the best lands, exploited labour by owning the tools of production, as ' best families ' normally and historically do, and who were now fighting the rise of the collective farms by arson, cattle-killing and murder. . . . The meetings I personally attended were more seriously judicial, more balanced in their discussion, than any court trial I have attended in America : these peasants knew they were dealing with serious punishments, and did not handle them lightly. . . . Those who envisage that the rural revolution which ended in farm collectivisation was a ' war between Stalin and the peasants ' simply weren't on the ground when the whirlwind broke. The anarchy of an elemental upheaval was its chief characteristic : it was marked by great ecstasies and terrors : local leaders in village township and province did what was right in their own eyes and passionately defended their convictions. Moscow studied and participated in the local earthquakes ; and, out of the mass experience, made, somewhat too late to save the live stock, general laws for its direction. It was a harsh, bitter and by no means bloodless conflict. . . . Township and provincial commissions in the USSR reviewed and cut down the lists of kulaks for exile, to guard against local excesses." [1]

Later, when the sabotage took the form of a widespread " general strike " against even cultivation of the collective farms, the Soviet Government found itself on the horns of the same dilemma that perplexed the administrators of the English Poor Law. To provide maintenance for able-bodied men whose refusal to work had brought them to destitution would merely encourage them, and their families, and eventually countless

[1] " The Soviet Dictatorship ", by Anna Louise Strong, in *American Mercury*, October 1934 ; *Dictatorship and Democracy*, by the same, 1934.

How one village came to its decision in 1930 to suppress the small minority which had persistently sought, by every kind of criminal act, to ruin the local kolkhos, is described in the artless recital of a peasant woman, *Collective Farm Trud*, told by Eudoxia Pazukhina (Moscow, 1932, pp. 60-61).

others, to repeat the offence. Yet deliberately to leave them to starve was an unacceptable alternative. The English Guardians of the Poor, early in the eighteenth century, invented the device, which was readopted in 1834, of relieving the able-bodied and their families only on condition that they entered the workhouse, and there performed whatever tasks of work could be set to them. The Soviet Government had no workhouses available and no time to build them. Its device was forcibly to remove the peasants who were found to be without food from the villages which they were demoralising to places at a distance where they could be put to work at the making of railways, roads or canals, at the cutting of timber, or at prospecting or mining for mineral ores— all tasks of discomfort and occasionally of hardship, by which they were enabled to earn the bare subsistence wage of relief work. It was a rough and ready expedient of " famine relief ", which undoubtedly caused much suffering to innocent victims. But candid students of the circumstances may not unwarrantably come to the conclusion that, when the crisis of possible starvation arrived, as the result largely of deliberate sabotage, the Soviet Government could hardly have acted otherwise than it did.[1]

With the characteristic Bolshevik habit of " self-criticism ", the Soviet Government blamed its own organisation for having let things come to such a pass. " The village Party and Young Communist organisation," declared Kaganovich in January 1933, " including the groups in state farms and machine-tractor stations, frequently lack revolutionary feeling and vigilance. In many places they not only do not oppose this anti-soviet work of hostile elements with class alertness and an everyday Bolshevik drive to strengthen soviet influence over the broad non-Party masses of the collective farmers and state farm-workers, but they them-selves sometimes fall under the influence of these sabotaging elements ; and some members of the Party, who entered for

---

[1] The enforced expropriation of these peasants has seemed to foreign critics an extreme injustice. Were not the peasants, in limiting their production, merely doing what they liked with their own ? In fact, the peasants in the USSR are not owners of the land they till, but merely occupants of nationalised land, for the purpose of cultivating it. But whether or not they are in the same position as the peasant proprietors of France or Flanders, there seems nothing unreasonable or inequitable in the view that, wherever the land is entrusted to a peasant class by the community, it is on the paramount condition that they should produce, up to their ability, the foodstuffs required for the maintenance of the community. Any organised refusal to cultivate must inevitably be met by expropriation.

careerist purposes, line up with the enemies of the collective and
state farms and the Soviet Government, and join with them in
organising thieving of seed at sowing time, grain at harvesting
and threshing time, hiding grain in secret granaries, sabotaging
state grain purchases, and really draw certain collective farms,
groups of kolkhozniks and backward workers of state farms into
the struggle against the soviet power.  It is particularly true of
state farms, where frequently the directors, under the influence of
anti-soviet elements, undergo a bourgeois degeneration, sabotage
the tasks set by the Soviet Government, enter upon out and out
treachery to the Party and Government, and attempt to dispose of
state farm products as if they were their own personal property."

But with no less characteristic Bolshevist persistence, the
occasion was taken to intensify the campaign, so as to ensure
that 1933 and 1934 should see better results than 1931 or 1932.
It was recognised, and frankly confessed, that a serious error
had been made, often owing to the mistaken zeal of local agents,
in making successive levies on the successful kolkhosi, when
these were found in possession of unexpectedly large crops.  Many
peasants had lost confidence in the government's financial
measures, always fearing that the results of their labours would
be taken away from them.  Hence the whole system was changed.
The government relinquished all right to take produce by contract any more than by requisition.  Henceforth nothing more
was to be exacted from the collective farms by way of agricultural
tax (apart from the agreed payment for the use of the tractors)
than the one official levy of grain, meat, milk and other produce,
definitely fixed in advance, in exact proportion so far as arable
produce was concerned, to the normal harvest on the number
of hectares that had to be sown and weeded and reaped.  Similar
assessments were made for other produce.  However great might
prove to be the yield, the government would claim no more.
Even if a larger area were sown than had been required, the
government pledged itself not to increase its demand upon the
zealous kolkhos.  As soon as this definitely fixed levy had been
paid for the whole district, each kolkhos was to be free to sell
the surplus to outsiders as it pleased ; even to selling it, in
the open market, to the highest bidder.[1]  At the same time the

---

[1] This single tax, as we may call it, was assessed in grain at three rates : the
normal on those kolkhosi which had the use of the government tractors, for which

whole organisation was drastically overhauled. Many hundreds of local officials were, during 1932, found guilty of gross neglect, or wanton mishandling of machinery, stores and crops. These were severely reprimanded and in many cases dismissed from office. Hundreds of the worst offenders were sentenced to imprisonment, and at least several dozens to be shot. The members of the kolkhosi themselves, including the managers and accountants, were also faithfully dealt with. What was most difficult to cope with was the deplorable general sullenness, in which many, and sometimes most, of the peasants had ceased to care whether or not the normal harvest was reaped. Where the ploughing had been only feebly performed ; the weeding left undone ; and the scanty growing grain filched from the fields by night, the whole kolkhos was drastically shaken up ; the most guilty of the sabotagers, often ex-kulaks, were expelled ; the negligent managers and peccant accountants were dismissed from office ; collective farms which had wilfully neglected or refused to till their land were sternly refused relief when they found themselves without food, so as not to encourage further recusancy ; and in some of the worst cases the inhabitants of whole villages, if only in order to save them from starvation, were summarily removed from the land that they had neglected or refused to cultivate, and deported elsewhere, to find labouring work of any sort for bare maintenance. It is not denied that in these summary removals, as in those of individual kulaks who had refused to conform to the government's requirements, great hardship was inflicted on a large number of women and children, as well as on the men. Without such cost in suffering, it is argued, the rapid reorganisation of peasant agriculture, which seemed the only practicable means of solving the problem of the national food supply, could not have been effected.

In the result there seems to us no doubt that this peculiar stiffening of the local rural administration by a chosen army of zealous and specially instructed Party members, in direct communication with Kaganovich and the special department for agriculture of the Central Committee of the Communist Party, was, during 1933 and 1934, remarkably effective. Kaganovich

a separate fee had to be paid ; a higher rate where no tractor fee had to be paid because none was used or desired ; and a still higher rate on the individual peasant or the kulak, whose very existence it was wished to discourage.

himself was during both these years constantly touring the country, looking minutely into everything, and giving orders which had to be obeyed.[1] The Soviet Government was lucky in a critical year (1933) in a harvest which, even if its excellence was exaggerated, was at least vastly better than those of the preceding years. But there would not have been anything like so great a yield if this extraordinary administrative activity had not seen to it, in practically all the 240,000 farms, that the sowing was actually undertaken and completed at the right time; that the harrowing was not scamped; that there was everywhere much more systematic weeding than had ever before been undertaken; that the tractors and harvesters were supplied to nearly every collective farm, and maintained in unwonted efficiency; that the harvest was got in without procrastination; and that the grain was guarded from theft and stored in safety. In the following year (1934) the harvest was apparently, on the average, not quite so great as in 1933; but the universal testimony was to the effect that the behaviour of the peasants had greatly improved. Some of the villages that had been among the most recalcitrant in cultivation during 1932, and had hungered most in the winter of 1932–1933, were among the most diligent in 1934, and abundantly reaped the reward of their increased labours. As a consequence it was reported that the government obtained in the aggregate almost as large an amount of grain, in return for its machinery and seed, as its share of the less abundant harvest of 1934, as it had received out of the bumper crops of 1933. And now that the worst members of the collective farms have been drastically expelled, whilst the others have been actually shown how the work should be done, and have been made to realise that, even after paying all that the government

[1] " An amusing turn was given to the congress when the speech of Tobashev, of Moscow Province, was interrupted by Kaganovich, Secretary of the Moscow Committee of the Party. ' When Kaganovich came to our farm,' declared Tobashev, ' our chairman said, " This is the way to the office ". Kaganovich replied, " It would be much better to see the barns and get an idea how you carry on work here ". He saw everything and everywhere pointed out shortcomings; our equipment, for instance, was kept in a shed, the door of which did not close properly.' ' I remember ', interjected Kaganovich, ' that snow came in through the roof.' (Laughter.) ' Quite right,' returned Tobashev, ' but now we have repaired it.' ' Very good,' returned Kaganovich, ' I'll return soon to find out.' ' We knew perfectly well ', concluded Tobashev, ' that you would not take our word for it. We are waiting for you to come back ' " (*Moscow Daily News*, February 18, 1933).

requires from them, *they have much more to their individual shares than they have ever in their lives made out* of their tiny holdings, they may perhaps be expected to be able to dispense with much of the hustling by which Kaganovich and his myrmidons in 1933 and 1934 pulled the USSR through a dangerous crisis.[1]

### Life on a Collective Farm

Let us now turn from the exciting campaign by which Kaganovich, as we think, saved the situation ; and relieved the Soviet Government from its grave anxiety as to the feeding of the city populations and the Red Army. What is the life that is normally led by the seventy millions of people in the USSR who make up the collective farms ?

" Superficially ", remarked the late Michael Farbman, " a collectivised village looks very like the traditional Russian village. But essentially it is something quite new. The life of a peasant in such a village differs almost entirely from that of the old-fashioned mujik. Instead of being confined to a petty world in which he had to till the various narrow strips that comprise his holding with the aid of a single horse, he has become a partner in a big estate and has to adapt himself to large-scale methods of cultivation and the use of all sorts of machines of which he had never even heard before. Moreover, he has suffered a social and political as well as an economic change. His share in the cooperative effort is involving him in various new experiences with his neighbours. Of these the organisation of work is naturally the most important." [2]

### The Members' Meeting

The basis of the administration of the collective farm, as in the soviet and trade union hierarchies, is the periodical meeting

---

[1] We may quote the testimony of an impartial Canadian expert : " Because of the increased area of holdings and higher yields in the collectives, as a result of the greater use of tractors and modern implements and production methods, the income per household on the average collectivised farm has increased at least 150 per cent as a nation-wide average, and by more than 200 per cent in numerous localities " (*Russia, Market or Menace*, by Thomas D. Campbell, 1932, p. 65). This author, who was in two separate years sent for by the Soviet Government to advise them how to cope with their agricultural difficulties, successfully conducts a 95,000-acre wheat farm in Montana, U.S.A.

[2] " Creating a New Agricultural System ", in *The Economist* (London), October 15, 1932.

of all the members over the age of eighteen. At such a meeting, at least once in every year, and in many cases more frequently, there is elected the chairman, and several other members to form the board of management (pravlenie), which constitutes the effective executive for all purposes. It is by this body, in the atmosphere of day-by-day discussion among all the members, and subject to periodical report and debate in the members' meeting, that all the necessary decisions are taken : what crops shall be raised on what parts of the farm ; when the various operations of ploughing, sowing, weeding and harvesting shall be undertaken ; which members shall be assigned to each of the innumerable separate tasks, and all the thousand and one detailed arrangements that even the smallest collective enterprise necessarily involves.

### *The Management of a Collective Farm*

The actual organisation of work within each collective farm, together with the arrangements for sharing the product among the members, vary from farm to farm. The 240,000 farms, indeed, differ indefinitely from each other in almost every respect, according to the local conditions and to the capacity and honesty of the leading members. At first, everything was of the simplest. All the members worked pretty well as they chose, at any of the varied tasks. It was often assumed that the year's product could and should be shared equally among all the little community, on the basis of the number of mouths to be fed, irrespective of age, sex, capacity or the work actually performed. Gradually this simplicity was abandoned in favour of a definite assignment of tasks and offices, by decision of the members' meeting, but on the recommendation of the responsible officers and the board of management. In all the well-organised kolkhosi the workers are allocated to brigades, to each of which is assigned a specific task. In order to fix responsibility each brigade has a particular area of land to cultivate, with its own set of implements, and is required to concentrate its work on a particular crop, whether wheat or rye, flax or beet, cotton or sunflower, throughout the whole agricultural year upon the same area, in the successive operations of ploughing, sowing, harrowing, weeding and harvesting. In the same way a specific brigade takes charge, throughout the whole year, of the horses, cattle, sheep or pigs that the kolkhos possesses in common, so that there may be no doubt as to responsibility for their maintenance in health.

Experience soon proved the necessity of changing the basis of sharing from mouths to be fed to days of work performed, often supplemented by an allowance for children under working age. The share for each day's work had then to be differentiated not by sex or age but according to the laboriousness or disagreeableness of the task.[1] The importance of the functions of management and accounting soon came to be increasingly recognised. But in order to keep down the overhead charges the number of members who may be employed otherwise than in actually productive work, such as management, secretarial duties, accounting and measuring, is strictly limited ; and it is laid down that their hours of work must be reckoned, in the sharing, at no more than the average per hour of the whole body of adult workers.

When it was found at the end of the harvest that a considerable surplus remained, after all the advances to members had been covered, and all the required transfers or payments to the government had been made—and this has undoubtedly been the case in successive years in many collective farms, and during 1933 and 1934 in, at least, many tens of thousands of them—the disposal of this surplus has been the subject of prolonged discussion among the members, leading up to a decision by the members' meeting.[2] How much should be devoted to capital improvement and how much to distribution as a bonus in money or in produce ; whether to build a new barn, a new cow-house, a new silo ; or a village hall, a club-house, or a cinema ; or a children's crèche, a primitive apartment house for the young

---

[1] " The value of work done by members of kolkhosi is reckoned in labour days. But what is a labour day ? A labour day is a fixed quantity and a fixed quality of work done by a member of the kolkhos " (Tataev, *The Distribution of Income in the Kolkhosi*, Partizdat, Moscow, 1932, p. 24, in Russian).

" In the Instructions issued by Kolkhoscentre as to rates of pay for work it is stated that no matter by whom the work is done—whether by a man, by a woman or a young person—this work, if equal in quantity and quality, must be reckoned as an equal number of labour days, and must be paid for in a corresponding share of the income " (*ibid.* p. 28).

[2] In order to ensure that nothing is decided without general consent, it has been prescribed by law that the objects of the proposed expenditure must be within the kolkhos itself ; and that no proposal shall be deemed to have been carried otherwise than by a clear majority in a meeting at which not less than two-thirds of the membership were present and voted.

and unmarried men, or a clinic for the visiting doctor—all these have been talked over, and here and there, one at a time, in whatever order desired, actually undertaken.

### How Disputes are Settled

In the working life of such a community there must inevitably occur disputes which even a vote cannot settle. For these, as in the factory, there is increasingly resort to " the Triangle ". " We have all heard ", writes a recent observer, " of the Triangle in the factories : management, Party and trade union. But on the collective farm there is no trade union. What then ? Have we forgotten the village soviet ? A village is occupied by collective farmers and a few artisans, the sales clerks in the cooperatives, school teachers, and so on. . . . The village soviet is the organ of government ; the kolkhos board the economic and labour control of the farm. Their interests can never clash ; they are complementary. The Triangle on the kolkhos . . . [is] composed of the chairman of the board, the chairman of the village soviet and the Party secretary. And this triangular form of representation is carried down through the farm structure. On each brigade there is also a member of the village soviet, elected from the brigade, who, with the brigadier and the brigade Party organiser, forms the brigade Triangle. Brigadiers are appointed by the farm board at a general meeting, when these appointments may be discussed, opposed or confirmed." [1]

### Democracy in Agriculture

No one can possibly visit all the 240,000 collective farms spread over an immense area ; and no visitor of half a dozen or so can form any useful idea of the extent to which such a sample —no larger than one-twenty-thousandth part—is typical of the enormous mass, either in general efficiency or in amount of product. What most impresses the political student is the vision of these 240,000 separate communities scattered throughout the length and breadth of the USSR, severally working out their own life-conditions, within the framework of the law and the

[1] Article by Charles Ashleigh describing collective farms in North Caucasus, *Moscow Daily News*, September 3, 1933. The Triangle is, however, not yet universal on collective farms, though it may be that it is tending to become so.

regulations common to them all, not as separate families but as members of a cooperative society in which all have a common interest.[1] What an education must be the endless discussions of the frequent members' meetings! How refreshingly novel must be the atmosphere in which the twenty or thirty million children of these collectivised peasants are now growing up!

At the same time the peasants are, with the aid of their families, also developing that part of the production which is left in their own hands. The magnitude and range of the individual enterprises of the members of the collective farms is seldom adequately realised. The "Model Constitution" recommended on February 17, 1935, states that "each household in collective farms in tilling districts which have a well-developed livestock industry may have at its personal disposal two or three cows, apart from calves, from two to three pigs with their offspring, a total of 20 to 25 sheep and goats, and an unlimited number of poultry, rabbits and up to 20 beehives. . . . The area of the land around the dwelling-place which is personally used by the kolkhos farmstead (exclusive of the land occupied by the dwelling) may range between a quarter and half an hectare, and in certain districts one hectare." (The hectare is 2·47 acres.)

### The Commune

We need say little, at this stage, of the completely collectivised settlement known as the commune. Here the little community has all its material possessions in common ownership, and unites all its activities under common management, very much as was done by the numerous societies formed during the past hundred years, in America and elsewhere, under the influence of Robert

---

[1] Competent observers testify to signs among the peasantry of a mental revolution. " Very striking tendencies can be observed in the buying activities of kolkhos peasants. None of them would think of buying a horse. He has no right to buy a horse. Here is a real farmer. But he would no more think of buying a plough than a factory working man would think of saving up to buy a turbine. The Russian peasant, in other words, can spend a decreasing amount of money on the acquisition of capital. He will use his money, instead, to eat more, clothe himself better and live more comfortably. This is another agent, Russians say, in undermining the capitalistic instincts of the mujik. I wish I could convey the momentousness of such psychological changes. They amount to a national mental revolution " (" The Evolution of Collectivisation ", by Louis Fischer, in *British Russian Gazette*, September 1933).

Owen, Cabet and Fourier, or among peculiar religious denominations such as the Shakers. In the USSR at least a couple of thousand communes have been established in various places during the past decade without any religious basis ; and many of them have now had several years' successful experience. We may cite as an example the commune named Seattle in the Salski district of North Caucasus province, which was founded in 1922–1923 by a group of Finnish Socialists, originally centred at Seattle in the State of Washington (U.S.A.). They were attracted to the USSR, as a country free from the oppressions of capitalism, in which they could apply, on a cooperative basis, the American agricultural machinery that they brought with them. Welcomed by Lenin, they were assigned 5291 hectares of unbroken steppe, twelve miles from the railway. Here the members, whose numbers had grown by 1935 to about 400, making a total population of approaching 1000, now comprising sixteen different nationalities, have erected substantial dwellings supplied with running water, provided nurseries and schools, sunk wells, built barns, granaries and silos, and brought under continuous cultivation more than 10,000 acres, selling the wheat annually to the Government Grain Trust.[1] The commune had, in 1933, over 100 cattle and nearly 200 pigs. It maintains a large wood-working shop and extensive brick-kilns, by which it is constantly adding to its buildings. An efficiently fitted machine shop not only keeps all the machinery of the neighbouring farms in repair, but also manufactures new parts and gears. The members of the commune enter freely into the local life of the district, take part in the elections to the village soviet (selosoviet), and send delegates to all the conferences and congresses that they are entitled to attend. All over the USSR the quarter of a million population of the couple of thousand communes take the same part in the civic organisation, local and

[1] An interesting article by Richard Gerbacy, a member of the commune, in the *Moscow Daily News*, October 20, 1933, described the celebration of the tenth anniversary of the foundation of the settlement. On our visit in 1932, we were not only freely supplied with information, but also presented with a lengthy pamphlet (in Russian) entitled *From the Country of the Capitalists to the USSR ; the American Commune Seattle*, by P. J. Thadeus (Moscow, Gosisdat, 1930), which, in translation, has enabled us to form a vivid picture of the early trials and the present organisation of this prosperous community.

The pamphlet *A Student in Russia*, by Paul Winterton (Cooperative Union, Manchester, 1929, 64 pp.), gives an attractive account of a commune in southern Ukraine, which had then enjoyed several years of prosperity and increasing civilisation, under enlightened leadership.

national, as do the kolkhosi. Whether or not these latter will gradually develop into communes, as many people suppose, but as the Soviet Government does not encourage, is a question of the future. At present it looks as if there was a tendency for individual ownership to reappear inside the commune. In order to increase the aggregate of livestock, the USSR People's Commissar of Agriculture has decreed that " every member of an agricultural commune has a right to acquire for his individual economy a cow, small producers' livestock and fowls." [1]

### The Hierarchy of Owner-Producers in Agriculture

The organisation of the owner-producer in agriculture stands plainly at a more rudimentary stage than that of the owner-producers in industry, which we described in the preceding section. The severe crisis of the past few years has stood in the way of any adoption of the hierarchical or pyramidal form of democratic centralism. No district councils representative of kolkhosi exist, nor is there any sign at present of the institution of an All-Union Congress of Collective Farmers. There is, accordingly, no central executive committee which such a congress would appoint. A preliminary stage to that of a representative "All-Union Congress of Collective Farmers " may have been the large gathering of " collective farm shock-brigaders " (udarniki) which was summoned to Moscow in February 1933. At this conference, attended by over 1500 local leaders of collective farm administrations from nearly all parts of the USSR, the difficulties and the prospects of these owner-producers were made the subject of stirring addresses by such outstanding ministers as Molotov, Kaganovich, Kalinin, Voroshilov and Yakovlev, together with Stalin himself. This conference at Moscow was followed during the spring of 1933 by others held for particular provinces.[2] A "Second All-Union

[1] "Collectivisation of Agriculture in the Soviet Union", by W. Ladejinsky, in *Political Science Quarterly*, March 1934.

[2] See the reports of speeches made at such conferences of udarniki in *Moscow Daily News*, February 15–20, 1933, and also February 1935; also *International Press Correspondence*, March 2 and May 26, 1933 ; *Speech at the First All-Union Congress of Collective Farm Shock Brigade Workers*, by J. Stalin (Moscow, 1933, 24 pp.) ; *The Great Offensive*, by Maurice Hindus, 1933, ch. vi., "Collectives", pp. 95-116.

At these conferences the delegates were invited, and their expenses were paid, by the USSR People's Commissar for the kolkhosi and peasantry, but invitations were issued in blank, a due proportion being sent to each pro-

Congress of Kolkhos Udarniks " held at the end of 1934 adopted a detailed and elaborate model constitution for all kolkhosi, which was formally approved by the Sovnarkom of the USSR and by the Central Committee of the Communist Party on February 17, 1935. This model constitution was strongly recommended for adoption by the members' meeting of each of the 240,000 kolkhosi ; now approaching 250,000.

The permanent central office in Moscow (Kolkhoscentre), from which was exercised some general supervision over all the collective farms in the USSR—or by which, at any rate, statistics were collected for the whole movement—has now been absorbed in the new commissariat, and is directly administered by the USSR People's Commissar for Agriculture (kolkhosi and peasantry). Probably one of the most important constitutional relations, apart from those with the Agricultural Commission of the Communist Party, are those with Gosplan, with which it must be frequently in consultation as to the annual formulation of the control figures of the General Plan, and the continued minor modifications which have to be made and adjusted.

Any hierarchical organisation of councils rising, tier after tier, from the members' meeting to an All-Union Congress of elected delegates is, in the case of the collective farms, frankly postponed. The authoritative regulation of such of the 240,000 farms as are imperfectly administered is, at present, more obvious than any organised expression of the desires and ideas of the fifteen million families who form the aggregate membership.

The vast majority of the 240,000 collective farms are, in fact, not yet wholly self-governing cooperative societies.[1] Such of them as have already made their agriculture successful, to the extent of maintaining their members, and their families, and of yielding to the government the amount of its levies for the agricultural tax, and in return for the use of its tractors and harvesters, its seeds and its fertilisers, do, in fact, manage their own affairs, by their own members' meetings ; and get from the government,

vince. The actual selection was made locally by vote among the whole number of udarniki. It was explicitly stated that many, if not most, of the delegates were non-Party men or women.

[1] But it seems ridiculous for a contributor to the pamphlet of the School of Slavonic Studies entitled *Collectivised Agriculture in the Soviet Union* (London, 1934, p. 30)—one who has been unable to visit the USSR to see for himself—to declare " that the legal status of the members of collective farms is for all practical purposes equivalent to bondage ".

beyond the machines that they hire, no more than supervision and advice. For the rest there has had to be devised an elaborate system of administration by which the members' meetings have been, by an ingenious combination of education and persuasion, economic pressure and, in the last resort, drastic coercion, shown how they should go.

### The Results in 1933

It is possibly useless to adduce aggregate figures of the yield of wheat during 1933 for the whole USSR—showing a considerable increase on any previous year—as evidence of the successful working of the system of collective farms. Nor can this success be proved by particular instances, any more than failure is proved by the most agonising letters of complaint, often of doubtful authenticity, which have been published abroad. It will, however, complete the picture if we give a summary of the report of one kolkhos, named " Successes of Stalin ", in the Middle Volga region. This collective farm, it will be seen, made a great success in 1932, without waiting for the campaign of the Policy Section or relying on the advice of the Machine and Tractor Stations. " This collective farm, comprising 234 families, had just completed the distribution of its income for the current year, after fulfilling the year's programme of grain deliveries by August 15. A total of 227 tons of grain was sold to the government out of a total grain crop of 619 tons.

" The gross income of the farm for the year, estimated on the basis of the official prices for agricultural products, is close to 95,000 roubles. In addition to 235 tons of rye, 337 tons of wheat, 26 tons of oats and 19 tons of millet, the farm produced 66 tons of potatoes, 18 tons of sunflower seed and 1000 tons of hay and straw. After selling to the government the set quantity of agricultural products, the farm proceeded to collect a seed supply to be used for next year's sowing. In addition, a supply of grain was collected for the feeding of the horses, sheep and hogs owned by the collective. Some grain was also set aside to supply those peasants who have left to work in the cities, under agreements signed with industrial organisations.

" The total net monetary income of the collective farm from the sale of grain to the government and from other sources, amounted to 50,000 roubles. From this sum, the farm paid agricultural taxes of 1750 roubles, and insurance 1700 roubles. A 3300 rouble loan was repaid to the State Bank: 10 per cent of the gross income of the farm was turned into a common fund, which is used largely for capital construction on the farm. By decision of the farm members, an additional 4 per cent of the gross income was set aside for cultural purposes, to pay bonuses and similar expenses. Two thousand roubles were invested in stocks of the Tractor Centre and Incubator Centre, which supply the farm with the required tractors and incubators. About 4000 roubles was spent for kerosene and lubricating oil for the tractors, for repairs, and for administrative expenditure.

" After all these expenses were met, the farm still had nearly 27,000 roubles in cash, as well as 185 tons of wheat and considerable quantities of other agricultural products.

" Up to September 20, when the distribution was effected, 26,000 working days had been put in by the members of the collective. It was estimated that in order to complete the work on hand some 8500 working days more will be required before the end of the year. The average pay for a working day will therefore be : 78 kopeks, plus 6·5 kilograms of grain, 2·0 kg. of hay, 14 kg. of straw, and various other farm products. *These amounts are from four to six times larger than the money and products received by the members per working day last year.*

" To stimulate better work, the two best field brigades (the groups in which the members work) received 10 per cent more per working day than the average, while two other brigades whose work was not up to the required level received 15 per cent less than average pay. . . . The collective farm members cultivate their own gardens and keep their own cattle and horses. This provides considerable additional income." [1]

Let us end this complicated analysis of the " campaign on the agricultural front " by a description by an eye-witness of one of the members' meetings when the harvest had been got in. " On September 7," writes the American student whom we have already quoted, " the collective farm ' Matvaeva ' celebrated the distribution of the first half of the grain shares. . . . The individual shares for the whole period ranged from 100 to 500 poods. Later in the day at the meeting . . . farmer after farmer rose to speak of the harvest, the problems that had been

[1] *Moscow Daily News*, October 15, 1932.

met and solved by the help of the head of the political section.
. . . One elderly woman rose, shook her finger at the meeting,
and reminded them ' *when we read in the papers how such a harvest
was possible we didn't believe it ; now it is an accomplished fact. . . .*'
As an example of what has been accomplished in a brief seven
months through the work of the political section, the collective
farm ' Bolshevik ' may be cited. Completely disorganised last
year by kulak sabotage, the Bolshevik farm failed to harvest all
its grain, failed in its grain deliveries, and the members themselves
were short of grain. This year that same kolkhos is one of the
leading farms in the district, and has been placed on the roll of
honour for the whole of the North Caucasus. . . . There is new
life in the villages." [1]

Such descriptive accounts by eye-witnesses of particular
collective farms, although they may be quite accurate, do not
enable us to come to any confident conclusion as to what is
happening in the whole 240,000 of them. They are doubtless
deliberately selected instances ; and, in fact, they make no pre-
tence of being anything else. Equally graphic descriptions can
be obtained of the complete failure of collective farms to obtain
any harvest at all, owing largely, as it is not denied, to the concerted refusal of the members to do any effective work at ploughing, weeding or harvesting, even to the extent of leaving themselves without seed, and occasionally without food during the
winter.[2] It is too soon to judge, on the one hand, whether the

---

[1] Article by F. E. Hurst on the Ustiabinsk Machine and Tractor Station,
North Caucasus, in *Moscow Daily News*, October 15, 1933. Other successful
kolkhosi are described and interesting descriptions of their working are given
in *Supply and Trade in the USSR*, by W. Nodel, 1934, pp. 95-100.

[2] We note that Mr. W. H. Chamberlin, who has now been transferred from
Moscow to Tokyo, continues to assert (in various magazine articles in 1934–1935,
and in his book *Russia's Iron Age*, 1935) that there was a terrible famine in
1932–1933, "one of the greatest human catastrophes since the world-war," which
caused, from disease and starvation, some four or five million deaths beyond the
normal mortality. After carefully weighing Mr. Chamberlin's various assertions
we can find no evidence of there having been any " natural " or " climatic "
famine in 1931–1934. There is abundant testimony from many sources that the
shortage in the crop was, for the most part, "man-made". It is, indeed, not
seriously disputed that in 1932 there was widespread refusal to sow, neglect to
weed, and failure to reap, just as there had been in previous years deliberate
slaughter of every kind of livestock, amounting to no fewer than 150 million
animals. This " man-made " shortage it was that Mr. Chamberlin calls a
famine. How far food scarcity was aggravated by undue exactions by the
government agents from a population manifestly guilty of sabotage may well
be a matter of controversy. We find, in the statements of Mr. Chamberlin and

successful kolkhosi will repeat, in less favourable years, when the official pressure is lightened, the material successes of 1933 and 1934 ; or, on the other, whether the stern measures taken against those who failed to cultivate the land entrusted to them can overcome the ingrained habit of mind of the individual peasant, incapable of recognising his own gain in any product, however considerable, which has to be shared with others. German expert observers declare that the agricultural difficulties in the USSR are not yet over, and that not for several years can the food position be declared to be safe. There are two principal grounds for this conclusion. Whatever may be done by drastic administration to compel the sullen farmers to cultivate effectively, this will not restore the slaughtered horses and cattle, sheep and pigs. The diminution of livestock had, in 1933, not yet stopped (except for pigs) ; although it is claimed that in 1934 the decrease was arrested in all but horses. Even if the aggregate total begins to rise during 1935, it must take several years to bring to maturity the animals now being born.

The second ground taken by those who know best the mind of a peasantry in any European country, is the sheer impossibility of persuading the elder kolkhos member to change his ideas and his habits. He has not yet got over his resentment at being deposed from his position of family autocrat,[1] nor will he easily

other believers in the famine, nothing that can be called statistical evidence of widespread abnormal mortality ; though it may be inferred that hardships in particular villages must have led, here and there, to some rise in the local death-rate. The continuous increase in the total population of the Ukraine and North Caucasus, as of the USSR as a whole, does not seem to have been interrupted, though the migration from the rural districts to the cities has continued, and may even have increased. The controversy is discussed in Louis Fischer's book *Soviet Journey*, 1935, pp. 170-172, in which he incidentally says, " *I myself saw, all over the Ukraine in October 1932, huge stacks of grain which the peasants had refused to gather in, and which were rotting. This was their winter's food. Then these same peasants starved.*"

[1] In many collective farms a way of dealing with the apathy and sullenness of the elderly peasants, who were frequently found sitting gloomily on the seat in front of their houses, whilst the young people were working in the fields, has been found. They have been formally appointed " inspectors of quality ", and given the duty of superintending the work and reporting on the quality of the crops harvested. They wear a badge, and walk about with an air of authority ! (see the cases cited in *Reise durch hundert Kollectivwirtschaften*, by L. F. Boross, Moscow, 1934, p. 176). This ingenious encouragement of the aged has been carried even further. In various districts, congresses of these inspectors of quality have been held, attended by hundreds of elderly peasants from the neighbouring kolkhosi, who have been addressed by leading statesmen, and treated as persons occupying key-positions in the local agriculture !

be weaned from his habit of seeking always to do less work than his fellow-members, on the argument that only in this way can he hope to " get even " with them, as they will, of course, be seeking to do less than he does !   It is not enough, such critics declare, to leave to the kolkhos member the full product of his own garden, his own poultry, his own beehives, his own pig and even his own cow.   This concession to individualism may, it is said, even make matters worse, by tempting the disloyal collective farmer to put all his energy into his private enterprise.   We do not ourselves pretend to a judgment.   But we suggest that the Bolshevik Government may not be wrong in putting its hopes, in the kolkhosi, as elsewhere, on the young people, who (as it is not always remembered) constitute about half the population.   These will have increasingly been nurtured in a collective atmosphere ; and, according to all accounts, they like it much better than the life of the individual peasant.   So, it seems, do most of the women. If the women and the children, and the young people, who together constitute three-fourths of the whole population, prefer the kolkhos, the kolkhos will endure.   This, at least, is the judgment of the observer who probably knows the Russian peasant better than any other writer.   " Of one thing we may be assured," declares Mr. Maurice Hindus, " so long as the soviets endure there will be no return to individual farming.   I have the feeling that, even if the soviets were to collapse, Russian agriculture would remain collectivised with control in the hands of the peasants instead of the government.   The advantages of collectivisation as a method of farming are indisputable.   There are even now scores of highly successful collective farms in the Black Earth region and in the Ukraine.   Collectivisation has within it the power to convert Russia from a backward to a progressive agricultural nation, as individual landholding with its inevitable small acreage never can." [1]

#### (c) MISCELLANEOUS ASSOCIATIONS OF OWNER-PRODUCERS

Needless to say, the advantages of association in the work of production are not confined to the cultivators and handicraftsmen, and other producers in agriculture or small scale industry.   We shall describe in the following chapter the entirely distinct con-

[1] *The Great Offensive*, by Maurice Hindus, 1933, p. 114.

sumers' organisation of the distribution of commodities, together
with the productive services incidental thereto. But even specifically within the sphere of production, where the two main types
of manufacturing artel and collective farm count by far the largest
numbers of members, we have to notice, as part of the social
structure of production in the USSR, various other kinds of " cooperatives ", often " mixed " in type, which are seldom described,
but which cannot be ignored.

We must, however, first write off, as superseded by subsequent
developments, practically all the array of independent agricultural
cooperative societies that existed in the USSR as recently as
1927.[1] At that date there were specialised societies for the assistance of the makers of butter and cheese and other milk products ;
societies for poultry and eggs ; for potatoes ; for grapes and
wine ; for horse- and cattle-breeding and the rearing of sheep ;
for tobacco ; for cotton ; for flax ; for sugar-beet ; for the production and distribution of various kinds of seed ; for bee-keeping
and what not. There were a number of credit societies on a
mutual basis. But most of these societies, or the various federations and unions that they formed among themselves, combined
the joint marketing of their members' produce with whatever
preparation for sale could conveniently be undertaken collectively.
Thus, there were cooperative creameries and cheese factories by
the thousand ; many hundreds of cooperative workshops and
mills for the preparation of flax ; hundreds of cooperative factories and distilleries for the manufacture both of food preparations and of alcohol from the extensive potato crop. In almost

---

[1] Apart from the voluminous Russian sources, the following more accessible
publications may be cited : *The Cooperative Movement in Russia*, by J. V.
Bubnoff (Manchester, 1917, 162 pp.) ; *The Cooperative Movement in Soviet
Russia*, by Elsie Terry Blanc (New York, 1924) ; *The Cooperative Movement
in Soviet Russia* (International Labour Office, 1925) ; *Die Konsumgenossenschaften in Sowjetrussland*, by Lubinoff (Berlin, 1926, 20 pp.) ; *Consumers'
Cooperation in the Union of Socialist Soviet Republics*, by P. Popoff (London,
1927, 46 pp.) ; *Die Genossenschaften in socialistischen Aufbau*, by W. Tikhomirov
(1927) ; *The Russian Cooperative Movement*, by N. Barou and E. F. Wise
(1927) ; *Die landwirtschaftlichen Genossenschaften in der Sowjetunion* (Berlin,
1928), translated as *Agricultural Cooperation in the Soviet Union*, by G. Ratner
(London, 1929) ; *The Cooperative Movement in Russia during the War*, by
Kayden and Antsiferov (1930); *Les voies du développement de la coopération de
production en URSS*, by W. Tikhomirov (1931) ; *The Year Book of Agricultural
Cooperation* (London, 1933) ; and, as to credit societies, *Economic Survey*
(Gosbank), November and December 1930, and *Russian Cooperative Banking*,
by N. Barou (London, 1931) ; and for all forms now existing, *Consumers'
Cooperation in the USSR*, by Leslie A. Paul (1934).

all cases the cooperative society supplied the technical instruction appropriate to the enterprise ; selected seed ; the best kinds of implements, and plans and models of improved buildings. It undertook the collection and storage of the produce ; arranged bulk sales to the consumers' cooperatives or the government trusts; opened up new markets; organised exhibitions in the cities, and concerted with the People's Commissar for Foreign Trade as to the widening of the range of the export trade. A large proportion of all the agricultural produce of the USSR, apart from cereals, was, in 1927, handled by these independent cooperative associations. In the cases of milk products, flax, potatoes, tobacco and sugar-beet, these associations dealt with 60 to 90 per cent of the whole production of the country.

This extensive development of voluntary and independent organisations of agricultural producers, which in 1927 numbered 80,000 separate societies, uniting as many as eight or nine million peasant households in voluntary cooperation, had, by 1932, completely disappeared from view. So far as the present writers could learn, all the 80,000 societies have ceased to exist as such ; their numerous federal associations have been " liquidated " ; and the various " centres " that they maintained at Moscow have been absorbed into the new USSR Commissariats of State Farms and of Agriculture respectively. A certain proportion of the local cooperative societies (including the Siberian creameries) have simply become collective farms (kolkhosi). Wherever the collective farms have been established, the credit societies have become unnecessary, as the individual members have little need of loans, whilst the State Bank supplies any credit required by the kolkhos itself. The great development of scientific institutes, which now place at the peasants' disposal all the facts and suggestions that he requires, may have rendered unnecessary much of the service of advice and instruction rendered by the specialist cooperative societies and federal unions. Yet it cannot be ignored that the summary " liquidation " of so extensive a growth of social tissue involves a loss to the peasantry which may not yet have been entirely made good to the whole twenty-five million households, by the more systematic organisation of state banks and commissariats, institutes and kolkhosi. Some miscellaneous developments of these we have now to describe.

*The Fishermen's kolkhosi.*—In no part of the organised structure of Soviet Communism do we find a more striking example of Lenin's principle of constitutional multiformity than in the industry of fishing, in which the USSR has now a greater annual output than Great Britain or Norway, and stands second only to Japan among all the nations of the world.[1] This industry is almost entirely a creation of the last fifteen years. Prior to the war there was practically no Russian deep-sea fishing, no other preserving than salting, no canning of the catch, and only an extensive but unorganised individual shore and river fishing, which sank under the disturbance of war and famine to its lowest point in 1921. In 1929 the Soviet Government began the establishment of deep-sea fishing (including whaling), with an ever-increasing development of refrigeration and other methods of preservation ; processing of various kinds ; various incidental manufactures, and, finally, canning on a large scale. The capital investment in up-to-date fleets of motor vessels, shore depôts and factories, and the canning industry, during 1929-1934, amounts to nearly 500 million roubles. At the present time (1935) there are at work more than 100 ocean-going trawlers, as well as larger vessels ; 8 shipbuilding wharves for repairing and increasing this fleet ; 21 refrigerating establishments ; 9 ice-making works ; 26 barrel factories; 250 radio transmitting and receiving stations; 27 fish-waste factories, and many incidental establishments. The annual catch of this state fishery department now amounts to nearly half a million tons of fish, or about twice as much as the total catch of all the fishermen of 1921 ; a remarkable achievement of only five years' constructive work.

But the Soviet Government, in establishing this great industry, in which all the workers are directly employed at salaries or wages, had no wish or intention to establish a monopoly, or to supersede the coast and river fisheries, by which some hundreds of thousands of fishermen are earning an independent living. On the contrary, these self-employing " owner-producers ", all round the coasts of

---

[1] The latest accessible information about the USSR fisheries is given in the article by Professor A. Petrov, entitled " The Fisheries of the Soviet Union, a New and Efficient Industry ", in the Supplement of *The Financial News* (London), November 5, 1934. This, however, says little about the fisher kolkhosi, for which should be consulted the decrees and regulations of July 1931 and September 1932, and an article by I. Ivanovsky, entitled " The Collective Fishery System in the USSR ", in *Voks Socialist Construction in the USSR*, vol. vi., 1934. See also *Das Fischerwesen Russlands*, by William F. Douglas (Berlin, 1930, pp. 206).

the USSR, and in all its great lakes and rivers, have been systematically encouraged ; helped in their equipment and marketing ; and finally brought together in a network of self-governing kolkhosi. The result has been that, concurrently with the rapid development of the state fisheries, the output of the self-governing owner-producers has also increased year by year, so that they can claim, in 1935, to be catching, in the aggregate, something like 60 per cent more weight of fish than they did in 1921, with a larger average income per head, and greater security and amenity.

We cannot recount all the stages in this friendly cooperation between the Soviet Government and the independent fishermen. The first few years after the revolution witnessed various not very successful attempts at a revival of the industry. In 1921 there began an apparently spontaneous organisation of the coastal fishermen in local artels, or communes, which presently established district and provincial unions for common purposes, and in 1923 the All-Russian Cooperative Industrial Union of Fishermen (Vsekopromrybaksoyus), with a centre at Moscow. But there was still comparatively little intercourse between the fishermen of the different coasts of the USSR, and many villages of fishermen remained untouched by the new movement of thought. In 1931, partly as a result of the growth of the new state fisheries, the various organisations of fisher kolkhosi were reorganised on a common plan, and united with some others which had meanwhile joined the hunters' associations, in an All-Union Congress of Fishing Kolkhosi (Rybakkolkhossoyus). Since that date nearly all the professional fishermen in the USSR, some 300,000 in number (other than the wage-earners of the state fishery department),[1] have joined one or other of the 1500 fisher kolkhosi which now form the federal association.

The special note of this federation seems to be the considerable autonomy retained by the several fisher kolkhosi, and their deliberate limitation of the functions entrusted to their delegates

---

[1] The wage-earners employed in the government fishing fleet are members of the Fishermen's Trade Union (in 1934 divided into the three trade unions of the fishermen of the northern, eastern and southern seas). There are still a small number of independent fishermen in the north and east of Siberia, who are mostly united in kolkhosi forming part of the " Integral " cooperative federation, presently to be described. It should be added that a few of the consumers' cooperative societies carry on, by employment at wages, small freshwater fisheries for their own needs.

to little more than marketing, the supply of equipment at wholesale prices, and the giving of technical instruction and advice. The 1500 kolkhosi elect delegates, roughly in proportion to membership, to the annual session of the congress of the particular regional union to which each of them belongs. The 42 regional union congresses (12 of them representing exclusively the kolkhosi fishing the fresh water of lakes and rivers) maintain each the smallest possible secretarial and accounting staff. The All-Union Congress, composed of delegates of the 42 union congresses, meets only once a year to re-elect its Executive Board of thirty-five members, and discuss the annual report. This Executive Board, which is unpaid, meets in Moscow only very occasionally, and leaves the daily work to the presidium of five members whom it appoints. These five salaried members, who give their whole time to their duties, regard themselves not as leaders or administrators of a great industry, but merely as organisers and technical advisers, two or three of whom, at all times, are on visit to the distant kolkhosi.

What, then, does the cooperative organisation provide for its members ? The writers had an opportunity, in 1932, of seeing, on the shores of the Sea of Azov, one of these fisher kolkhosi from the inside. The North Caucasus Krai included several regional fisher unions, to which, at that date, there belonged, 77 fisher kolkhosi,[1] with some 18,000 members, all working on the Sea of Azov or on the neighbouring shores of the Black Sea. The federal organisation provided the fisher kolkhosi with equipment, advice and instructions. It supplied its members with excellent thigh boots, nets and other equipment at wholesale prices. It provided advice in fishing methods, information as to weather and other prospects, and instruction in book-keeping. Each kolkhos, containing between one hundred and three hundred fishermen, owned collectively the boats, nets and other equipment, including sometimes a team of oxen to drag the heavily weighted net to land. It worked in brigades of several dozen men and boys each, who united in the operations under the direction of a leader of their own choice. Each catch, involving

[1] Only one of these kolkhosi, namely, that of Anaba, was in 1932 a completely collectivised commune.

Some of the fisher kolkhosi maintain their own subsidiary enterprises by wage labour, such as the weaving and repairing of nets, and even the raising of crops of foodstuffs for the members' households !

an hour or two's work, was straightway landed on the wharf
belonging to the state fish trust, or other purchaser, where the
fish were at once cleaned, salted or iced, packed and despatched.
The fisher kolkhos was thus concerned only with catching the
fish.   It was governed entirely by its own members' meeting,
which elected a president, as well as delegates to the regional
congress.[1]

The financial organisation was peculiar.   In 1932 each
kolkhos made its own contract for the sale of a specified proportion of the fish arising from its catch during the ensuing three
months.   Anything beyond the quantity contracted for, the
kolkhos might sell as and where it pleased.   These contracts
were, in 1932, made simultaneously for the whole district at a
meeting of representatives of the kolkhosi as sellers, and of the
state fish trust, as well as some consumers' cooperatives and large
factories as buyers.   It was usual, we were told, for the prices
for each weight of fish to be willingly raised for the seasons in
which the catch is normally least.   The kolkhos paid no subscription towards the expenses of the regional organisation, or
of the All-Union central office.   It was the buyer who paid a
fixed contribution for these purposes—in 1932 7½ per cent on
the price paid for the fish—to the regional organisation.   Thus,
the kolkhos was free to dispose of the whole of the contract price
as its members might determine.   What it habitually did was to
allocate 35 per cent of the proceeds of each catch to a fund for
renewal or increase of capital equipment (including amortisation
of any loan) ;   and the remaining 65 per cent to the members of
the brigade making each particular catch.   This lump sum was
shared according to a fixed ratio, among five grades of men and
boys, the lowest apprentice counting for one, and each of the
four higher grades getting one-fifth in excess of the grade below

---

[1] In the autonomous republic of the Crimea there were, in 1932, 13 fishing
kolkhosi along the coast between Eupatoria and the Sea of Azov, with 4500
members, supplying the land-dwellers with sturgeon, turbot, mullet, eels and
pilchards. " We no longer work for masters," said the seventy-three-year-old
leader ; " our boats, our nets, our fish are ours. We discuss our shortcomings
in production conferences. . . . The bad results of this year have been largely
our own fault. The youngsters in our collective must learn how to catch fish.
Again and again I tell them that there's no luck for a fisherman. It's all in
knowing how to do it. And we'll best serve the revolution when we know how
to provide the tons of fish needed by the country " (article on " Udarniks of
the Sea ", by Ed. Falkowski, in *Moscow Daily News*, October 15, 1932).

it ; the highest, therefore, counting for two. Of the commission of 7½ per cent on the price, payable by the purchaser direct to the secretary of the regional council, 4 per cent was retained for this council's expenses ; 2 per cent was allotted downward to the local council, whilst the remaining 1½ per cent was remitted upward to the Moscow centre.[1]

On the remodelling of the federation in 1932, the marketing arrangements were so far changed as to give the government the advantage of a systemised All-Union arrangement. Now the government annually enters into a simple contract to buy a specified uniform quota of the aggregate catch, from each kolkhos in membership, which is arranged by negotiation between the Commissariat of Supplies and the presidium of the All-Union Federation, and embodied in a general contract ratified by the Executive Board, specifying not only the amount, but also the price, the dates of delivery and the method of payment. In addition, each kolkhos negotiates supplementary conditions about details with the local state factories at which each catch is delivered.

The price paid by the government, which, it is claimed, the fishermen's board of thirty-five virtually fixes, with merely the concurrence of the government, is, roughly speaking, 20 per cent lower than could be obtained by the kolkhosi if they sold their catch in the open market by retail. But the kolkhosi get, for the government quota, the advantage not only of a fixed price all the year round without the trouble of obtaining transport, or the risk of waste, or the expense of retail selling, but also the privilege of obtaining the products of the state factories of equipment, etc., at wholesale prices.[2] If the Executive Board

---

[1] The financial arrangements have since been changed. The Government or other buyer now pays only the price agreed upon. The expenses of the organisation are met by levies on the kolkhosi, usually of no more than 3 or 4 per cent of the proceeds of sales.

[2] We understand that the Executive Board does not always find it easy to convince the separate kolkhosi that the price demanded for the government quota is as high as might reasonably be asked of so large a buyer. It is not always remembered that the government provides the motor engines and other equipment, thigh boots and special clothing, and many foodstuffs, at specially low prices. Sometimes a kolkhos will be exceptionally successful in its sales to other purchasers, and is reluctant to take into account its frequent losses by failure to get prompt transport, etc. When the catch has been unexpectedly small, appeals are made to the government to make an addition to the agreed price ; and this, we are told, is frequently conceded.

cannot agree with the government as to the price, this is settled by arbitration.  All fish in excess of the quota may be disposed of as each kolkhos pleases.  Supplies of fresh fish are eagerly sought by such independent buyers as the consumers' cooperative societies and the departments of " self supply " of factories, mines and railways ; and fresh fish finds also a ready sale at any accessible open market.  To these buyers the kolkhosi habitually charge a higher price than that obtained for the government quota, in order to compensate for the trouble and risk involved in such separate sales.  The associated kolkhosi have, since 1932, abandoned to the government all methods of " processing " the fish, whether by way of refrigeration or other ways of preserving, or by preparation of caviare, or by canning, all of which can most economically be conducted on a large scale.

The only tax levied by the government on the fishermen is one of 3 per cent on the aggregate value of the total year's catch, in return for the use of the public waters and for the fish taken therefrom.  The kolkhosi are all willingly cooperating with the Commissariat of Supplies in measures for protecting the fishing grounds from exhaustion, and now annually return to the water some fifteen billions of under-sized fish.

The 1500 fisher kolkhosi own over 65,000 fishing boats, mostly built by the members themselves, of which some 5000 are equipped with petrol motors supplied by the government on easy terms. The men are now demanding more powerful motors, even up to 150 horse-power, to enable them to fish at greater distances from shore.  Meanwhile they are assisted, in about thirty of the fishing-grounds, by motor-boat stations maintained by the government for service on payment by any brigade or kolkhos desiring them.

The earnings of the kolkhos members are said to be steadily rising.  In many districts they are reported to be between 2000 and 2500 roubles a year for the average man ; but in others they do not reach so high a sum.  Considerable " cultural " advances are reported.  In some districts hundreds of women take part in the work, and become kolkhos members.  There are floating clubs, with libraries and musical instruments, maintained by some of the kolkhosi.  There are crèches for the infants.  Nearly all the members join the local consumers' cooperative societies, whose recently rising demands for books and gramophones, wireless sets and bicycles, indicate an increasing margin of unbespoken income.

*Integral Cooperatives.*—This association, unique in con-stitutional form and in its peculiar combination of functions, was established only in July 1934, as the outcome of a decade of experience with organisations of other types.[1]

We trace its origin to the hierarchy of local associations estab-lished in 1924 by and for the large numbers of hunters and trappers of wild animals. The membership included hunters of different types, whether (a) " professional " hunters and trappers, who lived entirely by this vocation and formed only 15 per cent of the membership ; (b) semi-professionals, who accounted for another 50 per cent, and who pursued the vocation for gain or " for the pot ", but combined it with another occupation ; and (c) finally, also those " amateurs ", about one-third of the whole, who hunted only for amusement. The local associations and their regional unions set themselves to render the services that each of these classes required. They provided in some districts a certain amount of watching of the forests and the game. They supplied the hunters with all the implements of their vocation at little above wholesale prices. They stored and sold, when desired, the products of the chase. But the hunters' associations in some parts of the USSR did more than this. In the sparsely inhabited regions of the north (as, for instance, Tobolsk, Tomsk-Narym, Turukhansk, Kirensk and Priangarsk), where few other institu-tions exist, the hunters' societies united the features of other kinds of cooperatives ; developing fishing and the breeding of reindeer; providing fish canneries and meat factories; supplying all the necessities of the villages, and marketing all their dispos-able products. Practically the whole adult population of these areas belonged to the hunters' societies, to which they contributed several hundred thousand members. The hunters' cooperative societies in other areas of the USSR came to number nearly 1000, with some 600,000 members, organised in about 6000 groups. Each society was governed by general meetings of its members,

---

[1] Not much has been published, even (so far as we know) in Russian, upon Integral Cooperation ; and our information is derived mainly from personal enquiry. A volume (in Russian) entitled *The Far North, a Collection of Materials* (Moscow, 1934, 176 pp.), being a reprint of a special supplement of the journal *The Soviet North*, contains (p. 106, etc.) details and statistics as to Integral Cooperation.

who elected a president, and usually a small presidium. The societies were grouped in thirty-five regional federations, with councils of delegates from the societies within each region. These regional federations sent delegates to meet in occasional All-Union Congresses of hunters and trappers from all parts, and maintained an active central office in Moscow.

But this widespread cooperative organisation proved lacking in stability. Both its membership and its functions were too heterogeneous for lasting unity, over a geographical area so vast as the USSR. The divergence of interest between the professional hunters and trappers, on the one hand, and, on the other, the sporting amateurs and the peasants who hunted only occasionally, led to perpetual conflicts. In 1933, by decree of TSIK and Sovnarkom of the USSR of August 17, the " integral " societies of the Far North, consisting largely of " national minorities ", were set up as an independent system on the principle of the kolkhos. At last the All-Union Federation of Hunters was finally dissolved, and a new and more limited federal body, confined practically to Northern and Far-Eastern Siberia, but maintaining a central office at Moscow, was established on July 25, 1934, by a congress of delegates representing local cooperative societies in these areas.

The new body was, so far as hunting was concerned, from the first dominated by those for whom the pursuit of game is a constant means of livelihood, taking up at least half their time ; and these are now very largely concentrated in Northern and Eastern Siberia. The amateurs throughout the Union now find their wants supplied and their interests attended to by the voluntary organisations dealing with " sport " of every kind. The peasants, occasionally hunting " for the pot ", are now mostly members of collective farms, and dispose of their furs directly by communicating with the nearest agents of the Commissariat of Foreign Trade, or its Fur Trust.

The new federation, however, retains in membership the main bulk of the " mixed " cooperative societies within the geographical area with which it deals, whether these unite, in one and the same society, both production and distribution, or take on the form of kolkhosi, specialising either on agriculture or on fishing, or on reindeer breeding. We are told that, in this area, largely inhabited by different tribes of non-Russian stock, the people are at a stage of development too primitive to allow of their becoming members of various cooperative or other bodies having distinct and separate purposes. Whatever cooperative societies they establish almost invariably take on a " mixed " form, which is styled " integral ", and which permits them to include, in one and the same society, hunting, fishing, agriculture, stock-breeding, the marketing of produce of every kind, and the retailing of all the commodities that their members desire. It is a curious example of the feeling in favour of multiformity that the vast geographical area over which this form of cooperation prevails [1] is abandoned to the societies preferring it. Equally, it is an instance of the policy of " cultural autonomy " that no attempt is made by the USSR Government to impose on these " national minorities " what, in other parts of the USSR, has proved a superior form of organisation.[2] Neither Centrosoyus, representing the consumers' cooperative societies, nor Vsekorybaksoyus, representing the fisher kolkhosi, seeks to extend to this area, nor endeavours to entice away the local membership. The USSR Commissariat of the Timber Industries and the State Fishery Department of the USSR Commissariat of Supplies penetrate into this territory without competing with the " integral " societies, which sell their furs direct to the Fur Trust of the USSR Commissariat of Foreign Trade and their fish to the RSFSR Commissariat of Local Supplies, or to any other purchasers whom they can reach. The RSFSR Commissariat of Local Trade maintains in the area, principally in the more considerable centres of population, its own trading depots (Gostorgovlya) ; whilst the USSR Commissariat of Foreign Trade, through its Fur Trust, and the USSR Commissariat of Supplies, through such organs as Soyus Pushnina, Rybtrest, etc., contract with all or most of the local pro-

---

[1] The area of the activities of the Integral Cooperatives is described as including the Northern Krai, the Ostyak okrug, the Vogulsk okrug, the Narym Krai, the East Siberian Krai, Buriat Mongolia and the Far Eastern Krai. The membership, alike of the kolkhosi and of the primitive productive cooperative societies—amounting in all to something like 300,000 adults—is reported to be about half made up of " national minorities " (*The Far North* (in Russian), Moscow, 1934, p. 106, etc.).

[2] Thus the kolkhosi of the Far North are not pressed to assume the form in which all the land-holdings are merged in one undivided field. They are left in the stage in which each member retains his own instruments of production, and combines only for labour in specific operations of agriculture, or during the seasons for hunting or fishing.

ductive societies to buy a specified quota of their output at agreed prices.[1]

The Association of Integral Cooperatives included, in 1934, 869 societies termed simply "integral"; 610 consumers' societies, mostly more or less "mixed" in function; 243 cooperative productive associations, many of whom deal also in commodities for their members' consumption; and over 700 kolkhosi, predominantly for agriculture or reindeer breeding, but including some mainly for fishing. These separate societies are all governed by periodical meetings of their members, which elect a president or manager, and a small presidium. Nearly 1000 of them, which carry on retail trading in household commodities, have specific trading districts assigned to them, varying in extent from about 3000 square kilometres (Nenetsky okrug) up to about 23,700 square kilometres (Chukotsky okrug). But all the societies, including the kolkhosi, are united in 263 regional unions by rayons, okrugs, oblasts or krais (of which there are 239 for rayons, 21 for okrugs and 3 for oblasts and krais). It is presumably these 263 local unions that will elect delegates to the Congress of Integral Cooperative Societies that may be periodically summoned.

The organisational structure of the "Far North" of Siberia is plainly in an inchoate condition; unlikely, as it seems to the present writers, to remain long without substantial change, as to the nature of which no prediction is offered.

*War Invalids.*—The seven years of war, 1914–1920, left in the USSR an incalculable number of partially disabled men, whose existence imposed on the Soviet Government a problem transcending in magnitude and difficulty that of any other of the belligerents. It was dealt with on different lines from those followed by the other countries. The absence, in the USSR, of any vested interests of profit-making employers, and of any objection by soviet trade unionism, made it possible for the Soviet Government to set the partially disabled men to work, on their own account, upon any productive enterprise within their capacity. The form usually adopted was that of the artel. The "war invalids" capable of any productive work were invited to join a widespread federal association of owner-producers, largely self-

---

[1] The "plan" for fish in 1934 was fixed at 698,000 centners, whilst that for furs, etc., amounted to 9,980,000 roubles' worth (*The Far North* (in Russian), p. 106; Model Agreement (in Russian) for the supply and delivery of furs and skins: Moscow, Koiz, 1934).

governing in character, which in 1927 numbered 2861 little local
societies, with over 38,000 working members.  The association has
been liberally assisted from government funds, in order to enable
it to start a large number of industries for its members, usually on
a small scale, by which the disabled men are enabled to earn a
proportion of the maintenance allowed to them, the deficit being
met from public funds.  The separate enterprises, in 1927 numbering over 7000, are of the most varied kinds.  There are small
flour mills and oil factories, little distilleries and cheesemaking
centres, together with fruit and vegetable gardens, growing for the
local market.  There are bakeries making confectionery ; shoemaking and tailoring workshops, and furniture factories.  Some
men keep bees and poultry ; others man the numerous book and
newspaper stalls on the basis of a commission on sales ; or drive
carts and lorries in the execution of a succession of jobs of transportation.  The gross income of the association in 1925–1926 was
264 million roubles, of which rather more than one-third was the
net product of the members' own labour, the balance being found
from public funds.

In due course, as the number of war invalids capable of work
gradually decreased, the same organisation was utilised for the
" invalids of industry ", men or women partially disabled by
accident or industrial disease in the factory or the mine.  At the
present time these invalids of industry far outnumber, among
those at work, the men disabled in the war.  Out of a total of
about 100,000 members of the federation who are in one or other
form of employment, about 70,000 are members of manufacturing
artels, whilst the others are in artels of service, supplying part
of the personnel of hotels, theatres, cinemas, the large retailing
establishments and other government departments, clubs, hospitals and educational institutions.  All partially disabled men
are encouraged to join one or other of these artels and to continue
to perform such work as they can, as this is so much better for
them than vegetating in idleness on a meagre pension.  Such
workers are often trained free of charge in special technical institutes for the disabled.  They have often their own clubs for
suitable recreation, and their own sanatoria and rest-houses in the
Crimea or elsewhere.  There are special summer schools in the
country for the children of the disabled.  A few of these manufacturing artels of partially disabled men have become completely

self-supporting, and able to allow their members a small bonus in addition to their stipulated wages. Members may work in these artels whilst receiving the pensions awarded to them in respect of war disabilities, or those in respect of disabilities due to industrial accidents or diseases, or merely for old age after long service.[1] It is argued that the addition that they make to the aggregate supply of commodities and services is clearly a national gain, whilst the pensioners themselves benefit both physically and mentally by continuing to perform such work as is within their powers. This double advantage, it is claimed, far outweighs the cost to the public funds of the possible overlapping of pension and subsidy. There seems, in the USSR, no more reason for denying to any worker the wage that he earns, merely because he enjoys a pension awarded to him in respect of previous service, than merely because he owns a balance in the Savings Bank.

### (d) ASSOCIATIONS OF ARTISTIC AND INTELLECTUAL PRODUCERS

*Artistic and Intellectual Workers.*—It is difficult to keep account of the various other associations of owner-producers, of which there are possibly, in the wide expanse of the USSR, many hundreds. Incredible as it may seem to those who believe the USSR to be groaning in one all-pervading tyranny, these bodies form and dissolve and reform at the will of the members, with the least possible legal or official formalities. Equally difficult is it to discover which of them remain outside the federation of incops that has been already described. Thus, to cite only a few examples, the artists (chiefly painters, sculptors and architects) had, in 1931, an association of some 1500 members, called Khudozhnik (the Artist). This society provides its members a certain amount of accommodation in collective studios, runs for their service a small but efficient colour factory, organises exhibitions for the sale of their works, and even gives them credit when they are more than usually hard up ! The photographers, whose art is highly developed in the USSR, have an

---

[1] The pensions to war invalids and those to the widows and children of deceased men of war service, like allowances to the blind, the deaf and dumb, the crippled, etc., are awarded and paid by the Commissariats of Social Welfare of the several republics. The pensions payable in respect of disabilities due to industrial accidents and diseases, like those in respect of old age after long service, are payable from the social insurance funds, now administered by the trade union organisation.

artel of their own on similar lines. Those who are associated with the art side of the equipment of the theatre have another. A special group of artistic workers in wood and lacquer, largely concentrated in the little town of Palekh, who have for generations lived by carving and painting religious icons, have re-organised their industry in a cooperative society for the production of what is now in greater demand, namely, wooden boxes, trays and *plaques*, beautifully painted and lacquered, without religious associations.

The authors seem to have had from time to time, in addition to their professional associations of authors and journalists as such, a whole series of cooperative publishing societies of one sort or another. There is a society of scientists at Leningrad which publishes works on physical and biological science ; not in rivalry with the gigantic state publishing enterprise of the RSFSR, but in supplement of its work. There are similar publishing societies in one or more of the other constituent republics for works in their own languages. A separate enterprise at Moscow is that of the Cooperative Society of Foreign Workers in the USSR, which issues, for the instruction of the German, American and British residents, a series of books and pamphlets in their own language, most of them describing particular features of soviet industry, agriculture and social institutions.[1]

## The World of Labour in the USSR

The dominant impression made by the survey of the organisation of Man as a Producer will, we think, be one of multiformity. There could hardly be a wider divergence in constitutional structure than that between the 154 highly centralised trade unions (in round numbers eighteen million members), and the loosely federated twenty thousand cooperative societies of

[1] Publishing is a side-line of many of the other organisations that we have elsewhere described, from trade unions to universities, from the various kinds of cooperative societies to the multitude of voluntary associations with their extraordinary diversity of objects and purposes ; not excepting the Red Army and the Communist Party itself. Sometimes they have their own printing press. They always have to get paper from the People's Commissars in charge of the government paper mills and of all imports. All alike are subject, just as the government publishing houses themselves are, to the universal censorship. All of them, moreover, work in friendly cooperation with Ogiz (the principal state publishing house at Moscow) and with the publishing houses of the various constituent and autonomous republics.

owner-producers in industry (three million members) ; or between either of these bodies and, on the one hand, the 240,000 kolkhosi, or collective farms (thirty million members), or, on the other, the 1500 fisher kolkhosi (300,000 members). To add even further to the multiformity, there is still to be reckoned the strange breed of "Integral" cooperatives (300,000 members), whose chief peculiarity seems to be to jumble up together many of the characteristics in which all the rest differ from each other ; not to mention also the exceptional variety afforded by the federation of partially disabled men and women, who work at every conceivable occupation, and find their ground for separate association in the common feature of physical disability of one or other kind.

These fifty-odd million men and women working in the production of commodities and services are, it will be noted, of different kinds or grades. Some would be classed as brain workers, others as manual workers. Their personal remuneration, and, with it, their standards of living, vary considerably ; and whilst the level is undoubtedly rising all round, there is visible no tendency either to identity or to that equality which is stigmatised as a dead level. But amid all the multiformity of constitutional structure, and all the heterogeneity of work and grade, of wages and standard of living, there is one feature that is constant and ubiquitous in all the "productive" organisations. There is no segregation by wealth, or social class, or position in the hierarchy. In every enterprise, large or small, urban or rural, the directors and managers, the technicians and specialists, the book-keepers and the gate-keepers, the skilled mechanics and the general labourers are members of one and the same organisation, whether it be called a trade union, an industrial cooperative society, a collective farm, a fishermen's collective, an integral cooperative, or a society of war invalids. The ground for their common membership is their common interest in the enterprise in which they find themselves associated, and their similar common interest in the other enterprises engaged in the same branch of production throughout the USSR. Not only in their daily work and their monthly pay is there this common interest among all grades, but also in their other conditions of life. The hours of labour ; the safety and amenity of the place of work ; the provision of medical attendance and hospital treatment ; the whole range of social insurance ; the adequate provision and proper maintenance of dwelling-places ; the arrangements for the care and education of children ; the means of recreation, holidays, clubs and rest-houses, music and the theatre and endless other matters concern workers of all kinds.

What, in all this upgrowth of collective organisation, practically all new or remade since the Revolution, has happened to "workers' control" ?[1] Less than half the aggregate of "producers " in the USSR, it will be seen, are working under a contract of service at all (the eighteen million members of trade unions, together with the four million co-workers who, for one or other reason, are, as yet, non-members). Much more numerous are the various kinds of owner-producers for whom the trade union form is inappropriate. These owner-producers, whether in industrial artels (three millions), in collective farms (thirty millions) or in fishermen's associations (300,000), are themselves the owners of the commodities they produce, from the sale of which, after defraying all expenses and the government taxation, their remuneration is derived. They themselves direct, by their own members' meetings, their individual and combined labour, together with the conditions under which they work, and the speed and regularity of their exertions. But they have no monopoly. They have themselves to decide, in meeting assembled, and in constant competition with other forms of production, and other kinds of commodities, how they will satisfy the demands of the consumers of their products, and the users of the services that they are prepared to render. Their subjection is to the consumers whom they directly serve.

There is, of course, the further alternative to wage-labour of independent production by individual men or women, or by the family group. It is not usually realised that this still (1935) furnishes some sort of maintenance to as many as fifteen millions of adult men and women in the USSR. There are in the cities innumerable dressmakers and washerwomen ; droschky drivers and shoeblacks ; casual " handymen " of all kinds ; " freelance " journalists and authors, unsalaried artists and scientists.

[1] In a subsequent chapter on " The Liquidation of the Landlord and Capitalist ", we shall describe how, immediately after the revolution of October 1917, most of the factories in Petrograd passed under the management of workers' committees ; and how, in a very short time, this was found to be an unsatisfactory form of organisation.

In the vast rural districts between the Baltic and the Pacific the
independent peasants still number half a dozen million households, comprising perhaps twelve million adults, to say nothing
of the independent fishermen, the hunters, the " prospectors " of
minerals and what not, together with the nomads passing from one
grazing ground to another.  Those who regard work under a
contract of service as necessarily of the nature of " wage slavery "
may possibly imagine these fifteen million wholly independent
producers under Soviet Communism as enjoying complete control
over their own working lives !  But, however attractive such
complete control may be to some natures, and at some periods of
their lives, and however remunerative may be such independent
production in exceptional cases, it is the common experience of
mankind that it is not in such an isolated existence that the widest
freedom is found.  Work in combination with others nearly
always makes a larger product, and therefore affords a greater
width of opportunity, than isolated effort.  The question is in
which form of associated work does the worker obtain the most
control over his working life.

It seems to us clear that, in the great industrial establishments
that have for half a century been characteristic of Russian industry, the eighteen millions of trade unionists, whilst not actually
entrusted with the management of their several industries, do
control, to a very large extent, in their constant consultation with
the management, and with all the organs of government, the
conditions of their employment—their hours of labour, the exercise of factory discipline, the safety and amenity of their places
of work, and the sharing among themselves of the proportion of
the product that they agree should be allocated to personal wages.
In like manner, the trade unions not only control, and actually
manage by their own committees, the disposition of that other
part of the product which they agree should be allocated to the
whole range of social insurances, education, medical attendance,
holidays, and organised recreation of all kinds.  Only, this
" workers' control " is exercised, not by any worker as an individual, but jointly by the workers' committees; and, very largely,
not for one establishment by itself, but for each industry as a
whole ; and, in some cases, where this seems most appropriate,
for the whole body of producers in the USSR.  The influence,
upon every organ of government, of the eighteen million trade

unionists, is immeasurably great. It is, in fact, this which is acclaimed as the Dictatorship of the Proletariat ! [1]

Compared with the amount of control exercised by those workers who are enrolled in trade unions, that enjoyed by the different kinds of owner-producers is at once much less and much greater. It is much less at long range, and over a wide area. It is much greater over the particular farm or fishery, factory or workshop, in which the associated owner-producers work. It is not the thirty million men and women members of the kolkhosi or the three million members of the incops, or the 300,000 associated fishermen, who dominate the counsels of the USSR Sovnarkom or the Central Committee of the Communist Party, or carry weight with the State Planning Commission, but much more the smaller number of the trade unionists, whether factory workers, miners, railwaymen or labourers in the sovkhosi. But the superiority in control that the worker in the great industry enjoys over the larger area carries with it a lesser control within each particular workshop. Here the worker who is actually a partner with his fellows in the ownership and management of the little enterprise that is run as an industrial cooperative society may well feel that he enjoys a larger liberty to indulge his own caprices than the worker who has to obey the factory bell. In the Soviet Union the worker has an effective freedom to choose which form of associated labour he prefers. For nothing stands out more clearly from our survey of the World of Labour in the USSR than the inaccuracy of the assumption that Soviet Communism involves either universal state ownership of the instruments of production, or the existence of but one possible employer of labour, or of only one method of gaining a livelihood.

[1] With what accuracy this claim is made, and subject to what other influences, we examine in Chapter VI. of Part I., " Dictatorship or Democracy ? "

# CHAPTER IV

## MAN AS A CONSUMER

WE have seen how the inhabitants of the USSR are represented, in their capacity of citizens, in the soviet hierarchy. We have noted also that they are separately represented in their capacity of producers in three different ways. If they are wage or salary earners they are in the hierarchy of trade unionism. If they are not engaged at salary or wages, they are in one or other of the twin organisations of owner-producers, working respectively in manufacturing artels or incops and in collective farms. But, in all but the simplest societies, mankind has also a third capacity, in which wishes and ideas need a vehicle of expression, and individual activities a mechanism of collective control. As consumers, men and women think and act differently from what they do either as citizens or as producers. Moreover, in all but the smallest communities, to organise, with exact regularity, a daily distribution, among the whole body of consumers, of the innumerable commodities they desire, is a task of immense magnitude and difficulty, calling for its own distinct administration. Before assuming power, Lenin saw clearly and confidently that this task would have to be undertaken by the consumers' cooperative societies, with a membership becoming universal.[1] We may

[1] There is an extensive literature in Russian relating to the consumers' cooperative movement, whilst elaborate statistical and other reports are issued, chiefly by Centrosoyus. The following books in other languages may be more conveniently consulted : *The Cooperative Movement in Russia*, by V. V. Bubnov (Manchester, 1917) ; *The Russian Cooperative Movement*, by F. E. Lee (U.S. Government Printing Office, 1920) ; *The Cooperative Movement in Russia*, by Elsie Terry Blanc (New York, 1924) ; *Village Life under the Soviets*, by Karl Borders (New York, 1927) ; *Die Konsumgenossenschaften in der USSR* (Berlin, 1927, 72 pp.), translated as *Consumers' Cooperation in the USSR* (Manchester, 1927) by N. Popov (director of the Education Department of Centrosoyus) ;

doubt whether he, or anyone else, realised that, in the circumstances of the USSR, the organisation of distribution would prove at least as difficult as the organisation of production ; and that it would actually take longer to raise to any common standard of efficiency.

Let us consider, at the outset, some of the troubles that, in any country whatsoever, beset the organiser of a systematic distribution of foodstuffs and other household commodities. There is, first, the difficulty of getting an honest and efficient personnel. This matters far more in distribution than in production. The factory operative may contrive to be idle spasmodically, but this can be largely prevented. What is more to the point is that the materials and products that he handles are seldom such as to tempt him to purloin them for his own or his family's consumption. To the salesman or warehouseman in a cooperative store, on the other hand, or to the lorry driver or porter, at a time when food is scarce and his children at home are hungry, the provocation, if he happens to be pecuniarily distressed, to abstract something to take home is well-nigh irresistible. The temptation is increased by the practical difficulty of ensuring, in a vast number of separate stores, a demonstrably accurate audit of anything except money or stamps. Many kinds of goods in bulk cannot easily be checked on delivery from hand to hand, either by counting or by weighing ; whilst stocktaking is a process demanding for accuracy the highest skill and the utmost technical knowledge. Moreover, there must be an allowance for " waste " in retailing, and even in storing ; and no one can say with confidence how much. And nearly all commodities

*Soviet Russia in the Second Decade*, New York, 1928, ch. xi., " The Consumers' Cooperative Movement," by Paul Douglas, pp. 253-267 ; *Die Konsumgenossenschaften in Russland*, by S. Sapir, Berlin, 1928, 260 pp ; *The Cooperative Movement and Banking in the USSR*, by N. Barou (1928, 48 pp.) ; *The Cooperative Movement in the USSR and its Foreign Trade*, by N. Barou (1929, 30 pp.) ; *The Cooperative Movement in Russia during the War : Part I.— Consumers' Cooperation*, by Kayden (Oxford, 1929) ; *Consumers' Cooperation in Soviet Russia*, by E. F. Wise (Manchester, 1929) ; *The Consumers' Cooperative Movement in the Soviet Union*, by N. Nekrassov (Centrosoyus, Moscow, 1929) ; *Russian Cooperation Abroad : Foreign Trade 1912-1928*, by N. Barou (1930, 96 pp.) ; *Les Coopératives de consommation en l'URSS*, par A. E. Badeieff (Amiens, 1930) ; *Russian Cooperative Banking*, by N. Barou (1931, 82 pp.) ; *Cooperative Banking*, by N. Barou (1932, 350 pp.) ; *Russia : USSR*, edited by P. Malevsky-Malevich, New York, 1933, " Cooperation " pp. 572-83 ; and for the present position, *Cooperation in the USSR*, by Leslie A. Paul (1934, 160 pp.) ; and *Supply and Trade in the USSR*, by W. Nodel (1934, 176 pp.).

depreciate and spoil, to an extent that cannot easily be either checked or estimated. The vagueness in the ascertainment of how much there is produces a laxness in the disposing of it. Even the elected committeemen and the higher officials of the cooperative movement, just because they are always handling relatively large quantities of food and drink, are found—we think, in all countries—to be more disposed to treat themselves lavishly " out of the stores ", than are the corresponding committeemen and officials of the trade union movement.

Efficiency behind the counter involves, however, much more than honesty and precise accounting. The productive efficiency of the handicraftsman or factory operative is practically not lessened by occasional bad manners, nor even by habitual incivility or boorishness. For all that matters, these wage-earners can usually be stimulated to zeal and celerity, and continuity of effort throughout the whole working day, by systems of piecework remuneration. But the salesman behind the counter, like the cashier at the pay-desk, is required, all day long, whatever may be his own feelings, to manifest, to one customer after another, unfailing civility of manners and actual zeal in trying to suit the customer's desires, without a trace of resentment of the customer's stupidity or capricious changes of mind. When we cut adrift from the profit-making motive, this efficiency of service in the store cannot easily be pecuniarily stimulated or rewarded. Piecework rates of wages are often impracticable ; and even the system of more or less arbitrary bonuses for good conduct or smart salesmanship usually fails to effect any considerable improvement.

And there is a further trouble in organising distribution that is not always borne in mind. The man who actually makes cabinets or boots, or who joins with others in constructing a house or a colossal hydroelectric plant, may find joy in his work and pride in his production. But it is not easy for the most virtuous of salesmen to get up any enthusiasm for the daily service of handing out, to an indiscriminate crowd of purchasers, bread and potatoes, cabbages and groceries. It is not for nothing that retail shopkeepers have everywhere been despised by other vocations. In Russia, even more than in other countries, the little trader, often a Tartar or a Jew, or the village usurer or vodka seller, has long lived in an atmosphere of contempt, manifested alike by the handicraftsman and the factory operative, the

merchant and the brainworking professional. The result has been
a repugnance among the Russians to take to retail shopkeeping,
which has not been wholly removed by its transformation into
a public service. It has been noticed that relatively few active
socialists, and especially few members of the Communist Party,
have been at any time salesmen or clerks under the committees
of the consumers' cooperative societies.[1] All these considerations,
which apply even more to the Russian people than to some others,
make the construction of a satisfactory system of distribution
perhaps the most difficult of all the tasks to which Soviet
Communism has set its hand.

Unfortunately, the previous history of the Russian consumers'
cooperative movement and the position in which it stood in 1917
were not such as to facilitate its accomplishment of the task that
Lenin had, in thought, assigned to it. Consumers' cooperation
had been introduced into Russia from England and Germany
half a century before, but only in the way of paternal philanthropy
by exceptional employers, and in a form which may not have
remained entirely free from the evils of the truck system. Consumers' cooperation as a democratic outcome of independent
workmen's organisation may be said to have begun sporadically
in Russia with the twentieth century, and to have made headway
only with the revolutionary movement of 1905. As an independent organ of working-class opinion, it only barely survived
the tsarist repression of the subsequent years ; but the movement
continued to grow, in city and country, under watchful police
supervision, as a non-political outcome of enlightened " liberalism ", making for individual thrift. During the three years of
war (1914–1917), the consumers' cooperative societies in many
cases rendered great service, in association with the patriotic
efforts of the Zemstvos, in maintaining the supply of necessaries
both for the army in the field and for the civilian families at home.
When the 1917 revolution occurred, the consumers' cooperative
movement, which counted a quarter of the families in Russia
in its membership, was almost wholly under the influence of
anti-Bolshevik leadership. At any rate, the hundred or more
representatives whom the movement sent to the Democratic

---

[1] " The best Bolsheviks," we have been told, " despite a Party resolution
urging a change in spirit, have disdained to work in the cooperative stores,
manifesting a certain superior, one might almost say aristocratic attitude
towards the business of selling, buying and merchandising."

Conference (or " Pre-Parliament ") summoned by Kerensky's government in September 1917, ranged themselves " unanimously with the Kadets and Compromisers ".[1] Especially in the Ukraine had the cooperative movement an invidious intellectual heritage. At Kiev, and generally in the Ukrainian cities, the movement was frankly nationalist in spirit, desiring no connection with Moscow. In 1917 it supported the Menshevik uprising in the Ukraine and backed up Kerensky. In the following years it sided with Petlura, and supported Denikin and the counter-revolutionary efforts. Not until the population of the Ukraine had become disgusted with the reactionary character and the excesses of Denikin's army were there any overtures to Moscow. The leading cooperators of the Ukraine had, however, by this time so clearly indicated their intellectual position that they were naturally distrusted.

When the Bolshevik Government was firmly in the saddle, the cooperative societies went on struggling with the increasing difficulties of supplies ; and Lenin's administration, whilst noting their manifest lack of sympathy with its programme, took no immediate action against them. Presently, however, in the welter of war communism, the whole organisation of these societies was absorbed into the government machinery, their buildings and local organisation being autocratically utilised for the distribution of the state rations. This, however, was not the end. There is reason to believe that Lenin remained faithful to his conception of a voluntary organisation of consumers—a hierarchy of consumers' cooperative committees—as an essential part of the constitution, undertaking the whole distribution of household commodities. With the acceptance of the New Economic Policy (NEP), came the restoration to independence of the consumers'

---

[1] " Having up to this time (1927) occupied no place in politics, the cooperators . . . began to appear as the representatives of their 20 million members —or, to put it more simply, of some half the population of Russia. The cooperators sent their roots down into the village through its upper strata. . . . The leaders of the cooperators were recruited from the Liberal-Narodnik and partly the Liberal-Marxist intelligentsia, who formed a natural bridge between the Kadets and the Compromisers. . . . Lenin mercilessly denounced these ' chefs of the democratic kitchen '. . . . Trotsky argued in the Petrograd Soviet that the officials of the cooperatives as little expressed the political will of the peasants as a physician the political will of his patients or a Post Office clerk the views of those who send and receive letters " (*The History of the Russian Revolution*, by Leon Trotsky, vol. ii. (1933), pp. 331-332, 337 ; vol. iii. pp. 17-18, 31, 67).

cooperative societies. These were placed anew on a legal basis by the legislation of 1923-1924. On this revival of the voluntary societies, steps were taken to exclude from the leadership of the movement, as far as possible, those who had been prominent in it prior to 1919 and to bring to the front the Bolshevik members. The " activists " of the Communist Party nearly everywhere saw to it in the cities that the elections brought about the necessary preponderance of " well-disposed " cooperators on the committees, and the Central Board of Centrosoyus has ever since been in complete accord with the " General Line ".

In spite of all these inherent difficulties and temporary defects, the cooperative membership and turnover have, throughout the past decade, increased by leaps and bounds, because no family could wish permanently to forgo the advantage of belonging to a cooperative society. It became unnecessary to retain such attractions to recruiting as the dividend on purchases, and even the payment of interest on share capital.[1] The continuance of rationing, and the increasing limitation of purchases by the use of cards, issued to the producers as such, made it almost necessary for every member of the family over fourteen years of age to be separately enrolled in order to be eligible to share in the distribution of the commodities from time to time in short supply.[2] The result has been that, although membership of a consumers' cooperative society has remained legally quite optional, its practical advantages have made it—leaving out of account the " deprived " categories on the one hand, and the nomadic races and some still savage tribes on the other—almost coterminous with the adult population of the USSR. Unfortunately, as we shall relate, this astonishing increase in membership and turnover has sorely tried the capacity of the movement. Year after year the leaders and committees have been incessantly struggling to keep pace with the rapid multiplication of their customers, and at the same time to make good one defect after another that

---

[1] Any surplus is devoted, not to interest or dividend, but to some public object of use to the membership. But surpluses are not encouraged. Prices ought to be kept as low as possible.

" By a decision of Centrosoyus the normal profit of a village cooperative shop is limited to from 1½ to 2 per cent " (*Supply and Trade in the USSR*, by W. Nodel, 1934, pp. 98-99).

[2] We are informed that not all societies admitted members under eighteen, though many accepted them at fourteen, without power to vote until they reached the age of eighteen.

experience has revealed in the organisation. But we must first describe that organisation as it exists to-day.[1]

### The Hierarchy of Consumers' Cooperation in the USSR in 1935

The aggregate membership of consumers' cooperative societies in the USSR at the end of 1934 is stated as seventy-three millions, enrolled in 45,000 local or primary societies, which now extend to every part of this vast area. These societies are of three main types : namely, (1) the village store, which is by far the most numerous ; (2) the city society with a shareholding membership open to all comers (except such as may be individually excluded as belonging to the "deprived categories"); and (3)—a speciality of the USSR—the vocational society or " closed cooperative", in which membership is restricted to the persons employed, either in a particular establishment or in a particular vocation.[2]

A majority of all the cooperative members are to be found in the 41,000 relatively small village societies in the rural areas, and

---

[1] We take the following statistics from a detailed publication of Centrosoyus (in Russian) entitled *The Consumers' Cooperative Societies in 1929–1933* (Moscow, 1934, 215 pp.). Excluding the closed societies now transferred to the factory managements (ORS), the number of societies rose, in the cities, from 1403 in 1929 to 3782 on October 1, 1933 ; and in the villages from 25,757 in 1929 to 40,920 on October 1, 1933. The number of their trading units rose in the cities from 31,512 to 44,811 ; and in the villages to 122,632. The total sales in the cities rose from 5984 million roubles to 10,663 million roubles ; and in the villages from 3925 to 7814 million roubles—the aggregate total being nearly doubled

[2] At all times during the present century the workers employed in each of the gigantic establishments characteristic of modern Russian industry have tended to establish their own consumers' cooperative society, originating exclusively among their colleagues in work, and remaining practically confined to them. With the relatively large turnover among these workers, such societies came increasingly to include in their membership many who had left the establishment and were working elsewhere. In 1930, largely owing to the difficulty of obtaining sufficient supplies, a demand arose for making these societies definitely closed to any but persons actually in employment at the particular establishment, together with their dependents. This step was rapidly carried out during the next two years, until nearly every large factory had its " closed cooperative ". Meanwhile a similar policy had led to societies established exclusively for the members of particular vocations wherever they happened to be working. In 1933 and 1934 about 350 of the largest of these " Closed " cooperative societies, comprising nearly three million members, were converted into departments of the factory organisation with which they connected, and thus ceased to be cooperative societies. There still remain, in 1935, about 2300 cooperative societies that have a closed or restricted membership. This restriction of membership is regarded as a purely temporary measure, certainly destined to pass away when supplies become abundant, and at a date not more distant than a couple of years.

these, whilst adding branches in the neighbouring hamlets (averaging three per society), remain mostly of the simplest type. These are united in 2355 rayon Unions. These again, along with the 4000 city societies, having over 40,000 branches, are united in 32 provincial Unions for the six smaller constituent republics, and the 26 divisions of the RSFSR. From the councils of these 32 provincial Unions are drawn the representatives who constitute the Central Board of the Central Union of the USSR and RSFSR (Centrosoyus).

## The Members' Meeting

At the base of the cooperative pyramid is the open meeting of all the members over eighteen of each of the local or primary societies. These meetings, which are held as desired, usually every two or three months throughout the year, are reported to be well attended, even to the extent of 50 or even 75 per cent of the total membership,[1] women being almost as numerous as men. The officers and committeemen of the society are expected invariably to attend. They report the current business of the society, hear the members' complaints and give explanations. The meetings are reported to be usually very lively, many complaints and suggestions being made. Once a year the members have to elect the president and the members of the committee, and also the society's representatives to the rayon, together with a " control committee " or " revision committee", which has the important

[1] Members are usually admitted at fourteen if desired, but they do not become " active " until eighteen years old. It should, however, be said that the " deprived categories " already described are still statutorily excluded, not only from the soviet franchise but also from cooperative as from trade-union membership. The " open " societies freely sell to non-members any but " deficit commodities " or rationed goods. The share which members are required to take up and pay for, though the amount is always payable by easy instalments, is now usually equal to one month's earnings of the particular candidate. Since 1930 no interest is paid upon shares, any more than " dividend on purchases ", but the shares remain nominally withdrawable, and they are easily transferable to another society.

The whole surplus is now specifically devoted, according to the decision of the members' meeting, for various common purposes, such as educational work of different kinds, the provision of a library and reading-rooms, a benevolent fund for members falling into distress or needing help in sickness, and subscriptions to sundry patriotic associations.

In the rural districts the attendance at the members' meetings during the summer may fall to as little as 25 per cent, but rises to over 75 per cent in the winter. It is evidently pressure of work that keeps members away ; not severity of weather !

duties, not only of stocktaking and audit, but also of general supervision of the society's work. Except in the smallest village societies, it is the duty of the group of members of the Communist Party within the society to prepare a " slate", or list of candidates recommended, not excluding a due representation of outstanding " non-Party " men and women; and then to be active in securing its adoption by the election meeting. But in many of the smaller villages, the members of the Party are not numerous, and may, indeed, often be non-existent, and it is common for the committee to contain a large majority of non-Party members, whilst the president is frequently a non-Party man or woman.

### The Committee of Management

In all the rural societies the whole work of management is carried on by the directly elected committee or board, in consultation with the separately elected control committee or revision committee. The manager, as well as the secretary, is appointed by the committee of management, whilst the subordinate staff of salesmen, porters, drivers, etc., is selected by the manager subject to approval by the committee. It is the committee of management that appoints one or more representatives of the society to the meetings of the rayon Union. Membership of the rayon Union is not obligatory, but is almost universally found to be convenient; and the attitude of the rayon Union council to the local or primary society is one of helpfulness rather than control.

### The Rayon Union with the Rayon Council (Raisoyus)

The rayon council, representing all the consumers' cooperative societies that are members of the rayon Union, is elected annually, together with a revision or control committee, by a conference of delegates from these societies, which is attended also by the retiring rayon council. This rayon conference, at which, on an average, about a score of societies are represented by two or three times that number of delegates, is held either once a quarter or once every six months, to hear complaints and discuss the cooperative business of the rayon. The rayon council elects its own president and several other members of a presidium, who, with a separately elected revision committee, jointly constitute its only executive. The rayon council usually elects also the rayon representatives to the next higher authority, the conference of the oblast or republic Union to which the rayon belongs.

The rayon Union councils are now required to become members of the higher stages of the hierarchy, and to act under their instructions in carrying out the tasks prescribed by the General Plan. They also assist in the development and strengthening of another cooperative network, in which, over a large part of the movement, cooperative societies of all types—consumers'societies, manufacturing associations of owner producers (artels or incops) and agricultural associations of owner-producers (collective farms) —voluntarily come together in periodical local conferences to discuss the arrangements, such as those for the supply of commodities, that can be made for their common advantage.

## *The Oblast or Republic Union with its Council (Oblsoyus)*

Each of the six smaller constituent republics (not the RSFSR) gathers together in a republic Union the rayon councils within its area, and, along with each of them, the local or primary cooperative societies of the cities. In the case of the Ukraine (with Moldavia) this Union (Wickopspilka) represents a specially large body of cooperators, comprising over 400 rayons, in which are included some 12,000 local or primary societies, open or closed, for villages or cities or particular factories or industries ; having nearly twelve million members. In addition to the six republic Unions, there are similar Unions for the 26 separate divisions of the RSFSR, comprising 8 for its autonomous republics, 10 for its national minorities in other autonomous areas, 6 for its oblasts and 2 for the large cities of Moscow and Leningrad. In all these are included, not only the numerous village societies, but also the consumers' cooperatives in the cities, whether open or closed, including (down to 1932) some 350 of the largest closed societies confined to the workers in particular factories, establishments, industries or vocations. Each of these societies elects its representatives to an oblast conference, which the oblast Union council also attends. This oblast conference is held once or twice a year. It appoints annually the oblast Union council and also the oblast's representatives to the All-Union Cooperative Congress. The oblast council meets every few weeks throughout the year, and appoints annually its president and presidium by whom the work is mainly conducted.

### The All-Union Congress of Consumers' Cooperatives, with its Central Board for the USSR and the RSFSR (Centrosoyus)

The whole system culminates in the Central Board of Centrosoyus at Moscow, to which all the consumers' cooperative societies in the USSR are definitely affiliated. Two or three times a year the representatives of the 32 oblast or republic Unions, together with those separately elected for this purpose by the city societies, at the rate of one delegate for each 75,000 membership, meet in conference with the Central Board to discuss the whole course of its business. Periodically, too, the Central Board summons to a conference the presidents of all the oblast or republic Unions. Every two years the Central Board itself, together with a revision committee (whose business includes auditing), are elected at a specially summoned meeting of a much wider body, the All-Union Congress of Consumers' Cooperatives, comprising the authorised representatives of all the 2355 rayon Unions in the USSR, as well as of the 32 oblast or republic Unions. This congress elects the president of the Central Board, but the presidium of the Central Board is elected by the Central Board itself.

The business of Centrosoyus, combining as it does the functions of the English Cooperative Union with those of the English and Scottish Cooperative Wholesale Societies, and acting for a cooperative membership ten times as numerous as that of the United Kingdom or Germany, dispersed over an area many more times as extensive—is almost unimaginably gigantic and complex. With its extraordinarily rapid growth in membership, amid the obstacles of a constant inadequacy of production, the consumers' cooperative movement in the USSR, taken as a whole, has lived in a perpetual struggle to overcome its difficulties, whilst its structure has been almost continually in a state of readjustment and reorganisation which is never completed.

At present (1935) the work of Centrosoyus is organised as follows. The Board itself, composed of seventy members, must meet at least once a quarter, and in practice it sits about every ten days. Its prolonged sessions are usually attended by some forty members, together with a number of executive heads of departments without votes. Once a year it elects from among its own members a vice-president and ten others to form, with the president, a presidium which acts as an executive committee. These members meet almost daily, and give their whole time to the Board's service. The Board now elects from its own members also a " Committee of Control and Execution " which has its own official staff, and is charged with the duty of seeing that all the numerous decisions of the Board are actually carried out.

The large staff of officials is organised in seven autonomous sections and some forty distinct departments, all working under the close supervision of the presidium of the Central Board and its Committee of Control and Execution, as well as under the eyes of the entirely independent Revision Committee which is elected by and directly responsible to the All-Union Congress. Each of the seven sections specialises on a particular set of workers, as to whom it is deemed of particular importance that their supplies should be without interruption maintained at a high level, so as not to jeopardise the fulfilment of the General Plan. These sections have their several bank credits, and their several stock accounts. They comprise the following :

(*a*) The Transport Section, which coordinates the work of the railway employees' closed cooperative societies, according to the control figures and instructions supplied by the central board. It draws up plans for improving the supply of commodities to the various railway workshops, depots, locomotive centres, and particularly to the members of the shock brigades working therein.

(*b*) The Water Transport Section, which coordinates all the closed cooperative societies which cater for the workers employed in the sea and river transport service, in order to protect their interests as consumers ; making provision for cheap and good food for passengers and crews on board ships.

(*c*) The Fisheries Section, which controls the activities of the closed societies of the fishery workers, and makes itself responsible for satisfactory supplies of food and articles of prime necessity for all workers connected with sea, lake or river fisheries.

(*d*) The Timber Section, which caters through a network of lumbermen's cooperatives for all workers connected with the timber trade. It sends foodstuffs and manufactured goods to the places where the trees are felled, and seeks to raise the productivity of labour through improved supplies.

(e) The Peat Section, which supplies through the cooperative societies in the peat-producing districts, all the workers employed in this industry, in order to enable them to make the required output.

(f) The Cattle-Breeding and State Farm Section, which organises the work of the consumers' cooperatives in the cattle-breeding and grain state farms, and sees to the carrying out of the price policy.

(g) The Central Army Cooperative Administration, which sees to the network of closed cooperatives wherever the defence forces are stationed.

Apart from this specialised sectional supervision of particular groups of closed cooperatives, the vast Centrosoyus office has the following forty-odd departments, styled " associations ", sections, groups or sectors, and each of them enjoying a large measure of autonomy under its own manager, who is directly responsible to the Central Board and its Committee of Control and Execution. The following summary of this extraordinary organisation is of interest as indicating not only the immense size and range of its operations, but also the characteristic way in which it has grown up by the addition of a new department to cope with each new emergency.[1]

1. CENTRAL DEPARTMENTS AND GROUPS.

*Departments* :

(a) Purchase of stocks of goods.

(b) Accounting.

(c) Training of new staff.

(d) Planning and finances.

(e) Foreign affairs.

(f) Cooperative upbuilding and recruiting of new members.

(g) Administrative department.

(h) Secretariat of the Presidium.

*Groups* :

(a) Transport.

(b) Capital constructions.

(c) Industrial enterprises.

---

[1] The list of departments, under various designations, is constantly changing, and usually increasing in complexity ; see *Cooperation in the USSR*, by Leslie A. Paul, 1934, pp. 70-74.

(*d*) Recording and distribution of cooperative workers.

(*e*) Central arbitration.

(*f*) Sanitary service.

2. BOARDS OF TRADE (INDUSTRIAL GOODS).

*Departments* :

(*a*) Textile.

(*b*) Ready-made clothing.

(*c*) Leather goods.

(*d*) Planning.

(*e*) Circulation of goods and inter-district bases.

(*f*) Inspection.

3. BOARD OF COOPERATIVE RESTAURANTS (VSEKOOPIT).

4. BOARD OF COOPERATIVE BREAD-BAKING.

5. ALL-UNION COOPERATIVE ASSOCIATIONS.

*A. Trade* :

(*a*) Haberdashery.

(*b*) Educational goods.

(*c*) Handicraft goods.

(*d*) Groceries.

(*e*) Matches.

(*f*) Shop equipment.

(*g*) Import Department.

(*h*) Parcels Department.

(*i*) Sale of non-planned goods.

(*j*) Bureau of supply and demand.

(*k*) Containers and warehouses.

(*l*) Supplies, repairs of cars, etc.

*B. Production* :

Tea Association.

*C. Purchase and storing of goods* :

(*a*) Fruits and vegetables.

(*b*) Milk, dairy products, poultry and eggs.

(*c*) Raw goods.

(*d*) Purchase of meat.

(*e*) Grain and flour.

(*f*) Fisheries.

6. AUDITING COMMITTEE.

## The Mechanised Bakeries

Perhaps the most outstanding single achievement of the consumers' cooperative organisation in the USSR is the abolition of the primitive and insanitary cellars and hovels in which was baked the bread that forms so large a part of the diet of all the inhabitants. These small hand bakeries, which were universal in all the cities of Europe a century ago, and still persist, to a greater or less extent, in all countries except the USSR, have been replaced in nearly all the cities of European Russia by large, new and completely mechanised plants. Those in Moscow and Leningrad are not only the largest in the world, but also the most magnificent in their equipment and arrangements, exciting the unstinted admiration of those who are acquainted with the best that other countries can show. They are also, what is not always the case in the USSR or elsewhere, both economically and financially successful; reducing the cost of production to such an extent as to permit not only of increases of wages and reductions of hours to all the workers employed, and successive reductions in the price to the consumer, but also the reimbursement of the whole capital outlay within less than five years.[1]

The first partly mechanised bakery was hastily established under the stress of war by the St. Petersburg Municipal Council in 1915. This was successively enlarged and improved by the Bolshevik Government, but not for a whole decade was it found possible to decide to supersede the hand bakeries. Meanwhile they were in Moscow and Leningrad gradually concentrated by amalgamations and extensions into half their former number. In about a score of cases partial mechanisation was effected, sometimes in new buildings. In March 1925 the Council of Labour and Defence (STO) adopted, in principle, the plan of complete supersession by newly erected and entirely mechanised establishments. Leading administrators, accompanied by engineers, were sent to the principal cities in Western Europe and the United States to inspect the latest achievements in bakery

[1] The best account of these bakeries is that by their chief administrator in Moscow, who was awarded the Order of Lenin (*Mechanised Baking in Moscow*, by A. Badayev, with a foreword by I. Dobrynin, Cooperative Publishing Society of Foreign Workers, Moscow, 1934, 84 pp.). See also *Supply and Trade in the USSR*, by W. Nodel, 1934, pp. 145-152.

equipment, and to purchase all the necessary machinery, none of which was at that time produced in the USSR. During the years 1926–1929 the first three completely mechanised bakeries were constructed in Leningrad and Moscow. Meanwhile considerable improvements were invented by the Soviet engineer Marsakov, notably in the conveyer system, which enabled much more labour to be dispensed with than in even the most advanced American, Dutch or British bakeries. The whole of the machinery was then constructed in the soviet machine-making establishments. By the end of 1932 there were at work in the principal cities of the USSR more than 300 more or less mechanised bakeries of large size (including eleven claiming to be " entirely automatic ") turning out daily over 15,000 tons of bread of several varieties. Moscow and Leningrad, with a combined population exceeding six millions, are now (1935) wholly supplied by a score of gigantic completely mechanised bakeries, which are palaces of scientific sanitation, in which the workers enjoy not only the seven-hours day and regular holidays on full pay but also all sorts of amenities. Not only the industry but also the conditions of labour have been revolutionised to such an extent as to render almost incredible the descriptions in the English Parliamentary Papers of a century ago, and what Maxim Gorky himself experienced half a century ago. This has been one of the most successful achievements of the soviet administrators, in which L. M. Kaganovich played a large part ; and which stands to the credit of the Leningrad and Moscow Cooperative Unions, as well as to that of the members of the Board of Cooperative Breadmaking of Centrosoyus, by whom the whole network of mechanised bakeries is directed.

## Cooperative Education

Special mention must be made of the extensive network of educational organisations maintained by the consumers' co-operative movement. Whilst elementary education is left to the schools everywhere maintained by the soviets, the cooperators apply themselves to providing the additional education required by an active cooperator, and still more by every committeeman and employee in the service of the movement. There are, accordingly, a whole array of vocational classes and even schools, devoted to subjects which every cooperator ought to know. These were

reported, in 1933, to have some 60,000 pupils.  In every oblast
there is at least one cooperative "technicum" (institute of secondary grade) under the supervision of the cooperative Union of the
oblast.  These cooperative technicums have now something like
10,000 students.  At Moscow there is a cooperative academy, and
at Leningrad a cooperative institute, both of them claiming university rank, and restricted, by entrance examinations, to students
over 18 qualified to enter on advanced studies.  Each oblast or
rayon in the USSR has the privilege of nominating its quota of
students to these cooperative universities, paying for them in fees
covering all the instruction, and in stipends meeting the cost of
maintenance of each student.  From the graduates of these two
institutions are drawn an increasing proportion of the principal
officers of Centrosoyus, and the managers of many of the more
important primary societies.  The system of cooperative education in the USSR is by far the most extensive in the world.[1]

## The Results Achieved

The cooperators of the USSR pride themselves, not without
warrant, on the marvellous growth of their movement, in turnover
as well as in membership, and in the range and variety of the
commodities supplied, now comprising at least 70 per cent of the
total retail trade within the Union.  There seems to be scarcely a
centre of population west of the Urals, and none of any magnitude
in Siberia or Transcaucasia, which is not served by a local consumers' cooperative society, usually covering several villages and
hamlets.  Every year the membership, the trade turnover, the
capital employed, and the numbers of separate buildings or other
" selling points " and of the persons engaged in the work, goes on
increasing, apparently without check.  The range and variety of
the commodities supplied, at any rate by Centrosoyus, and in the
central stores of the city societies, has steadily increased, and
many of the local or primary societies, especially in the cities,
have taken increasing advantage of this widening of the range of
supplies.

Thus the large Leningrad City society, which has some 400
branch shops for its 980,000 members, opened in 1933 a magnificent
central store, stocked with 25,000 different commodities, the

[1] See *Cooperation in the USSR*, by Leslie A. Paul, 1934, pp. 113-131.

contents alone being insured against fire for 25 million roubles ; including, for instance, a score of different penknives, and forty different varieties of boots and shoes, in a dozen different sizes. Nor is this provision of variety in any way unique. The children's toy department in a central Moscow store was found, in 1934, to have 400 kinds of toys in stock, and was severely rebuked for having so limited a variety ! The stock was immediately increased to 1500 kinds of toys, and in 1935 it is to have 2000. Already in 1932 various cooperative societies in the cities were advertising their willingness to supply clothing made to measure and specially fitted to each customer's figure. This refinement will be facilitated by the promised establishment of a separate department of the government clothing factories, which is to specialise in " bespoke tailoring", and expects to employ a staff of 1500 expert cutters and fitters and coatmakers, to execute individual orders upon the measurements taken by the local societies. In all sorts of ways the convenience of the customer is being increasingly studied. Thus, it could be authoritatively claimed in 1934 that " delivery of goods to the home has been developed on a large scale in recent years. In Leningrad over 200,000 persons have their orders delivered to their homes ; in Moscow there is a similar number ; at Dnieprostroi 16,000 families (or 50,000 persons) have theirs delivered; at Kuznetskstroi 16,000 persons, and so on. Delivery orders are executed by special warehouses or branches of the big retail shops. . . . The system of subscription books for the purchase of staple commodities such as bread, milk, vegetables, etc., has lately become quite popular. . . . In Leningrad, since the beginning of 1933, nearly half the bread has been sold on monthly subscription books purchased at the beginning of each month. The subscription book covers the quantity . . . required for the month ; its use eliminates daily cash purchases, and speeds up the sale of the bread to each customer." [1] Meanwhile, in various cities, " vigorous efforts have been made, in recent years, to establish so-called house-shops in the big workers' apartment houses. The house-shops aim at organising the supply of food products and other necessaries to the tenants of the house. These shops, as a rule, are open only a few

---

[1] *Supply and Trade in the USSR*, by W. Nodel, 1934, pp. 51-52. The numbers stated for Leningrad and Moscow seem exaggerated. The difficulty of obtaining sufficient motor-lorries has stood in the way of extending this service.

hours a day, and the tenants themselves help in the work (the salesmen generally work only part of their time in the shop and are elected from among the tenants of the house)." [1]

This multiplication of retailing points and increasing attention to the customers' varying demands has gone hand in hand with concentration of mass production in a smaller number of gigantic factories. Thus, as we have mentioned, the making of bread in nearly all large cities, and also throughout the Donbas coal-mining area, has been practically monopolised by highly mechanised cooperative bakeries on a gigantic scale. From these huge bread factories a fleet of motor-lorries deliver several varieties of bread several times a day to hundreds of bread shops in each large city. The concentration of production permits of the most systematic and prompt distribution of the staple article of Russian diet, through a vast network of selling points, which, in Moscow and Leningrad, reaches the high figure of one in the midst of each 400 families.

Another extension of the past few years has been the development of communal feeding, by the provision of cooperative dining establishments, supplying plain meals at low prices. This has gone very far. Not only does every factory, every large office, and every educational institution, from the elementary school to the university college, provide meals for its own people, on its own premises, but there are also large public dining-halls open to all comers. The work is too great to be undertaken under a single direction. " Communal feeding ", we are told, " is carried on by two organisations ; Soyusnarpit, a special trust subordinated to the People's Commissariat of Supply, and Vsekopit, a trust subordinated to the Centrosoyus. Soyusnarpit controls communal feeding establishments in Moscow, Leningrad, Donbas, Kharkov and the Urals. In all other cities, and in villages, communal feeding is organised by Vsekopit . . . [through] the cooperatives operating in the given factory, town or village." [2]

There has been a corresponding development of cooperative supplies in the villages, but less generally in operation. Village cooperative societies are sharing in the wider range of supplies offered by Centrosoyus. In many cases the village has organised

<hr />

[1] *Supply and Trade in the USSR*, by W. Nodel, 1934, p. 51.
[2] *Ibid.* pp. 140-141.

its own communal feeding arrangements, either through the collective farms or through the village cooperative society. Usually they work together. " The aim of a village cooperative society in the USSR ", it has been said, " is not merely to sell goods, but to sell them in a way which will strengthen the collective farm ; help to complete the sowing, harvesting, threshing as speedily as possible ; help to carry out all agricultural operations in the best manner. That is why, in the spring, all cooperatives carried part of their work into the field ; that is why, during reaping and threshing, tens of thousands of stalls are opened in the fields, so that the collective farmer does not have to go to the village for goods, but can get them on the spot where he is working." [1]

Enterprise of this kind is, however, not universal. Some of the village committees of management, and their managers, are still content to obtain only the commonest kinds of customary necessaries, ignoring the steadily widening of range of available supplies and not giving scope for their members' new wants. The oblast cooperative councils are accordingly now trying to " educate the demand ". Experimental shops are being opened by these councils in local centres of population, in which goods of better quality, and in greater variety, are exposed for sale, for the purpose of bringing to the notice of committee-men, managers and members alike how greatly the range of cooperative supplies has increased. The increasing prosperity of the peasantry, in tens of thousands of collective farms, is (1935) leading to novel demands for wireless sets, gramophones, books, bicycles, watches, fur coats, leather jackets, and especially leather boots and shoes, in kinds and qualities heretofore outside the experience of the manager of a village cooperative society. It is a sign, not necessarily of any worsening of the service, but, more frequently, of an awakening of new desires and of a consciousness of higher standards, that the members continue to grumble at the shortcomings of the distributing organisation that they themselves control.

The popular dissatisfaction with the cooperative societies has arisen in the past very largely from the inadequacy of the supplies to meet the constantly growing demands of the consumers. The severe rationing of this or that foodstuff ; the limitation on the

[1] *Ibid.* p. 100.

amount of this or that commodity that may be supplied by the society to any one member within each year; even the total failure, at this point or that, of the supply of certain commodities —all this has been plainly not so much the fault of the consumers' cooperative movement as one of the shortcomings of the organisation for production, caused, in the main, not by any falling off in the supply either of food or of household commodities, which, in the aggregate, goes on steadily increasing year after year, but by the enormous growth in the effective demand, with which it is almost impossible to keep pace. The popular complaints have, however, this amount of justification, that the Central Board has never yet wholly succeeded in preventing unnecessary delays and stoppages in the transmission of supplies from farm or factory to the store counter. There have been not a few occasions when village and even city stores have been clamouring in vain for particular supplies, when these have been lying unopened, and even forgotten, at some intermediate point. More usually the manager and even the committee-men of the village store are found to be sunk in a routine of repeating their old orders, strictly limited in range to a few commodities that they know will go off quickly, rather than seek to fulfil their customers' unexpressed yearning for a wider choice. Whatever inspection the Central Board maintains over the working of the 41,000 village stores, this has apparently not yet succeeded in stirring to a livelier imagination the minds of those who ought to be on the alert to satisfy the customers' desires.

In the cities much of the complaints have, in the past, related to the queues, and the frightful amount of time that shopping requires. This is not due so much to the inadequacy of supplies— which the consumers' cooperative movement cannot completely amend—as to the working of the whole distributive apparatus of the Soviet Union; and particularly the primitive cooperative arrangements for selling, which have been in constant course of improvement, but at a rate never quite keeping pace with the growth of population. In the large cities, there have hitherto been not enough shops. Inside the shops there is, even now, not enough length of selling counter; indeed, at times, not even enough standing room for the customers. There are often not enough salesmen and cashiers to avoid the formation of queues within the shops; and, on the commodities, not enough legible price-tickets visible to the customers, so as to enable them promptly to make up their minds.[1]

Behind all the complaints to which the shortcomings of the consumers' cooperative movement have, from time to time, given rise, there is a popular suspicion that the movement has not yet been able wholly to rid itself of elements out of sympathy with the Communist Party, and that such unfriendly influences may even intentionally lessen efficiency at all points.[2]    Until a

---

[1] It is to this inadequate selling accommodation and staffing, which is constant and ubiquitous, rather than to the merely local and periodical short supply of particular commodities, that is to be attributed the characteristic feature of Soviet shopping, namely, the queue, with its invariable accompaniment of extraordinarily slow service at the counter and at the pay desk.    It is not usually any short supply of commodities that causes a queue, but the failure to dispose of each customer's shopping as quickly as additional customers arrive. Where any such delay occurs, a queue will inevitably be formed, even if supply is more than adequate to the whole demand, or (as in the sale of postage stamps, at the principal post office) even unlimited.    The queue phenomenon is not confined to Soviet Russia, but may be witnessed at any British railway station when numerous passengers arrive nearly simultaneously at the window of one ticket-issuing clerk.    As soon as additional windows are opened, enabling additional clerks to issue tickets, proportionately to the gathering crowd, the queue quickly disappears, quite irrespective of the adequacy of the supply of tickets.

It should be added that, in the USSR in 1934, queues had become rare, even in the largest cities ; and had come to be most obvious at the railway ticket offices, the post offices, and some of the public dining-halls, in none of which were they due to any shortage of supply.

[2] In a few cases members of the Communist Party or of the League of Youth (Comsomols) have taken complete charge of a consumers' society, by request of the members.    These have sometimes been run as model stores.    Thus we learn that " Cooperative store No. 41 of the October district, Moscow, staffed entirely by Comsomols, is known as the best shop in the district, thanks mainly to the efforts of Boris Levit, Comsomol manager.    With a previous record of embezzlements, queues and underweighing, for the ten months that the Comsomols have been in charge of the store there has not been a single complaint.

" Levit himself does not wait for goods to be brought to the store—he goes out to get them.    There had been no cigarettes—Levit went direct to the tobacco trust and saw to it that the store was supplied with cigarettes.    He did the same regarding fruit.    When food of poor quality is sent in, this Comsomol shop does not pass it on to the consumer but sends it back with complaints.

" The 3300 consumers attached to this shop—no small number to cater to —are workers employed in two printshops.    The Comsomol store keeps in touch with the workers, informing them when new assortments are received, and arranges that the stuff be sold immediately after work-hours.    Levit himself has made reports in departments of the printshop and has succeeded in fulfilling demands and doing away with defects that were pointed out.

" Salesmen of the vegetable department were awarded premiums amounting to 40 per cent of their wages during August and September for good work.    All vegetables were carefully handled, the winter supply of potatoes was quickly and carefully unloaded.    Not only did the Comsomols stop after work hours to see that the vegetables were properly unloaded, but they attended subotniks

few years ago, the movement certainly retained on the staff an unusually high proportion of persons disaffected towards the communist régime. In 1930 it was found that Centrosoyus was employing no fewer than " 136 former Mensheviks, members of the Bund, Social Revolutionaries, Kadets (constitutional democrats), Popular Socialists, anarchists and others ; 11 ministers of former governments ; 109 former merchants ; 82 ex-officers, of whom 34 served in the White Army. . . . Those figures were obtained only during the special purge that was carried out in 1930." [1] The total personnel employed by the movement now reaches one million ; and it has so far proved impossible to enrol anything like that number of trained and zealous, honest and industrious salesmen, cashiers and accountants. " The cooperative personnel ", it has been said, " has been distinctly inferior ; bureaucrats on top ; slow, indifferent and rude employees on the bottom. . . . There have been more speculators, embezzlers, thieves and bureaucrats in the cooperative system than in any other branch of soviet enterprise." Nor are there available in the USSR the 40,000 or 50,000 competent store managers that are requisite. In the four-fifths of the cooperative societies that operate in the villages, it is still usual for the committees of management to fill all the salaried posts from among the village residents, very largely from members of the committee-men's own families.[2] It is against much local opposition that the Central

in other warehouses. This store is spotless. Each salesman takes turn in superintending the cleaning. Accounts are in perfect order. Each worker has passed the technical norm examination, and all are active in social and political work " (*Moscow Daily News*, October 3, 1933).

There are, we fear, very few cooperative societies of which such an enthusiastic report could be made, even by their warmest admirers.

[1] *Fifteen Years' Soviet Building* (in Russian), 1932, p. 256.

[2] Drastic measures are being taken to raise the standard of these cooperative employees. Thus it was reported in June 1933 that " About 100,000 workers employed in 6500 stores of the consumers' cooperative system have recently undergone an examination by special committees set up to decide their fitness for work in cooperatives. Over 12,000 of them have been found unfit and will be dismissed.

" In some regions the percentage of misfits was found to be extremely high. In the Odessa Province 57·7 per cent of the cooperative workers were disqualified by the examination committees ; in Baku 38 per cent of the workers were dismissed ; in Northern Ossetia 21 per cent.

" The cleaning was accompanied in many cities by special meetings called in the factories and offices to discuss the work of the cooperative stores. Here the store committees reported on their work and in a number of cases the complaint books were read to ascertain the quality of the service rendered by the cooperative workers " (*Moscow Daily News*, June 15, 1933).

Board strives continually to improve the training, and even the manners, of the huge staff of the movement. For the higher positions of greater responsibility than salesmen, for whom, as we have mentioned, an elaborate scheme of cooperative education exists, reliance has still to be placed, to a great extent, upon men and women qualified only by their long experience in the movement, some of whom have only reluctantly accepted the Bolshevik régime, and are only very doubtfully in sympathy with the policy embodied in the successive Five-Year Plans.[1] There is accordingly ample explanation of the inability of the consumers' cooperative movement to undertake, at present, the whole vast service of distribution of commodities.

## *The Rivals of the Consumers' Cooperative in Retail Distribution*

The task of the consumers' cooperative movement in the USSR has not been made easier by the fact that a whole series of encroachments upon what might have been considered its sphere have been made. In 1930 the USSR Commissariat of Trade was reorganised into a Commissariat of Supplies, with a view to the more systematic regulation of the whole internal trade

---

[1] It is certainly widely believed in the USSR that " ever since the beginning of the revolution, the enemies of the soviets have given a great deal of their attention to the food supplies, that is, to the most vulnerable spot in the soviet organisation, attacking it on two fronts—on the production front in the kolkhosi, and on the distribution front in the cooperatives ". Thus *Pravda*, in commenting on the decree of December 4, 1932, referred to the " anti-soviet elements of the consumers' cooperative movement, who have unfortunately not yet been expelled from Centrosoyus ".

The following quotation from the local newspaper of Nivastroy in October 1932, given in the *New Republic* (New York) of May 24, 1933, typifies the readiness to attribute evil to the cooperative personnel, but it must not be taken for truth. " At the very moment that our Communist Party is making a determined effort to improve workers' food supplies, class enemies are penetrating into our cooperatives, undermining their work and creating endless food difficulties. . . . The impudence of our class enemies is boundless. They overcharge, pocketing the money, thus disrupting the price policy of the government. They steal and privately sell foodstuffs of which there is a shortage—butter, meat, sugar. . . . Of the nineteen persons now on trial, almost every one is a lishenets (one deprived of his right of citizenship), or a kulak, or a former merchant who had concealed his identity and wormed himself into the workers' cooperative of Nivastroy. . . . The harm they have done is enormous, and, under present conditions, especially grave. There should be no mercy. The sentence of the proletarian court must remind all those who would misappropriate public [socialist] property, who would try to attack us from the rear, that the punitive arm of the proletarian dictatorship will bring down upon them in every instance the extreme penalty provided by the law of August 7."

within the USSR, whether wholesale or retail (as distinguished from production, which was, at that date, left to the control of the Supreme Economic Council). Primarily, it seems, the duties of the People's Commissar of Supplies were to be concentrated on the distribution of foodstuffs (including sugar) from the farm or the factory right down to the consumer, who was to be increasingly served in the cities by a system of food factories, mechanised kitchens and public dining-halls. Six great combines were at once established as independent financial entities, but under the direct superintendence of the People's Commissar, for bread, meat, fish, vegetable oils, conserves and refrigerating stores. These combinations were to be joined by all undertakings large enough to be of " All-Union " or even of " republic " significance ; whilst all smaller ones had to submit to the general direction and control of the combines in order to ensure that the whole area was properly served. The Commissariats of Trade already existing in the republics, and the oblast councils of the consumers' co-operatives, became, within the several spheres, the representatives and agents of the USSR People's Commissar of Supplies. It is not easy to ascertain to what extent this ambitious scheme of coordinating under a People's Commissar all the agencies engaged in trade came practically into operation. In September 1934 this commissariat was divided into two. The People's Commissar of Supplies will now devote himself entirely to managing and increasing the supplies of all foodstuffs (including vodka and tobacco) which require any kind of preservation or " processing ". When ready for retailing to the consumer, these supplies will pass under the direction of a new People's Commissar of Internal Trade, who will exercise a general control over all arrangements for retailing, by whatsoever organisations. He will be responsible for sanctioning the number of retail shops in each area, and for determining schedules of maximum prices. Under these two new USSR Commissariats there has begun a great development of direct government retailing of all sorts of commodities in most of the large cities. " During the two years 1931 and 1932 the Government commercial system was extended almost five times (from 14,700 shops on January 1, 1931, to 70,700 on January 1, 1932)." [1] These " commercial shops ", which vary from great department stores down to the smallest kiosk or market counter,

[1] *Supply and Trade in the USSR*, by W. Nodel, p. 31.

selling a limited range of foodstuffs, or a particular line of goods
in demand, charge relatively high prices, considerably above those
of the " closed " cooperatives, but often below those prevailing
in the " bazaar ", or open market, which it is desired to bring
down.

In addition to these new " government shops ", there have
been, from time to time, various other retail shops for which the
USSR Sovnarkom is ultimately responsible, namely, those opened
in Moscow, Leningrad and some other cities, by various manufacturing trusts or combines, for the supply directly to the public
of their own products. We may instance the shops selling textile
fabrics opened by Textorg, a subsidiary of the Textile Combine ;
and those selling goloshes and other rubber goods, opened by the
Rubber Trust. This undisguised encroachment on the sphere of
the consumers' cooperative societies was much resented ; and as
it produced an obvious duplication of effort, its extension was not
encouraged. Much of the retailing by the trusts has therefore
been abandoned. Some of the trusts have, however, persisted,
finding this independent access to the consumers of great use in
enabling them to follow more closely the variations in their
desires.

A newer rival in the field of retailing, maintained by the USSR
People's Commissar for Foreign Trade, is that of Torgsin—the
name given to the extensive chain of shops in prominent positions,
together with sales counters in hotels and tourist offices, now
opened to the number in the aggregate of over one thousand, in
scores of cities and towns, for the sale of all sorts of commodities,
exclusively for foreign valuta, gold and silver, or precious stones.
This enterprise, begun in 1930 on a small scale in Moscow and
Leningrad, and at first restricted to foreign customers, had for its
object, not so much the making of profit for the state, as the
collection of foreign valuta for use in paying for imports. It
proved so successful, and seemed to meet such a keenly felt need,
that the doors of the Torgsin shops were presently opened to all
comers, irrespective of nationality, provided only that they were
able to pay for their purchases in gold, silver or precious stones,
as well as foreign valuta, including drafts on Torgsin resulting
from deposits made abroad—thus affording to foreign friends a
convenient alternative to the despatch of parcels containing
presents.

The consumers in Moscow, Leningrad and Kiev are even promised, at an early date, probably in 1936, the opening of "one-price stores", after the model of the Woolworth establishments in the American and western European cities. These will be maintained by the Administration of Department Stores Department of the USSR Commissariat of Supplies. They will begin by retailing household necessities, haberdashery, knitted goods, perfumes and cosmetics, in one, three and five rouble departments. There will also be 50 kopek counters for ribbons, pins, rubber bands, pencils and shoe laces. There will also be a cafeteria, where purchasers will purchase special slot coins to enable them to help themselves to iced coffee, hot rolls and various pastries.

We come now to retailing enterprises of particular local bodies. We may mention first the huge retail trade long done by the Commissariat for Supplies of the RSFSR in some of the larger cities of that republic. Though these shops and kiosks are organised according to oblast or city boundaries, and usually bear a local name, they do not usually belong to the local governing bodies but to the RSFSR People's Commissar of Supplies. In Moscow he has an enormous department store in the centre of the city, which is extremely well equipped and liberally stocked with every conceivable commodity for household use. Smaller departmental stores exist in streets in other quarters of the city, together with special shops for the sale of shoes, clothing, wine and tobacco, and a large number of kiosks and street-stands selling candy, cigarettes, etc.—making a total of over 500 selling points, at which the People's Commissar for Trade deliberately competes with the consumers' cooperative societies; not, indeed, by lower prices but by more varied stocks, and chiefly, it is said, with intent to supply models in organisation and methods of retail distribution.

Second in magnitude only to the extensive retail trading of the RSFSR People's Commissar himself, is that conducted by various local authorities in the RSFSR. Much the most important of these enterprises is that called "Mostorg", which was originally organised as a joint-stock company to retail the products of Moscow producing trusts, in which the executive committee of the Moscow oblast had, in 1928, 77·2 per cent of the stock, whilst 10·3 per cent was held by certain trusts in the oblast, 11·2 per cent by the Moscow Municipal Bank and 1·3 per cent by the USSR

People's Commissar of Finance—thus entirely owned by public authorities. It was managed by a board of five directors, elected by the corporate shareholders, and assisted by a larger council on which the trade unions and the local governing bodies were represented. Already in 1929 its total capital was over 10 million roubles. It had then nine wholesale divisions, which supplied its retail departments with hardware, technical equipment, chemicals, building supplies, knitted goods, textiles, clothing, office equipment and jewellery. It supplied materials for all building works in the oblast, and contracted with factories for the supply of working-clothes and overalls of their staffs. It long had a monopoly of the supply of the Moscow public offices with lead pencils ! Its total turnover in 1928–1929 was 288 million roubles ; at a working cost of under 8 per cent. Already in 1929 it had 225 shops and stores (about half in Moscow city), and over 5000 employees. In 1933 it was entirely reorganised and placed immediately under the administration of the Moscow City Soviet.[1] On the other hand, the Leningrad City Soviet does not itself maintain any retail stores.

Another type of retailing organisation is that undertaken for their own products by trusts of local significance, and thus under the direction of the municipal or other local soviet. " Mossel-prom ", for instance, was long a Moscow trust, employing some 15,000 persons in factories producing candies, macaroni, fancy confectionery, beer, tobacco, toys and other small articles. Half its product was taken wholesale by the consumers' cooperative organisation, the USSR trusts or the state export organisation. But the other half Mosselprom marketed itself in Moscow through its own 40 stores and 400 kiosks, and a large number of agencies in restaurants, hotels, etc. It has now ceased to exist as a separate entity, and its production and distribution have been taken over by different commissariats and the Moscow City Soviet.

The Ukraine stands second only to the RSFSR in the magnitude and range of the retail trading conducted practically by its own Sovnarkom under various commissariats.

---

[1] We may mention here the seldom described commission shops maintained in most cities by the municipal authorities for offering for sale all sorts of miscellaneous articles, at prices fixed by the owners, on a commission of 25 per cent. These take the place of the pawnbrokers' establishments of western Europe as an easy means of disposal of unwanted oddments of personal belongings, misfits, discarded ornaments, cast-off clothing and " white elephants " of every kind.

In another field we have to notice the district pharmacy or drug-store, which, as a part of the public medical service, is everywhere conducted by the People's Commissar of Health of the particular constituent or autonomous republic. These district pharmacies are, however, to be found only in the urban areas. In the rural areas drugs are dispensed by the visiting medical practitioner or his assistants.

Nor do all these shopkeeping enterprises of the USSR and republic governments, or of the oblast or municipal governments, or of the trusts and combines that they control, exhaust the list of rivals in retailing with which the consumers' cooperative movement has to contend. Other forms of cooperation also compete for the consumers' shopping. Some retail shops in the cities are maintained by the manufacturing associations of owner-producers (incops), for the sale of linen, embroidery, toys and small articles of wood or leather. There are artels of bakers who keep retail shops for confectionery. Much more important, however, is the competition to which we shall recur in our subsequent chapter entitled " In Place of Profit ", of the collective farms in entering into contracts directly with particular factories, as well as of the individual peasants, in the direct supply of city customers with all sorts of foodstuffs ; from stalls in public markets or even from baskets in the streets, down to the ubiquitous offering for sale to travellers of cooked food at every provincial railway station.[1] This direct supply of the consumer was, during 1932, greatly widened, so far as concerns the two-thirds or four-fifths of the peasants who are members of collective farms, by the definite instructions of the USSR People's Commissar for Agriculture that the whole surplus of the collectivised product, over and above the fixed quota due to the government and after all the government exactions had been duly met, together with everything produced individually by the members, may be freely sold anywhere, at any price, to the consumers, either individually or collectively, in the open market [2] or direct to the factories or trusts, or to the public

---

[1] The restaurants at the railway stations, and the supply by trolley cars on the platforms, are provided by the local cooperative societies. The dining-cars on the trains are administered by the USSR People's Commissariat for Internal Trade.

[2] This " open market " selling has been the subject of ever-varying decrees and municipal regulations. At times both before and after NEP, it has been encouraged and even stimulated, in order to supplement the insufficient supplies brought forward by the cooperative organisation. Then it has been discouraged

restaurants and hotels, or to any of the consumers' cooperative organisations either in separate transactions or on standing contracts.[1] Nothing is forbidden to the sellers except purchase for resale at a profit, and sale to known speculators.

### Recent Encroachments on the Sphere of the Consumers' Cooperative Movement

Apart from the maintenance and even the increased development of the various rival distributing agencies that we have described, the last three or four years have witnessed a series of definite encroachments on the sphere heretofore assigned to the consumers' cooperative movement. It has become definitely part of the policy of the government to relieve both Centrosoyus and the local societies of part of the burden of their ever-increasing work. Although they have come to deal with over 70 per cent of the retail distribution of commodities in the USSR, there is no longer any idea of their eventually undertaking the whole of it. It is doubtless on other grounds that the associations of owner-producers, whether in manufacturing artels or in collective farms, have lately received, as already mentioned, so greatly enlarged a freedom to sell their products directly to the consumers, either in their own shops or at the public markets, instead of this supply necessarily going through the consumers' cooperative societies. There were other grounds, too, for the steady expansion of retailing by the central or local government that we have described. Possibly the most important of the recent encroachments on the actual or potential sphere of the consumers' cooperative move-

and even repressed, partly because the market operations could not practically be restricted to direct sales from producer to consumer, and " speculation " (meaning buying in order to resell at a profit) became rampant ; partly because the crowds of peasants were not only dirty and disorderly, but also obstructive to traffic ; and partly because, in times of short supply, outrageous prices were asked, as the beginning of the bargaining characteristic of the Oriental bazaar. These were naïvely cited by foreigners as if they were the actual prices at which the commodities changed hands ! One distinguished expert, sent out to discover the state of the crops, varied his agricultural investigations by spending an hour in the open market of every city he visited, making no purchases, but asking the price of everything, and carefully noting whatever he was *asked*, in due course reporting this as being the actual price level !

[1] Centrosoyus itself makes large purchases by standing contracts with kolkhosi and incops. But what stands in the way of an indefinite extension of this system of wholesale supply with regard to foodstuffs is the necessity for submitting any large stocks to some process of drying or preservation, or else of constructing and maintaining huge cold-storage establishments.

ment has been the transfer to the factories themselves by decree
of December 4, 1932, of the whole property and all the functions
of the closed cooperative societies (ZRK) attached to the larger
and more important factories, usually those having more than
2000 employees.[1]   Under this decree, in which the Central Board
of Centrosoyus reluctantly acquiesced, some 350 of the larger
consumers' cooperative societies, with something like three million
members, have been transformed.   All their buildings and equipment, with their farms and other enterprises, have been transferred to the factories for the employees of which they catered,
with no other compensation for the capital expenditure that had
been incurred by the cooperative organisation than the nominal
creation of loans to the factories, bearing no interest and without
any term for repayment, which Centrosoyus may include in its
balance sheet among the cooperative assets.   The members of the
transformed cooperative societies suffer, indeed, no pecuniary loss,
not even that of the small sums paid up on their shares in the
societies now dissolved, as these sums, bearing no interest, still
benefit the same individuals as trade union members working in
the particular factories concerned.   But they now participate in
the management of their food and other supplies, not as cooperative shareholders, but as factory workers who are members of
their trade union ; they attend the shop, brigade or shift meetings
of their co-workers, in lieu of those of the cooperative society ;
and instead of voting for the committee of management of that
society, they vote for the shop, brigade or shift representatives on
the factory commission for supplies, and other committees, as

[1] The decree of December 4, 1932, applies a similar principle to all the other
closed cooperative societies (such as those for particular vocations and industries,
those for the state farms (Sovkhosi) and those for the factories having fewer
than 2000 employees), but not so drastically as in the case of the 262 factories,
having each over 2000 employees, which were then specified.   In other cases,
the closed cooperative societies are to continue in existence, and in connection
with the cooperative hierarchy headed by the Central Board of Centrosoyus,
but to be also subject to the authority of the factory management.
   " In all the factories where the closed workers' cooperatives were left intact
(and these constitute a majority) the position of the factory director in regulating
the utilisation of the products assigned by the State for the workers of the
particular factory has been considerably strengthened.   The factory administration provides transport facilities for the closed workers' cooperative, helps
to organise vegetable gardens and invests considerable sums in the cooperative.
The form in which the factory administration participates in the work of the
cooperatives, and the financial aid given by it, are laid down in special agreements concluded between Centrosoyus and the People's Commissariats of each
industry " (*Supply and Trade in the USSR*, by W. Nodel, 1934, p. 87).

they do for their main factory committee (FZK). The production and distribution of food and the retailing of other commodities continues as before, but it now becomes an integral part of the work of the factory management. The superintendent or director of the factory, subject to the combine or trust and of the Sovnarkom, takes over the responsibility for these functions from the former cooperative society's committee of management, including the administration of farms and other cooperative departments, hitherto under the authority of the cooperative hierarchy, headed by the Central Board of Centrosoyus. The intention and object of this momentous decree was avowedly this very supersession of consumers' cooperative management by factory management. It was believed that greater efficiency in food supply and retail distribution, and a more exact issue of ration cards,[1] would be secured by cutting away these large factory retailing establishments (ORS) from their dependence on the overburdened Centrosoyus, whilst leaving them free to purchase what they chose, whether directly from state or municipal departments acting either as wholesalers, manufacturers or agricultural producers, or from the manufacturing associations of owner-producers (incops), or the consumers' cooperative movement itself. A special commission or sub-committee of the factory committee for supplies is appointed to replace the cooperative committee of management. To manage what has become the new department of factory supplies, a deputy director, who will usually be the past president of the closed cooperative society, is appointed by the factory director, subject to the consent of this special commission of supplies. From the constitutional standpoint, in short, what has happened is a transfer of these 350-odd important enterprises from the consumers' cooperative hierarchy to the two hierarchies of the trade union and the soviets.[2]

---

[1] " A scrutiny of the persons formerly supplied through [74 of] these shops established the fact that, out of two million persons supplied by them, 273,000 persons had no connection with the 74 factories concerned, and no right to be supplied with factory rations " (*Supply and Trade in the USSR*, by W. Nodel, 1934, p. 86).

[2] The decree of December 4, 1932, is available in English in various summaries, such as that in the *Slavonic Review* for the first quarter of 1933 ; *Moscow Daily News*, November 18, 1932, December 23, 1932 ; *Manchester Guardian*, December 6, 1932. The lengthy memorandum (in Russian) " On the Organisational Structure of the Consumers' Cooperative System ", issued by the Central Board of Centrosoyus in January 1933, gives a significantly extenuating explanation of the decree.

## The Principle of Self-Supply

On the other hand, the consumers' cooperative societies have been repeatedly pressed, during the last four years (1932–1935), to extend their operations from distribution to agricultural production. Why should not every one of the forty or fifty thousand separate societies, instead of contenting itself with handling the commodities supplied to it by Centrosoyus, endeavour to make its members independent of the vagaries of the transport system, independent of the shortcomings of the central organisation, and, to a large extent, independent also of the sovkhosi and kolkhosi on which they could not always count ? Hence each of the various societies of consumers was urged to take on the task of producing for its own members such things as vegetables and fruit, and the produce of piggeries and dairies, with which to eke out and vary the sometimes exiguous ration to which their cards as producers entitled them. We have here one more instance of that multiformity to which the USSR constitution is so much addicted. Many of the larger consumers' societies, and a few of the smaller ones, accordingly took to " self-supply " in this sense, with the result not only of making a perceptible addition to the nation's supplies, but also of satisfying more of their members' desires. Some idea of the magnitude already attained in this independent production by the consumers' societies may be gathered from the following statistics. At the end of the year 1933 no fewer than 4029 consumers' cooperative societies had their own *koopkhosi* or farms (excluding 1689 others maintained by the factory supply departments (ORS), representing former closed cooperative societies). The cooperative societies' farms sowed 305,800 hectares with potatoes, and 163,100 hectares with other vegetables. They produced 1,682,200 tons of potatoes, and 703,200 tons of other vegetables. They possessed 663,500 pigs and 299,300 horned cattle—truly a considerable addition to the nation's food supply ! [1]

## The Extent of the Market

It is not easy to forecast the future sphere of the consumers' cooperative movement in the USSR. With regard to the principal

---

[1] Article by Centrosoyus on " International Cooperative Day in the USSR ", in International Cooperative Alliance *Review of International Cooperation*, October 1933, p. 375.

issue there is, however, no doubt. The service of distribution will certainly remain under the control not of the producers of the particular commodities and services but of the consumers and users thereof. What cannot be foreseen is how this control will be shared among the various forms that may be taken by the consumers' organisation. There is to be considered the necessary provision for the needs of the future generations of citizens, which cannot logically or safely be entrusted to the representatives of the actual consumers of to-day. There are some kinds of commodities and services—we may instance the manufacture of requisites for the defence forces and the postal service—of which the government itself is the only consumer or user. There are others, such as railway transportation and road maintenance, and nearly all kinds of municipal activities, for which there can scarcely be any practicable voluntary organisation of individual consumers as such, as distinguished from municipal citizenship. Finally, there is the problem of supplying the needs of such agglomerations of consumers as the workers in particular factories or other establishments, or persons engaged in particular vocations, when the distribution of commodities and services can perhaps be most conveniently administered by these particular agglomerations of "producers", as distinguished from geographically defined associations of consumers at large. As we have already described, the trade unions are, in the USSR, assuming not only the control but also the actual administration of vast services enjoyed by their members, such as social insurance. Thus there is certainly a place in the organisation of distribution for the state department and the municipality on the one hand, and for administration by industrial or other establishments on the other, or even by associations of producers such as the trade unions. How exactly the relative spheres of each of these, and of the various consumers' cooperative societies, can best be demarcated, in different communities, at different stages of social development, remains, we think, for the future to decide. It may be suggested that the answer to the enquiry may turn on the conditions in which it proves possible to secure, from one or other kind of social institution, the most efficient management of particular branches of distribution. The consumers' cooperative society may well continue to be the best alternative to the profit-making shopkeeper for the supply of household commodities to all the residents in the rural village, and, indeed, to all but closely segregated or exceptionally specialised groups of residents in the cities. It may be that, in the cities, some special groups of consumers may be able to secure more efficient management than a consumers' cooperative society is likely to supply, if the distribution of household commodities to such groups is dealt with (by the aid of advisory committees concerned only with supplies) as part of the administration of the establishments in which their members are employed. In either case it is distribution under the direction of the consumers of the commodities and services they desire, not under the direction of the producers of those particular commodities. Similarly, where the government or the municipality undertakes vast services for common use, or in the interests of future generations, it does so as a universal association of consumers, under the control of the citizens ; and not under that of the particular workers who produce these services.

# CHAPTER V

## THE VOCATION OF LEADERSHIP

In the constitution of Soviet Communism, as we have seen, the adult inhabitant, apart from specific legal disqualifications, finds separate provision made for his or her participation and representation in three distinct capacities, namely, as a citizen, as a producer and as a consumer. We have now to add, to this unparalleled elaborateness of the representative system, an artificially constructed category that we can best describe as one of super-citizens. These men and women are not withdrawn from ordinary life or common citizenship. They have a conscious responsibility greater and deeper than that of the plain man or woman. They are held to a higher standard of behaviour, under a more stringent discipline. They are, in fact, selected out of the mass for the exercise of a special vocation,[1] and the fulfilment of a particular duty based upon a definite creed, namely, that of " Marxism " as authoritatively interpreted from time to time. This select body, universally known as the Communist Party, or simply as " the Party "—everyone else being " non-Party "— may easily be deemed the most important part of the effective constitutional structure of the USSR.[2] It must, however, be

---

[1] The English word " vocation " was, for the first few centuries of its use, limited to a " calling by God or by Jesus Christ ". Since the sixteenth century it has increasingly been used indiscriminately for any specialised occupation, although usually with reference to one having some sort of professional organisation or qualification. Thus Hobbes could assert, in 1651, that " Some laws are addressed . . . to particular provinces ; some to particular vocations, and some to particular men " (*The Leviathan*, by Thomas Hobbes, II. xxvi. 137). But political or any other public leadership has, in England, seldom been recognised as a specialised occupation.

[2] Innumerable manuals and pamphlets are to be had in Russian describing the constitution, principles and duties of the Communist Party, and its junior

noted that, unlike those parts of the constitution of the USSR
that we have already described—the multiform democracy of
Man as a Citizen, Man as a Producer and Man as a Consumer—
the Communist Party has no organic connection with the Soviet
Government by statute or other form of law. Neither the
organisation nor the activities of the Communist Party are so
much as mentioned in the "Fundamental Law", or in any
statutory amendments of it. Nor has the Party any legal
authority over the inhabitants of the USSR, not even over its
own members! The only sanctions that the Party can use to
control its members are those of reprimand and expulsion; and
these entail no legal disability. The Party members enjoy no
statutory privileges. They are individually under the same
obligation as other citizens to obey the law of the land; and they
can be, and are, prosecuted and punished, like other people, for
any action condemned by the law. The Communist Party
appears, in fact, to have practically the same status under the
law as a Roman Catholic order, such as the Society of Jesus,
has, or used to have, in a Roman Catholic country. If the Party
influences or directs the policy of individuals or public authorities,
it does so only by persuasion. If it exercises power, it does so by
" keeping the conscience " of its own members, and getting them
elected to office by the popular vote. Even when not holding
public office, the Party members act as missionaries among the
non-Party citizens in the organisations of every kind throughout
the USSR. It is in this way that the Party secures the popular

subsidiaries (Comsomols, Pioneers and Octobrists). There are also histories of
the Party in Russian, such as *History of Russian Social Democracy, 1898-1907*,
by L. Martov, Moscow, 1923; and *History of the Russian Social Democratic
Party*, by M. N. Lyadov, Moscow, 1906, 1925. Among sources more accessible
may be mentioned *Civic Training in Soviet Russia* and *Making Bolsheviks*,
both by S. N. Harper, University of Chicago, 1931; the good chapter entitled
"The Communist Party", by Jerome Davis, in *Russia in the Second Decade*,
edited by Stuart Chase and others, New York, 1928; *Histoire du parti communiste de l'URSS (Parti bolchevik)*, by E. Yaroslavsky, Paris, 1931 (which
is stated to have been translated from the Russian also into German, Spanish,
Turkish, Tartar, Chinese and Yiddisch); *Geschichte des Bolshevismus*, by A.
Rosenberg, 1932, translated as *History of Bolshevism*, 1933; *La Révolution
russe*, by Henry Rollin, vol. ii. entitled "Le Parti bolcheviste", Paris, 1931;
*Soviet Rule in Russia*, by W. R. Batsell, 1929; *The Soviet State*, by B. W.
Maxwell, 1934, pp. 38-47; *Outline History of the Communist Party of the Soviet
Union*, by N. M. Popov, 1935, translated from the 16th Russian edition;
*The Seventeenth Conference of the CPSU in Questions and Answers*, compiled
by S. Sheftel (Cooperative Publishing Society of Foreign Workers, Moscow,
1933), affords a convenient view of present policy.

consent to, or at least the popular acquiescence in, the policy that it promotes.

The Communist Party has, since its establishment, changed not only its name but also its function. It was created, as the Bolshevik section of the Social Democratic Party of Russia, primarily as the instrument of revolution. It was continued and strengthened, after the seizure of power, in October 1917, as the organ by which the revolution could be maintained and directed. It exists to-day, as the student of political science will realise, chiefly as the means by which the people of the USSR, in all their multiform participation in government that we have described, are continuously supplied with intellectual leadership. To give this leadership, not merely at the centre or from the heights, but ubiquitously, in the factory or on the farm, no less than at election meetings, is the service which the voluntarily recruited membership of this remarkable companionship adopts as its life-duty. There has, in fact, been created, as part of the constitutional structure of the USSR, a highly organised Vocation of Leadership.

## How the Communist Party arose

The student of the numerous books and pamphlets, articles and letters, emanating from the little groups of Russian revolutionary exiles during the first fifteen years of the present century will have no doubt about the origin and purpose of this organisation. Though the Social Democratic Party — the definitely Marxian successor to half a dozen waves of revolutionary activity since 1825—was inaugurated at Minsk in 1898, it was Vladimir Ilych Ulianov, at that time not yet widely known as N. Lenin, who, from 1900 onward, gradually gave the nascent party its unique form. Unlike his Russian predecessors—unlike every other party organiser—Lenin had no use, within the Party, for mere sympathisers, for partially converted disciples, for adherents who based their acts on Christianity or a general humanitarianism, or on any other theory of social life than Marxism, nor even for those whose interpretation of Marxism differed from his own. It was not a body of electors prepared to give him their votes that he was collecting. Popular election had practically no place in tsarist Russia. For the instrument of revolution that he was forging he needed something different from an electoral force, namely, a completely united, highly disciplined and relatively small body of "professional revolutionists", who should not only have a common creed and a common programme but should also undertake to give their whole lives to a single end, the overthrow of the entire governmental structure of the autocratic "police state". The creation of such a body was no easy task. In interminable controversies between 1900 and 1916, we watch Lenin driving off successively all whom he could not persuade to accept his model; all whom he considered compromisers or temporisers; opportunists or reformists; half-converted sympathisers who clung to one or other form of mysticism for which Karl Marx had found no place; the Mensheviks who accepted alliances with liberalism or had other "bourgeois" tendencies, and the Social Revolutionaries who, as he thought, dreamt that individual acts of terrorism would eventually evolve a new society out of the peasant community of the Mir. With all these elements it cannot rightly be said that Lenin was intolerant. He allowed that they were fully entitled to go their own way. His attitude was one of patiently explaining to them the superior efficiency of his own line of action, and of insisting on taking his own course, with however small a fragment of disciples. It was, as he was always demonstrating, neither he nor they, nor any group whatsoever, that would make the revolution, but the proletarian mass, which had to be inspired to the necessary action, and then guided and led in the social reconstruction that must follow. For this supreme purpose what was needed was a membership, whether small or great, that was devoid not only of division but also of dubiety; so disciplined as to be able to take combined action without hesitation as soon as the word was given; and so united in their socialism as to be capable of patiently embodying it in practical administration when the time for reconstruction came. If the reader will think of this membership, provisionally, as a united confraternity, a widely spread companionship, or as a highly disciplined order, professing a distinct and dogmatic political creed, and charged with a particular vocation, rather than as a political party, he will approach nearer to an understanding of its present-day characteristics and of its sociological significance.

During the Great War the cleavage between Lenin's party

and all the other revolutionary sections became ever more acute. Lenin, from the first, took up the attitude that the war was, on both sides, an "imperialist" quarrel, with which the socialists of every country had nothing to do, except in so far as, by opposing their several governments, they could, in every country, convert the war between different groups of nations into a revolutionary upheaval of the workers against the landlords and capitalists, probably entailing civil war. All the other sections in Russia rejected this "defeatist" attitude, and supported the government, more or less consistently, in the defence of the country. The growing unpopularity of the war among all classes played into Lenin's hands. The narrowly restricted band of "professional revolutionists" that he had been slowly forming during the preceding decade had grown, by February 1917, to what then seemed the respectable number of about 30,000, dispersed throughout the cities of the tsarist empire. That all these were in earnest about the matter was to some extent guaranteed by the constant danger of prosecution, imprisonment and exile that the mere membership of a revolutionary party had involved.[1]

[1] To the efficiency of the organisation, and to the amazing success of the Party that Lenin had organised, Mr. H. G. Wells bore eloquent testimony in 1920 : "From end to end of Russia, and in the Russian-speaking community throughout the world, there existed only one sort of people who had common general ideas upon which to work, a common faith and a common will, and that was the Communist Party. While all the rest of Russia was either apathetic like the peasantry, or garrulously at sixes and sevens, or given over to violence and fear, the Communists believed and were prepared to act. Numerically they were and are a very small part of the Russian population. . . . Nevertheless, because it was in those terrible days the only organisation which gave men a common idea of action, common formulas and mutual confidences, it was able to seize and retain control of the smashed Empire. It was and it is the only sort of administrative solidarity possible in Russia. These ambiguous adventurers who have been and are afflicting Russia, with the support of the Western Powers, Denikin, Kolchak, Wrangel and the like, stand for no guiding principle and offer no security of any sort upon which men's confidence can crystallise. They are essentially brigands. The Communist Party, however one may criticise it, does embody an idea, and can be relied on to stand by its idea. So far it is a thing morally higher than anything that has yet been brought against it. It at once secured the passive support of the peasant mass by permitting them to take land from the estates and by making peace with Germany. It restored order—after a frightful lot of shooting—in the great towns. For a time everybody found carrying arms without authority was shot. This action was clumsy and brutal but effective. To retain its power the Communist Government organised Extraordinary Commissions with practically unlimited powers, and crushed out all opposition by a Red Terror. Much that that Red Terror did was cruel and frightful, it was largely controlled by narrow-minded men, and many of its officials were inspired by social hatred and the fear of counter-

But the unobtrusive recruiting, and the secret admission by local groups scattered all over Russia, were incompatible, alike with any scrupulously careful selection of members and with the elaboration of party machinery. During the eight months of the Provisional Government in 1917, the membership of the party, still called the Russian Workmen's Social Democratic Party (Bolshevik), grew rapidly to nearly 200,000. In 1918, after its accession to power, the highly disciplined Party changed its name to the Russian Communist Party (Bolshevik). In 1922, on the formation of the Soviet Union, the Party became the Communist Party of the USSR (Bolshevik). By the end of 1932 its numbers (including "candidates" or probationers) had, without any lessening of the obligations of membership, and in spite of continuous "cleansing" and repeated purges, risen to more than 3,300,000. At the Seventeenth Party Congress of January 1934 considerable changes were made in the Party organisation, and in the nomenclature of some of its organs, the terms cell, nucleus and fraction being dropped. We have now to describe the Party of to-day, which, after the last drastic purge of 1933, counts, in 1935, nearly three million members and probationers.

## The Party Membership

Admission to Party membership is, and has always been, conferred as a privilege, to which no one has any prescriptive right, and in conformity with definite rules, to which no exception is allowed. Applicants for admission must, of course, profess whole-hearted acceptance of the communist creed, as laid down by Marx and as interpreted by Lenin and Stalin. They must manifest this adhesion in their lives by being habitually politically " active " in their respective spheres ; not only by displaying zeal in their daily work of production or service, but also by spontaneously undertaking extra duties of social influence. They must be warranted entirely free from Christian or any other

revolution, but if it was fanatical it was honest. Apart from individual atrocities, it did on the whole kill for a reason and to an end. Its bloodshed was not like the silly aimless butcheries of the Denikin régime, which would not even recognise, I am told, the Bolshevik Red Cross. And to-day the Bolshevik Government sits, I believe, in Moscow as securely established as any government in Europe ; and the streets of the Russian towns are as safe as any streets in Europe " (*Russia in the Shadows*, by H. G. Wells, 1920, pp. 61-64).

religious or metaphysical " ideology ", regarded as inconsistent with whole-hearted adhesion to Marxian communism. No member of the " deprived categories ", such as ministers of religion or monks, kulaks or former landlords, capitalist employers or traders, can be admitted under any circumstances.[1] Nor must applicants have a " petty bourgeois ideology ", nor, indeed, any marked attachment to private property. A desire to live without work, or any considerable amount of personal possessions, would certainly be a bar to admission. Would-be members have to be formally recommended for admission to probationary membership (in which stage they are known as " candidates ") by two, three or five Party members, who know them personally and who are held responsible for their recommendations, even to the extent of being summarily expelled from the Party for any negligence or improper partiality. Even on the highest recommendation, candidates are not finally accepted as members until they finish a probationary period of at least one year or two years, according to their class status at the date of application. During this period of probation the candidate pays the full membership dues, varying according to his salary or other income, and he is summoned to all open meetings ; he is assigned tasks and generally treated as a member, except that he is not allowed to vote on Party decisions. More important is the fact that he is watched by his new comrades ; his conduct is periodically reported on, and his character is carefully studied. If he is not considered in all respects satisfactory, his application will either be summarily rejected, or his period of probation will be extended.

The requirements for admission as candidates differ in detail according to age, occupation and social heritage.[2] Admission is

---

[1] " Former members of other parties [meaning particularly the Mensheviks and the Social Revolutionaries] are admitted in exceptional cases on the recommendation of five Party members, three of whom must be of ten years' Party standing and two of pre-revolutionary Party standing ; and only through an industrial primary organisation ; the admission of such a candidate must be endorsed by the Central Committee of the Communist Party irrespective of the social status of the applicant. . . . They have to go through a three years' period of probation " (Rules, I (c) and note to II. 12, in *Socialism Victorious*, 1934, pp. 693, 696). Such admissions are now extremely rare and entirely exceptional.

[2] Thus, whilst there is a universal minimum age for admission of eighteen years, youths of either sex under twenty years of age, if not actually serving in the Red Army, are admitted only after training and service in the League of

most easily gained either by young people between eighteen and twenty, of workman or peasant parentage, who have been serving as Comsomols ; or, with a similar parentage, by conscripts actually serving in the Red Army ; or by outstanding manual-working wage-earners in productive industry. It is, in fact, from these three sources that the great majority of candidates now come. The preponderance in the Party membership of actual manual workers is carefully maintained, although not without some difficulty. Whilst it is comparatively easy, even with ubiquitous work in recruiting, to keep the aggregate of admissions duly balanced, so many of those of workman or peasant parentage, entering from the ranks of the Comsomols, the Red Army or the factory operatives, presently become salaried organisers or office workers, or obtain promotion in due course as administrators, lecturers or technicians, that the proportion of Party members at any one time actually working at the bench or the forge is always in danger of dropping below 50 per cent. To ensure a substantial majority to such industrial manual workers was one of the motives that led, in 1924–1925, to the simultaneous admission of the " Lenin contingent ", in commemoration of the death of the great leader, when no fewer than 200,000 of the outstanding wage-earning men and women in the factories and mines, chosen very largely by their non-Party fellow-workers, were accepted as candidates within a few months.[1]

Communist Youth (Comsomols), to be subsequently described. Industrial workmen with a production record of not less than five years must submit recommendations from three Party members of five years' Party standing, and are subject only to a year's probation. Industrial workers with a production record of less than five years ; agricultural workers ; Red Army men from among workers or collective farmers ; and engineers and technicians working directly in shops or sectors must have five recommendations from Party members of five years' Party standing, and are subject to two years' probation. Collective farmers ; members of handicraft or artisan artels ; and elementary school teachers, must have five recommendations from Party members of five years' Party standing, and also the recommendation of a representative of the political department of the Machine and Tractor Station or of the Party District Committee, and are subject to two years' probation. Other employed persons must have five recommendations from Party members of ten years' Party standing, and are subject to two years' probation. In the case of a Comsomol of any of the above categories, the recommendation of the Comsomol District Committee is treated as equivalent to those of two Party members. The new class of sympathisers are admitted to Sympathisers' Groups by the local Party Committee on the recommendation of two Party members.

[1] Of this mass-recruiting, Stalin remarked in April 1924 as under : " Our Party has recently added 200,000 new working-class members to its ranks. The remarkable thing about these new members is that they have not, for the

In connection with the general " cleansing " of the Party in 1933, which we shall presently describe, there was instituted a new class of associates, called " sympathisers ", being those who, although loyal and zealous, proved to be intellectually incapable of explaining or expounding Marxism, or the General Line of the Party, in such a way as to make it plain to the outside enquirer. Such persons are excluded from the roll of Party members, and thus deprived of a decisive vote in Party meetings ; they are to be formed into " Sympathisers' Groups ", who are to be attached to the Primary Party Organs, the meetings of which these sympathisers are required to attend, and in which they may have a consultative vote.

## The Rules of the Order [1]

Apart from a relatively high standard of personal behaviour, there are three fundamental requirements that are strictly enforced. The first concerns unity of doctrine and practice. The Party member must unhesitatingly adhere to the " General Line " in communist theory and soviet policy, as authoritatively laid down from time to time ; and must be guilty neither of " right deviation " nor " left deviation ". There is, indeed, laid upon the Party member an obligation of union and loyalty far beyond that imposed on the non-Party masses. On new issues, and, in fact, in all matters not yet authoritatively decided on, there is,

most part, entered the Party on their own initiative, but have been sent by their non-Party fellow workers, who took an active hand in proposing the new members, and without whose approval no new members would have been admitted " (*Leninism*, by J. Stalin, vol. i., 1928, p. 164).

[1] The rules of the Communist Party will be found in English in various publications ; see, for instance, that entitled *Resolutions and Decisions* [of the Seventeenth Party Congress] *including Party Rules* (Cooperative Publishing Society of Foreign Workers, Moscow, 1934, 84 pp.) ; or the volume published in London entitled *Socialism Victorious* (Martin Lawrence, 1934), pp. 689-711.

The Party dues are as under :

20 kopeks per month on an income up to 100 roubles
60    ,,      ,,        ,,      101 ,, 150    ,,
1 rouble    ,,        ,,      151 ,, 200    ,,
1.50 roubles  ,,        ,,      201 ,, 250    ,,
2    ,,      ,,        ,,      251 ,, 300    ,,
2 per cent on incomes 301 to 500 roubles
3  ,,      ,,     over 500  ,,

In addition, there is an initiation fee of 2 per cent of the current wage payable on admission as a candidate.

even for the Party member, complete freedom of thought and full liberty of discussion and controversy, private or public, which may continue, as in the series of Trotsky debates in 1925–1927, even for years.[1] But once any issue is authoritatively decided by the Party, in the All-Union Party Congress or its Central Committee, all argument and all public criticism, as well as all opposition, must cease ; and the Party decision must be loyally accepted and acted upon without obstruction or resistance, on pain of expulsion ; and, if made necessary by action punishable by law, also of prosecution, deportation or exile.

The second requirement from the Party member is that of implicit and complete obedience to the corporate Party authority. He must take up and zealously perform any task or duty entrusted to him. In the exercise of this duty he must go wherever he is ordered, pursue any occupation assigned to him, reside wherever required, and, in the service of the establishment of soviet communism throughout the world, generally submit himself to whatever course of conduct is thought best by his superiors in the Party hierarchy. In this respect the position of the Party member seems to resemble that of the member of a typical religious order in the Roman Catholic Church.

The third requirement of the Party member is also analogous to that of the member of a religious order. He does not actually take a vow of poverty, but in applying for and in accepting Party membership he knowingly accepts the regulation bringing every Party member under strictly defined limits of salary or other

---

[1] Rule IX. 57 declares that " the free and positive discussion of questions of Party policy in individual organs of the Party, or in the Party as a whole, is the inalienable right of every Party member, derived from internal Party democracy. Only on the basis of internal Party democracy is it possible to develop Bolshevik self-criticism and to strengthen Party discipline, which must be conscious and not mechanical. But extensive discussion, especially discussion on an All-Union scale, of questions of Party policy, must be so organised that it cannot lead to attempts by an insignificant minority to impose its will upon the vast majority of the Party, or to attempt to form factional groupings which break the unity of the Party ; to attempts at a split which may shake the strength and endurance of the dictatorship of the proletariat to the delight of the enemies of the working class. Therefore a wide discussion on an All-Union scale can be regarded as necessary only if (a) this necessity is recognised by at least several local Party organisations whose jurisdiction extends to a region or a republic each ; (b) if there is not a sufficiently solid majority on the Central Committee itself on very important questions of Party policy ; (c) if in spite of the existence of a solid majority on the Central Committee which advocates a definite standpoint, the Central Committee still deems it necessary to test the correctness of its policy by means of a discussion in the Party."

earnings, which are based on the principle that his income should be not substantially greater than that of the skilled and zealous manual worker. This regulation, which embodies the communist objection to the usual practice of allowing, and even desiring, the work of government to fall into the hands of a wealthy class, or at least of a class of administrators having a markedly different standard of life from that of the people they are governing, was first made by the Paris Commune of 1871. It was at once approved by Karl Marx, and was, a whole generation later, adopted by Lenin for his nascent party of revolutionists, who in tsarist times, with very few exceptions, necessarily lived abstemious lives, whether as almost destitute exiles or as persecuted proletarians in " underground Russia ". It has, from the first, been the rule of the Bolshevik Party; a rule which, though varying in details from time to time and even from place to place, is reported, even by hostile critics of the Party, to have been continuously maintained and substantially enforced.[1] There is a corresponding provision relating to extraneous earnings, such as those from authorship or journalism, which are much affected by Party members. Of all such earnings, in addition to the ordinary progressive income tax to which all residents in the USSR are liable, Party members have to surrender to the Party funds 20 or 30 per cent of the total, and in extreme cases even 50 per

[1] Until recently, the regulation appears to have been that the Party member may not take for himself in Moscow any salary higher than 300 roubles per month. With the rise in both wages and prices, this has lately been raised to 600 roubles per month. If his office carries a higher salary, the balance has to be surrendered to the Party. In some districts, assumed to have lower costs of living, the permissible maximum may be even lower. To this rule an exception was made in 1932, apparently by private Party circular ; an exception which has led to the mistake, eagerly disseminated by enemies of the régime, that the Party maximum had been abolished. Where a Party member is employed as a technician, actually in the works, not merely in administration, he may now receive a salary equal to that paid to any non-Party technician in that establishment, not being a foreigner serving on a special contract. The highest case is said to be 900 roubles per month. The motive for this exception is said to have been a desire to encourage Party members to qualify themselves to replace in due course both the foreign and the non-Party specialists, whose services are at present indispensable. It should be added, as a possible further exception, that the latest arrangements allow the governing body of a trust or combine, having a surplus on the year's production in the nature of profit, to allocate a fixed proportion of this surplus not exceeding one per cent to any way of improving the enterprise that may seem to them expedient. There may thus be, in some cases, an extra payment to the responsible technicians by way of premiums for some exceptional device for extra production. These exceptions, which affect only a tiny proportion of the Party members, and these not the highest in authority, illustrate the stringency of the rule.

cent.[1] It need not be said that this prescribed maximum of personal income by way of salary or extraneous earnings is exclusive of all " functional expenses ", which are provided to any extent that the task or duty appears to require.[2] Thus, officials, whether or not Party members, have all travelling expenses paid, proceeding frequently by aeroplane. They have at their disposal a liberal supply of motor-cars, which are not supposed to be used for pleasure. They very naturally enjoy, though as officials in the overcrowded cities and not as Party members, a valuable preference in the allocation of apartments (though without any privilege in the permissible extent of accommodation) ; and they, like many million industrial workers, are, again as government officials and not as Party members, entitled to shop at the retail stores maintained at their several establishments (the " closed cooperative societies "), with less restricted supplies of " deficiency " commodities, and more carefully limited prices, than are available to the unfavoured citizen. But, subject to all these necessary qualifications, it is a fact that the administrators of Soviet Communism in the USSR, even of the highest grades, including the People's Commissars in the Sovnarkom, and the heads of the great consumers' cooperative movement, unlike the leading administrators of every other great nation, are found occupying flats of three or four rooms, with their wives often going out to work for wages, and altogether living a life not substantially differing, in the total of personal expenditure, from that which is open to the most highly skilled manual workers of their own country.

### The Meaning of Leadership

What, then, is the vocation that the two or three million Party members undertake on these terms in the USSR of to-day ? They constitute, it is said, the vanguard of the proletariat, or, varying the metaphor, the spearhead of its activity, in the main-

[1] If a Party member wins a high prize in the state lottery loans, the Party authorities decide what proportion of it he should surrender to the Party—in this case the sum being allocated to a special fund for pensioning superannuated members. Party members awarded a premium for a valuable industrial invention or winning a prize in the lottery loan often cede the whole of it to the Party, or to some public fund.

[2] Thus, soviet embassies or legations in foreign countries may be maintained at any standard of expenditure, and with as much diplomatic entertaining, as is deemed expedient.

tenance of the Bolshevik revolution and the building up of the socialist state.[1] But what does this mean in practice ?

At all times more than half the Party membership, as we have mentioned, continues at its manual labour in the factory or the mine, in the oil-fields or at the hydro-electric plants, on the farms or in the railway or postal service, with the mercantile marine or the river-transport vessels. The specific Party duty of these million or more members is so to lead their manual-working lives as to be perpetually influencing the minds of the ten or twenty times as numerous non-Party colleagues among whom they work. They must set themselves to be the most zealous, the most assiduous, the most efficient workers of their several establishments. They must neglect no opportunity of raising their own qualifications and increasing their technical skill. They must make themselves the leaders among the wage-earners, employing every means of educating the non-Party mass in communist doctrine and soviet policy. In the meetings of the trade union and the consumers' cooperative society, as in the manufacturing artel and the collective farm, they must, in concert with their comrades in the concern, constantly take an active part, using their influence to guide the whole membership towards the most complete fulfilment of the function of the organisation in the socialist state, along the lines from time to time authoritatively prescribed. We see them, accordingly, filling the " shock brigades " and " cost-accounting brigades ", by means of which the output is increased, " scrap " is diminished, waste prevented and the production cost per unit reduced to a minimum. With the same object they lead their shifts, teams, brigades or whole establishments into successive " socialist competitions " with others working in the same field. They freely undertake the

---

[1] The preamble to the Rules, as adopted in 1934, declares that " The Party *effects the leadership* of the proletariat, the toiling peasantry and all toiling masses in the struggle for the dictatorship of the proletariat, for the victory of socialism. . . . The Party is a unified militant organisation held together by conscious iron proletarian discipline. The Party is strong because of its coherence, unity of will and unity of action, which are incompatible with any deviation from the programme, with any violation of Party discipline or with informal groupings within the Party. The Party demands from all its members active and self-sacrificing work to carry out the programme and rules of the Party, to fulfil all decisions of the Party and its organs, to ensure unity within the Party, and the consolidation of the fraternal international relations among the toilers of the nationalities of the USSR, as well as among the proletarians of the whole world " (Preamble to Rules in *Socialism Victorious*, 1934, p. 691).

numerous "spare time" offices connected with their various organisations, which are either wholly unpaid or only slightly remunerated, such as insurance officers, dues collectors, social club officials, or secretaryship of this or that committee ; realising that such service increases their influence upon their fellow-workers. It is to be noted that their power over the workers has to be entirely educational and persuasive in character, not authoritative. The Party members in any establishment cannot, as such, give any orders, either to the management or to their fellow-workers. They can impose no policy. They can change nothing but the minds of the men and women among whom they work. This persuasive training of the non-Party mass, continuously effected by a million of the principal manual-working leaders, unobtrusively organised in tens of thousands of Party cells, represents a social influence of incalculable potency.

For some 40 per cent or more of the Party membership, the vocation takes the form of salaried service in the innumerable kinds and grades of public administration, including trade union and cooperative, and even the voluntary organisations that we shall hereafter describe. These offices are by no means confined to Party members, or even to persons of communist opinions. It seems that, in various important branches of public administration, Party members are actually in a minority among those in receipt of departmental pay. In the factory operatives and villagers taken by conscription for the Red Army ; among the band of nearly a million salaried employees of the consumers' cooperative societies ; in the staff of half a million teachers in the elementary and secondary school service ; among the eighty thousand members of the medical profession, and even in the tiny membership of the College of Advocates (corresponding to the British or American lawyers) ; in the host of subordinate civil servants, typists and attendants, even in the Moscow Kremlin itself, there is reported to be, for various reasons, an overwhelming non-Party majority. In the directly elected soviets, as we have mentioned, the proportion of Party members is increasing, but except in the cities they are usually in a minority ; and in the more remote or more primitive villages—largely from sheer lack of a sufficient number of Party candidates—they seldom fill more than a quarter of the seats. Out of nearly two million elected members of primary soviets in city and country in the whole

USSR, it seems as if three-quarters of a million are Party members or Comsomols. In 1934 the Party members constituted 18·9 per cent, and the Comsomols, 11·5 per cent. of all the village soviets ; whilst in the city soviets their percentages were 42·0 and 11·9.

### *The Party Group* (*late fraction*)

On the other hand, it is to be noticed that the Party members elected to any soviet, or finding themselves members of any other body in which there are non-Party colleagues, are definitely instructed, whenever there are as many as three of them together, invariably to form a private caucus among themselves, which is called a Party Group. This caucus is imperatively directed to hold regular private meetings, in order to consider every subject coming before the whole body ; and always to decide, by a majority, what shall be " the Party line " on each issue. Every Party member is then peremptorily required, as an incident of his Party obedience, to adopt as his own the decision thus arrived at. For the Party members on any public body to split among themselves, and vote otherwise than as their own majority decides, is one of the most heinous of Party offences, and one which is practically never committed. The Party rules prescribe, as the specific tasks of the Party Group " the strengthening of every side of the influence of the Party, the execution of its policy outside the Party, and Party control of the work of all the particular institutions and organisations concerned ". For its current work the group may appoint a bureau and a secretary. With this universal organisation of Party Groups, the Party members obtain far greater weight in any public body than any other section ; greater, even, than the usual superiority of these picked professionals to the bulk of the non-Party members would otherwise secure to them. For this as well as for other reasons, Party members will now usually be found in a majority in the various higher councils, and in the committees that the primary soviets elect ; and this preponderance steadily increases, tier after tier, up each hierarchy, whether soviet, trade union, consumers' cooperative movement or manufacturing association of owner-producers (artels or incops). The highest governing bodies in all these hierarchies are found to be almost wholly composed of Party members, though even in these (excluding, of course, that of the Communist Party itself) there are usually a few non-Party persons.[1]

This preponderance of Party members in administration is even more marked in the higher executive offices to which appointments are made by the congresses, conferences and councils. Thus, the People's Commissars (ministers of state), constituting the sovnarkoms (cabinets), alike of the USSR and of the constituent and autonomous republics of the Union, are invariably Party members, together with their assistants or deputies.[2] The various control commissions are invariably made up of Party members. Nearly all the trusts and combines are directed by boards composed (except for a few non-Party technicians), exclusively of Party members. All the higher commanders (officers) of the Red Army, together with a majority of the junior commanders (subalterns) are Party members. Most of the directors of industrial establishments of all kinds are Party members, although the technicians whom they control still include a considerable proportion of non-Party persons. The same may be said of the institutions of higher education, whether university colleges or " technicums " ; and likewise of the various medical institutions, and even of nearly all the " cultural " institutions, such as libraries, theatres and " parks of culture and rest ". In short, the Party members who are office-bearers, and who are all pledged to complete obedience to the dictates of the Party authorities, have assumed as their main vocation the supreme direction of policy and the most important parts of its execution, in every branch of public administration in the USSR, where public administration covers a much larger part of the common life than it does in any other country. And just as the Communist Party cell in the factory or the institution co-ordinates and directs the influence which the Party members exercise among their fellow-workers, so the Communist Party Central Committee, and especially the inner Politbureau which it appoints, not only prescribes the general

[1] It should be noted that the Party rules expressly prescribe that, "irrespective of their importance, the Groups are completely subordinated to the corresponding Party organisations. In all questions the Groups must strictly and undeviatingly adhere to the decisions of the leading Party organisations."

[2] We hear of only one exception. Mr. Winter, the universally respected and trusted Russian engineer of Dnieprostroy, though not a Party member, has been appointed Deputy People's Commissar of Heavy Industry (*Moscow, 1911-1933*, by Allan Monkhouse, 1933). He has since joined the Party.

line to be pursued by all the Party cells throughout the USSR,
but also co-ordinates and directs the policy and executive action
of the Sovnarkom of People's Commissars, and of all the Party
members who constitute the most important part of the staffs
of these commissariats. It is in this way, in fact, that is exercised
the dictatorship of the proletariat.[1]

## The Primary Party Organ (late cell or nucleus)

It is interesting to find the Communist Party in the USSR
organised on substantially the same hierarchical or pyramidal
pattern of Democratic Centralism as that we have described as
common to the soviets, the trade unions, the consumers' cooperative societies and the incops or associations of owner-
producers in industry. The base of the Party organisation is
what used to be called the cell, or nucleus, but which the 1934
Rules call the Primary Party Organ. This is cónstituted among
the members employed in any enterprise, whatever its object or
character, or residing in any village where as many as three
members of the Party are found. Thus, every industrial establishment, whether factory or mine, electric plant or poultry incubat-
ing enterprise, newspaper office or state farm, has at least one
Primary Party Organ in each of its departments. Every other
social institution, whether university, college or " technicum ",
hospital or maternity clinic, trade-union office or cooperative
store, kustar artel or collective farm, has its Primary Organ.
The same may be said of every depot or centre of the railway and

---

[1] We may notice, as one of the numerous " projections " of the central Party
organisation, the implicit obligation imposed on individual Party members to
support, in any emergency, the constituted public authority, to maintain order,
and to protect public property. Thus it is the duty of Party members travelling
on the Volga steamboats to report themselves immediately to the captain, so
that he may be able to invoke their assistance whenever required. If anything
is going wrong, the Party members will consult together, as if they were a fraction ; and they may collectively press the captain to take appropriate action (as,
for instance, the summary dismissal of a steward or other member of the ship's
company who is so drunk as to cause annoyance to the passengers). A Party
member travelling on a train, or even passing along the road, will feel bound to
intervene to maintain public order, and to prevent assault or robbery, or the
destruction of public property. On announcing his Party membership, he will
usually be able to secure obedience, or, if not, he can command any militiaman
(police constable) or local official to take action. In many ways his position
towards the public, and especially towards ill-doers, is not unlike that of an
English " special constable ", if not of a Justice of the Peace in the eighteenth
century.

postal services, of every branch of the provincial and municipal administration and of every department of the central government. Every vessel in the growing mercantile marine and every soviet agency in foreign countries is similarly equipped. Apart from all enterprises and specific organisations, there are Primary Party Organs for units, areas such as villages in which there are few Party members or none employed in agriculture for wages or salary, but in which members of the Party reside as school or post-office or railway employees, or as peasant agriculturists (not being kulaks), especially in collective farms, or as independent handicraftsmen. In fact as many as one-half of all the cells (comprising, however, a very much smaller proportion of the entire Party membership) are to be found in such villages. In 1933, on the institution of " politotdeli " or " policy sections " (which we have described in our chapter on Collective Farms) to cope with the crisis in agriculture, the Central Committee sought to reorganise the cells in the rural districts. " Very frequently ", it was observed, " the village Party groups, consisting chiefly of communists employed in rural institutions such as the village soviet, the post office, the militia [local police], the schools, and so on, have little contact with the collective farms, and give little attention to their work. . . . In the future the communists working directly on collective farms will form a distinct nucleus, to be controlled by the policy sections; while those members of the Party who are employed in village institutions which have no immediate connection with the collective farms will be organised separately and be subordinated to the district committee. Where the number of communists in the collective farm is too small to be formed into a nucleus, they will be grouped together with the comsomols and sympathisers, and formed into a communist comsomol unit of the collective farm. . . . For purposes of further coordination of the work of the policy sections and district committees, the chiefs of the policy sections will act as members of the district committee bureau." [1]

In normal times the procedure of formation of new primary organs is simple enough. A meeting is called of all the known Party members; a resolution constituting the cell is passed; a secretary and president are elected (who must be of at least a

[1] Decree of the Central Committee of the Communist Party; in *Moscow Daily News*, July 17, 1933.

year's standing as Party members) ; and formal sanction for the
new organ is sought and obtained from the next higher unit of
Party organisation, the district committee. It is the duty of
every Party member to accept membership of the Party Organ
in the body in which he works, or in the village in which he resides,
and to attend its meetings. As soon as the membership of the
cell exceeds a dozen or a score, a bureau or standing committee
will be elected for a term of six months. In great industrial
works and extensive establishments of other kinds, there may be
as many as hundreds of Party members, and in a few cases, of
thousands, but in such cases separate organs are formed for the
several departments, workshops, brigades, teams or shifts, among
which the work is divided. All the organs in a single large factory
or other establishment nominate representatives to a factory or
institute Party committee, which is responsible for common
action within the enterprise. In such cases permission may be
obtained for one member—occasionally more than one—to be
appointed at a salary, paid from Party funds, not exceeding the
average of his past earnings, to give his whole time to the secretarial and organisation work of the organ. The three million Party
members and candidates are, with few exceptions,[1] distributed

---

[1] In 1926, when there were about 30,000 cells, about one-fourth, or 7315, of
them were in industrial establishments such as factories or mines ; one-half, or
15,819, were in rural villages ; 5167 were in government departments and
institutions ; 566 were in the Red Army ; and 573 were in educational institutions. Out of more than a million members and candidates at that date there
were only about 4000 classed as " solitary Communists ", not in a position to be
members of cells (*Civic Training in Soviet Russia*, by S. N. Harper, 1929, p. 23).
The total number has greatly increased. " At the time of the Sixteenth Party
Congress (1930) the number of primary Party organisations and candidate
groups was 54,000 : by October 1, 1933, the number had risen to 130,000."
Kaganovich added, " I can give you data concerning 150 shop organisations in
85 of the largest enterprises in which a total of 700,000 workers are employed,
of whom 94,000 are communists. Almost half the number of secretaries of
shop Party organisations in these enterprises joined the Party after 1929, and
only one-fourth joined the Party before and in 1925 " (*Report on the Organisational Problems of Party and Soviet Construction*, by L. M. Kaganovich, 1934,
pp. 115-116).

The few thousand Party members who are entirely isolated, and not attached
to any establishment or enterprise of any sort, include such exceptional persons
as those working in unsalaried independence as writers, artists or scientific
researchers, or doctors confining themselves to private practice. There may
also be a few of them among the surviving independent peasants, not being
kulaks, outside the collective farm areas. But a much more considerable
exception numerically is afforded by those who are superannuated and retired
from work, whilst not abandoning Party membership, though excused from
paying Party dues.

among these organs, the number of which in the USSR now exceeds 130,000, giving an average of about a score of members and candidates to each Primary Party Organ. In the large factories, there may be hundreds of members in each organ.[1]

The duties of the Party organ are precisely formulated and universally understood. It has no formal authority in the enterprise within which it has established itself. Neither the organ nor its standing committee, nor the factory or institute Party committee representing all the cells in the enterprise, nor any of their officers or members, can give any orders to the director or manager, or to the other workers, or to the trade union or cooperative officials or committees, or to the municipal soviet or officials. The organ cannot impose any policy or make any regulation for the enterprise. What the cell and its members have to do is to carry on a persistent education of the other workers, and, by persuasion and personal example, to be perpetually influencing the whole organisation within which it lives, familiarising everyone with the slogans and latest decisions of the Communist Party ; in such a way as to attract, as new candidates for membership of the Party, the most suitable men and women ; and, above all, in such a way as to ensure that all the operations of the enterprise conform in all respects to the " General Line ".

For further elucidation of the working of the Primary Party Organ in every kind of industrial establishment in the USSR, we give general descriptions by two competent and well-informed American observers, who naturally used the former name of cell.

" After the General Line has been mapped out by the Party Congress and the Congress of Soviets, the government depart-

---

[1] The following explanation of the utility to the Party of the cell organisation is of interest. " Nuclei are set up in factories, enterprises, offices, departments, in shops, shifts and so on. What are the advantages of this ? They lie in the fact that all members of a nucleus are occupied in the same work, premises or locality. They meet every day at work, know each at work as well as at meetings. All members share its interests. The nucleus and individual members have opportunities for a thorough study of all aspects of work, of the whole administrative staff in their factory, and of the non-Party members there. The nucleus carries on daily, hourly work among the masses bringing them nearer to the Party and to communism. Through its members the nucleus can find out the spirit of the masses, their dissatisfaction with the system of shifts, ventilation, etc., can carry on lively discussion of political questions, such as Stalin's letter on the collective farms, and so on " (Bolshevism for Beginners, by P. Kerzhentsev, 1931, pp. 19, 20).

ments, combines, trusts and factories work out the detailed application of these policies. It is then the task of the Party cells in the factories and villages to see that instructions are carried out. They must call attention to defects in production and administration, and make special efforts to overcome difficulties. They attempt to accomplish this, not by direct interference with the management, but by working through the Party members who are in the factory management, the board of the trust or combine, the factory committees and the trade unions. Whenever necessary the cell can appeal to the higher economic and trade union instances. The Party cell, consisting primarily of workers in industry and agriculture, plays a leading rôle in increasing production, attaining higher labour productivity, improving labour discipline, and obtaining better labour conditions. Among other tasks, it is the duty of the Party cell to counteract bureaucracy and to protect the interests of the workers against any infringement on the part of the administration. The dominating elements in the individual management are the Party cell, the [trade union] factory committee and the management. This combination is known as the ' triangle of factory control '.[1]

" The Party cell . . . holds meetings and decisions are reached in these meetings as to the position which the Party members are to take on any question which has arisen or is likely to arise. Then in trade union or other factory meetings the Party members vote unanimously for the previously agreed-upon decision. Its power therefore is very great. The Fabkom [trade union factory committee], since it is elected in a meeting in which the guidance has been given by the Party, is an organ which the Party cell not only dominates, but which is actually an organ of the cell. In other words, the Party cell is greatly superior in importance to the Fabkom. The Party cell is represented always by its secretary, and in practice it is he rather than the chairman of the Fabkom who is able to be a counterweight to the factory management. If any conflict arises, it is usually between the management of the factory and the secretary of the Party cell, who is naturally supported by the Fabkom. Conflicts between the Party cell and the management are not as likely to happen as might be thought, however, for the director of the factory is almost certain to be a communist (Party member) himself, and

---

[1] *The Soviet Worker*, by Joseph Freeman, 1932, pp. 96, 98.

to have been appointed with the consent or even direction of the higher Party authorities. The Party cell, therefore, is by no means in a position to ride rough-shod over the decisions of the management. Furthermore, the point of view of the Party cell is not likely to be as antagonistic to that of the management, as would be true if the Fabkom were a counter-weight independent of the Party. All orthodox members of the Party must support, heart and soul, the movement for rationalisation of industry, and for increasing the productivity of labour. The Party cell cannot, therefore, openly oppose the management in any move that it makes towards improving the efficiency and productivity of the factory. In this way the position of the Party in the factory organisation is an earnest that conflicts over attempts to increase productivity will be reduced to a minimum. . . . Indeed, the influence of the Party organisation in the whole structure cannot be overestimated. It is a force which works directly among the personnel of industry to obtain support for official industrial policies, and welds the management and the Party labourers into an organisation whose responsibilities and duties as Party members are of more importance to them than their position in industry, be it as officers of labour unions, managers of factories, directors of trusts and syndicates, or even members of the Supreme Economic Council itself." [1]

Among the 130,000 cells, in some tens of thousands of enterprises of the most varied kinds, working under all sorts of conditions, there must necessarily be an almost endless variety. We give a few examples of cell activity or inactivity.

In October 1932, when some alarm was felt about the crisis in agriculture, a correspondent of the *Moscow Daily News* gave a detailed account of the work being done by the two Party cells among the hundreds of persons employed on a particular state farm (sovkhos). "The two sections into which the farm was divided had each its cell, with 12 and 8 Party members respectively. These members, besides performing all the regular duties of a cell, had joined forces to drive their fellow-workers into a higher productivity. The twenty Party members had formed themselves into five unofficial committees, two undertaking special responsibility for the care of the two herds of cattle, two seeing to the management of the tractors and the building of the

[1] *The Economic Life of Soviet Russia*, by Calvin B. Hoover, 1931, p. 36.

necessary barns, whilst the fifth conducted the persistent education and agitation. The cattle committees had set up milk recording, with the result of demonstrating that the cows milked by Party members yielded, on an average, 5·1 litres per cow, as against only 4·2 litres per cow in non-Party hands. After getting the subject discussed at several meetings, 71 non-Party milk-women pledged themselves to increase cleanliness and regularity of feeding, with the intention of reaching an average daily yield of 6·5 litres. The committee on tractors held discussions with all the tractorists, who ultimately promised to reduce the average idle time of each machine from 45 to 20 per cent, and so carry out the plan of autumn ploughing well ahead of schedule time. Meanwhile all Party members and comsomols have led extemporised brigades of non-Party workers of all ages in expeditions for collecting leaves, weeds and young shoots, which can be converted in the silo into fodder for the winter. The committee on education and agitation had got established two day schools for candidates on probation and an evening political school for all comers, working on a definite programme." [1]

Another vision of a cell is given in a resolution of severe reprimand passed by the central committee of the Communist Party in the Ukraine, about the failure of the cells and the Party factory committee in a great steel-works to get carried out the administrative reforms demanded by the Party authorities. " The Party organisation in the Stal steel-works has not yet introduced the principle of single manager in industry ; it has not yet abolished the threefold intervention by the director of the works, the secretary of the works committee and the secretary of the communist factory cell in the administrative and technical management of work. It has not yet stopped the unjust persecution of technicians and the interference of the People's Commissariat of Labour (SIC). The plenary session of the CC of UCP hereby declares that all local branches of the CP shall hereafter prohibit all kinds of interference by the administrative and judicial authorities in the industrial life of factories and workshops ; they shall discontinue the intolerable triple interference in the management of works ; and shall guarantee to the technical staff complete freedom in exercising their duties and

[1] " How the Communist Party functions in lifting the Output on a State Farm ", in *Moscow Daily News*, October 28, 1932.

free play to their initiative, for which they alone shall henceforth be responsible." [1]

In offices and institutions of every kind, in the kustar artel and in the consumers' cooperative society, in the kolkhos and the sovkhos, what we have now to call the Primary Party Organ has substantially the same functions as in the factory or the mine. Everywhere it is an organ of persistent political education of the masses among which its members work, and at the same time a persuasive instrument of extraordinary potency in securing—in the main, silently and unobtrusively—the putting in operation, by every kind of social or economic institution in the length and breadth of the USSR, of the policy as from time to time centrally determined. But, as the base of the hierarchy of committees and conferences of the Communist Party itself, the organ fulfils two other functions. It formulates and transmits the feelings and views of its own members, who, taken together, make up the entire Party, to the central directing authorities thereof. And it affords opportunities for members to prove their qualifications for the responsible work of government, whilst at the same time providing an avenue for promotion in the necessarily extensive staff of salaried officials in all the various branches of public work which is increasingly recruited from among the Party membership of proletarian or poor peasant extraction.

### The District (Rayon) Conference

All the Primary Organs within a geographical area, usually coincident with the soviet administrative district called a rayon, annually elect in general meeting delegates to the Party rayon conference. This elects a president and secretary (who must have three years' Party standing, and his election has to be approved by the next higher Party unit), together with a presidium or standing executive committee. The Party rayon conference chooses delegates to the Party republic conferences.

The periodically meeting Party district or rayon conference, together with the district committee, has the duty of supervising

---

[1] Resolution of CC of UCP, June 25, 1931, included in article by Sergius Prokopovich in *The Slavonic Review*, September 1931. The order which the guilty cells had ignored was that by the All-Union CC of the Communist Party relating to factory discipline described in *Russia in Transition*, by Elisha M. Friedman, 1933, p. 217.

and directing the work of all its constituent organs. It sanctions the establishment of new ones. It is expected that the work of each district committee will take up the whole time of two members in addition to the secretary, who receive salaries from Party funds.[1]

### The Republic Congress

Each of the six smaller republics, excluding the RSFSR, has its own Party congress, that of the Ukraine being of special importance and influence. In the Ukraine the republic Party congress is formed by delegates elected by the region Party conferences of that republic, and it elects, along with the inevitable Control Commission, a central committee of the Ukraine Communist Party, which supervises and directs all the Party work. In the five smaller republics there may be Party congresses called for the whole republic, but they are of considerably less importance.

### The USSR and RSFSR Party Congress

The supreme Party congress for the whole USSR, including the RSFSR, consists of delegates elected by all the region conferences throughout the whole area, together with delegates elected directly by the republic Party congress of each republic.

The USSR Party congress used to meet annually, then usually every two or three years, and now apparently only every four years, when over a thousand delegates and alternates assemble at Moscow. So large and so infrequent a congress can do little but listen to set speeches, and formally ratify what has been done by the Central Committee of the Party (CC of CP) which it elects. It is, however, usefully supplemented by a less formal gathering, called an All-Union Party Conference, not mentioned in the Rules, but meeting prior to each congress—latterly one or two years before—and attended only by the presidents or secretaries of the local Party organisations.

[1] In both city and village the cells are also grouped geographically by local neighbourhood for coordination of work and mutual helpfulness. Thus, the larger cities have ward committees, uniting the cells within each ward. In the rural areas there is a committee representing all the cells of each district containing at least three cells. These committees are enjoined to meet regularly, not less than once a fortnight, in order to prevent inconsistent or uncoordinated action by individual Primary Party Organs.

The distinction in function between the All-Union Party congresses and the All-Union Party conferences is not clear to us, except that it is the congress which elects the Central Committee, together with the Commission of Party Control, and which ratifies their actions; and that it is only the decisions of the congress which are formally binding, those of the conference, if in the nature of new departures, requiring ratification by the Central Committee. The alternating congresses and conferences are both numbered successively; thus the Seventh Party Conference of 1918 preceded the Seventh Party Congress of 1919, and so on, the interval gradually widening until the Seventeenth Party Conference of 1932 preceded the Seventeenth Party Congress of 1934 by nearly two years. But we cannot detect any difference between the usual business, or the subjects dealt with, by the one and the other. Both listen to long and elaborate accounts of the progress made in various departments of administration, together with ambitious projects for the future. Neither spend much time, if any, in dealing with Party, as distinguished from soviet, affairs. During the years 1924–1928 both were the scene of heated discussions on principles or theories of public policy between the spokesmen of opposing factions, which always ended in resolutions on matters of fact being passed by overwhelming majorities, or even unanimously. Both congress and conference serve, in reality, the same purpose of wide and resounding demonstrations of policy and progress; and both are made the means of impressing upon the local representatives the common policy of the Party, against which only theoretical objections have usually been made. Moreover, both are useful in bringing representatives from distant parts into touch with the supreme administrators at Moscow. It is to be noted that, whereas both these bodies originally met annually, and then biennially, each of them now meets only every four years, the congress two years after the conference.[1]

---

[1] The proceedings of all the successive All-Union Party congresses and conferences can be most conveniently followed in *Histoire du parti communiste de l'URSS*, by E. Yaroslavsky, Paris, 1931; or in English, in the *Outline History of the Bolshevik Party of the Soviet Union*, by N. Popov, 2 vols, London, 1935, translated from the 16th Russian edition. (Neither of these works is free from bias in describing the factional differences.)

At the Seventeenth Party Congress in 1935 there were 1225 delegates with full powers, and 736 candidates with only consultative voice. Among those with full powers, 598, or 48·5 per cent, attended for the first time. About 80 per cent of the whole had entered the Party before 1920, nearly a quarter of

## The Central Authority

The Central Committee (CC of CP), consisting in 1935 of 70 members, with 68 substitutes or alternates, is the real governing authority of the Party. But as it meets at most only about a dozen times a year, its authority is practically exercised by the president, the general secretary (Stalin), the three assistant secretaries, and the two influential committees that it elects, together with the elaborately organised series of departments now developed under their supervision. The committees are (*a*) the Politbureau, now composed of 10 members and 5 candidates ; and (*b*) the Orgbureau having 10 members and 2 candidates. The Party Congress also elects the Central Control Commission (now called Commission of Party Control), and the Auditing (formerly Central Revision) Commission, both of members not included in the above, who must be of ten years' Party standing. The duty of these commissions is to see that the decisions of the Party congress are carried out, and also to organise and direct the constant " cleansing " (chistka) and periodical " purging " of the Party membership. The Party Control Commission, which often meets jointly with the plenum of the Central Committee in order to become fully acquainted with its policy,[1] maintains the record of every Party member in the USSR, and deals with every accusation or suspicion of delinquency. Its operations locally were, until 1934, practically merged with the organisation of the Workers' and Peasants' Inspection, which are elsewhere described.[2]

---

whom had done " underground work " prior to 1917. Three-quarters of the whole had fought in the Civil War. The number of delegates from among the workers in agriculture and transport was greater than ever before (*Moscow Daily News*, February 3, 1934).

[1] Thus it did so in January 1933 in what Kaganovich termed " a truly historical plenum. This plenum was held on the border-line between the First and Second Five-Year Plans. It summed up the tremendous construction of the First Five-Year Plan, gave an analysis of the political significance of these results, mapped out the roads for to-morrow, raised fundamental problems before our Party for a complete and lengthy phase of development. The plenum discussed four questions . . . the first the results of the Five-Year Plan. The second about the political sections of the machine-tractor stations, or essentially about the current tasks of the Party in the villages. The third, the inner Party situation, about the anti-Party grouping of Smirnov, Eismont and Tolmachev. Finally, the fourth question, about the cleansing of the Party " (*Moscow Daily News*, January 24, 1933).

[2] See Appendix VI. to Part I.

### The Central Committee

In the Central Committee, to which the periodically meeting All-Union Congress of the Communist Party entrusts complete powers between Congresses, we come very near to the heart of the whole constitutional organism of the USSR.[1] The Central Committee varies slightly in numbers from time to time. As elected in January 1934, it comprised nearly as many alternates or substitutes as members. These candidates may attend the meetings, but do not vote unless they are chosen to fill vacancies. The committee must meet every three months, and now meets usually for two or three days monthly, when its members are supplied beforehand with reports and drafts for their consideration. These papers are prepared, and policy and decisions are provisionally formulated, by the standing sub-committees, the Politbureau and the Orgbureau, having at their command an extensive and highly trained secretariat, and consisting each of nearly a dozen members, at whose incessant meetings the current business is attended to. The Central Committee has a presidium of four members and four alternates, which consults with the Politbureau. It is agreed on all hands that it is in the Politbureau, which has always included the principal national leaders for the time being, nearly all of whom hold important executive offices in the Soviet Government, that the real power resides. This is, however, true only in the sense that the Politbureau, in consultation with the presidium of the Central Committee, can normally count on the support of the plenum of the Central Committee, the next meeting of which is at most only a few weeks off ; just as the Central Committee itself presumes on the support of the All-Union Congress of the Party, whose next meeting may be three or four years off. But this support has not been (and

[1] *The Rules of the Communist Party*, edition of 1934, gives the following reference to the Central Committee : " The Central Committee during the interval between congresses, guides the entire work of the Party ; represents the Party in its relations with other Parties (the Communist Parties of other countries), organisations and institutions ; forms various Party institutions and guides their activities ; appoints the editorial staffs of the central organs working under its control and confirms the appointments of the editors of the Party organs of big local organisations ; organises and manages enterprises of public importance ; distributes the forces and resources of the Party, and manages the central funds. The Central Committee directs the work of the central soviet and public organisations through the Party Groups in them " (*Rules*, par. 33).

even to-day is not) invariably forthcoming. "There has always been opposition within the Communist ranks", writes a careful observer.[1] In 1917, in 1921, in 1923, in 1926 and 1927, to say nothing of minor quarrels, there were, at the Central Committee and Party Congress, definite factions led by successive leaders advocating rival theories, which were fought out in repeated debates and oratorical controversies. There have been, at all times since 1917, not only differences of opinion within the Party, but even hot controversies among the leaders as to policy ; sometimes, as in the struggle with the Trotskyists, extending over years, and arousing considerable public discussion.[2] Thus, whilst the majority among the little group of leaders normally gets its way, it does not do so without having to take seriously into account whatever conflicting opinions may be entertained among the colossal Party membership, as voiced by particular leaders on controversial points, and occasionally not without having to introduce into its policy the modifications necessary to secure unanimity.[3]

What in the USSR is exceptional, and even unique, is the fact that the Central Committee of the Communist Party, and its most important sub-committee, the Politbureau, which are not known to the written constitution, or to the codes, and are nominally not organs of the government at all, are constantly occupied, not with the internal business of the Communist Party itself, but mainly, and sometimes almost exclusively, with the policy and the practice, the legislation and the administration of every department of the soviet state. The members of the Politbureau

---

[1] Jerome Davis, in *Soviet Russia in the Second Decade*, edited by Stuart Chase and others, New York, 1928, p. 157, where a useful summary of these factions is given.

[2] As we have mentioned, the Party *Rules* actually prescribe discussion in the All-Union Party Congress in certain cases.

Moreover, there is provision for discussion in every local committee or cell, in connection with each successive Party Congress, first of the theses, on reports, which the Central Committee proposes to lay before the Congress, and, subsequently, of the resolutions and decisions passed by the Congress. This wide circulation among the entire Party membership is deliberately promoted as the best means of securing active concurrence in policy.

[3] The plenum of the Central Committee will even go so far in support of the majority of the Politbureau, as summarily to remove from the Politbureau any member who persistently and obstinately sets his will against that of the majority. Thus in 1929, after Bukharin had been removed by the Comintern from the presidium of its own executive committee, " the plenum [of the Central Committee of the Party] decrees the removal of comrade Bukharin, who is the ideologist of Right Deviation, from the Politbureau "

plainly feel themselves to be personally responsible for the whole government of the country. Although the Party *Rules* declare (No. 28) that " the Central Committee regularly informs the Party organisations of its work ", the committee naturally keeps its internal proceedings strictly confidential, and no account of the discussions is ever published.[1] But in April 1928 the widely circulating newspaper *Izvestia* gave, possibly by inadvertence, the prospective agenda for the ensuing half-year, not only of the plenum of the Central Committee, but incidentally also of the Politbureau, as confirmed by the Central Committee, in conjunction with the Central Control Commission. This skeleton agenda for the ensuing six months, which naturally does not include the matters of urgency demanding consideration at each meeting, makes evident how comprehensive is the control that the Party maintains, as a matter of course, over every part of soviet policy and its execution. We give the complete text, although we are unfortunately not in a position even to enumerate the elaborate reports which were evidently prepared for circulation before each meeting.[2]

## The Agenda

1 April.  Crop movement.
2  „     Programme of the Communist International.
3 May.   Improvement of higher and middle technical educational institutions with a view to the training and use of " red " specialists and economic workers.
4  „     Radio and cinema betterments.
5  „     Universal obligatory primary education.

---

[1] What is given to the press is a bare statement of the subjects considered. Thus, " the Plenum assembled on November 17, 1929. The Plenum examined the following questions : (1) instructions as regards the control figures of the national economy for 1929–30; (2) problems and further tasks of Kolkhos construction ; (3) report of the Central Committee of the Communist Party of the Ukraine on work in the village ; (4) Union of the Commissariat of Agriculture ; (5) the fulfilment of the decisions of the July 1928 plenum of the Central Control Committee on the preparation of technical cadres."

[2] In October 1927 it appeared that a member of the Central Committee, who dissented from the proposals of the Politbureau, complained—as such members in all bodies frequently do—that " the theses have been distributed to us, members of the Central Committee, only a few hours before the plenary meeting of the Central Committee. . . . To undertake a serious discussion of these theses . . . it is necessary to give more time to them than has been given by will of the Politbureau " (*Soviet Rule in Russia*, by W. R. Batsell, 1929, p. 715).

6 June.  State and financial conditions of the railways.

7 ,,  Position and betterment of construction.

8 ,,  Seven-hour work day.

9 July.  Reorganisation of the People's Commissariat for Trade of the USSR.

10 ,,  Rationalisation of industry.

11 Aug.  National defence.

12 ,,  Collective and soviet estates.

13 Sept.  Control figures of people's economy for 1928–1929.

14 ,,  Industrial and financial plan for 1928–1929.

15 ,,  Execution of export and import and foreign exchange plans for 1927–1928, and plans for 1928–1929.

16 Oct.  Execution of 1927–1928 budget and the budget plans for 1928–1929.

17 ,,  Results of bank mergers and reorganisation of the State Bank.

18 ,,  Political and economic work in the Ukraine.

19 Nov.  Struggle with bureaucratism in the state and economic machine.

20 ,,  The Five-Year economic plan.[1]

After confirmation by the plenum of the Central Committee, the decisions of the Politbureau are often published broadcast in the newspapers, either in the speeches of the leaders, or as long and detailed schemes of administrative reform in particular departments. Or they may take the form of actual decrees avowedly binding upon every member of the Communist Party, whether in his public capacity as people's commissar, member of a trust or combine, director or works manager; or in his private capacity as a citizen. Such decrees sometimes bear only the signature of Stalin, as General Secretary of the Party. Sometimes they are signed also by Molotov, as president of the Sovnarkom (or cabinet) of the USSR. Sometimes the co-signatory will be Kalinin, who has for so many years been the president of the presidium of the All-Union Central Executive Committee (TSIK), who may be taken to represent the All-Union Congress of Soviets, the supreme legislative authority. We have been unable to

---

[1] *Izvestia*, April 12, 1928; *Soviet Rule in Russia*, by W. R. Batsell, 1929, pp. 714-715. It may be doubted whether any Cabinet of a Parliamentary Democracy organises so completely in advance its consideration of the subjects to which it can be foreseen that special attention will have to be given.

understand on what basis these signatures are chosen for particular documents ; or what exactly is the distinction between them and laws formally enacted by the All-Union Congress of Soviets with the concurrence of the two chambers of its Central Executive Committee.[1]  But there can be no doubt that Stalin correctly described the situation when he referred to " the supreme expression of the guiding function of our Party.  In the Soviet Union, in the land where the dictatorship of the proletariat is in force, *no important political or organisational problem is ever decided by our soviets and other mass organisations, without directives from our Party.*  In this sense, we may say that the dictatorship of the proletariat is, *substantially*, the dictatorship of the Party as the force which effectively guides the proletariat." [2]

It must be emphasised that the Central Committee does not limit its intervention in the government of the USSR to what may be considered legislation, even in its widest sense.  Acting with the Control Commission, now the Commission of Party Control, which is separately elected by the Party Congress, the Central Committee, at the instance of both its subcommittees, is perpetually directing the executive work of the far-flung Party membership.  This we have already noticed with regard to the Primary Party Organs and Party Groups, through which the supervision and control are exercised over the lower stages of the soviet hierarchy ; and through the district committees of the Party, with the aid of the extensive salaried staff maintained by the Party itself at every nodal point throughout the USSR.[3]

---

[1] An American observer notes this issue of decrees as a change of practice. " With the resumption of the socialist offensive under the leadership of the Party, the line between Party and government has all but disappeared.  The Five-Year Plan was a Party plan, later formally sanctioned by the government. Then gradually the Party has adopted the practice of issuing orders which become legislative without any formal action by a government body " (*Making Bolsheviks*, by S. N. Harper, 1931, p. 8).

To the constitutional student it is no less interesting to find these decrees often signed also by the leading official of the organisation chiefly affected by them, signifying the concurrence of its own governing committee.  Thus, a decree affecting the consumers' cooperative organisation will be signed also by Zelenski, the president of Centrosoyus ; and one transforming trade-union organisation or policy also by Shvernik, the general secretary of the All-Union Central Council of Trade Unions (AUCCTU).

[2] *Leninism*, by J. Stalin, vol. i., 1928, p. 33.

[3] The staff of full-time salaried officers employed directly by the Party, and paid from Party funds, is both extensive and varied.  The staff at headquarters alone now approaches a thousand persons.  Throughout the USSR the Party staff was stated in 1927 as 24,000 (*Soviet Russia in the Second Decade*,

During the years 1932 and 1933 there were three new developments, in what may be called direct " projections " of the authority of the Central Committee, outside the Party hierarchy, by which groups of Party members were placed actually within the administrations conducted by People's Commissars, in order to control them in the direction of reform. One of these developments, the establishment of Machine and Tractor Stations, throughout a large part of the agricultural area, we have already described in connection with the newly appointed USSR People's Commissar of Agriculture. Here we need only notice that all the chiefs of these Machine and Tractor Stations, and the majority of their working staffs, numbering altogether many thousands of men and women, were chosen from among trusted Party members of long standing and good reputation, by the responsible officers of the Orgbureau, under the direction of the Central Committee, by whom also their allocation to the several districts was determined. It should be said that the newly appointed USSR People's Commissar of Agriculture, himself a Party member, to whom the chiefs of the Machine and Tractor Stations were made nominally responsible, warmly welcomed this intervention of the Central Committee in the difficult administrative task that he had undertaken.

In the following year (May 1933) the Central Committee, again in concert with the USSR People's Commissar of Agriculture, suddenly made the appointment of about 25,000 selected Party members to constitute a new staff of " policy sections ",[1] which were placed in virtual control of a large proportion of the state and collective farms, with instructions to " clean up " the mass of inefficiency, negligence and positive damage to public

edited by Stuart Chase and others, New York, 1928, p. 150). It has since considerably increased ; although the fifty thousand or so members who were, in 1930 and 1933, " sent to the agricultural front ", and in the latter year, also to the " transport front ", are probably borne on the budgets of the commissariats for agriculture and railways.

The Party receipts from fees on a membership of between two and three millions must be somewhere in the neighbourhood of 50 million roubles a year. No accounts have ever been published, even to the Party members themselves.

[1] What is often translated as " political sections " (politotdeli) has nothing to do with " politics ", in the ordinary usage of that word. What the politotdel is appointed for, is to put in operation a given " policy ", which may relate to agriculture or railway administration or anything else. It corresponds most closely in England with a " government commissioner " sent by the Cabinet to a Crown Colony or to a provincial centre in order to " get done " certain specific things.

property into which the sullenness and individual greed of the
" old man peasant ", who had been pressed into the new collective
organisations—if not also the factor of deliberate sabotage by
disaffected citizens—had brought some of the sovkhosi and many
of the kolkhosi. All these policy sections were placed under a
special chief, very carefully selected by the Central Committee,
who was to work in the Commissariat of Agriculture itself, and
be second only to the People's Commissar. Under the direction
of this Chief of the Policy Sections, assisted by the new Assistants
also selected by the Central Committee, the " policy sections "
were to have charge of all the Party work on the farms ; they
were to " distribute the Party forces " as might be required ;
and they were to coordinate their activities with the territorial
Party committees, which were instructed to render all possible
assistance in their work. It is to be noticed that the blame for
the inefficiency was placed on Party members and non-Party
workers alike. The task of the new policy sections was generally
to spur the Party members and the active non-Party men to higher
achievements ; to enforce " proletarian discipline " ; to combat
" absenteeism and loafing " ; to raise the technical qualifications
of both Party and non-Party workers ; and to " conduct a
systematic struggle against class enemies, kulaks and wreckers
who are at present rather being encouraged by the easy-going
attitude taken towards them by the Communists ".[1]

The third of these developments concerned the Commissariat
of Railways, where a similar mass of inefficiency had become
apparent, with the result that the lines had become overwhelmed
with the continually increasing passenger and freight traffic. In
June 1933 the Central Committee decreed the appointment of
some thousands of trusted Party members as " policy sections "
in the railway administration, stationing them at every railway
depôt, warehouse, engine-house and important junction. Here,
under the orders of a newly selected Chief of the Railway Policy
Sections, who took up his abode in the Commissariat of Railways,
as second only to the People's Commissar, the Party members
detailed for the policy sections were instructed peremptorily to
" cut out red tape ", to put an end to delays and stoppages, to

[1] See the lengthy resolution of the Joint Plenum of the Central Committee
and the Central Control Committee of the Communist Party, in the Report of
L. M. Kaganovich, which filled eight columns of the *Moscow Daily News*,
January 16, 1933.

expose and dismiss employees of any grade who are guilty of idleness or negligence, or even of failure to improve their technical qualifications ; whilst new scales of pay were to be introduced, finally " liquidating the petty bourgeois ideal of equality of wages, which stands in the way of effective organisation of an efficient service ".

At the Seventeenth Party Congress in 1934 the temporary projections of the Party into the agricultural districts were regularised by being absorbed into the regional Party organisations themselves. The policy sections (politotdeli) attached either to the Machine and Tractor Stations, or to the kolkhosi and sovkhosi, cease to exist as such, and their memberships are added to those of the Primary Party Organs and the regional Party committees, which have to be reorganised into half a dozen separate branches corresponding with those of the Central Party organisation. The policy sections were considered to have successfully accomplished the task assigned to them of changing the mentality of the kolkhos members and of ensuring the protection of public property. But experience had proved that the policy sections were no longer sufficient to conduct the greatly increased and more complex work of the present-day kolkhos village. It was no longer a question of organising sowing, harvesting and grain collection, for which the policy sections were formed, and it was felt that the normal Party and soviet organisations were more competent to deal with all the political, economic, educational, social and other work of the villages.[1]

### The Motives for Party Membership

Those who are sceptical about the achievements of Soviet Communism, and, indeed, all students of social organisation, will naturally ask what can be the motives that induce large and ever-increasing numbers of men and women—throughout 1930–1934 to the number of thousands every week—voluntarily to join the Communist Party. Why should they seek membership of a body

---

[1] *Report on the Organisational Problems of Party and Soviet Construction*, by L. M. Kaganovich, to the Seventeenth Party Congress, 1934, 156 pp. With regard to the policy sections (politotdeli) assigned to the railway system, it may be inferred that, as Kaganovich in 1935 became People's Commissar for this service, these will be gradually absorbed either into the railway service itself, or into the local Party organisations connected therewith.

which requires of them a relatively high standard of personal behaviour; a life of implicit obedience to the commands of superior authorities; perpetual submission to a discipline enforced by penalties which are often severe; and the abandonment of individual acquisitiveness of pecuniary wealth? First, we may place the impulse of a faith—to be subsequently described—which communists will not allow us to call a new religion, but which has all the impelling force that religions have elsewhere possessed. Whatever may be thought of Soviet Communism, it certainly seems to give to its adherents not only a sure and certain conviction of absolute truth, but also the consciousness of a special mission for the improvement of humanity, a mission intensely attractive, in the twentieth century, to young and ardent spirits. Of its eventual success, in the complete transformation of human society throughout the world, they entertain no doubt. Difficulties do not daunt them. Hardships and suffering, even on the largest scale, do not slacken the recruiting.

Secondly, there is the desire, much more widely spread than is commonly supposed, for fuller opportunity to exercise one's personality; the wish to wield influence in the little world in which every individual lives; the ambition to rise to work of " greater responsibility " — in short, the craving, even of the ordinary man or woman, for power. It is noteworthy that, as will be subsequently described, the main object and purpose of public education in the USSR, from the nursery school up to the highest technical institute and university college, is to arouse in the pupils, even those of the poorest parents, this desire for individual expansion, and in every way to foster its development in as large a proportion of the population as possible. With the accumulation of personal wealth barred, membership of the Party offers, in the USSR, at any rate to all but the infinitesimal number of artistic or intellectual geniuses, the only opportunity of " rising in the world ".

These motives, it will be allowed, are not in themselves unworthy of respect. With the statistics of the past eighteen years before us, we cannot doubt their proven efficacy in securing the recruiting of millions of members. But does the incentive last? Can a Party grown to such magnitude maintain throughout its colossal membership Lenin's standard of personal conduct; devotion to Party duty; implicit obedience to the common will, and pecuniary self-abnegation ? Communists freely admit the frequent presence, in the Party membership, of backsliding and sloth ; of hypocrisy and self-seeking ; of disgraceful personal misconduct ; of " right " and " left " deviations from the General Line ; of jealousies and perverted ambitions, leading to intrigues and factionalism. These evil influences, they suggest, cannot be wholly excluded. But they can be kept down by vigilant and perpetual scrutiny of the behaviour of all the members, and by the drastic disciplining, even to peremptory expulsion from the Party, that is constantly going on, of members found guilty of offences against communist ethics.

This disciplining, and removal of offenders against communist ethics, and the periodical " purging " of the lists, is carried on in a manner and to an extent which is, we think, unknown in any other organisation in the world. Any member of the Party who falls below the standard set for a Party member is dealt with, first by the Party organ to which he belongs, and further by the Central Commission of Party Control, which investigates every accusation or report that is received. There is, accordingly, in the present gigantic membership, a constant hail of cautions and reprimands, private or public, followed if necessary by disciplinary removal or demotion ; suspension from membership for a year or more ; or summary expulsion from the Party, coupled in serious cases, by notification throughout the departments that the delinquent is to be refused employment in any responsible position ; or, where necessary, by communication of the offence to the department of the procurator with a view to criminal prosecution.[1]

[1] Seibert gives the following table " compiled from figures published by the Party " :

|  | 1922 | 1923 | 1924 | 1925 | 1926 | 1927 |
|---|---|---|---|---|---|---|
| Expulsion . . . | 25,900 | 25,500 | 25,622 | 20,004 | 24,589 | 16,718 |
| Voluntary and Mechanical withdrawals | 14,100 | 15,300 | 7,501 | 12,094 | 21,088 | 27,340 |

" The Party press publishes an accurate list giving the names of the expelled and the causes of expulsion. Tabulating these lists for the first quarter of the year 1928 I found that nearly half of all the expulsions had been effected on the ground of ' official derelictions ' (embezzlement and venality), and on account of drunkenness, or (a special head) ' systematic drunkenness ' I do not think that the frequency of these offences in the expulsion list signifies that such offences are really very common in Bolshevik party life, for I hold, rather, that the figures indicate the importance the party attaches to the good behaviour of its

The misconduct of the Party member to which serious attention is called may be of various kinds. Any manner of life habitually inconsistent with "communist ethics" will lead to trouble. Thus, drinking is not forbidden, nor a failure to live continuously up to the highest sexual standards. But habitual drunkenness which impairs health and judgment, or a loose living that causes public scandal, is severely dealt with. Peculation or embezzlement, involving public loss, not only entails expulsion from the Party but is also referred to the Procurator for criminal prosecution ; as may also a high degree of negligence causing waste or damage. Ostentatious expenditure, or a luxurious standard of life incurs criticism, and may easily lead to censure as being "inconsistent with communist ethics". On the whole, there appears to be a steadily rising standard of personal conduct from one end of the USSR to the other. With the increasing influence of the comsomols, there seems even to be a growing " puritanism " in manners and morals expected from the Party member. This we describe in our subsequent Chapter XIII., entitled "The Good Life ".

### The Purging of the Party

In addition to this perpetual Party " cleansing " in detail, the entire membership, the whole of the millions, are periodically subjected, one by one, to a simultaneous public inquisition into their individual character and conduct, with the intention and result of eliminating, even by the hundred thousand, those who are deemed unworthy of retention in the Party.

Of these systematic and simultaneous Party purgings there have already been several. The first was made on Lenin's suggestion in 1921, "when the Party consolidated its ranks at the time of the transition to the New Economic Policy"; and some 250,000 members and candidates—about one-third of the then total— were excluded.[1] This first Party purging was followed in the

members. Certainly, in view of the general frequency of alcoholism in Russia, the number of drunkards in the list of the expelled is not large. I want to emphasise the fact that nowhere have I met so large a number of fanatical teetotallers as among the Bolsheviks, whose ranks likewise contain an increasing proportion of non-smokers—which also means a great deal in Russia " (*Red Russia*, by Theodor Seibert, 1931, p. 143).

[1] The Control Commission was established . . . in 1920, when it became evident that communists in important positions were becoming involved in actions that compromised their political principles. At first a communist

subsequent years by a series of partial measures. Thus, in 1924, there was a systematic testing of the members and candidates in all the cells not engaged in productive industry, then comprising about one-fourth of the Party membership ; and of this number about 60 per cent were expelled from the Party. In 1926 there was a similar but less complete testing of the cells in the villages, with numerous exclusions. A complete re-registration of members was made in 1927, when some 46,000—chiefly persons guilty of " deviation " from the General Line—were quietly dropped. The second complete Party purging, mainly directed against industrial malingerers or persons of disgraceful conduct, together with those who had neglected or refused to carry out the Party policy, was decided on at the November plenum of the Central Committee in 1928, and undertaken in 1929, on the inauguration of the first Five-Year Plan and the campaign for the development of the collective farms ; when the exclusions numbered over 100,000, or nearly one-tenth of the whole. The third purging of the Party took place in the first year (1933) of the struggle for the Second Five-Year Plan, when about a quarter of a million, or one-eighth of the whole, were removed from the membership roll. This " third Party purging ", so the Central Committee of the Party declared, " must be thoroughly organised . . . its main intention must be directed to improving the qualitative composition of the organisation. Only those comrades can remain in the Party who are wholly devoted to the working class : who place the interests of communism and the Party above everything."

The special features of the purge of 1933 appear to have been (*a*) the attention paid to ensuring that every member should have a competent knowledge of the Party programme and the most important decisions, so as to be able to explain them to the non-

convicted of taking bribes, of drunkenness or of misuse of power would be summarily shot. But when the promulgation of the New Economic Policy greatly increased the number of communists who were actively concerned in the management of trade and industry, and so put additional temptations in their way, the earlier method of summary discipline was abandoned in favour of a judgment pronounced in the Party court, the Control Commission. The first act of this unique commission was to require all members of the Party to apply for re-registration. Every one of its 600,000 members had therefore to submit to an investigation before he was readmitted to the Party. In this way more than 250,000 members considered to be of the arrivist and careerist type lost their Party ticket in 1921. Since then the watch kept by the Control Commission and the periodical cleansings of the Party have been considered the surest way of countering the changed psychology and outlook of members " (*After Lenin*, by Michael Farbman, 1924, p. 63).

Party masses ; *(b)* the strict examination, in " the nuclei attached to the non-productive undertakings ", of the conduct of those who " abuse the Party position for personal ends, embezzlement, nepotism, careerism, bureaucratic attitude towards the masses " ; and *(c)*, in the rural districts, the sharp scrutiny of the way each member " is fighting for the . . . fulfilling of the obligations of the collective farms . . . against the kulak and his agents ", and " how he is protecting the socialist common property ", especially on the sovkhosi and the kolkhosi. But it was recognised by the Party authorities, apparently for the first time, that not every one of the three million members and candidates could successfully demonstrate a complete understanding of Marxism ; and many were relegated to a new category of subordinate connection with the Party, under the designation of " sympathisers ". " It not infrequently happens ", reported *Pravda*, " that a comrade, although he may be personally quite loyal to the soviet power, as a Party member may damage the movement in practice, even without willing it, if he is not yet in a position to lead the collective peasants or the non-Party workers in the interests of the Party. Here is the case, not of a Party member, but of a comrade who sympathises with the Party. Such sympathising comrades often hasten to join the organisation, not understanding that there is a difference between a comrade who wishes to help the Party, and a Party member, who must possess the necessary preparation in order to be able to lead the non-Party masses under the slogans of the Party." [1]

How is so huge an operation as the individual testing and examination of more than three million members carried out ? The whole purging is conducted under a Central Cleansing Commission, specially appointed by the Central Committee, which forms cleansing commissions for each RSFSR province and each

---

[1] " The Party purging in the USSR ", *Pravda*, December 12, 1932, summarised in *International Press Correspondence*, December 15, 1932 ; *Civic Training in Soviet Russia*, by S. N. Harper, 1929, pp. 20-21 (a previous account); many references in *Moscow Daily News* during May and June 1933 may be referred to. An illuminating address by L. M. Kaganovich to a meeting of active Party members at Moscow on May 27, 1933, was published (in English) under the title *Purging the Party* (Cooperative Publishing Society of Foreign Workers, Moscow, 1933, 32 pp.). A fuller account will be found in *Bolshevik Verification and Purging of the Party Ranks*, by E. Yaroslavsky (Moscow, 1933, 66 pp., same publisher). This gives, for each year, 1921-1932, the statistics of recruiting, resignations and expulsions ; and also, for 1905, and for each year 1917-1932, the percentage of workers, peasants and others in the membership.

of the smaller republics, consisting of half a dozen tried and trusted members of long standing. These provincial commissions appoint district cleansing commissions of three members each. If the Party membership in a given district is less than 500, these district commissions take direct charge of the cleansing. If the membership is more than 500, the district commission appoints cell or nucleus commissions, also of three members each, who must be of at least seven years' standing, and never having belonged to any other Party, or to any of the former factions within the Party. Factories employing 2000 or more Party members have their own cleansing commissions, similar in functions to the district commissions, and setting up separate commissions for departments or branches. These commissions choose their own chairmen, who have to be approved by the provincial commission. Before the general cleansing starts, the members of the district cleansing commission must go through their own cleansing at open meetings of the cells or nuclei to which they belong, together with any members of the public who choose to attend the meetings taking place before members of the provincial commission. Similarly, members appointed to the nucleus cleansing commissions have to go through their own cleansing before members of the district cleansing commissions at public meetings of their own nuclei. The cleansing commissions may decide on Party expulsion, transfer of members to candidature, or from candidature to the new category of sympathisers. They have no right to remove people from employment, or to shift them from one employment to another.

A widespread campaign was, in the spring of 1933, ordered throughout the newspaper press and at public meetings, in order to make the whole population, and not merely the Party membership, aware of the objects and methods of the testing and purging. The testing, according to the formal instructions of the Party congress in 1928, and of the central commission in 1929, takes place in public, in the presence, not only of each member's immediate colleagues, but also, as it is expressly required, " openly before non-Party workers or the poor-peasant village masses ". Anyone may put questions to the member " on the stand ", as to anything relating to his duties as a member ; including therefore, his knowledge and his opinions on " Marxism " ; his attitude towards current " deviations ", left or right ; his " activeness ", whether in tasks imposed on him, or in his daily work, or in voluntary social duties ; his zeal and performances as a " shock-brigader " ; even on his irregularity of attendance at Party meetings ; his obedience to Party decrees and decisions ; his work on committees or commissions, or as member of a " fraction " ; and, last, but by no means least, on alleged unconformity between his manner of life or personal behaviour and " communist ethics ". It should be added that the Central Commission, " having presented every member of the Party with definite demands in respect of his moral level, his connection with the masses, his active participation in the work of the Party, in the construction of socialism, etc.", went on, in 1929, to " offer a warning against distorting the testing into a trivial and captious burrowing into the Party member's private life "—a warning which, it is to be feared, is never likely to be scrupulously observed by every one of the 50,000 crowds before which the two or three million members have individually to submit themselves for examination. It should, however, be said that there is a wide range of graduated penalties for those found guilty of one or other grade of imperfection or delinquency. Expulsion from the Party, with or without criminal prosecution or future exclusion from responsible public employment, is reserved for serious offenders. Others may be suspended from membership for a term of a few months or a year, or relegated to the lower grade of candidates, or merely have their period of probation extended. Others, again, may be found to fall short, not in character or conduct, but merely in knowledge of Marxist doctrines, or in ability to expound soviet policy to the non-Party masses ; and these may either be relegated to the new category of sympathisers, or only be directed to attend the educational classes organised by the Party. Every decision regarding a Party member must be concisely " motivated ", and the minute has to be accompanied by documentary evidence of the charges brought against the member. Membership cards must not be taken away from those expelled until the expulsion has been approved by the district cleansing commission.[1] Moreover, there is, from every

[1] Instructions of the Central Cleansing Commission, in *Moscow Daily News*, May 22, 1933.
These instructions were ratified by the following paragraph in the Party *Rules* of 1934. " By periodic decisions of the Central Committee . . . purgings are held for the systematic cleansing of the Party of class-alien and hostile

local decision, an effective right of appeal within one month ; or, more correctly, to a rehearing, before a higher tribunal, and this appeal may be pursued, without payment of any fees, right up to the Central Cleansing Commission at Moscow. In fact, the final decision lies nominally with the ensuing All-Union Congress of the Communist Party, which may be appealed to if the decision of the Central Cleansing Commission is unsatisfactory.

We may conclude this account of the purgings by a few scenes from that of 1933, as reported in the newspapers. " About 1500 Moscow Communists have already gone through the Party cleansing since the beginning of the month, and a similar number in Leningrad, according to the latest reports. The cleansing has roused the masses of Party members and of non-Party people to greater political activity and study.

" Among the first to go through the cleansing were the local leaders. In Moscow, for example, the political secretaries of province, city and district Party committees passed through the cleansing at open meetings of their organisations.

"The cleansing commission for province and city leaders consists of Knorin, Chairman of the Moscow Cleansing Commission ; Stasova, one of the oldest members of the Bolshevik Party and an associate of Lenin, now internationally known for her activity in the International Labour Defence ; and Pyatnitsky, known for his work in the Communist International.

" The political secretaries of the district committees of the Party passed the cleansing at factory meetings." [1]

At Moscow, for instance, " in the meeting hall of the Society of Old Bolsheviks ", two of the most venerated members went on the stand, before taking up their duties as members of the district cleansing commission. " The entire cleansing commission of Moscow province, headed by Knorin, presided. Knorin opened the meeting by stating that the life and political activity

---

elements ; double-dealers who deceive the Party and who conceal their real views from it, and who disrupt the policy of the Party ; overt and covert violators of the iron discipline of the Party and of the state ; degenerates who have coalesced with bourgeois elements ; careerists, self-seekers and bureaucratised elements ; morally degraded persons who by their improper conduct lower the dignity of the Party and besmirch the banner of the Party ; passive elements who do not fulfil the duties of Party members, and who have not mastered the programme, the rules and the most important decisions of the Party " (*Rules*, I. 9 ; p. 695 of *Socialism Victorious*, 1934).

[1] *Moscow Daily News*, June 10, 1933.

of the two appointees are well known to all present. . . . Knorin thereupon declared that the meeting had not been called to hear the biographies of the two Old Bolsheviks who had to go through the cleansing, but in order to find out whether the society had any objection. . . . A member of the society, Enisian, took the floor and declared he did not believe anyone would have any objection to raise. . . . After several other members of the society had spoken, the chairman asked whether anyone still had any objections to raise. The reply was a unanimous ' No '. ' In this case we can consider Comrades Smidovich and Samoilovich as having passed the cleansing,' announced the chairman." [1]

## " The Cleansing starts at Moskvoshvei.

" There was great excitement the other day at Moskvoshvei No. 3 Clothing Factory. ' We are beginning the chistka [Party cleansing] to-day ', I was told in the factory Party office. The first to be questioned was Bugacheva, secretary of the Party cell. She came into the office while we were talking, dressed in black skirt and white blouse. ' Look how she dressed up ', someone commented. ' Watch out, don't be cleansed.' We all smiled. She blushed.

" The workers of the second and fourth floor met in the dining-room to listen to the report on the purpose of the cleansing and to participate in it.

" ' Let me speak, let me speak ', insisted a tall girl with a red kerchief around her head. ' We have some Party members on our floor who don't care a bit for our department. If a machine gets out of order or something happens, they don't pay any attention. On the other hand, we have some Party members who raise hell when anything interferes with production. These keep up the good record of our department, but the others I think should be

---

[1] *Moscow Daily News*, May 30, 1933.

The Society of Old Bolsheviks was an unofficial social organisation open to all Party members whose membership dated from before 1917. It had excellent premises assigned for its use, and was long a pleasant club in which pre-revolutionary memories were revived and exchanged. Latterly its steadily ageing membership showed signs of developing into a coterie not always in sympathy with modern decisions on policy of the Central Committee, which naturally came to include an increasing proportion of Party members who had grown up since 1917. Possibly in order to prevent its becoming a centre of perpetual criticism, the society, and also the similar society of Old Exiles, were summarily dissolved by the Central Committee in 1935.

cleansed out. They care only for themselves. A good Party member should care for all of us, for our department and for the whole factory.'

" Her statement was greeted with applause. During the discussion the district cleansing commission arrived and was given a rousing ovation.

" The chairman called upon Bugacheva to tell her story, to explain how long she had been in the Party and what she is doing as a Party member. Everybody listened attentively.

" ' I was born in 1886 in the village in Pskov district. My father was a poor peasant. In 1905 I was married and soon ran away with my husband to Moscow. At first I worked as a servant in the houses of the rich. You don't know what it meant to be a servant under the régime of the tsars. I was unable to stand it very long and went to work in a tailor shop. In 1912 I joined the union. I learned quite a bit. During the war I learned still more. In 1917 I joined the Party. During the October days I participated in the struggle in the Krasnaya Presnya district. Later on I was elected a member of the district soviet. Was a member of the control commission of the soviet. Was sent to work by the Party to different institutions.

" ' Since 1928 I am back in the tailor shop. First as a machine worker. Now working as Party secretary on the fourth floor. Our floor carried out the production plan 119 per cent. This month we expect to exceed this figure. There is no ' brak ' on our floor. The loan went over big. I may say that our department is one of the leading in the factory. Don't know what else I may tell you. Better ask questions.'

" The chairman stood up.

" ' Does anybody want to ask any questions or does anybody want to say anything about Bugacheva ? '

" Several hands were raised. A non-Party worker was given the floor.

" ' I have known Natalia Bugacheva for several years. She is one of the best communists we have in our factory. If you ask her a question, whether political or on production, she will always explain in detail and in such language that we non-Party workers can understand. During the loan campaign she used to come to the factory at seven in the morning and remained in the factory till eleven at night. I wish others would take an example from her.'

" Another stood up.

" ' I am secretary of the factory MOPR.  Last year Bugacheva won some money in the MOPR lottery, but when I informed her about it she refused to take the money and donated it back to the MOPR.  It is not the money part that I want to mention, but the fact that Bugacheva acted in this case as she always does, as an example to other workers.  She is worthy of the honour of being a member of the Bolshevik Party.'

" ' We are not asking for praise, we want criticism of Bugacheva ', declared the chairman.

" ' But we can't say anything wrong about her ', shouted a red-haired girl.  She was supported with applause.  An old Party worker took the floor.

" ' I have known Bugacheva from the first day she came to our factory.  At that time we had a group of Right-wingers and Trotskyites on the fourth floor.  We sent her to that floor.  She fought them, annihilated them.  From a backward department, always lagging, she led it to the front, over-fulfilling the production plan.  She always carried out successfully the work entrusted to her.  I know I can recommend her in the name of the whole factory as a good Bolshevik Party member.'  Thunderous applause.

" The chairman got up again.  ' This is a very serious business. The Party wants to weed out all who are in the Party but really don't belong there.  There are many weaklings, many two-faced people who are trying to misuse the trust put in them by the Party.  We call upon the non-Party workers to disclose all these things among the Party members.  We want to know all the bad things even about good Party members.  To-day we hear only praises.  Isn't there anyone who wants to say anything against Bugacheva ? '

" ' No !  No ! ' came a chorus of voices.

" The commission discussed the matter for a few minutes and the chairman announced the decision :

" ' We consider Bugacheva worthy of membership in the All-Union Communist (Bolshevik) Party.'  Again thunderous applauses shook the hall.  The meeting was declared closed and almost everybody rushed to the platform to shake hands with the excited Bugacheva.  The first Party member at Moskvoshvei No. 3 had come through the ' chistka ' (cleansing)." [1]

[1] *Moscow Daily News*, June 3, 1933.

A CULPRIT EXPOSED

" The Party cleansing is taking place in the engineers' and udarniks' dining-room in the Kalinin (Fraise) Cutting-Tool Plant. . . . Darting a sharp, hurried glance at the microphone that is to carry all his words to thousands of listeners-in throughout the Moscow province, Gorachev begins to speak. He holds himself calmly, even jokes a bit. But one is instantly aware that he has thought over carefully beforehand every word that he is saying now. He speaks slowly and weighs each word before it leaves his mouth. . . . ' I was the son of a fitter who later quit his trade and sold fish for 20 years. After the October Revolution he opened up a hardware stand in the Danilov market.'

" Gorachev is going to be honest and straightforward. He will tell frankly everything of the past. ' But why did you hide your social origin when you entered the Party ? ' interrupts Sakhat-Muratov, a Turkoman, the chairman of the cleansing commission. ' Why did you write in the application you filled out before entering the Party that you were the son of a worker ? '

" ' Oh yes, a mistake crept in there,' says Gorachev. ' I should have written " worker-trader ".' Everybody laughs.

" After a cross-fire of questions, the audience learns that, for hiding his social origin during the 1929 cleansing, the cleansing commission had deemed it necessary to keep him in a lower position for five years. But Gorachev does not like lower positions. After wandering from factory to factory looking for the best job, he finally lands at the Fraise, where he secures the important post of secretary of the factory trade union committee.

" How did Gorachev hold down this position ? Several of the workers get up to speak. . . . One tells of the incident when Morozov, technical director, rudely upbraided and discharged the lathe hand Chernov because he forgot to turn off the motor on his lathe one day. It was a secret to no one that Morozov repeatedly assumed a haughty attitude towards the workers. The factory paper and social opinion in the plant rose in defence of Chernov. But despite this, Gorachev backed up Morozov in discharging Chernov.

" Another speaker reveals the curious method of giving out premiums that was sanctioned by Gorachev. When on the fifteenth anniversary of the October Revolution, premiums were granted to the best udarniks in the Fraise plant, thanks to the 'blessing' of Gorachev, premiums were given to 30 members of the engineering and technical staff and . . . one worker !

"'He did not protect the interests of the workers,' said another, 'but protected, instead, the interests of his own pockets.' The funds of the factory trade union committee were a 'mutual aid society' for Gorachev and his cronies. Loans that were not returned, and thefts, were part of the heritage that was received from Gorachev by the staff of the trade union committee. Six thousand roubles were squandered in a short time by him. A significant portion of this sum went directly into his pockets.

"Here is an example of how Gorachev managed the trade union money. He was tired. He decided to take a rest. So he got a hospital bulletin and went to a sanatorium as a sick man. As a sick worker is entitled to his wages in the Soviet Union during the period of his illness. Gorachev received his money. But this was not enough. On coming back, he took a vacation for himself. This was enough, it would seem ? No ! In addition, he took a large sum of money for an unused vacation. Semenov, a worker in the trade union organisation, gets up and says that no decision was passed by the trade-union committee ratifying the giving of any . . . money for unused vacation to Gorachev. . . . 'I was finally removed from my post for mismanagement,' says Gorachev. . . .

"Gorachev got married. Now getting married is a big event. One ought to celebrate it properly. But to celebrate properly one needs a bountiful feast with plenty of good things to eat. . . . So Gorachev gets one of the factory trucks one night, goes down to the store, and piles into the truck a small mountain of cookies, apples, sugar, butter, candy.

"The factory [news] paper caught him red-handed, and after a long denial Gorachev finally confessed to his guilt. He was relieved of his position of secretary of the factory trade union committee and sent to work on the production line at a lathe.

"But Gorachev, as we have seen, does not like lower positions. And a short while later we see a new figure : Gorachev—assistant personnel manager of the milling cutter department. His Party job is Comsomol organiser. . . . 'Here,' admits Gorachev, 'my leadership was not efficient.'

"'That's not quite correct,' says a Comsomol. 'You didn't

give us any leadership at all.' Others get up and put the finishing touches to the portrait of Gorachev, as the careerist, cheat, self-supplier, squanderer of trade union funds.

"When Gorachev steps down from the stand two and a half hours later, he is no longer smiling. His career is ended. Once more he is sent back to the production line. This time he will stay there . . . until he becomes a different man." [1]

### The Results of the 1933 Purging

The "Party Cleansing" of 1933 was practically completed before the opening of the Seventeenth Party Congress, to which one of the two vice-presidents of the Sovnarkom reported its results. He described its special objects, therein differing from previous "cleansings", as the discovery of (1) the extent to which the members, admittedly loyal in theory, were still actively taking part as "fighters at the front of socialist construction"; and (2) the degree in which such members were intellectually equipped to explain to the non-Party masses the Marx-Lenin-Stalin faith that they held. True to soviet custom, Rudzutak found much for outspoken criticism. He complained that, in many cases, the local Party organisation had failed to maintain contact with their individual members. Party education was far from adequate. The directives and decisions of the Central Committee were often neglected, or else acted on in a formal and lifeless way. The percentage of members expelled by decision of the district and primary cleansing commissions was 17, whilst 6·3 per cent more had been reduced to the new grade of sympathisers. These percentages would be somewhat reduced after the hearing of the appeals. Leningrad and Moscow had the smallest averages of exclusions, at 12·7 and 13·6 per cent; whilst East Siberia had no less than 25·2 per cent; the Urals, 23·1 per cent; Odessa, 21·9 per cent; the Far Eastern, 21·9 per cent; and Karelia, 20·3 per cent. [2]

### The Internal Reorganisation of 1934

In the course of the year 1934, following the decision of the Seventeenth All-Union Congress of the Party upon proposals

---

[1] *Moscow Daily News*, September 3, 1933.
[2] See Rudzutak's report in *Moscow Daily News*, February 6, 1934.

presented by L. M. Kaganovich,[1] considerable alterations were
made in the administrative structure of the central Party
authority. The Central Control Commission of the Party[2] was
reappointed, but under the new name of Commission of Party
Control, and with a membership reduced to 61, whilst its
functions were, as we understand it, very largely transformed.
Whilst retaining its duty of continuous supervision of the whole
Party membership, and the investigation of all complaints and
accusations against individual members, it ceased to act in close
conjunction with the Workers' and Peasants' Inspection, which has
hitherto been represented by an officer of the standing of a
People's Commissar in the several Sovnarkoms of the USSR, the
constituent republics and the autonomous republics. All these
were, in the course of the year, simply abolished, whilst the work
of the specially commissioned juries of inspection and enquiry
was transferred to the trade union organisation, under the All-

[1] See the lengthy exposition in *Moscow Daily News,* January 6 to 10, 1934 ;
also *Forward to the Second Five-Year Plan of Socialist Construction—the Resolution of the XVII Party Conference* (Moscow, 1934, 40 pp.).

[2] The Central Control Commission, established by Lenin in 1920, had
increased steadily in magnitude and influence. Its membership grew from 7 in
1922 to 50 in 1923, to 151 in 1925, to 163 in 1926, and to 195 in 1927. Since
1927 it has remained at about 200. These carefully chosen members do not
hold office in conferences or committees, but attend all Party meetings as
observers, reporting to an executive committee of about 25 members, which is
responsible to a plenary meeting held in Moscow every four months.

At the Party Congress in 1935 Stalin gave the following account of the
Commission, and reason for the change. " As for the Central Control Commission, it is well known that it was set up primarily, and mainly, for the
purpose of averting a split in the Party. You know that at one time there
really was a danger of a split in the Party. You know that the Central Control
Commission and its organisations succeeded in averting the danger of a split.
Now there is no longer any danger of a split. But there is an imperative need
for an organisation that could concentrate its attention mainly on the work of
supervising the fulfilment of the decisions of the Party and of its Central Committee. The only organisation that could fulfil this function is a Commission
of Party Control of the Central Committee of the CPSU working on the instructions of the Party and of its Central Committee and having its representatives
in the districts, who will be independent of the local organisations. It goes
without saying that such a responsible organisation must wield great authority.
And in order that it may wield sufficient authority, and in order that it may be
able to take proceedings against any responsible worker, including members of
the Central Committee, who has committed any misdemeanour, the members
of this Commission must be elected and dismissed only by the supreme organ of
the Party, viz. the Party Congress. There cannot be any doubt that such an
organisation will be quite capable of securing the control of the fulfilment of
the decisions of the central organs of the Party and of tightening up Party
discipline " (*Report to Seventeenth Party Congress on the Work of the Central
Committee of the CPSU*, by Josef Stalin, Moscow, 1935, pp. 93-94).

Union Central Committee of Trade Unions (AUCCTU). In place of the Workers' and Peasants' Inspection in the several Sovnarkoms, there was established, as we have already described, a new Commission of Soviet Control for the whole USSR, nominally appointed by and directly responsible to the Sovnarkom of the USSR as a whole. For the first appointment of this central Commission of Soviet Control of the USSR Sovnarkom, the All-Union Congress of the Communist Party took upon itself to nominate the entire membership of 70, from tried and trusted Party members. It is with this body, in substitution for the abolished Workers' and Peasants' Inspection, that the reorganised central Commission of Party Control acting for the Communist Party will act in the closest concert. We understand that, whilst the information obtained will be at the disposal of both sides, the division of duties will be the following : Any changes required in the constitutional organisation, or in the personnel of the various offices, will be made, formally, by the appropriate authority in the soviet hierarchy, from the USSR Sovnarkom down to the village soviet. On the other hand, any disciplinary action against Party members as such, and the issue to them of any necessary " directives ", will be matters for the Commission of Party Control, acting for the Communist Party.

But the most important change in the new arrangements is not so much in the manner in which any necessary action will be formally taken, as in the reorganisation of what has gradually become an extensive array of central departments of the Communist Party itself. What we may describe as the internal office administration of the Communist Party has been completely transformed. The recent extensive developments of " policy sections " (politotdeli) in the machine and tractor stations and collective farms, and at every railway or water-transport centre, in which possibly as many as 50,000 of the most zealous and active of the Party members are now employed, have made necessary a sweeping rearrangement of departmental administration.

Under the Central Committee of the Communist Party and its two main committees there are now to be no fewer than nine separate departments, namely, (1) the Agricultural Otdel ; (2) the Industrial Otdel ; (3) the Transport Otdel ; (4) the Planning, Finance and Trade Otdel ; (5) the Political-Administrative Otdel ; (6) the Otdel of the Leading Centres ; (7) the Otdel of Culture and

Propaganda of Leninism, and two other "sectors"; (8) the Administrative Sector; and (9) a Special Sector not yet otherwise designated. In May 1935 the Otdel of Culture and Propaganda of Leninism was subdivided into five branches, namely, (a) the Otdel of Party Propaganda and Agitation; (b) the Otdel of the Press and the Publishing Houses; (c) the Otdel of Schools and Universities; (d) the Otdel of Educational Work, dealing with libraries, clubs, sport organisations, radio, cinemas, theatres and authorship; and (e) the Otdel of Scientific and Technical Inventions and Discoveries. All these departments are to be accommodated at the enlarged Moscow offices of the Communist Party.

The Party's departments in the provinces are being reorganised along similar lines. Under the Party Committees of the republics and lesser authorities, there will be, in each case, six separate departments, namely, (1) the Agricultural Otdel; (2) the Transport and Industrial Otdel; (3) the Soviet Trade Otdel; (4) the Otdel of Culture and Propaganda of Leninism; (5) the Otdel of the leading Party organs (cities and rayons); and (6) a Special Sector. The existing secretariats under the oblast or krai Party Committees and those under the various Executive Committees of the Party in the constituent and autonomous republics will be abolished; and only two secretaries in each case will be allowed. " All questions which require discussion must be raised direct in the bureaux, and the working out of practical problems must be entrusted not to special commissions, but to the heads of departments, and to the responsible workers in the soviet, trade union, cooperative, comsomols and other organisations."

The Party administrations in the rayons and smaller cities are being similarly reorganised, so that they may be directly concerned with the various branches of production. They are to be specifically and intimately connected with the local Party organisation, such as the primaries and groups in the village soviets (selosoviets), collective farms (kolkhosi), and state farms (sovkhosi); and with all the " policy sections " that are in the field (politotdeli).

Instead of the otdeli hitherto existing under the rayon Party committees (raycom) and those (gorcom) of all but the largest cities, there are to be appointed responsible travelling instructors or organisers, who are to be *ex officio* members of the raycom or

gorcom ; and who are each to be attached to a group of primary
Party organisations, where they are expected to deal with all
branches of the Party work, whether cultural, political propaganda,
mass agitation, organisation, etc. It will be for the secretary
and his deputy or assistant to control and supervise the work
of these travelling instructors or organisers, their distribution
in the field, and the carrying out of the instructions given
to them.[1]

What is the motive and intention, or the governing idea,
behind these sweeping measures of what we might at first sight
regard as essentially office reorganisation ? As we understand it,
the reform is intended to set up, from one end of the USSR to
the other, a double system of inspiration, direction, inspection,
criticism, and especially of continuous " check up " of the actual
putting in operation of all the various decrees and " directives "
of the Soviet Government. The student of political science will
be interested to trace, in this reorganisation, the proposed
establishment not of one but of two separate centralisations.
The USSR Sovnarkom of People's Commissars, with its elaborate
hierarchy of soviets from the All-Union Congress down to the
selosoviet of the village ; and its corresponding hierarchy of
departments, federal or provincial, unified or non-unified, all
subject to the new Commission of Soviet Control, represents the
Temporal Power. Henceforth there will be, alongside this
Temporal Power, another hierarchy, equally penetrating and
ubiquitous ; headed by the new Commission of Party Control ;
directed not from the Moscow Kremlin but from the adjacent
central offices of the Communist Party ; having no statutory or
other legal authority ; and using only its influence on the minds
of the Party members. Nearly one-half of all these Party members
happen, indeed, to have been elected or appointed to most of
the key positions of either the local or the central government.
Provision is made, in a way which we do not doubt will be
successful, for consistent unity in the decrees and directives

[1] We gather that, at the outset, the work of the two commissions will be
carried on in 28 specially demarcated divisions of the USSR. There seem to
have been appointed, as a start, 22 divisional officers of the Commission of
Soviet Control and 11 of the Commission of Party Control. In 5 of these divisions there are to be officers of both commissions ; in 6 others only officers of the
Commission of Party Control ; and in the other 22 only officers of the Commission of Soviet Control. There is to be an organised office in each division,
and perhaps more than one, to which complaints may be sent.

emanating from either of these parallel authorities ; and for complete harmony in the action taken.[1]

## The Comsomols

Second in importance only to the Communist Party itself, is its multiform junior organisation headed by the " All-Union Leninist Communist League of Youth " (YCL), which we shall refer to under its common appellation of Comsomols.[2] This latter is an entirely voluntary body of some five millions of young people between fourteen and twenty-three, with an extension of term for those elected to office, and (as consultants merely) for such others as may be locally desired.

Perhaps the most striking feature is the magnitude of the growth and the width of development of this army of Comsomols. As long ago as 1903, Lenin proposed and carried at the Social Democratic Party Conference a resolution recommending special party organisation among young men and women. In the following decade of industrial development the total number of young people employed in the ever-growing factories rose, by the

---

[1] The political science student cannot but be reminded of Auguste Comte's proposals for the establishment of a " Spiritual Power ", devoid of any " authority " ; parallel with the whole corps of officials of the government, having all the " authority " in their hands. We must point out, however, that Comte's Spiritual Power, though excluding all reference to the supernatural, was to be a hierarchy in the old ecclesiastical sense of the word, wholly directed and appointed from above. The Communist Party of the USSR, however great and far-reaching may be its corporate influence, is, as we have explained, itself dependent on the whole body of its members, who vote in their primaries and their Party groups, and in the rayon committees, right up to the All-Union Congress of the Communist Party, which acts as a final Court of Appeal and can at any time change the whole policy.

[2] We have found the fullest account in English of the Comsomols in Professor S. N. Harper's *Civic Training in Soviet Russia* (1929) and *Making Bolsheviks* (1931), on which we have drawn freely. *In Place of Profit*, by Harry F. Ward (1933), incidentally affords a vivid account of the spirit manifested by the Comsomols. See also *Die Jugend in Sowjetrussland*, by Klaus Mehnert, Berlin, 1932, translated as *Youth in Soviet Russia*, 1933 ; and *New Minds New Men*, by Thomas Woody, 1932. *The Rules of the All-Union Leninist League of Youth* (in Russian), a booklet of which over a million copies have been issued, gives precise details. Descriptions of meetings and other proceedings of the Comsomols are frequently given in the *Komsomol Pravda* (in Russian), the principal organ of the organisation, and less frequently (in English) in the *Moscow Daily News*. A (Russian) pamphlet, *The Cell in the Kolkhos* : *Days and Works of the Savrukhinsk Cell of the YCL*, by S. Kolesnichenko and T. Ussachev (published by Ogiz, Moscow, 1932), gives a vivid description of successful work by the Comsomol cell of a large collective farm. Similar publications dealing with the concerns of the organisation are innumerable.

end of 1916, to what was for Russia the large total of 300,000. During the revolutionary months of 1917 these young people, especially in Moscow and Petrograd, spontaneously formed political groups of their own, which played a prominent part in the meetings and demonstrations. The various revolutionary sections sought to attach these youthful groups to themselves, but success lay with the Bolsheviks, who, towards the end of 1917, were able to incorporate many of their members in the Red Guard. In October 1918 the first congress of Bolshevik youth organisations was held at Moscow, when 22,000 members were represented, and the Communist League of Youth was formally instituted. At the second congress in 1919 the membership had risen to 96,000. The third congress in 1920 counted no fewer than 400,000, including many recruits from the peasantry. Down to this date the note had been that of active service on the military even more than on the political front. Now that victory had been achieved, the membership fell away. Then came the command for study ; study to fit themselves for membership of the Party, as well as active participation in industrial and political work ; and, as new duties, energetic assistance in the education of the younger children, on the one hand, and, on the other, the promotion of the young workmen's interests on the economic front.

The consolidation of the organisation, and also the inception of its extraordinarily wide growth and varied development, may be dated from the fifth annual congress of 1922 with its institution of " class pride " and a Comsomol code of conduct. In all directions the organisation broadened out. Every form of communist training was developed and pursued ; the promotion of all healthy forms of recreation, from athletics to theatre-going ; every kind of intellectual study, from discussions and lectures to contributing to newspapers and publishing poems ; every branch of " activeness ", from " liquidating illiteracy " and clearing away rubbish, to joining " shock brigades " and taking part in " cleansing raids " for checking " bureaucratism ". By 1924 the membership, including candidates, had reached 632,000 ; by 1926, 1,612,372 ; by 1927, 2,250,000. The lists were then more strictly scrutinised, but in 1928 the membership was reckoned at 2,000,000 ; and by 1935 it had risen to something like 5,500,000, one-third from the industries of the cities and two-thirds from the agricultural villages ; being approximately 90 per cent of the total industrial

youth, and 20 per cent of all the peasant youth, of the entire
USSR, about one-fourth of all the members being girls and young
women.

The Comsomols adopt the pattern of organisation common
throughout the USSR.  The whole membership is grouped in
cells, formed not only among the employees of factories and other
industrial establishments, or of offices and institutions of all kinds,
but also among the students enrolled in the higher educational
institutions, and among the young people of the agricultural
villages.  The number of these cells in the USSR is now over
100,000, a majority of them either in the kolkhosi or in the villages.
These cells are grouped geographically in districts (city or rayon),
for which they elect district committees and officers.  These district committees are, in the RSFSR and the Ukraine, united by
provinces (oblast or krai), and elsewhere by the smaller five
republics, each with its own committee and officers.  These
local committees send their officers every two years to an All-
Union Conference at Moscow, specially for organisational purposes,
and in the alternate years they elect delegates from the membership to a still more imposing All-Union Congress, which is much
more than a glorified picnic.  This congress listens to elaborate
speeches, passes resolutions and appoints a standing central committee by which the whole organisation is practically governed.
So close is the parallelism with the organisation of the Communist
Party that Comsomols who find themselves serving on mixed
committees, or belonging to non-Party organisations or institutions, invariably form themselves unobtrusively into a " fraction "
or group, which decides a common policy, and is responsible to
the Comsomol committee of the district or province in which
the committee, organisation or institution works.  At the lowest
stage (the cell) the offices are all filled gratuitously, the personnel
frequently changing, thus affording useful training to a large
proportion of the junior membership, the duties being performed
outside school or working hours.  But already in the district
committees and secretaryships the duties are sufficiently onerous
to require the full-time service of one or more salaried officers in
each case, and these become more numerous in the higher ranges
of the organisation.  These places are practically all filled from
the ranks of the Comsomols themselves, but they tend to fall into
the hands of the abler and more experienced of them.

The reorganisation of the League of Youth is to follow other lines than those of the Party itself. It was decided by the Comsomol Central Executive Committee (June 18, 1935), and declared by A. V. Kosarev, the Comsomol secretary, on behalf of Stalin himself, that their corporate activity is henceforth to be concentrated upon education—education of their own members, of the Pioneers, and of such workers, peasants and students as they can influence. Separate subcommittees are to direct the work among these several groups. The Comsomols are henceforth not to busy themselves so much with assisting production ; and, above all, they are not to concern themselves about possible developments of the policy of the Party itself.

Hitherto no express confession of faith has been called for from the young applicant for membership. For youthful workmen or peasants of poor parentage, no recommendations are required, and not even any period of probation, whilst there is no assumption that the applicant will have had any political training or experience. The children of middle peasants (seredniaks), however, or of parents of any occupation reputed to be relatively wealthy, are not invited to join, nor are they, indeed, easily admitted, whilst those of kulaks are usually refused. Young people employed in soviet institutions, and the children of such employees, and any others not of workmen or peasant parentage, are required to present a recommendation from a member of the Party of two years' Party standing, together with two recommendations from Comsomol members. Young people who are the children of shopkeepers or other definitely " bourgeois " classes find some difficulty in joining, but may be admitted on good Party recommendations, and (unlike other applicants) subject to six months' probationary membership (the so called candidates), during which they pay dues, attend meetings and participate in all activities except voting, and are watched and reported on as to conduct, character, and " civic activity ". There is no attempt to maintain in the Comsomol membership a numerical preponderance of the industrial workmen. But the direction of the organisation is kept in the hands of the workmen and the kolkhos members, as well as secured to the Communist Party, by additional qualifications for holding office above the primary organ. Thus, the secretary of the district committee must anyhow be, not only a Comsomol of at least a year's standing, but also a Party member of a year's standing ; and if he is a peasant, he must have two years' standing as a Comsomol, whilst, if he is one of the intelligentsia, he must be not only of three years' standing as a Comsomol but also of two years' standing as a Party member. For secretaryship of a provincial committee the required qualifications are still more stringent, and also similarly differentiated, so as to put barriers in the way of all but avowed and tried communists of working-class parentage.

The most important features of the Comsomol organisation are its educational purpose and the extent to which it disciplines its members. There is plainly no seeking to attract recruits under false pretences, or by any concealment of aims. The " tasks and duties of members of the YCL " as laid down by the ninth All-Union Congress, and embodied in the rules, expressly require that " the Comsomoletz [member] must be worthy of the name of his great teacher [Lenin]; he must be the most "energetic, honourable, daring fighter, supremely loyal to the revolution, and an example to all youth and all workers. He must work every day to enlist new members in the League. . . . The best members of the YCL will be admitted to the ranks of the Party. . . . The Comsomoletz fights persistently for the general line of the Party. He is obliged to study systematically the teaching of Marx, Engels, Lenin, Stalin. . . . He is a loyal assistant to the Party in the struggle for the socialist reconstruction of the national economy, and the industrialisation of the USSR. . . . Every Comsomoletz is obliged to equip himself with essential technical knowledge, to master a leading technique and to work systematically for the raising of his qualifications. . . . The Comsomoletz who works for wages must be a member of a trade union and must take an active part in its work. . . . The Comsomoletz in the village is an organiser of the socialist reconstruction of agriculture. He must work for the realisation of the great task of liquidating kulakism. He must be an organiser and member of a kolkhos . . . and must work with all his energy for the strengthening of the union of the working class with the peasantry. . . . For heroic self-sacrificing struggle on the socialist construction front, the Comsomoletz is awarded the Order of the Labour Red Banner. . . . The Comsomoletz is an active worker on the cultural revolution front. He fights for the polytechnicisation of the schools.

He is an active physical culturist. He must be prepared at any moment to defend the Soviet Union with arms. He must study military matters, and master one form of military discipline. . . . The YCL is the patron of the Red fleet and Red air force. . . . Every Comsomoletz must help the Pioneers to take part in socialist construction."

These high and varied obligations of Comsomol membership are persistently enforced. " Self - criticism " is as constant a feature in the Comsomol cells and district organisations as in every other form of soviet activity. The pressure of public opinion in the Comsomol cell is reinforced by frequent admonitions from the higher authorities of the organisation, and made still more effective by the Comsomol newspaper press, the principal organ of which is the *Komsomol Pravda* published by the Comsomol Central Committee, which has a circulation running into many hundred thousands, from end to end of the USSR. This Comsomol press, which includes literally hundreds of local and specialist journals, though edited and directed by salaried officers, is largely filled with unpaid contributions from the vast membership, in which the exuberant vitality and enthusiasm is as marked as the youthful fanaticism.

Discipline is, however, also maintained within each cell by more direct means. Votes of censure on individual members, for breaches of rules or offences against communist ethics, are frequent. Many things that are not actually prohibited are " bad form " among Comsomols. Voluntary withdrawals of slack or unwilling members are common. Those who fail to attend meetings, or participate in the activities of the body, or neglect to pay the dues,[1] are quickly dropped. Actual expulsions are reported to be even more numerous than from the Communist Party itself, and mainly for similar grounds. " Conduct unbecoming a Comsomol ", if persisted in, may in itself lead to expulsion ; whilst habitual drunkenness or sexual looseness, and any form of behaviour deemed indecent or disgraceful, will certainly be so punished. The requirements of " political literacy " is insisted

[1] The Comsomol membership dues are small, as many of the members are not yet self-supporting. A common rate is one-half of one per cent of the monthly wage. Many are excused on account of poverty. Those older ones who are also members of the Communist Party pay dues only to the Party. Thus the restricted money income of the Comsomols both necessitates and evokes a very large amount of individual service from the whole membership, extending even to unpaid organising and secretarial duties.

on. The young Comsomol must attend a " political circle " or a special school until he has acquired a knowledge of the main principles of Leninism ; and if after three years he is adjudged to be still " politically illiterate ", he will usually be removed from the membership roll.[1] Nor may he neglect his share of " political activeness ". Any member not performing a due amount of voluntary social service, in one or other form, is cautioned, reprimanded and eventually expelled.

An effective expedient for continual guidance of the whole communist youth is found in the frequent conferences and congresses. One of the authors' most vivid impressions was derived from attendance at a session of the seventh All-Union Conference of Comsomols, when 1200 young men and women, of many different races, leaders of Comsomol cells from all over the USSR, were brought to Moscow for eight days of strenuous attendance (varied by organised games, dances and visits to the opera) to be criticised and instructed by their own spokesmen and by distinguished academic professors and Party leaders. It was impossible not. to be impressed with the enthusiasm and energy, the joy of new freedom and the eagerness for improvement of this exuberant youth. The official congratulations on their really considerable achievements were interspersed with warnings that discussion on theoretic issues must not interfere with practical productive work, especially in shock brigades ; that they must not neglect the duty of answering the letters of the younger Pioneers ; and that the practice of passing resolutions in the exact terms of others that they had received was not calculated to secure respectful attention. It was not by such means that they had already been influential in raising the position of the Comsomols. Their advice as to educational curriculum had been an important factor in such legislative reforms as the raising of the

[1] In 1932–1933 the YCL " political schools " were opened throughout the USSR from October 15 to April 15, with a curriculum varying according to local conditions. All young communists who had not previously passed through such courses were peremptorily required to attend, whilst those who had completed the elementary work were directed to continue their studies by attending Party schools or, where these are not accessible, by correspondence. The Central Committee of the YCL set aside 100,000 roubles as a prize fund, from which to provide rewards in cash or gifts of libraries from 1000 to 10,000 roubles for cells and district committees that organise the best schools. Secretaries and other officers will be awarded prizes of books, bicycles, watches or holiday trips, whilst groups of successful members will be sent on tours (*Moscow Daily News*, September 17, 1932).

school-leaving age to fifteen ; the development of factory schools
with three and a half hours' theoretic instruction and three and a
half hours' applied science and practical work for those joining
the factory before sixteen ; and the institution of the seven-hour
work-day.  They might well demand that their factory earnings
should not, as was occasionally the case, be kept back as arrears ;
and that even second-year apprentices should be entitled to
transfer from time work to piecework.  They should insist everywhere on the carrying out of the Central Committee's decision
allotting to young persons 15 per cent of all the places in the
Houses of Rest and 50 per cent of all those in the Sanatoria.
Their concentration on the full execution of the Five-Year Plan
need never be pressed in such a way as to prejudice their own
economic or hygienic interests as young workers.  We could not
help feeling that the practice of the Soviet Government of calling
up to Moscow, for a general conference, the representatives from
all over the vast area of the USSR—representing a considerable
annual expense—was, in this, as in so many other branches of the
public service, a most potent instrument alike of education and of
administration.[1]

The following description of a successful Comsomol cell at
work inside a kolkhos is abbreviated from the account given in a
general report prepared by the Middle Volga Krai committee of
the Comsomols, in conjunction with the *Komsomolskaya Pravda*,
on the measures taken locally to carry out the Central Committee
of the Party's (TSIK) decree of April 1, 1931.  The cell began by
working as a separate brigade in the fields, doing 15 per cent more
than the other brigades.  " Then, on the instructions of the local
Party cell," the twenty-five Comsomols distributed themselves
among all the brigades, for the purpose of " giving a lead to all
the various farm sections ", with a result that the whole " productivity was raised to a marked degree " . . . the YCL membership on the farm was increased threefold—the system of organising
work with four to ten YCL members at the head of each brigade
became more and more efficient . . . dependent on the vigour
with which the YCL cell promotes ' consciousness ' among the
non-Party mass of workers." [2]

[1] See description of this conference in *Moscow Daily News*, July 3, 1932.

[2] From a Russian work entitled *The Cell in the Kolkhos : Days and Works of
the Savrukhinsk Cell of the YCL*, by S. Kolesnichenko and T. Usachev, Ogiz,
Moscow, 1932.

In 1932–1933, when " the agricultural crisis " was at its height, a large number of Comsomols were selected for service in the Ukraine, the Volga Basin and the North Caucasus, as " harvesting overseers ". They were to protect the grain from pilfering peasants or marauding bands ; to organise and lead " gleaning detachments " so that nothing should be lost, and generally to " increase productivity ". With regard to the sugar-beet harvest, the YCL All-Union Conference called for " socialist competition " among all Comsomol units, as to which could organise and conduct the most efficient arrangement. A prize fund of 200,000 roubles was to be formed with the aid of the Sugar Trust for distribution among the successful organisations.[1]

But for this agricultural work not all urban Comsomols proved themselves worthy. In May 1933 the newspapers reported the expulsion of seven young men as " deserters from the most important front of the class struggle ". As young mechanics in the Stalin Auto Plant (AMO), they had volunteered for work on a state farm in North Caucasus. They were provided with railway tickets, and given a public send-off by the Moscow Comsomol Committee as heroes of the day. But before actually getting to the sovkhos, they heard such a discouraging account of " life on a farm ", that they took fright and returned to Moscow. Brought before the Moscow Committee, they frankly explained that they were told " that wages on the farm were lower than in the factory ; farm life was too dull for them ; there were very few people around in the village . . . that work would be very hard . . . we thought it would be tough out there ; we simply took fright, and thought we might as well return ". . . . The Moscow Comsomol Committee decided that " the whole group should be expelled as cowards and deserters, and factory organisers should be warned to be more careful in choosing volunteers for work ".[2]

### The Pioneers and the Octobrists

The organisation of the younger population is undertaken by two junior bodies, " the Children's Communist Organisation of Young Pioneers in the name of Comrade Lenin "—universally known as the Pioneers—and less definitely, by what are called the

---

[1] *Moscow Daily News*, September 8, 1932.
[2] *Ibid.*, May 16, 1933.

" Little Octobrists ", in honour of the month of 1917 in which the Bolsheviks achieved power. The " Little Octobrists " are children between 8 and 11, who act under the guidance of the Pioneers ; whilst the Pioneers, between 10 and 16, are helped and directed by the Comsomols, aged 14 to 23, who are themselves, as we have seen, steered and controlled by the Communist Party itself, which may be joined at 18.[1]

## The Pioneers

The communist organisation of children of an age below that of the Comsomols did not take form until 1923. It was preceded by various attempts of the nature of the " Boy Scout " movement, the first of no great duration, definitely militarist, and under capitalist and conservative influences (the "poteshny", 1906–1910) ; and the second, more pacifist, under " liberal " influences (1907–1919), which, after various attempts at adjustment to the new conditions, was gradually " liquidated " under " war communism ". In 1921–1923 sporadic efforts were made to adapt the useful parts of the Boy Scout idea to the requirements of the Communist Party ; and at the fifth Comsomol Congress in October 1922 the present pioneer organisation was founded. By October 1923 it had still under 5000 members, but the Soviet Government and the Communist Party then joined the Comsomols in helping the new body, and it sprang rapidly into colossal magnitude, having by 1925 no fewer than a million members. The name of Lenin was then taken into the title. The scope of the organisation was enlarged, and at the same time the Pioneers were given the task of bringing their younger brothers and sisters, as young as eight years old, into groups of Little Octobrists. By 1926 the two junior organisations had over two million members (1,800,000 Pioneers and 250,000 Octobrists), actually exceeding in combined membership the numbers of the Comsomols at that date ; and the two younger

---

[1] These ages, it will be seen, overlap, and, as it is said, by design ; in order that each of the lower organisations may continue to include some who have already joined the next higher one, and who may therefore supply both leadership and encouragement in progression. Some Little Octobrists do not become Pioneers, and many Pioneers prefer not to undertake the onerous responsibilities of Comsomols ; whilst only a selection from these are admitted to Party membership.

bodies have since kept pace in an expansion which has now (1935) reached six millions. Thus the Pioneers have enrolled about 8 per cent of all the children between ten and sixteen in the USSR, just over one-half of the members being the children of peasants, one-third being the children of industrial workmen, and one-sixth being of other parentage, including office-workers, " toiling intelligentsia " and the new bourgeoisie of NEP. About two-fifths of the members are girls and three-fifths boys.

The members are organised in brigades, of which there are probably 100,000, two-thirds in the villages and one-third in the cities and urban areas. In the cities each factory has its brigade, and this basis is preferred, so as to ensure proletarian influence. Other brigades are formed in or around workmen's clubs or children's homes, and, failing other nuclei, even in schools (but it is provided that in such cases the leader of the brigade must be an industrial workman, and not a member of the school staff). In the villages, on the other hand, the school nearly always has to be made the base of the brigade. The desire is, wherever possible, to base the Pioneers' brigade on a place in which material production is carried on.

The object and intention of the Pioneer organisation is stated with studied moderation by Madam Krupskaya, the widow of Lenin, who has always taken great interest in the movement. " The Pioneer Movement ", she wrote, " reaches the children at that age when the personality of the individual is still being formed, and it promotes the social instincts of the children, helping to develop in them civic habits and a social consciousness. It places before the children a wonderful goal, that goal which has been brought to the fore by the period through which they are living, and for which the workman class of the whole world is fighting. This goal is the liberation of the toilers and the organisation of a new order in which there will be no division into classes, and no exploitation, and where all people will lead a full and happy life." [1]

The *Guide for the Young Pioneer*, the official manual which is placed in the hands of every applicant for membership, puts the matter candidly and explicitly. The right to wear the red star of membership and the red kerchief, and to give the Pioneer's salute, is acquired only after making the solemn promise re-

[1] Quoted in *Civic Training in Soviet Russia*, by S. N. Harper, 1929, p. 61.

quired of every full member. " I, a young Pioneer of the USSR, in the presence of my comrades, solemnly promise that (1) I shall stand steadfastly for the cause of the workman class in its struggle for the liberation of the workmen and peasants of the whole world ; (2) I shall honestly and constantly carry out the precepts of Ilych [Lenin], and laws and customs of the Young Pioneers."

The five " laws " and the five " customs " are summarised as follows :

## THE LAWS

(1) The Pioneer is faithful to the cause of the workman class and to the precepts of Ilych [Lenin].

(2) The Pioneer is the younger brother and helper of the Young Communist and the Communist [Party member].

(3) The Pioneer organises other children and joins with them in their life. The Pioneer is an example to all children.

(4) The Pioneer is a comrade to other Pioneers, and to the workmen and peasant children of the whole world.

(5) The Pioneer strives for knowledge : knowledge and understanding are the great forces in the struggle for the cause of the workman.

## THE CUSTOMS

(1) The Pioneer protects his own health and that of others. He is tolerant and cheerful. He rises early in the morning and does his setting up exercises.

(2) The Pioneer economises his own time and that of others. He does his task quickly and promptly.

(3) The Pioneer is industrious and persevering, knows how to work collectively under all and any conditions, and finds a way out in all circumstances.

(4) The Pioneer is saving of the people's property, is careful with his books and clothes, and the equipment of the workshop.

(5) The Pioneer does not swear, smoke or drink.[1]

---

[1] The Little Octobrists have also their own laws and customs, viz.: " The Little Octobrists help the Pioneers, the Young Communists, Communists, Workmen and Peasants. The Little Octobrists strive to become Young Pioneers. Little Octobrists are careful to be neat and clean in body and clothes. Little Octobrists love to work."

Admission to the Little Octobrists or to the Pioneers is easy. Any child within the limits of age, whatever its parentage, may be proposed and admitted to the grade of candidate, in which it must pass at least two months. The practice now is to accept, as members, candidates from any social class—even those of priests or of the new bourgeoisie, if they are, after probation, deemed likely to make good Pioneers. As candidates they are required to learn the " laws and customs " of the organisation, and show to their new comrades that they are observing them. Very often they are required to pass a formal examination on them. Only after such a period of testing is a candidate allowed to take the solemn promise, wear the badge and kerchief, and carry the membership card.

The organisation of the Pioneers is, as far as possible, closely attached to production in the factory or in the farm. Ten members constitute a " link ", four or five of which make a brigade. There are general meetings of each link and also of the brigade, to elect officers and discuss schemes of work. Each brigade is attached to a Comsomol cell, one of the members of which—young, physically active, full of life and a proletarian— is nominated to act as brigade leader. This is one of the ways in which Comsomols discharge their duty of civic activity. Each brigade has its own soviet, consisting of the four or five link leaders, the brigade leader and a representative of the Comsomol cell. Each district committee of the Comsomols has a committee, the " Section on Pioneers ", which directs and supervises the work of all the brigade leaders within its area ; and the work of all the " Sections on Pioneers " is supervised by the corresponding committee on Pioneers which is appointed by the Central Committee of the whole organisation in the USSR, chosen at its biennial All-Union Comsomol Congress at Moscow.

The Little Octobrists have a parallel but simpler organisation. Five members form a link, which is given a Pioneer as leader. Five links form a group, to which is assigned a Comsomol as special group leader, appointed by the Comsomol cell to which the Pioneer unit is attached. Each Octobrist group forms an integral part of the Pioneer brigade. It should be added that the members of each link choose from among their own number an assistant leader to work with the Pioneer leader of the link and the Comsomol leader of the group.

It will be seen that from the bottom to the top of this organisation of youth, from 8 to 23 years of age, careful provision is made for unity of action, a graded leadership, continuous supervision by the seniors and control by the Party itself, through a special assistant secretary. Yet at the same time there is a constant stress upon initiative and independent activity by the links, cells, groups and brigades. Every member is expected and persistently urged to be an " activist ", to be always doing something, and in particular to be constantly participating in the work undertaken by his unit. Games of all kinds, especially if of athletic nature, are not objected to, but each link or cell is expected to be actually performing some work useful in the building up of the socialist state. There is no end to the jobs that Pioneers find to do, or that Comsomols are pressed to undertake. They may clear away litter, sweep a street or help in a building operation. They may help to put down private as well as public drunkenness, and to " liquidate illiteracy " in their own or someone else's family. In the summer, where parties camp out in the woods, they will find it as good fun to help to get in the harvest as " to play at Indians ". The elder boys and girls may form " shock brigades " in farm or factories, and thus usefully raise productivity. They swell the processions at demonstrations, and audiences at meetings, ready to help in any way required. And everywhere they march about behind their own skeleton bands, with much community singing and mutual speech-making.[1]

[1] What is described as a " rousing address " was delivered by Madam Krupskaya at a conference of Comsomol workers among Pioneers in November 1933. " Lenin ", she said, " always insisted on the need of seizing upon the main link in any given situation. The main link in the Pioneer detachment is its leader, who is appointed by the Comsomol cell. The leader should be able to exercise an influence on the children in his charge. Sound knowledge, political as well as general ; social activity and the ability to approach children are the main qualifications for a Pioneer leader. The Young People should not rest satisfied with formal education. Study must be continued in later life. In particular, they should learn how to study, how to extract the maximum benefit from books and newspapers, as well as from observation. As a rifle is in battle, so is knowledge in general life. . . . The Pioneer should be an active social worker, thus providing an example for the children. He should firmly grasp the meaning of Lenin's words that the essence of communist morality is a readiness to sacrifice everything, one's life if needed, for the good of the working class. . . . The Pioneer leader should so approach an unruly child as to find out what interests him ; then to stimulate and encourage that interest and so transfer his energy to new lines. . . . Their disdain for bourgeois child movements, especially the Boy Scouts, causes many Pioneer leaders to miss much that is instructive in their approach to the child. Their experience should be studied, of course, with discrimination. . . . It was not enough for the Com-

Most foreign observers are enthusiastic about this growing army of 10 or 12 million young people. It is not always remembered that they are the self-chosen *élite* of a much larger mass. Moreover, even among this *élite* there are numerous backsliders, who are constantly being weeded out. Those who persist and thrive under the discipline of organised association with their equals in age, manifest, as it seems, some significant shortcomings or defects, at any rate in manners. They may be thought " uppish " with their elders, and fanatically intolerant. It is very good to be devoted to hygienic living, but the habit of " opening windows in other people's houses " is complained of ! In short, the enthusiastic Pioneer is apt to be, at any rate during certain years, a bit of a prig !

" These young people ", says a recent American observer, " are formulating the answer to the question of what will happen when the older generation of revolutionaries, with their self-forgetting enthusiasm, is gone. They are engaged in a continuous revolution—destroying and replacing ancient ideas, attitudes and habits. . . . Soviet educators are saying that the youth who have grown up since the revolution constitute a new type. . . . They certainly have much clearer-cut mentality ; they think more concretely and concisely. When you seek information from them, these younger men and women take out a pencil and ask for your exact question. Then rapidly they formulate their answers according to an exact outline, and usually you get precisely what you are after in the minimum of time. . . . Remembering the hours spent with small companies of these leaders of the masses in many places, one still feels the impact of their vitality ; one realises also that it is as different from that of European students, as they, in their turn, are different from the students of the United States. The latter, with their doubting fear of life or their inability to find enjoyment unless it is paid for and provided by others, seem strangely world-weary alongside

somol cells to appoint the Pioneer leader, and to rest at that. The cell should provide him with facilities for self-improvement, and care for his material well-being " (*Moscow Daily News*, November 24, 1933).

Latterly, there has been some authoritative criticism of the magnitude of the demands for " social work " on the Pioneers and younger Comsomols. The young people, it was said, were being overstrained, and even over-excited, with the result that their education suffered, and even their health. It seems to have been directed that the pressure should be lightened ; and that a watch should be kept for any evil result of excess.

exuberant youth of more ancient lands, with their hikes and rest-houses ; their unaffected group-singing and folk dances. This quality of exuberance the Russians share ; but they work while they study, and study while they work, uniting theory and practice, not in minor jobs whose outcome is private profit, but in a vast social upbringing. . . . They are enjoying life while they are changing it. . . . There shines from their eyes a con-centrated and eager intensity such as I have never seen before outside a religious revival or a strike meeting. . . . Every American to whom I have talked, who has taught these youthful builders of socialism, agrees that the first and main difference between them and the more serious section of American college students lies in the fact that they are dominated by a great purpose. As a soviet educator put it, " they know where they are going ; they know how ; and they know why ". . . . They know not only the transitional nature of the present period but to what it leads. . . . They regard the present conquest of the material means of life through new forms of organisation as the necessary preliminary to the opening up of a new freedom for the continuous development of all human capacities. . . . They have survived . . . the lean years of famine. . . . Their ruggedness has been filled with the greatest purpose that can enter into man. One feels that in them the life force has once again come to full floodtide. It is with this fact that those who dream of destroying what they are building must reckon." [1]

## *The Comintern*

Opposite the Moscow Kremlin, not inside its walls, and not to be confused, either, with the extensive offices of the Communist Party of the USSR, the visitor sees a considerable office building which is occupied by the " Comintern " or " Communist Inter-national ". This Communist or " Third " International, dating from 1919, is—unlike its first and second predecessors [2]—neither

[1] " Soviet Russia—Land of Youth ", in *The Nation* (New York), August 3, 1932, by Harry F. Ward ; see also his book *In Place of Profit* (1933).

[2] The first " International working men's association " was formed in London in 1864, under the influence of Karl Marx. It was considerably dislocated following on the suppression of the Paris Commune in 1871, but lingered on until a formal dissolution in 1876 (*The History of the First International*, by G. M. Stekloff, 1928). It was reformed at Paris in 1889 (the " Second International ") and soon attracted the affiliation of nearly all the Social Democratic Parties, as

in form nor in substance, a mere federation of national bodies, but an avowedly unified world organisation of the proletariat of all nations, all its members pledged to obey the orders of the central headquarters, wherever this may be situated. It is essential that the student should constantly bear in mind that it was not the government of a particular territory that the Bolsheviks had in view, or the dominion of a particular race. As we have described in a preceding chapter,[1] the conception of a territorial state, or of an empire extending over particular territories, was absent from their interpretation of Marxism.[2] What Lenin and his friends visualised was the establishment, in one country after another, almost as a continuous process, of a particular organisation of human society, what they termed the classless society. This was to be a new civilisation for the whole human race, in which the organisation of industry by the capitalist's employment of wage-labour for his own profit would be completely abolished, to be replaced by collective ownership and administration for the common good, on the basis of as near

well as that of the principal trade unions of the world (except the United States). The Great War of 1914–1918, together with the ensuing dictatorships in Hungary, Poland, Italy, Germany, etc., have seriously damaged its influence. But already at the Prague Socialist Congress in 1912, Lenin was concerting, with the various " left-wing " sections, a new international organisation ; and in March 1915 he expounded to a conference of Russian Socialists at Berne the necessity for a " proletarian " International. In September 1915, and April 1916, small conferences at Zimmerwald and Kienthal in Switzerland brought together representatives of socialist groups which had refused to support their governments in the war, and which wished to convert the struggle into one of proletarians against governments dominated by Imperialist Capitalism. In these conferences Lenin, with other Russian exiles, played a leading part in developing the idea of a new world organisation to replace the Second International. In January 1919, fifteen months after the Bolshevik conquest of power, the " first Communist International Congress " was summoned by wireless telegraphy from Petrograd, to meet at Moscow in March 1919 in order to " lay the foundation of a common fighting organ, which will be a uniting link and methodically lead the movement for the Communist International, which subordinates the interests of the movement in every separate country to the common interests of the revolution on an international scale " (*Soviet Rule in Russia*, by W. R. Batsell, 1919 ; *L'Internationale ouvrière et socialiste,* vol. i., 584 pp., 1907, issued by Le Bureau socialist international ; *Secret History of the International Working Men's Association*, by Onslow Yorke (W. H. Dixon), 1872, 166 pp. ; *The Worker's International*, by R. W. Postgate, 1920, 125 pp. ; *The Two Internationals*, by R. Palme Dutt, 1920 ; and see the section entitled " Contradictory Trends in Foreign Policy " in our subsequent Chapter XII. on " The Good Life ").

[1] See pp. 139-140, 153-155.

[2] For this reason we chose as the title of this book *Soviet Communism*, and not " Soviet Russia ", or " The USSR ".

an approach to complete communism as might prove practicable for the time being.

It was with this view that the " Communist International " was established at Moscow in 1919 as a " general staff of world revolution ", by a congress to which working-class organisations of all the world had been, by wireless telegraphy, summoned to send representatives. About 60 delegates were present when the congress assembled in March 1919 ; but the only body effectively represented was the Russian Communist Party, the few non-Russians being mostly individuals without mandate or influence. At subsequent congresses, down to the latest in 1935, always held at Moscow, delegates from the Party groups in scores of different countries have attended, and various of them have been placed upon the large executive committees by which the organisation is, in form, governed. In fact, however, the total membership even professedly represented from other countries has never reached as much as one-fourth of the membership of the Communist Party of the USSR. The congress and all its committees have always been completely dominated by the principal representatives of the Central Committee of the Communist Party of the USSR, who, as we have seen, also concentrate in their hands the supreme direction of the government of their own country.

It is therefore not without reason that writers on the constitution of the USSR include the Comintern in their description of its constitutional structure,[1] as they do the Sovnarkom.

The formal constitution of the Comintern puts the relation in quite a different way. The supreme authority rests, not with the Soviet Union, but with the world congress of the Comintern, meeting every two, four or seven years, and composed of delegates of all the various affiliated Communist Parties throughout the world. The delegates of the Communist Party of the USSR have proportionately no greater representation, and nominally no more authority, than those from any other country. All alike are peremptorily required, under penalty of expulsion, to obey the orders from time to time issued by the Executive Committee which the Congress elects. The " Twenty-one Points " that Lenin expounded to the Second Congress of the Communist Inter-

---

[1] For instance, *Soviet Rule in Russia*, by W. R. Batsell, 1929, chap. xiii. ; who also quotes *Konstitutsia SSSR i RSSR*, by S. Dranitsyn.

national, as the indispensable conditions on which alone membership could be allowed, are on this subject even more than usually incisive. " All decisions of the congresses of the Communist International, as well as the decisions of its Executive Committee, are binding upon all the parties belonging to the Communist International. . . . The programme of every party belonging to the Communist International must be sanctioned by the regular congress of the Communist International, or by its Executive Committee." [1] Members, who have to pay regular small dues, are admitted by the several affiliated " sections " of the Comintern, which are required to describe themselves as Communist Parties. Every member in such a Party is supposed to belong to a nucleus or cell, formed in the factory or other establishment in which he is employed. The primary duty of the nucleus is to convert the workers to communism by demonstrating the futility of every other form of organisation, especially the trade unions under their present leadership ; nevertheless to urge them to remain members of these useless unions in order to upset their futile action ; and, in particular, to foster " mass strikes ", without much regard for the likelihood of their immediate success, as a means of " educating " the workers into revolutionary " class consciousness ".[2]

It need not be said that the periodical congress of the Communist International is as little fitted to act as a deliberative or legislative body as the All-Union Congress of the Communist Party of the USSR, or as that of the All-Union Congress of Soviets. The crowd of so-called delegates from many countries, which at the congress in 1928 numbered not far short of a thousand and at that of 1935 about half that number, are necessarily, for the most part, unacquainted with each other. They meet only every

---

[1] " Conditions of Membership " (The " Twenty-one Points of Lenin ") as adopted by the Second Congress of the Communist International (*Soviet Rule in Russia*, by W. R. Batsell, 1929, p. 766).

This complete centralisation of authority in Moscow has been maintained. In 1928 it was reaffirmed. " Unlike the Social Democratic Second International, each section of which submits to the discipline of its own national bourgeoisie and of its own fatherland, the sections of the Communist International submit to only one discipline, viz. international proletarian discipline, which guarantees victory in the struggle of the world's workers for world proletarian dictatorship " (Statement of " the strategy and tactics of the Communist International in the struggle for the Dictatorship of the Proletariat ", adopted by the Congress of 1928 ; *Programme of the Communist International*, New York, 1929).

[2] *Bolshevism for Beginners*, by P. Kerzhentsev, 1931, pp. 115-117.

few years for a week or two. Such an assembly could be no more than a parade or a demonstration. The Congress, in fact, was summoned to listen to a series of lengthy declamatory speeches by the leading members of the. Party in the USSR, who entirely dominated the proceedings ; whilst duly selected speakers from other countries came to the platform, sometimes to make complaints, but usually to fire off similar orations. Long statements of general policy called theses or programmes, couched in revolutionary phraseology, and specially abusive of every other kind of socialist or labour organisation, either national or international, were prepared in committees, to be submitted to the congress, to be adopted without detailed examination[1] or dissent, chiefly in order that they might be published in several languages in the *International Press Correspondence*, from which they were copied in the hundreds of little journals throughout the world that are under communist control.

The Executive Committee (IKKI) or (ECCI) that the Congress appoints, and to which it delegates all its authority until the next Congress, is, we think, less well-informed, less well served by its agents, and therefore as a whole less effective than the corresponding standing executives of the USSR Communist Party and Soviets. It is composed, we were told, of between one and five delegates from each country, the USSR having no more than the number allowed to France, Germany and Great Britain. We have the opinion that it is, and has always been, dominated by the same little group of old-revolutionary Bolsheviks. One of them has always been its president.[2] It meets as a plenum only every six months, when half the membership constitutes a quorum, so that the current administration, and even the frequent decisions as to policy, are in practice committed to the standing presidium of which Stalin himself is a member. This inner executive, which should meet at least once a fortnight, and which appoints the political secretariat, is even more completely dominated by the representatives of the Kremlin than the plenum of the Executive

[1] " Foreigners ", said Lenin at the Fourth Congress in 1923, " have to learn how to understand all that we have written about the organisation and up-building of the Communist Parties, *which they have subscribed to without reading and without understanding it* " (*Fourth Congress of the Communist International* (November 1923), *Abridged Report*, London, p. 119 ; see *Soviet Rule in Russia*, by W. R. Batsell, 1929, p. 761).

[2] From 1919 to 1927 it was Zinoviev ; since then D. Z. Mannilsky, a member of the Central Committee, has acted.

Committee or the Comintern congress itself.[1]   The so-called
representatives, on the executive committee and on its presidium,
of the foreign sections of the Communist International are for
the most part, and have hitherto always been, persons of little
public standing among the wage-earners of their own countries.
Most of them find it impossible to attend the six-monthly meetings
in Moscow, at which they are represented by substitutes resident
in that city, who may speak but not vote.[2]

We shall deal in a subsequent chapter [3] with the relations
between the Comintern and the Soviet Foreign Office (Narko-

[1] According to the invariable pattern in the USSR, the Comintern Congress
also appoints a Control Commission, independent of the Executive Committee,
which is supposed to investigate " matters concerning the unity of the sections
affiliated ", as well as the conduct of individual members—that is to say, to
enforce the orthodox doctrine.

[2] The published materials for an account of the Communist International,
are, in half a dozen languages, abundant, so far as concerns manifestos,
programmes, theses and " directives " to the Communist Parties of all countries.
But the internal administration of the Comintern, and the actual proceedings
of its control commission, Executive Committee and presidium remain entirely
secret.   The best single source for published documents is *International Press
Correspondence*, issued by the Party almost weekly, in English as well as in other
languages, primarily as free " copy " for the hundreds of little communist
journals throughout the world, but supplied also to individual subscribers.   The
proceedings (abridged) of most of the Comintern congresses have been published
as separate volumes in English and other languages.   Batsell (*Soviet Rule in
Russia*) and S. N. Harper (*Civic Instruction in Soviet Russia*) contain the most
useful descriptons of the Comintern in volume form known to us ; but for early
history see also *The Second and Third Internationals and the Vienna Union* (1922),
and *The Two Internationals*, by R. Palme Dutt, 1920, together with the histories
cited above.

The finances of the Comintern for 1931 were thus summarised in dollars and
cents, for publication by the Executive Committee :

|  | Income |  | Expenditure |
|---|---|---|---|
| Brought forward . | 61,089.30 | Administrative expenses .   .   . | 372,347.80 |
| Membership dues from | | Postage and telegraph | 38,387.75 |
| 41   parties   and | | Subsidies   to   party | |
| 3,700,788 members . | 1,128,236.40 | newspapers,   publishing houses and | |
| Collections and donations   .   .   . | 46,371.80 | cultural work   . | 756,900.00 |
| Receipts from publications, etc.   .   . | 59,618.30 | Travelling expenses . | 52,732.00 |
| | | Carried forward . | 74,948.25 |
| TOTALS | 1,295,315.80 | .. | 1,295,315.80 |

YCL and 17 Parties were exempted from payment.
(*International Press Correspondence*, October 26, 1932, p. 1007.)

[3] See " Contradictory Trends in Foreign Policy ", in Chapter XII. in Part
II., " The Good Life ".

mindel). Here we need only express the opinion that the importance of the Comintern, whether in its international aspect, or as a part of the working constitution of the USSR, is no longer what it was. Its proceedings do not fit in so well with a policy of world peace as they may have done with a policy of world revolution. In a subsequent chapter we shall discuss how far the fundamental aim of a world revolution has been abandoned or substantially modified by the proceedings of the Seventh Congress, held, after many postponements, at Moscow in August 1935. Meanwhile the subventions that Moscow used to supply, under various designations, to many of the sections in other countries, appear to have dwindled down to almost insignificant amounts, chiefly for legal defence of manual workers prosecuted for their communist opinions.

## The Nature of the Communist Party

We have done our best to set out precisely the constitution and functions of the Communist Party. Merely as a social institution, it is a specimen of the greatest interest to the student. Is it a new type in the world, and what are its characteristics ?

As we indicated at the opening of this chapter, the Communist Party in the USSR, in its structure and in some of its leading features, has a distinct resemblance to the religious orders established in past ages in connection with Buddhism, Christianity and other world religions. It is literally outside of the legal constitution of the secular state, and professedly independent of it. It repudiates any national boundaries, and claims a sphere that is world-wide, and independent of nationality, race or colour. It is self-selective in its recruitment, in that it augments its membership exclusively by co-option. It is pyramidal in form, broadly democratic at the base, but directing its self-management from the top downwards. Its test for membership is fundamentally that of acceptance of an ideology of the nature of a creed, from which is evolved an exceptional code of conduct, not imposed on the ordinary citizen, which all its members must obey, the ultimate sanction being expulsion from membership. It has even added, in its new category of " sympathisers ", something analogous to the " lay brothers " of the religious orders. It has in substance, though not in name, a " holy writ ", the authority and veracity of which must not be questioned, but which is subject at all times to authoritative imterpretation. By means of this interpretation the organisation, through an elaborate hierarchy, directs the ideology and conduct of a membership of colossal magnitude. This membership has a distinct vocation to which it is pledged; accompanied by what are equivalent to vows of obedience and poverty, and by authoritative customs constituting a penumbra around the ordinary citizen's creed and code of conduct, a penumbra which may or may not be enforced by the legislature and judiciary of the country in which the organisation exists. Of the intensity of faith of the Party, and the strength of the devotion of its members, often leading to the greatest self-sacrifice and even martyrdom, no candid student can have any doubts. Finally, it tends to erect one man as its head, who is nominally no more than an ordinary member, and may not hold the highest or any office at all in the State, but who reaches the apex of the pyramid by popular acclamation, based on election, at first direct and afterwards indirect; but who, once chosen, is professedly the chief director, and who becomes, in time, practically irremovable by the membership.

There are, however, other features in the Communist Party which definitely mark it off from any of the religious orders that have ever existed in the world; and which make it an entirely new and original type of social institution. In particular, there is one great unlikeness of the Communist Party which accounts for the indignation always manifested, by communists on the one hand and by Christians on the other, whenever it is suggested that this new organisation is of the nature of a religious order. Its purpose and its ideology (which we must not call a creed) are not only different from those of the religious orders past or present, but also fundamentally antagonistic to every one of them. The Communist Party flatly rejects, not only Christianity and Islam, but also every form of Deism or Theism. It will have nothing to do with the supernatural. It admits nothing to be true which cannot be demonstrated by the " scientific method " of observation, experiment, ratiocination and verification. Unlike any religion in the world's history, Soviet Communism, as we shall describe in a subsequent chapter,[1] is whole-heartedly

[1] Chapter XI., Part II., " Science the Salvation of Mankind ".

based on science, the newest and most up-to-date science, meaning man's ever-expanding knowledge of the universe, which it
eagerly adopts and confidently applies to every task or problem,
and to the advancement of which it gives all honour and devotes
considerable public funds. In fact, in the nature of its mentality,
as in the direction of its activities, the Communist Party reminds
us less of a religious order than of the organisation of the learned
professions of Western Europe, such as those of the lawyers and
doctors, engineers and public accountants. Like these and many
other professional bodies, the Communist Party concerns itself
exclusively with the affairs of this world. It resembles these
bodies also in constituting an exclusive corporation, selecting,
training, disciplining and expelling its own members, according
to a code of conduct of its own invention. Where it differs from
these organised professions is in standing outside the constitution
of its country, and, whilst its members are individually subject
to the law of the land like other citizens, in the corporate body
itself being entirely free from outside control. Moreover, unlike
the vocations of the lawyers and dòctors, that which the Communist Party assumes, namely, public leadership, puts the
ordinary citizen under no obligation to invoke the services of
its members, even where these are most needed !

### Why, in Soviet Communism, National Leadership requires an elaborate Organisation

The political student may ask what it is in the USSR that
calls for such an elaborate organisation of leadership. No other
country, whether governed by an autocrat or by a committee of
Parliament, has felt it necessary to provide, in this way, deliberately and avowedly, for the continuous intellectual guidance, not
merely of its people as a whole, but of all the people.

Thoughtful communists point out, as part of the explanation,
that the Soviet Government differs from every other government
in the world, in that it has a fanatically held and all-overriding
purpose of social and economic change. Most governments have
had no purpose of change of any sort. Their object is primarily
the " maintenance of order "—which means the existing order—
together with defence, or the repelling of any attack from within
or without. The Soviet Government, on the other hand, avowedly

exists for the deliberate purpose of changing the existing order, not eventually, at some distant date, but actually, and within the present generation ; and that not in mere generalities but in the most intimate circumstances of the people's lives. In the USSR, if the mass of the population is to be lifted out of barbarism to an advanced civilisation, it is held that the whole people must be freed from the subjection and control inevitably associated with the private ownership of the means of production. No less necessary is it that the aggregate wealth production of the whole community should be greatly and continuously increased ; that, to this end, the primitive processes of agriculture, as of manufacturing industry, must be transformed by the universal application of mechanical, physical and chemical science ; and that manual labour must be, as far as possible, superseded by power-driven machinery, without the toll elsewhere levied on production by functionless " owners " of either land or capital, or other " parasitic " consumers. How gigantic is the task thus undertaken by the Soviet Government can be realised only by those who take the trouble to estimate what nine-tenths of the population between the Baltic and the Pacific were like in 1913 ; or what were the economic and social conditions of the country as a whole after the Civil War of 1918–1920 and the famine of 1921.

Now, it is a feature of this task—a task such as no government has ever before dreamt of undertaking—that it cannot be completely accomplished without the active cooperation of practically every family in the land. Just as in a modern war it is not only the armies whose energies must be coordinated to the common end, but nearly the whole working population ; so the great struggle with nature for an immediate increase in economic productivity, without the so-called automatic adjustment of supply and demand on which capitalism so disastrously relies, cannot afford the luxury, either of non-participants, or of disunity among the executants. In war-time complete national coordination is sought by autocratic commands, to which obedience is secured by drastic penalties. The task of transforming the social and economic life of all the people is, however, different and more difficult than that of repelling an invading army ; and it cannot be achieved by peremptory commands and prohibitions. It involves changing the content of the minds of the whole people. It demands universal education and persistent propaganda, patient argument and personal example, brought to bear on every individual, at every age, in every place.

Such a transformation of society is, it is clear, not a change that is within the capacity of a mere dictatorship, even if this is exercised by the greatest of men. It is, in fact, not a case of creating " a leader " or " the leader ". It demands the active participation of millions of instructors. The lives to be influenced, the minds to be changed, the personal habits to be taught, can be dealt with, for the most part, only by direct personal contact in the hours of work as in the hours of leisure. In the USSR it is not the statesmen at the top who actually exercise this peculiar power, though they may direct it ; but the million or more of picked working men and working women members of the Communist Party, whose ubiquitous personal intercourse with their fellows never ceases.

Western students will recognise that something can be done by the expedient of allowing and inducing practically the whole adult population to participate in the administration, in one way or another, so that the changes to which they are led come as the outcome of their own discussions, and are gradually embodied in the local regulations that they themselves formulate. That is one great advantage of the extraordinary multiformity of the constitutional structure of the USSR, with its millions of small meetings during each year of fellow-workers or neighbours asking questions or passing resolutions ; and of its threefold representation, in the several elected councils, of Man as a Citizen, Man as a Producer and Man as a Consumer. But a public meeting, large or small, without intellectual leadership, is but a mob. Such a meeting, in countries of long political experience, often spontaneously throws up its own temporary leader. But such transient leaders, the outcome of a million meetings, will, of themselves, certainly not create any uniform current of public opinion. It is the business of the members of the Communist Party everywhere to proffer to the crowd the guidance that it needs.

It has sometimes been argued that this persistent persuasion and personal example may be supplied, in capitalist countries, by the well-disposed members of superior social classes, such as the landed aristocracy, the retired officers of the army and navy, or the commercial community. Such superior social classes have ceased to exist in the USSR ; and there is no reason to believe that, if they did exist, they would honestly and loyally cooperate with the purpose of the Soviet Government, which demands, indeed, their complete elimination.

There seemed, to the Bolshevik authorities, no alternative. There would be no leadership given to the people, such as was required—a guidance continuous, persuasive, ubiquitous and consistent—unless it was deliberately planned and provided by an organisation for the purpose. Communists to-day believe that the Communist Party, with half its members always at the bench or in the mine, and its schemes of policy carefully worked out after elaborate debate in the various representative committees and conferences, often with prolonged publicity to allow of widespread criticism, is an organisation well suited to its purpose. Its leadership is plainly not less persuasive, but actually more persuasive, in that it is exercised less by peremptory laws, or even by universal schooling, than by personal example, intellectual argument and continuous propaganda. Whether or not a community under such guidance—a community so markedly unlike any other that has ever existed—can properly be described as a Democracy, will be considered in the next chapter.

# CHAPTER VI

## DICTATORSHIP OR DEMOCRACY?

ONE difficulty of accurately assessing and defining the essential characteristics of the constitutional structure of the USSR is the rapidity with which it changes. Even the so-called "Fundamental Law" defining the rights and obligations of citizenship has nothing of the rigidity of a formal constitution embodied in a special instrument, unchangeable except by some elaborate process. Any alteration that seems to be required need not wait for a plebiscite, or even a general election. Much of it is independent of any action by a legislative body. Whether or not the All-Union Congress of Soviets is in session, there are always at work standing committees empowered to make without delay any alterations, in any part of the constitution, affecting any section of the population, in any part of the country, that changing circumstances require. And in so vast a territory, with so huge and so varied a population, going through so tremendous an economic development, the circumstances are always changing. Hence the constitution of the USSR is far and away the most mobile of any known to political science. We cannot to-day simply take it for granted that it is supremely important that a constitution should be rigid. It is certainly not clear that the mobility of the working constitution in the USSR during the past decade has been, in itself, detrimental to the progress of its inhabitants in health or economic prosperity; or that it has incurred popular disapproval.[1]

[1] It is interesting to notice that many of the advantages claimed for rigidity in constitutions have to do either (a) with the private ownership of land or other forms of personal wealth, which it is thought desirable to defend against confis-

The characteristic mobility of the constitution of Soviet Communism is, however, all the more perplexing to the student in that the several parts of the constitution change independently of each other ; and change, moreover, at different rates and in different directions. Thus, the hierarchy of soviets seemed relatively stable in form and in substance. It grew, indeed, in volume. The continually increasing electorate, the constantly rising total of votes cast at the innumerable electoral meetings, and the perpetual multiplication of councils of one or other kind, and of councillors to man them, involves the personal participation in government by an ever-increasing number of the citizens, women as well as men. To this characteristic of an ever-widening participation we shall recur. In 1935 another kind of widening was announced for adoption before the next general election ; namely, the substitution, for indirect election upon a not quite equal franchise, of direct election by an entirely equal franchise, in an electorate that may then approach the colossal total of one hundred millions.

The continual growth in the volume of manufacturing industry, mining, transport, electrification, mechanised agriculture, social services and governmental departments, with the corresponding increase in the number of wage or salary receivers, has led, not only to an ever-mounting trade union membership, but also to a continuous advance in trade union functions. The great work done by trade union committees in the administration of accident prevention, labour recruiting, factory schools and technical classes, social clubs, recreation and holiday arrangements, and all forms of social insurance, was emphasised in 1933 by the abolition of the office of People's Commissar of Labour, directly controlled by the Sovnarkom ; and the transfer of the direction of the actual administration of the huge ministerial departments concerned with every branch of social insurance to the All-Union Trade Union Council (AUCCTU).

An analogous growth is to be noted during the past few years

catory legislation or executive action ; or else (*b*) with the making of private profit, which might be hampered by unexpected or frequent changes in social institutions ; or else (*c*) with the maintenance of the privileges of a privileged class, whether aristocrats, landed proprietors, or a " superior " race. In a community in which neither personal wealth nor private profit-making exists, and no class has legal privileges, constitutional rigidity loses many of its supporters.

in the less completely organised hierarchies of the manufacturing artels and of the widespread kolkhosi of the shore fishermen. During the same years an enormous extension has been made in the collectivisation of agriculture, on the one hand into sovkhosi, or state farms, and on the other into kolkhosi, or collective farms, principally of the artel type. Among the collective farms only the base of the pyramid has yet been laid, and the development of tiers of congresses of delegates for rayon, oblast, republic and All-Union deliberations has been postponed. In the consumers' cooperative movement, the rate and kind of change is difficult to assess with precision. Whilst continuing to increase its colossal membership, and even its aggregate volume of transactions, it has been losing ground in various directions, partly to those manufacturing trusts which do their own retailing ; partly to the " commercial " shops set up by the government itself ; partly to the republic and municipal soviets which multiply their retail " selling points " ; and partly, as elsewhere described, to the trade union hierarchy so far as concerns not only the retailing of household commodities but also the production of foodstuffs for the workers in the larger establishments. Moreover, a marked feature of the last few years, to be described in a subsequent chapter,[1] has been the growth and encouragement of wholesale trading between these different forms of organisation, in order that each of them may be in a better position to supply its individual customers. This has resulted in a vast network of free contracts, based on competition in an open market, among collective farms and trade unions and industrial artels and consumers' cooperative societies, each of them functioning alternately as an association of producers and an association of consumers.

Amid this unending flux, the student must note the significance of the universal adoption and continuous retention, often without legislative prescription, for all the various parts of the constitution, of the common and nearly unchanging pattern of organisation which we have described, termed by its originators democratic centralism. This pattern, now pervading the whole social structure of the USSR, is not found in any other part of the world, nor in any previous constitution. Another characteristic of this pattern of social organisation is its extreme fluidity. The different

[1] Chapter IX. in Part II., " In Place of Profit ".

parts of the constitution have often been set going one by one, by spontaneous activity, in areas hitherto without government —and, for that matter, also in areas professedly under other governments—without proclamation or formal authority, and irrespective of other parts of the USSR constitution, which have sometimes followed at later dates. Thus, in various popular accounts of the gradual organisation of primitive regions in the northern forest districts or in the recesses of Kamchatka we see the holding of a village meeting which elects a soviet, linking up with other soviets, and eventually sending delegates to the congress of soviets at Moscow. Presently the local residents coagulate as consumers into a cooperative society which gets eventually into communication with Centrosoyus. Stray members of the Communist Party form a nucleus or cell, now styled a primary Party organ, and presently constitute themselves a Party Group in the local soviet or in the cooperative society's committee ; and they conform their activities to the latest " directives " from the Politbureau or Central Committee at Moscow. When mining or transport or manufacturing industry creates a class of wage-earners, these join their several trade unions, irrespective of municipal frontiers or racial differences ; and they then begin to send delegates to the hierarchy of indirectly elected trade union councils, conferences and congresses, of which the highest periodically assembles at Moscow. The constitution formed on this pattern may, we suggest, appropriately be termed a multiform democracy, organised on the basis of universal participation with democratic centralism ; a constitutional form so loose as to be exceptionally mobile and, for that reason, endowed with an almost irresistible quality of expansiveness.

In describing, in separate chapters, the organisation in the USSR of Man as a Citizen, Man as a Producer, Man as a Consumer and Man in the Vocation of Leadership, we may have seemed sometimes to imply that all these separate parts of the constitution of Soviet Communism are of equal status, each exercising supreme authority in its own sphere. This is not so. The Central Executive Committee (TSIK) of the All-Union Congress of Soviets, representing the totality of the inhabitants in the USSR, and not merely any fraction of them, stands supreme over all the ramifications of the trade unions, the consumers' cooperative movement and the various kinds of associations of owner-

producers, just as it does over the tier upon tier of soviets.[1]  As
for the relation in which the All-Union Congress of Soviets stands
to the All-Union Congress of the Communist Party in the USSR,
what can be said is that there has been no attempt by the
soviet legislature to make laws for, or to interfere with the
activities of, the Communist Party.   The practical independence
of the soviet authorities is not so apparent.   Since 1930 all
important decrees of the USSR Central Executive Committee or
the Sovnarkom, whether legislative or administrative, have been
issued over the signature, not of their president (Kalinin or
Molotov) alone, but also over that of Stalin as General Secretary
of the Communist Party.   It is, moreover, significant that these
decisive acts are, in all important cases, initiated within the
Politbureau of the Communist Party ;  and they receive in due
course the endorsement either of the Central Committee or of
the All-Union Congress of the Communist Party.   Indeed, as we
explained in the preceding chapter, the Communist Party is
perpetually issuing " directives ", great or small, to its members
exercising authority or influence within all the other organisations
of the state.   In the present connection it must be recalled that
this remarkable companionship is not, in theory, an organisation within the USSR.   It professes to be an organisation of
the vanguard of the proletariat throughout the world, knowing
neither racial nor geographical limits.   Its highest authority is
the periodical congress of the " Third International ", representing the Communist Parties of all the countries of the world.
This body acts normally by the directives which the Comintern
issues to the faithful in all countries.   It aims, in fact, at a
world supremacy over all the administrations established by the
proletariat of the several nations or countries.   The historical
student will be reminded of the supremacy which the Pope, as
the head of the Catholic Church, for centuries maintained over
Christendom.   Whether, on the occasion of some great crisis,
there will arise any effective rivalry, or any disturbing friction,
between the secular government of the USSR and the ideological

---

[1] It is, however, significant of the persistent striving towards participation
and consent, that when alterations are made in the constitution or statutory
obligations of either the trade union hierarchy or the consumers' cooperative
movement, these authoritative decrees are normally discussed, decided and
actually signed, not only by Kalinin or Molotov or other authorities representative of the soviet, but also by the leading official representing the trade unions
or the consumers' cooperative movement respectively.

companionship or order which to-day dominates the situation, may be left as a fascinating problem for the sociologist of the future.[1]

We have to add, as a further elaboration of the constitution of the USSR, some reference to the circumambient atmosphere of voluntary organisation which it is perpetually creating and developing as a part of itself. Some people have asserted that government activity kills voluntaryism. In the USSR, on the contrary, every government activity seems to create a vastly greater voluntary activity, which the people themselves organise up to a high point, always along the lines and in support of the government's own purpose and plan ; always and everywhere led and directed by members of the Communist Party. We despair of conveying in a few pages any adequate idea of the magnitude, the variety or the range of action of these voluntary organisations linked up or intertwined with one or other government department.[2]  We need not repeat our description of the ten million or more young people voluntarily enrolled as Little Octobrists,

---

[1] The question of the possibility of the governmental organisation becoming emancipated from the control of the Communist Party has more than once been discussed within the Party. "In 1925", so the French historian Henry Rollin puts it, Stalin himself pointed out the "danger of the disappearance of the tutelage of the Party". He showed how greatly the governmental organs, both administrative and economic, steadily increased in magnitude and influence with the reconstruction of the country. "The more they grow in importance, the more their pressure on the Party is felt, the more they take up an attitude of resistance to the Party. Hence the danger of the state apparatus shaking itself free from the Party." Against this danger Stalin pressed for a regrouping "of forces, and a redistribution of directing active members among the governmental organs, so as to ensure the directing influence of the Party in this new situation. This was the origin of the disgrace of Rykov, president of the Council of Commissars, and of Tomsky, president of the trade unions, as well as of the purging of the soviet apparatus that was completed in June 1929, in order to seat firmly the domination that Stalin exercised in the name of the Party" (*La Révolution russe*, vol. i., "Les soviets", by Henry Rollin, Paris, 1931, pp. 269-270).

"The Party makes no concealment of the tutelage in which it holds the soviet organs. Thus, on the check to collectivisation in March 1930, the Central Committee of the Party issued direct instructions of a purely governmental kind by a circular addressed to all the Party organisations and published in the entire soviet press on March 15. The official governmental organs could do more than put these decisions in a more official form a few days later" (*Ibid.* p. 278).

[2] More detailed accounts of voluntary organisations in the USSR will be conveniently found in *Civic Training in Soviet Russia* (1929) and *Making Bolsheviks* (1931), both by S. N. Harper ; *New Minds, New Men*, by Thomas Woody (1932) ; *Die Jugend in Sowjetrussland*, by Klaus Mehnert (1932), translated as *Youth in Soviet Russia* (1933).

Pioneers and Comsomols, in subordination to the extensive membership of the Party. We may more conveniently begin with the specifically patriotic society, formed " to cooperate in defence of the revolution " (OSO), and another " for aviation and chemical industries " (Aviakhim), both now merged in one huge contributing membership of a dozen millions (Osoaviakhim). These millions of members in village or city form cells, or sections, or circles, or corners, coordinated in a whole series of provincial and central councils. They are all pledged to active personal cooperation in the defence of the country, in peace-time as well as in war, against foreign invasion or external pressure. They seek to arouse general interest in foreign affairs by lectures, literature and discussion. They study military science, especially aerial bombing and chemical warfare. They form clubs for rifle practice and aviation. They maintain specialist museums and libraries, and " defence homes ", which are practically social clubs. They have collected considerable sums for building additional aeroplanes for presentation to the Red Air Force. Organised bands of members have participated in the training manœuvres of the Red Army. Other bands have, with equal zeal, undertaken the clearing of particular districts from noxious insects. Out of the vast membership, several thousand local societies for regional study have emerged, devoting themselves to exhaustive surveys of the physical and economic characteristics of their own neighbourhood, partly for the benefit of the local schools, in which regional study has its place.

Vying in size with Osoaviakhim is the League of the Godless, for the emancipation of the backward part of the population from the religion that seems to the Marxist mere superstition, benumbing or distracting the spirit of man. This entirely voluntary organisation, made up for the most part of young people of either sex, corresponds essentially to the nineteenth-century National Secular Society of Great Britain ; but enormously transcends it in activity, as well as in magnitude and range of operations. Its millions of members, organised in cells or branches from one end of the USSR to the other, campaign actively against the various churches and their religious practices ; circulating atheistic literature ; pouring scorn on any but a scientific interpretation of nature ; clearing the icons out of the homes, and weaning the boys and girls alike from churchgoing and from the celebration of religious festivals.[1] We should fail to appreciate either the magnitude or the dogmatic intolerance of the crusade against supernaturalism in the USSR, conducted by these militant atheists, if we compared it with anything less than the campaign against atheism and heathendom carried on in all their fields of action by all the missionary societies and religious orders of all the Christian churches put together.

Another society of colossal magnitude, claiming indeed many millions of members, is the International Society for Assistance to Revolutionaries in other countries (MOPR). This has for its object, not only to bring " the broad masses into contact with the world-revolution ", but also " to enable them to come to the assistance of those who are fighting for it ". It disseminates information of doubtful accuracy about the progress of communism in all countries, but it is most interested in rebellions and riots, strikes and the various kinds of " martyrdom " to which, as it is alleged, the ruling classes everywhere condemn their working-class victims. The tens of thousands of branches of MOPR collect funds for the assistance of sufferers all over the world, from those in the prisons of Hungary or Poland to " Sacco and Vanzetti " and " the Scottsborough negroes ". We could mention dozens of other voluntary organisations of the most varied nature. There is a " Down with Illiteracy " society, and a " Hands off China " society ; a " Friends of Children " society (ODD), and a " Society for settling Jews on the Land " (OZET) ; a gigantic " Peasant Society for Mutual Assistance " (KOV), and a whole movement of working women's and peasants' conferences, to which tens of thousands of villages send delegates, and in which everything specially interesting to women is discussed and assisted and promoted. Nor must we omit the immense membership of all the various societies arranging every kind of athletic sports, under the supervision and with the constant encouragement of the Supreme Council for Physical Culture in the USSR, appointed by the Central Executive Committee (TSIK), and the People's Commissars for Education in all the constituent and autonomous republics. It is active personal participation in games and competitions that is promoted, among an aggregate membership of all

---

[1] See the detailed account in *Religion and Communism*, by J. F. Hecker (1933) ; and see our Chapter XI. in Part II., " Science the Salvation of Mankind ", especially the section headed " Anti-Godism ".

races running into tens of millions, in Asia as well as in Europe ; not merely the organisation of spectacles at which the members look on, although this factor in the habit of athleticism is not neglected. Gigantic stadiums are being built out of public funds in many of the cities, including a " Middle Asian Central Stadium " at Tashkent. Even more remarkable is it to learn that the members of the sports associations include in their activities the rendering of personal assistance to the agricultural and transport departments, whenever required. "Uzbek, Tadjik and Turkoman athletes ", we read, " have helped considerably in the repairing of locomotives, in cotton planting and in harvesting, in the re-election of the soviets and in the quick response to the new internal loan." [1]

Whilst unable to exclude from our statement of the constitution some account of these auxiliary voluntary activities, we hesitate to make any estimate of their net worth. They take up time and energy. They may even distract attention from more urgent problems. But their colossal magnitude and ubiquitous activities make the voluntary organisations a very important part of the social structure. There can be no doubt about their enormous educational effect upon the half-awakened masses which still make up so large a part of the population of the USSR —especially upon the " deaf villages " of the interior, and upon what Marx and Lenin termed the " idiocy of village life ". The sharing in public affairs which the vast membership of these voluntary organisations secures, and the independent action which each cell or section, group or corner, learns to take in cooperation with the various departments of the soviet administration, constitute an essential part of that widespread " participation " in government which seems to us one of the most character-istic notes of Soviet Communism. It is, more than anything else, this almost universal personal participation, through an amazing variety of channels, that justifies the designation of it as a multiform democracy.

## The Meaning of Dictatorship

Can the constitution of the USSR, as analysed in the pre-ceding chapters, be correctly described as a dictatorship ? Here

[1] *Moscow Daily News*, June 29, 1933.

we must deal one by one with the various meanings given to this word.  In the popular British use of the term, a dictatorship means government by the will of a single person ; and this, as it happens, corresponds with the authoritative dictionary meaning, in strict accord with the undoubted historical derivation.[1] It is clear that, in form, there is nothing in the constitution of the USSR at all resembling the Roman office of dictator ; or, indeed, any kind of government by the will of a single person.  On the contrary, the universal pattern shows even an exaggerated devotion to collegiate decision.  In the judicial system, from the highest court to the lowest, there is nowhere an arbitrator, a magistrate or a judge sitting alone, but always a bench of three, two of whom at least must agree in any decision or judgment or sentence.[2]  In municipal administration there is no arbitrary mayor or burgomaster or " city manager "—not even a high salaried official wielding the authority of a British Town Clerk— but always a presidium and one or more standing committees, the members of each of which have to be continuously consulted by its president ; or else a specially chosen commission, all the members of which have equal rights.  Moreover, all of them have to be incessantly reporting in person their proceedings to the larger elected soviet, or its standing executive committee, from which they have received their appointment.  From one

[1] The *New English Dictionary* gives the following meanings : *Dictator*—" A ruler or governor whose word is law ; an absolute ruler of a state . . . a person exercising absolute authority of any kind or in any sphere ; one who authoritatively prescribes a course of action or dictates what is to be done ". *Dictatorship*—" The office or dignity of a dictator ".

" A dictatorship is the most natural government for seasons of extraordinary peril, when there appears a man fit to wield it " (Arnold's *History of Rome*, vol. i. p. 446, 1838).

[2] It may be added that even the Ogpu was not governed by the will of a single person.  It was a commission of persons, appointed annually by the USSR Sovnarkom (or Cabinet).  Its last president was reported to be somewhat infirm, who, far from being even as much of a personal influence as his predecessor Djerdjinsky, was reported to leave the control rather too much to the other members of the commission.  Its practice was never to condemn people to death, exile or imprisonment without formal trial by a collegium of three judges ; and even then the sentences had to be confirmed by the commission as a whole, whilst clemency could always be exercised by a decision of the Central Executive Committee (TSIK) of the All-Union Congress of Soviets.  The fact that the Ogpu trials, and all its other proceedings, were behind closed doors—like the British proceedings against spies in war-time—may be abhorrent to us, but is not relevant to the question of whether or not it was in the nature of a dictatorship, in the strict sense of government by a single person.  We refer to this in Chapter VII. in Part II., " The Liquidation of the Landlord and the Capitalist "

end of the hierarchy to the other, the members of every council
or committee, including its president, can always be " recalled "
without notice, by a resolution passed by the body (or at a
meeting of the electorate) to which they owe their office.
At any moment, therefore, anyone taking executive action may
find himself summarily superseded by his collectively chosen
successor.

And if we pass from the soviet hierarchy, with all its tiers of
councils, and its innumerable proliferations of committees, and
commissions, and People's Commissars, and other executive
officers—which collectively exercise the supreme authority in the
state—to the semi-autonomous hierarchies finally subject to this
supreme authority, whether they are composed of trade unions
or of consumers' cooperatives, or of manufacturing artels or
collective farms, or of cooperative hunters or fishermen, we find,
as we have shown, always the same pattern of organisation.
Nowhere, in all this vast range of usually autonomous, but finally
subordinate authorities, do we discover anything involving or
implying government by the will of a single person. On the
contrary, there is everywhere elaborate provision, not only for
collegiate decision, but also, whether by popular election or by
appointment for a given term, or by the universal right to recall,
for collective control of each individual executant. Thus, so
far as the legally constituted legislative, judicial and executive
authorities of the state are concerned, at any stage in the hierarchy, or in any branch of administration, it would, we think,
be difficult for any candid student to maintain that the USSR
is, at any point, governed by the will of a single person—that is
to say, by a dictator.

### Is the Party a Dictator?

But, admittedly, the administration is controlled, to an
extent which it is impossible to measure, but which it would be
hard to exaggerate, by the Communist Party, with its two or
three millions of members. On this point there is complete
frankness. " In the Soviet Union," Stalin has said and written,
" in the land where the dictatorship of the proletariat is in force,
no important political or organisational problem is ever decided
by our soviets and other mass organisations, without directives

from our Party.  In this sense, we may say that the dictatorship
of the proletariat is substantially the dictatorship of the Party,
as the force which effectively guides the proletariat." [1]  [How
the Bolsheviks do love the word dictatorship !]  It must, however, be noted that the control of the Party over the administration is not manifested in any commands enforceable by law on the
ordinary citizen.  The Party is outside the constitution.  Neither
the Party nor its supreme body can, *of itself*, add to or alter the
laws binding on the ordinary citizens or residents of the USSR. [2]
The Party can, by itself, do no more than " issue directives "—
that is, give instructions—*to its own members*, as to the general
lines on which they should exercise the powers with which the law,
or their lawful appointment to particular offices, has endowed
them.  The Party members, thus directed, can act only by persuasion—persuasion of their colleagues in the various presidiums,
committees, commissions and soviets in and through which, as we
have seen, the authority over the citizens at large is actually
exercised.  The 50 or 60 per cent of the Party members who
continue to work at the bench or in the mine can do no more
than use their powers of persuasion on the ten or twenty times
more numerous non-Party workers among whom they pass
their lives.  By long years of training and organisation this
Party membership exercises a corporate intellectual influence on
the mass of the population which is of incalculable potency.  But
the term dictatorship is surely a misnomer for this untiring
corporate inspiration, evocation and formulation of a General
Will among so huge a population.  For it is, as we have seen, the
people themselves, and not only the Party members, who are
incessantly called upon to participate personally in the decisions,
not merely by expressing opinions about them in the innumerable
popular meetings ; not merely by voting for or against their

---

[1] *Leninism*, by J. Stalin, vol. i., 1928, p. 33.

[2] Presumably this is the reason why, as already indicated, specially important
" directives " to the Party membership which are in the nature of decrees or
laws, to be obeyed also by the non-Party mass, though emanating from the
Central Committee of the Communist Party, bear the signature (in addition to
that of Stalin) of Kalinin, signifying the concurrence of the Central Executive
Committee (TSIK) of the All-Union Congress of Soviets ; or that of Molotov,
expressing the concurrence of the USSR Sovnarkom, each of which bodies
can constitutionally enact new laws, subject to their subsequent ratification by
the All-Union Congress of Soviets and its two-chambered Central Executive
Committee.

exponents at the recurring elections; but actually by individually sharing in their operation.

## *Is Stalin a Dictator?*

Sometimes it is asserted that, whereas the form may be otherwise, the fact is that, whilst the Communist Party controls the whole administration, the Party itself, and thus indirectly the whole state, is governed by the will of a single person, Josef Stalin.

First let it be noted that, unlike Mussolini, Hitler and other modern dictators, Stalin is not invested by law with any authority over his fellow-citizens, and not even over the members of the Party to which he belongs. He has not even the extensive power which the Congress of the United States has temporarily conferred upon President Roosevelt, or that which the American Constitution entrusts for four years to every successive president. So far as grade or dignity is concerned, Stalin is in no sense the highest official in the USSR, or even in the Communist Party. He is not, and has never been, President of the Presidium of the Central Executive Committee of the All-Union Congress of Soviets—a place long held by Sverdlov and now by Kalinin, who is commonly treated as the President of the USSR. He is not (as Lenin was) the President of the Sovnarkom of the RSFSR, the dominant member of the Federation; or of the USSR itself, the place now held by Molotov, who may be taken to correspond to the Prime Minister of a parliamentary democracy. He is not even a People's Commissar, or member of the Cabinet, either of the USSR or of any of the constituent republics. Until 1934 [1] he held no other office in the machinery of the constitution than that, since 1930 only, of membership (one among ten) of the Committee of Labour and Defence (STO). Even in the Communist Party, he is not the president of the Central Committee of the Party, who may be deemed the highest placed member; indeed, he is not even the president of the presidium of this Central Committee. He is, in fact, only the General Secretary of the Party, receiving his salary from the Party funds and holding his office by appointment by the Party Central Committee, and,

---

[1] In 1934 he was elected a member of the presidium of the Central Executive Committee (TSIK).

as such, also a member (one among nine) of its most important subcommittee, the Politbureau.[1]

If we are invited to believe that Stalin is, in effect, a dictator, we may enquire whether he does, in fact, act in the way that dictators have usually acted ?

We have given particular attention to this point, collecting all the available evidence, and noting carefully the inferences to be drawn from the experience of the past eight years (1926–1934). We do not think that the Party is governed by the will of a single person ; or that Stalin is the sort of person to claim or desire such a position.   He has himself very explicitly denied any such personal dictatorship in terms which, whether or not he is credited with sincerity, certainly accord with our own impression of the facts.

In the carefully revised and entirely authentic report of an interview in 1932, we find the interviewer (Emil Ludwig) putting the following question :  " Placed around the table at which we are now seated there are sixteen chairs.  Abroad it is known, on the one hand, that the USSR is a country in which everything is supposed to be decided by collegiums ; but, on the other hand, it is known that everything is decided by individual persons.  Who really decides ? "   Stalin's reply was emphatic and explicit. He said :  " No ; single persons cannot decide.  The decisions of

---

[1] He is also a member of the Executive Committee of the Third International (Comintern), which is, like the Communist Party of the USSR, formally outside the state constitution.

A very critical, and even unfriendly, biographer gives the following characterisation of him :  " Stalin does not seek honours.  He loathes pomp.  He is averse to public displays.  He could have all the nominal regalia in the chest of a great state.  But he prefers the background. . . . He is the perfect inheritor of the individual Lenin paternalism.  No other associate of Lenin was endowed with that characteristic.  Stalin is the stern father of a family, the dogmatic pastor of a flock.  He is a boss with this difference :  his power is not used for personal aggrandisement.  Moreover, he is a boss with an education.  Notwithstanding general impressions, Stalin is a widely informed and well-read person. He lacks culture, but he absorbs knowledge.  He is rough towards his enemies but he learns from them " (*Stalin : a Biography*, by Isaac Don Levine, 1929, pp. 248–249).

An American newspaper correspondent, who has watched both Stalin and the soviet administration in Moscow for the past decade, lately wrote as follows : " Somebody said to me the other day—'Stalin is like a mountain with a head on it.  He cannot be moved.  But he thinks.'  His power and influence are greater now than ever, which is saying a great deal.  He inspires the Party with his will-power and calm.  Individuals in contact with him admire his capacity to listen and his skill in improving on the suggestions and drafts of highly intelligent subordinates.  There is no doubt that his determination and wisdom have been important assets in the struggles of the last few years " (Louis Fischer, in *The Nation*, August 9, 1933).

single persons are always, or nearly always, one-sided decisions. In every collegium, in every collective body, there are people whose opinion must be reckoned with. From the experience of three revolutions we know that, approximately, out of every 100 decisions made by single persons, that have not been tested and corrected collectively, 90 are one-sided. In our leading body, the Central Committee of our Party, which guides all our soviet and party organisations, there are about 70 members. Among these members of the Central Committee there are to be found the best of our industrial leaders, the best of our cooperative leaders, the best organisers of distribution, our best military men, our best propagandists and agitators, our best experts on soviet farms, on collective farms, on individual peasant agriculture, our best experts on the nationalities inhabiting the Soviet Union, and on national policy. In this areopagus is concentrated the wisdom of the Party. Everyone is able to contribute his experience. Were it otherwise, if decisions had been taken by individuals, we should have committed very serious mistakes in our work. But since everyone is able to correct the errors of individual persons, and since we pay heed to such corrections, we arrive at more or less correct decisions." [1]

This reasoned answer by Stalin himself puts the matter on the right basis. The Communist Party in the USSR has adopted for its own organisation the pattern which we have described as common throughout the whole soviet constitution. In this pattern individual dictatorship has no place. Personal decisions are distrusted, and elaborately guarded against. In order to avoid the mistakes due to bias, anger, jealousy, vanity and other distempers, from which no person is, at all times, entirely free or on his guard, it is desirable that the individual will should always be controlled by the necessity of gaining the assent of colleagues of equal grade, who have candidly discussed the matter, and who have to make themselves jointly responsible for the decision.

We find confirmation of this inference in Stalin's explicit description of how he acted in a remarkable case. He has, in fact, frequently pointed out that he does no more than carry out the decisions of the Central Committee of the Communist Party. Thus, in describing his momentous article known as " Dizzy with

[1] *An Interview with the German Author, Emil Ludwig*, by J. Stalin, Moscow, 1932, pp. 5, 6.

Success ", he expressly states that this was written on " the well-known decision of the Central Committee regarding the ' Fight against Distortions of the Party Line ' in the collective farm movement. . . ." " In this connection ", he continues, " I recently received a number of letters from comrades, collective farmers, calling upon me to reply to the questions contained in them. It was my duty to reply to the letters in private correspondence ; but that proved to be impossible, since more than half the letters received did not have the addresses of the writers (they forgot to send their addresses). Nevertheless the questions raised in these letters are of tremendous political interest to all our comrades. . . . In view of this I found myself faced with the necessity of replying to the comrades in an open letter, *i.e.* in the press. . . . *I did this all the more willingly since I had a direct decision of the Central Committee to this purpose.*" We cannot imagine the contemporary " dictators " of Italy, Hungary, Germany and now (1935) the United States—or even the Prime Minister of the United Kingdom or France—seeking the instructions of his Cabinet—as to how he should deal with letters which he could not answer individually. But Stalin goes further. He gives the reason for such collegiate decision. He points out that there is a " real danger " attendant on the personal " decreeing by individual representatives of the Party in this or that corner of our vast country. I have in mind not only local functionaries, but even certain regional committee members, and even certain members of the Central Committee, a practice which Lenin had stigmatised as communist conceit. " The Central Committee of the Party ", he said, " realised this danger, and did not delay intervening, *instructing Stalin to warn the erring comrades in an article* on the collective farm movement. Some people believe that the article ' Dizzy with Success ' is the result of the personal initiative of Stalin. That is nonsense. Our Central Committee does not exist in order to permit the personal initiative of anybody, whoever it may be, in matters of this kind. It was a reconnaissance on the part of the Central Committee. And when the depth and seriousness of the errors were established, the Central Committee did not hesitate to strike against these errors with the full force of its authority, and accordingly issued its famous decision of March 15, 1930." [1]

[1] *Leninism*, by Josef Stalin, vol. ii. pp. 294-295.

The plain truth is that, surveying the administration of the
USSR during the past decade, under the alleged dictatorship
of Stalin, the principal decisions have manifested neither the
promptitude nor the timeliness, nor yet the fearless obstinacy that
have often been claimed as the merits of a dictatorship.  On the
contrary, the action of the Party has frequently been taken after
consideration so prolonged, and as the outcome of discussion sometimes so heated and embittered, as to bear upon their formulation
the marks of hesitancy and lack of assurance.  More than once,
their adoption has been delayed to a degree that has militated
against their success ;  and, far from having been obstinately and
ruthlessly carried out, the execution has often been marked by a
succession of orders each contradicting its predecessor, and none
of them pretending to completeness or finality.  Whether we take
the First Five-Year Plan, or the determination to make universal
the collective farms ;  the frantic drive towards " self-sufficiency "
in the equipment of the heavy industries, and in every kind of
machine-making, or the complete " liquidation of the kulaks as a
class ", we see nothing characteristic of government by the will of
a single person.  On the contrary, these policies have borne, in
the manner of their adoption and in the style of their formulation,
the stigmata of committee control.  If the USSR during the past
eight or ten years has been under a dictatorship, the dictator has
surely been an inefficient one !  He has often acted neither
promptly nor at the right moment ;  his execution has been
vacillating and lacking in ruthless completeness.[1]  If we had to

[1] It is not easy to get hold of copies of the pamphlets surreptitiously
circulated in opposition to the present government of the USSR, which is
personified in the alleged dictatorship of Stalin.  One of the latest is described
as entitled *The Letter of Eighteen Bolsheviks* and as representing the combined
opposition to the dictatorship of both " right " and " left " deviationists.  The
specific accusations are reported as relative, not so much to the manner in which
policies are framed, or to their origin in a personal will, as to the policies themselves, which are now alleged to have been faulty on the ground that they have
failed !  These policies were (a) the stifling of the activities of the Comintern,
so that no world revolution has occurred ;  (b) the confused and vacillating
execution of the faulty Five-Year Plan ;  (c) the ruinous failure of so many of the
collective farms ;  (d) the weak half-measures adopted towards the kulaks ;
(e) the making of enemies, not only among the peasants and intelligentsia, but
also within the inner governing circle, by failing to get them to combine on
policy !

It will be seen that these criticisms of the USSR Government are exactly
parallel in substance and in form with those that are made by a Parliamentary
opposition to the policy of a Prime Minister in a parliamentary democracy.
They do not reveal anything peculiar to a dictatorship as such.

judge him by the actions taken in his name, Stalin has had many of the defects from which, by his very nature, a dictator is free. In short, the government of the USSR during the past decade has been clearly no better than that of a committee. Our inference is that it has been, in fact, the very opposite of a dictatorship. It has been, as it still is, government by whole series of committees.

This does not mean, of course, that the interminable series of committees, which is the characteristic feature of the USSR Government, have no leaders ; nor need it be doubted that among these leaders the most influential, both within the Kremlin and without, is now Stalin himself. But so far as we have been able to ascertain, his leadership is not that of a dictator. We are glad to quote an illustrative example of Stalin's administration, as described by an able American resident of Moscow : " Let me give a brief example of how Stalin functions. I saw him preside at a small committee meeting, deciding a matter on which I had brought a complaint. He summoned to the office all the persons concerned in the matter, but when we arrived we found ourselves meeting not only with Stalin, but also with Voroshilov and Kaganovich. Stalin sat down, not at the head of the table, but informally placed where he could see the faces of all. He opened the talk with a plain, direct question, repeating the complaint in one sentence, and asking the man complained against : ' Why was it necessary to do this ? '

" After this, he said less than anyone. An occasional phrase, a word without pressure ; even his questions were less demands for answers than interjections guiding the speaker's thought. But how swiftly everything was revealed, all our hopes, egotisms, conflicts, all the things we had been doing to each other. The essential nature of men I had known for years, and of others I met for the first time, came out sharply, more clearly than I had ever seen them, yet without prejudice. Each of them had to cooperate, to be taken account of in a problem ; the job we must do, and its direction became clear.

" I was hardly conscious of the part played by Stalin in helping us to reach a decision. I thought of him rather as someone superlatively easy to explain things to, who got one's meaning half through a sentence, and brought it all out very quickly. When everything became clear, and not a moment sooner or later,

Stalin turned to the others : ' Well ? ' A word from one, a phrase
from another, together accomplished a sentence. Nods—it was
unanimous. It seemed we had all decided, simultaneously,
unanimously. That is Stalin's method and greatness. He is
supreme analyst of situations, personalities, tendencies. Through
his analysis he is supreme combiner of many wills." [1]

There is, in fact, a consensus of opinion, among those who have
watched Stalin's action in administration, that this is not at all
characteristic of a dictator. It is rather that of a shrewd and
definitely skilful manager facing a succession of stupendous
problems which have to be grappled with.[2] He is not conceited
enough to imagine that he has, within his own knowledge and
judgment, any completely perfect plan for surmounting the
difficulties. None of the colleagues seated round the committee
table, as he realises, has such a plan. He does not attempt to bully
the committee. He does not even drive them. Imperturbably
he listens to the endless discussion, picking up something from each
speaker, and gradually combining every relevant consideration
in the most promising conclusion then and there possible. At
the end of the meeting, or at a subsequent one—for the discussions are often adjourned from day to day—he will lay before his
colleagues a plan uniting the valuable suggestions of all the other
proposals, as qualified by all the criticisms ; and it will seem to
his colleagues, as it does to himself, that this is *the* plan to be
adopted. When it is put in operation, all sorts of unforeseen
difficulties reveal themselves, for no plan can be free from shortcomings and defects. The difficulties give rise to further discussions and to successive modifications, none of which achieves

---

[1] *Dictatorship and Democracy in the Soviet Union*, by Anna Louise Strong,
New York, 1934, p. 17.

[2] Mussolini describes very differently his own statutory dictatorship. He
once said : " There is a fable which describes me as a good dictator but always
surrounded by evil counsellors to whose mysterious and malign influence I
submit. All that is more than fantastic : it is idiotic. Considerably long
experience goes to demonstrate that I am an individual absolutely refractory
to outside pressure of any kind. My decisions come to maturity often in the
night—in the solitude of my spirit and in the solitude of my rather arid (because
practically non-social) personal life. Those who are the ' evil counsellors of
the good tyrant ' are the five or six people who come each morning to make
their daily report, so that I may be informed of all that's happening in Italy.
After they have made their reports, which rarely takes more than half an hour,
they go away " (*Through Fascism to World Power*, by Ion S. Munro, 1935,
p. 405).

perfect success. Is not this very much how administration is carried on in every country in the world, whatever may be its constitution ? The "endless adventure of governing men" can never be other than a series of imperfect expedients, for which, even taking into account all past experience and all political science, there is, in the end, an inevitable resort to empirical "trial and error".

At this point it is necessary to observe that, although Stalin is, by the constitution, not in the least a dictator, having no power of command, and although he appears to be free from any desire to act as a dictator, and does not do so, he may be thought to have become irremovable from his position of supreme leadership of the Party, and therefore of the government. Why is this ? We find the answer in the deliberate exploitation by the governing junta of the emotion of hero-worship, of the traditional reverence of the Russian people for a personal autocrat. This was seen in the popular elevation of Lenin, notably after his death, to the status of saint or prophet, virtually canonised in the sleeping figure in the sombre marble mausoleum in Moscow's Red Square, where he is now, to all intents and purposes, worshipped by the adoring millions of workers and peasants who daily pass before him. Lenin's works have become "Holy Writ", which may be interpreted, but which it is impermissible to confute. After Lenin's death, it was agreed that his place could never be filled. But some new personality had to be produced for the hundred and sixty millions to revere. There presently ensued a tacit understanding among the junta that Stalin should be "boosted" as the supreme leader of the proletariat, the Party and the state.[1] His portrait and his bust were accordingly distributed by tens of thousands, and they are now everywhere publicly displayed along with those of Marx and Lenin. Scarcely a speech is made, or a conference held, without a naïve—some would say a fulsome— reference to "Comrade Stalin" as the great leader of the people.

---

[1] Trotsky relates in elaborate detail what he describes as the intrigues aiming at his own exclusion from among those who, at public meetings, were given popular honours as leaders. Presently, he continues, "then the first place began to be given to Stalin. If the chairman was not clever enough to guess what was required of him, he was invariably corrected in the newspapers. . . . It was as the supreme expression of the mediocrity of the apparatus that Stalin himself rose to his position" (*My Life*, by Leon Trotsky, 1930, pp. 499, 501).

Let us give, as one among the multitude of such expressions of whole-hearted reverence and loyalty, part of the message to Stalin from the Fifteenth Anniversary Celebration of the Leninist League of Young Communists (the five million Comsomols). " In our greetings to you we wish to express the warm love and profound respect for you, our teacher and leader, cherished in the minds and hearts of the Leninist Comsomols and the entire youth of our country. . . . We give you, beloved friend, teacher and leader, the word of young Bolsheviks to continue as an unshakable shock-detachment in the struggle for a classless socialist society. We swear to stimulate the creative energy and enthusiasm of the youth for the mastery of technique and science and in the struggle for Bolshevik collective farms and for a prosperous collective farm life. We swear to hold high the banner of Leninist internationalism, fearlessly to fight for the elimination of exploitation of man by man, for the world proletarian revolution.

" We swear to continue to be the most devoted aids to our beloved Party. We swear with even more determination to strengthen our proletarian dictatorship, to strengthen the defence of the socialist fatherland, to train hundreds of thousands of new exemplary fighters, super-sharp-shooters, fearless aviators, daring sailors, tank operators and artillery corps, who will master their military technique to perfection. We swear that we shall work to make the glorious traditions of Bolshevism part of our flesh and blood. We swear to be worthy sons and daughters of the Communist Party. The Leninist Comsomol takes pride in the fact that under the banner of Lenin, the toiling youth of the country which is building socialism has the good fortune freely to live, fight and triumph together with you and under your leadership." [1]

It seems to us that a national leader so persistently boosted, and so generally admired, has, in fact, become irremovable against his will, so long as his health lasts, without a catastrophic break-up of the whole administration. Chosen originally because he was thought more stable in judgment than Trotsky, who might, it was felt, precipitate the state into war, Stalin is now universally considered to have justified his leadership by success; first in overcoming the very real difficulties of 1925 ; then in surmounting the obstacle of the peasant recalcitrance in 1930–1933 ; and finally

[1] *Moscow Daily News*, November 1, 1933.

in the successive triumphs of the Five-Year Plan. For him to be dismissed from office, or expelled from the Party, as Trotsky and so many others have been, could not be explained to the people. He will therefore remain in his great position of leadership so long as he wishes to do so. What will happen when he dies or voluntarily retires is a baffling question. For it is a unique feature in Soviet Communism that popular recognition of pre-eminent leadership has, so far, not attached itself to any one office. Lenin, whose personal influence became overwhelmingly powerful, was President of the Sovnarkom (Cabinet) of the RSFSR, or, as we should say, Prime Minister. On his death, Rykov became President of the Sovnarkom of the USSR, to be followed by Molotov, but neither succeeded to the position of leader. Stalin, who had been People's Commissar for Nationalities and subsequently President of the Commissariat for Workers' and Peasants' Inspection, had relinquished these offices on being appointed General Secretary of the Communist Party. It is Stalin who has, since 1927, " had all the limelight ". No one can predict the office which will be held by the man who may succeed to Stalin's popularity ; or whether the policy of " boosting " a national leader will continue to be thought necessary when Soviet Communism is deemed to be completely established. For the moment the other dominant personalities seem to be L. M. Kaganovich, one of the Assistant Secretaries of the Communist Party of the USSR and Secretary of the Party in Moscow, in 1935 appointed People's Commissar of Railways ; Molotov, the President of the USSR Sovnarkom ; and Voroshilov, the popular People's Commissar of Defence.

### The Dictatorship of the Proletariat

We have yet to discuss the most ambiguous of so-called dictatorships, the " dictatorship of the proletariat ". This high-sounding phrase, used more than once by Karl Marx,[1] and re-

---

[1] See, for instance, his statement of 1852 : " What I added (to the conception of the existence of the class struggle) was to prove : (1) that the existence of classes is only bound up with certain historical struggles in the development of production ; (2) that the class struggle necessarily leads to the dictatorship of the proletariat ; (3) that this dictatorship is itself only a transition to the ultimate abolition of all classes and to a society without classes " (Marx to Weydemeyer, March 12, 1852 ; see Beer's article in *Labour Monthly*, July 1922).

It may be helpful, in the interpretation, to consider what, in the view of Marx, was the opposite of the dictatorship of the proletariat. This was

peatedly and vehemently endorsed by Lenin, has been accepted by those in authority as an official designation of the constitution of the USSR, in preference to any reference to the leadership of the Communist Party or to the early slogan of " All Power to the Soviets ". We frankly confess that we do not understand what was or is meant by this phrase. As rendered in English it seems to mean a dictatorship exercised *by* the proletariat, *over* the community as a whole. But if the terms are to be taken literally, this is the union of two words which contradict each other. Dictatorship, as government by the will of a single person, cannot be government by the will of an immense class of persons. Moreover, if by the proletariat is meant the mass of the population dependent on their daily earnings, or as Marx frequently meant, the whole of the workers engaged in industrial production for wages, the dictatorship of the proletariat would, in highly developed capitalist societies like Great Britain, where three-quarters of all men of working age are wage-earners, mean no more than the rule of an immense majority over a minority. Why, then, should it be termed a dictatorship ?

We do not pretend to any competence in determining what Marx may have meant by the dictatorship of the proletariat. More relevant is what Lenin meant by the phrase when he made it one of the cardinal principles of his revolutionary activity. This meaning we can best discover in the successive stages leading up to the first formulation of the constitution in 1918, and to its subsequent elaboration.

Lenin had long held that the revolution in Russia could never be carried out by, literally, the masses of the people. He differed profoundly from both the rival sects of revolutionaries, the Social Revolutionaries and the Mensheviks, as to the correct interpretation of the Revolution of February 1917, which they accepted as a " bourgeois " revolution, but which he insisted on making into a socialist revolution. But Lenin never believed that the actual transformations of social structure involved in the socialist revolution that he desired could be effected either by the hordes of peasants, whether still grouped in villages, or

emphatically not democracy in any of its meanings, but the " dictatorship of the bourgeoisie ". One or other dictatorship was, Marx thought, inevitable, during the transition stage, which might last for a whole generation. See the useful book *Towards the Understanding of Karl Marx*, by Professor Sidney Hook, 1933, pp. 250-269.

driven off their little holdings ; or even by a mass movement in the cities. In Lenin's view, the socialist revolution could be carried into effect only by the long-continued efforts of a relatively small, highly disciplined and absolutely united party of professional revolutionists (which became the Communist Party), acting persistently on the minds of what he called the proletariat, by which he always meant the manual-working wage-earners in the factory and the mine, in mere alliance with the vastly more numerous, but for this purpose inert, peasantry, whether poor, middling or relatively well-to-do.

Thus Lenin expected and meant the social transformation itself to be, like all social changes, designed and promulgated by a minority, and even by only a small minority of the whole people. On the other hand, he had in view no such personal *coup d'état* as Louis Napoleon perpetrated in December 1851. He steadfastly refused to countenance any attempt at an overthrow of the Kerensky Government until he was convinced that an actual majority of the manual-working wage-earners in the factories of Leningrad and Moscow had become converted to the support of the growing Bolshevik Party. It may, indeed, be said that all three stages of the Russian revolution, and, most of all, that of October 1917, enjoyed wide popular support, whilst the last was effected by a widespread upheaval among the city populations, supported by the mass of the disintegrating soldiery, and willingly acquiesced in by such of the peasantry as became aware of what was happening. The Russian revolution may therefore fairly be described as democratic rather than dictatorial.

But Lenin had long pondered over what Marx had come to realise after 1848, that it was much more difficult to maintain a revolutionary government than to put it into office. Whilst believing firmly in government by the people, much more firmly and more sincerely than most parliamentary democrats of the time, Lenin knew that the revolutionary enthusiasm of the mass of the people quickly subsides. The force of old habits of thought is rapidly reasserted. Long before the new government could possibly effect any improvement in material conditions, there must inevitably be an ebbing of the tide. Reactionaries within the city and without would promptly influence the mob, as well as the timid *petite bourgeoisie*, to sweep away a government which had brought only disillusionment. Hence it was indispensable

that, if the revolution was to be maintained, there should be no
immediate resort to popular election of the executive government.
The members of the Constituent Assembly were accordingly
promptly sent about their business, and all attempts to maintain
their position were drastically suppressed by force. Pending
the formulation of a constitution, Lenin and his colleagues
undoubtedly ruled the state as an autocratic junta, ruthlessly
suppressing all opposition, irrespective of the momentary popular
feeling, whatever it was. The peasants, whom it was impracticable to consult, were induced to acquiesce by being left free to
continue the anarchic seizure of the landlords' estates, and their
redistribution among all those belonging to the village. To
please the soldiery as well as the urban proletariat, the war was
brought to an end as speedily as possible, on whatever terms
could be obtained from the triumphant German army. Everything, even popular control, was temporarily sacrificed to the
maintenance in power of an executive resolute enough, and strong
enough, to prevent a popular reaction. This was the heyday of
what had been foreseen as " the dictatorship of the proletariat ".
Lenin was quite frank about it. " The essence of dictatorship ", he had written, " is to be found in the organisation and
discipline of the workers' vanguard, as the only leader of the
proletariat. The purpose of the dictatorship is to establish
socialism, to put an end to the division of society into classes, to
make all the members of society workers, to make the exploitation
of one human being by another for ever impossible. This end
cannot be achieved at one stride. There will have to be a transitional period, a fairly long one, between capitalism and socialism.
The reorganisation of production is a difficult matter. Time is
requisite for the radical transformation of all departments of life.
Furthermore, the power of custom is immense ; people are
habituated to a petty-bourgeois and bourgeois economy, and will
only be induced to change their ways by a protracted and arduous
struggle. That was why Marx, too, spoke of a transitional period
between capitalism and socialism, a whole epoch of the dictatorship of the proletariat."[1] Nor was this authoritarian control of
the transition period to be in any sense partial or half-hearted.

[1] Lenin, *Works* ; Russian edition, vol. xvi. pp. 226-227 ; adopted by Stalin
in his " Problems of Leninism " in *Leninism*, by Josef Stalin, Russian edition,
1926 ; English translation, 1928, vol. i. p. 27.

What Lenin meant by the oft-quoted phrase is clear. " The dictatorship of the proletariat ", he said, " is a resolute, persistent struggle, sanguinary and bloodless, violent and peaceful, military and economic, pedagogic and administrative, against the forces and traditions of the old society.   The force of habit of the millions and tens of millions is a formidable force." [1]

But this autocratic executive action of the transition period had nothing to do with the constitution, which was adopted for the RSFSR at the earliest possible moment.   Historical students habitually think of representative institutions, especially when based on popular election, as providing a check upon autocratic executive action.   But every politician knows that there is no more powerful bulwark of a government than representative institutions which provide it with popular support.   Lenin and his colleagues, whilst summarily dismissing the Constituent Assembly, actually hurried on the enactment of a constitution, deliberately as a means of strengthening the central executive authority.   For their purpose there was no need for the constitution to create a dictatorship.   Indeed, as enacted by the Fifth All-Russian Congress of Soviets on July 10, 1918, within nine months from the seizure of power, this Fundamental Law contained no trace of anything that could possibly be termed a dictatorship.   It vested " all power in the soviets ", directly chosen by the people.   Each soviet freely chose its delegates to the district and provincial councils, and these finally to a national assembly, which appointed not only the Cabinet of Ministers but also a standing Central Executive Committee and its presidium to control them.   And though the city populations were given proportionately larger representation than the peasantry—at about twice the rate [2]—the numerical preponder-

---

[1] *The Infantile Disease of Leftism in Communism*, by N. Lenin (1920); English edition, 1934.   Marx had clearly predicted a prolonged transition period. " Between the capitalist and communist systems of society lies the period of the revolutionary transformation of one into the other.   This corresponds to a political transition period, whose state can be nothing else but the revolutionary dictatorship of the proletariat " (from Marx's " Critical Analysis of the Gotha Programme of the German Social Democratic Party ", translated in *Towards the Understanding of Karl Marx*, by Sidney Hook, 1933, p. 255).

[2] This habitual numerical over-representation of the cities in the USSR is usually over-stated.   The representation of the cities is at so many per thousand *electors*.   That of the rural districts is at so many per thousand *population*, only about half of whom are over eighteen, and qualified as electors.   We have analysed elsewhere the number and nature of the deprived categories excluded

ance of the rural population was so enormous—more than four times that of the cities—that the delegates deriving their mandates ultimately from the village soviets at all times constituted the majority of the All-Union Congress of Soviets.

It is difficult to assert that the system of popular soviets and indirect election was deliberately chosen by Lenin or anyone else. This was the form into which representative institutions inevitably flowed in the Petrograd and Moscow of 1917, whilst the peasantry knew no other. But we may well believe that Lenin was alive to the fact that, whilst this " soviet system " satisfied the popular aspirations and provided for the constitution an invaluable basis of direct election on the widest known franchise, this same system gave the national executive the necessary protection against being swept away by a temporary wave of popular feeling. The soviet system left no room for a referendum, or even for a parliamentary general election. It was the reverse of government by the mob ! The very multiplication into millions of the election meetings, and the interpolation of tier upon tier of councils, gave the fullest opportunity for the persuasive action of the highly disciplined companionship into which the Bolshevik party was shaped. We may say that, if the " dictatorship of the proletariat " continued after 1918 to be indispensable for the maintenance of the revolutionary government, as was undoubtedly thought to be the case, it was perpetuated, not in the representative structure, which might fairly claim to be a particular species of popular constitution, in fact just as truly " democratic " as the parliamentary government of Great Britain or the United States ; but in the actual use made by the executive, with the aid of the Communist Party, of the powers entrusted to it under the constitution. Any government, whatever the form of the constitution, can use the powers entrusted to it in a manner that people will term dictatorial. As democrats confess with shame, it is undeniable that governments professedly the most democratic, in countries enjoying the blessings of parliamentary government and universal suffrage, have, on occasions, in peace as in wartime, distinguished themselves by their drastic use of force, and even of physical violence, against their opponents, just like the

from the franchise—analogous, it may be suggested, to the exclusion of the women, the negroes, the paupers, the illiterate, the nomadic, and various other classes in this or that country counting itself civilised and democratic !

most dictatorial of the personal dictators that history records. Thus, if we must interpret the " dictatorship of the proletariat ", as exercised in the USSR since 1918, we might say that it is not in the constitutional structure, nor even in the working of the soviets and the ubiquitous representative system, that anything like autocracy or dictatorship is to be found, but rather in the activities that the constitution definitely authorises the executive to exercise.

### Is the USSR an Autocracy ?

How far, and in what sense, the habitual action of the executive government of the USSR is in the nature of autocracy we have now to examine.  A government is usually said to be an autocracy, or a dictatorship, if the chief authority enacts laws or issues decrees without submitting them beforehand to public discussion and criticism by the people themselves or their authorised representatives, in order to be guided by their decision.  This safeguard of debate can, of course, only be obtained in the case of fundamental or important legislation.  It would plainly be impracticable, in any populous country, to submit for public discussion the thousands of separate decisions that every government has to take from day to day throughout the year.  In the USSR, as we have seen, the amount of public discussion of government decisions, before they are finally made, is plainly very considerable.  From the trade union or cooperative society or village meetings, up to the frequent sessions of the Central Executive Committee (TSIK) and the biennial All-Union Congress of Soviets, the systematic discussion of public affairs, from one end of the USSR to the other, and in terms which are regularly communicated to the highest authorities, appears, to the citizen of the western world, simply endless.[1]  But, in addition, there are

---

[1] " Under what form shall social ownership be manifested—municipal, federal or voluntary cooperative ?  Which industries are better handled by state-appointed managers ?  Which by small groups of workers selecting their own management ?  What relations shall exist between various forms of socially owned production, between city and rural districts ?  What relative attention shall be given to each of a thousand factories, trades, localities ?  Over this daily stuff of government, discussion and struggle goes on ; and change and experiment. . . . Political life in rural districts starts around the use of the land.  Sixty peasants in council—the collective farm of a small village— meeting with the representatives of the township [(rayon) land] department, or the farm expert from the tractor station, to draw up their ' farm plan '. Number of households, of people, of horses, ploughs, tractors, extent and type of

occasions on which the highest legislative and executive authorities
will publicly call upon the whole population to help in the solution
of a difficult problem of government. We may cite two remarkable examples. In October 1925, after seven years' experience of
the great freedom in sex relations which the revolution had
inaugurated, when the proposals of the People's Commissar for
Justice for an amendment of the law as to marriage were brought
before the Central Executive Committee (TSIK), a heated controversy arose. What did this practically supreme legislature do ?
It resolved to submit the draft law, which excited so much
interest, for discussion by the whole people throughout the
length and breadth of the USSR. " The whole country ", we are
told, " was shaken to its depths by the question. In countless
discussion meetings—from gatherings of thousands of workers
in the large cities to the tiny debates in the peasant [village]
reading-rooms—the separate points of the new draft were threshed
out again and again. The People's Commissariat [for Justice]
received reports of more than 6000 meetings of this kind, but, of
course, the number of debates actually held was much larger.
The point about which the discussion chiefly revolved was the
question whether an unregistered, so-called ' factual ' marriage
should be placed in its legal consequences on an equality with
one that had been legally registered. . . . There were, in the
Soviet Union, some 80,000 to 100,000 couples whose ' marriages '
in no wise differed from those officially contracted, either in
substance or form, except in the absence of registration. . . . The
legal protection which the law provides in the case of registered
marriages—which is of particular importance to the wife—ought
certainly not to be withheld from the partners in these ' factual '
marriages. A number of arguments were arrayed against this

land, must be included. The plan must take account of the little community's
food and fodder needs, the past crop rotations, the marketable crop recommended by the State for their locality. Certain general directions come down
from the central Commissariat of Agriculture, filtered through the provincial
[oblast] land office, and adapted to their region ; a two per cent increase in
grain, or a rise in industrial crops is asked for. The sixty peasants in council
consider by what concrete means they will expand or rearrange their fields for
all these purposes ; discussion after discussion takes place all winter through
till the ' plan ' is accomplished. Consciously they are settling problems of
government on which country-wide, province-wide, nation-wide plans will be
issued. From this simple base all other tasks of government spring " (*Dictatorship and Democracy in the Soviet Union*, by Anna Louise Strong, New York,
1934, pp. 7-8).

view. . . . But the other additional provisions and changes in
the new code—the question of divorce, alimony and women's
property—were also fiercely contested . . . especially . . . the
provision of the new law that women's domestic work should be
placed on an equal footing with men's work. . . . The discussion
brought [to the Government] a flood of letters, largely from
working women, as is usually the case in such circumstances in
Russia. . . . The general discussion of the new marriage law
lasted a whole year : doubtless the first case in which a whole
people, a people of 160 millions, made a law for itself, not through
elected representatives [nor yet, we may add, by mere assent or
dissent to a finished law formally announced to them on refer-
endum], but by all expressing their opinion. And when, in
December 1926, the draft (revised in the light of the opinions
popularly expressed) was introduced for the second time in the
TSIK . . . the debate raged once more before it was finally
decided, and for the last time the various opinions clashed." The
new draft was adopted by a large majority, and came immediately
into force (on January 1, 1927).[1]

The popular discussion on the marriage law concerned a
matter in which the people's interest was probably more intense
than that of the legislators. We therefore take as a second
example a difficult problem of statesmanship, in which only
persons of trained and well-informed judgment could usefully
pronounce an opinion. We have already described in our section
on Collective Farms how the problem arose. The momentous
decision to solve the problem of the national food supply mainly
by what has been called the Second Agrarian Revolution—the
brigading of the millions of individual peasants into some hundreds
of thousands of collective farms, and the " liquidation of the
kulaks as a class "—was not taken until after more than two
years of public discussion and heated controversy, as well as
long-continued debate in the legislative bodies. Moreover, the
decision eventually arrived at, and announced by Stalin in 1928,
was not exactly any one of the proposals which had been put
forward at the outset of the debate in which the whole thinking
and reading population, and not merely the members of the
Communist Party, had been participating. It was itself the

[1] See the lengthy description in *Woman in Soviet Russia*, by Fannina W.
Halle, published in German in 1932, and in English in 1933, pp. 109-136.

outcome of the debate, combining what seemed to be the best features of several of the proposals with safeguards against the dangers which discussion had revealed. Our own conclusion is that, if by autocracy or dictatorship is meant government without prior discussion and debate, either by public opinion or in private session, the government of the USSR is, in that sense, actually less of an autocracy or a dictatorship than many a parliamentary cabinet.

### In whose Interest does the Government act ?

There is, however, yet another view of the much-debated phrase, the Dictatorship of the Proletariat, which must not be overlooked ; and which may well be thought to be wholly applicable to the government of the USSR from 1917 to 1927, and, in a wider sense, to that of the present day. It may be suspected that, when socialists or communists talk about the Dictatorship of the Proletariat, with some "dynamic passion" in "downing" a former ruling class, what they really mean is a government which, irrespective of its form, provides a strong and resolute executive, acting unhesitatingly in the interests of the manual-working wage-earning class. When such socialists or communists talk about the Dictatorship of the Bourgeoisie (or of the Capitalist), it is clearly not the form of the government that they have in mind, but merely its strong and resolute administration in the interests of the proprietary class. In the same sense, it is exactly accurate to describe the government of the USSR, at any rate from 1917 to 1927, as a Dictatorship of the Proletariat, meaning the urban or industrial manual-working wage-earners. Since 1928, that government may be deemed to have in view also the interests of the kolkhosniki, the owner-producers in agriculture who have joined together in collective farms. Perhaps the scope of the word proletariat is becoming enlarged, so that it now includes all those, whether mechanics or agriculturists, who will admittedly be qualified for citizenship of the future " classless state ".

### A New Social Form ?

We add a final comment. We have discussed, as a current controversy, the question whether the government of the USSR is a dictatorship or a democracy. But there is no more fertile source of error in sociology, as in any other science, than posing a question in the terms of ancient categories, or even of yesterday's definitions. Can we wisely limit our enquiries by such alternatives as " aristocracy, oligarchy and democracy " ; or "dictatorship versus democracy"? History records also theocracies, and various other " ideocracies ", in which the organised exponents of particular creeds or philosophic systems have, in effect, ruled communities, sometimes irrespective of their formal constitutions, merely by "keeping the conscience" of the influential citizens. This dominance may be exercised entirely by persuasion. The practical supremacy at various times of the Society of Jesus in more than one country was of this nature. The Communist Party of the USSR frankly accepts the designation of " keeper of the conscience of the proletariat ". Have we perhaps here a case —to use a barbarous term—of a " creedocracy " of a novel kind, inspiring a multiform democracy in which soviets and trade unions, cooperative societies and voluntary associations, provide for the personal participation in public affairs of an unprecedented proportion of the entire adult population ? The Union of Soviet Socialist Republics does not consist of a government and a people confronting each other, as all other great societies have hitherto been. It is a highly integrated social organisation in which, over a vast area, each individual man, woman or youth is expected to participate in three separate capacities : as a citizen, as a producer, and as a consumer ; to which should be added membership of one or more voluntary organisations intent on bettering the life of the community. Meanwhile, leadership is carried on by a new profession, organised, like other professions, as a voluntarily enlisted and self-governing unit ; the only part of the constitution of Soviet Communism, by the way, that has no foundation in any statute. In short, the USSR is a government instrumented by all the adult inhabitants, organised in a varied array of collectives, having their several distinct functions, and among them carrying on, with a strangely new " political economy ", nearly the whole wealth production of the country. And when, in addition, we find them evolving a systematic philosophy and a new code of conduct, based upon a novel conception of man's relation to the universe and man's duty to man, we seem to be dealing with something much greater than a constitution. We have, indeed, to ask whether the world may not be witnessing in the USSR the emergence of a new civilisation. But before we can adequately deal with this question, in the final pages of this book, we have first to study the social institutions in action, in order to discover, by an analysis of " social trends ", in what directions this huge population is moving.

# APPENDICES

## APPENDICES TO PART I

PAGE

I. DIAGRAM OF THE ADMINISTRATIVE STRUCTURE OF THE USSR, WITH EXPLANATORY TABLES . . . . . 457

II. DIAGRAM OF THE POLITICAL STRUCTURE OF THE USSR, WITH EXPLANATORY TABLES . . . . . . 461

III. THE DECLARATION OF THE CENTRAL EXECUTIVE COMMITTEE OF THE UNION OF SOVIET SOCIALIST REPUBLICS OF JULY 13, 1923 . . . . . . . . 462

IV. THE POWERS AND AUTHORISED FUNCTIONS OF THE VILLAGE SOVIET . . . . . . . . 465

V. THE SECTIONS AND COMMISSIONS OF THE CITY SOVIETS . 471

VI. NOTE RELATING TO THE COMMISSARIAT FOR WORKERS' AND PEASANTS' INSPECTION . . . . . . 474

VII. THE INTERNAL ORGANISATION OF THE NARKOMAT OF SOV-KHOSI . . . . . . . . 479

VIII. THE INTERNAL ORGANISATION OF THE NARKOMAT OF AGRI-CULTURE . . . . . . . . 485

IX. LIST OF THE 154 TRADE UNIONS AMONG WHICH THE MEMBER-SHIP OF THE 47 TRADE UNIONS OF 1931 WAS DISTRIBUTED IN 1934 . . . . . . . . 492

X. THE DUTIES AND FUNCTIONS OF THE FACTORY COMMITTEES 496

XI. THE COLLECTIVE AGREEMENT (KOL-DOGOVOR) OF THE FRAIS-ING-LATHE WORKS AT GORKI FOR THE YEAR 1933-1934 . 505

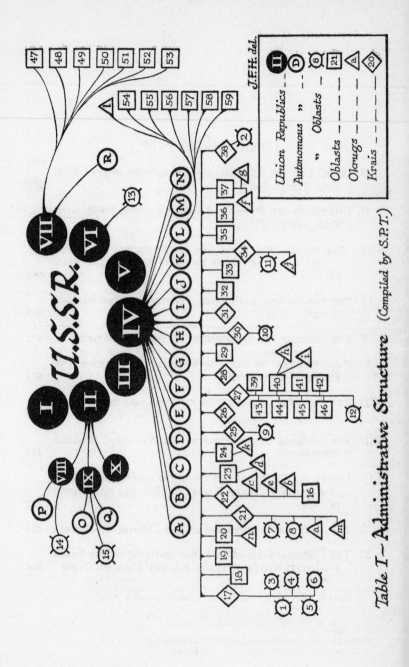

Table I — Administrative Structure (Compiled by S.P.T.)

# I

## Diagram of the Administrative Structure of the USSR

(Compiled by S.P.T. from the *Whole USSR*, 1931, *Ten years of the Constitution of the USSR*, 1933, and *Collections of Laws and Regulations*, 1934, 1935)

### TABLE I

#### Administrative Structure

Seven Union Republics, 3 Soviet Socialist Republics in Transcaucasia, 14 Autonomous Republics in the RSFSR, 3 Autonomous Republics in Transcaucasia, 1 Autonomous Republic in the Ukraine, 12 Autonomous Oblasts in the RSFSR, 1 Autonomous Oblast in Tadzhik and 2 Autonomous Oblasts in Transcaucasia, 11 Krais and 24 Oblasts in the RSFSR (including 8 Oblasts in the Far-Eastern Krai and 6 Oblasts in the Kazak Autonomous Republic), 7 Oblasts in the Ukraine and 14 Okrugs in the RSFSR.

Seven Union Republics—

| | | *Capital* |
|---|---|---|
| I. | The White Russian SSR · | Minsk |
| II. | The Transcaucasian SFSR | Tiflis |
| III. | The Turkoman SSR | Ashkhabat |
| IV. | The RSFSR | Moscow |
| V. | The Uzbek SSR | Samarkand (now Tashkent) |
| VI. | The Tadzhik SSR | Stalinbad |
| VII. | The Ukrainian SSR | Kharkov (now Kiev) |

Three Soviet Socialist Republics in Transcaucasia—

| | | |
|---|---|---|
| VIII. | The SSR of Azerbaijan | Baku |
| IX. | The SSR of Georgia | Tiflis |
| X. | The SSR of Armenia | Erivan |

Fourteen Autonomous Republics in the RSFSR—

| | | |
|---|---|---|
| A. | Daghestan | Makhach-Kala, January 20, 1921 |
| B. | Bashkir | Ufa, March 24, 1919 |
| C. | Buryat-Mongolian | Verkhneudinsk (now Ulan-Uda), June 4, 1923 |
| D. | Karelian | Petrozavodsk, July 27, 1923 |
| E. | Chuvash | Cheboksary, April 21, 1925 |
| F. | Kirghiz | Frunse, February 1926 |
| G. | Tartar | Kazan, May 27, 1920 |
| H. | Crimean | Simferopol, October 18, 1921 |
| I. | German Volga | Petrovsk (now Engels), July 19, 1923 |
| J. | Kazak | Alma-Ata, October 1924 |
| K. | Yakut | Yakutsk, April 20, 1922 |
| L. | Kara-Kalpak | Turtkul (now Nukus), May 11, 1925 |
| M. | Mordovsk | Saransk, December 20, 1934 |
| N. | Udmurtsk | Izhevsk, December 28, 1934 |

Three Autonomous Republics in the Transcaucasian SFSR—

| | | |
|---|---|---|
| O. | Abkhaz (by convention within Georgia SSR) | Sukhum |
| P. | Nakhichevan (within Azerbaijan SSR) | Nakhichevan |
| Q. | Adzharistan (within Georgia SSR) | Batum |

457

One Autonomous Republic in the Ukraine—

                                         *Capital*

    R. Moldavian                   Balta (now Tiraspol), October 12, 1924

Twelve Autonomous Oblasts in the RSFSR—

| | |
|---|---|
| 1. Kabardino-Balkarsk | Nalchik, January 1, 1921 |
| 2. Adygeisk | Krasnodar, July 27, 1922 |
| 3. Karachaevsk | Mikoyan-Shakhar, January 12, 1922 |
| 4. Chechen-Ingush | Grosny, September 20, 1923 |
| 5. North-Ossetinsk | Vladikavkaz (now Ordzhonikidze), July 7, 1924 |
| 6. Cherkess | Batalpashinsk (now Sulimov), July 27, 1922 |
| 7. Khakass | Abakan, 1930 |
| 8. Oirat | Ulala (now Oirat-Tura), June 1, 1922 |
| 9. Mariisk | Ioshkar-Ola, November 4, 1920 |
| 10. Kalmyk | Elista, November 4, 1920 |
| 11. Komi (Zyryan) | Syktyvkar, January 12, 1921 |
| 12. Jewish | Biro-Bidzhan, May 7, 1934 |

One Autonomous Oblast in the Tadzhik SSR—

    13. Gorno-Badakhshansk         Khorog

Two Autonomous Oblasts in Transcaucasia—

| | |
|---|---|
| 14. Nagorno-Karabakh | Stepanakert |
| 15. South Ossetin ' | Zkhinvali (now Stalinir) |

Eleven Krais and 12 Oblasts in RSFSR—

| | |
|---|---|
| 16. Chita Oblast | Chita |
| 17. North Caucasian Krai | Pyatigorsk |
| 18. Leningrad Oblast | Leningrad |
| 19. Moscow Oblast | Moscow |
| 20. Kalinin Oblast | Kalinin |
| 21. West Siberian Krai | Novosibirsk |
| 22. East Siberian Krai | Irkutsk |
| 23. Sverdlovsk Oblast | Sverdlovsk |
| 24. Chelyabinsk Oblast | Chelyabinsk |
| 25. Gorki Krai | Gorki |
| 26. Kirov Krai | Kirov |
| 27. Far-Eastern Krai | Khabarovsk |
| 28. Kuibyshev Krai | Kuibyshev [1] |
| 29. Orenburg Oblast | Orenburg |
| 30. Stalingrad Krai | Stalingrad |
| 31. Saratov Krai | Saratov |
| 32. Kursk Oblast | Kursk |
| 33. Voronezh Oblast | Voronezh |
| 34. Northern Krai | Arkhangel |
| 35. Western Oblast | Smolensk |
| 36. Ivanovo-Industrial Oblast | Ivanovo-Vosnessensk |
| 37. Obsko-Irtysh Oblast | Tumen' |
| 38. Asovo-Chernomorsky Krai | Rostov-Don |

Eight Oblasts in the Far-Eastern Krai—

| | |
|---|---|
| 39. Amur | Blagoveshchensk |
| 40. Kamchatka | Petropavlovsk |
| 41. Primorsk | Vladivostok |
| 42. Sakhalin | Alexandrovsk |
| 43. Khabarovsk | Khabarovsk |
| 44. Zeyisk | Rukhlovo |
| 45. Ussuriisk | Nicholsk-Ussuriisk |
| 46. Nizhni Amur | Nickolaevsk on Amur |

Seven Oblasts in the Ukrainian SSR—

| | |
|---|---|
| 47. Chernigov | Chernigov |
| 48. Kiev | Kiev |
| 49. Odessa | Odessa |
| 50. Donetz | Stalino |
| 51. Dniepropetrovsk | Dniepropetrovsk |
| 52. Kharkov | Kharkov |
| 53. Vinitza | Vinitza |

[1] Formerly Samara and Middle Volga Krai

Six Oblasts in the Kazak Autonomous Republic—

|  |  | *Capital* |
|---|---|---|
| 54. | South Kasak | Chimkent |
| 55. | West Kasak | Uralsk |
| 56. | East Kazak | Semipalatinsk |
| 57. | Karagandin | Petropavlovsk |
| 58. | Aktubinsk | Aktubinsk |
| 59. | Alma-Ata | Alma-Ata |

Fourteen Okrugs in the RSFSR—

| | | |
|---|---|---|
| *a.* | Narym | Kolpashev |
| *b.* | Vitimo-Olekmino | Kalakan |
| *c.* | Taymyrsk | Dudinka |
| *d.* | Komi-Permyak | Kudymkar |
| *e.* | Ebenkinsk | Turinsk Kultbase |
| *f.* | Ostyako-Vogul'sk | Samarovo |
| *g.* | Jamal'sk | Salegard |
| *h.* | Koryansk | Penzhinsk Kultbase |
| *i.* | Chukotsk | Anadyr |
| *j.* | Nenetsk | Nar'yan-Mar |
| *k.* | Argayash | Argayash |
| *l.* | Karkaralinsk | Karkaralinsk |
| *m.* | Tarsky | Tara |
| *n.* | Velikie Luki | Velikie Luki |

## CHANGES MADE BY THE NEW CONSTITUTION OF 1936

THE seven Union Republics have become eleven by the dissolution of the Transcaucasian SFSR into its three constituent republics and the promotion to Union Republics of two of the Autonomous Republics of the RSFSR, namely, those of Kirghiz and Kazak.

The fourteen Autonomous Republics of the RSFSR have become seventeen by (*a*) the above-mentioned promotion to Union Republics of Kirghiz and Kazak ; (*b*) the transfer to the Uzbek SSR of the Autonomous Republic of Kala-Kalpak ; and (*c*) the promotion to be Autonomous Republics of six Autonomous Oblasts, namely, Kabardino-Balkarsk, Kalmyk, Komi, Mariinsk, Chechen-Ingush, and North-Ossetinsk.

The eleven Krais of the RSFSR have been reduced to five, namely, North Caucasian, West Siberian, Far-Eastern, Asovo-Chernomorsky, Krasnoyarsk (formerly the Chita Oblast).

The twelve Oblasts of the RSFSR have become nineteen by (*a*) the change from Krai to Oblast of the six above mentioned ; (*b*) the addition of one new Oblast, namely, Yaroslavl ; whilst (*c*) the Olsko-Irtysh Oblast is renamed Omsk Oblast.

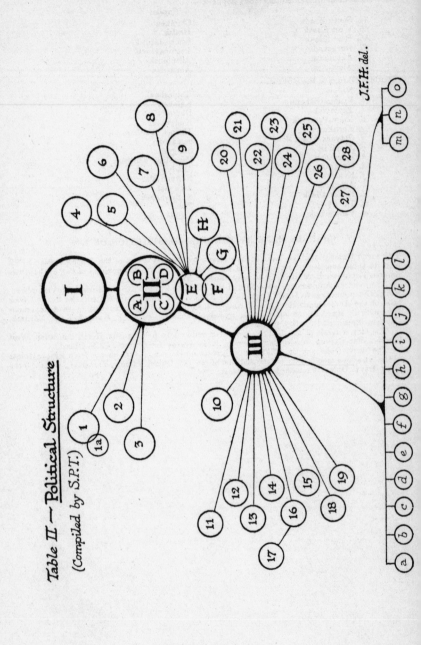

Table II — Political Structure

(Compiled by S.P.T.)

J.F.H. del.

# II

*Diagram of the Political Structure of the USSR*

## TABLE II

*Political Structure*

I. All-Union Congress of Soviets (AUCS).
II. Central Executive Committee of the USSR (TSIK).
III. Council of People's Commissars (Sovnarkom).

A. Council of the Union.  (Union of Soviets.)
B. Presidium.
C. Soviet of Nationalities.
D. Presidium.

E. Presidium of the TSIK.
F. Presidents of the TSIK.
G. Secretariat of the TSIK.
H. State Credits and Savings Commission.

1. Supreme Court (Verkhsud).
1a. Procurator.
2. Supreme Council of Physical Culture.
3. Budget Commission.
4. Supreme Council for Communal Economy.
5. Central Archives.
6. Committee of Higher Technical Education.
7. Scientific Research Institutions Committee.
8. Central Election Committee.
9. Organisation and Soviet Construction Commission.
10. Permanent Representatives of the Union's Republics.
11. Yield of Crops Commission.
12. Council of Labour and Defence (STO).
13. Soviet Central Commissions.
14. Government Arbitration Commission.
15. Chief Concession Committee.
16. Gosplan.
17. Central Board of Economic Calculation (Khosuchet).
18. Central Board of Roads and Transport.
19. Central Board of the Civil Air Fleet.
20. Central Board of the North Sea Route.
21. Committee for the Supply of Agricultural Products.
22. Central Commission for Special Freights.
23. Central Convention Bureau for Decentralised Supply.
24. Radio-Broadcasting Committee.
25. Commodity Funds and Trade Regulation Committee.
26. Handicraft Industry Committee.
27. Land Settlement Committee.
28. Central Board of Cinema and Photo Production.

### 12 All-Union People's Commissariats (Narkomats)

a. State Farms (NKSovkhos).
b. Foreign Affairs (NKID).
c. Defence (NKOborony).
d. Internal Affairs (NKVnutdel).
e. River Transport (NKVod).
f. Heavy Industry (NKTyazh).

g. Foreign Trade (NKVneshtorg).
h. Means of Communication (railways) (NKPS).
i. Posts and Telegraphs (NKSvyas).
j. Forest Industry (NKLes).)
k. Light Industry (NKLegprom).
l. Food Industry (NKPISHCH).

### 3 Unified Narkomats

m. Agriculture (NKZem).
n. Finance (NKFin.).
o. Internal Trade (NKVnutorg).

461

# III

## APPENDIX TO CHAPTER I (see p. 9)

*The Declaration of the Central Executive Committee of the Union of Soviet Socialist Republics of July 13, 1923* [1]

To all governments and to all the peoples of the earth : From the first moment of their existence the soviet republics were united by the bonds of close cooperation and mutual assistance, which subsequently assumed the form of treaties of alliance. The power of the workers and peasants united them into a single unit, with common needs, in their struggle against the attacks of foreign capitalist states and against the internal counter-revolutionary attacks on the soviet form of society. The solidarity of the labouring masses united them in their common task of establishing fraternal cooperation between the liberated peoples. Together they emerged from the victorious proletarian revolution, having overthrown the power of their landowners and capitalists. Together they passed through the dire experiences of intervention and blockade, and emerged triumphant. Together they started the enormous task of restoring the national economy, on the basis of the new economic structure of society, after it had passed through unprecedented calamities.

Whilst rendering to one another constant fraternal assistance

---

[1] We take this translation from *Soviet Rule in Russia*, by W. R. Batsell, New York, 1929, a volume of lasting usefulness (in spite of the aberrations of its author) because of its extensive reproduction of texts. Nearly the same translation of part of the document was included in the British Government Stationery Office paper of 1924 entitled *Soviet Russia : a description of the various political units existing on Russian territory, to which is appended the Constitution of the USSR of July 6, 1923.* A pamphlet (56 pp.) was published in English at Moscow in 1932 entitled *The Fundamental Law (Constitution) of the USSR, together with the Constitution (Fundamental Law) of the RSFSR.* A French translation, with some comments, will be found in *La Constitution de l'Union des Républiques Socialistes Soviétiques*, par Stefan Yaneff (Bibliothèque de l'Institut du Droit Comparé de Lyon), Paris, 1929, vol. xv. Another will be found in the official *Annuaire diplomatique du Commissariat du Peuple pour les affaires étrangères*, distributed annually at Moscow.

An interesting summary of the subsequent changes will be found in the pamphlet (in Russian) edited by E. Pashukanis, and entitled *Ten Years of the USSR Constitution*, Moscow, Ogiz, 1933, p. 96.

with all their strength and resources, they nevertheless for a long time remained separate states only united by treaties of alliance.

The further development of their mutual relations and the requirements of the international position have now led them to combine into one united state.

The strength of the world reaction and the aggressive aims of the imperialistic governments, with the consequent dangers of renewed attacks, made it imperative to unite the defensive forces of all the soviet republics in one central union government.

At the same time economic reconstruction in the soviet republics, ruined as they are by war, intervention, and blockade, is an impossible task unless they combine their forces, and can only be successfully realised by properly ordered guidance from one economic centre for the whole union.

The very nature of the workers' and peasants' state, in the gradual development and strengthening of the new structure of society in the soviet republics, is driving them increasingly towards union and towards the fusion of their forces for the realisation of their common aim.

At the soviet congresses held recently in the various soviet republics the peoples of these republics decided unanimously to form a Union of Soviet Socialist Republics, a single united state. This union of peoples with equal rights remains a purely voluntary union, which excludes all possibility of national oppression or the compulsion of any nation to remain within this united state, every republic enjoying the right to leave the union if it so desires. At the same time the door is left open for the voluntary entry into the union of other socialist republics that may be formed in the future.

The declaration and treaty of union accepted by the contracting soviet republics were ratified, and brought into operation on July 6 by the Union Central Executive Committee.

In view of the necessity to unite the defensive forces of the soviet republics against external attacks, an inter-union military and naval people's commissariat has been set up.

In view of the common needs and problems facing the soviet republics in their relations with the capitalist states, an inter-union commissariat for foreign affairs has been formed. The necessity for complete centralisation in the conduct of foreign trade on the basis of the state's monopoly, and to defend the soviet republics against the attempts of the capitalist states to bring about their economic subjection, has made it necessary to set up a single inter-union commissariat for foreign trade.

Further, the proper regulation of their national economy demands a united transport and postal and telegraph system, that is to say, the formation of inter-union commissariats for transport and for posts and telegraphs.

Other branches of state activity in the separate republics forming the Union are partly subordinated to the Union central institutions, while at the same time each republic retains its own corresponding central institution ; and partly they remain exclusively in the hands of the separate republics.

The direct administration of national economy and finance, the organisation of the food supply, the state defence of the rights and interests of hired labour, the control over the whole state apparatus of the workmen's and peasants' inspection, will be in the hands simultaneously of the inter-union centre, in so far as guidance from a single centre is required, and of the separate centres of each republic, in so far as special control in the territories of the latter is essential.

Commissariats dealing with special national questions of ordinary daily life, such, for instance, as education, agriculture, internal affairs, justice, etc., will exist only in the separate republics, and will be under their sole control.

The unity of will of the labouring masses of the whole Union will be expressed in its supreme authority, the Union Congress of Soviets, but at the same time each nationality will have special representation in the Soviet of Nationalities, which will cooperate on equal rights with the Union Soviet elected by the Congress.

The Union of Soviet Republics, thus established on the basis of the fraternal cooperation of peoples, will place before itself the aim of preserving the peace with all nations. All the nationalities, with equal rights, and working together in close cooperation, will together develop their culture and prosperity, and work out the problems facing the workers' government.

As the natural ally of oppressed peoples, the Union of Soviet Socialist Republics seeks to live in peace and friendly relations with all peoples and to establish economic cooperation with them. The Union of Soviet Socialist Republics places before itself the aim of furthering the interests of the labouring masses of the whole world. Over the enormous territory stretching from the Baltic, the Black and the White Seas to the Pacific Ocean, the Union is already realising the fraternity of nations and the triumph of labour, but it is striving at the same time to bring about friendly cooperation between the peoples of the whole world.

Chairmen of the Union Central Executive Committee : M. I. Kalinin, G. E. Petrovsky, N. N. Narimanov, A. G. Cherviakov. Members of the presidium of the Union Central Executive Committee : A. S. Enukidze, L. B. Kamenev, F. Y. Kon, D. I. Kursky, D. Z. Manuilsky, A. F. Miasnikam, K. G. Rakovsky, Y. I. Rudzutak, A. I. Rykov, T. V. Sapronov, P. G. Smidovich, J. V. Stalin, M. P. Tomsky, M. G. Tskhakaya, Khibir-Aliev.

Secretary of the Union Central Executive Committee : A. Enukidze.

KREMLIN, MOSCOW, *July* 13, 1923

# IV

## APPENDIX TO CHAPTER II (see pp. 28-31)

### *The Powers and Authorised Functions of the Village Soviet*

THE powers and authorised functions of the village soviet in the USSR are elaborately set forth in the decree of the Central Executive Committee of January 1, 1931,[1] of which the following is a summarised translation :

We have, first, the general functions stated :

1. A Selosoviet is the supreme organ of power within its territory, through which the proletariat performs its dictatorship.

2. A Selosoviet carries out, in accordance with the laws and with the regulations of its higher authorities, the following tasks :

(*a*) It organises the poor-batraks and the middle-peasants masses of the village, carries out the work of social-economic life of the village, participates in the industrialisation of the country, and combats the kulaks and other class enemies and liquidates the kulaks as a class, by means of mass collectivisation.

(*b*) It carries resolutions on all questions connected with the village and discusses problems of the krai, oblast, republic, and of the entire Union of Republics, submitting its considerations to the higher authorities.

(*c*) It controls the activities of all its own institutions, enterprises and organisations, supervises the work of the institutions on its territory which are not subordinated to it, and renders assistance to all institutions on its territory.

(*d*) It takes the necessary steps to supervise the work of the institutions and citizens for the State.

(*e*) It combats all the activities which are contrary to the class proletarian policy and attends to the obedience of every citizen and official to the laws and regulations of the Soviet power.

[1] Decree of the VTZIK of January 1, 1931 ; published in the Collection of Laws and Regulations, No. 11. Part I. of March 26, 1931.

The decree then enumerates an incredibly lengthy list of functions which the village soviet is supposed to fulfil :

6. In the election of the Selosoviet :

(*a*) It organises the election commission and controls the entire election campaign.

(*b*) It prepares a list of persons who ought to be deprived of the right of election, and keeps up to date the list of deprived persons, sanctioned by the Rayon Ispolkom.

(*c*) It elects delegates to the Rayon Congress of Soviets.

7. In the sphere of mass organisation :

(*a*) It attracts to its work workmen, batraks, kolkhosniks and the poor-middle elements of the village.

(*b*) It takes necessary steps to attract women to soviet construction work and facilitates their promotion to responsible posts.

(*c*) It conducts systematic work amongst the batraks and poor, improves conditions of work of their groups, and discusses with them all important questions of the agenda of the Selosoviet meeting.

(*d*) It conducts political and economic propaganda amongst the vast masses of labouring people.

(*e*) It forms the soviet and kolkhos cadres.

(*f*) It convokes general meetings of electors (not less than three times a year), reports there on its activities, and discusses all important problems of the soviet economic and cultural construction.

8. In the sphere of the national policy, the Selosoviet takes necessary measures in protecting the national minorities, in raising their political, economic and cultural standard, and in attracting them to the Soviet construction.

9. In the sphere of planning and statistics :

(*a*) It prepares a plan of the economic and social-cultural construction of the village and submits it to the Rayon Ispolkom.

(*b*) It sanctions the plans of its own institutions and controls their execution.

(*c*) It discusses the plans of other institutions on its territory, gives its opinion on them and collaborates in their execution.

(*d*) It elects the village statisticians-representatives and carries on all statistical work.

(*e*) It keeps the register of village households.

10. In the sphere of the socialist reconstruction and of the development of agriculture :

(*a*) It takes necessary steps to preserve the existing kolkhoses and to form the new ones.

(*b*) It discusses and sanctions the plans of collective farms and other cooperative organisations.

(*c*) It periodically arranges meetings for hearing the reports of the institutions dealing with the kolkhoses as well as the reports of the kolkhoses themselves, which are situated on its territory.

(*d*) It gives its conclusions as to requests for credits and equipment for the kolkhoses.

(*e*) It assists in the introduction of new methods in the collective farms.

(*f*) It supervises the distribution of labour and technical staff in the collective farms and attends to the discipline in the collective and soviet enterprises.

(*g*) It pronounces its veto on any illegal decisions of the collective farms and other cooperative institutions and reports immediately on this to the Rayon Ispolkom.

(*h*) It takes necessary steps to develop the collectivisation of farms and assists the batraks and the individual peasants in forming kolkhoses.

(*i*) It renders assistance to sovkhoses and to the M.T.S. (Motor and Tractor Stations).

(*k*) It takes all necessary measures in increasing the area sown, and in raising the yield, and encourages the development of all kinds of farming and the introduction of agricultural improvements.

(*l*) It assists the government in the nationalisation of lands and reports on all lands and fields which are in possession of collective farms or individual peasants and advises, if necessary, on their confiscation.

(*m*) It controls the activities of agricultural societies and liquidates them in the areas of mass collectivisation, with the sanction of the Rayon Ispolkom.

11. In the sphere of industry :

(*a*) It runs its own industry.

(*b*) It controls the use of sandstone and clay on its territory.

(*c*) It supervises its home industry and assists kustars in creating artels.

(*d*) It supervises all enterprises on its territory and renders them the necessary assistance.

12. In the sphere of forestry :

(*a*) It looks after the forests which have a local use.

(*b*) It develops timber and the wood-chemical industry.

(*c*) It supervises all woods and forests on its territory and renders assistance in preserving woods of national importance and protects all woods and forests from fire, damage, etc.

13. In the sphere of supply, cooperation and trade :

(*a*) It attracts the local population to cooperative organisations and improves their activities.

(*b*) It collects and controls funds for the purpose of cooperation and collectivisation of batraks (landless peasants).

(*c*) It controls the local trade and prices.

(*d*) It supervises local markets, fairs, etc.

(*e*) It fixes rents for shop premises and stalls.

14. In the sphere of finance and budget :

(*a*) It drafts the Selosoviet Budget and submits it to the Rayon Ispolkom.

(*b*) It deals with the approved credits.

(*c*) It collects taxes and rates.

(*d*) It deals with the deductions of local taxes and rates, with the terms of payment, etc.

(*e*) It collects fines and sells by auction the property of persons who have not paid them.

(*f*) It makes inventories of inheritances and communicates them to the Rayon Ispolkom.

(*g*) It takes part in building up the state credit system and in the floating of state loans, etc.

(*h*) It deals with the self-taxation of the population.

(*i*) It cooperates with the insurance schemes.

15. In the sphere of local government :

(*a*) It deals with all housing questions, school and hospital buildings, etc.

(*b*) It repairs local roads, bridges, etc.

16. In the sphere of communications the Selosoviet collaborates with the Norkompochtel.

17. In the sphere of labour :

(*a*) It attends to the strict fulfilment of the Labour Code.

(*b*) It registers and controls all collective agreements of batraks with their employers.

(*c*) It attracts, if necessary, the local population to public works in making roads, organising transport, etc.

18. In the sphere of education :

(*a*) It liquidates illiteracy and opens all kinds of educational institutions.

(*b*) It supervises the public education of children, takes care of the homeless waifs, appoints trustees to them, etc.

(*c*) It assists the government in establishing agricultural and technical education, distributes young persons amongst different schools and factories, etc.

(d) It sees to the supply of boots, clothing and food to the poorest children.

19. In the sphere of health :

(a) It supervises all the hospitals and sanitary establishments, which are maintained on the Selosoviet Budget.

(b) It takes all necessary steps to the organisation of sanitary inspection and combats venereal diseases.

(c) It advances the knowledge of personal hygiene and develops physical culture.

(d) It appoints trustees to insane persons.

20. In the sphere of social insurance :

(a) It keeps the register of insured persons and pays out the benefits.

(b) It forms artels of invalids.

(c) It takes a special care of the Red Army invalids, veterans of the Civil War, and of all persons who suffered from the kulaks and contra-revolutionaries. It forms them into collective farms.

(d) It supervises the activities of the societies for mutual aid.

(e) It appoints trustees to blind and dumb persons, etc.

21. In the sphere of the defence of the country :

(a) It keeps the register of all persons liable for military service.

(b) It registers horses, carriages and other requisites of war.

(c) It assists in recruiting.

(d) It takes care of the families of persons serving in the Peasants-Workers Army.

(e) It undertakes all kinds of useful military training.

(f) It participates in organisation of military training courses.

(g) It deals suitably with persons avoiding military compulsory service.

22. In the sphere of judicial prosecution:

(a) It forms a village judicial court.

(b) It supervises the election of judges.

(c) It attends to the strict fulfilment of the decisions of the court.

(d) It deals with notarial acts.

(e) It finds employment for persons sentenced to compulsory work.

23. In the sphere of revolutionary activities :

(*a*) It attends to the maintenance of revolutionary order and combats all anti-soviet elements.

(*b*) It arrests suspected persons.

(*c*) It deals with domiciliary searches and inspection of documents.

(*d*) It combats drunkenness, hooliganism and secret sale of alcoholic drink.

(*e*) It appoints village executive officers (ispolnitel).

(*f*) It collects administrative fines.

24. In the sphere of administration:

(*a*) It registers deeds, issues identity cards, etc.

(*b*) It keeps the register of all voluntary organisations on its territory and supervises their activities.

(*c*) It attends to the strict fulfilment of the laws regulating religious societies.

# V

APPENDIX TO CHAPTER II (see pp. 51-54)

*The Sections and Commissions of the City Soviets*

(Extract from the Regulations as to City Soviets of October 24, 1925, published by the Communist Academy, Moscow, 1927)

45. IN order to attract all members of the Soviet, and also wide masses of workers to the practical work of the city soviets and its organs, the city soviets are divided up into sections according to separate branches of municipal economy and administration. The sections assist in the work of the city soviet in general, and also supervise the work of the executive organs of the Soviet.

46. The number of sections and the functions of each are determined by the Soviet.

47. The following sections are compulsory for each city soviet :

(*a*) Communal economy, (*b*) finance and budget, (*c*) education, (*d*) public health, (*e*) cooperative trading. Other sections (administrative, legal, housing, labour, industry, social insurance, military, workers' inspection, etc.) are created by Resolution of the Soviet as required.

48. Members join any section from choice, but every member of the Soviet must work in one section.

49. In addition to members of the Soviet, membership of a section may include representatives of trade unions, of factory-works and local committees, of delegate meetings of women workers, of the Red Army and separate social organisations, as well as individual workers whose collaboration in the work of the section appears desirable.

*Note.*—The person in charge of the corresponding organ (the head of the department or of the sub-department) must necessarily be included in the membership of the section.

50. The Soviet, or its presidium, may temporarily relieve individual deputies from work in the sections.

51. All members of the section have a casting vote in its work.

*Note.*—Persons invited to attend separate meetings of the section such as experts, specialists and others, have a consultative vote.

52. A section—

(*a*) Considers the plans of work in its branch of economy and administration.

(*b*) Hears the reports of the corresponding organs and gives their conclusions upon them to the plenum or presidium.

(*c*) Considers the fundamental problems of the current work of the executive organs and gives its conclusions upon them.

(*d*) Studies the work in institutions, undertakings, etc., in the corresponding branch of economy and administration.

(*e*) Attaches members of the section to undertakings and institutions, who serve the city in their branch of work, in order to supervise and assist their work.

(*f*) Hears the report of the bureau as to the carrying out of the plan and of the resolutions of the section.

(*g*) Appoints standing commissions (sub-sections) to ensure closer contact with separate branches of the executive apparatus in the corresponding department of administration and economy.

(*h*) Appoints temporary commissions to work on separate problems.

(*i*) Considers the proposals, resolutions, etc., brought up by individual members of the section on their own initiative, and relating to the given branch of work.

(*j*) Considers similar projects and resolutions brought forward by various institutions, organisations and individuals in the corresponding branch of work.

(*k*) Takes part in the working-out of plans and projects relating to the fundamental problems of the work of corresponding executive organs in meetings and conferences, etc., called by them.

53. The resolutions of the sections are confirmed and executed by the presidium of the city soviet.

54. In cases where the section does not agree with the decision of the presidium of the city soviet it may put the matter before the plenum of the Soviet for their discussion.

55. Problems which require preliminary working-on are forwarded by the presidium of the city soviet to the corresponding sections.

56. The section meets at times fixed by the plenum or presidium of the Soviet and by the bureau of the section.

57. The section elects a bureau from among its members for the period during which it holds office; the person in charge of the corresponding branch of work in the city must be included in this.

58. The bureau elects a chairman and also a deputy-chairman and a secretary of the section.

*Note.*—The person in charge of the corresponding executive organ must not hold office as chairman of the section.

59. The bureau is the executive and administrative organ of the section, and is responsible to the section for the preparation of matters to be laid before the plenum of the section ; it collects and systematises material, keeps the registers of members of the section and of its commissions, keeps registers of attendances at meetings, makes reports as to the activities of the section, forwards the resolutions of the sections to the proper quarters, sees that they are executed, and takes part in the meetings of the presidium of the city soviet through its delegates, who have a consultative vote in it.

60. The general direction of the work of the section is in the hands of the plenum and of the presidium of the city soviet.

61. For the consideration of general questions which affect two or more sections, the presidium of the city soviet may call joint meetings of the bureaux or plenums of these sections.

# VI

APPENDIX TO CHAPTER II (see p. 365)

*Note relating to the Commissariat for Workers' and Peasants'*
*Inspection (Rabkrin, or RKI)*

ONE of the most remarkable of the executive departments of the
USSR Government was the standing Commission of Workers' and
Peasants' Inspection, which ranked as a USSR Commissariat under
its president, who was always a member of the USSR Sovnarkom.
A similar organisation existed in all the constituent and autonomous
republics, the local head always sitting in the local sovnarkom.
This unique department was instituted in 1919 and reorganised at
the instance of Lenin himself and entrusted for the first few years
to Stalin, when his special task of arranging relations with the non-
Russian nationalities and other " cultural minorities " in the USSR
had been practically completed. Lenin's object was to counteract
the tendencies to an invidious " bureaucratism " which were becoming visible in the rapidly developing collectivism to which Soviet
Communism was committed. To do this he wished to call in the
ordinary citizens—the workers and peasants—as inspectors and
critics of the working of every public department, great or small,
so that they might eliminate the " red tape " characteristic of official-
dom, and check the growing separation in habits and manners
between the bureaucrats and the public at large. For this important
service Lenin relied on the common sense and intuitive judgment
of the mechanics and the villagers ; but Stalin apparently realised
that, for any accurate appraisement of the organisation of a great
enterprise, whether in the office or in the factory, trained observation
and administrative experience was requisite, if only to direct the
criticisms of the ordinary citizen, and to formulate wisely the reform-
ing proposals in which the criticism eventuated.

The USSR Commission for Workers' and Peasants' Inspection
came to have no fewer than five assistants, each at the head of a
considerable department—so true is the common Russian joke that
the only remedy for bureaucracy is the creation of more bureaucracy !
It gradually accumulated in the service of the juries of laymen on

474

its extensive staff, either at Moscow or at its numerous local offices, highly trained inspectors and auditors, including, we are told, " many of the oldest, most educated and most experienced Communists ". It was closely connected and actually intertwined in work with the Control Commission of the Communist Party, which maintains a constant watch upon the conduct and the careers of every member of the Party, receiving complaints and accusations, and investigating every suspicion and rumour. The Workers' and Peasants' Inspection was actually carried out all over the USSR by specially appointed committees or delegations of men and women who took " time off " from their own factories, farms or offices, to visit other departments ; interrupting the business of these, sometimes without notice, in order to ascertain how much work is actually being performed by the constantly increasing staffs, to detect instances of unnecessary forms and duplication of effort, and to suggest improvements.

The investigations of the Workers' and Peasants' Inspection became an important basis for the " chistka " or cleansing, to which every public department was from time to time subjected. This must not be confused with the " chistka " to which the members of the Communist Party, wherever they are employed, are subjected every three or four years. The "chistka " with which the Workers' and Peasants' Inspection was concerned was irrespective of Party membership and related only to the persons employed in a particular establishment. " Periodically ", records Mr. Calvin B. Hoover, " the technical and administrative staffs of industry are required to face the cleaning commission. . . . When hearings are held before the cleaning commission, all the workers of the industry are invited and expected to be present. As a matter of fact anyone can be present, and anyone can ask questions of the person who is being ' cleaned '. The process is not a pleasant one for the person ' at the bar ', for every possible criticism which can be raked up is usually fired at his unlucky head. Every questionable act which he may have done, any indiscreet conversation, any part of his private life may be hauled out into the pitiless light of publicity. The janitor may accuse the director of the trust of having a bourgeois taste in neckties or of not providing proper safeguards for workmen in dangerous occupations. The ancestry of the victim is particularly examined into, and happy is he who can answer that his mother ' came from the wooden plough ' and his father ' came from the loom ', and thrice damned is he whose ancestry includes either kulak, bourgeois, or landlord. . . . Nevertheless, this institution gives a sense of power even to the individual workman, and it does serve to lessen any tendency on the part of the administrative personnel to be tyrannical in any special personal cases, lest the victim attain his revenge at the next chistka." [1]

[1] *Economic Life of Soviet Russia*, by Calvin B. Hoover, 1930, pp. 262-263.

It should be added that the victims of the " chistka " had a right of appeal to superior authorities ; and any unduly drastic decision of the commission was often reversed.

The Workers' and Peasants' Inspection as a whole was described by Mr. W. H. Chamberlin, who had watched its operation over a number of years, as " a sort of permanent super-commission for audit and control ; it is continually combing the other state departments for traces of graft, bureaucratism and other abuses. The Rabkrin has a far-flung net ; its inspectors look into everything, from the management of the Moscow Art Museum to the building of a new industrial plant, from the civil service qualifications of the officials in Daghestan to the conditions of the peasant farms in the Kuban ".[1] Naturally, such investigations are not popular in the offices subjected to them ; and the mere cost of so extensive a service is a serious drawback. But the common opinion is that the Rabkrin ". . . seems to make out a good cause for its activity on the ground that the savings which it has recommended far outweigh the cost of its upkeep ".[1]

Whatever doubts may be expressed about the technical efficiency of its inspections, or of the net advantage of the retrenchments that it recommends, it is clear that the activity of such a popular tribunal did much to maintain the conviction of the common people that they were in command. Its peripatetic inspections were also a potent instrument of popular education in public administration. It earned an enthusiastic eulogium from one of few British economists who have troubled to investigate the government structure of the USSR. Mrs. Barbara Wootton, writing in 1934, declared that " It is much to be hoped that, even should the Russians relax their fierce repression of the now unpopular social classes, they will not lightly abandon their institution of Workers' and Peasants' Inspection. Undoubtedly the price of this meddlesome interference of the rank and file into affairs of which they must, in ninety-nine cases out of a hundred, understand nothing at all, is a considerable sacrifice of efficiency. But, even at that price, it may be argued that the safeguard which this affords against the odious vulgarities of class distinctions is well worth having. For those who are accustomed by the nature of their work to give commands, or are divorced from the crude physical realities of farm and mine and factory, what can be more salutary than some such direct personal reminder that they are no better than their fellows ? The official intrusion of those who perform the simplest, the dirtiest or the most tedious jobs into the secret places of those whose work is skilled, responsible and interesting (and paid for as such) provides a means of contact between the one group and the other that might never be established in any other way ; and it makes at the same time a magnificent

[1] *Soviet Russia*, by W. H. Chamberlin, 1930, p. 119.

assertion that none shall judge the one superior to the other. Nor is it unreasonable to hope that, as the standard of proletarian education rises, the price of this intrusion, even in terms of economic efficiency, may be gradually diminished. The better educated the rank and file become, the more will they realise and respect the province of the expert ; the less will such criticisms as they make be directed to technical matters, on which their opinion is valueless, and the more to human issues on which their judgment stands equal with that of others—on which those, upon whom their inspections descend, are no better qualified to pronounce than they ; the more, in fact, will they concern themselves, not with the currency policy of the central bank, or the rotation of crops on a collective farm, but with the detection of those signs of personal ostentation and arrogance on the one hand, and of subservience on the other, which mark the insidious growth of class distinctions." [1]

This interesting institution was, after fifteen years' existence, brought to an end in 1934, at the instance of the Communist Party. There seem to have been complaints that, in many parts of the country, the department was insufficiently organised to deal with anything like all the complaints that reached its local offices. There were excessive delays in remedying grievances. But the main purpose, as explained in the speeches of Kaganovitch and Kuibyshev to the plenum of the Party Control Commission (as reported in the *Moscow Daily News*, July 5 and 11, 1934), seems to have been a more thorough and continuous " checking up " of the loyalty, promptitude and efficiency of the subordinate officials of the various ministries, especially in the districts remote from Moscow, in carrying out the decisions of the Central Government. It was apparently the method of inspection by the workers and peasants that was objected to. *Pravda*, July 4, 1934, in an editorial, explained that " the method of inspection, which was the basic principle of the work of the Control Commission, is now replaced by the method of control and verification of fulfilment of the Party and Government decisions. The control becomes now the inseparable part of the administration. . . . The control of the reconstruction of the Narkomzen, Narkomput and of the Narkomvod has proved that the reconstruction was achieved only partially, and that it was concerned with the central organs and their staffs, and did not yet affect the secondary and primary organisations of the Narkomats themselves or their local branches."

Whatever may have been the reasons, the Central Committee of the Communist Party, at its session of June 28, 1934, called for the complete supersession of the RKI department throughout the USSR, with a view to its functions being more efficiently organised. A separation was made between the work of inspection or detection

[1] *Plan or no Plan*, by Barbara Wootton, 1934, p. 265.

of abuses, on the one hand, and on the other the duty of taking disciplinary action against officers found to be to blame, or other administrative action to remedy grievances. The work of inspection and detection has since continued under the direction of the trade union hierarchy, headed by the All-Union Central Committee of Trade Unions. The duty of continuous " verification " to ensure that each new decree or directive is promptly carried out, and that of taking disciplinary or other administrative action was entrusted to a new Commission of Control, appointed by and responsible to the Sovnarkom of the USSR, the first members being nominated or suggested by the Central Committee of the Communist Party.[1] This new commission, which will have its own agents in all parts of the USSR, is to work in close collaboration with a separate Commission of Party Control, responsible to the Central Committee of the Communist Party, whose function it is to maintain a constant scrutiny of the conduct of all the members of the Party. The whole area of the USSR has been divided into 28 districts, in each of which will be stationed either a member of the Commission of Soviet Control, or a member of the Commission of Party Control, or a member of each body. To local offices under such direction, all complaints and criticisms of any branch of public administration are to be directed ; and to these offices the reports of the inspections by trade union local committees are to be sent. It remains to be seen whether, under the new system, these inspections will continue to be made.

[1] *Membership and Regulations of the Commission of Party Control and the Commission of Soviet Control* (in Russian) (Moscow, 1934), 34 pp.

# VII

## APPENDIX TO CHAPTER II (see pp. 97, 250)

*The Internal Organisation of the Narkomat of Sovkhosi*

(Resolution of the Central Executive Committee and of the Council of People's Commissars of the USSR. *Izvestia*, 23.4.34)

In order to do away with the shortcomings of organisation in the work and structure of the apparatus of the Narkomsovkhos of the USSR and of its local organs, and in order to improve their work, and strengthen individual responsibility, the TSIK and Sovnarkom of the Union of SSR decree the reorganisation of the Narkomat of Sovkhosi of the USSR on the following lines :

### I. Central Apparatus of the Narkomat of the Sovkhosi

1. The following departments and sections of the People's Commissariat of Grain and Livestock Sovkhosi are to be abolished :

(a) The Chief Department of Work and Repairs.
(b) The Department of Organisation of Territory.
(c) The Department of Registration and Distribution of the Labour Force.
(d) The Department of Labour and Living conditions.
(e) The Department of Accounting and Statistics.
(f) The Fuel Department.
(g) The Finance Department.
(h) The Department of Book-keeping.
(j) The Department of Workers' Supplies.
(k) The Scientific and Technical Department.
(l) The Veterinary Department.
(m) The Stock-breeding Department.
(n) The Control and Disposals Section.
(o) The Seed-cultivation Section.
(p) The Protection from Fire Section.
(q) The Law Section.

(*r*) The Section for verifying execution.

(*s*) The Section of Zernostroy (grain accumulation).

2. The following structure of the central apparatus of the Narkomsovkhos is laid down :

(*a*) The Chief Administration of Grain Sovkhosi, to carry out all functions relating to the management of the Grain-producing Sovkhosi of the Narkomsovkhos.

(*b*) The Chief Administration of Cattle and Dairy Sovkhosi, to carry out all functions relating to the management of Dairy and Cattle Sovkhosi of the Narkomsovkhosi.

(*c*) The Chief Administration of Pig-breeding Sovkhosi, to carry out all functions relating to the management of the Pig-breeding Sovkhosi of the Narkomsovkhosi.

(*d*) The Chief Administration of Sheep-breeding Sovkhosi, to carry out all functions relating to the Sheep-breeding Sovkhosi of the Narkomsovkhosi.

(*e*) The Chief Adminstration of Education, to which all higher educational institutions, technical schools and schools on the special register of the Narkomsovkhosi are to be subordinated.

(*f*) Policial Administration.

3. The Chief Administration of the Grain-producing Sovkhosi to consist of the following Departments :

(*a*) Agrotechnical and Rotation of Crops.

(*b*) Machine-technical.

(*c*) Seeds.

(*d*) Cattle-breeding.

(*e*) Supply for workers.

(*f*) Finance and Book-keeping.

Sections :

(*a*) Planning.

(*b*) Construction.

(*c*) Labour Force.

(*d*) Scientific and Research Institutions.

The Chief Animal-breeding Administrations are to contain the following departments :

(*a*) Zoo-technical.

(*b*) Veterinary.

(*c*) Machine-technical.

(*d*) Agrotechnical.

(*e*) Breeding.

(*f*) Finance and Book-keeping.

Sections :
(a) Planning.
(b) Construction.
(c) Labour Force.
(d) Scientific and Research Institutions.

In order to improve contact between the Chief Administrations with the Trusts and the Sovkhosi and in order to ensure proper guidance of the work of Trusts and of Sovkhosi, the Chief Administration of the Animal-breeding Sovkhosi delegates Assistant Chiefs of Administration to inspect the following groups of rayons :

(a) Chief Administration of Grain Sovkhosi :

*1st Group.*—Trusts situated in the territory of USSR, the Crimea, Northern Caucasus, and of the Azov-Black-Sea Krais.

*2nd Group.*—Trusts situated in the territory of the Stalingrad, Saratov, and of the Middle Volga Krais, of the Bashkir ASSR and of the Central Black Earth Oblast.

*3rd Group.*—Trusts situated in the territory of the Far Eastern Krai, of the Eastern Siberian and Western Siberian Krais, of the Kazakstan, and of the Chelyabinsk Oblast.

(b) Chief Administrations of the Cattle and Dairy and Sheep-breeding Sovkhosi :

*1st Group.*—Trusts situated in the territory of USSR, the Crimea, Northern Caucasus, Azov-Black-Sea Krais, Stalingrad, and Saratov Krais and of the Central Black Earth Oblast.

*2nd Group.*—Trusts situated in the territory of the Western Siberian, Eastern Siberian, Northern and Middle Volga Krais, of the Sverdlovskaya Oblast, and of the Bashkir and Tartar ASSR.

*3rd Group.*—Trusts situated in the territory of the Chelyabinsk Oblast, of Kazakstan and Kirghizia.

(c) Chief Administration of Pig-breeding Sovkhosi :

*1st Group.*—Trusts situated in the territory of the USSR, Northern Caucasian and Azov-Black-Sea Krais. •

*2nd Group.*—Trusts situated on the territory of the Saratov and Middle Volga Krais, Central Black Oblast, and of the Bashkir and Tartar ASSR.

*3rd Group.*—Trusts situated on the territory of Eastern Siberian and Western Siberian Krais, of the Chelyabinsk Oblast and Kazakstan.

4. The following central Departments of the Narkomsovkhosi of the USSR are to be organised :
(a) Planning and Financial.
(b) Accounting and Statistics.

(c) Specialists.

(d) Administrative and Management.

(e) Secretariat of the Narkomat.

5. To create and attach to the Narkom :

(a) A section for the registration and selection of the labour force.

(b) A central Arbitration Court.

(c) A Scientific Technical Council.

(d) A group of inspectors to verify execution.

6. To reorganise " Sovkhossnab " into an office called " Supplies for Sovkhosi ", to retain its function of supplying the Sovkhosi with machines, implements and mineral manures, according to the classification passed by the Sovnarkom of the USSR.

## II. The Union Trusts of Grain-producing and Animal-breeding Sovkhosi

1. The following departments to be organised in the Union Grain Trusts :

(a) Agro-field (crop rotation ?).

(b) Machine—technical.

(c) Seeds.

(d) Cattle-breeding.

(e) Planning.

(f) Supplies for workers.

(g) Finance and Book-keeping.

(h) Cost Accounting office with warehouses and shops for the sale of equipment and materials to the Sovkhosi.

(i) Building Office.

(j) Administrative and Management Section.

2. In the Union Animal-breeding Trusts the following Departments are to be organised :

(a) Zoo-technical.

(b) Veterinary.

(c) Breeding.

(d) Machine-technical.

(e) Agro-field.

(f) Planning.

(g) Finance and Book-keeping.

(h) Building.

(i) Cost Accounting office with warehouses and shops for the sale of equipment and materials to the Sovkhosi.

(j) Administrative and Management Section.

3. At the head of the Trust is the Director of the Trust with two deputies—of these one is a Deputy for the political work.

### III. The Sovkhosi

1. At the head of the Sovkhosi is a Director appointed and dismissable by the People's Commissar.

The Director of the Sovkhos has one Deputy (in addition to his deputy for the political work) and one assistant for workers' supplies.

2. The following typical structure for Grain Sovkhosi is to be confirmed :

(*a*) Director of the Sovkhos.

(*b*) Political Department of the Sovkhos.

(*c*) Manager of the Department (according to the number of departments) with a Deputy for the political part.

(*d*) Senior Agronome of the Sovkhos and junior agronomes, according to the number of departments.

(*e*) Manager of the tractor park, who is directly responsible for the proper use and good condition of tractors and machines.

(*f*) Mechanics, according to the number of departments.

(*g*) Manager of the petrol station.

(*h*) ORS (Department of Workers' Supplies).

(*i*) Book-keeping Department.

The automobile column, road detachment and repair workshop are constituent parts of the Sovkhos and are directly subordinate to the Director of the Grain Sovkhos.

3. The following typical structure for Animal-breeding Sovkhosi is to be confirmed :

(*a*) Director of the Sovkhos.

(*b*) Political Department of the Sovkhos.

(*c*) Manager of each farm (according to the number of farms).

(*d*) Senior zoo-technician, and junior zoo-technicians, according to the number of farms.

(*e*) Veterinary surgeon and veterinary *feldschers*, according to the number of farms.

(*f*) Zoo-technician for breeding-work.

(*g*) Agronome for the Sovkhos.

(*h*) Mechanic.

(*i*) Manager of petrol station.

(*j*) Book-keeping Department.

### IV. Representatives of the Narkomat of Sovkhosi

1. The Narkomat of Sovkhosi has its own representatives on the Sovnarkoms of the Union Republics.

2. The existing departments of representatives of the Narkomat of Sovkhosi in krais, oblasts and autonomous republics are to be abolished.

It is to be left to the sovnarkoms of autonomous republics, and to the krai and oblast ispolkoms, to have the right of control over the activities of the sovkhos trusts of the Narkomsovkhosi.

It is to be made the duty of the Commissariat of Grain and Animal Sovkhosi of the USSR to carry out the reorganisation of the organs of management of sovkhosi on the basis of the present decree not later than June 1, 1934.

| | |
|---|---|
| Chairman of the Central Executive Committee of the Union of SSR : | M. KALININ |
| Chairman of the Soviet of People's Commissars of the Union of SSR: | V. MOLOTOV |
| Secretary of the TZIK of the Union of SSR : | A. ENUKIDZE |

MOSCOW, KREMLIN, *April* 22, 1934

# VIII

## APPENDIX TO CHAPTER II (see pp. 97, 250)

### *The Internal Organisation of the Narkomat of Agriculture*

(Resolution of the Central Executive Committee and of the Council of People's Commissars of the Union of SSR, *Pravda*, 5.4.34)

In order to do away with the shortcomings of organisation in the work and structure of the apparatus of the Narkomzem of the Union of SSR and of republican and local organs, and in order to improve their work and strengthen personal responsibility, the TSIK and Sovnarkom of the Union of SSR decree the reorganisation of the system of the agricultural organs of the Union of SSR on the following lines :

### I. Central Apparatus of the Narkomzem of the USSR

1. To liquidate in the Narkomzem of the USSR the following departments and sections, associations and trusts :

(a) The Chief Grain Department of the MTS.
(b) The Chief Department of Cotton MTS.
(c) The Chief Department of the Beet MTS.
(d) The Chief Department of Flax and Hemp MTS.
(e) The Chief Department of Vegetable and Potato MTS.
(f) The Chief Department of machine-haymaking stations.
(g) The Department of Organisation of Kolkhos Labour and Distribution of Income.
(h) The Department of technical propaganda.
(i) The Fodder Department.
(j) The Department of Chemicalisation, and Lime Bureau.
(k) The Fuel Department.
(l) The Department of Repairs and Work.
(m) The Section of Control and verification of execution.
(n) The Chief Department of Capital Construction.
(o) The Department of Livestock Kolkhos goods Farms.

(*p*) The Section of Economics of Labour and of Production Quotas.

(*q*) The Union of Cotton Sovkhosi.

(*r*) The " Glavvodkhos " Association.

(*s*) The Association " Novlub ".

(*t*) The " Soyussmenovod " Association.

(*u*) The Association of Fight Wreckers.

(*v*) The Flax Sovkhos Centre.

2. To organise the following Chief Administrations of the NKZ of the Union of SSR :

(*a*) Chief Administration for grain and oil-producing cultures, to carry out all functions for management of machine tractors and agro-field service for grain and oil production in all republics, krais and oblasts of the USSR.

(*b*) The Chief Beet Administration—to carry out all functions for the management of the machine tractors and the agro-field service for production.

(*c*) The Chief Flax and Hemp Administration.

(*d*) The Chief Cotton Administration.

The following Departments are formed within the Chief Administration for Grain and Oil-producing Cultures, the Chief Beet Administration, the Chief Cotton Administration, and the Chief Flax and Hemp Administration :

Agro-technical and Rotation of Crops.

Machine-technical.

To Fight Wreckers.

Seed.

Financial and Book-keeping.

Sections :

Planning.

Labour Force.

For Scientific Research Institutions.

In addition to this, the following Departments are formed in these Administrations :

In the Chief Grain Administration—a Rice Department.

In the Chief Cotton Administration—a Department of Cotton Sovkhosi, an Irrigation Department, a Department of new textile cultures, and a Department of mineral manures.

In the Chief Flax and Hemp Administration—a Department of Flax and Hemp Factories, a Department of Flax and Hemp Sovkhosi and a Department of mineral manures.

In the Chief Beet Administration—Department of Mineral Fertilisers.

(*e*) The Chief Administration for Livestock-breeding, within which the following Departments are formed :
Horned cattle breeding.
Pig-breeding.
Sheep-breeding.
Sections :
Veterinary.
Fodder.
Planning and Financial.

(*f*) The Chief Administration for Horse-breeding : to carry out all functions relating to the management of horse-breeding sovkhosi, horse-breeding farms, and the breeding and maintenance of the number of horses in the country.

(*g*) The Chief Veterinary Administration.

(*h*) The Chief Administration for Sub-tropical Cultures.

(*i*) The Chief Department for Afforestation and Protective (?) Forests.

(*j*) The Chief Administration for Tobacco.

(*k*) The Chief Administration for Silk-worm Culture.

(*l*) The Chief Administration for Higher Technical Educational Institutions and Technical Schools.

(*m*) Political Administration.

3. In order to improve the contact of the Chief Administrations with the krais and oblasts and in order to ensure proper guidance for grain production and livestock-breeding so that they may be adapted to the peculiarities of the principal regions of the USSR, Assistant Heads of Administrations are detailed in the Chief Administrations for Grain and Oil-producing cultures and the Chief Administration for Livestock-breeding, to inspect the following groups of rayons :

*1st Group of Rayons.*—Ukrainian SSR, Crimean ASSR, the Central Black Earth Oblast, Azov-Black-Sea Krai, the Northern Caucasus Krai, the Trans-Caucasian FSR, the Middle Asiatic Republics.

*2nd Group of Rayons.*—The Moscow Oblast, the Gorki Krai, the Ivanovskaya Oblast, the Leningrad Oblast, the White Russian Oblast, the Northern Krai, the Tartar ASSR, the Sverdlovskaya Oblast, the Ob-Irtysh Oblast, the Western Oblast.

*3rd Group of Rayons.*—The Stalingrad Krai, the Saratov Krai, the Middle Volga Krai, the Bashkir ASSR, the Kazak ASSR.

*4th Group of Rayons.*—The Chelyabinsk Oblast, the Western Siberian, Eastern Siberian and Far-Eastern Krais.

4. The following Departments are to be formed within the NKZ of the Union of SSR :

(a) Planning and Financial.
(b) Accounting and Statistical.
(c) Specialists.
(d) Administrative and Management.
(e) Secretariat of the Narkomat.

5. To lay down that the following are attached directly to the Narkom of Agriculture of the Union of SSR :

(a) Section for Registration and Selection of Labour Force.
(b) A group of inspectors to verify execution.
(c) Central Arbitration Court.

6. To reorganise the Association " Selkhossnabjenie " into an office called " Selkhossnabjenie ", this office to retain the functions of supplying the MTS and the sovkhosi of the NKZ of the USSR with machines, implements and mineral manure according to a limited list, confirmed by the Sovnarkom of the USSR ; the krai and oblast offices of the Association " Selkhossnabjenie " with all their warehouses and shops are to be handed over to the krai and oblast Land Administrations.

## II. Apparatus of the Narkomzem of the RSFSR

The work of the Narkomzem of the RSFSR is to be concentrated upon guidance as regards production of vegetables and potatoes, orchards, land utilisation and improvement, local forests, poultry farming, rabbit-breeding and beekeeping ; the responsibility for guidance in this work in the krais, oblasts and autonomous republics of the RSFSR is to lie with the Narkomzem of the RSFSR.

In accordance with this, the following structure of the Narkomzem of the RSFSR is laid down :

(I) Administrations :

(a) Vegetable.
(b) Potato.
(c) Fruit-growing.
(d) Land Utilisation.
(e) Local Forests.
(f) Poultry Farming, Rabbit-breeding and Beekeeping.
(g) Special Higher Educational Institutions and Technical Schools for training cadres of mass qualifications (?) for breeding small live-stock, fruit-growing, vegetable-growing and land utilisation.
(h) Industrial Sovkhosi.

(II) Departments :

(a) Planning and Financial.
(b) Local Land Improvement and Peat.

(*c*) Agriculture in the Far North.

(*d*) Administrative and Management.

(*e*) Secretariat of the Narkomat.

(III) Attached to the Narkom of Agriculture of the RSFSR :

(*a*) Land Commission.

(*b*) Section for Selection and Registration of Labour Force (Cadres).

(*c*) Arbitration.

III. APPARATUS OF THE NARKOMZEMS OF REPUBLICS AND OF THE LAND ADMINISTRATIONS OF KRAIS AND OBLASTS (NKZ OF THE RSFSR EXCLUDED)

1. In the Narkomzems of Republics and in the Oblast and Krai Land Administrations the following Administrations are created :

(*a*) Grain (in all oblasts, krais and republics), Beet (in all oblasts, krais and republics which grow beet), Cotton (in all republics, krais and oblasts which grow cotton), and other Administrations (flax and hemp, vegetable, potato, forestry, orchard) according to the special bias of a given republic, krai and oblast.

(*b*) Livestock-breeding.

(*c*) Horse-breeding.

(*d*) Veterinary.

(*e*) Political Section.

2. Departments :

(*a*) Planning and Finance.

(*b*) Accounting and Statistics.

(*c*) Land Utilisation and Improvement.

(*d*) Training of Labour Force.

(*e*) Management.

3. Attached to the Narkoms for Agriculture in the republics and to the chiefs of krai and oblast Land Administrations :

(*a*) Section for Selection and Registration of Labour Force.

(*b*) Land Commission.

(*c*) Arbitration.

(*d*) " Selkhossnabjenie " Office.

## IV. THE RAYON LAND APPARATUS

It must be recognised that the tendency which exists in certain krais, oblasts and republics towards the liquidation of the Rayon Land Departments is an erroneous one.

In order to strengthen the Rayon Land organs :

1. The Rayon Associations of stock-breeding farms are to be abolished as independent economic organs, and are to be made into sections of the Rayon Land Departments for stock-breeding.

2. The Rayon Land Departments are made responsible for operative guidance in agriculture in the kolkhosi which are not served by the MTS, and in individual homesteads; operative guidance as regards stock-breeding in the rayon; general planning [summary planning] of agricultural production in the rayon; state supervision as regards quality of agricultural work in all kolkhosi and individual homesteads; operative guidance in fruit-growing; compilation of summary reports as to agricultural campaigns in the rayon; management of state property and of forests of local importance.

3. To establish in accordance with this the following typical structure of the Rayon Land Department:

Manager of the Rayon Land Department.

Deputy Manager of the Rayon Land Department; he also to act as manager of the section of Livestock-breeding.

The Rayon Land Departments are to have no section beyond the Livestock-breeding section.

The Rayon Land Department have:
Senior Agronome.
Senior Land Arranger.
Senior Forester.
Senior Inspector for Accounting.
Technician for Construction.

4. To establish the following structure for the Section of Stock-breeding:

Manager of the Livestock-breeding section.
Senior Zoo-technician.
Senior Veterinary Surgeon.
District Zoo-technicians and Veterinary Surgeons, attached to definite kolkhosi.
Zoo-technician for Horses.

5. A Land Commission is established and attached to each Rayon Land Department.

6. The incubator stations are directly subordinate to the Rayon Land Departments.

### V. Machine and Tractor Stations

1. The post of Manager of MTS district is to be abolished, so that the tractor brigades are directly subordinate to the Director of the MTS, and so that agronomes and travelling mechanics should be attached to definite groups of kolkhosi and tractor brigades, and should be directly subordinate to the Senior Agronome and Senior Mechanic.

2. The following typical structure of the MTS is fixed :

(*a*) Director of MTS.

(*b*) Polit-otdel of the MTS.

(*c*) Senior Mechanic (he is also manager of the tractor garage, and is held wholly responsible for the proper use and condition of tractors) and Travelling Mechanics.

(*d*) Senior Agronome, Agronomes for Special Cultures and Seeds, according to the bias of the work of the MTS, and Agronomes attached to definite Groups of Kolkhosi.

(*e*) Manager of the Petrol Station.

(*f*) Book-keeping.

The MTS to contain also, directly subordinate to the Director of the MTS, working on cost-accounting basis :

Motor Columns.

Road Detachment.

Repair Workshop.

## VI

It is made the duty of the Narkomzem of the USSR to complete the reorganisation of land organs, according to the present decree, by May 15, 1934.

Chairman of the Central Executive
Committee of the Union of SSR :   M. KALININ

Chairman of the Council of People's
Commissars of the Union of SSR :   V. MOLOTOV

Secretary of the Central Executive
Committee of the Union of SSR :   A. ENUKIDZE

MOSCOW, KREMLIN, *April* 4, 1934

# IX

## APPENDIX TO CHAPTER IV (see p. 174)

*List of the 154 Trade Unions among which the Membership of the 47 Trade Unions of 1931 was distributed in 1934*

| Old Unions | New Unions |
|---|---|
| Black metallurgy | 1. Black metallurgy of the South |
|         ,, | 2.   ,,     ,,     ,,   East |
|         ,, | 3.   ,,     ,,     ,,   Centre |
| Transport machinery | 4. Transport machinery |
|         ,, | 5. Shipbuilding |
| Electrical workers | 6. Electrical machinery |
|         ,, | 7. Electrical low-tension current industry |
|         ,, | 8. Electro-stations |
| Auto-tractor industry | 9. Aviation industry |
|     ,,       ,, | 10. Automobile industry |
|     ,,       ,, | 11. Tractor industry |
| General machinery | 12. Tool and instrument makers |
|     ,,       ,, | 13. Machinery of fine precision |
|     ,,       ,, | 14. Heavy machinery |
|     ,,       ,, | 15. Military metal industry |
|     ,,       ,, | 16. Ordinary machinery |
|     ,,       ,, | 17. Metal goods |
| Non-ferrous metallurgy | 18. Gold and platinum extraction |
|     ,,       ,, | 19. Non-ferrous extraction |
|     ,,       ,, | 20.     ,,     manufacture |
| Mining | 21. Iron ore mining in the South |
|     ,, | 22.   ,,     ,,     ,,   East |
|     ,, | 23. Mining of non-metallic ores |
|     ,, | 24. Salt industry |
|     ,, | 25. Geological research workers |
| Coal-mining | 26. Coal-mining in the Centre |
|     ,, | 27.   ,,       ,,   East |
|     ,, | 28.   ,,       ,,   Donbas |
| Petroleum | 29. Petroleum in the Caucasus |
|     ,, | 30.     ,,       ,,   East |
|     ,, | 31. Petroleum distillation |
| Construction workers | 32. Heavy industry of the Centre and South |
|     ,,       ,, | 33. Heavy industry of the Far East |
|     ,,       ,, | 34. Heavy industry of the Urals and Western Siberia |

| Old Unions | New Unions |
|---|---|
| Construction workers | 35. Light industry (timber and food products) |
|      ,,     ,, | 36. Housing and communal industry |
| Railway, posts and road workers | 37. Railways and metropolitan works |
|      ,,     ,, | 38. Macadam road workers |
| Cement and ceramic | 39. Fireproof clay workers |
|      ,,     ,, | 40. Cement workers |
|      ,,     ,, | 41. Brick workers |
| Timber and forestry industry | 42. Timber and forestry industry of the South and Centre |
|      ,,     ,, | 43. Timber and forestry industry of the North |
|      ,,     ,, | 44. Timber and forestry industry of the East |
| Woodworking industry | 45. Woodworking industry of the North |
|      ,,     ,, | 46. Woodworking industry of the Centre and South |
|      ,,     ,, | 47. Woodworking industry of the East |
|      ,,     ,, | 48. Furniture and musical instruments |
|      ,,     ,, | 49. Matches and plywood |
| Chemical industry | 50. Coke-chemical industry |
|      ,,     ,, | 51. Nitrates and special chemicals |
|      ,,     ,, | 52. Soda products and mineral mixtures |
|      ,, .     ,, | 53. Paint and pharmaceutical products |
| Glass and porcelain | 54. Glass |
|      ,,     ,, | 55. Porcelain |
| Cotton manufacture | 56. Cotton manufacture in Moscow, Leningrad and elsewhere |
|      ,,     ,, | 57. Cotton manufacture in Ivanovo oblast |
|      ,,     ,, | 58. Manufacture of other fibres |
| Wool, silk and knitting industries | 59. Woollen industry |
|      ,,     ,, | 60. Knitting industry |
|      ,,     ,, | 61. Silk industry |
| Linen and hemp industry | 62. Linen industry |
|      ,,     ,, | 63. Hemp industry |
| Sugar industry | 64. Sugar-making |
|      ,,     ,, | 65. Beet sugar—sovkhosi workers |
| Leather industry | 66. Leather goods |
|      ,,     ,, | 67. Boots and shoes |
|      ,,     ,, | 68. Fur goods |
| Needlework | 69. Needlework in the North |
|      ,, | 70.    ,,    ,,   South |
| Printing and publishing | 71. Printing in the Centre and South |
|      ,,     ,, | 72.    ,,    ,,   North |
|      ,,     ,, | 73. Publishing industry |
| Flour-milling, baking and confectionery | 74. Baking |
|      ,,     ,, | 75. Confectionery |
|      ,,     ,, | 76. Flour-milling and Elevator Service in the South and Centre |
|      ,,     ,, | 77. Flour-milling and Elevator Service in the East |

| Old Unions | New Unions |
|---|---|
| Fish | 78. Fisheries in the Far East |
| „ | 79. „　　„　　North |
| „ | 80. „　　„　　South |
| Workers in agricultural products | 81. Tobacco workers |
| „　　　„ | 82. Wine and distillery workers |
| „　　　„ | 83. Brewery and starch-making workers |
| Workers in agricultural sovkhosi (state farms) | 84. Grain sovkhosi |
| „　　　„ | 85. Vegetable sovkhosi |
| „　　　„ | 86. Garden crop sovkhosi |
| „　　　„ | 87. Cotton sovkhosi |
| Workers in animal-breeding sovkhosi (state farms) | 88. Pig sovkhosi |
| „　　　„ | 89. Sheep sovkhosi |
| „　　　„ | 90. Horse sovkhosi |
| „　　　„ | 91. Other animal and game sovkhosi |
| „　　　„ | 92. Milk and Meat sovkhosi of the Centre and South |
| „　　　„ | 93. Milk and Meat sovkhosi of the Urals and Siberia |
| „　　　„ | 94. Milk and Meat sovkhosi of Kazakstan and Middle Asia |
| Machine and tractor stations | 95. MTS in the South and Centre |
| „　　　„ | 96. „　　„　　East |
| „　　　„ | 97. Agricultural institutions |
| Meat and tinned food industries | 98. Meat industries and refrigeration |
| „　　　„ | 99. Tinned food industries |
| „　　　„ | 100. Butter and fat-making |
| „　　　„ | 101. Milk industry |
| Railway workers | 102. Railway workers of the Centre |
| „　　　„ | 103. „　　„　　„　South |
| „　　　„ | 104. Railway workers of the East and Far East |
| „　　　„ | 105. Railway workers of Middle Asia |
| „　　　„ | 106. Railway workshops |
| Water transport workers | 107. Sea transport |
| „　　　„ | 108. River transport |
| Auto drivers and avion workers | 109. Aviation workers |
| „　　　„ | 110. Auto drivers in Moscow and Leningrad |
| „　　　„ | 111. „　　in the South |
| „　　　„ | 112. „　　„　　East |
| Post and telegraph | 113. Postal workers |
| „　　　„ | 114. Telegraph, telephone and radio workers |
| Communal workers | 115. Tramway workers |
| „　　　„ | 116. Workers in communal enterprises |
| Municipal enterprises | 117. Housing administration |
| „　　　„ | 118. Municipal administration |
| „　　　„ | 119. Fire brigades |
| „　　　„ | 120. Haircutters |
| Public feeding workers | 121. Consumers' cooperative public feeding enterprises |
| „　　　„ | 122. State enterprises of public feeding |

| Old Unions | New Unions |
|---|---|
| Cooperative and state distributive trades | 123. Consumers' cooperative employees of the Centre |
| ,,            ,, | 124. Consumers' cooperative employees of the Ukraine |
| ,,            ,, | 125. Consumers' cooperative employees of the Caucasus |
| ,,            ,, | 126. Consumers' cooperative employees of Siberia and the Urals |
| ,,            ,, | 127. Consumers' cooperative employees of the East |
| ,,            ,, | 128. Employees in state trading |
| ,,            ,, | 129.     ,,     in foreign trade |
| ,,            ,, | 130.     ,,     in bookshops |
| Workers in state institutions | 131. Workers in state institutions |
| ,,            ,, | 132. Workers in administrative institutions |
| ,,            ,, | 133. Workers in the Courts of Justice |
| ,,            ,, | 134. Workers in the institutions of National Economy |
| Cinema and other artistic workers | 135. Photo-cinema industry |
| ,,            ,, | 136. Artistic industries |
| Medico-sanitary workers | 137. Workers in medico-sanitary institutions of RSFSR |
| ,,            ,, | 138. Workers in medico-sanitary institutions of Ukraine |
| ,,            ,, | 139. Workers in medico-sanitary institutions of Middle Asia |
| ,,            ,, | 140. Workers in medico-sanitary institutions of Transcaucasus |
| ,,            ,, | 141. Workers in medico-sanitary institutions of White Russia |
| Workers in educational institutions | 142. Workers in colleges, high schools and scientific institutes |
| ,,            ,, | 143. Workers in primary and secondary schools of RSFSR |
| ,,            ,, | 144. Workers in primary and secondary schools of Ukraine |
| ,,            ,, | 145. Workers in primary and secondary schools of White Russia |
| ,,            ,, | 146. Workers in primary and secondary schools of Transcaucasus |
| ,,            ,, | 147. Workers in primary and secondary schools of Middle Asia |
| ,,            ,, | 148. Workers in pre-school institutions |
| ,,            ,, | 149. Workers engaged in institutions of political education |
| Finance and banking | 150. Finance and banking |
| Paper-making | 151. Paper-making |
| Rubber manufacture | 152. Rubber manufacture |
| Peat workers | 153. Peat workers |
| Agricultural machinery makers | 154. Agricultural machinery makers |

# X

*The Duties and Functions of the Factory Committees* (see p. 182)

(Resolution of the II Plenum of the Central Executive Committee
of the All-Union Congress of Trade Unions (AUCCTU), on the
Report of Comrade Shvernik, *Trud*, December 11, 1932)

(SUMMARY only. After a general introduction, there follow the paragraphs summarised below) :

1. The collective agreement must, in fact, become the basis of
the whole of the trade union work of the FZK (factory committee)
in the undertaking. The FZK must so organise its work in the
undertaking that the fight for the carrying out of the conditions laid
out in the collective agreement—by management and workers alike—
and the systematic watch that the collective agreement is being
carried out, become the daily concern and the main subject of the
activities of the Factory and Workshop Committees.

2. The FZK must increase their share in the work of planning
and regulating wages in the undertaking by taking an active part
in the classification of workers so that they can be put on wage-
scales, and in determining technically possible quotas of output and
payment in accordance with the Wage-Scale Schedule and the
collective agreement. The FZK must see to it that the greatest
possible use is made of piecework and that payment for work done
is made on the basis of progressive premiums. Workers doing
particularly important or difficult work must be dealt with separately.

The FZK must watch over the spending of the wages fund and
prevent any waste or overspending which may occur as the result
of the employment of excessively large staffs, of the use of overtime
to any large extent, and to increases of wages paid to individual
workers in breach of the collective agreement.

The FZK must keep watch that correct wages are paid to the
workers, and must make a determined fight against the under-
payment of workers and wrong entries of wages in the workers'
wages books.

The FZK must watch strictly that the quotas of output should correspond to the technical conditions of production obtaining in the industry at the time.

3. The Plenum notes the quite inadmissible diminution of the part played by the RKK (Workers' and Peasants' Inspection)[1] and the slackening of their activities. The RKK must become the most important and authoritative organ in the settlement of conflicts in the field of fixing rates of pay and rates of output. The Plenum advises that membership of the RKK should consist of truly responsible representatives of the FZK and of the management—of persons who know the conditions of production and enjoy the confidence of the workers.

The activities of the RKK must be freed from all elements of red-tape and from a heartless attitude to the workers. The RKK must ensure the speedy consideration of the workers' statements, and the workers concerned must be allowed to take part in this. The RKK must see to it that exhaustive and accurate decisions as to the problems raised are reached, and that the workers are informed of these decisions in good time by means of a compulsory display of these decisions in the workshops.

4. The Plenum draws attention to the fact that the decision taken by the Ninth All-Union Congress of Trade Unions as to the strengthening of Technical Rate-Fixing Bureaux (TNB) has not yet been carried out. This is quite inadmissible at the present time, when the technique of rate-fixing is becoming increasingly complex, and when its importance in the regulation of wage-rates is constantly growing.

The Plenum advises the FZK to see that this decision of the Ninth All-Union Congress of Trade Unions is carried out at the earliest possible moment.

5. In view of the fact that spoliage and stoppages disorganise production, and thereby lead to the lowering of wages of the workers, the Plenum advises the FZK to carry out unwaveringly any decree of the Government as to payment for bad work and stoppages, and to combat energetically the causes which lead to this ; the broad masses of the workers must be drawn into dealing with this most urgent problem.

6. The Plenum completely and wholly endorses the resolution of TSIK and of the Sovnarkom of the USSR, as to the fight against absenteeism, regarding this as a most important measure in strengthening labour discipline.

All trade union organisations are to have this decision of the

---

[1] For the abolition of the Workers' and Peasants' Inspection as an independent commissariat, and the transfer of its functions partly to the All-Union Central Committee of Trade Unions, and partly to the new Commission of Soviet Control, see Appendix VI, pp. 474-476.

Government explained to them at their meetings, so that it is really carried out.

Greater use is to be made of the Comrades' Courts, so that they become the most important weapon in the class education of workers and in the strengthening of socialist labour discipline.

7. While noting great advances in the activities of conferences to discuss production in groups and brigades, the Plenum observes a slackening in the work of workshop and factory conferences for the discussion of production.

The Plenum makes it the duty of the FZK to strengthen the activities of the workshops and of the factories in this respect, so that the conferences become practical schools for the training of broad masses of workers in the management of production.

8. In a number of undertakings the decision of the Party, of the Government, and of the All-Union Central Committee of Trade Unions as to the part of Assistant Directors in production conferences has been distorted. The purpose of this measure was to raise the authority of production conferences within the undertaking, and to ensure the speedier carrying out of the workers' proposals. In many undertakings the managements (with the cognizance of the FZK and of the higher trade union organisations) have made use of the appointment of the chairman of production conferences as Assistant Director in order to make him do purely administrative work.

The chairman of the production conference (the Assistant Director) may be set free from all work which does not follow from his duties as organiser of production conferences, and the person dealing with the workers' suggestions. His part as one of the most important workers in the FZK in the field of directing factory, workshop and group production conferences must be strengthened, as well as his share in the entire work of the factory and workshop committees.

9. The Plenum notes that the FZK are paying less attention than before to the simple form of socialist competition between workers, namely, udarnichestvo (shock brigades) ; this must be improved.

A number of FZK are not taking their duties as regards making up lists of udarniks (shock-brigaders) sufficiently seriously, and include in them persons who are unworthy of the name. While fighting false udarnichestvo the FZK must achieve the systematic payment of premiums to the udarniks and also make sure that they get preferential treatment in the way of better food in the factory dining-rooms, and are allowed to buy goods the sale of which is unprofitable in the factory shops, etc.

10. The Plenum approves the decision of the TSIK of the Party as to the transfer of ZRK (closed cooperatives) of the larger undertakings to the managements, and as to the appointment of the

chairmen of the ZRK as Assistant Directors in the remainder of the undertakings.

The Plenum draws attention to the fact that in this respect the work of the FZK will also increase. The FZK must detail their best workers into the supply organisations of the management ; they must ensure their participation in the committees of supply in the undertakings, and work for the greatest possible increase of the stocks of supplies by factory managements, the ZRK and the dining rooms.

The FZK must mobilise the masses for the fight against waste and criminal abuses in connection with the workers' food supplies ; these are meant only for the workers in the given undertaking. The numbers to be supplied, and the quantities of supplies to be issued, must be checked by the FZK, and they must also keep a check on the issue of shopping books and food cards.

11. The FZK must give systematic help to the managements and to the ZRK in developing suburban farms and farm-yards ; the FZK must see to it that at the earliest possible moment piggeries, dairy farms, rabbit farms, fishponds, etc., become of real value in supplying the workers and their families with foodstuffs.

The experiment of the more advanced factories in attaching villages to themselves for the purpose of getting food supplies should be emulated ; and the workers must themselves help in getting direct supplies from these attached villages, and also in establishing stores of food in the factories.

The FZK must also give every possible assistance to the workers and their families in organising their own allotments or gardens (vegetable, rabbit-breeding, piggeries, etc.), which would provide additional sources for the improved feeding of workers.

12. The Plenum considers that the work of the FZK, in so far as housing is concerned, is not satisfactory. They are recommended to make use of the experience of the campaign for the October Housing Fund, which has shown that by concentrating material and men in the most important sectors of building ; by preliminary allotment of dwellings to workshops and individual workers' families ; by mobilising local supplies of building materials ; and by utilising the voluntary labour of the future occupiers, the supply of living accommodation in the undertakings can be largely increased. Special attention must be paid to better construction, and to the greatest possible use of local building material.

The FZK must increase the attention paid to the correct use of the living accommodation available ; the best workers on the regular staff and the udarniki (shock-brigaders) must have first claim upon this. The FZK must see to it that care is taken of the dwellings, and that they are repaired in good time, etc.

The FZK must also see to it that the workers' villages, apartments and lodging-houses are kept in good and sanitary order, and that day-nurseries and kindergartens are established in connection with these ; expenditure on establishments for children must be carefully watched.

13. The Plenum notes that a number of FZK do not direct and do not systematically watch the work of the paying-out centres of Social Insurance in the undertakings. . . . The Plenum recommends to the FZK to strengthen the paying-out centres by appointing within a month their most active workers to act on them ; their work must be carefully watched and special attention must be paid to the improvement of the medical service ; to a more rational use being made of the insurance fund ; to social service for the workers (crèches, kindergartens, the feeding of school children) ; to a wise and timely sending off of workers to sanatoria, houses of rest and watering-places ; and to a full use being made of the travelling facilities allotted for these purposes.

14. The Plenum draws attention to the fact that the work of the FZK in the field of protection of labour and of safety appliances is clearly unsatisfactory, and that they do not work in conjunction with the inspectors ; the Plenum advises the FZK to carry out a daily direction of the work of the inspectors, and to watch over the expenditure of funds set aside for improving safety appliances.

15. The Plenum puts before the FZK the task of improving radically and effectively, within the shortest possible time, the cultural work within all links of the trade union organisation in the undertaking without any exceptions.

They must concentrate their attention on the general and technical instruction of adults ; the instruction of children and young people ; technical propaganda ; political education. Special attention must be paid to new workers. The recreation of the workers must also be dealt with.

16. In the field of technical propaganda the FZK must take an active part in the measures taken by the technical propaganda departments of the management led by the Assistant Directors in the production conferences ; they must do this by explanatory and organising work among the masses, and supplement this by technical propaganda in Red Corners and Clubs ; by the distribution of technical literature, and by working with the authors of useful books and pamphlets. In all work among the masses in the field of technical propaganda the FZK must seek the support of the voluntary workers among societies of the workers themselves, and of the engineers and technicians (the society " To Master Technique " ; and the scientific societies of engineers and technicians).

17. In their work among the masses the trade union organisations must see to the carrying out of the slogan " Every factory is a fortress of defence " ; they must concentrate their attention, in the first place, on problems of anti-aircraft defence, rifle-shooting and gliding (?).

At the same time the defence work of the FZK must be still more inspired with the problems of the international education of the working masses.

The FZK must also increase their assistance in the development of physical culture.

18. The clubs must be considered by the FZK as one of the greatest levers in communist education, and they must therefore reorganise their club work according to the resolution of the All-Union Central Committee of the Trade Unions of September 2, 1932. The FZK must direct the work of clubs and Red Corners primarily to explaining to the masses the policy of the Party and of the Government, the successes of socialist construction and the difficulties encountered ; they must systematically raise the socialist class-consciousness, especially of the new workers. This political agitation work, which is also explanatory and which it is the duty of every trade union organisation and trade unionist to perform, must be built on concrete examples from their own undertaking (the execution of the promfinplan, examples of competition, the fight against absenteeism, spoilage, stoppages, carelessness with factory property, etc.). This work must systematically raise the consciousness of new workers to the level of understanding the interests of the workers' socialist state as a whole.

19. The Plenum notes that the FZK have not fully carried out the estimates for the spending of funds for cultural work ; the Plenum puts before the FZK, and the leading trade union and inter-trade-union organisations, the task of systematic control over the correct and full spending of the funds for cultural service among the workers.

20. The FZK must give systematic help and real direction to the workshop committees and to the trade union group organs, and show them by precept how they must work in the field of dealing with the workers' complaints, of directing the activities of production conferences, of the regulation of wages, of directing socialist competition, the improvement of dining-rooms, the communist education of workers, etc.

The Plenum advises that the practice of fussing and disturbing the workers in workshop committees and group organs, in order that they may carry out functions which are in no wise connected with their service to the working masses and to production, should be stopped. Greater initiative and independence in deciding separate problems is to be given to the organs of the union in the workshop and in the group.

21. In order to attract wider masses of workers into the active work of the union and the discussion of measures affecting the entire factory and all the workshops, the Plenum advises that conferences of trade union group organs be called regularly and periodic-

ally ; general workshop meetings not less than once a month, and general factory meetings not less than once in two months. The Plenum empowers the presidium of the executive committees of the trade unions to determine accurately the rights and duties of group organisers.

22. The Plenum demands from the FZK an unconditional carrying out of the directions of the Ninth All-Union Congress of Trade Unions as to proletarian democracy and election rights, and demands a most determined fight with those who contravene them.

The general meetings and conferences of workers in the factories are the highest leading organs of the trade union in the undertaking. The Plenum advises that these meetings and conferences be carefully prepared, that the most important problems, those which most interest or trouble the workers, be put before them ; their decisions must be carried out as soon as possible.

The Plenum considers it necessary to have in the undertakings not less than one " Trade Union Day " a month in order to carry out mass trade union work.

23. The Plenum attaches special importance to the speedy and painstaking resolution of problems raised in the letters and complaints of workers which come to the FZK. The Plenum recommends that personal responsibility for this work be put upon one member of the presidium or of the plenum of the FZK. It is necessary to attract voluntary active workers to this activity, and to conduct the most determined fight against a red-tape official attitude to the letters and statements of workers. The Trade Union Press must lead in the fight for due attention being paid to the workers' letters.

24. The Plenum underlines the fact that one of the most important methods of fighting the bureaucratisation of the trade union work and of attracting the broad masses of their members to social work is to draw into the work of the FZK in all its aspects, into the work of the workshops committees and into the work of the group organs, of a large number of active volunteers ; without these the FZK could not cope with the tasks before them. The Plenum accordingly advises all trade union organisations to increase their work in this field, to widen the circle of active volunteers by raising their political and cultural level and by directing and helping their work. In calling systematically conferences of the active volunteers to discuss separate problems (the collective agreement, the protection of labour, the organisation of the work of the trade union, etc.) the FZK must teach them by concrete examples how the work must be done.

25. The Plenum notes that the decision of the Ninth All-Union Congress of Trade Unions as to the work of the FZK in respect of the leading trades is not being carried out satisfactorily by the FZK.

The Plenum advises that delegate workers in the leading trades be selected in the workshops, and that workshop and factory meetings of these workers be called systematically; help is to be given to them in satisfying the needs of the workers in the leading trades.

26. The Plenum advises the FZK to conduct a daily and determined fight for the inclusion of new members into the trade unions; all forms of mass work are to be used in this—(meetings with non-members, patronage of regular workers over new workers, the press, the work of the Clubs, of Red Corners, etc.).

Special attention is to be paid to improving trade union discipline among the members of the unions. In particular, the FZK must fight arrears in the payment of membership fees; this is to be done by means of explanatory work among the masses and a better organisation of the work of collectors of membership fees. Present arrears in membership fees must be liquidated by January 15, 1933.

27. The Plenum notes the excessive number of investigations of undertakings carried out by the higher trade union organs, and advises the Presidium of the VTSIK of the Trade Unions to establish a system which would diminish the number of these investigations to a considerable extent.

In order to avoid duplication in the guidance of the work of the FZK by the union and inter-union organs, the Plenum underlines that the immediate direction of the FZK is the province of the oblast (krai) departments of the union. The oblast soviets of the trade unions guide the activities of the FZK through oblast departments, rayon trade union soviets, and concentrate their work upon the control and checking of what has been accomplished and upon help in the work of the FZK.

28. The Plenum notes that frequent changes in the personnel of the FZK are extremely detrimental to the work; the Plenum advises all trade union organisations to stop this practice and to keep for long periods the better workers in the FZK and in the workshop committees, as well as group organisers. A change of personnel should, as a rule, occur only during re-elections.

All trade union organisations must use the present campaign of re-elections into the FZMK in order to maintain in office the better workers, and in order to verify whether the decisions of the Ninth All-Union Congress of Trade Unions are being carried out.

29. The most important task of the oblast departments and of the TSIKS of the Unions is the selection of chairmen of the FZK. For this work must be put forward trusty persons, who enjoy the unquestioned support and authority of workers in the factory; their level must constantly be raised, they must be freed from petty supervision and from functions which are alien to them; constant care must be taken of them and help must be given to them in their work.

After the conclusion of the re-elections of the FZK in the undertakings, short courses (without taking them away from their work) must be started for trade union group organisers, for members of the workshop committees and of the FZK. As from January 1933 a network of primary trade union circles for new members of the trade unions is also to be started.

# XI

## APPENDIX TO CHAPTER III (see p. 190)

*The Collective Agreement (Kol-dogovor) of the Fraising-Lathe
Works at Gorki for the Year 1933–1934*

THE elaborate collective agreements (Kol-dogovor) annually entered
into between the managements of the industrial enterprises in the
USSR and the trade union organisations are unknown to the western
world ; and have apparently never been translated.  We therefore
print, nearly in full, the translation that we have had made of a
characteristic specimen from our own collection, which no one but
a student of trade unionism, or of industrial organisation, need
trouble to read !  It may be explained that the unfamiliar word
" fraise " means (*New English Dictionary*) " a tool used for enlarging a circular hole ;  also, in watchmaking, for cutting teeth in a
wheel".  A "fraising-lathe" is presumably a lathe bearing such a tool.

COLLECTIVE AGREEMENT OF THE WORKERS, THE ENGINEERS AND
 TECHNICAL PERSONNEL (ITR) AND THE EMPLOYEES OF THE
 FRAISING-LATHE WORKS AT GORKI (NIZHNI-NOVGOROD), FROM
 MARCH 1, 1933, TO MARCH 1, 1934

I. *Mutual Obligations as to the Carrying out of the Industrial and
Financial Plant*

1. It is the fundamental aim of the present agreement to carry
out the six instructions of Comrade Stalin, the resolutions of the
Ninth Congress of Trade Unions, and of the January Plenum of
the Central Committee and the Central Control Commission of the
All-Russian Communist Party ;  to ensure the most successful fulfilment of the industrial and economic duties of the undertaking during
1933—the first year of the Second Five-Year Plan—and, upon this
basis, the continuous improvement in the material and cultural
condition of its workers, engineers and technical personnel (ITR)
and employees.

2. In order to carry out these tasks the Administration, the Factory Committee (zavkom), the workers, the engineering and technical personnel and the employees undertake to ensure the unconditional fulfilment of the qualitative and quantitative indices of the industrial and financial plan by strengthening the proletarian labour discipline, by the further development of socialist forms of labour such as socialist emulation, shock brigades (udarnichestvo), counter industrial and economic plans and cost-accounting brigades, and by the most speedy mastering of the technique and of the planned capacity of the equipment.

[Here follow detailed tables of Indices of Output, Indices for Increase of Productivity, and Statistics of the Factory Wage Fund and its distribution.]

3. The Administration undertakes :

(*a*) To transfer the basic productive workshops to the system of cost-accounting not later than June 1.

(*b*) To give instructions as to production to the workshops for the following month not later than the 25th of each month, and to each working-place not later than the 30th. The Chief of PPS is responsible for this.

(*c*) For bringing not later than the 20th of each month, before the Factory Committee (zavkom), a plan showing the proposed productivity of labour, and the wages of the piece-rate categories of workers, with information as to the execution of the financial plan of production of the undertaking. The Chief of TES is responsible for this.

(*d*) For carrying out measures for instituting personal responsibility at all points of the work, and for establishing the clear responsibility of each worker and employee for the work given to him, and for the property entrusted to him. For this purpose, not later than May 1 :

(1) Workers must be allotted to definite working-places and definite shifts. The chiefs of workshops are responsible for this.

(2) Definite equipment and tools are to be attached to each worker, and a definite task fixed for him. Chiefs of workshops are responsible for this.

(3) Definite members of the administrative and technical personnel and of the serving personnel are to be attached to definite groups and shifts of workers. Chiefs of workshops and of the Departments of the Works Management are responsible for this.

(4) Individual responsibility is to be established for damaged goods, spoilt material and breakages of equipment, for the quantity and quality of the finished product, and of the semi-finished goods which are passed from one section to another, and from one work-

shop to another. Chiefs of workshops, and of OTK, OGM and OPP, are responsible for this.

(5) Preventive repairs are to be carried out according to plan, and the repairing staff is to be attached to the objects to be repaired. The Chief of OGM is responsible for this.

(*e*) To consider within ten days all proposals for rationalisation sent in by production conferences, workers, engineering and technical personnel (ITR) and employees, and to inform within the same period the author of each proposal as to the results of the proposal.

Within twenty days after a proposal has been accepted, to determine its economic effects and the premium to be given to the author of the proposal, in pursuance of the ruling as to premiums.

To establish the period within which each accepted proposal is to be introduced into the scheme of production, and to fix the persons who are to be responsible for its carrying out. The Zav. Briz. (factory invention committee) is responsible for this.

(*f*) To start keeping systematic records of the work done by shock brigades and by those engaged in socialist competition : and to present to the Factory Committee information as to the results of their work not later than the 10th of each month. The Department of Mass Works is responsible for this.

(*g*) Not later than within twenty days from the moment of receiving notice from a brigade that they wish to be transferred to cost-accounting, to determine from the point of view of the conditions of the technological process the possibility of transferring the brigade to cost-accounting ; and, within the same period, to prepare the necessary conditions for this, and to take the necessary official steps for the transfer of the brigade to cost-accounting, including the making of the cost-accounting agreement.

The premiums are paid to cost-accounting brigades in accordance with the typical ruling as to cost-accounting brigades by the Commissariat of Labour and All-Union Central Committee of Trade Unions.

The calculations of economics of premiums for the brigade are done every month. The premiums are paid at the same time as the wages.

(*h*) To give premiums to the udarniks (shock-brigaders) and to the engineering and technical personnel (ITR) of the udarnik and cost-accounting brigades, and of separate workshops, for the best productive results of their work ; for exceeding quantitatively and qualitatively their tasks ; for showing initiative in developing socialist competition ; and for exceeding the productive and financial plan.

Premiums are given to pupil udarniks in the same way as to adult workers for best progress at school and in production, for carrying out ahead of time the cost-productive programmes, etc. Nominations for receipt of premiums are brought forward by the Administration and the Factory Committee, and are discussed at the workshop conferences and at production conferences.

(*i*) To ensure the provision of technical guidance for night shifts, and the provision of services to the workers, in the same way as it is done for day shifts.

4. The Factory Committees undertake :

(*a*) To organise their political mass work and productive work in such a manner that, by means of proper regulation of wages, regulation of labour and daily care for the living and cultural needs of the worker, the carrying out of the productive tasks of the undertaking is ensured.

(*b*) To ensure the carrying out, in workshops and among groups of workers, of cultural-political work, and of social disciplinary action as regards persons who break the rules.

(*c*) To mobilise the revolutionary watchfulness of workers as regards the penetration of alien class elements into production ; to mobilise the workers for fighting every kind of theft, and to organise, in the workshops, brigades for the protection of socialist property.

(*d*) To take an active part, and to give direct help to the Administration, in carrying out measures for the organisation of labour and fixing of technical quotas, and to organise brigades in the workshops for assisting in the fixing of such quotas.

(*e*) To ensure systematic direction of, and instructions for, the organisers of udarniks and cost-accounting brigades ; to organise technical help by the ITR to the udarniks and cost-accounting brigades, and to workmen engaged in socialist competition ; to organise the work of production conferences according to groups and trades, making sure of the full participation in them of the workers, of the engineering and technical personnel (ITR) and of the Administration.

(*f*) Systematically, not less than once a quarter, to check the correct expenditure of the funds for the payment of premiums for socialist competition, for udarnik work and for inventions.

5. The workers, the ITR, including the foreign workers (INS), and foreign specialists, and also the employees, undertake :

(*a*) To strengthen labour discipline in every way, to liquidate absenteeism and late arrival ; to get the utmost out of the workingday ; to achieve the fulfilment and even the exceeding of the tasks set, while simultaneously improving the quality of the output ; and liquidating stoppages and damaging of goods.

(*b*) To take an active part in the production conferences as regards technical problems, and in the improvement of production and organisation of labour.

(c) The ITR and skilled workers undertake to pass on their knowledge and experience as regards production to new cadres of workers.

## II. *Labour Discipline*

6. In order to strengthen the socialist discipline of labour and to ensure the fulfilment and the exceeding of the industrial and financial plan, and of the tasks laid down by the Joint Plenum of the Central Committee and Central Control Commission of the All-Union Communist Party as regards the improvement in the quality of the output, lowering costs of production and increased productivity of labour, the Administration and the Factory Committee take upon themselves the following obligations :

(a) The Administration and the Factory Committee undertake, as from May 1, to verify the measures necessary to adjust the registers of attendance ; of lateness at work ; of absenteeism ; and early leaving of work, bearing in mind the instruction of the Commissariat of Labour (Narkontrud) as to registration of records.

(b) The Administration undertakes to put in operation without demur the decision of the Sovnarkom of the USSR of 15.xi.32 as to dismissals for absenteeism without sufficient reasons.

(c) The Administration undertakes, with the corresponding organisations, to take measures in order to improve the means of communication between the undertaking and the workers' residences ; to abolish queues in the dining-rooms and cafeteria of the closed cooperative society (ZRK), etc.

7. The Factory Committee undertakes to carry out the mass political educational work for genuinely socialist labour discipline ; to organise workers' brigades; to verify, in the homes of the workers, the reasons given for absenteeism ; to make the persons guilty of encouraging absentees responsible for their actions. The Factory Committees are held responsible if they ignore or fail to carry out in full the law as to absenteeism ; together with the Administration, the Factory Committee undertakes to cooperate in the improvement of the personnel of register-keepers.

8. The Administration and the Factory Committee undertake the following obligations as regards the creation of favourable conditions for Comrades' Courts : the Administration is to provide the necessary accommodation and the necessary material for the consideration of cases ; the Factory Committee is to carry out concrete direction ; to give regular instructions ; to provide the personnel of the Comrades' Courts from the best udarnik workers ; and to free the chairmen of the courts from too many other onerous social duties.

### III. *Hiring of Labour, Transfers, Dismissals*

9. The Administration and the Factory Committee undertake to adopt drastic measures in order to discover and dismiss immediately alien class elements, not allowing them to penetrate into production.

10. The recruiting of labour is carried out in an organised way by the Administration, through making agreements with kolkhoses or organs of labour, and by attracting to production members of the families of the workers, of the engineering and technical personnel (ITR) and of the employees.

The Administration makes the Head of the Department of Labour Recruiting responsible for taking on and dismissing workers.

The Administration must, within three days, inform the Factory Committee of every new worker taken on ; and the Factory Committee has the right to lodge a reasoned objection within three days of being so informed.

11. The Administration undertakes to specify, in their quarterly plans as to the recruiting of labour, those employments in which women should be taken on in preference to men.

12. In filling vacancies the Administration undertakes to promote to the most skilled work, in the first instance, those udarniks, workers and employees who have completed their studies at the professional technological courses, and persons who have the longest records of work at the given undertaking.

13. The Administration undertakes to organise introductory courses, and to train in them all newly-taken-on workers and employees, both with a view to acquainting them with the peculiarities of production and to their obtaining the technical knowledge which is necessary for work in the establishment ; the programme to be agreed in consultation with the Factory Committee.

Attendance at these courses is compulsory for all persons on their being newly taken on to work. The Technical Propaganda and the Staff Department are responsible for this.

14. A worker who, for reasons of production, is transferred to work paid at a lower rate has a preferential right to return to his old work if that is resumed within two months from the day of his transfer. A person who is transferred on account of illness to lighter work has, on convalescence, the same right. The Heads of Workshops and Departments are responsible for this.

15. Workers and employees who have been absent from work during not more than two months on account of illness, and then return to work, cannot be refused employment (this is exclusive of leave of absence for pregnancy and confinement).

Workers who have lost their capacity to work as a result of injuries received at work, and workers who are being pensioned, may be dismissed only after their incapacity for employment has been established by a medical control commission, and only when a leaving grant is issued to them according to law. The Chief of Labour Recruiting and Dismissals is responsible for this.

16. Members of factory, workshop and shift committees, workers of the workers' part of the Workers' Control Commission (RKK), members of the factory bureau of the engineers' and technicians' section (ITS) and members of the Comrades' Courts cannot be dismissed or transferred to other work without the sanction of the higher trade union organisation. The Chiefs of Workshops and Departments are responsible for this.

17. In dismissals of superfluous labour force the following are given preference in being allowed to keep their jobs, other things being equal : udarniks, members of the trade union, women who have dependents, members of families of persons called up to the Red Army, workers who have given long service in production, and persons to be called up to the Red Army in 1933.

### IV. *Training of Staff and Technical Education*

18. Within the limits of the funds allocated for this in the industrial and financial plan, the Administration undertakes :

(*a*) To impart to the workers the compulsory minimum of technical knowledge within the periods set out in the plan, making sure that these courses are provided with premises, leaders of study circles, and the necessary teaching equipment and materials. The workers in their turn undertake to attend these courses, according to the technical minimum programme, not less than once in six days. Absence from courses is considered to be equal to disregard of the rules of internal order and labour discipline.

(*b*) To provide adequate accommodation and upkeep for a mass technical library.

(*c*) To bear the expenses of production excursions [educational visits] of workers up to the sum of 1000 roubles, and to agree the list of persons to be sent in each case in consultation with the Factory Committee.

(*d*) To pay the fees of 15 workers at technical correspondence courses, and to organise constant technical advice for all workers.

(*e*) To subscribe to technical publications in their own language for foreign workers.

To provide with interpreters those production conferences in which foreign workers and specialists and workers belonging to national minorities participate.

To provide with leaders the circles of foreign workers and of workers belonging to national minorities.

19. The Administration undertakes, during the course of 1933, to train in the factory school (FZU) 120 pupils as below :

(*a*) To train and give refresher courses in the factory and works courses, and in the workers' evening schools, within the scope of the funds agreed by the industrial and financial plan.

(*b*) In order to improve the fixing of production quotas the Administration undertakes, within the limits of the funds agreed in the industrial and financial plan, to train and give refresher courses, during 1933, in special classes, to specialist clerks for calculating production quotas.

(*c*) Within the limits of the funds agreed in the industrial and financial plan, to send workers for instruction to courses outside the undertaking.

The selection of persons to be sent is made in consultation with the Factory Committee.

*Note.*—This undertaking is to be given official form in a supplementary agreement to be made between the Administration and the Factory Committee not later than May 1, 1933.

20. The Administration undertakes to use the 10,000 roubles allotted according to the industrial and financial plan for completing the enlargement of the factory school (FZU) and the production workshops attached to it, during the second quarter of the year.

The Administration undertakes to employ in production the pupils who have completed their course of studies, according to their speciality, ensuring to them on their leaving the school the means necessary to raise their qualifications (attaching them to a definite working-place, giving them promotion as their qualifications improve).

The pupils of the factory school (FZU) undertake to improve the quality of their theoretical and practical work ; not to miss wilfully any practical work or theoretical instruction ; to carry on an unreconcilable fight with those who despoil socialist property (steal and spoil tools, materials, equipment, workshops and lecture-rooms, teaching equipment, books, copy-books, etc.); to combat the spoiling of goods and stoppages ; to take an active part in the social and production life of the undertaking, in shock brigades, socialist competition, rationalisation and inventions, and in the work of production conferences.

The Administration undertakes, not later than June 1, to create instructional conditions for pupils in the practical work of production. It must attach them to highly skilled workers.

## V. *Wages*

21. The wage-rate for workers of the first category, for a seven-hour working day, is fixed at 35·4 kopeks per hour for time-work; at 44·5 kopeks per hour for piece-work; and at 48 kopeks per hour for workers on piece-rates employed in operations of tempering.

The hourly day-rate for workers of the remaining categories is fixed in accordance with the following coefficients of the wage-rate scale :

| Category : | 1 | 2 | 3 | 4 | 5 | 6 | 7 | 8 |
|---|---|---|---|---|---|---|---|---|
| Coefficients : | 1 | 1·2 | 1·45 | 1·75 | 2·1 | 2·5 | 3·0 | 3·6 |

22. Piece-rates are calculated in accordance with the wage-scales for piece-workers fixing new rates for 1933, as soon as quotas are reconsidered. Until the reconsideration of quotas the existing piece-rates remain in force. The new scale makes no automatic change in rates.

23. Workers are placed in the various categories according to the work they perform. When allocating work, care must be taken to give it to the appropriate categories of workers.

Individual allocation of workers to the categories of the wage-scale is carried out independently by the chiefs of departments and workshops, within the limits of the average coefficient of the given department and workshop, in accordance with the Rates-and-Grading Directory in force in the machine-building industry for lathe-making. Disputes between workers and chiefs of workshops and departments as regards grading are dealt with by the Scales-conflicts Commissions of the department or workshop; if no agreement is reached, they are passed on to the Factory Control Commission (RKK).

If for thirty consecutive days a worker has done work of a higher category than his own, and if he has produced the quota appropriate to that category, and if there is sufficient work in that higher category, he must be transferred to the higher category, except when he has been replacing a worker absent owing to illness, or on holiday or on an official mission.

If, however, for two months out of two and a half a worker has been doing work of a higher category, and continues to be so employed after that period has elapsed, he must be transferred to the higher category without having to make application, provided that he has fulfilled the quota and that his work is of the quality appropriate to that category.

In cases where there is enough work for a worker in his own grade, but he has, as an exception, been given urgent work of a lower grade, he has no right to refuse it; but wages in such cases are paid according to the worker's category.

In cases where a worker of a lower grade temporarily replaces a worker of a higher grade who is absent owing to illness, or on holiday or on an official mission, or is attending the *tersbor* (? terri torial militia), the worker of the lower category is paid for the work he is actually doing, without being transferred to the higher category. When the person whom he has been replacing returns to work, the lower-paid worker does not, when he returns to his former work in his own grade, retain the right to the higher wage that he had been temporarily receiving. When a worker does work only one category lower than his own, he receives only the payment of that category.

24. For special categories of time-rate workers who do specially skilled and responsible work of a category not below that of category 6, the rate of category 1 is fixed at 40 kopeks per hour. But when their work is poor in quality or not sufficiently productive, the chiefs of their workshops have the right to pay them according to the general rate for time-workers.

For special categories of time-workers a special system of premium payments is to be introduced to correspond with the actual output of their labour, and in pursuance of a regulation to be worked out by the management together with the responsible Technical Expert Section (TES) by May 1.

In work where it is impossible to keep a record of the output of time-workers, they may be paid premiums based on valuation of their output by foremen and workshop engineers. The premiums are paid to time-workers only within the limits of the moneys saved as a result of their labour, and from a fund specially set aside for this purpose, within the limits of the wages fund sanctioned by the plan. The amount of this special fund is fixed by the management before the beginning of the month or quarter.

25. Hourly day-rates for pupils of the factory school (FZU), and also for individual and brigade instruction of the first category, are fixed at 18·3 kopeks. The hourly rates for other categories are fixed in accordance with the coefficients given in the following wage-rate scale :

| Category : | 1 | 2 | 3 | 4 |
|---|---|---|---|---|
| Coefficients : | 1 | 1·2 | 1·5 | 1·9 |

26. The management undertakes to admit pupils of the factory school (FZU) to piece-work as from the second year of their instruction, and at rates equal to those of adult piece-workers.

27. Skilled workers who have pupils attached to them for instruction in production, and who combine this work with their own work in production, receive a monthly compensation by way of additional payment equal to 25 per cent of the pupil's rate. Half of this is paid monthly, and the rest at the end of six months if the

pupil passes his test. If the instruction is given in a brigade of piece-workers, the skilled workers who have pupils attached to them are compensated in the same way. The same system of payment applies also to the training of adult workers. In training in brigades the management undertakes to attach all pupils to skilled workers. The output of pupils is credited to the Staff Department of the works.

28. Workers in the undertaking who are undergoing instruction with a view to changing their skilled occupation, or to improving their qualifications, are paid at the rate fixed for time-workers of category 1.

29. The engineering and technical personnel are paid according to the Grading Directory for Engineering and Technical Personnel of the Central Executive Committee of the Machine-Building Union for maximum and minimum salaries. The minimum rate for the first category is 130 roubles. The salaries for each separate post between the fixed minimum and maximum rates are fixed by the chiefs of departments and workshops in accordance with the wages fund. Differences of opinion are settled by the Workers' Control Commission (RKK).

Premiums for members of the engineering and technical personnel and for employees in workshops and works departments for over-fulfilling the plan are to be paid in accordance with a regulation to be made by the works management by May 15. The Technical Expert Section (TES) is responsible for this.

30. Until such time as state regulation is adopted, the salaries of employees and of the subordinate staff (MOP) will be according to the scales of 1932, and in pursuance of the classification of employment attached to the present collective agreement. Within the limits of the wage-fund for this group of workers, their salaries are fixed by the chiefs of departments and workshops. Conflicts are settled by the RKK.

31. The Administration undertakes to place on a piece-rate basis all work suitable for the application of the production quota system, and to raise the percentage of piece-work to the total time worked according to the table given below :

Percentage of piece-work, 1.vii.33 . . − 75 per cent
,,          ,,          1. xi.33 . . − 80  ,,
,,          ,,          1. i.34 . . − 85  ,,

A plan for the effective introduction of piece-rates in workshops, and for different kinds of work, is appended.

Piece-work must be carried out in conjunction with the obligatory calculation of the individual output and earnings of each worker.

32. Piece-work rates for work done by brigades are calculated on the principle of division of labour according to the kind of opera-

tion and to the grade and skill of the workers involved. The earnings are divided among the members of the brigade in proportion to the hours worked and to the wage-rate scales of the several workers.

Work will be undertaken by brigades whenever the conditions of the technical process, the close interlocking of the equipment used, or the best use of the skill of the workers available, makes this advisable.

33. If the time necessary for making appliances, equipment or tools for a piece of work has not been allowed for in fixing the quota, or has not been included in calculating the piece-rates for this work, the price of the extra work entailed will be paid to the workers over and above their piece-rate wages, as if it were a separate piece of work.

34. When a piece-rate worker is transferred to other work within his own workshop, in his own trade and category and to the same kind of bench, his work is paid at the rate proper for the new work. No notice need be given of such transfer.

When a worker is moved from highly specialised work to other work, although it be of a lower grade, payment is made according to the work done.

35. In return for the wages paid to them in pursuance of the present agreement, the workers undertake to achieve the quota of production laid down by the works management, the work done corresponding in quality to the technical conditions. Repeated failure to fulfil the quota of output without good reason, or a product inferior in quality to that made possible by technical conditions, due to the worker's negligence, will lead to reduction to a lower category, or to dismissal.

36. Disputes between workers and the Administration about quotas of output, or calculation of wage-rates, are dealt with by the RKK. Until the dispute has been dealt with, the worker has no right to refuse to do the work allotted to him, though he may disagree with the wage-rate or the quota of output.

37. The Administration undertakes to carry out to the letter the conditions as regards the calculation of wage-rates; it undertakes not to permit over-spending of the wage-fund, and not to make any additional payments which have not already been provided for by the law or the collective agreement.

The Factory Committee (ZK) undertakes to keep systematic watch, and to establish the most rigid control, over the correct use of the wage-fund, both as regards separate groups of workers and workshops and the works as a whole. In all cases where the wages-scale discipline has been broken, or where the wage-fund has been over-spent, the Factory Committee undertakes to take all measures to stop these irregularities and to report them to the higher trade union organisation, while at the same time seeing that the culprits are brought to justice.

38. The factory management (ZU) undertakes to pay from its own resources the salary of one wage-rate clerk for the Factory Committee (ZK) and one clerk to calculate the output quotas.

39. Wages are paid twice a month, outside working hours ; on the 25th of each month for the first half of the month, and on the 10th of the following month for the second half. Payments will be made first to those workshops which have over-fulfilled or fulfilled the programme of production.

## VI. *Production Quotas*

40. Production quotas are worked out by the Administration as for a shock-worker, upon a basis of maximum utilisation of equipment, and of making allowance for unavoidable stoppages, for a normal percentage of spoilt goods and for time lost in necessary rest during working hours.

41. In order to ensure the proper organisation of labour, the Administration undertakes :

(*a*) To introduce during 1933 the production quota system, according to the table given below, in the following percentages of work :

|  |  |  |  |  |
|---|---|---|---|---|
| By 1.vi.33 | . | . | . | − 45 per cent |
| ,, 1.xi.33 | . | . | . | − 55 ,, |
| ,, 1. i.34 | . | . | . | − 60 ,, |

(*b*) To organise instruction in production, so that for each new production quota the worker is properly trained in the methods upon which the quota to be fulfilled is based.

(*c*) To keep count of the carrying out of the quotas in kind (not according to the wages paid), and also to keep count of the time taken to carry out the quota. To analyse daily the carrying out of the quotas, and to keep watch over the conditions upon which the quotas were calculated ; simultaneously, to let the workers have their instruction cards, taking care that these are issued for mass work in the first place.

(*d*) To complete the records of each item of equipment not later than by July 1. The Section of Technical Norms (STN) is responsible for this.

42. Quotas of production and piece-rates calculations will be constantly revised for planning purposes during the entire period that this collective agreement is in force ; and this must ensure the complete fulfilling of the indices given in the plan, and an increase

in the productivity of labour at wages fixed by the plan. The plan of revision of quotas will be prepared by the management of the works and is to be agreed in consultation with the Factory Committee (ZK) not later than the 15.iv.33, and is attached to the collective agreement. Reduced quotas must be revised immediately, in order that their consideration should be completed not later than 1.iv.33.

The revised planned quotas are fixed for one year. Earlier reconsideration of quotas is permissible only where some technological process has been changed, where methods of rationalisation have been adopted, and where technical improvements and improvements in organisation have been introduced, so that the productivity of a worker's labour has been increased. For work to which the production quota system is being applied for the first time, the quotas of production and the wage-scales will be reconsidered by the Administration after they have been checked in practice for a period of not more than three months, after which they will be fixed for one year. Quotas of production and wage-scales fixed by the works management for basic and repetition work will be brought to the notice of the workers in the workshops and communicated to the Factory Committee (ZK) before being introduced. After seven days these quotas become operative.

43. Where output is increased as a result of improvements introduced by a worker on his own initiative, the Administration has the right to reconsider the quota of production with a view to raising it; and the inventor, irrespective of the premium already paid to him, will work on at the old wage-rate for three months after the improvement has been carried out. For all other work in this, the wage-rates will be reconsidered at the same time as the production quotas.

44. In giving out piece-work to the workers, the Administration must accompany it by an instruction, showing the piece-rate wage and the time to be taken. When he receives new work, the workman must hand over his instruction, showing the work he has finished, together with that which he has not yet completed, to the foreman.

If additional payments have to be made as a result of changes in the conditions upon which the quota of production was originally calculated, they must be made in accordance with an additional payment sheet, showing the reasons for the additional payment, the sum payable and the time for which the additional payment is being made.

45. The working of overtime, as a rule, is not permitted. Task work is not allowed. All work outside regular working hours, by whomsoever initiated, and irrespective of the payment to be made,

is permitted only in exceptional cases, in the order and for the reasons laid down by law (such as shipwreck, and disasters due to the forces of nature, etc.). Overtime work is permitted only after the passing of the relevant resolution by the all-factory Workers' Control Commission (RKK) and after sanction for this has been obtained from the workers' inspectorate. It is not permitted to compensate for overtime by taking time off during working hours.

46. Payment for spoilt goods and time lost owing to breakdowns in machinery is made in accordance with the existing legislation dealing with this subject.

47. Supplies for workers and their living conditions : the Administration undertakes :

(*a*) To give financial assistance to the closed cooperative society (ZRK) within the limits of the sums ear-marked in the industrial and financial plan, in order to enlarge its circulating capital, to increase self-supplies and to improve the food provision.

(*b*) To give the accommodation necessary for dining-rooms and cafeterias, and to provide—according to the lists made out for the suburban farm—the means necessary for help in building a store-house for keeping vegetables, for building piggeries and rabbit hutches (see section relating to building of living accommodation).

(*c*) To give active help to the closed cooperative society (ZRK) during the whole period of the operation of the collective agreement, by providing traction power for sowing operations in connection with the works.

(*d*) By April 15 the works management will put one motor-car at the disposal of the closed cooperative society (ZRK), the latter being responsible for paying for the staff required and for repairs.

(*e*) To help, within the limits of the sums set aside for this purpose, in repairing the premises occupied by the canteen quarters (kitchen, dining-room, store-houses), and to give every assistance in adapting and re-equipping these premises with a view to providing the best possible service to the workers.

To give regular and timely information to the closed cooperative society (ZRK) as to the carrying out of the industrial and financial plan in the workshops, and to find the necessary means, from the internal resources of the works, in order to ensure priority in supplying the shock-workers. The mobilisation of such means to be worked out in consultation with the shock-workers.

48. The Administration undertakes :

(*a*) To give help and assistance in the organisation of collective and individual non-subsidised farms.

(*b*) To organise dining-rooms and cafeterias for evening and night shifts in the same way as for day shifts.

(*c*) The works management undertakes to inform the organisations which supply wood for fuel of their requirements in good time, so as to ensure adequate supplies of wood to the workers for the winter, at rates fixed by the higher organisations ; they further undertake to give every help to the workers' collective efforts in organising self-supplies of fuel. The management undertake to make sure that the residences for single workers and for pupils of the factory school (FZU) are adequately heated.

(*d*) Within the limits of the estimates, the management undertake to make sure that the pupils of the factory school (FZU), who live in the residences attached to the works, are supplied with bedding, tea equipment, etc. ; that they have baths free of charge, not less than twice a month, in the works baths. They undertake to have the pupils' linen washed free of charge, not less than twice a month, and to continue to provide free breakfasts for poor pupils, twenty in number.

49. The Factory Committee undertakes :

(*a*) To establish effective supervision of workers over shops, dining-rooms and other undertakings, and to select thirty workers to strengthen the personnel of the ZRK for this purpose.

(*b*) To give practical assistance to the Administration in the organisation of self-supplies, by attracting to this the workers and their families, on a large scale.

(*c*) To improve the sowing, weeding and collection of the harvests in suburban farms by organising an extensive participation in this work of workers and their families. The suburban farms as a whole must produce 749 tons of vegetables and 20 tons of meat, so as to improve the provision of food for the workers.

(*d*) To give every help to the Administration in raising money for increasing the turnover and for increasing the financial strength of the closed cooperative society (ZRK) (share reserves, reserve funds, etc.).

(*e*) To establish social control over the selling prices of goods and over the issue of ration cards, thus helping the Administration to withdraw these documents from slackers and offenders against social discipline.

50. The Administration undertakes :

(*a*) To build dwelling-houses, out of the sum of 1,260,000 roubles allocated for building of dwellings and cultural and social buildings, as follows :

| | | |
|---|---:|---|
| Repairs to house No. 2. To be completed by 1.vii.33 . . . . . . | 35,000 | roubles |
| Repairs to house No. 3. To be completed by 1.vii.33 . . . . . . | 40,000 | ,, |
| Completing the building of house No. 4, by 1.vii.33 | 2,000 | ,, |
| Completing the building of house No. 5, by 1.x.33 | 23,500 | ,, |
| Erection of new 8-apartment stone house, by 1.i.34 . . . . . . | 150,000 | ,, |
| Erection of four new barracks, by 15.ix. . . | 260,000 | ,, |
| Repairs to barracks and lathe houses (list given) . | 30,000 | ,, |
| Road and street planning and construction (list given) . . . . . . | 40,000 | ,, |
| Outhouses and usual offices (details given) . | 20,000 | ,, |
| Piggery, vegetable barn and rabbit hutches for suburban farm . . . . . | 50,000 | ,, |
| Water supply and canalisation (details given) . | 100,000 | ,, |

Social and Cultural Construction :

| | | |
|---|---:|---|
| Adaptation of premises for crèche, to be completed by 1.vi. . . . . . | 10,000 | ,, |

The allocation of apartments in houses belonging to the works management will be carried out by the Administration in agreement with the Factory Committee (ZK).

Shock-workers, and members of the engineering and technical personnel who are shock-workers, workers in cost-accounting brigades, inventors, and workers of long service in the undertaking, will be given priority in the allocation of dwellings.

Apartments in houses which are being built will be allocated to the workers in good time, so that the future tenants may share in the social control over the completion of the building at the appointed date.

The Factory Committee (ZK) undertakes to organise systematic control and ample help to the working masses in carrying out measures which would ensure in full the execution of the plan of construction.

51. The Administration undertakes to bear the full cost of the organisation and maintenance of the crèche—as regards heating, lighting, supply of equipment, cleaning, medical consultations concerning the children of workers, within the limits of the allocation made for this purpose.

52. To disinfect periodically the residences attached to the works.

The Factory Committee (ZK) undertakes to give active help in ensuring the smooth running of institutions for the children of workers, and to enlist the cooperation of the paying-out centres of the social insurance in the undertaking for this purpose.

53. The families of workers, of members of the engineering and technical personnel, and of employees who have died as a result of an accident at work, will be given assistance by the Administration in one lump sum, equal to the monthly earnings of the deceased.

## VII. *Improvements in Conditions of Labour as regards Health*

54. The Administration undertakes :

(*a*) To observe strictly all requirements of preventive care as regards safety technique and industrial hygiene in the erection of new premises and in the reconstruction of existing workshops.

(*b*) To carry out all the measures necessary for the improvement of the conditions of labour as regards health (safety technique, industrial hygiene) in accordance with the agreement made with the inspectorate of labour, and at the times stated in the agreement.

(*c*) To provide all workshops with tanks of cooled, boiled drinking water, with mugs to them.

(*d*) To provide washstands for workers in workshops.

The Factory Committee (ZK) undertakes to establish daily supervision over the use of means allotted for the improvement of the health conditions of work, and over the proper utilisation of the materials issued for this purpose.

55. Working clothes will be issued, as laid down by the Commissariat of Labour (NKT) of the USSR. Washing, mending and disinfection of working clothes, and repairs to working boots, will be done at the expense of the establishment. Workers who are engaged in injurious occupations will have milk issued to them in the quantities fixed by the NKT of the USSR. Working clothes and all neutralising preparations are issued to pupils in the same measure as they are issued to adults.

56. The Administration undertakes to provide special accommodation with separate compartments for clothes, so that each of the workers may keep both his own clothes and his working clothes in his own compartment. The establishment will replace, either in cash or in kind, all clothes lost, if they have been handed over for safekeeping.

57. The workers undertake to take care of the working clothes and boots issued to them, and also to hand over for safe-keeping their own clothes, as well as their working clothes and boots, according to established order. When working clothes and boots are done with, or when a worker leaves the establishment, they must be returned. No new working clothes or boots will be issued until the old ones are returned.

58. The Administration and the Factory Committee (ZK) undertake to submit to a preliminary professional test all pupils to be admitted, and to have them medically examined regularly during their period of instruction.

59. The Administration undertakes to organise special short-term courses of instruction in safety technique, as applied to the peculiarities of the given processes, for new workers taken on. The workers undertake to carry out the rules relating to safety technique, and to observe the necessary requirements as to hygiene in working places and places of common use ; also to notify the Administration in good time of unprotected machinery, or of faulty protection of moving parts.

60. The Administration undertakes to apply measures for the reduction of accident and sickness.

The Factory Committee (ZK) undertakes to mobilise the workers for a struggle against accidents and sickness, and to keep watch—through specially selected individuals and the social inspector of labour—that the Administration carries out the measures necessary for improving the health conditions of work and safety technique.

61. The Administration and the Factory Committee undertake to adopt within a month all measures necessary to improve the working conditions of the evening and night shifts, in order to ensure :

(a) That the evening and night shifts have adequate administrative and technical guidance.

(b) That they are supplied, without any break, with materials, tools and lighting.

(c) That the ventilating installations, cloakrooms and safety devices function properly.

(d) That the medical centre, the dining-rooms and cafeterias function properly.

62. The Factory Committee and the Administration undertake to organise the distribution of admissions to sanatoria, health resorts and houses of rest—both those allotted to them and those bought out of the premium fund—so as to satisfy the workers, the engineering and technical personnel (ITR), the shock-workers and the inventors, in the factory, who carry out the requirements of the plan and who stand in need of medical attention or rest.

VIII. *Duties as regards Cultural Work and Trade Union Organisations*

63. The Administration undertakes :

(a) To provide premises suitable for office work, properly equipped and furnished, for the Factory Committee (ZK), the various workshop committees and the office of the engineering and technical section (ITS), and to pay the cost of heating, telephone service, cleaning, repairing and guarding, out of the moneys of the establishment; and also to bear the cost of lighting, heating and cleaning the Red Corners in the workshops and in the dormitories.

(*b*) The Administration undertakes to bear the cost of repairing, lighting, heating and protection against fire, of the club of the works, within the limits laid down for this purpose by legislation.

(*c*) The works management undertakes to organise Red Corners in No. 1 workshop, in the SGM and the factory school (FZU), in addition to those already existing.

64. The Administration undertakes to provide, within the limits sanctioned in the industrial and financial plan, the means for health work among the workers' children, and to take part in this work; it also undertakes to provide accommodation for work among the Pioneers.

The Administration undertakes to make monthly payments, simultaneously with the payment of wages, to the funds of the Factory Committee (ZK), amounting for the first thousand workers to 1·5 per cent of the total wages paid, and for the rest of the workers to 1 per cent of the total wages paid, towards the upkeep of the factory school (FZU), and 1 per cent of the total wages paid towards cultural work.

IX. *The Conditions of Work of the Engineering and Technical Personnel*

65. In order to ensure the active influence of the entire body of the engineering and technical personnel (ITR) upon the practical solution of the problems of production, connected with the struggle for the new technique and for improving production, the engineering and technical section undertakes to achieve in 1933 the utilisation to capacity of all lathes, machines and aggregates thereof; to mechanise all labour-absorbing processes; to see that workers and members of the engineering and technical personnel (ITR) are placed in the workshops to the best advantage: for this purpose the assistance of the appropriate highly trained specialists of the NITS, of the scientific research institutes and of the higher technical educational institutions must be enlisted.

66. The Administration undertakes:

(*a*) To issue by 1.vi. an instruction which would determine the rights and duties of every member of the engineering and technical personnel according to the post occupied by him, so that the engineering and technical personnel (ITR) should be doing only technical and production work. The instruction as to the rights and duties of the engineering and technical personnel (ITR) in workshops must be worked out not later than May 1 of this year; the responsibility for this rests with the Department of Rationalisation in the works, and with the chiefs of workshops.

(b) To enlist the participation of the engineering and technical personnel (ITS) in the solution of problems of planned recruiting and of rational utilisation of the engineering and technical personnel (ITR).

67. In cases of dismissal according to paras. (a) and (b) of article 47 of the KZOT, the members of the engineering and technical personnel (ITR) must have a month's notice in writing given to them. When members of the engineering and technical personnel (ITR) are dismissed for causing material loss in production, the Administration undertakes to appoint an expert commission consisting of the representatives of the Administration, of the Factory Committee, of the local body of the engineering and technical personnel (ITR) and of specialist experts, according to the recommendation of the higher organisations of the ITS.

68. Members of the engineering and technical personnel (ITR) who work in workshops injurious to health have a right to additional holidays, and to the issue of working clothes and neutralising preparations as laid down by the Commissariat of Labour (NKT).

69. The Administration will provide the necessary sums, within the limits allocated for the purpose, for improving the qualifications of the engineering workers as follows : journeys and excursions within the USSR and abroad ; refresher courses and attendance at scientific and technical conferences and congresses ; to aid the work of the NITS ; for study of foreign languages ; for organisation and provision of technical libraries and technical literature, including foreign publications (in agreement with the engineering and technical section (ITS and NITS)); for the publishing work of the engineering and technical section (ITS and NITS), etc.

When it is contemplated to send members of the engineering and technical personnel (ITR) abroad or elsewhere for the purpose of improving their qualifications, their candidatures will be agreed by the Administration and the Factory Committee (engineering and technical section) in consultation.

The Administration undertakes to put at the disposal of the engineering and technical personnel (ITR) archives, research studies, etc.

The moneys allocated for the work of the NITS will be handed over to the NITS within a month of their allocation.

70. The Administration undertakes :

(a) To provide the necessary residential accommodation, for those members of the engineering and technical personnel (ITR) who have either not got any at all or are badly in need of it, in houses which have been newly built or purchased, in addition to those houses which have already been specially set aside for the engineering and technical personnel (ITR).

(*b*) To make a plan not later than 5.v. in agreement with the Factory Committee (engineering and technical section) ZK(ITS), setting aside residential accommodation for the engineering and technical personnel (ITR) month by month, together with a list of members of the engineering and technical personnel (ITR) to whom such residential accommodation must be allotted.

(*c*) To make sure beforehand that the necessary residential accommodation is available for those members of the engineering and technical personnel (ITR) who are to be taken on, or transferred from other places.

(*d*) The Administration undertakes to provide six vacations in health resorts, with pay for railway expenses, out of the premium reserve fund, and to allocate them in accordance with achievements in production, according to the premium system, in consultation with the engineering and technical section (ITS).

(*e*) The Administration undertakes to increase the funds for food supplies in cases where persons who are not members of the ITR are attached to the ITR dining-rooms, so as to make sure that the increase in numbers fed does not lead to a deterioration in the feeding of the ITR.

71. The Administration and the ZK(ITS) undertake to see that the best possible use is made of the capacities of foreign specialists in their own fields, by providing them with suitable conditions for their work, by developing cultural and political activities among them, and by giving them appropriate cultural services.

72. In the summer time the Administration undertakes to provide boat transport for the workers and members of the engineering and technical personnel across the river Oka to the Mysa.

73. The Administration undertakes to provide by May 1 accommodation for cultural services to the ITR in dwelling-house No. 1 ; to equip and organise a cafeteria on a cost-accounting basis ; and to arrange for supplies out of the self-supply of the closed co-operative society.

74. The works management undertakes to provide regularly, not less than once in six days, hot water for baths, and to arrange for the cleaning of apartments of the unmarried members of the ITR.

### X. *The Duties of the ITR*

75. To fulfil the industrial and financial plan as regards its quantitative indices, *i.e.* to ensure that the planned increase of

productivity reaches 138 per cent ; to lower the cost of production ; and to make sure that the output is of the requisite quality.

76. To bring about an economy of not less than 500,000 roubles during 1933, by using rationalisation methods and inventions of the ITR.

77. To assist in lowering the percentage of spoilt goods in basic production.

78. To lower stoppages due to breakdowns of machinery to 3-3·5 per cent of that set aside for repairs, by making compulsory the introduction of planned preventive repairs.

79. To appoint 50 ITR as social technical leaders to all production brigades in the works, with an undertaking that they will give constant guidance and instruction and that they will ensure the use of cost-accounting in the brigades.

80. To make sure that all basic production workshops have completely mastered in all details the established technological process of lathe 682, with use of all appliances and special tools as planned.

81. To give guidance in raising the qualifications of the workers (technical minimum), and to select from the members of the ITR forty trained leaders, having organised a seminar for them ;· to make sure that the teaching is given systematically, according to programme.

82. To take the greatest possible part in preparing technological instructions as to care of equipment and in the continuous elaboration of these instructions.

### XI. *Work of the RKK and Checking of the Carrying out of the Collective Agreement*

83. The Factory Committee (ZK) and the Administration undertake to create all the conditions necessary for the normal working of the Workers' Control Commission (RKK), and for the immediate consideration (within three days) of all communications received.

In order to improve the work of the RKK, the ZK undertake to improve the qualifications of the workers' part of the RKK, by giving them short-term courses of instruction in labour legislation and calculation of production quotas, so that by giving systematic instructions the workers and employees will be rallied round the RKK.

The Administration undertakes to provide technical services to the RKK by its own staff, and to let the RKK have all the materials necessary for settling particular problems ; further, to provide expert advice when required.

84. The Administration and the ZK undertake to organise a systematic check upon the carrying out of their mutual obligations. When the collective agreement is infringed, the Administration and the ZK must take immediate steps to stop the infringement.

85. Every three months a mass checking of the carrying out of the collective agreement is undertaken.

Individual members of the works management who are actually guilty of offences against this collective agreement are liable to criminal proceedings under article 134 of the UK. Each worker, ITR or employee will be punishable according to the table of fines and penalties, and will also be responsible to the Comrades' Court and, as members of the trade union, to their trade union organisation.

86. The Administration undertakes to print this collective agreement with all its appendices, and to distribute it to the workers by May 1.

87. New legislation passed during the period of the operation of this collective agreement will be binding upon both the contracting parties.

| | |
|---|---|
| Chairman of the Factory Committee (Zavkom) : | KAZAKOV |
| Director of the Works : | TARANKOV |
| Chairman of the Workers' Control (RK) : | SEVRIDOV |
| Chief of the STP and ST : | MINERVIN |

15.iv.33

# XII

## APPENDIX TO CHAPTERS II and VI (see pp. 84-87, 419-451)

### *The New Constitution of 1936 (complete text, with a summary setting forth the Rights of Man)*

WE are indebted for this admirable translation of the Russian text to Mrs. Anna Louise Strong, who has given a dozen years to the USSR. It is curious that there is no official version in English of the Soviet Constitution, but English is not one of the eleven official languages in the USSR. Mrs. Strong has examined seven translations, all made by staffs of experts : The *Moscow News* translation (MN), the Cooperative Publishers (CO), the International Publishers (IP), the Lawrence and Wishart (LW), the Inprecor (INP), a translation made by the Soviet Embassy in Washington (SE) and a translation made by an English-speaking embassy in Moscow for official use (LEG). The first five vary considerably among themselves but tend towards a sovietized English not always clear to the average reader ; the SE translation has improved on much of their phrasing, but not on all. (Note the ungrammatical use of " Union Republic " for constituent republic.) The LEG makes important improvements from the standpoint of legal English, but tends occasionally towards a too-legal phrasing which violates the clear simplicity of the Russian text. Mrs. Strong has earned our thanks by preserving the feeling of the original in a simple, direct and readable translation, meantime giving footnotes to show the chief differences. The layman should thus be able to read it without confusion, while the student may trace possible shades of interpretation as shown by different texts.

Amendments made by the Constitutional Congress after popular discussion have been indicated in the indented portions of the text.

The footnotes are those of Mrs. Strong. Her book, *The New Soviet Constitution* [New York, 1937, 164 pp.], affords the best account of the coming of the constitution.

# CHAPTER I

## THE STRUCTURE OF SOCIETY [1]

ARTICLE 1 : The Union of Soviet Socialist Republics is a socialist state of workers [2] and peasants.[3]

ARTICLE 2 : The political foundation of the USSR consists of soviets [4] of working people's [5] deputies, which grew up and became strong as a result of the overthrow of the power of landlords and capitalists and the winning of the dictatorship of the proletariat.

ARTICLE 3 : All power in the USSR belongs to the working people of town and country as represented by soviets of working people's deputies.

ARTICLE 4 : The economic foundation of the USSR consists of the socialist economic system and the socialist ownership [6] of the tools and means of production, firmly established as a result of the liquidation of the capitalist economic system, the abolition of private ownership [6] of the tools and means of production, and the abolition of the exploitation of man by man.

ARTICLE 5 : Socialist property [6] in the USSR has either the form of state property (the wealth [7] of the whole people) or the form of cooperative-collective property (property of separate collective farms, property of cooperative associations).

---

[1] In other translations " Social Organization ", " The Organization of Society ".

[2] " Workers " means industrial workers, contrasted both with peasants and with white-collar employees. Proposals made during the nation-wide discussion to recognize " intellectuals " in this article—there were various suggested phrasings—were rejected on the ground that this article gives the class basis of Soviet society and that intellectuals are not a separate class. Intellectuals are, however, included in all powers and privileges of the Soviet state, under the word " trudyashchikhsya ", here translated " working people ".

[3] I should like to use " farmer " as that is the generic term in America, as " krestyanin " is in Russian, for all persons working in agriculture, but I don't venture to oppose all seven translators.

[4] " Soviet " means " council ".

[5] All other translations say " toilers " which in English implies heavy, exhausting labour; the Russian word means all persons, including artists and scientists, who do useful work of hand or brain. There is no good English equivalent.

[6] " Sobstvennost ", i.e. " ownership " or " property ". I have chosen now one, now the other, according to the English sense.

[7] " Dostoyaniye "—not the same word as " sobstvennost "—implies wealth rather than ownership.

ARTICLE 6 : The land, its deposits, waters, forests, mills, factories, mines, railways, water and air transport, banks, means of communication, large state-organized farm enterprises (state farms, machine-tractor stations, etc.) and also the basic housing facilities in cities and industrial localities are [8] state property, that is, the wealth of the whole people.

ARTICLE 7 : Public enterprises in collective farms and cooperative organizations, with their livestock and equipment, products raised or manufactured by the collective farms and cooperative organizations, as well as their public structures, constitute [8] the public, socialist property of the collective farms and cooperative organizations.

Aside from the basic income from socialized collective farm husbandry, every collective farm household shall have for personal [9] use a plot of land attached to the house and, as personal [9] property, the subsidiary husbandry [10] on the plot, the house, productive livestock, poultry, and small farm tools—according to the statutes of the farming artel.

> Words " aside from the basic income from socialized collective farm husbandry " were added by the Constitutional Congress.

ARTICLE 8 : The land occupied by collective farms is secured to them without payment and without time limit, that is, for ever.

> The words " without payment and " were added.

ARTICLE 9 : Alongside the socialist system of economy, which is the dominant form of economy in the USSR, the law allows small-scale private enterprise of individual peasants and handcraftsmen based on their personal labour, provided there is no exploitation of the labour of others.

ARTICLE 10 : The right of personal property of citizens in their income from work and in their savings, in their dwelling house and auxiliary husbandry, in household articles and utensils and in articles for personal use and comfort, as well as the right of inheritance of personal property of citizens, is protected by law.

> " As well as the right of inheritance of personal property of citizens " was added in amendment.

[8] LEG gives " shall be ", to conform to English legal use ; I retain the present tense to conform with Stalin's emphasis that the constitution represents attainments to date. In later paragraphs referring to government procedure I follow LEG and also use " shall ".

[9] " Its own ", " individual ", " private " in various translations.

[10] " Auxiliary establishment, or enterprise " in other translations is too pretentious.

ARTICLE 11 : The economic life of the USSR is determined and directed by a state plan of national economy in the interests of increasing the public wealth, of steadily raising the material and cultural standard of the working people, and of strengthening the independence of the USSR and its capacity for defence.

ARTICLE 12 : Work in the USSR is a duty and a matter of honour for every able-bodied citizen, on the principle : " He who does not work shall not eat ".

In the USSR the principle of socialism is realized : " From each according to his ability, to each according to his work ".

"And a matter of honour " was added.

## CHAPTER II

## THE STRUCTURE [11] OF THE STATE

ARTICLE 13 : The Union of Soviet Socialist Republics is a federal state, formed on the basis of the voluntary union [12] of the following Soviet Socialist Republics equal in rights :

The Russian Soviet Federated Socialist Republic ;
The Ukrainian Soviet Socialist Republic ;
The White Russian Soviet Socialist Republic ;
The Azerbaijan Soviet Socialist Republic ;
The Georgian Soviet Socialist Republic ;
The Armenian Soviet Socialist Republic ;
The Turkmen Soviet Socialist Republic ;
The Uzbek Soviet Socialist Republic ;
The Tajik Soviet Socialist Republic ;
The Kazakh Soviet Socialist Republic ;
The Kirghiz Soviet Socialist Republic.

ARTICLE 14 : Within the jurisdiction of the Union of Soviet Socialist Republics, as represented by its highest organs of power and organs of state administration, shall lie : [13]

(a) Representation of the Union in international relations; conclusion and ratification of treaties with other states ;

(b) Questions of war and peace ;

(c) Admission of new republics into the USSR ;

[11] Other translations " State Organization ", " The Organization of the State ".

[12] IP translation; others give " association ".

[13] " Shall " from LEG translation, correct legal form implying compulsion. Other translations use present tense. See note 8.

(*d*) Supervision of the observance of the constitution of the USSR and ensurance of the conformity of the constitutions of the constituent republics [14] with the constitution of the USSR ;

(*e*) Confirmation of changes of boundaries between constituent republics ;

(*f*) Confirmation of the formation of new territories and provinces [15] as well as new autonomous republics within the constituent republics ;

> This paragraph (*f*) was added.

(*g*) Organization of the defense of the USSR and the direction of all the armed forces of the USSR ;

(*h*) Foreign trade on the basis of state monopoly ;

(*i*) Protection of the security of the state ;

(*j*) Establishment of national economic plans of the USSR ;

(*k*) Confirmation of the unified state budget of the USSR as well as of the taxes and revenues which go to form the All-Union,[16] the republic and the local budgets ;

(*l*) Administration of banks, industrial and agricultural establishments and enterprises and also of trading enterprises of All-Union importance ;

(*m*) Administration of transport and communications ;

(*n*) Direction of the monetary and credit system ;

(*o*) Organization of state insurance ;

> The original draft had " of property " added ;
> these words were struck out.

(*p*) Contracting and granting of loans ;

(*q*) Establishment of the fundamental principles for the use of land as well as for the exploitation of its deposits, forests and waters ;

(*r*) Establishment of the fundamental principles in the domain of education and public health ;

(*s*) Organization of a single [17] system of national economic accounting ;

(*t*) Establishment of the principles of labour legislation ;

(*u*) Legislation governing the organization of courts and judicial procedure ; criminal and civil codes ;

---

[14] LEG translation. All others use " union republic ", which is not only confusing but inaccurate, as " soyuznaya " is an adjective, the same incidentally, as is translated " federal " in Article 13. " Federated republic " is a possible translation, but " constituent " is the English word for " belonging to and making up the Union ", the exact meaning of " soyuznaya ".

[15] " Krai " given as " territory ", " oblast " as " province ", following majority of translations.

[16] All-Union, the equivalent of " Federal " in America.

[17] " Unified " in most translations.

(*v*) Laws regarding citizenship of the Union ; laws concerning the rights of foreigners ;

(*w*) Passing All-Union acts of amnesty.

ARTICLE 15 : The sovereignty of the constituent republics shall be [18] restricted only within the limits set forth in Article 14 of the constitution of the USSR. Outside of these limits, each constituent republic shall exercise state power independently. The USSR shall protect the sovereign rights of the constituent republics.

ARTICLE 16 : Each constituent republic shall have its own constitution, which shall take into account the peculiarities of the republic and be drawn up in full conformity with the Constitution of the USSR.

ARTICLE 17 : The right freely to secede from the USSR is reserved to each constituent republic.

ARTICLE 18 : The territory of the constituent republics may not be altered without their consent.

ARTICLE 19 : The laws of the USSR shall have like force in the territories of all constituent republics.

ARTICLE 20 : In case of conflict between a law of a constituent republic and a law of the Union, the All-Union law shall prevail.

ARTICLE 21 : A single Union citizenship is established for all citizens of the USSR. Every citizen of a constituent republic is a citizen of the USSR.

ARTICLE 22 : The Russian Soviet Federated Socialist Republic shall consist of the following territories : Azov-Black Sea, Far-Eastern, West Siberian, Krasnoyarsk and North Caucasus ; of the provinces : Voronezh, East Siberia, Gorky, Western, Ivanovo, Kalinin, Kirov, Kuibyshev, Kursk, Leningrad, Moscow, Omsk, Orenburg, Saratov, Sverdlovsk, Northern, Stalingrad, Chelyabinsk and Yaroslavl; of the autonomous soviet socialist republics : Tatar, Bashkir, Daghestan, Buryat-Mongolian, Kabardino-Balkarian, Kalmyk, Karelian, Komi, Crimean, Mari, Mordovian, Volga German, North Ossetian, Udmurtsk, Chechen-Ingush, Chuvash and Yakut ; and of the autonomous provinces : Adygei, Jewish, Karachai, Oirat, Khakass and Cherkess.

ARTICLE 23 : The Ukrainian Soviet Socialist Republic shall consist of the following provinces : Vinnitsa, Dniepropetrovsk, Donetz,

---

[18] " Shall " from LEG translation. See notes 8 and 13. Henceforth this legal form will be used without comment. The other translations use present tense throughout.

Kiev, Odessa, Kharkov and Chernigov and the Moldavian Autonomous Soviet Socialist Republic.

ARTICLE 24 : The Azerbaijan Soviet Socialist Republic shall include the Nakhichevan Autonomous Soviet Socialist Republic and the Nagorno-Karabakh Autonomous Province.

ARTICLE 25 : The Georgian Soviet Socialist Republic shall include the Abkhazian ASSR, the Ajar ASSR and the South Ossetian Autonomous Province.

ARTICLE 26 : The Uzbek Soviet Socialist Republic shall include the Kara-Kalpak ASSR.

ARTICLE 27 : The Tadjik Soviet Socialist Republic shall include the Gorno-Badakhshan Autonomous Province.

ARTICLE 28 : The Kazakh Soviet Socialist Republic shall consist of the following provinces : Aktyubinsk, Alma-Ata, East Kazakhstan, West Kazakhstan, Karaganda, Kustanai, North Kazakhstan, South Kazakhstan.

ARTICLE 29 :· The Armenian SSR, the White Russian SSR, the Turkmen SSR, and the Kirghiz SSR shall contain no autonomous republics or territories or provinces.


CHAPTER III


THE HIGHEST [19] ORGANS OF STATE POWER OF THE
UNION OF SOVIET SOCIALIST REPUBLICS


ARTICLE 30 : The highest organ of state power of the USSR is the Supreme Soviet [20] of the USSR.

ARTICLE 31 : The Supreme Soviet of the USSR shall exercise all the rights vested in the Union of Soviet Socialist Republics in accord-

---

[19] SE translation; others have "Supreme". The Russian word is "Vysshy", not the same as in "Supreme Soviet".

[20] "Verkhovny Soviet." Translated "Supreme Council" except in LEG translation. Since all translations use "Soviet" everywhere else the same Russian word occurs, as "village soviet", "Union of Soviet Socialist Republics", "soviets of working people's deputies", "the political foundation of the USSR consists of soviets", it is politically confusing to change suddenly to "Council" for the supreme body of the land, consisting of more than a thousand elected representatives. "Council" implies a small appointed body, accentuates the contrast with the previous "Congress of Soviets", and gives the impression of a group of dictators or a return to capitalist democracy. I therefore follow LEG in retaining the word "Soviet", the form universal throughout the entire structure of Soviet power.

ance with Article 14 of the Constitution, insofar as they do not, by virtue of the Constitution, fall within the competence of organs of the USSR accountable to the Supreme Soviet of the USSR, i.e., the Presidium of the Supreme Soviet of the USSR, the Council [21] of Peoples' Commissars of the USSR and the Peoples' Commissariats of the USSR.

ARTICLE 32 : The legislative power of the USSR shall be exercised exclusively by the Supreme Soviet of the USSR.

ARTICLE 33 : The Supreme Soviet of the USSR shall consist of two chambers : the Soviet [22] of the Union and the Soviet of Nationalities.

ARTICLE 34 : The Soviet of the Union shall be elected by the citizens of the USSR by electoral districts on the basis of one deputy for every 300,000 of the population.

ARTICLE 35 : The Soviet of Nationalities shall be elected by the citizens of the USSR by constituent and autonomous republics, autonomous provinces and national regions [23] on the basis of twenty-five deputies from each constituent republic, eleven deputies from each autonomous republic, five deputies from each autonomous province and one deputy from each national region.

> In the original draft this read : " The Soviet of Nationalities shall consist of deputies appointed by the Supreme Soviets of the constituent and autonomous republics and the soviets of working people's deputies in the autonomous provinces : on the basis of ten deputies from each constituent republic, five deputies from each autonomous republic and two deputies from each autonomous province ".

ARTICLE 36 : The Supreme Soviet of the USSR shall be elected for a term of four years.

ARTICLE 37 : The two chambers of the Supreme Soviet of the USSR, the Soviet of the Union and the Soviet of Nationalities, shall have equal rights.

ARTICLE 38 : The legislative initiative shall belong in equal degree to the Soviet of the Union and the Soviet of Nationalities.

ARTICLE 39 : A law shall be considered adopted if passed by both

---

[21] " Soviet Narodnykh Kommissarov." I retain " Council " here since it is a small appointed body.
[22] See note 20. Same word here.
[23] " Okrugs ", also " districts ". Cf. note to Article 94.

chambers of the Supreme Soviet of the USSR by a simple majority in each.

ARTICLE 40 : Laws passed by the Supreme Soviet of the USSR shall be published in the languages of the constituent republics over the signatures of the Chairman [24] and Secretary of the Presidium of the Supreme Soviet of the USSR.

> " In the languages of the constituent republics " was added.

ARTICLE 41 : The sessions of the Soviet of the Union and the Soviet of Nationalities shall begin and terminate simultaneously.

ARTICLE 42 : The Soviet of the Union shall elect a Chairman [24] of the Soviet of the Union and two Vice-Chairmen.

ARTICLE 43 : The Soviet of Nationalities shall elect a Chairman of the Soviet of Nationalities and two Vice-Chairmen.

ARTICLE 44 : The Chairmen of the Soviet of the Union and of the Soviet of Nationalities shall preside over the meetings of the respective chambers and regulate their internal procedure.

ARTICLE 45 : Joint sessions of both chambers of the Supreme Soviet of the USSR shall be presided over alternately by the Chairman of the Soviet of the Union and the Chairman of the Soviet of Nationalities.

ARTICLE 46 : Sessions of the Supreme Soviet of the USSR shall be convened by the Presidium of the Supreme Soviet of the USSR twice a year.

Special sessions shall be convened by the Presidium of the Supreme Soviet of the USSR at its discretion or on the demand of one of the constituent republics.

ARTICLE 47 : In case of disagreement between the Soviet of the Union and the Soviet of Nationalities the question shall be referred for settlement to a conciliation commission formed on a parity basis. If the conciliation commission does not come to an agreement, or if its decision does not satisfy one of the chambers, the question shall be considered a second time in the chambers. Failing an agreed decision of the two chambers, the Presidium of the Supreme Soviet of the USSR shall dissolve the Supreme Soviet of the USSR and shall fix [up] new elections.

ARTICLE 48 : The Supreme Soviet of the USSR shall elect at a joint sitting of both chambers the Presidium of the Supreme Soviet

[24] LEG uses " President ".

of the USSR, consisting of the Chairman of the Presidium of the Supreme Soviet of the USSR, eleven Vice-Chairmen, the Secretary of the Presidium and twenty-four members of the Presidium.

> Original draft had four Vice-Chairmen and thirty-one members.

The Presidium of the Supreme Soviet of the USSR shall be accountable to the Supreme Soviet of the USSR in all its activities.

ARTICLE 49 : The Presidium of the Supreme Soviet of the USSR shall :

(*a*) Convene the sessions of the Supreme Soviet of the USSR ;

(*b*) Interpret existing laws of the USSR and issue decrees ;

(*c*) Dissolve the Supreme Soviet of the USSR in conformity with Article 47 of the Constitution of the USSR and fix [up] new elections ;

(*d*) Hold consultations of the entire people (referendums) on its own initiative or on the demand of one of the constituent republics ;

(*e*) Rescind decisions and orders of the Council of Peoples' Commissars of the USSR and the Councils of Peoples' Commissars of the constituent republics in case they do not conform to the law ;

(*f*) In the intervals between sessions of the Supreme Soviet of the USSR, remove from office and appoint Peoples' Commissars of the USSR at the instance of the Chairman of the Council of Peoples' Commissars of the USSR, subject to subsequent confirmation by the Supreme Soviet of the USSR ;

(*g*) Award decorations of the USSR and bestow honorary titles of the USSR ;

> " Bestow honorary titles " was added.

(*h*) Exercise the right of pardon ;

(*i*) Appoint and replace the high command of the armed forces of the USSR ;

(*j*) In the intervals between sessions of the Supreme Soviet of the USSR, declare a state of war in case of an armed attack upon the USSR, or in case of the need of fulfilling international treaty obligations of mutual defence against aggression ;

> The phrase " or in case of the need of fulfilling international treaty obligations of mutual defence against aggression " was added amid applause, the only applause greeting the reading of any amendment.

(*k*) Declare general or partial mobilization ;

(*l*) Ratify international treaties ;

(*m*) Appoint and recall plenipotentiary representatives of the USSR to foreign states ;

(*n*) Receive the credentials and letters of recall of diplomatic representatives of foreign states accredited to it.

> The original draft read, " Accepts the credentials of diplomatic representatives of foreign states ".

ARTICLE 50 : The Soviet of the Union and the Soviet of Nationalities shall elect credentials committees [25] which shall verify the credentials of the members of the respective chambers.

On representation of the credentials committee the chamber shall decide either to recognize the credentials or to declare invalid the elections of individual deputies.

ARTICLE 51 : The Supreme Soviet of the USSR shall appoint, whenever it deems necessary, investigating and auditing commissions on any matter.

All institutions and officials are bound to comply with the demands of these commissions and to submit to them the necessary materials and documents.

ARTICLE 52 : A deputy of the Supreme Soviet of the USSR may not be prosecuted or arrested without the consent of the Supreme Soviet of the USSR, and during the period when the Supreme Soviet of the USSR is not in session, without the consent of the Presidium of the Supreme Soviet of the USSR.

ARTICLE 53 : On the expiration of the term of office of the Supreme Soviet of the USSR, or on its dissolution before the expiration of its term, the Presidium of the Supreme Soviet of the USSR shall retain its powers until the formation of a new Presidium of the Supreme Soviet of the USSR by the newly elected Supreme Soviet of the USSR.

ARTICLE 54 : On the expiration of the term of office of the Supreme Soviet of the USSR, or on its dissolution before the expiration of its term, the Presidium of the Supreme Soviet of the USSR shall fix new elections to be held within a period of not more than two months from the date of expiration of the term of office or the dissolution of the Supreme Soviet of the USSR.

ARTICLE 55 : The newly elected Supreme Soviet of the USSR shall be convened by the Presidium of the former Supreme Soviet of the USSR not later than one month after the elections.

ARTICLE 56 : The Supreme Soviet of the USSR at a joint session of both chambers shall set up the executive [26] of the USSR—the Council of Peoples' Commissars of the USSR.

[25] Following LEG ; others use " commissions ".
[26] All other translations " government ", in the European sense, i.e. executive branch.

## CHAPTER IV

## THE HIGHEST ²⁷ ORGANS OF STATE POWER OF THE CONSTITUENT REPUBLICS

ARTICLE 57 : The highest organ of state power of a constituent republic shall be the Supreme Soviet of the constituent republic.

ARTICLE 58 : The Supreme Soviet of a constituent republic shall be elected by the citizens of the republic for a term of four years.

The rates of representation shall be fixed by the constitutions of the constituent republics.

ARTICLE 59 : The Supreme Soviet of a constituent republic shall be the only legislative organ of the republic.

ARTICLE 60 : The Supreme Soviet of a constituent republic shall :

(*a*) Adopt the constitution of the republic and amend it in accordance with Article 16 of the Constitution of the USSR ;

(*b*) Approve the constitutions of the autonomous republics included in it and define the boundaries of their territories ;

(*c*) Approve the economic plan and budget of the republic ;

(*d*) Exercise the right of amnesty and pardon of citizens sentenced by the judicial organs of the constituent republic.

ARTICLE 61 : The Supreme Soviet of a constituent republic shall elect the Presidium of the Supreme Soviet of the constituent republic consisting of : the Chairman of the Presidium of the Supreme Soviet of the constituent republic, Vice-Chairmen, a Secretary of the Presidium and members of the Presidium of the Supreme Soviet of the constituent republic.

" Secretary of the Presidium " was added.

The powers of the Presidium of the Supreme Soviet of a constituent republic shall be defined by the constitution of the constituent republic.

ARTICLE 62 : To conduct its sessions, the Supreme Soviet of a constituent republic shall elect its Chairman and Vice-Chairmen.

ARTICLE 63 : The Supreme Soviet of a constituent republic shall set up the executive ²⁶ of the constituent republic—the Council of Peoples' Commissars of the constituent republic.

²⁷ From SE translation ; others have " Supreme ".

## CHAPTER V

## ORGANS OF STATE ADMINISTRATION OF THE UNION
## OF SOVIET SOCIALIST REPUBLICS

ARTICLE 64 : The highest executive and administrative organ of state power of the Union of Soviet Socialist Republics shall be the Council of Peoples' Commissars of the USSR.

ARTICLE 65 : The Council of Peoples' Commissars of the USSR shall be responsible to the Supreme Soviet of the USSR and accountable to it ; and between sessions of the Supreme Soviet, to the Presidium of the Supreme Soviet of the USSR.

> " And between sessions of the Supreme Soviet, to the Presidium of the Supreme Soviet of the USSR " was added.

ARTICLE 66 : The Council of Peoples' Commissars of the USSR shall issue resolutions [28] and orders on the basis of, and in execution of, the existing laws and shall verify their execution.

ARTICLE 67 : Resolutions and orders of the Council of Peoples' Commissars of the USSR shall be binding throughout the entire territory of the USSR.

ARTICLE 68 : The Council of Peoples' Commissars of the USSR shall :

(*a*) Co-ordinate and direct the work of the All-Union and Union-Republic Peoples' Commissariats of the USSR and of the other economic and cultural institutions subordinate to it ;

(*b*) Take measures to carry out the national economic plan and state budget and to strengthen the credit-monetary system ;

(*c*) Take measures to secure public order, to defend the interests of the state, and to safeguard the rights of citizens ;

(*d*) Exercise general supervision in the sphere of relations with foreign states ;

(*e*) Fix the annual contingent of citizens to be called for active military service and direct the general organization of the armed forces of the country ;

(*f*) Set up, when necessary, special committees and central administrations attached to the Council of Peoples' Commissars of the USSR for economic, cultural and defence construction.

> This paragraph (*f*) was added.

ARTICLE 69 : The Council of Peoples' Commissars of the USSR shall have the right, in respect to those branches of administration

[28] LEG wording ; others give " decisions ".

and economy which come within the competence of the USSR, to suspend resolutions and orders of the Councils of Peoples' Commissars of the constituent republics and to annul orders and instructions of Peoples' Commissars of the USSR.

ARTICLE 70 : The Council of Peoples' Commissars of the USSR shall be formed by the Supreme Soviet of the USSR and shall consist of :

The Chairman of the Council of Peoples' Commissars of the USSR ;
The Vice-Chairmen of the Council of Peoples' Commissars of the USSR ;
The Chairman of the State Planning Commission of the USSR ;
The Chairman of the Soviet Control Commission ;
The Peoples' Commissars of the USSR ;
The Chairman of the Committee on Agricultural Products ; [29]
The Chairman of the Committee on [the] Arts ;
The Chairman of the Committee on Higher Education.

ARTICLE 71 : The Executive of the USSR or a Peoples' Commissar of the USSR to whom any question by a member of the Supreme Soviet of the USSR is addressed shall be obliged to give a verbal or written reply in the respective chamber within a period of not more than three days.

ARTICLE 72 : The Peoples' Commissars of the USSR shall direct the branches of state administration which come within the competence of the USSR.

> The word " vedayut ", " has charge of ", in original draft was changed to " rukovodyat ", " directs ". The same change was also made in Articles 75, 76, 84, 87.

ARTICLE 73 : The Peoples' Commissars of the USSR shall issue, within the limits of the competence of the respective Peoples' Commissariats, orders and instructions on the basis of, and in execution of, existing laws as well as of resolutions and orders of the Council of Peoples' Commissars of the USSR, and shall verify their execution.

ARTICLE 74 : The Peoples' Commissariats of the USSR shall be either All-Union or Union-Republic.

ARTICLE 75 : The All-Union Peoples' Commissariats shall direct the branches of state administration entrusted to them throughout the territory of the USSR either directly or through organs appointed by them.

---

[29] LEG has " procurements " ; SE has " stocks " ; others have " for purchasing agricultural products " [in the Russian text, zasotovok].

ARTICLE 76 : The Union-Republic Peoples' Commissariats shall direct the branches of state administration entrusted to them, as a rule, through like-named Peoples' Commissariats of the constituent republics, and shall directly administer only a definite limited number of enterprises according to a list confirmed by the Presidium of the Supreme Soviet of the USSR.

> " As a rule " and " and shall directly administer only a definite limited number of enterprises according to a list confirmed by the Presidium of the Supreme Soviet of the USSR " were added.

ARTICLE 77 : The following Peoples' Commissariats shall be All-Union Peoples' Commissariats :

Defence ;
Foreign Affairs ;
Foreign Trade ;
Railways ; [30]
Communications ;
Water Transport ;
Heavy Industry ;
Defence Industry.

> " Defence Industry " was added.

ARTICLE 78 : The following Peoples' Commissariats shall be Union-Republic Peoples' Commissariats :

Food Industry ;
Light Industry ;
Timber Industry ;
Agriculture ;
State Grain and Livestock Farms ;
Finance ;
Internal Trade ;
Internal Affairs ;
Justice ;
Health.

### CHAPTER VI

### ORGANS OF STATE ADMINISTRATION OF THE CONSTITUENT REPUBLICS

ARTICLE 79 : The highest executive and administrative organ of state power of a constituent republic shall be the Council of Peoples' Commissars of the constituent republic.

ARTICLE 80 : The Council of Peoples' Commissars of a constituent

[30] Literally " Ways of Communication " but refers [mainly] to railways.

republic shall be responsible to the Supreme Soviet of the constituent republic and accountable to it, and in the intervals between sessions of the Supreme Soviet of a constituent republic, to the Presidium of the Supreme Soviet of the constituent republic.

> " And in the intervals between sessions of the Supreme Soviet of a constituent republic, to the Presidium of the Supreme Soviet of the constituent republic " was added.

ARTICLE 81 : The Council of Peoples' Commissars of a constituent republic shall issue resolutions [28] and orders on the basis of, and in execution of, the existing laws of the USSR and of the constituent republic, and of the resolutions and orders of the Council of Peoples' Commissars of the USSR, and shall verify their execution.

ARTICLE 82 : The Council of Peoples' Commissars of a constituent republic shall have the right to suspend the resolutions and orders of the Council of Peoples' Commissars of the autonomous republics and to rescind the decisions and orders of the executive committees of the soviets of working people's deputies of territories, provinces and autonomous provinces.

ARTICLE 83 : The Council of Peoples' Commissars of a constituent republic shall be formed by the Supreme Soviet of the constituent republic and shall consist of :

The Chairmen of the Council of Peoples' Commissars of the constituent republic ;
The Vice-Chairmen ;
The Chairman of the State Planning Commission ;
The Peoples' Commissars for :
  Food Industry ;
  Light Industry ;
  Timber Industry ;
  Agriculture ;
  State Grain and Livestock Farms;
  Finance ;
  Internal Trade ;
  Internal Affairs ;
  Justice ;
  Health ;
  Education ;
  Local Industry ;
  Municipal Economy ;
  Social Welfare ;
A representative of the Committee on Agricultural Products ;
Chief of the Administration for [the] Arts ;
Representatives of the All-[Union] Peoples' Commissariats.

ARTICLE 84 : The Peoples' Commissars of a constituent republic shall direct those branches of state administration which come within the competence of the constituent republic.

ARTICLE 85 : The Peoples' Commissars of a constituent republic shall issue, within the limits of the competence of the respective Peoples' Commissariats, orders and instructions on the basis of, and in execution of, the laws of the USSR and the constituent republic, of resolutions and orders of the Council of Peoples' Commissars of the USSR and of the constituent republic, and of orders and instructions of the Union-Republic Peoples' Commissariats of the USSR.

ARTICLE 86 : The Peoples' Commissariats of a constituent republic shall be either Union-Republic or Republic.

ARTICLE 87 : Union-Republic Peoples' Commissariats shall direct the branches of state administration entrusted to them and shall be subordinate both to the Council of Peoples' Commissars of the constituent republic and to the corresponding Union-Republic Peoples' Commissariat of the USSR.

ARTICLE 88 : Republic Peoples' Commissariats shall direct the branch of state administration entrusted to them and shall be subordinate directly to the Council of Peoples' Commissars of the constituent republic.

## CHAPTER VII

## THE HIGHEST [27] ORGANS OF STATE POWER OF THE AUTONOMOUS SOVIET SOCIALIST REPUBLICS

ARTICLE 89 : The highest organ of state power of an autonomous republic is the Supreme Soviet of the ASSR.

ARTICLE 90 : The Supreme Soviet of an autonomous republic shall be elected by the citizens of the republic for a term of four years, according to rates of representation fixed by the constitution of the autonomous republic.

ARTICLE 91 : The Supreme Soviet of an autonomous republic shall be the only legislative organ of the ASSR.

ARTICLE 92 : Each autonomous republic shall have its own constitution, which shall take into account the peculiarities of the autonomous republic and which shall be drawn up in full conformity with the constitution of the constituent republic.

ARTICLE 93 : The Supreme Soviet of an autonomous republic shall elect the Presidium of the Supreme Soviet of the autonomous republic and shall form the Council of Peoples' Commissars of the autonomous republic in accordance with its constitution.

## CHAPTER VIII

## LOCAL ORGANS OF STATE POWER

ARTICLE 94 : Soviets of working people's deputies shall be the organs of state power in territories,[31] provinces, autonomous provinces, regions, districts, cities and rural localities [32] (stanitsa, village, khutor, kishlak, aul).

ARTICLE 95 : The soviets of working people's deputies of territories, provinces, autonomous provinces, regions, districts, cities and rural localities (stanitsa, village, khutor, kishlak, aul) shall be elected by the working people in the respective territories, provinces, autonomous provinces, regions, districts, cities and rural localities for a term of two years.

ARTICLE 96 : The rates of representation for the soviets of working people's deputies shall be fixed by the constitution of the constituent republic.

ARTICLE 97 : The soviets of working people's deputies shall direct the activity of the organs of administration subordinate to them, ensure the maintenance of public order, the observance of the laws and the protection of the rights of citizens, direct the local economic and cultural construction and draw up the local budget.

> " Carry out local economic and cultural construction " in the original draft was changed to " direct the local economic and cultural construction ".

ARTICLE 98 : The soviets of working people's deputies shall make decisions and issue orders within the limits of the powers conferred on them by the laws of the USSR and the constituent republic.

ARTICLE 99 : The executive and administrative organs of the soviets of working people's deputies of territories, provinces, autonomous provinces, regions, districts, cities and rural localities shall

---

[31] " Krai ", territory ;
" oblast ", province ;
" okrug ", region ;
" rayon ", district ;
" stanitsa ", Cossack village ;
" khutor ", hamlets of a few farms [in Ukrainia] ;
" kishlak ", village in Central Asia ;
" aul ", mountain or desert village, especially in the Caucasus.
[32] " Villages " in all translations except SE ;  a rural administrative unit including several villages or hamlets.

be the executive committees elected by them consisting of a Chairman, Vice-Chairman, Secretary and members.

> " And rural localities " and " Secretary " were added.

ARTICLE 100 : The executive and administrative organs of rural soviets of working people's deputies in small settlements, in accordance with the constitutions of the constituent republics, shall be the Chairman, Vice-Chairman and Secretary elected by them.

> " Secretary " was added.

ARTICLE 101 : The executive organs of the soviets of working people's deputies shall be directly accountable both to the soviet of working people's deputies which elected them and to the executive organ of the higher soviet of working people's deputies.


CHAPTER IX

THE COURT AND THE ATTORNEY-GENERAL'S ³³
OFFICE

ARTICLE 102 : Justice in the USSR shall be administered by the Supreme Court of the USSR, the Supreme Courts of the constituent republics, territorial and provincial courts, courts of autonomous republics and autonomous provinces, regional courts, special courts of the USSR created by resolution of the Supreme Soviet of the USSR, and peoples' courts.

> " Regional [okrug] courts " was added to original draft. Russian text uses different word for " resolution " in the original and final drafts.

ARTICLE 103 : Cases in all courts shall be tried with the participation of peoples' associate judges ³⁴ except in cases specially provided for by law.

ARTICLE 104 : The Supreme Court of the USSR shall be the highest judicial organ. It shall be charged with supervision of the judicial activities of all the judicial organs of the USSR and of the constituent republics.

> The word " judicial " was inserted before the word " activities ".

³³ Also given " State Prosecutor ", " State Attorney ". I have used Attorney-General for American readers, with state and district attorneys for the subordinate divisions.
³⁴ Literally " co-sitters "; several versions use " assessors ".

ARTICLE 105 : The Supreme Court of the USSR and the special courts of the USSR shall be elected by the Supreme Soviet of the USSR for a term of five years.

ARTICLE 106 : The Supreme Courts of the constituent republics shall be elected by the Supreme Soviets of the constituent republics for a term of five years.

ARTICLE 107 : The Supreme Courts of the autonomous republics shall be elected by the Supreme Soviets of the autonomous republics for a term of five years.

ARTICLE 108 : Territorial and provincial courts, courts of autonomous provinces and regional courts shall be elected by the soviets of working people's deputies of the territories, provinces, regions and autonomous provinces for a term of five years.

" Regional " [okrug] was added.

ARTICLE 109 : The peoples' courts shall be elected for a term of three years by the citizens of the district, by secret vote, on the basis of universal, direct and equal suffrage.

ARTICLE 110 : Court proceedings shall be conducted in the language of the constituent or autonomous republic or autonomous province with the guarantee to persons not knowing the language of full acquaintance with the material of the case through an interpreter, and also of the right to speak in court in their native language.

ARTICLE 111 : In all courts of the USSR cases shall be heard in public unless otherwise provided by law, and the accused shall be guaranteed the right to defence.

ARTICLE 112 : The judges are independent and shall be subordinate only to the law.

ARTICLE 113 : The highest supervision over the strict observance of laws by all the Peoples' Commissariats and institutions subordinate to them, as well as by individual officials and also by citizens of the USSR, is vested in the Attorney-General of the USSR.

ARTICLE 114 : The Attorney-General of the USSR shall be appointed by the Supreme Soviet of the USSR for a term of seven years.

ARTICLE 115 : State attorneys of republics, territories and provinces, as well as state attorneys of autonomous republics and autonomous provinces shall be appointed by the Attorney-General of the USSR for a term of five years.

ARTICLE 116 : District attorneys of regions, districts and cities shall be appointed for a term of five years by the state attorneys of the constituent republics and confirmed by the Attorney-General of the USSR.

> " Regions, districts and cities " in final draft replaced " district " in original draft.

ARTICLE 117 : The state and district attorneys' offices shall perform their functions independently of any local organs whatsoever and be subordinate solely to the Attorney-General of the USSR.

## CHAPTER X

## BASIC RIGHTS AND DUTIES [35] OF CITIZENS

ARTICLE 118 : Citizens of the USSR have [36] the right to work, that is, the right to guaranteed employment and payment for their work in accordance with its quantity and quality.

The right to work is ensured by the socialist organization of the national economy, the steady growth of the productive forces of Soviet society, the elimination of the possibility of economic crises, and the abolition of unemployment.

> " That is " in the final draft replaced a dash in the original draft. " Elimination of the possibility of economic crises " replaced " the absence of economic crises ".

ARTICLE 119 : Citizens of the USSR have the right to rest.[37]

The right to rest is ensured by the reduction of the working day to seven hours for the overwhelming majority of the workers, the institution of annual vacations with pay for workers and other employees, and the provision of a wide network of sanatoria, rest homes and clubs serving the needs of the working people.

ARTICLE 120 : Citizens of the USSR have the right to material security [38] in old age and also in case of sickness or loss of capacity to work.

This right is ensured by the wide development of social insurance of workers and other employees at state expense, free medical service for the working people, and the provision of a wide network of health resorts at the disposal of the working people.

> " For the working people " was inserted after " free medical service ".

[35] Some translations use " Fundamental " for " Basic " ; and " Obligations " for " Duties ".

[36] LEG " shall have ", but I here revert to present tense for Articles 118-122 in common with all the other translations, having employed the LEG form throughout all discussions of government structure.

[37] SE adds " and leisure ".                    [38] SE gives " maintenance ".

ARTICLE 121 : Citizens of the USSR have the right to education.
This right is ensured by universal compulsory elementary education, by education free of charge including higher education, by a system of state stipends [39] for the overwhelming majority of students in higher schools, by instruction in schools in the native language, and by the organization in factories, state farms, machine-tractor stations and collective farms of free industrial, technical and agricultural education for the working people.

ARTICLE 122 : Women in the USSR are accorded equal rights with men in all spheres of economic, state, cultural, social and political [40] life.
The realization of these rights of women is ensured by affording women equally with men the right to work, payment for work, rest, social insurance and education, and by state protection of the interests of mother and child, pregnancy leave with pay, and the provision of a wide network of maternity homes, nurseries and kindergartens.

ARTICLE 123 : Equal rights for citizens of the USSR, irrespective of their nationality or race, in all spheres of economic, state, cultural, social and political life, shall be an irrevocable law.
Any direct or indirect limitation of these rights, or, conversely, any establishment of direct or indirect privileges for citizens on account of their race or nationality, as well as any propagation of racial or national exclusiveness [41] or hatred and contempt, shall be punished by law.

ARTICLE 124 : In order to ensure to citizens freedom of conscience, the church in the USSR shall be separated from the state, and the school from the church. Freedom of religious worship [42] and freedom of anti-religious propaganda shall be recognized for all citizens.

ARTICLE 125 : In accordance with the interests of the working people, and in order to [43] strengthen the socialist system, the citizens of the USSR are guaranteed by law :

(*a*) Freedom of speech ;
(*b*) Freedom of the press ;
(*c*) Freedom of assembly and meetings ;
(*d*) Freedom of street processions and demonstrations.

These rights of citizens are ensured by placing at the disposal of the working people and their organizations printing shops, supplies

[39] SE gives " scholarships ".
[40] Strictly, " social-political ".
[41] " Exceptionalism " in many translations.
[42] SE translation ; others give " to perform religious rites ". Literally, " to perform the activities of the religious cult ".
[43] All except SE give " for the purpose of ".

of paper, public buildings, the streets, means of communication and other material requisites for the exercise of these rights.

" By law " was inserted.

ARTICLE 126 : In accordance with the interests of the working people, and for the purpose of developing the organized self-expression and political activity of the masses of the people, citizens of the USSR are ensured the right to unite in public organizations—trade unions, cooperative associations, youth organizations, sport and defence organizations, cultural, technical, and scientific societies ; and the most active and politically conscious citizens from the ranks of the working class and other strata of the working people unite in the All-Union Communist Party (of Bolsheviks), which is the vanguard of the working people in their struggle to strengthen and develop the socialist system and which represents the leading nucleus of all organizations of the working people, both social [44] and state.

> " The All-Union Communist Party (of Bolshe-
> viks)," i.e., the official name, in the final draft re-
> placed " the Communist Party of the USSR " of the
> original draft.

ARTICLE 127 : Citizens of the USSR are guaranteed inviolability of the person.   No one may be subject to arrest except by an order of the court or with the sanction of a state attorney.[45]

ARTICLE 128 : The inviolability of the homes of citizens and secrecy of correspondence are protected by law.

ARTICLE 129 : The USSR grants the right of asylum to foreign citizens persecuted for defending the interests of the working people or for scientific activity or for their struggle for national liberation.

ARTICLE 130 : It is the duty [46] of every citizen of the USSR to observe the constitution of the Union of Soviet Socialist Republics, to carry out the laws, to maintain labour discipline, honestly to perform his public duties [47] and to respect the rules of the socialist community.

ARTICLE 131 : It is the duty of every citizen of the USSR to safeguard and strengthen public socialist property as the sacred and inviolable foundation of the Soviet system, as the source of the wealth and might of the fatherland, as the source of the prosperous and cultural life of all the working people.

[44] SE ; others give " public ".
[45] Includes district attorneys and Attorney-General.
[46] SE ; others give " Every citizen—is obliged. . . .''
[47] " Honestly to regard his social duties ", or " to take an honest attitude towards ".

Persons making attacks [48] upon public socialist property shall be [49] regarded as enemies of the people.

ARTICLE 132 : Universal military duty shall be the law.
Military service in the Workers' and Peasants' Red Army represents an honourable duty of the citizens of the USSR.

ARTICLE 133 : The defence of the fatherland is the sacred duty of every citizen of the USSR. Treason to the homeland [50] : violation of the oath, desertion to the enemy, impairing the military might of the state, espionage : shall be punished with the full severity of the law as the gravest crime.

> The original draft contained " on behalf of a foreign state " after " espionage ".

## CHAPTER XI

## THE ELECTORAL SYSTEM

ARTICLE 134 : Elections of deputies to all the soviets of working people's deputies ; to the Supreme Soviet of the USSR ; to the Supreme Soviets of the constituent republics ; to the territorial and provincial soviets of working people's deputies ; to the Supreme Soviets of the autonomous republics ; to the soviets of working people's deputies of autonomous provinces ; to the soviets of working people's deputies of the regions, towns and rural districts (stanitsas, villages, khutors, kishlaks, auls) [31] shall be effected by the voters on the basis of universal, equal and direct suffrage, by secret ballot.

ARTICLE 135 : The elections of deputies shall be universal : all citizens of the USSR who have reached the age of 18, irrespective of race and nationality, religion, educational qualifications, residence, social origin, property status or past activity, shall have the right to take part in the elections of deputies and to be elected, with the exception of insane persons and persons condemned by court with deprivation of electoral rights.

> Article 135 in the original draft read as follows :
> " Elections of deputies are universal : all citizens in the USSR who in the year of the elections reach the age of 18 have the right to participate in elections

---

[48] " Attempting to violate ", " to infringe " are other versions.
[49] LEG ; all others say " are ".
[50] All other translations give " fatherland ", but " rodina " is a more intimate term than " otechestvo ", translated " fatherland " just above.

of deputies and to be elected, with the exception of the mentally deficient and persons deprived of electoral rights by the courts."

ARTICLE 136 : The elections of deputies shall be equal : every citizen shall have one vote ; all citizens shall take part in the elections on an equal basis.

> Article 136 in the original draft read :
> " Elections of deputies are equal : every citizen has the right to elect and be elected irrespective of race or nationality, religion, educational qualifications, residence, social origin, property status or past activity."

ARTICLE 137 : Women shall have the right to elect and to be elected on equal terms with men.

ARTICLE 138 : Citizens who are in the ranks of the Red Army shall have the right to elect and to be elected on equal terms with all citizens.

ARTICLE 139 : The elections of deputies shall be direct : the elections to all the soviets of working people's deputies, beginning with the rural and city soviets of working people's deputies and up to and including the Supreme Soviet of the USSR shall be directly effected by citizens through direct elections.

ARTICLE 140 : The voting at elections of deputies shall be secret.

ARTICLE 141 : Candidates for elections shall be nominated by electoral districts.

The right to nominate candidates shall be ensured to public [51] organizations and societies of working people ; Communist Party organizations ; trade unions ; cooperatives ; organizations of youth ; cultural societies.

ARTICLE 142 : Every deputy shall be obliged to report to the electors on his work and on the work of the soviet of working people's deputies and may at any time be recalled by decision of a majority of the electors in the manner prescribed by law.


CHAPTER XII

EMBLEM, FLAG, CAPITAL

ARTICLE 143 : The state emblem of the Union of Soviet Socialist Republics shall consist of a sickle and hammer on the globe of the earth depicted in rays of the sun and surrounded by ears of grain,

[51] " Social " in several versions.

with the inscription : " Workers [52] of all lands unite ", in the languages of the constituent republics.   Above the emblem shall be a five-pointed star.

ARTICLE 144 : The state flag of the Union of Soviet Socialist Republics shall be of red cloth with a sickle and hammer depicted in gold in the upper corner near the staff and above them a red five-pointed star bordered in gold.   The ratio of the width to the length shall be one to two.

ARTICLE 145 : The capital of the Union of Soviet Socialist Republics shall be the city of Moscow.

## CHAPTER XIII

### PROCEDURE FOR AMENDING THE CONSTITUTION

ARTICLE 146 : Amendments to the Constitution of the USSR shall be effected only by decisions of the Supreme Soviet of the USSR, adopted by a majority of not less than two-thirds of the votes in each of its chambers.

PRESIDIUM OF THE EIGHTH EXTRAORDINARY CONGRESS OF SOVIETS OF THE UNION OF SOVIET SOCIALIST REPUBLICS

N. Aitakov

V. Akhun-Babayev

I. Akulov

A. Andreyev

V. Bluecher

S. Budyonny

A. Chervyakov

V. Chubar

R. Eiche

L. Kaganovich

M. Kalinin

N. Khrushchev

A. Kiselev

S. Kosior

M. Litvinov

P. Lyubchenko

A. Mikoyan

V. Molotov

G. Musabekov

G. Ordjonikidze

G. Petrovsky

P. Postyshev

A. Rakhimbayev

Y. Rudzutak

N. Shvernik

J. Stalin

D. Sulimov

K. Voroshilov

N. Yeznov

A. Zhdanov

THE KREMLIN, MOSCOW

*December 5, 1936*

[52] Strictly, " proletarians ".   I follow the English slogan.

## CHIEF CHANGES FROM PREVIOUS SOVIET CONSTITUTIONS

### CHAPTER I

ARTICLES 1 TO 4 :

The RSFSR Constitution of 1918 declared " the establishment (in the form of a strong Soviet government) of the dictatorship of the urban and rural workers, combined with the poorer peasantry, to secure the complete suppression of the bourgeoisie, the abolition of the exploitation of man by man, and the establishment of socialism ".

The present Constitution assumes that these objectives have been obtained and declares that the USSR " is a socialist state of workers and peasants ". Its political foundation is given as " soviets of working people's deputies ", a much more conclusive term than earlier.

ARTICLES 5 AND 6 :

The RSFSR Constitution of 1918 declared the abolition of private ownership of land " in order to establish the socialization of the land ". It ratified the law on workers' control in industry and that on the Supreme Economic Council . . . " as a first step towards the complete transfer to the Workers' and Peasants' Soviet Republic of all factories, workshops, mines, railways and other means of production and transport ". It " ratified the transfer of all banks " to the government.

The present Constitution expresses the completion of those processes of which the 1918 Constitution was a first step.

ARTICLES 7 TO 12 :

All this detail regarding collective farm property and private property is absent from the first two Constitutions.

### CHAPTER II

ARTICLE 13 :

The present Constitution contains eleven constituent republics of which only one—the RSFSR—existed in 1918, and four—the RSFSR, the Ukraine, White Russia and Transcaucasia—in the 1924 Constitution. The Uzbek SSR and the Turkmen SSR were added at the end of 1924 ; the Tajik SSR in 1929, making seven.

The present Constitution dissolves Transcaucasia into three separate constituent republics—the Armenian, Georgian and Azerbaijan—and forms two new republics—the Kazakh and Kirghiz.

This means a considerable raising of status for many minor nationalities.

ARTICLE 14 :

The Constitution of 1924, passed at the beginning of the " new economic policy ", which permitted private trade and concessions to foreign capital, spoke of " laying the foundations of, and establishing a general plan for, the entire national economy of the Union, the definition of branches of industry . . . the conclusion of concessionary agreements ". It included also " the direction " of foreign trade and " the establishment " of a single monetary and credit system.

The present Constitution gives to the Union Government " administration of banks, industrial and agricultural establishments, as well as trading establishments " and also " foreign trade on the basis of state monopoly ".

### CHAPTER III

The 1924 Constitution gave supreme power to the " All-Union Congress of Soviets " of some two thousand members indirectly elected and convening once a year. Between sessions power was vested in the Central Executive Committee of somewhat more than four hundred members in two chambers which convened three times a year. This, in turn, elected a Presidium which had " supreme legislative, executive and administrative " power in the interim.

The present Constitution vests the supreme power more simply and directly in the Supreme Soviet of slightly more than a thousand members, meeting twice a year, and consisting of two chambers roughly equal in number. Between sessions a Presidium of thirty-six members continues with strictly prescribed functions but without legislative power.

### CHAPTER V

ARTICLES 70, 77, 78 :

Contrast these eight All-Union Commissariats, ten Union-Republic Commissariats, and five Chairmen of Commissions—total twenty-three main departments—with the five All-Union Commissariats and six " Unified Peoples' Commissariats " of 1924.

Of the former All-Union Commissariats—Foreign Affairs, War and Marine, Home and Foreign Trade, Transport, Posts and Telegraphs—Transport has been divided into Railways and Water Transport ; Home and Foreign Trade have become two separate Commissariats.

The former " Unified Peoples' Commissariats " were : Supreme

Economic Council, which has given birth to Heavy Industry, Defence Industry, Food Industry, Light Industry, Timber Industry ; Agriculture, which is now supplemented by State Grain and Livestock Farms ; Labour, which is now abolished, its functions having been transferred to the trade unions ; Finance, which remains ; Workers' and Peasants' Inspection, now replaced by the Soviet Control Commission ; Central Statistical Department, now replaced by the State Planning Commission. The present Commissariats of Justice and Health are a centralization of functions formerly performed locally. The functions of the OGPU, formerly an independent department to which a special chapter of the 1924 Constitution was devoted, are now included in the Commissariat of Home Affairs. The Committees on Agricultural Products, Art and Higher Education are completely new additions.

CHAPTER IX

The present Constitution gives greater independence to the courts than formerly. Under the 1924 Constitution, the Supreme Court, if faced with a conflict between the laws of a constituent republic and the Union, could only " appeal " to the Central Executive Committee to set this right. Now it has " supervision of the judicial activities of all judicial organs of the USSR and of the constituent republics ".

Formerly the judges were appointed and removable by the Central Executive Committee ; now they are appointed for a fixed term of five years, i.e., longer than the life of the appointing body.

The Attorney-General is appointed for seven years and appoints all state and district attorneys, who are thus independent of local governments. Formerly similar independence was enjoyed by the OGPU but its functions went beyond those of investigation and prosecution to which the Attorney-General's office is limited.

CHAPTER X

The earlier constitutions had no list of " basic rights and duties ". The right to work did not appear since unemployment was not abolished until 1931. The right to rest and to material security were not included in earlier constitutions although the eight-hour day, paid holidays and sickness insurance were introduced by law at an early stage. The Constitution of 1918 did not guarantee the right to education but " set before itself the task of providing for the workers and poorer peasants a complete, universal and free education ".

Equal rights for women and for all nationalities were part of the earlier constitutions.

" Freedom of religious and anti-religious propaganda " was recognized in the text of 1918 but was changed to the present formulation in the revised constitution of the RSFSR of 1927.

Freedom of the press and of assembly were recognized in the Constitution of 1918 ; their material guarantees—printing shops, meeting halls and other technical resources—were transferred " to the working class and to the peasants ".  The present Constitution widens this to include all " the working people and their organizations ".

" Full liberty of association for the workers " was ensured in the Constitution of 1918, the government pledging itself to " lend to the workers and peasants all its material and moral assistance to help them to unite and organize themselves ".  The present Constitution defines the types of organizations which have arisen and specifically mentions the Communist Party.

" Inviolability of homes and secrecy of correspondence " were not guaranteed in previous constitutions.

The right of asylum was granted in 1918 to " all foreigners persecuted for political and religious offences ".  The present Constitution reads " for defending the interests of the working people or for scientific activity or for their struggle for national liberation ", a clear indication of the historical changes which have taken place in world pressures.

In 1918 the " honour of bearing arms " was " granted only to the workers ; the leisured sections of the population will fulfill other military duties ".  In the present Constitution all citizens are equal.

### CHAPTER XI

ARTICLE 134 :

According to previous constitutions, deputies to the town and rural soviets were elected by the voters by a show of hands at meetings.  Larger areas were governed by Congresses of Soviets elected by the lower soviets.  In the All-Union Congress the cities were represented by one delegate for every 25,000 electors, and the provinces by one delegate for every 125,000 inhabitants.

The present elections are direct to both local and central governing bodies on an equal basis of representation and by secret ballot.

ARTICLE 135 :

Previous constitutions gave lists of disfranchised persons includ-

ing those who employed others for the sake of profit—a category that
no longer exists—clergy and former Tsarist officials.

The present Constitution grants the suffrage to all citizens except
the mentally deficient and persons condemned by law with deprivation of electoral rights.

CHAPTER XIII

The All-Union Congress of Soviets could change the constitution
by a majority vote.

Now a change requires two-thirds of the votes in each of the
chambers of the Supreme Soviet.

SUMMARY

So far we have quoted Mrs. Strong.  We now add our own
summary of the constitution, not in the Russian phraseology, but
in terms enabling the British or American reader more easily to
comprehend its purport; and not following the order of the legal text
but rearranged so as to bring out its character as a new Declaration
of the Rights of Man.

*The Twelve Tables of the Law*

   I. The Right to work, and to be enabled to live by the work that
must be found for all able-bodied adults, with their own option,
alternatively, to join in independent cooperative productive
societies, either in industry, agriculture or fishing, or to work
individually on their own account, without the employment of
hired labour.

  II. The Right to leisure, by statutory limitation of the hours of
employment in office, factory, mill or mine ; together with
the provision of paid holidays and of all approved means of
happily using the leisure so ensured.

 III. The Right of those who work at wages or salary by hand or by
brain, and of their incapacitated dependants, collectively, to
the entire net product of the labour so employed throughout
the whole USSR, as annually ascertained.

 IV. The Right to positive health of body and mind, so far as this
can be secured by the widest possible use of preventive and
curative medicine and surgery, and of public sanitation, with

wages in sickness and incapacity without waiting interval or time limit ; and the ensuring of adequate nutrition and physical as well as mental training of all infants, children and adolescents.

V. The Right of Women to fulfil the function of motherhood with all possible alleviation of the physical suffering involved ; without pecuniary sacrifice or burden, and further aided by universally organized provision for the care of infants and children.

VI. The Right to education equally for all races, without limit or fee, for persons of any age and either sex, with maintenance in suitable cases.

VII. The Right to prompt and adequate provision for the family on the death of any breadwinner or pensioner ; with universally gratuitous funeral, and instant succour of the home.

VIII. The Right to superannuation at a definite age before senility or upon previous breakdown, with adequate non-contributory pension.

IX. The Right to freedom of speech, freedom of assembly and of holding mass meetings, freedom of street processions and demonstrations and freedom of the press [from domination by capitalist, financial or counter-revolutionary ownership or control]. These " rights of the citizens " by Article 125 " are ensured *by placing at the disposal of the toilers and their organizations* " [including trade unions, cooperative societies, sport and other voluntary societies] printing presses, supplies of paper, public buildings, and other material requisites for the exercise of these rights ; as well as by the prohibition of private profit-making and exploitation.

X. The Right to criticize every branch of the public administration, and to agitate for its improvement, by groups and associations of divers kinds, such as trade unions, cooperative societies and cultural associations, by speeches at public meetings and by printed matter—yet without any organization of merely political groups having no other common interest than public criticism or opposition, and without permission to individuals or factions to obstruct the *execution* of what has been finally decided on by the supreme elected legislature.

XI. The Right to elect, irrespective of nationality, race, sex or colour ; freely, directly, secretly, equally and universally ; from 18 years of age ; to all governing assemblies from the lowest to the highest, without pecuniary, residential or other limiting qualification ; candidates being put forward by non-party groups of every description, as well as by the Vocation of Leadership known as the Communist Party. This will produce an electorate numbering actually 55 per cent of the census population, as compared with one of less than 40 per cent in the United States and Great Britain, reduced as those are by requirements of residence and specific registration.

XII. The Right to inviolability of the person, and of his correspondence. The right to be free from arbitrary arrest, as in other continental administrations, will not have what is so much cherished in England, the special protection of that unique British peculiarity, the Habeas Corpus Act. But (Article 127) " the citizens of the USSR are guaranteed inviolability of person. No person may be placed under arrest except by decision of a court or with the sanction of the judicial department of the State Attorney ", which is now made independent of the executive.

## ELECTION REGULATIONS

The necessary regulations for the elections, which are to take place in the autumn of 1937, are not completely formulated in the code published in July 1937. The constituencies were then not defined. So far only certain points have been decided. Among these are (a) that the elections will take place everywhere on the same day; (b) that the poll will be open from 6 A.M. to midnight; (c) that polling districts will be provided for each one or two thousand electors in the cities, and for each five hundred in the country, or even for each hundred in sparsely inhabited districts; (d) that no candidate may stand for more than one constituency; (e) that if no candidate polls an actual majority of the votes cast, there will be a Second Ballot confined to the two candidates heading the list; (f) that lists of electors in alphabetical order will be posted up in each polling district; (g) that the ballot papers will be officially provided with envelopes in which the elector will place his ballot paper, after crossing out all but one name.

END OF VOL. I